Lanier
Leading Edge Computer
Levi Strauss & Co.
Lincoln Electric Company

Marlow Industries
Marriott Corporation
Mary Kay Cosmetics
Matsushita
Mazda
McDonald's Corporation
McDonnell Douglas
McKinsey & Company
Merck & Co.
Merisel
Microsoft Corporation
Milliken & Co.
Minolta
Mitsubishi
Mobil Chemical
Moody's
Motorola

New Balance
Nissan
Nordstrom
Northwest Airlines

Packard Bell
PepsiCo, Inc.
Pioneer Hi-bred International
Pizza Hut
Prudential-Bache

Quaker Oats

Reebok
Reynolds Tobacco
Rice Aircraft Company
Ricoh
Ritz-Carlton Hotel Co.
RJR-Nabisco
RKO Warner Video
Robert Plan Corporation

Salomon Brothers
O. M. Scott & Sons Company
Sealed Air Corporation
Sears Roebuck
Sharp
Solectron Corp.
Sterling Chemicals, Inc.
Systematics Financial Services Inc.

Taco Bell
Texas Instruments
Towers Perrin Company
Toyota Motor Company

United Airlines (UAL)
United Technologies

Wainwright Industries Inc.
Wal-Mart
Wallace Co.
Walt Disney Company
Warburg Asset Management
Western Electric
Westinghouse

Xerox

Zytec Corp.

Managerial Economics and Organizational Architecture

THE IRWIN SERIES IN ECONOMICS

Appleyard and Field
International Economics
second edition

Appleyard and Field
International Economics: Trade Theory and Policy
second edition

Appleyard and Field
International Economics: Payments, Exchange Rates, and Macro Policy
second edition

Aslanbeigui and Naples
Rethinking Economic Principles: Critical Essays on Introductory Textbooks

Baily and Friedman
Macroeconomics, Financial Markets, and the International Sector
second edition

Barron and Lynch
Economics
third edition

Baye
Managerial Economics and Business Strategy
second edition

Bornstein
Comparative Economics Systems: Models and Cases
seventh edition

Brickley, Smith, and Zimmerman
Organizational Architecture: A Mangerial Economics Approach

Brown and Moore
Readings, Issues, and Problems in Public Finance
fourth edition

Callan and Thomas
Environmental Economics and Management: Theory, Policy, and Applications

Colander
Economics
second edition

Colander
Microeconomics
second edition

Colander
Macroeconomics
second edition

Fisher
State and Local Public Finance
second edition

Hadjimichalakis and Hadjimichalakis
Contemporary Money, Banking, and Financial Markets

Hyman
Economics
fourth edition

Hyman
Microeconomics
fourth edition

Hyman
Macroeconomics
fourth edition

Hyman
Modern Microeconomics: Analysis and Applications
third edition

Katz and Rosen
Microeconomics
second edition

Lehmann
Real World Economic Applications: The Wall Street Journal Workbook
fifth edition

Lindert and Pugel
International Economics
tenth edition

Maurice and Thomas
Managerial Economics: Applied Microeconomics for Decision Making
fifth edition

O'Sullivan
Urban Economics
third edition

O'Sullivan
Essentials of Urban Economics

Roger and Daniel
Principles of Economics Software Simulation

Rosen
Public Finance
fourth edition

Schwarz and Van Dyken
Manager: Managerial Economics Software

Rosser and Rosser
Comparative Economics in a Transforming World Economy

Santerre and Neun
Health Economics: Theories, Insights, and Industry Studies

Sharp, Register, and Grimes
Economics of Social Issues
twelfth edition

Slavin
Economics
fourth edition

Slavin
Microeconomics
fourth edition

Slavin
Macroeconomics
fourth edition

Walton and Wykoff
Understanding Economics Today
fifth edition

Managerial Economics and Organizational Architecture

JAMES A. BRICKLEY

CLIFFORD W. SMITH, JR.

JEROLD L. ZIMMERMAN
William E. Simon Graduate
School of Business Administration
University of Rochester

Boston, Massachusetts   Burr Ridge, Illinios   Dubuque, Iowa
adison, Wisconsin   New York, New York   San Francisco, California   St. Louis, Missouri

Irwin/McGraw-Hill

A Division of The McGraw·Hill Companies

Irwin Book Team

Publisher: *Michael W. Junior*
Senior sponsoring editor: *Gary Nelson*
Developmental editor: *Ellen Cleary*
Marketing manager: *Katie Rose*
Project supervisor: *Susan Trentacosti*
Production supervisor: *Laurie Sander*
Prepress buyer: *Jon Christopher*
Designer: *Crispin Prebys*
Compositor: *Quebecor Printing/Dubuque*
Typeface: *10/12 Times Roman*
Printer: *Quebecor Printing/Dubuque*

Library of Congress Cataloging-in-Publication Data

Brickley, James A.
   Managerial economics and organizational architecture / James
A. Brickley, Clifford W. Smith, Jr., Jerold L. Zimmerman
      p. cm.
   ISBN 0-256-15825-8
   Includes index.
      1. Managerial economics. 2. Organizational effectiveness. I.
   Smith, Clifford W.   II. Zimmerman, Jerold L., 1947-   III. Title
   HD30.22.B729   1997
   658—dc20   96-09324

Printed in the United States of America
   3 4 5 6 7 8 9 0   QD   3 2 1 0 9 8 7

Dedicated to our wives—Cindy, Bernie, and Dodie

Preface

Managerial problem solving and decision making benefit from the use of an important set of economic tools. Yet, except for a few esoteric works generally inaccessible to MBA and undergraduate students, existing textbooks fail to present economic principles managers can use in actually managing their organizations. Until recently, economists paid little attention to *organizational architecture*. Rather than base the analysis on models from psychology and sociology as has been typical in management books analyzing the design of organizations, we have written a new management book with its foundation based on recent economics research that focuses on the internal structure of the firm. We employ basic yet powerful economic tools of analysis such as optimization and equilibrium to examine how managers can design organizations to motivate individuals to *make choices* that *increase firm value*.

We believe the design of the organization is of fundamental importance. Until now, there has been little comprehensive coverage of such important topics as developing effective performance-evaluation systems and compensation plans, assigning decision-making authority among employees, or managing transfer pricing disputes among divisions. This omission is both significant and problematic, given the increased pressures on management to structure more effective organizations. That's why our first objective in writing this book has been to provide managers and aspiring managers with a systematic, comprehensive framework for addressing organizational problems.

Reflecting the expansion of the academic research base, a number of business schools have begun teaching courses based on this emerging literature or incorporating this material within existing courses. However, the available teaching materials for these courses, primarily academic articles, are accessible only to the most determined students. This severely limits the breadth of topics that can be covered in such a course. We encountered this problem in our own teaching experiences and realized we were unlikely alone in the need to make the available research more accessible to a larger audience. To that end, we have strived to write the underlying theoretical concepts in simpler, more intuitive terms and illustrate them with numerous examples, most drawn from actual company practices.

Another reason for writing the book has been to provide a multidisciplinary, cross-functional approach to organizational economics. Our interests span economics, finance, accounting, information systems, and financial institutions; this has allowed us to draw examples from several functional areas to demonstrate how this underlying economic framework can be used to analyze a variety of problems managers regularly face. Given the pressures from the business environment on today's classroom, this represents an important aspect of our efforts.

The Conceptual Framework

Although the popular press and existing literature on organizations are replete with jargon—TQM, reengineering, outsourcing, teaming, venturing, empowerment, and corporate culture—they fail to provide managers with a systematic, comprehensive framework for examining organizational problems. This book uses economic analysis to develop such a framework. In this book we present this important material in an organized, integrated, accessible manner.

Through this text, students will gain an understanding of the basic tools of economics and how to apply them to solve important business problems. While the book covers the standard managerial economic problems of pricing and production, it pays special attention to organizational issues. In particular, the book will help students better understand:

Decision rights assignment

Performance evaluation

Rewards

The components of organizational architecture are like three legs of a stool. It is important that all three legs be designed so that the stool is **balanced.** Changing one leg without careful consideration of the other two is typically a mistake.

- The firm's business environment and strategy as important determinants of organizational design.
- Changes in environment and strategy and their affect on appropriate design.
- How to structure more effective organizations using a unifying conceptual framework.
- The three key features of *organizational architecture*—the assignment of decision-making authority, the reward system, and the performance-evaluation system—which allow managers to structure organizations to achieve their desired results.
- The interrelations among corporate policies such as strategy, financing, accounting, marketing, information systems, operations, compensation, and human resources.

Organizational architecture, in turn, provides a more integrated and comprehensive view of material presented elsewhere in the business curriculum.

Changing Nature of the Curriculum

Increasing global competition and technological change are prompting firms to undertake major organizational restructurings as well as producing fundamental industry realignments. Furthermore, the pace of change does not appear to be slowing within the foreseeable future. Business and economics students recognize these issues and consequently want to develop skills that will better prepare them to manage organizational change as well as making them more effective managers. Thus, these changes within the business community have had an important effect on the curriculum offered by business schools.

Many firms are shifting from functional organizational structures (manufacturing, marketing, and distribution) to a more process-oriented, cross-functional organization. Curricula are evolving to reflect this change. Many business school programs have been revised to address these concerns; narrow technical expertise in a single functional area (whether accounting, finance, information management, or marketing) is not sufficient. To be effective managers in this environment, students must develop cross-functional skills. To meet these challenges, business schools are becoming more integrated. Courses build on each other. Problems faced by managers are not just finance problems or operations problems or marketing problems; rather, most business problems involve elements that cut across traditional functional areas. And for that reason, the curriculum must encourage students to apply concepts they have mastered across a variety of courses. One of our overriding objectives in writing this book has been to ensure that students can identify problems and apply important analytical skills they will need when making decisions within firms.

Our View of Content and Pedagogy

There are many topics that could be covered in an economics textbook. This book focuses on those topics that we believe are most relevant to managers. For instance, the book provides an in-depth treatment of compensation policy, outsourcing, transfer pricing, and business-process reengineering. We spend little time on public policy topics, such as minimum-wage legislation, antitrust policy, and income redistribution through the welfare system or the tax code. There are a number of other important features that differentiate this book from others currently available.

- This book provides a comprehensive, cross-functional framework for organizational problems. It does this by first describing and integrating important research findings that have been published in a variety of functional areas. It then demonstrates how to apply the framework to actual organizational problems.
- We have tried to write a readable book. Reviewers, instructors, and students found the forerunner edition accessible and interesting. Technical mathematics and statistics are replaced with intuitive descriptions and simple examples. More technical material is provided in appendices for those who wish to pursue it.
- Numerous examples drawn from the business press and our experiences illustrate the theoretical concepts. These examples, many highlighted in boxes, reinforce the underlying principles and help the student better visualize the application of more abstract ideas. Each chapter begins with a specific case history that is used throughout the chapter. This provides an important pedagogical device that unifies the chapter and aids the reader in recalling the key constructs.
- Nontraditional economics topics dealing with outsourcing, leadership, business reengineering, total quality management, and ethics are examined. Business school curricula are often criticized for being slow in covering topics of current interest to business, such as ethics, reengineering, and TQM. The last four chapters examine these recent management trends and demonstrate how the book's framework can be used to analyze and understand topical current issues.
- End-of-chapter problems and cases are drawn from real organizational contexts. From the business press as well as our contact with executive MBA students and consulting experiences, we have structured exercises that provide students with rich opportunities to apply the framework to problems like the ones they might encounter as managers.

Alternative Uses for the Text

This book is based on the existing literature dealing with the economics of organizations. It also contains basic material on managerial economics, which we discuss in three chapters. All the tools necessary for understanding and applying the organizational economic framework we develop throughout this text have been selected for their managerial relevance. In our experience, these managerial-economic tools are invaluable for those students who have been out working (and hence not in a classroom) for some time, or for those who didn't major in business or economics as an undergraduate. Those with an economics background may choose to forgo this material. We have structured these discussions of demand, production/cost, and market structure to be optional. That is, if you don't want to cover these tools fully, you can skip Chapters 4 through 6 without loss of continuity. The inclusion of this material enables you to use the book in either an introductory managerial economics course or in a course on organizations, where students would have had a prior economics course.

Our book is an effective tool in a variety of classes at the MBA, executive MBA, or undergraduate level. We strongly recommend that all students read Chapters 1–3 and 7; they are the chapters which provide the underlying tools and framework for the text. Chapters 4–6, as we mentioned before, cover the basic managerial-economics material of demand, costs, production, and market structure. Chapters 8–14 provide the comprehensive framework to understand organizational architecture, and we recommend, again, that these be covered in sequence. Finally, Chapters 15–18 cover four special managerial topics: outsourcing, leadership, TQM/reengineering, and ethics. They are capstone chapters—chapters that apply and illustrate the framework. Instructors can assign them based on available time and their specific interests.

Developing This Book for an Emerging Discipline

Over the past two decades, we have learned much from teaching this material and helping others to implement these concepts in practice. We observe growing interest in this subject, as more journal articles, academic meetings, and courses appear around the globe. And in the process of developing this book over the past several years, we have learned a great deal more.

Meeting the demands of instructors and students, many of which are driven by an ever-changing business environment, requires input from numerous individuals. The development process that provided that feedback was extensive and instrumental in making this book market driven. Over 20 individual instructors reviewed the manuscript throughout the writing process. In addition, three separate market surveys garnered responses from over 400 individuals. Their feedback helped shape the direction of this text.

Instructors consistently asked for a modern book based on sound theory with solid applications. The response from our reviewers to the text organization, topic coverage, and pedagogical program has been quite positive. In fact, in response to the demands of an unusually vocal marketplace, we published a forerunner edition of this work entitled, *Organizational Architecture: A Managerial Economics Approach,* released in Fall of 1995. Although we had a definite objective in mind as we set out to write this book, we welcomed the extensive feedback we received from many readers. The generous comments from reviewers and users of the forerunner edition have substantially improved this text.

The development process is a time-consuming and tricky undertaking. Authors have to be open to criticism and willing to learn from others who are traveling a similar yet distinct highway. Although we are unlikely to please everyone, we have worked to critically evaluate suggestions and to be responsive where consistent with our mission.

This book represents the current state of the art. Development is on-going as research continues to evolve and as we continue to learn. *Managerial Economics and Organizational Architecture* covers an exciting, dynamic area of study and work. We hope that a small portion of that excitement is communicated through this text. Reviewers, instructors, and students frequently mentioned the relevance of material to the business community, the accessibility of the prose, and the logical flow within the framework we have developed. However, in the final analysis, it is instructors and their students who will determine the true value of our efforts. We welcome, in fact urge, feedback. If readers would like to share their thoughts on this work or their classroom experiences, please feel free to contact to any of us at the University of Rochester. Many thanks in advance for the assistance.

Brickley@mail.ssb.rochester.edu
Smith@mail.ssb.rochester.edu
Zimmerman@mail.ssb.rochester.edu

Acknowledgments

No textbook springs from virgin soil. This book especially owes its intellectual roots to the work of dozens toiling to develop, test, and explain organization theory to their students. It is important that readers understand the historical precedents of this work, how it developed, and continues to evolve.

At Rochester in the 1970s, William Meckling and Michael Jensen began teaching a course on the economics of organizations. Their course, initially based on the writings of Armen Alchian, Ronald Coase, Harold Demsetz, John Gould, Frederick Hayek, and Jack Hirshleifer, explored how economics can help managers better structure and manage organizations. In 1976 Mike and Bill published their influential paper on agency costs.[1] This paper attracted much attention and encouraged related research in economics, finance, and accounting.

Bill's and Mike's teaching and research stimulated our interest in the economics of organizations. Much of our research focused on organizational issues. For example, Brickley worked on franchise contracts, corporate control, and executive compensation contracts. Smith worked on corporate debt, executive compensation contracts, the organization of insurance firms, and ethics. Zimmerman worked on agency theory problems in accounting, performance evaluation, and cost allocations. Most of this work was coauthored with our colleagues: Ray Ball, Michael Barclay, Sanjai Bhagat, Jeffrey Coles, Frederick Dark, Greg Jarrell, Ronald Lease, David Mayers, Shehzad Mian, Kevin Murphy, Lee Wakeman, Jerold Warner, Ross Watts, and Michael Weisbach.

Over the years, the organizations course developed a basic analytic structure: self-interested behavior of individuals, the role of knowledge in decision making, agency theory, and organizational design. While many of these ideas existed in the literature, Mike and Bill organized them in a quite powerful way. Of particular importance is their focus on three critical features of organizational design: (1) the assignment of decision rights within the organization, (2) the reward system, and (3) the performance-evaluation system. These three elements, which we call *organizational architecture,* serve as an important organizing device for this book. As you will discover, this structure makes this rich body of knowledge more useful for managerial decision making.

---

[1]M. Jensen and W. Meckling (1976) "The Theory of the Firm: Managerial Management Behavior, Agency Costs and Ownership Structure," *Journal of Financial Economics 3,* 305–60.

The organizations course at the Simon School evolved over the last 25 years. As other faculty began teaching the course, each contributed to enriching the analysis and course structure. Ronald Schmidt especially helped to ensure the course's acceptance with the students. His energy and pedagogical insights demonstrated the power of the analysis to address managerial problems. In the mid-1980s, after 19 years as Dean at Rochester, Bill retired. Mike moved to Harvard and continued his work on organizations. With his colleagues, George Baker, Michael Gibbs, Kevin Murphy, and Karen Wruck, additional insights and in-depth clinical studies were produced.

Research both at Rochester and other schools expanded our understanding of organizational phenomena. Mike and Bill wrote a series of papers that summarized the basic framework used in the organization course, and which elaborate on certain key building blocks. The following papers were of particular importance in the development of this book:

- W. Meckling (1976) "Values and the Choice of the Model of the Individual in the Social Sciences," *Schweizerische Zeitschrift fur Volkswirtschaft und Statistik,* (December).
- M. Jensen (1983) "Organization Theory and Methodology," *Accounting Review* 58, 319–39.
- E. Fama, and M. Jensen (1983) "Separation of Ownership and Control," *Journal of Law & Economics* 26, 301–26.
- M. Jensen and W. Meckling (1986) "Divisional Performance Measurement," Harvard Business School working paper.
- M. Jensen and W. Meckling (1991) "Specific and General Knowledge, and Organizational Structure," *Main Currents in Contract Economics,* L. Werin and H. Wijkander, eds. (Blackwell, Oxford), Chapter 9.
- K. Wruck and M. Jensen (1994) "Science, Specific Knowledge and Total Quality Management," *Journal of Accounting and Economics* 18, 247–87.

The intellectual genesis of this book lies in this body of work. No amount of citation or acknowledgments can adequately reflect the encouragement and stimulation that Bill and Mike provided, both in person and through their writings.

During the last two decades important contributions to the literature on the economics of organizations were made by scholars such as: Eugene Fama, Oliver Hart, Bengt Holmstrom, Edward Lazear, Paul Milgrom, John Roberts, Sherwin Rosen, and Oliver Williamson. Moreover, our colleagues Ray Ball, Kevin Murphy, Ronald Schmidt, Ross Watts, and Michael Weisbach also made substantial contributions to this effort. Through the work of these individuals and others, we have learned a significant amount about the economics of organizations.

In the late 1980s at Rochester, the organizations course was moved from a second-year elective to a first-year required course. This highlighted the importance of this course in the curriculum. By this time, many of the concepts in the course had begun to permeate the school's curriculum. Agency problems were now discussed in accounting, information systems, finance, marketing, and operations courses, thereby better integrating the Rochester curriculum. More faculty became involved in the course and contributed to its development—especially Ray Ball, Scott Keating, Kevin Murphy, Karen Van Nuys, and Michael Weisbach.

Four other individuals also contributed to the development of the book. Stacey Kole, Lawrence Matteson, and Glenn MacDonald at Rochester provided many suggestions and thoughtful comments which helped to clarify our thinking on key issues. Don

Chew, Editor of the *Journal of Applied Corporate Finance,* greatly assisted us in writing a series of articles for his journal based on the book. Writing these articles enormously improved the exposition of the book.

This project has benefited from an extensive development effort. In addition to generations of Simon School students, many colleagues both in the United States and overseas formally reviewed the manuscript and gave us detailed feedback, for which we are very grateful.

John H. Brown	Richard R. Pace
Georgia Southern University	*University of Dayton*
Luke Froeb	David Parker
Vanderbilt University	*University of Birmingham, UK*
Michael Gibbs	Tim Sorenson
University of Chicago	*Seattle University*
Charles M. Gray	Martin Stahl
University of St. Thomas	*Empire State College*
Daniel R. LeClair	Michael Sykuta
University of Tampa	*University of Pittsburgh*
Robert Maness	Steven Tomlinson
Louisiana State University	*University of Texas at Austin*
Stephen E. Margolis	Roger Tutterow
North Carolina State University	*Kennesaw State College*
J. Peter Mattila	Walter Verdon
Iowa State University	*Tiffin University*
Daniel L. McConaughy	Mike Williams
Rosary College	*Bethune Cookman College*
Seth W. Norton	Huizhong Zhou
Wheaton College	*Western Michigan University*

We owe special thanks to Luke Froeb, Scott Keating, and Chris James, all of whom used early drafts of this material in class and provided us with valuable comments.

In addition, meeting with more than 60 faculty (from a variety of academic and industry backgrounds) at the Conference on Market-Based Management at the University of Kansas in May 1995 provided additional feedback and encouragement about this project. This face-to-face interaction improved our work materially. We would like to thank Henry Butler for organizing the conference and providing this opportunity as well as the attendees listed below for their input:

Professors Urton Anderson, Ronald A. Ash, Jay Barney, Barry Baysinger, Bruce O. Bublitz, Keith Chauvin, Jerilyn Coles, Deepak Datta, Louis DeAlessi, Robert J. De-Fillipi, Ken Eastman, Yar M. Ebadi, Jerry Ellig, Ali M. Fatemi, Allen Ford, Charles R. Greer, Constanza Hagmann, William Halal, Bill Hesterly, Clifford Holderness, Doug A. Houston, Robert Jacobson, Kissan Joseph, Maurice Joy, Danny A. Klinefelter, Charles E. Krider, Michael D. Kull, Dwight Lee, Murray Levin, Floyd Lilley, Richard K. Litherland, Lee L. Manzer, Juliann Mazachek, Cynthia McCahon, Sanjay Mishra, Ronald L. Moomaw, V. K. Narayanan, Brian Niehoff, David O'Bryan, David A. O'Dell, Guy Owings, Laura Poppo, H. Joseph Reitz, Barbara E. Rytych, John E. Schoen, William F. Shughart II, Vernon L. Smith, Daniel G. Spencer, Michael Sykuta, Marilyn L. Taylor, Steve Thomas, Jim Waegelein, Doug Whitman, and Todd Zenger.

In addition, we are grateful for the feedback from over 400 individuals who completed three separate surveys. Their thoughts served to guide us in the refinement of this work.

We appreciate the efforts of Michele Cox and Kathy Jones who provided secretarial support and Rachna Prakash who provided research assistance.

Finally, we wish to thank our colleagues at Richard D. Irwin: Michael Junior, Ellen Cleary, and Gary Nelson. They encouraged us to pursue this project. Through their vision and publishing expertise, they provided us with insights and feedback to help expand our audience while adhering to our mission.

James A. Brickley
Clifford W. Smith, Jr.
Jerold L. Zimmerman

Feedback from the Business Community

Joel Stern, Managing Partner, Stern Stewart & Co.

Managerial Economics and Organizational Architecture is the first systematic attempt to apply the insights of financial economics to the design of large organizations. Given the current business environment of near-continuous change, the central message of this book—that the assignment of decision-making authority must be consistent with performance measurement and incentive compensation systems—can only become more valuable to managers in thinking about the right structure for their companies.

Mark S. Greenstein, Consultant of Arthur D. Little

You've produced more than an academic textbook. *Managerial Economics and Organizational Architecture* is also effective as a reference manual for analysis and design of organizations. I've used this material on numerous occasions in my consulting career, for example:

- To understand why a systems development organization was more interested in reliability than in meeting the needs of its customers.
- To determine how an internal service organization grew larger and busier yet provided deteriorating value to its stakeholders.

The framework provided in the book provides me with questions that lead me to realize my client's capabilities and their limitations.

Gerald P. Concannon, Manager of Customer & Technical Support, Xerox Corporation

At Xerox, as with most dynamic companies, the tempo of significant change is increasing every day. This puts constant pressure on managers to maintain a fundamental approach to the principles of organizational architecture. Without such a compass, managers will most surely flounder on the rocks of chaos and lost productivity. In our business we no longer have a choice as to whether to allocate decision rights lower in the organization. We manage customer and technical support analysts with highly specialized technical knowledge. When a problem is escalated from a customer or one of our field employees, immediate decisive action must be taken. People in these support positions are highly interdependent. The range of systems technical knowledge is simply too broad for one individual to comprehend. It may take two and on occasion three people with complementary technical skills to handle a problem.

The customer environment is also dynamic with regard to the information technology products employed in document production. Platforms and software applications for document creation change frequently; network topologies and connectivity software also change; and the number and complexity of third-party products connected to our equipment is constantly on the rise. Therefore decisions must be made constantly to adapt to these changes. Who gets trained on what? Where do they get trained? How do we group people into teams with complementary skills and knowledge? If we had management involvement in these decisions, we'd suffer the critical time loss of constantly gathering and moving specialized knowledge.

Decision rights to answer these questions are allocated to the analysts themselves. By applying the principles of *Organizational Architecture* covered in your book we have structured the work environment to accommodate rapid change with minimal agency problems. The reward and the performance evaluation systems are dynamic. All work can be observed and team and individual performance results are public knowledge. We find that peer review is a strong contributor to maintaining a positive business focus. Of course team and individual results are also included in periodic performance reviews.

People are rewarded by their peers in many ways. For example, the desire for advanced technical training is constant. Tom Peters says that learning is the motivator of the nineties. That's certainly true in our department. Analysts choose who gets trained on what. So, stronger contributors to work performance get preference. The workers also select their own team members. Since performance evaluations include work group performance, strong performers are chosen more for their job skills and knowledge than their social attributes.

The Xerox Customer Support Center recently received the 1996 award for Continued Excellence in Customer Support from the Software Support Professionals Association. Having a management team well grounded in the principles of organizational architecture played a major role in this achievement. We approach the challenges of change with confidence. Best wishes for continued success in the publication of this outstanding book. My copy of the forerunner edition is already on the bookshelf in my office.

Christian W. Hafner, Director, Swiss Bank Corporation, Zurich

Now that I apply the determinants of the organizational structure as an analysis tool, I am substantially more confident in my decisions. With this approach to integrate the studies and research of economics and management as well as finance and accounting, the authors have created a complete guide to lead managers to success.

Paul H. McAfee, Director, Eastman Kodak Company

Although you wrote your book *Managerial Economics and Organizational Architecture* as a textbook, it is equally useful as a day-to-day management guidebook and reference.

An MBA program delivers an enormous amount of information, and a wealth of quantitative analytic processes, to its graduates. A manager can apply this learning to almost any element of business management. But the graduating student usually is left on her own to determine how to integrate her learning so that she contributes most effectively to her business goals.

Your book is unique. It integrates sound analytic economic processes with a solid framework for understanding—and positively influencing—organizational design.

Your text sits by my desk at work. I use it regularly to review fundamental management principles. I use it to help me find the right words to explain a new idea to my management colleagues and to senior management. And I use it to bring a heightened awareness of the importance of the assignment of decision rights, and the processes of evaluating and rewarding performance, to the management teams in which I participate.

Mark Babunovic, Managing Director, The Chase Manhattan Bank, N.A.

Thank you for the advance copy of *Managerial Economics and Organizational Architecture.* It was a compact refresher course (one London/New York round-trip) as well as a chance to think about the overlap between the concepts in the book and what I have seen work—or not work—in business management. The following examples came first to mind:

1. One of our bigger challenges in the wholesale financial services industry is promoting the sale of multiple products through single-product salespeople. *Managerial Economics and Organizational Architecture* suggests an approach that recognizes salespersons' incentives to protect both their customer relationships and their stake in product-specific knowledge and success. Consistent with this, clearly measuring and compensating salespeople on the basis of customer rather than product sales is often an effective solution. Conversely, compensation systems that ignore these motives end up promoting behavior that ignores the distributional efficiency and customer service benefits of cross-marketing.

2. In the derivatives industry, successful performance evaluation and reward systems are often among a firm's most jealously guarded secrets—evidence of the strategic value of applying the principles of this book.

3. *Managerial Economics and Organizational Architecture* derives conditions for the optimal use of teams in performing tasks or functions within a business. In my experience, delegating appropriate decision rights to teams under these conditions, with team-defined objectives, evaluation, and compensation, results in consistently improved performance and better communication (and a virtually automatic process of underperformers being weeded out by the team itself).

4. Running an expense center (in this case a service bureau providing analytical and programming services to different trading businesses) highlighted the problem described in this book of users understanding demand at budget allocation time and overconsuming the rest of the year. Consistent with this analysis, effective partial solutions included encouraging users wherever appropriate to "in-source" by taking on dedicated resources (recruiting if necessary from expense center personnel). Another was to assign a "relationship manager" from the center to each user with joint accountability to the user's manager and myself. This made the relationship manager more responsive to the user (by giving her the sense of being a part of the line business she supported) and making it more difficult for the user to understate demand or overconsume (or overcomplain).

Thinking about business organizations as rational individuals responding to incentives and new information simply fits the facts. The three basic elements developed in *Managerial Economics and Organizational Architecture* allow managers to translate this thinking into operational decisions: allocating decision rights, measuring performance, and compensating individuals and groups. The power of this approach in analyzing problems common to managing organizations equips the reader with a rich set of tools for identifying and solving them.

Dr. Tomlinson G. Rauscher, Manager of Systems Reprographics Family Group, Xerox Corporation

These concepts have had a profound effect on my management thinking and career. I have used the concepts you present in addressing the problem of reducing the time to market in a firm's product development process. My theory is that organizational architecture is the primary determinant of the time required to design and deliver a new product. Using these principles I directed a team that delivered a product to market in 30 weeks compared to a benchmark of 77 weeks.

It is the book I wish I had written.

Contents in Brief

Part 3

Applications of Organizational Architecture

Contents

chapter 3   Markets, Organizations, and the Role of Knowledge   37

chapter 4   Demand 62

chapter 5   Production and Cost 87

Part 2

Designing Organizational Architecture

chapter 9   Decision Rights: The Level of Empowerment   192

chapter 10   Decision Rights: Bundling Tasks into Jobs and Subunits   218

Part 3

Applications of Organizational Architecture

chapter 15 Vertical Integration and Outsourcing 350

chapter 18   Ethics and Organizational Architecture   435

Part I

Basic Concepts

chapter 1

Introduction*

CHAPTER OUTLINE

*Portions of this chapter were published in J. Brickley, C. Smith, and J. Zimmerman (1995), "The Economics of Organizational Architecture," *Journal of Applied Corporate Finance* 8:2, 19–31.

Francis Baring, with his brother John, established Barings Bank in London in 1762. Their bank prospered by facilitating international trade. Barings helped finance the British effort in the American Revolutionary War, and thereafter, Barings credit reopened trade with the United States. In 1803, Barings helped the United States finance the Louisiana Purchase and helped Britain finance its wars against Napoleon. In 1818, the bank's influence was such that Duc de Richelieu observed, "There are six great powers in Europe: England, France, Prussia, Austria, Russia, and Barings Brothers."

The bank almost failed in 1890 when loans that it had made in Argentina defaulted. But it survived with the help of a bailout engineered by the Bank of England. The family rebuilt the bank over the following decades. Although it never regained its former preeminence, Barings retained its reputation as a gilt-edged institution run largely by members of the family and owned primarily by a charitable foundation. In the first half of the 1990s, its influence expanded significantly, in part due to its substantial Far East securities business.

In late February 1995, Barings's board of directors met to review the 1994 results. The bank had a small rise in profits—a quite reasonable result in what had been a dreadful year for most of its competitors. One big contributor to those results had been a very profitable securities operation in Singapore. But that afternoon, things changed dramatically. The Singapore office trading star, Nick Leeson, unexpectedly walked out of the office and disappeared. As senior management examined the bank's records, it became clear that something was very wrong.

In principle, Leeson engaged in a simple operation—arbitraging security prices between the Osaka Stock Exchange and the Singapore International Monetary Exchange (SIMEX).[1] Leeson should have been able to lock in a virtually riskless profit by selling the security on the exchange with the higher price while simultaneously buying it on the exchange with the lower price. And although price differences are typically small, arbitraging in enough volume can produce a substantial profit. In this arbitrage business, although Barings might accumulate large positions on both exchanges, those securities it bought and those it sold should balance. The bank was supposed to face no net exposure to price changes.

Yet what management found as they reviewed the bank's records was that Leeson had bought securities in both markets. In effect, he had made an enormous bet that the security price would rise. But it had fallen, and now the solvency of the bank was threatened.

How could this have happened? It appears that Leeson circumvented the bank's internal controls. The Singapore branch was small, and Leeson had effective authority over both trading as well as the bank's back office systems (bookkeeping, clearing, and settlement). He used that power to conceal losses and disguise the true nature of his activities—and thus he was able to "cook the books." For example, he apparently told senior management that a number of his trades were on behalf of clients and not the bank. And the bank's internal control systems did not uncover the deceit.

By early March, the bank's aggregate losses totaled $1.4 billion. Leeson was arrested by German police at the Frankfurt Airport. Eventually Leeson was returned to Singapore where he was tried and sentenced to three years in prison. And Barings, Britain's oldest merchant bank, had been sold to ING (the large Dutch financial institution) for £1. Thus, Barings's owners had lost their entire investment.

---

[1]The specific securities Leeson traded were futures contracts on the Nikkei 225—the main Japanese stock market index.

The Barings collapse was ultimately caused by a poorly designed organization. As *The Wall Street Journal* noted:

> *What is emerging from the documents and from interviews with current and former Barings executives is a fatally flawed organization: one that ignored at least several warning signs going back not just weeks and months, but years; one that so wanted to ensure the continuation of profits from Singapore—which boosted bonuses—that it was reluctant to impose tight controls; one that had a deeply split staff, which ultimately may have contributed to its downfall.[2]*

Three general aspects of the bank's organization contributed to the failure: (1) the broad range of authority and responsibilities granted to Leeson; (2) aspects of the firm's compensation system; and (3) gaps in the bank's systems for evaluating, monitoring, and controlling its employees. Let's examine each in more detail.

First, Leeson had responsibility for both proprietary and customer trading as well as effective control of the settlement of trades in his unit. This broad assignment of decision-making authority created the opportunity to circumvent the bank's internal controls. As the *Financial Times* noted:

> *In Singapore, Mr. Leeson was in the process of settling transactions as well as initiating them. A watertight line between dealing and operational responsibility, crucial to internal control, was missing.[3]*

In reaction to the Barings collapse, SIMEX changed its rules to require that member firms ensure that proprietary traders not handle customer business and that the head of the dealing section not take charge of the settlement process.

Second, the bank's compensation system encouraged Leeson to speculate while providing senior managers with limited incentives to exercise tight control over their star trader. Barings traditionally had paid out approximately 50 percent of gross earnings as annual bonuses. Yet a system where managers participate in annual profits—but not in losses—can encourage excessive risk taking. This perverse incentive can be most pronounced when a small bet loses and the employee tries to make it up by doubling the bet. If this second bet also loses, there can be a strong incentive to double up again and "go for broke."

Third, Leeson compromised the firm's performance-evaluation system. He misrepresented trades for the bank as customer trades and hid losses. A better designed and executed monitoring system would have identified these problems long before the solvency of the institution was threatened.

Managerial Economics and Organizational Architecture

Standard managerial economics books address a number of questions that are important for organizational success:

- What markets will the firm enter?
- How differentiated will the firm's products be?
- What mix of inputs should the firm use in its production?

---

[2]M. Branchli, N. Bray, and M. Sesit (1995), "Barings PLC Officials May Have Been Aware of Trading Position," *The Wall Street Journal* (March 6), 1.

[3]"The Box that Can Never Be Shut," *Financial Times* (February 28, 1995), 17.

Changing Architecture Exposes Fraud

While Leeson's actions are unusual in that they resulted in the insolvency of his employer, others have engaged in similar deception. Toshihide Iguchi of Daiwa Bank's New York office, allegedly hid $1.1 billion of trading losses from more than 30,000 unauthorized trades in U.S. treasury securities over 11 years. Like Leeson, Iguchi had responsibility for both trading and back-office operations for the bank. Daiwa's decisions in 1993 to separate these operations and to bolster internal audits led to the uncovering of the fraud. In July 1995, Iguchi, then in charge only of settlements, wrote a letter to the bank's president confessing his misrepresentation. He noted it had become increasingly difficult to maintain the deceit. Thus, although Iguchi's unauthorized trading resulted in the loss of 10 percent of the total regulatory capital of one of Japan's largest banks, these problems were uncovered and stopped before the bank was ruined.

Source: J. Sapsford, M. Sesit, and T. O'Brien (1995), "Daiwa Bank Executive Is Charged in New York in $1.1 Billion Debacle," *The Wall Street Journal* (September 22), A2.

- How should the firm price its products?
- Who are the firm's competitors and how are they likely to respond to the firm's product offerings?

Addressing these questions is certainly important—and in this book, we do—yet this tale of Barings's untimely end suggests that this list is seriously incomplete. It is also important to address questions about the internal organization of the firm. A poorly designed organization can result in lost profits and even in the failure of the institution.

With the benefit of hindsight, it seems easy to identify elements of the Barings organization that if changed might have prevented this debacle. But the critical managerial question is whether one could reasonably have identified the potential problems before the fact and structured a more productive organization. Barings's management did not. We believe the answer to this fundamental managerial question is a resounding *yes*. To examine these issues, a rich framework that can be consistently applied is required.

We are not, of course, the first to recognize the importance of corporate organization or to offer advice on how to improve it. The business section of any good bookstore displays a virtually endless array of prescriptions: *Benchmarking, Empowerment, Total Quality Management, Reengineering, Outsourcing, Teaming, Corporate Culture, Venturing, Matrix Organizations, Just-In-Time Production, Downsizing.* The authors of all these books would strongly agree that the firm's organization and the associated policies chosen by management can have profound effects on performance and firm value. And they all buttress their recommendations with selected stories of firms that followed their advice and achieved fabulous successes.

The problem with such approaches, however, is that each tends to focus on a particular facet of the organization—whether it be quality control, or worker empowerment, or the compensation system—to the virtual exclusion of all others. As a consequence, the suggestions offered by the business press are often inconsistent. These publications tend to offer little guidance as to which tools are most appropriate in which circumstances. The implicit assumption of most is that their technique can be successfully adopted by all companies. This assumption, however, is usually wrong. Ultimately, this literature fails to provide managers with a productive framework for resolving organizational problems.

Organizational Architecture

In contrast to the approach of most business best-sellers, we seek to provide a systematic framework for addressing such issues, one that can be applied consistently in analyzing organizational problems and structuring more effective organizations. In this book, we offer a framework that identifies three critical aspects of corporate organization: (1) the assignment of decision rights within the company; (2) the methods of rewarding individuals; and (3) the structure of systems to evaluate the performance of both individuals and business units. (Not coincidentally, these are the same three aspects of the organization we identified in the Barings case.)

We introduce the term *organizational architecture* to refer specifically to these three key aspects of the firm. We hesitate to simply use "organization" to refer to these three corporate features because common usage of that term refers only to the hierarchical structure—that is, decision-right assignments and reporting relationships—while it generally ignores the performance-evaluation and reward systems. We thus use organizational architecture to help focus attention on all three of these key aspects of the organization.

Stated as briefly as possible, our argument is that successful firms assign decision rights in ways that effectively link decision-making authority with the relevant information for making good decisions. When assigning decision rights, however, senior management must also ensure that the company's reward and performance-evaluation systems provide decision makers with appropriate incentives to make value-increasing decisions.

Depending on the firm's specific circumstances, it will assign decision-making authority differently (some will decentralize particular decisions but centralize others) and will tailor its reward and performance-evaluation systems. Even though no two firms might adopt precisely the same architecture, successful firms ensure that the three critical aspects of organizational architecture are coordinated.

Our approach is integrative in the sense that it draws on a number of disciplines: accounting, finance, information management, marketing, management, operations, political science, and strategy. But what also distinguishes this approach most clearly from that of the best-sellers is its central reliance on the basic principles of economics.

Economic Analysis

Economics has long been applied to questions of pricing policy—for example, "How would raising the price of the firm's products affect sales and firm value?" This book addresses standard managerial-economics questions involving pricing, advertising, scale, and the choice of inputs to employ in production. In addition, we apply these same tools to examine questions of organizational architecture. For example, "How would changing a division from a cost center to a profit center change employee decisions and impact firm value?"

In essence, economics provides a theory of how individuals make choices. For example, in designing organizations, one must always keep in mind that individuals respond to incentives. Managers and employees can be incredibly resourceful in devising methods to exploit the opportunities they face. This also means, however, that when their incentives are structured improperly, they can act in ways that reduce firm value. In choosing corporate policies, it is critical that managers anticipate potential responses by customers, suppliers, or employees that might produce undesirable outcomes. Failure to do so invites individuals to "game" the system and can result in the complete failure of well-intentioned policies.

R&D and Executive Turnover

Suppose a firm links the CEO's bonus to earnings and the CEO will be retiring in two years. The CEO might reduce the firm's research and development budget to boost earnings this year and next. Five years down the road, earnings will suffer with no new products coming on stream. By then, however, this CEO will be long gone. In fact, research suggests that this can be a problem for some R&D-intensive firms.

Source: P. Dechow and R. Sloan (1991), "Executive Incentives and the Horizon Problem," *Journal of Accounting and Economics* 14, 51–89.

We use economics to examine how managers can design organizations to motivate individuals to make choices that enhance firm value. For example, the evidence suggests that the problem of chief executive officers (CEOs) slashing R&D budgets prior to their retirement is not widespread.[4] The research suggests that these perverse incentives can apparently be controlled by basing the CEO's incentive compensation on stock prices and by managing CEO succession so that decision rights are gradually transferred to the successor over the years prior to the final departure.

Traditional economic analysis generally characterized the firm simply as a "black box" that transforms inputs (labor, capital, and raw materials) into outputs. Little consideration was given to the internal architecture of the firm.[5] In recent years, economists have focused more on questions of organizational architecture.[6] But there has been little effort devoted to synthesizing the material in an accessible form that emphasizes the managerial implications of the analysis. We apply the basic tools of economics to examine the likely effect on firm value of decisions such as centralization versus decentralization, the bundling of tasks into specific jobs and jobs into business units within the firm, the use of objective versus subjective performance measures, compensating employees through fixed versus variable (or "incentive") compensation, and retaining activities within the firm versus outsourcing. In sum, we examine how managers can structure organizational architecture to motivate individuals to make choices that increase firm value.

In this analysis, ideas of equilibrium—the interplay of supply and demand in product, labor, and capital markets—represent important constraints on managerial decisions. Understanding how prices and quantities change in response to changes in costs, product characteristics, or the terms of sale is a critical managerial skill. For example, 1990 increases

[4]K. Murphy and J. Zimmerman (1993), "Financial Performance Surrounding CEO Turnover," *Journal of Accounting and Economics* 16, 273–315.

[5]Of course, there are several notable exceptions: F. Knight (1921), *Risk, Uncertainty, and Profit* (London School of Economics: London); R. Coase (1937), "The Nature of the Firm," *Economica* 4, 386–405; and F. Hayek (1945), "The Use of Knowledge in Society," *American Economic Review* 35, 519–530.

[6]For example, R. Coase (1960), "The Problem of Social Cost," *Journal of Law and Economics* 3, 1–44; S. Cheung (1969), "Transaction Costs, Risk Aversion, and the Choice of Contractual Arrangements," *Journal of Law and Economics* 12, 23–42; A. Alchian and H. Demsetz (1972), "Production, Information Costs, and Economic Organization," *American Economic Review* 62, 777–795; K. Arrow (1974), *The Limits of Organization* (W. W. Norton: New York); M. Jensen and W. Meckling (1976), "Theory of the Firm: Managerial Behavior, Agency Costs and Ownership Structure," *Journal of Financial Economics* 3, 305–360; Y. Barzel (1982), "Measurement Costs and the Organization of Markets," *Journal of Law and Economics* 25, 27–48; O. Williamson (1985), *The Economic Institutions of Capitalism: Firms, Markets, Rational Contracting* (Free Press: New York); and B. Holmstrom and J. Tirole (1989), "The Theory of the Firm," in R. Schmalensee and R. Willig, eds., *Handbook of Industrial Economics* (North-Holland: New York).

in petroleum prices accompanying the Gulf War prompted oil companies to increase production, encouraged petrochemical companies to alter their input mix to economize on a now more expensive input, made salespeople reevaluate their decisions about contacting potential customers by phone rather than in person, and encouraged auto producers to focus more on gas economy in the design of new models. Yet these incentives to change depend on the structure of the organization. For instance, a salesperson is less likely to switch to greater reliance on telephone and mail if the firm reimburses all selling expenses than if salespeople are responsible for the costs of contacting potential customers.

Economic Darwinism

Survival of the Fittest[7]

The collapse of Barings, Charles Darwin might have noted, is an example of how competition tends to weed out the less fit. As described in *The Origin of the Species,* natural history illustrates the principle of "survival of the fittest." In industry, we see *economic Darwinism* in operation as competition weeds out ill-designed organizations that fail to adapt. Competition in the marketplace provides strong pressures for efficient decisions—including organizational decisions. Competition among firms dictates that only those firms with low costs survive. If firms adopt inefficient, high-cost policies—including their organizational architecture—competition will place strong pressures on these firms to either adapt or close.

Fama and Jensen suggest that "the form of organization that survives in an activity is the one that delivers the product demanded by customers at the lowest price while covering costs." This survival criterion helps highlight that while a well-crafted organizational architecture can contribute to a firm's success, it is not sufficient for success. The firm must have a business strategy that includes products for which the prices customers are willing to pay exceed costs. The potential for value creation by a company that only manufactures buggy whips is quite limited no matter how well structured the firm's organizational architecture.

Nevertheless, given a firm's business strategy and product mix, its choice of organizational architecture can have an important impact on profitability and value. An appropriate architecture can lower costs by promoting efficient production; it also can raise the prices customers are willing to pay by helping to assure high-quality production, reliable delivery, and responsive service.

Economic Darwinism and Benchmarking

In the biological systems that Darwin analyzed, the major forces at work were random mutations in organisms and shocks to the external environment (for instance, from changes in weather). But in the economic systems on which we focus, purposeful voluntary changes—like GM copying Chrysler—occur. In fact, this practice has been formalized in the process of *benchmarking.* Benchmarking generally means looking for those

---

[7]This section draws on the analysis in A. Alchian (1950), "Uncertainty, Evolution, and Economic Theory," *Journal of Political Economy* 58, 211–221; G. Stigler (1951), "The Economics of Scale," *Journal of Law and Economics* 1, 54–71; and E. Fama and M. Jensen (1983), "Separation of Ownership and Control," *Journal of Law and Economics* 26, 301–325.

Economic Darwinism: General Motors and Chrysler

In the U.S. auto industry at the beginning of 1994, two different organizational architectures compete in new model development. General Motors places strong emphasis on functional specialties. GM has established small teams that consist of experts from the same functional field. Each team is charged with a particular assignment that relates to its area of specialization. For example, one team might have the primary responsibility for the design of the body of the vehicle while another team might be charged with developing the drive train. These teams work simultaneously on their specific tasks. Some of the individuals on these teams also serve on additional cross-functional teams that are charged with coordinating the development process across the functional areas.

In contrast to GM, Chrysler Corporation places nearly all decisions about the development of a new vehicle in the hands of a single cross-functional product team. Chrysler's platform teams include engineers, designers, financial analysts, marketing experts, and manufacturing people who all report to a single project leader. This leader has authority over each of the team members and their work.

General Motors's CEO, Jack Smith, attributed important differences in the operation of Chrysler and GM to these differences in organization. Chrysler took three years to bring the new Viper to market; GM regularly takes more than five. And at the bottom line—Chrysler earned about $7 for every $100 in sales for 1994; GM earned 70 cents.

GM and Chrysler offer but two illustrations of how firms differ when they make fundamental decisions about the organization of their activities. Fortunately, for firms like GM, this decision-making process is ongoing. In 1995, GM reorganized its product development process along lines that more closely resembles the Chrysler model. Thus, economic Darwinism is a major force at work in industries around the globe.

Source: A. Stertz (1992), "Detroit's New Strategy to Beat Back Japanese Is to Copy Their Ideas," *The Wall Street Journal* (October 1).

companies that are doing something best and learning how they do it in order to emulate them. But this process also occurs in less formal ways. As Alchian argued, "Whenever successful enterprises are observed the elements common to those observed successes will be associated with success and copied by others in their pursuit of profits or success."[8] For example, if the cover article in the next *Fortune* reports an innovative inventory control system at Toyota, managers across the country—indeed, around the globe—will see it and ask, *Would that work in my company too?* Undoubtedly, the managers with the strongest interest in trying it will be those in firms with current inventory problems.[9] Some will achieve success, but others may experience disastrous results caused by unintended though largely predictable organizational 'side effects' (like Leeson's unchecked incentive for risk taking).

Although competition tends to produce efficiently organized firms over the longer run, uncritical experimentation with the organizational innovation *du jour* can expose the firm to an uncomfortably high risk of failure. Successful organizations are not just a collection of "good ideas." The elements of a successful organization must be carefully coordinated—the different elements of the firm's architecture must be structured to work together to achieve the firm's goals. For this reason, it is important to be able to analyze the likely consequences of a contemplated organizational change and forecast its impact on the entire firm.

[8]Alchian (1950), 218.

[9]This raises the question of why any firm with an innovative idea would voluntarily disclose it. Perhaps the free publicity outweighs the lost competitive advantage.

This concept of economic Darwinism thus has important managerial implications. First, existing architectures are not random; there are sound economic explanations for the dominant organization of firms in most industries. Second, surviving architectures at any point in time are optimal in a *relative* rather than an *absolute* sense; that is, they are best among the competition, not necessarily the best possible. These two observations together suggest that, although improvements in architecture are certainly always possible, a manager should not be too quick to condemn the prevailing organization without careful analysis. Before undertaking major organizational changes, senior managers should therefore have a good understanding of how the firm arrived at its existing architecture and, more generally, why particular types of organizations work well in particular settings.

Purpose of the Book

The primary purpose of this book is to provide a solid conceptual framework for analyzing organizational problems and structuring a more effective organizational architecture. The book also provides basic material on managerial economics and discusses how it can be used for making operational decisions—for example, input, output, and pricing decisions. This material additionally supplies a set of tools and an understanding of markets that is important for making good organizational decisions.

Our Approach to Organizations

We begin with two basic notions: People act in their own self-interest, and information is often asymmetric—individuals do not all share the same information. As we have indicated, this framework suggests that the three critical elements of organizational architecture are the assignment of decision rights, the reward system, and the performance-evaluation system. Successful organizations assign decision rights in a manner that effectively links decision-making authority with the relevant information to make good decisions. Correspondingly, successful organizations develop reward and performance-evaluation systems that provide self-interested decision makers with appropriate incentives to make decisions that increase the values of their organizations.

It is also important to note that modern organizations are very complex, and developing an understanding of how people within them behave is difficult. As in any book that addresses this set of topics, we face difficult tradeoffs between adding more institutional richness to embrace more real world reality versus omitting details to keep the analysis more focused and manageable. At certain points (especially where little prior formal analysis of the problem exists), we take quite complex problems and discuss them in terms of simplified examples. Nonetheless, we believe that in these cases, we can provide important managerial insights to these topics through the admittedly simple examples.

Finally, we believe that a powerful feature of this economic framework is that it can be readily extended to incorporate many other managerial policies such as finance, accounting, information systems, operations, and marketing policies. In this sense, the book can play an important integrating role across the entire business curriculum. This type of integration is becoming increasingly important with the expanded use of cross-functional teams.

Overview of the Book

The book is organized as follows.

Part 1: Basic Concepts lays the groundwork for the book. Chapter 2 summarizes the economic view of behavior, stressing management implications. Chapter 3 presents an overview of markets, provides a rationale for the existence of organizations, and stresses the critical role of the distribution of knowledge within the organization. Chapters 4 through 6 cover the traditional managerial-economics topics of demand, production and cost, and market structure. These three chapters provide the reader with a fundamental set of microeconomic tools and use these tools to analyze basic operational policies such as input, output, and product-pricing decisions. These chapters also provide important background material for the subsequent chapters on organizations—a good understanding of the market environment is important for making sound organizational decisions.[10] Chapter 7 examines conflicts of interest that exist within firms and how contracts can be structured to reduce or control these conflicts.

Part 2: Designing Organizational Architecture develops the core framework of the book. Chapter 8 provides a basic overview of the organizational-design problem. Chapters 9 and 10 focus on two aspects of the assignment of decision rights within the firm—the level of decentralization chosen for various decisions, and the bundling of various tasks into jobs and then jobs into subunits. Chapters 11 and 12 examine compensation policy. First we focus on the level of compensation necessary to attract and retain an appropriate group of employees. Then we discuss the composition of the compensation package, focusing on how the mix of salary, fringe benefits, and incentive compensation affects the value of the firm. In Chapters 13 and 14, we analyze individual and divisional performance evaluation.

Part 3: Applications of Organizational Architecture uses the framework that we have developed to provide insights into contemporary management issues. Chapters 15 through 18 discuss outsourcing, leadership, total quality management, reengineering, and ethics.

Suggested Readings

A. Alchian (1950), "Uncertainty, Evolution, and Economic Theory," *Journal of Political Economy* 58, 211–221.

M. Jensen (1983), "Organization Theory and Methodology," *The Accounting Review* 58, 319–339.

M. Jensen and W. Meckling (1992), "Specific and General Knowledge, and Organizational Structure," *Journal of Applied Corporate Finance* 8:2, 4–18.

---

[10]Chapters 2 and 3 should be read by all. A reader familiar with microeconomics can proceed directly to Chapter 7 to focus on organizational issues. (Such a reader, however, might find the material in Chapters 4 to 6 a helpful review.) Others should read Chapters 4 to 6 before proceeding to the material on organizations.

Review Questions

1–1. What are the three aspects of *organizational architecture?*

1–2. Xerox has developed an expert system to assist employees who answer the company service center's 800 number to help callers who have problems with their photocopy machines. The system is designed to lead the employee through a set of questions to diagnose and fix the problem. If the machine operator cannot fix the problem with the assistance of the input from the service center employee, a service representative is dispatched to make a service call. This expert system is designed to evolve more effective prompts as experience accumulates. This will be accomplished by having service representatives call the service center after a service call. The nature of the problem and the actions taken are to be entered into the system. Xerox bases pay for the individuals who answer the 800 number on the number of service calls they handle; it bases compensation for service representatives on the number of service calls they make. What incentives does this create?

1–3. Briefly describe *economic Darwinism.*

1–4. *The Wall Street Journal*[11] reports:

> *Franchisees, who pay fees and royalties in exchange for using franchisers' business formats, have become much more militant in recent years about what they see as mistreatment by franchisers. In general, Ms. Kezios is seeking federal and state laws to give franchisees more power in franchise arrangements. Among her goals: creating legally protected exclusive territories for franchisees.*

How would you expect existing franchisees to react to this proposed regulation? How would you expect a potential new franchisee to react to this proposed regulation?

1–5. In the process of benchmarking, a colleague of yours notes that Lincoln Electric, a producer of electric arc welders, has much higher productivity than does your company. Unlike your firm, Lincoln has an extensive piece-rate compensation system; much of its employees' total compensation is simply the number of units produced times the piece rate for that type unit. Your colleague recommends that our company adopt a piece-rate compensation system to boost productivity. What do you advise?

1–6. In the life insurance industry, we see two major ownership structures—common stock insurers and mutual insurers. In the common stock companies, the owners—its stockholders—are a separate group from its customers—the policyholders. In a mutual, the policyholders are also the owners of the company. It has been argued that mutual insurance companies are dinosaurs—they are large, slow, bureaucratic, and inefficient. How would you respond to such an argument?

---

[11]J. A. Tannenbaum (1995), "Activist Fights for the Rights of Franchisees," *The Wall Street Journal* (May 22).

chapter 2

The Economist's View of Behavior

I n June 1992, the state of California filed charges alleging that Sears Auto Centers were overcharging customers an average of $230 for unneeded or undone repairs. These charges were followed by similar allegations by the state of New Jersey. Ultimately, Sears admitted that "some mistakes did occur" and agreed to a settlement for an amount up to $20 million. Sears maintained that its senior management had been unaware of the problem and neither condoned nor encouraged defrauding customers. This auto-repair scandal imposed significant costs on Sears. As the complaints became public, the price of Sears stock declined by about 6 percent, while sales at the auto centers declined significantly.

To limit these costs, it was important for Sears's management to act quickly to address the problem. As a first step, management had to decide what motivated employees to recommend unneeded repairs. Only then could management choose a policy to redress the situation. If management thought the problem was caused by a few dishonest employees, the likely response would have been to try to identify and fire these employees. If, instead, management thought the problem was caused by unhappy workers taking out their frustrations on customers, a potential response would have been to adopt a job-enrichment program to increase worker satisfaction and, it would be hoped, customer service. Many alternate assumptions and responses are possible.

The example of Sears illustrates a general point. Managers' responses to problems are likely to depend on their forecast of people's reactions—on their underlying model of behavior. Most managerial actions involve trying to affect the behavior of individuals such as employees, customers, union officials, and subcontractors. Managers with different understandings (or models) of what motivates behavior are likely to take different actions and make different decisions.

We begin this chapter by briefly summarizing the general framework economists use to examine individual behavior. Some graphical tools are introduced to aid our analysis. Next, we use this economic framework to analyze the problem at Sears Auto Centers. The managerial implications of this analysis are discussed. We contrast the economic view of behavior with alternative views and discuss why the economic framework is particularly useful in managerial decision making. Finally, we discuss decision making under uncertainty.

Economic Behavior: An Overview

Unlimited Wants and Limited Resources

Individuals have unlimited wants. People generally want more money, better houses, cars, clothing, and other personal material items. Many people also want to improve the plight of the less fortunate—starving children and the homeless. People are concerned about religion, mortality, and gaining the respect and love of others.

In contrast to wants, resources are limited. Households face limited incomes that preclude all the purchases and expenditures that individuals in the households would like to make. There are a finite number of trees and fixed amounts of land and other natural resources. There are only 24 hours in the day. People do not live forever.

Economic Choice

Economic analysis is based on the notion that individuals assign priorities to their wants and choose the most preferred options available. If Kathy Jones is confronted with a choice between a laptop or a desktop computer, she can tell you whether she prefers one to the other or is indifferent between the two. She correspondingly purchases the preferred alternative. If Kathy has a $400 per week budget, she considers the many ways to spend the money and then chooses the package of goods and services that maximizes her personal happiness. She cannot make all desired purchases on a limited budget. However, the choice is personally optimal given her limited resources.

Economists do not assert that people are selfish in the sense that they care only about their own personal wealth. Within the economic paradigm, people can also care about such things as charity, family, religion, and society. For instance, Kathy might donate $100 to a church, if the donation brings her greater happiness than alternative uses of the money.

Economists also do not contend that individuals are supercomputers that make infallible decisions. Individuals are not endowed with perfect knowledge and foresight, nor is additional information costless to acquire and process.[1] For example, Kathy might order an item from a restaurant menu only to find that she does not like what she ordered. Within the economic paradigm, she does the best she can in the face of imperfect knowledge; she learns from her experience and does not repeat the same mistakes in judgment time after time.

Marginal Analysis

Marginal costs and benefits are the incremental costs and benefits that are associated with making a decision.[2] It is the marginal costs and benefits that are important in economic decision making. An action should be taken when the marginal benefits of the action exceed the marginal costs. Mary Winters has a contract to help sell products for an office supply company. She is paid $50 for every sales call that she makes to customers. Thus, Mary's marginal benefit for making each extra sales call is $50. Mary enjoys playing tennis more than selling. If she places a marginal value of more than $50 on the tennis that she would forgo by making an extra call, she should not make any more sales calls—the marginal costs are more than the marginal benefits. She should make additional sales calls if the reduction in tennis playing is valued at less than $50.

Marginal analysis is a cornerstone of modern economic analysis. In economic decision making, "bygones are forever bygones." Costs and benefits that have already been incurred are *sunk* (assuming they are nonrecoverable) and hence are irrelevant to the current economic decision. Mary paid $5,000 to join a tennis club five years ago. This cost does not affect her current decision of whether to make an extra sales call or play tennis. That expenditure is past history and does not affect Mary's current trade offs.

---

[1]Economists sometimes use the idea of *bounded rationality*. Under this concept, individuals act in a purposeful and *intendedly rational* manner. However, they have cognitive limitations in storing, processing, and communicating information. It is these limitations that make the question of how to organize economic activity particularly interesting. H. Simon (1957), *Models of Man* (John Wiley & Sons: New York).

[2]For the technically inclined: *Marginal* costs and benefits are typically defined as changes in costs and benefits associated with very *small changes* in a decision variable. For instance, the marginal costs of production are the additional costs from producing an additional small quantity of the product (for instance, one more unit). Often decisions involve discrete choices, such as whether or not to build a new plant. In these cases, it is not possible to define a small change in the decision variable. *Incremental* costs and benefits are those costs and benefits that vary with such a decision. For our present discussion, the technical distinction between marginal and incremental is not important.

Marginal Analysis: An Example

Ludger Langer owns a company that installs wood floors. He is offered $20,000 to install a new floor. The opportunity cost of his labor and other operating expenses (excluding the wood) are $15,000. He has the wood for the job in inventory. It originally cost him $6,000. Price declines have reduced the market value of the wood to $2,000, and this value is not expected to change in the near future. Should he accept the contract?

He should compare the marginal costs and benefits from the project. The marginal benefit is $20,000. The marginal cost is $17,000—$15,000 for the labor and operating expenses and $2,000 for the wood. The historic cost for the wood of $6,000 is not relevant to the decision. He can replace the wood used for the job for $2,000. The $4,000 drop in the value of the inventory is a sunk cost that is irrelevant to the decision (ignoring the tax considerations). Since the marginal benefits exceed the marginal costs, he would be better off accepting the contract than rejecting it. This example illustrates that in calculating marginal costs, it is important to use the opportunity cost of the incremental resources, not the historic cost.

Opportunity Costs

Since resources are constrained, individuals are faced with *tradeoffs*. Using limited resources for one purpose precludes their use for something else. For example, if Larry Matteson uses four hours to play golf, he cannot use the same four hours to paint his house. The *opportunity cost* of using a resource for a given purpose is its value in its best alternative use. The opportunity cost of using four hours to play golf is the value of using the four hours in the next best alternative use.

Marginal analysis frequently involves a careful consideration of the relevant opportunity costs. If Larry starts a new pizza parlor and hires a manager at $30,000 per year, the $30,000 is an *explicit* cost (a direct dollar expenditure). Is he better off managing the restaurant himself, since he can avoid the explicit cost of $30,000 by not paying himself a salary? The answer to this question depends (at least in part) on the opportunity cost of his time. If he can earn exactly $30,000 in his best alternative job, the *implicit* cost of self-management is the same as the explicit cost of hiring an outside manager—he forgoes $30,000 worth of income if he manages the parlor himself. Both explicit and implicit costs are opportunity costs that should be considered in the analysis. Suppose that Larry's gross profit from the pizza parlor, before paying the manager a salary, is $35,000, and that he can earn $40,000 in an outside job. Hiring a manager for $30,000 yields a net profit of $5,000 from the pizza parlor. He also earns $40,000 from the outside job, for total earnings of $45,000. If he manages the pizza parlor himself, he earns only $35,000. In this example, it is better for him to work at the outside job and hire a manager to run the restaurant.

Opportunity Costs and V-8

The Campbell Soup Company used the idea of an opportunity cost to create a successful ad campaign for its V-8 vegetable juice. Upon finishing a soft drink, the fellow in the ad would slap his forehead and exclaim, "Wow—I coulda had a V-8." Since one is unlikely to drink both a soft drink and a V-8, the opportunity cost of the soft drink is the foregone V-8—a cost that the commercials sought to convince the audience is quite high.

The Economic Framework and Criminal Behavior

Criminals are often considered to be psychologically disturbed. Evidence, however, suggests that criminal behavior can be explained, at least in part, by the economic framework. This framework predicts that a criminal will consider the marginal costs and benefits of a crime and will commit the crime only when the benefits exceed the costs. Under this view, increasing the likelihood of detection and/or the severity of punishment will reduce crimes. In a pioneering study, Ehrlich (1973) examined whether the incidence of major felonies varied across states with the expected punishment. He found that the incidence of robberies decreased about 1.3 percent in response to each 1 percent increase in the proportionate likelihood of punishment. The incidence of crime also decreased with the severity of the punishment. Since Ehrlich's study, scholars have conducted extensive research on this topic. In general, the results support the conclusion that the economic model is useful in predicting criminal activity.

Source: I. Ehrlich (1973), "Participation in Illegitimate Activities: A Theoretical and Empirical Investigation," *Journal of Political Economy* 81:3, 521–565.

Creative Nature of Individuals[3]

In the economic framework, individuals maximize their personal happiness given resource constraints. Indeed, people are quite creative and resourceful in minimizing the effects of constraints. Consider the government's imposition of the 55-mile-per-hour speed limit. This regulation constrained drivers by increasing the fines for fast driving. Individuals responded by developing radar detectors and other technology that allowed drivers to reduce the likelihood of getting caught and receiving fines. This technology reduced the effect of the legal constraint. Similarly, when the government increases tax rates, almost immediately accountants and financial planners begin developing clever ways to reduce the impact of the new taxes. Some self-employed individuals were able to reduce the impact of recent tax increases by changing the status of their incorporation. The creative nature of individuals has important managerial implications, which we discuss later in this chapter.

Creative Responses to a Poorly Designed Incentive System

A manager at a software company wanted to find and fix software bugs more quickly. He devised an incentive plan that paid $20 for each bug the Quality Assurance people found and $20 for each bug the programmers fixed. Since the programmers that created the bugs were also in charge of fixing them, they responded to the plan by creating many more bugs in software programs. This action increased the payoffs under the plan, since there were more bugs to detect and fix. The plan was canceled in only one week after one employee netted $1,700 under the new program.

Source: S. Adams (1995), "Manager's Journal: The Dilbert Principle," *The Wall Street Journal* (May 22).

[3]This section draws on the analysis in M. Jensen and W. Meckling (1994), "The Nature of Man," *Journal of Applied Corporate Finance* 7, 4–19.

Graphical Tools

Economists often use a set of graphical tools to illustrate how individuals make choices. We use these tools throughout this book. They also are used in other courses in the typical business school curriculum, such as in finance, labor economics, and marketing courses. (Our intent is to introduce these tools so that the reader is comfortable in using them in simple applications; we avoid discussion of the more technical considerations that underlie their development.) We subsequently use the tools to analyze the problems at Sears Auto Centers.

Individual Objectives

Goods are things that people value. Goods include standard products like food and clothing, services like haircuts and education, as well as less tangible emotions such as love of family and charity. The economic model of behavior posits that people purchase goods that maximize their personal happiness, given their resource constraints (such as a limited income). Economists use the term *utility* in referring to personal happiness.

To provide a more detailed analysis of how people make choices, economists represent an individual's preferences by a *utility function.* This function expresses the relation between total utility and the level of goods consumed. The individual's objective is to maximize this function, given the resource constraints.[4] The concept can be illustrated most conveniently through the simple example, where the individual cares about only two goods. The insights from the two-good analysis can be extended readily to the case of additional goods such as food, housing, clothing, respect, and charity.

Suppose that Terry Rasmussen only values food and clothing. In general form, his utility function can be written as follows:

$$\text{Utility} = f(\overset{+}{\text{food}}, \overset{+}{\text{clothing}}) \qquad (2.1)$$

Terry prefers more of each good—thus, his utility rises with both food and clothing. In Terry's case, his specific utility function is:

$$\text{Utility} = \text{Food}^{1/2} \times \text{Clothing}^{1/2} \qquad (2.2)$$

For instance, if Terry has 16 units of food and 25 units of clothing, his total utility is 20 (Utility = $16^{1/2} \times 25^{1/2}$ = 4 × 5 = 20). Terry is better off with 25 units of both food and clothing. Here, his utility is 25 (Utility = $25^{1/2} \times 25^{1/2}$ = 5 × 5 = 25).

Utility functions rank alternative bundles of food and clothing in the *order* of most preferred to least preferred, but they do not indicate how much one bundle is preferred to another. If the utility index is 100 for one combination of food and clothing and 200 for another, Terry will prefer the second combination. The second bundle does not necessarily make him twice as well off as the first bundle. This formulation does not allow one person's utility of a bundle to be compared to another person's utility.

[4]Clearly, most individuals do not actually consider maximizing a mathematical function when they make consumption choices. However, this formulation can provide useful insights into actual behavior to the extent that it *approximates* how individuals make choices. Mathematicians have shown that if an individual's behavior is consistent with some basic "axioms of choice" (comparability, transitivity, nonsatiation, and willingness to substitute), the individual will make choices *as if* he or she were trying to maximize some utility function.

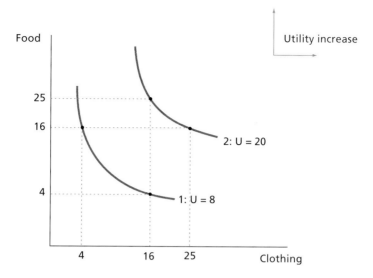

Figure 2.1   Indifference Curves

These indifference curves picture all combinations of food and clothing that yield the same amount of utility. The specific utility function in this example is $U = F^{1/2} \times C^{1/2}$, where F is food and C is clothing. Northeast movements are utility increasing. Indifference curve 2 represents all combinations of food and clothing that yield 20 units of utility, while 1 pictures all combinations that yield 8 units of utility. Other indifference curves could be drawn for different levels of utility.

Indifference Curves

Preferences implied by the utility function can be illustrated graphically through *indifference curves.* An indifference curve pictures all the combinations of goods that yield the same utility. Given his utility function in equation 2.2, Terry is indifferent between either 16 units of food and 25 units of clothing or 25 units of food and 16 units of clothing. Both combinations yield 20 units of utility, and are on the same indifference curve. Figure 2.1 shows two of Terry's indifference curves. Terry is indifferent between the combinations of food and clothing along a given curve. For example, if given a choice between any two points on curve 1, Terry would say that he does not care which one is selected. In either case, he would obtain 8 units of utility.

The slope at any point along one of Terry's indifference curves indicates how much food he would be *willing to give up* for a small increase in clothing (his utility remains unchanged by this exchange).[5] Standard indifference curves have negative slopes. If Terry obtains a smaller amount of food, the only way he can be equally as well off is to obtain more clothing. If the slope at a point along an indifference curve is -2, Terry is willing to

[5]Recall that the slope of a line is a measure of steepness, defined as the increase or decrease in height per unit of distance along the horizontal axis. Slopes of curves are typically found geometrically by drawing a line tangent to the curve at the point of interest and determining the slope of this tangent line. The slope at a point along one of Terry's indifference curves indicates how the quantity of food changes for small changes in the amount of clothing in order to hold utility constant. Since Terry is by definition indifferent to this exchange (he remains on the same indifferent curve), he is *willing* to make the exchange.

give up two units of food to obtain one unit of clothing. Alternatively he is willing to give up one-half unit of clothing to obtain one unit of food. This *willingness to substitute* has important implications, which we discuss below.

North and east movements in graphs like Figure 2.1 are utility increasing. Holding the amount of food constant, utility increases by increasing clothing (an eastward movement). Holding the amount of clothing constant, utility increases by increasing the amount of food (a northward movement). Thus, in Figure 2.1, Terry would rather be on indifference curve 2 than 1. He obtains 20 units of utility rather than 8.

Economists typically picture indifference curves as convex to the origin (they bow in, as in Figure 2.1). Convexity implies that if Terry has a relatively large amount of food, he would exchange a relatively large quantity of food for a small amount of additional clothing. Thus, the indifference curves in Figure 2.1 are steep when the level of food is high relative to the level of clothing. In contrast, if he has a relatively large amount of clothing, he would be willing to substitute only a small amount of food for additional clothing. Correspondingly, the indifference curves in Figure 2.1 flatten as Terry has less food and more clothing. The behavior implied by the convexity of indifference curves is consistent with the observed behavior of many individuals—most people purchase a balanced combination of food and clothing.

Constraints

Terry would like to have large quantities of both food and clothing. Unfortunately, he faces a budget constraint that limits his purchases. Suppose that he has an income of I, and the prices per unit of food and clothing are P_f and P_c, respectively. Since he cannot spend more than I, he faces the following constraint:

$$I \geq P_f F + P_c C \tag{2.3}$$

where F and C represent the units of food and clothing purchased. The constraint indicates that only combinations of food and clothing that cost less than I are feasible. Rearranging terms, this constraint can be written as:

$$F \leq I/P_f - (P_c/P_f)C \tag{2.4}$$

Figure 2.2 pictures this constraint—sometimes called a *budget line*. All combinations of food and clothing on or below the line are possible. Combinations above the line are not possible given income of I. The F-intercept (on the vertical axis) of the line, I/P_f, indicates how much food Terry can purchase if his entire income is spent on food and no clothing is purchased. The C-intercept is correspondingly I/P_c. The slope of the line $(-P_c/P_f)$ is -1 times the ratio of the two prices. We refer to the ratio, P_c/P_f, as the *relative price* of clothing. It represents how many units of food must be given up to acquire a unit of clothing (the opportunity cost of clothing). For example, if the price of clothing is \$8 and the price of food is \$2, the relative price of clothing is 4. To keep total expenditures constant, four units of food must be given up for every unit of clothing purchased. The relative price of food is P_f/P_c (in this example, 0.25). One quarter unit of clothing must be given up for each unit of food purchased.

The constraint changes with changes in Terry's income and the relative prices of the two goods. As shown in Figure 2.3, changes in income result in parallel shifts of the constraint—the slope is not affected. An increase in income shifts the constraint outward (to the right), while a decrease in income shifts the constraint inward. The slope

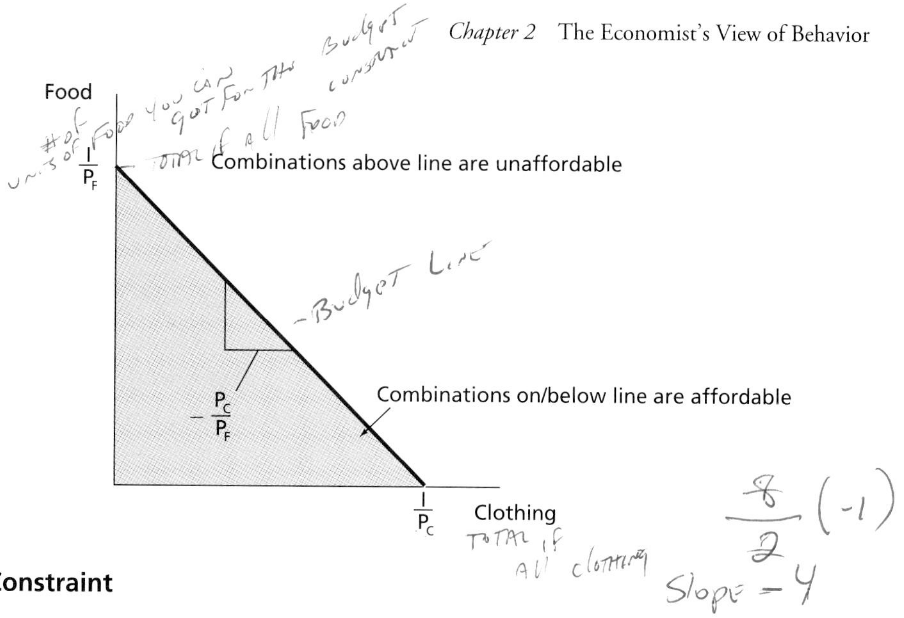

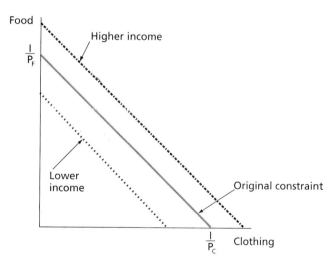

Handwritten annotations: # of Food you can got for the Budget consumed — Total of all Food — Budget Line — Total if all clothing — Slope = 4 — $\frac{8}{2}(-1)$

Figure 2.2   Constraint

The constraint reflects the feasible combinations of food and clothing that are available given the person's income (I). The vertical and horizontal intercepts, respectively, show the amounts of food and clothing that can be purchased if no income is spent on the other good. The slope of the constraint is equal to −1 times the ratio of the prices of the two goods. For instance, if the price of clothing is $8 and the price of food is $2, the slope will be −4. This slope implies that four units of food must be given up for one unit of clothing. If both goods are priced the same, the slope will be −1.

Figure 2.3   Income Changes

This figure shows that there is a parallel shift in the constraint when income changes. The slope of the constraint does not change because there is no change in the prices of the two goods. The slope is −1 times the ratio of the prices.

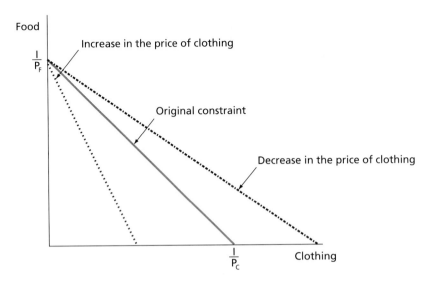

Figure 2.4   Price Changes

This figure shows how the slope of the constraint changes with changes in the price of clothing. The slope of the line is $-(P_C/P_f)$. Thus, an increase in the price of clothing produces a steeper line, while a decrease produces a flatter line. Changes in the price of food also affect the slope of the line.

of the constraint changes with the relative prices of the two goods. As shown in Figure 2.4, if the price of clothing increases relative to the price of food, the constraint becomes steeper. If the price of clothing falls relative to the price of food, the constraint becomes flatter.

Individual Choice

Within this economic framework, Terry's goal is to maximize utility given the constraint. Utility is maximized at the point of tangency between the constraint and an indifference curve.[6] Figure 2.5 portrays the optimal choice. Terry could choose points like A and B on indifference curve 1. However, point A on curve 2 is preferred. Terry would prefer to be at any point on curve 3. These points are not possible given his income.

The graphical solution to Terry's choice problem has a simple intuitive interpretation. At the point of tangency, the indifference curve and the constraint have equal slopes. Recall that the slope of the indifference curve represents Terry's willingness to trade food for clothing, while the slope of the constraint represents the terms of trade dictated by the marketplace. At the optimal choice, the *willingness and ability to trade are equal*. At other feasible combinations of food and clothing, Terry's utility could be increased by making substitutions. For instance, if Terry were at a point where he was willing to trade five units of food for one unit of clothing and the relative price of clothing were 4 (the slope of the indifference curve is steeper than the constraint), Terry would be better off purchasing less

---

[6]For simplicity, we ignore the possibility of corner solutions—the points where the budget constraint intersects the axes. With corner solutions, the individual spends all income on only one good.

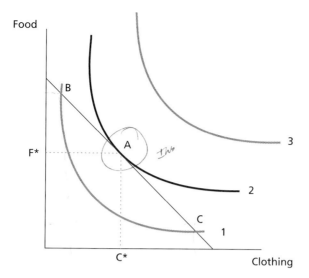

Figure 2.5   Optimal Choice

The individual is best off by choosing point A where the constraint is tangent to indifference curve 2. This optimal combination of food and clothing yields higher utility than other feasible alternatives (for example, points B and C). The individual would prefer points on indifference curve 3, but these points are not feasible given the constraint.

food and more clothing. (He is willing to trade five units of food for one unit of clothing, but only has to give up four units of food to obtain one unit of clothing in the market-place.) Alternatively, if Terry were at a point where he was only willing to give up one unit of food for one unit of clothing (the slope of the indifference curve is flatter than the con-straint), he would be better off purchasing more food and less clothing—since he receives five units of food for each unit of clothing given up.

Changes in Choice

Terry's constraint will change whenever prices or income change. Correspondingly, he will make different choices. Recall that changes in relative prices alter the slope of the constraint. Typically, when the relative price of a good increases, individuals choose less of that good.[7] Figure 2.6 shows how Terry will purchase less food as its relative price increases—food is more expensive and so less attractive than it was at a lower price. Due to the particular utility function used in this example, the amount of clothing purchased remains unchanged. More generally the amount of clothing purchased can either go up or down. It depends on the location of the new tangency point. Even though the price of clothing is relatively more attractive, the increase in food prices can limit available in-come so as to reduce the amount purchased of both goods. Changes in Terry's income motivate parallel shifts in the constraint and will change his optimal choice. In Chapter 4, we examine how changes in income affect consumption choices. We also elaborate on the effects of price changes.

[7]Conceptually, some individuals might purchase more of a good as the price increases. However, this outcome is not very likely.

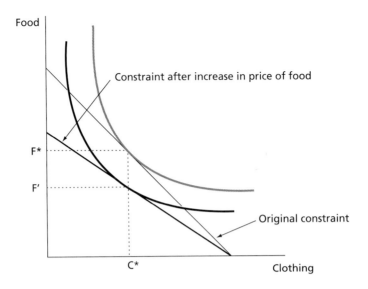

Figure 2.6   Optimal Choice and Price Changes

This figure shows how the optimal choice changes with an increase in the price of food. In this example, the individual chooses less food (F′ rather than F*). This is the typical case—usually, an individual will purchase less of a good when its price increases. Due to the particular utility function used in this example, the amount of clothing purchased remains unchanged (C*). More generally, the amount of clothing purchased can either go up or down. It depends on the location of the new tangency point.

Motivating Honesty at Sears

Often, economists focus on consumption goods such as food and clothing. This focus is natural given the interests economists have in understanding consumer behavior. The analysis can easily be extended to consider other goods that people care about, such as love and respect.[8] Such an extension can be used to analyze the problem at Sears Auto Centers.

Suppose that Sue Lawler, like other employees at Sears, values two goods—money and integrity. Her utility function is:

$$\overset{+}{}\qquad\overset{+}{}$$
$$\text{Utility} = f(\text{money, integrity}) \tag{2.5}$$

Money is meant to symbolize general purchasing power; it allows the purchase of goods such as food, clothing, and housing. Integrity is something Sue values for its own sake—being honest in the dealings with other people makes Sue feel good and is valued for that reason. (The analysis in this chapter is framed in a simple one-period context and does not consider future monetary returns from developing a good reputation; in Chapters 7 and 18, we extend the analysis and consider these multiperiod effects.)

Suppose that integrity can be measured on a numerical scale, with Sue preferring higher values. For example, 5 units of integrity provide more utility than 4 units of

---

[8]G. Becker (1993), "Nobel Lecture: The Economic Way of Looking at Behavior," *Journal of Political Economy* 101, 385–409.

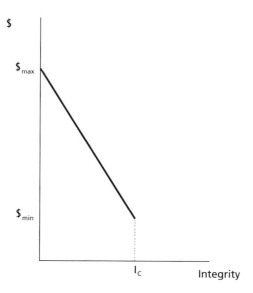

Figure 2.7   Hypothetical Constraint Facing a Worker at Sears Auto Center

The constraint pictures the maximum amounts of money and integrity that are possible for the worker given the compensation scheme and conditions at the store. If the employee sacrifices all integrity and recommends many unnecessary repairs, the employee earns a maximum of $\$_{max}$ a month. Fewer sales are made if the employee recommends fewer unnecessary repairs (selects a higher level of integrity), and income is lower since the worker is paid a commission on sales. I_C represents complete honesty.

integrity. (In actuality, measuring a good like integrity on a numerical scale may be very difficult. Yet this complication does not limit the qualitative insights that are gained from the analysis.)

Salespeople at Sears Auto Centers were paid a commission based on total sales. In addition, they had sales quotas for particular products and services. Missing these quotas could result in job loss as well as lower pay. Individual sales apparently could be increased and sales quotas met by being dishonest (for example, telling customers that they needed new shock absorbers when they did not).

Given the customer volume at the store and the commission rate, there is some maximum amount that Sue can earn even if she recommends repairs to all customers. If she recommends fewer repairs, income will decline. If she is completely honest and recommends no unnecessary repairs, sales quotas would be difficult to meet, resulting in potential job loss and less income. Figure 2.7 pictures Sue's implied constraint. This constraint depicts the maximum amounts of money and integrity that are possible given the compensation plan and conditions at the store.[9] If Sue sacrifices all integrity, she earns $\$_{max}$ a month. If she is perfectly honest, she earns much less (there is some floor on income that depends on the traffic from customers with legitimate problems). Intermediate options along the constraint are possible. While Sue would like to earn more than $\$_{max}$, higher earnings are not feasible.

[9]For simplicity, we draw the constraint as linear. Linearity is not necessary for our analysis.

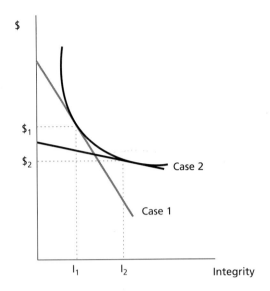

Figure 2.8   Optimal Choices of a Worker at Sears Auto Center under Two Different Compensation Plans

Case 1 reflects the original compensation plan. In this case, compensation consists of a high sales commission and the constraint is relatively steep. In Case 2, the firm pays a higher portion of the wage as a fixed salary and a lower commission rate. The slope of the constraint is flatter. The result is that the individual chooses a higher level of integrity in Case 2 than Case 1.

Sue chooses a combination of integrity and compensation that places her on the highest indifference curve. This choice occurs at the point of tangency between her indifference curve and the constraint. Sue ends up selecting relatively low amounts of integrity because the Sears management has made integrity expensive—if Sue chooses more integrity, she must forfeit a relatively large amount of income.

Management can alter the constraint facing Sue and other salespeople by changing the compensation scheme. In the Sears case, lowering the sales commission (in favor of a fixed hourly wage) reduces the monetary gains from selling more products through dishonest behavior and thus flattens the constraint. Changes in the slope of the constraint result in a different tangency point and thus a different choice. Figure 2.8 shows how Sue's optimal choice changes when the sales commission is decreased.[10] The result is more honest behavior. In essence, Sue "purchases" more integrity because it is less expensive. Consistent with this analysis, Sears actually responded to the problem by changing the compensation scheme from commission to straight salary. It also eliminated sales quotas and introduced a program to reward personnel for high levels of customer satisfaction.

[10]We have altered the compensation scheme in a manner that places Sue on the same indifference curve. The rationale for doing this is as follows. Sears must provide Sue with sufficient utility to retain her at the firm. Below this level of utility, Sue will quit. Sears is unlikely to want to pay Sue more than this minimum utility because it reduces firm profits. Thus, Sears has an incentive to adjust compensation in a manner that keeps her on the same indifference curve. Sue's indifferences curve in Figure 2.8 can be viewed as this "reservation" utility. This topic is covered in more detail in Chapter 11.

Managerial Implications

The analysis illustrates how the economic framework can be used to analyze and address management problems. Managers are interested in affecting the behavior of individuals such as workers, customers, union leaders, and subcontractors. Understanding what motivates individuals is critical. The economic approach views individual actions as the outcomes of maximizing personal utility. People are willing to make substitutions (for example, less leisure time for more income) if the terms of trade are advantageous. Managers can affect behavior by appropriately designing the constraints faced by individuals. The design of the constraints affects the tradeoffs that individuals face and hence their choices. For example, management can motivate workers through compensation plans and customers through pricing decisions.

The outcome of individuals making economic choices is a function of both constraints and preferences. Individuals try to achieve their highest level of satisfaction given the constraints they face. Our discussion of management implications, however, intentionally focuses on constraints, not preferences. As a management tool, the usefulness of focusing on personal preferences is often limited. Preferences are not generally observable, and virtually anything can be explained as simply a matter of personal tastes. Also, it is difficult to change what a person likes and does not like. A preference-based explanation for why employees were dishonest at Sears is that these workers gained personal utility from being dishonest (or compared to employees at other firms, Sears employees were willing to trade large amounts of personal integrity for small financial rewards). This explanation is not very helpful in giving management guidance on how to address the problem. It suggests that Sears might try to fire dishonest workers and replace them with workers who care more about personal integrity. The inability to observe personal preferences limits the viability of this approach. How would Sears know if, as a group, the new hires would be any less dishonest than the old employees? You cannot just ask applicants if they are honest; if they are not, they will have no qualms about claiming that they are.

The fact that individuals are clever and creative in minimizing the effects of constraints greatly complicates management problems. Changing incentives will affect employee behavior, though sometimes in a perverse and unintended manner. Consider the Soviet Union's early attempts to adopt incentive compensation to motivate workers. Taxi drivers were rewarded for total miles traveled (with or without passengers), while lamp manufacturers were rewarded on their production measured in kilograms. In response to these incentive plans, taxi drivers started driving empty cabs at high speeds on highways outside Moscow, while lamp manufacturers started producing light fixtures that would pull out of ceilings (because the manufacturers substituted lead for lighter-weight inputs). Sears initially adopted a commission plan to motivate salespeople to work harder. The dishonest behavior was a side effect that probably was unanticipated at the time the plan was adopted.

In summary, the economic approach to behavior has important managerial implications. The framework suggests that a manager can motivate desired actions by setting appropriate incentives. However, the manager must be very careful because improper incentives can motivate perverse behavior.

It is worth noting that economic analysis is limited in its ability to forecast the precise choices of a given individual because individual preferences are largely unobservable. The focus is on aggregate behavior or what the typical person tends to do. For example, an economist might not be very good at predicting which of several people will work harder under a new incentive plan. The economist will be successful in predicting that the average

---

Perverse Incentives at Lincoln Electric

Lincoln Electric is a successful company that manufactures arc welding equipment. It is famous for a strong emphasis on incentive compensation. This incentive program appears to be a primary source of the high productivity of Lincoln's production workers. At one point, Lincoln Electric decided to extend its incentive compensation program to clerical workers. Counters were installed on typewriters and secretaries were paid on the number of characters typed. This policy resulted in an increase in the amount of typing. The program, however, was discontinued when it was discovered that a secretary spent her lunch hour typing worthless pages in order to increase her compensation.

Source: N. Fast and N. Berg (1975), "The Lincoln Electric Company," Harvard Business School Case #376–028.

---

employee will work harder when compensation is tied to output than when a fixed salary independent of performance is paid. Managers are typically interested in structuring an organizational architecture that will work well and does not depend on specific people filling particular jobs. Individuals come and go, and the manager wants an organization that will work well as these changes occur. In this context, the economic framework is likely to be very useful. For management problems where the characteristics of a specific individual are more important, other frameworks may be more valuable. For example, if the board is interviewing potential new CEOs, insights into an individual's behavior derived from psychology might be extremely useful.

Alternative Models of Behavior[11]

We have shown how the economic view of behavior can be used in managerial decision making. We now discuss three other models that are commonly used by managers (either explicitly or implicitly) to explain behavior. Our discussion of each of these models is simplified. The intent, however, is to capture the essence of a few of the more prominent views that managers have about behavior and to illustrate how managerial decision making is affected by the particular view. We contrast these alternative views with the economic view and argue why the economic framework is particularly useful for managers.

Happy-Is-Productive Model

Managers sometimes assert that happy workers are more productive than unhappy workers. Managers following this happy-is-productive model see as their goal the designing of work environments that satisfy workers. Psychological theories, such as Maslow's and Herzberg's, are frequently used as guides in efforts to increase job satisfaction.[12]

A manager adhering to the happy-is-productive model might suggest that the problem at Sears was motivated by disgruntled employees who took out their frustrations on

---

[11]This section draws on the analysis in Jensen and Meckling (1994).

[12]F. Herzberg, B. Mausner, and B. Snyderman (1959), *The Motivation to Work* (John Wiley & Sons: New York); and A. Maslow (1970), *Motivation and Personality* (Harper and Row: New York).

Happy-Is-Productive versus Economic Explanations of the Hawthorne Experiments

Seven productivity studies were conducted at Western Electric's Hawthorne plant over the period 1924–1932. All seven studies focused on the response of assembly workers' productivity when different independent variables were manipulated (for example, length of break times and workday). Surprisingly, productivity rose virtually regardless of the particular manipulation. For example, it is claimed that productivity increased whenever illumination of the work area was changed, regardless of the direction of the change. When the lights were turned up, productivity increased, and when they were turned down, productivity increased, as well. This result, known as the Hawthorne Effect, is among the most discussed findings in psychology, and is often taken as support for the happy-is-productive mode. The workers in the experiment were given special attention and nonauthoritarian supervision relative to other workers at the plant. Also, the affected workers' views on the experiments were solicited by management, and the workers were given more responsibility. These actions, it has been argued, increased job satisfaction and performance.

Parsons (1974) presents evidence that the findings of the Hawthorne experiments can be explained by accompanying changes in the compensation system. Prior to the experiment, all workers were paid based on the output of a group of about 100 workers. During the experiment, the compensation plan was changed to base pay on the output of only five workers. In this case, a given worker's output more directly affects her own pay, and economic theory predicts increased output. Interestingly, the last of the original Hawthorne experiments observed workers where the compensation system was not changed. In that experiment, there was no change in output.

Source: H. Parsons (1974), "What Happened at Hawthorne?" *Science* 183, 922–932.

customers. This view implies that Sears could reduce the problem by promoting employee satisfaction through such actions as designing more interesting jobs, increasing the rates of pay, and improving the work environment. Happier employees would be expected to provide customers with better service.

The economic and happy-is-productive models do not differ based on what people care about. The economic model allows individuals to value love, esteem, interesting work, and pleasant work environments, as well as more standard economic goods such as food, clothing, and shelter. The primary difference in the models is what motivates individual actions. In the happy-is-productive model, workers exert high effort when they are happy. In the economic model, workers exert effort because of the rewards.

To contrast the two models, consider offering an employee guaranteed lifetime employment plus a large salary, which will be paid to the worker independent of performance. The happy-is-productive model suggests the worker will be more productive, as the additional job security and high salary are likely to increase job satisfaction. The economic model suggests the worker would exert less effort (since the worker receives no additional rewards from working harder and will not be fired for exerting low effort).

Good-Citizen Model

Some managers subscribe to the good-citizen model. The basic assumption is that employees want to do a good job; they take pride in their work and want to excel. Under this view, managers have three primary roles. First, they need to communicate the goals and objectives of the organization to workers. Second, they need to help workers discover how to achieve these goals and objectives. Finally, managers should provide feedback on performance so that workers can continue to enhance their efforts. There is no reason to have incentive pay, since individuals are intrinsically interested in doing a good job.

This view suggests that the problems at Sears occurred because employees misunderstood what was good for the company. Employees might have thought that increasing sales was in the company's interests, even if it required a certain amount of dishonesty. Under the good-citizen view, the management of Sears could motivate employee honesty by clearly communicating to the employees that Sears would be better off in the long run if its salespeople did not lie to customers. Managers of each automotive center might be instructed to hold a series of employee meetings to stress the value of employee honesty and customer service.

In the good-citizen model, employees place the interests of the company first. There is never a conflict between an employee's personal interest and the interest of the company. In contrast, the economic model posits that employees maximize their own utility. Potential conflicts of interest often arise. The economic view predicts that pleas from Sears management for employees to be more honest would have little affect on behavior unless the reward system was changed to make it in the interests of workers to be more honest.

Product-of-the-Environment Model

The product-of-the-environment model argues that the behaviors of individuals are largely determined by their upbringings. Some cultures and households promote positive values in individuals, such as industry and integrity, while others promote negative traits, such as laziness and dishonesty. This model suggests that Sears had dishonest individuals in its automotive centers. A response would have been to fire these workers and replace them with honest workers from better backgrounds.

Which Model Should Managers Use?

Behavior is a complex topic. Any behavioral model is unlikely to be useful in all contexts. For example, the economic model is unlikely to be helpful in predicting whether a given individual will prefer red shirts to blue shirts (selling at the same price). But our focus is on managerial decision making. In this context, there are reasons to believe that the economic model is particularly useful.

Managers are frequently interested in fostering *changes* in behavior. For example, managers want consumers to buy more of their products, employees to exert more effort, and labor unions to reduce their demands for wage increases. In contrast to other models, the economic framework provides managers with concrete guidance on how to alter behavior. Desired behavior can be encouraged by changing the relevant costs and benefits facing the decision maker. For example, incentive compensation can be used to motivate employees, while price changes can be used to affect consumer behavior.

There is ample evidence to support the hypothesis that this economic framework is useful in explaining changes in behavior. The most common example is that consumers tend to buy fewer products at higher prices. The evidence suggests that the model is also useful in explaining behavior in many other contexts, including voting; the formation, dissolution, and structure of families; drug addiction; and the incidence of crime.[13]

[13]Becker (1993).

The Economics of Voting Behavior

Economics has proven useful in explaining behavior in many contexts, including corporate voting. Economics implies that shareholders who own large blocks of stock have a stronger incentive to vote on corporate issues than nonblockholders for two reasons. First, blockholders are more affected by changes in stock price since they own more shares. Second, they are more likely to affect the outcome of the election. Consistent with this prediction, Brickley, Lease, and Smith (1988) find that blockholders are more likely to vote in elections on antitakeover amendments than nonblockholders. Interestingly, they also find that financial institutions such as banks and insurance companies, which frequently derive benefits from lines of business under management control (for example, by providing banking services or insurance to the firm), are less likely to oppose management on management-sponsored proposals than are other shareholders without potential business relationships. This outcome is also predicted by the economic framework.

Source: J. Brickley, R. Lease, and C. Smith (1988), "Ownership Structure and Voting on Antitakeover Amendments," *Journal of Financial Economics* 20, 267–291.

The good-citizen model appears less successful in predicting behavior in business settings. Management would be an easy task if employees would work harder and produce higher quality simply on request. The happy-is-productive model also has significant limitations. Most importantly, the existing evidence suggests that there is little relation between job satisfaction and performance (see W. R. Scott's Criticisms of the Happy-Is-Productive Model in the following box). Happy employees are not necessarily more productive. Sometimes, managers might want to follow the implications of the product-of-the-environment model and fire employees with undesirable traits. This approach is unlikely to be useful in solving most managerial problems. Also, given laws that limit discrimination, this approach can subject the firm to potentially serious legal sanctions.

Criticisms of the Happy-Is-Productive Model

W. Richard Scott summarizes some of the major concerns about the happy-is-productive model (sometimes referred to as the human-relations movement):

Virtually all of these applications of the human-relations movement have come under severe criticism on both ideological and empirical grounds. Paradoxically, the human-relations movement, ostensibly developed to humanize the cold and calculating rationality of the factory and shop, rapidly came under attack on the grounds that it represented simply a more subtle and refined form of exploitation. Critics charged that workers' legitimate economic interests were being inappropriately deemphasized; actual conflicts of interest were denied and "therapeutically" managed; and the roles attributed to managers represented a new brand of elitism. The entire movement was branded as "cow sociology" just as contented cows were alleged to produce more milk, satisfied workers were expected to produce more output.

The ideological criticisms were the first to erupt, but reservations raised by researchers on the basis of empirical evidence may in the long run prove to be more devastating. Several decades of research have demonstrated no clear relation between worker satisfaction and productivity.

Source: W. Scott (1981), *Organizations: Rational, Natural and Open Systems* (Prentice Hall: Englewood Cliffs, NJ), 89–90.

Decision Making under Uncertainty

Throughout this chapter, we have considered cases where the decision maker has complete certainty about the items of choice. For instance, Terry Rasmussen knew the exact prices of food and clothing, and Sue Lawler knew the precise tradeoff between integrity and compensation at Sears. Decision makers, however, often face uncertainty. For instance, in choosing among risky investment alternatives (such as stocks and bonds), an individual must forecast the likely payoffs. Even so, there can be significant uncertainty about the eventual outcomes. The analysis presented in this chapter can readily be extended to incorporate decision making under uncertainty.[14] A detailed analysis of decision making under uncertainty is beyond the scope of this book. This section introduces a few concepts that we will use later in this book.

Expected Value

Taylor Scroggin sells real estate for RealCo. He receives a sales commission from his employer. For simplicity, suppose that Taylor has three possible incomes for the year. In a good year, he sells many houses and earns $200,000, while in a bad year he earns nothing. In other years, he receives $100,000. Probability refers to the likelihood that an outcome will occur. In this example, each outcome is equally likely, and thus has a probability of ⅓ of occurring. The *expected value* of an uncertain payoff is defined as the weighted average of all possible outcomes, where the probability of each outcome is used as the weights. The expected value is a measure of central tendency—the payoff that will occur on average. In our example, the expected value is:[15]

$$\text{Expected value} = (\tfrac{1}{3} \times 0) + (\tfrac{1}{3} \times 100,000) + (\tfrac{1}{3} \times 200,000) = \$100,000 \qquad (2.6)$$

Variability

While Taylor can expect average earnings of $100,000, his income is not certain. The *variance* is a measure of the variability of the payoff. It is defined as the expected value of the squared difference between each possible payoff and the expected value. In this example, the variance is:

$$\text{Variance} = \tfrac{1}{3}(0 - 100,000)^2 + \tfrac{1}{3}(100,000 - 100,000)^2 + \tfrac{1}{3}(200,000 - 100,000)^2$$
$$= 6.7 \text{ billion} \qquad (2.7)$$

The *standard deviation* is the square root of the variance:

$$\text{Standard deviation} = (6.7 \text{ billion})^{1/2} = 81,650 \qquad (2.8)$$

Variances and standard deviations are used as measures of risk. It does not really matter which we use, since one is a simple transformation of the other (higher standard deviations correspond to higher variances). In this example, we focus on the standard deviation. An event with a definite outcome has a standard deviation of zero. Higher standard deviations reflect more risk.

---

[14]For example, E. Fama and M. Miller (1972), *The Theory of Finance* (Dryden Press: New York), Chapter 5.

[15]Note that the expected value need not equal one of the possible outcomes. As a weighted average, it can be a value between outcomes. In this example, it happens to correspond to one of the possible outcomes, $100,000.

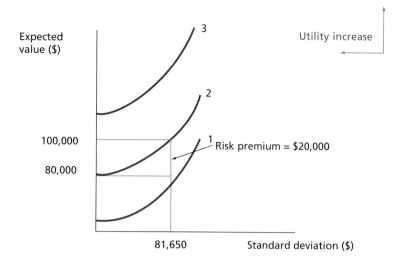

Figure 2.9   Indifference Curves for Expected Value and Standard Deviation

This figure displays three indifference curves for a *risk-averse* individual. The individual prefers higher expected value but lower standard deviation. Standard deviation is a measure of risk. Since risk is a "bad," the indifference curves are positively sloped. Northwest moves are utility increasing. Currently, the individual has a compensation package that has an expected value of $100,000 and a standard deviation of $81,650. The *certainty equivalent* of this package is $80,000. The *risk premium* is $20,000.

Risk Aversion

Like most people, Taylor is *risk averse*—holding the expected payoff fixed, he prefers a lower standard deviation. He, therefore, gains utility from an increase in expected value, but he experiences a reduction in utility from increases in standard deviation. Figure 2.9 shows three of Taylor's indifference curves. Each curve shows all combinations of expected value and standard deviation that give Taylor equal utility. In contrast to our previous analysis, one of the objects of choice is a "bad"—Taylor does not like risk. Thus, in this figure, the indifference curves have positive slopes and northwest movements are utility increasing (recall in the standard analysis that the curves have negative slopes and northeast movements are utility increasing). The slopes of the indifference curves indicate Taylor's degree of risk aversion. Steeper slopes translate into higher risk aversion. (If the slopes of the indifference curves are steep, Taylor must receive a relatively large increase in expected value for each additional unit of risk to maintain a given level of utility.) If his indifference curves were totally flat, he would be *risk neutral*. A risk-neutral person cares only about expected value and is indifferent to the amount of risk. Indifference curve 3 is associated with the highest level of utility, while curve 1 is associated with the lowest utility. Taylor is currently on curve 2. Given a choice among compensation plans with different expected payoffs and risk, Taylor will choose the combination that places him on the highest indifference curve.

Certainty Equivalent and Risk Premium

Figure 2.9 indicates that Taylor is indifferent between the risky commission scheme, which has an expected payoff of $100,000, and a certain income of $80,000. The $80,000 is Taylor's *certainty equivalent* for the risky income stream—he is willing to trade the uncertain income of $100,000 for a certain income of $80,000. The difference between the expected value of the risky income stream and the certainty equivalent is called the *risk premium*. This $20,000 premium, which comes in the form of a higher expected payoff, must be paid to keep Taylor indifferent between the risky income stream and his certainty equivalent.

Suppose that Taylor receives a job offer from another real estate company that would pay him a fixed salary of $90,000 per year. Taylor considers the new job to be the same as his current job in all dimensions other than the compensation plan. Taylor's current compensation plan will not motivate him to continue to work for RealCo. Even though his current plan has a higher expected payoff, he would prefer the certain $90,000 to the risky commission plan. If RealCo wants to retain Taylor, it must offer him a compensation package that provides the same level of utility as the $90,000 for certain. We expand on this issue in more detail later in the book.

CASE STUDY
Interwest Healthcare Corp

Interwest Healthcare is a nonprofit organization that owns 10 hospitals located in three western states. Cynthia Manzoni is Interwest's chief executive officer. Robert Harris, Interwest's chief financial officer, and the administrators of the 10 hospitals report to Manzoni.

Harris is deeply concerned because the hospital staffs are not being careful when entering data into the firm's management information system. This data involves information on patient intake, treatment, and release. The information system is used to compile management reports such as those relating to the costs of various treatments. Also, the system is used to compile reports that are required by the federal government under various grant programs. Harris reasons that without good information, the management and government reports are less useful and potentially misleading. Harris is worried about the managerial implications and the potential loss of federal grants. The federal government periodically audits Interwest and might discontinue aid if the reports are deemed inaccurate.

Harris has convinced Manzoni that a problem exists. She also realizes the importance of an accurate system both for management planning and maintaining federal aid. Six months ago, she invited the hospital administrators and staff members from the corporate financial office to a retreat at a resort. The purpose was to communicate to the hospital administrators the problems with the data entry and to stress the importance of doing a better job. The meeting was acrimonious. The hospital people accused Harris of being a bureaucrat who did not care about patient services. Harris accused the hospital staffs of not understanding the importance of accurate reporting. By the end of the meeting, Manzoni thought that she had a commitment by the hospital administrators to increase the accuracy of data entry at their hospitals. However, six months later, Harris claims that the problem is as bad as ever.

Manzoni has hired you as a consultant to analyze the problem and to make recommendations that might improve the situation.

Discussion Questions

1. What are potential sources of the problem?
2. What information would you want to analyze?
3. What actions might you recommend to increase the accuracy of the data entry?
4. How does your view of behavior affect how you might address this consulting assignment?

Summary

This chapter summarizes the way economists view behavior. In the economic model, individuals are seen as having unlimited wants and limited resources. They rank alternative uses of limited resources in terms of preference, and choose the preferred alternative. Individuals are clever in figuring out ways of maximizing their utility (happiness) in the face of resource constraints. Individuals are not necessarily selfish in the sense that they care only about their personal wealth. They can care about charity, family, religion, and society. They are not infallible supercomputers.

The *opportunity cost* of using a resource is the value of the resource in the best alternative use. For example, the cost of having a manager use five hours to work on a project is the value of the manager's time in working on the next best alternative project. Economic decision making requires careful consideration of the relevant opportunity costs.

Marginal costs and benefits are the incremental costs and benefits that are associated with the decision. In calculating marginal costs, it is important to use the opportunity costs of the incremental resources. For example, in deciding whether to purchase a new laptop computer, the marginal cost is the price and the marginal benefit is the value that the person places on the new computer. It is the marginal costs and benefits that are important in economic decision making. Action should be taken when the marginal benefits are greater than the marginal costs. *Sunk costs* that are not affected by the decision (for example, unrecoverable funds previously spent on computers) are not relevant.

A *utility function* is a mathematical function. It relates total utility to the amounts that an individual has of whatever items that the individual cares about (*goods*). Preferences implied by a utility function are pictured graphically by *indifference curves*. Indifference curves picture all combinations of goods that yield the same amount of utility. Individual choice involves maximizing utility given resource *constraints*. Graphically, the constraint shows all combinations of goods that are feasible to acquire. The optimal choice is where the indifference curve is tangent to the constraint. At this point, the individual is at the highest level of utility possible given the constraint.

Changes in the constraint result in changes in the optimal choice. An important implication is that managers can affect behavior by affecting constraints. Managers, however, have to be careful. Individuals are clever at maximizing their utility, and setting the wrong incentives can have perverse consequences.

We contrast the economic model with three other models of human behavior that managers often use. We argue that the economic model is likely to be particularly useful in managerial decision making.

The analysis in this chapter can be extended to the case where the decision maker faces uncertainty about the items of choice. An example of decision making under uncertainty is choosing among risky investment alternatives. One concept that we will rely on later in this book is *risk aversion*. When confronted with a risky and a certain alternative, with the same expected (or average) payoff, a risk-averse person will always choose the certain outcome. A *risk premium* must be offered to entice the person to choose the risky alternative.

Throughout this chapter, we focus primarily on how managers might use the economic view to analyze and influence the behavior of employees. As we will see, the economic view is very powerful and is useful in explaining behavior in a variety of different contexts.

Suggested Readings

G. Becker (1993), "Nobel Lecture: The Economic Way of Looking at Behavior," *Journal of Political Economy* 101, 385–409.

M. Jensen and W. Meckling (1994), "The Nature of Man," *Journal of Applied Corporate Finance* 7, 4–19.

Review Questions

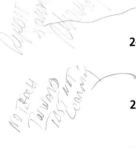

2–1. Which costs are pertinent to economic decision making? Which costs are *not* relevant?

2–2. **a.** Briefly describe the four models of behavior presented in this chapter.

   b. What are the implications of these models for managers attempting to influence their employees' behavior?

2–3. Workers in a plant in Minnesota are observed to be industrious and very productive. Workers in a similar plant in Southern California are observed to be lazy and unproductive. Discuss how alternative views of human behavior and motivation might suggest different explanations for this observed behavior.

2–4. Employees at a department store are observed engaging in the following behavior: (a) they hide items that are on sale from the customers, and (b) they exert little effort in designing merchandise displays. They are also uncooperative with one another. What do you think might be causing this behavior, and what might you do to improve the situation?

2–5. Travelers commonly tip shoe shiners at airports. The tips are made after the shoe shine is complete and the traveler has no legal obligation to make the tip. Is the existence of tips to shoe shiners consistent with the economic view of behavior? If a study were to compare tips earned by shoe shiners at commuter airports (which tend to serve the same passengers on a routine basis) with the tips earned by shoe shiners at airports at resort locations, what would you expect to find? Explain.

2–6. Several school districts have attempted to increase teacher productivity by paying teachers based on the scores their students achieve on standardized tests (administered by outside testing agencies). The goal is to produce higher quality classroom instruction. Do you think that this type of compensation scheme will produce the desired outcome? Explain.

2–7. A company recently raised the pay of workers by 20 percent. The productivity of the workers, remained the same. The CEO of the company was quoted as saying, "it just goes to show that money does not motivate people." Provide a critical evaluation of this statement.

2–8. One physician who worked for a large health maintenance organization was quoted as saying:

> One day I was listening to a patient's heart and realized there was an abnormal rhythm. My first thought was that I hoped that I did not have to refer the patient to a specialist.

Indeed, HMO physicians have been criticized for not making referrals when they are warranted. How do you think the physician was paid by the HMO? Explain.

2–9. Insurance companies have to generate enough revenue to cover their costs and make a normal profit—otherwise, they will go out of business. This implies that the premiums charged for insurance policies must be greater than the expected payouts to the policyholders. Why would a person ever buy insurance, knowing that the price is greater than the expected payout?

2–10. Critically evaluate the following statement: "Risk averse people never take gambles."

2–11. Suppose that an investment can yield three possible cash flows: $5,000; $1,000; or $0. The probability of each outcome is ⅓.

   a. What is the expected value and standard deviation of the investment?

   b. How much would a risk-neutral person be willing to pay for the investment?

   c. How much would a risk-averse person be willing to pay for the investment?

chapter 3

Markets, Organizations, and the Role of Knowledge

Duria the greater part of the 20th century, the Soviet Union and the United States were involved in an acrimonious debate over the merits of free-market versus centrally planned economies. The Soviet belief in the superiority of central planning was summed up in Premier Nikita Khruschev's famous prophecy, "We will bury you." During the 1990s, however, the world witnessed the rapid collapse of many of the centrally planned economies in the world. The Soviet Union broke apart. The Berlin Wall was dismantled, and East and West Germany were reunited. Communist governments throughout Eastern Europe were replaced, while the market economies in countries like Japan and Singapore thrived.

These events appear to support the contention that central economic planning does not work as well as free markets. However, on closer inspection, it is evident that a substantial amount of central economic planning is conducted within free-market economies. Indeed, most of the production in modern economies occurs within firms, where resource-allocation decisions are made by managers in a manner that is often closely akin to central planning. Management, through administrative actions, dictates the output mix of the firm, as well as the methods of production. These decisions can involve billions of dollars of resources and thousands of employees. Indeed, the size of the largest firms in the world exceeds that of many national economies. For instance, the 1991 gross national products of Egypt, Peru, and Portugal were $30 billion, $47 billion, and $65 billion, respectively. The 1991 net sales at General Motors was $109 billion. If central planning is so bad, why do firms in free-market economies rely so heavily on it?

In this chapter, we examine three questions: How do free-market systems work? What are the relative advantages of free-market systems compared to central planning in large economies? Why do we observe so much economic activity conducted within firms in market economies?

Answers to these questions are particularly important to managers for two reasons. First, management must have an understanding of how markets work to make good input, output, and pricing decisions. Second, national economies are like firms in that they are human creations to organize economic activity. Understanding the relative advantages and disadvantages of markets, central planning, and firms is directly relevant to understanding firm-level issues such as whether or not to decentralize decision rights to workers and whether to make or buy the firm's inputs.

Goals of an Economic System

Every economic entity—be it a national economy, firm, or household—is confronted with three basic issues:

- What to produce.
- How to produce it.
- How to allocate the final output.

Economic entities can organize in alternative ways to address these issues. For instance, national economies can rely on either central planning or free markets. Similarly, firms and households can use centralized decision making, where the CEO or head of household makes all major decisions. Alternatively, other people in the firm or household can be granted significant decision-making authority.

Given the alternatives, what is the best way to organize economic activities? To answer this question, we need some criterion for comparing alternative systems. Unfortunately, there is likely to be disagreement over such a criterion. For instance, you might argue that the optimal system would produce your preferred mix of products and give them all to you, while your neighbor is likely to disagree. Given these differences in opinion, economists focus on a relatively uncontroversial but narrow criterion for comparing the effectiveness of economic systems, *Pareto efficiency*.[1] A distribution of resources is said to be Pareto efficient if there is no alternative allocation that keeps all individuals at least as well off but makes at least one person better off. If an economic system is not producing an efficient allocation of resources, its members can be made better off by making Pareto-improving changes (changes that benefit some of the members without hurting others).

As an example, assume that the economy produces 1,000 personal computers and no VCRs. This distribution of resources is not Pareto efficient if there is a subset of individuals who want to convert their computers to VCRs and can do so without reducing the utility of other individuals in the society. Based on the concept of Pareto efficiency, its citizens are better off if the economy produces more VCRs and fewer computers. If this action adversely affects even one person, the move is not Pareto improving and an economist cannot say whether the move is good or bad from a societal viewpoint.[2] Pareto efficiency also requires that goods be produced in an efficient manner. The resource allocation is not Pareto efficient if production could be rearranged so that more VCRs are produced without lowering computer production (and vice versa).

In centrally planned economies, government officials decide what to produce, how to produce it, and who obtains the final output. In free markets, these decisions are decentralized to individuals in the economy. At least in concept, a central planner could order any feasible production and distribution of goods. Thus, any allocation of resources that can be achieved by a free-market economy can in principle be achieved by a centrally planned economy. We begin by discussing how free-market systems work and how they can produce a Pareto-efficient allocation of resources. We then discuss why in large economies a free market is more likely to produce an efficient resource allocation than central planning .

Property Rights and Exchange in a Free-Market Economy

Property Rights

A *property right* is a socially enforced right to select the uses of an economic good. A property right is *private* when it is assigned to a specific person. Private property rights are *alienable* in that they can be transferred (sold or given) to other individuals. For example, if Valerie Fong owns an automobile, she can use the automobile as she sees fit (within some limits), and can restrict others from using the vehicle. She also can sell the automobile (transfer to another person whatever property rights she has in the vehicle). The government maintains police and a court system to help enforce these property rights.

An important feature of a free-market economy is the use of private property rights. Owners of land and other resources have the legal rights to decide how to use these resources and frequently trade these rights to other individuals. They are free to start new businesses and to close existing businesses. In contrast, in centrally planned economies, property tends to be owned by the state; government officials decide how to use these resources.

---

[1]The term is named after Vilfredo Pareto, 1848–1923, an Italian economist and sociologist.

[2]Therefore, economics does not address the question of which of the many possible efficient resource allocations is best for a society. Producing your preferred set of products and giving them all to you is efficient (the allocation cannot be changed without making you worse off). However, others will argue that the allocation is not fair or equitable. Economists typically do not attempt to settle these types of debates.

Dimensions of Property Rights

Ownership involves two general dimensions: *use rights* and *alienability rights.* These aspects of ownership do not always move in lockstep. You own your body in the sense that you can decide what activities to pursue. Yet, there are significant legal restrictions on alienability. For instance, you cannot enter a legally enforceable contract to sell one of your kidneys, despite the fact that you have two, can live comfortably with one, and might value your second kidney much less than a wealthy individual dying because of kidney failure. Due to this restriction, there is no free market in kidneys. In some transactions, it is possible to sell use rights while retaining alienability rights. In a rental contract, the renter obtains the rights to use an apartment, but does not have the right to sell the unit. Conversely, the landlord has the right to sell the apartment, but does not have the right to use it while the lease is in force.

Gains from Trade

To understand how a market economy works, it is necessary to understand the motives for trading property rights. Why do people buy and sell? The answer is to make themselves better off.

Tom Sawyer, Huckleberry Finn, and the Gains from Trade

An example of the gains from trade is provided by Mark Twain in a dialogue between Tom Sawyer and Huck Finn:

"Say—what's that?"

"Nothing but a tick."

"Where'd you get him?"

"Out in the woods."

"What'll you take for him?"

"I don't know. I don't want to sell him."

"All right. It's a mighty small tick, anyway."

"Oh, anybody can run a tick down that don't belong to them. I'm satisfied with it. It's good enough for me."

"Sho, there's ticks a-plenty. I could have a thousand of 'em if I wanted to."

"Well, why don't you? Becuz you know mighty well you can't. This is a pretty early tick, I reckon. It's the first one I've seen this year."

"Say, Huck—I'll give you my tooth for him."

"Le's see it."

Tom got out a bit of paper and carefully unrolled it. Huckleberry viewed it wistfully. The temptation was very strong. At last he said:

"Is it genuwyne?"

Tom lifted his lip and showed the vacancy.

"Well, all right," said Huckleberry, "it's a trade."

Tom enclosed the tick in the percussion-cap box that had lately been the pinch bug's prison, and the boys separated, each feeling wealthier than before.

Source: M. Twain (1944), *The Adventures of Tom Sawyer* (Whitman: Racine, WI), 54–55.

Strategic-Business Planning: Ignoring the Economics of Trade

During the 1970s, many firms adopted a particular form of strategic business planning. All projects of the firm were ranked based on growth potential and market share. Projects with high growth potential and high market share were called stars, while projects with low growth potential and market share were referred to as dogs. Dogs were sold, while stars were kept. Funding for the stars came from cash cows, projects with high market share and low growth potential.

The idea behind this process is to treat the projects of a firm like stocks in a portfolio. Through systematic analysis, winners are to be kept and losers sold. Money is invested in the winners to enhance the firm's competitive advantage. While the idea sounds intriguing, its underpinnings are inconsistent with the basic economics of trade—sell if, and only if, you can get a price that exceeds the value of keeping the item yourself. This principle implies that, contrary to the process, dogs should be kept unless they can be sold at sufficiently high prices. Similarly, stars should be sold if the price is sufficiently high.

By the 1980s, many firms found that violating the basic economics of trade had led them to accumulate suboptimal collections of projects. Large increases in stock prices were observed as these firms reshuffled plants, divisions, and subsidiaries through sell-offs, spin-offs, and divestitures.

Source: "The New Breed of Strategic Planner," *Business Week,* September 17, 1984, 62–68.

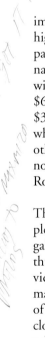

In the economic framework, people order their preferences and take actions that maximize their level of satisfaction (utility). Trade takes place because the buyer places a higher value on the item than the seller. The corresponding *gains from trade* make both parties better off—voluntary trade is *mutually advantageous.* For example, if Jose Coronas is willing to pay up to $16,000 for a particular automobile and Rochester Motors is willing to sell the automobile for as little as $10,000, the potential gains from trade are $6,000 ($16,000 − $10,000). If the automobile trades at $13,000, both parties are $3,000 better off. Jose gives up $13,000 to buy something that he values at $16,000, while Rochester Motors obtains $13,000 for something it values at only $10,000. At other prices between $10,000 and $16,000, the total gains are still $6,000 but they are not split evenly. For example, at a price of $15,000, Jose gains $1,000 in value, while Rochester Motors gains $5,000.[3]

Where do the gains from trade come from? One source is differences in preferences. The buyer and seller may simply place different values on the item of trade. For example, some people value new automobiles more than others. Another important source of gains is that the seller may be able to produce the item more cheaply than the buyer and thus may have a *comparative advantage* in its production. In advanced economies, individuals specialize in producing goods where they have a comparative advantage and make trades to acquire other goods. Specialization greatly enhances the standard of living of a society. Imagine that you had to be completely self-sufficient (making your own clothing, growing your own food, building your own house, and producing your own vehicles for transportation). Your overall standard of living would be much lower than it is living in a modern, specialized economy.

A common misconception is that trade takes place because people have too much of some goods—people sell to others what they cannot use themselves. This view, however, does not explain why individuals sell houses, cars, jewelry, land, and other resources

[3]Sometimes, individuals regret a trade after the fact. For instance, Jose might be unhappy that he purchased a particular automobile from Rochester Motors. On average, he must find it advantageous to purchase automobiles or else he would quit purchasing them (at least from Rochester Motors). Jose's ability to say no limits the extent to which he can be exploited in a trade.

Gains from Trade: The Story of McDonald's

McDonald's Corporation, with over 13,000 restaurants in 65 countries, is the largest fast-food company in the world. Its worldwide sales in 1992 were over $20 billion. While Ray Kroc is often given credit for founding this company, the history of the restaurant goes back to 1937 when two brothers, Dick and Mac McDonald, opened a drive-in restaurant. It was these brothers who conceived of the idea of a clean, highly efficient, quick-service restaurant with a limited menu centered around hamburgers and french fries. It was Kroc, however, who had the vision and the ability to take this idea and expand it nationwide. Taking advantage of the potential gains from trade, the McDonald's brothers sold Kroc the exclusive rights to franchise copies of their operation all over the United States. This transaction resulted in one of the most successful business operations of all time.

Source: C. Shook and R. Shook (1993), *Franchising: The Business Strategy that Changed the World* (Prentice Hall: Englewood Cliffs, NJ).

(such as Tom's tooth and Huck's tick) that they value highly and have in short supply. The economic explanation for trade argues that trade does not take place because people have too little or too much of a good. Trade takes place whenever a person is willing to pay a higher price for a good than it is worth to the owner. While you might love your new sports car, you would sell it if someone offered you a high enough price.

It is important to recognize that trade is an important form of value creation. The act of trading produces value that makes individuals better off. Gains from trade also provide important incentives to move resources to more productive uses. If Irene Nichols can make the most productive use of a piece of land, she will be willing to pay a higher price for the land than other potential users. The current owner, Jody Crowe, has the incentive to sell the land to Irene, since she gets to keep the proceeds from the sale. It is these incentives that help to promote a Pareto-efficient allocation of resources in a free-market economy. If all mutually advantageous trades are exhausted, it is impossible to change the allocation without making someone worse off.

Basics of Supply and Demand

Gains from trade explain why individuals buy and sell. But what coordinates the separate decisions of millions of individuals in a free-market economy to prevent chaos? Why aren't there massive surpluses produced of some goods and huge shortages of other goods? What restricts the amounts demanded by the public to the amounts supplied? The answers to these questions lie in the market price system.

The Market Price Mechanism

The basic economics of a price system can be illustrated through standard supply and demand diagrams. Figure 3.1 displays a supply and demand diagram for a particular model of personal computer (PC)—for example, a 486 machine with standard quality and features. The vertical axis on the graph shows the price for a PC, while the horizontal axis shows the total quantity of PCs demanded and supplied in the market for the period (for example, a month).

The market includes all potential buyers and sellers of this type of PC. Suppose that in this market there are many buyers and sellers and that individual transactions are so

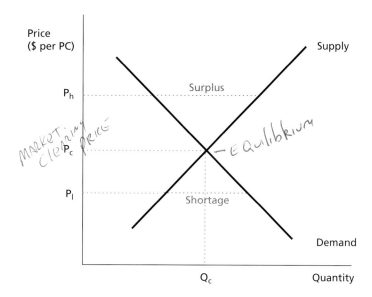

Figure 3.1   Supply and Demand in the PC Industry

The demand curve shows the number of PCs that consumers want to purchase at each price. The supply curve shows the number of PCs that producers want to sell at each price. Equilibrium is where the two curves cross. Here, the quantity supplied equals the quantity demanded. If the price is above the market-clearing price of P_c, there is a surplus of PCs. Producers supply more PCs than consumers want to purchase. If the price is below the market-clearing price, there is a shortage. Producers supply fewer PCs than consumers want to purchase. Surpluses and shortages put pressure on prices and quantities to move to the equilibrium levels of P_c and Q_c.

small in relation to the overall market that the price is unaffected by any single sale or purchase. In this case, no buyer or seller has market power—all trades are made at the going market price. We label this type of market as *competitive*. (In Chapter 6, we extend our analysis of competitive markets. We also examine *noncompetitive* market structures.)

The *demand curve* (D) shows how many total PCs consumers are willing to buy at each price. The demand curve slopes downward because consumers typically buy more if the price is lower. For example, consumers are likely to buy more PCs if the price is P_l (say, $500) than if the price is P_h (say, $1,500).

The *supply curve* (S) shows how many PCs producers are willing to sell at each price. The curve slopes upward—at higher prices, producers are able and willing to produce and sell more units. For example, at a price of $500, most potential producers cannot cover their costs and refrain from production. At a price of $1,500, more units are manufactured and brought to market.

The two curves cross at the *market-clearing* price, P_c, and quantity, Q_c. At the market-clearing price, the quantity of PCs demanded is exactly equal to the quantity supplied. Here, the market is said to be in *equilibrium.*

There are strong pressures in markets that push prices and quantities toward their equilibrium levels. To see why, suppose that the market price is above the equilibrium price, such as P_h in Figure 3.1. At this higher price, there is a *surplus* of PCs—suppliers produce more PCs than consumers are willing to purchase. As inventories of unsold PCs build, this surplus places downward pressure on prices as suppliers compete to try to sell their products. As prices fall, fewer PCs will be produced and more will be demanded, thus reducing the surplus. In contrast, if the price is below the market-clearing price,

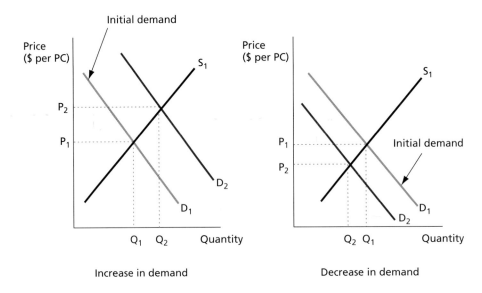

Figure 3.2   The Effects of a Shift in Demand on the Equilibrium Price and Quantity of PCs

The initial equilibrium is where the demand curve, labeled D_1, intersects the supply curve, labeled S_1. The left panel shows the effects of an increase in demand. The result is a higher equilibrium price and quantity. The right panel shows the effects of a decrease in demand. The result is a lower equilibrium price and quantity.

such as P_1 in Figure 3.1, there is a *shortage* of computers. Here, consumers will bid up the price of PCs as they compete for the limited supply. As prices rise, producers will increase their output and consumers will demand fewer PCs, thus reducing the shortage. When the market is in equilibrium, there is no pressure on prices and quantities—the quantity demanded exactly equals the quantity supplied. The market price is stable at this point.

Supply and demand diagrams like Figure 3.1 are snapshots at a point in time. As time passes, both supply and demand curves are likely to change. Figure 3.2 shows the effects of a shift in demand in the PC market. The left panel pictures a shift in demand to the right. Here, there is an increase in demand, since at each price consumers demand more PCs. Demand for PCs might increase for a variety of reasons, including an increase in the purchasing power of consumers and a decline in the prices of supporting software.

Shifts in Demand, Quantity, and Price at the Ryder Cup

The Ryder Cup features competition between top American and European golfers. It has become one of the most prominent golfing events in the world. In 1995, the Ryder Cup was held in Rochester, New York, at Oak Hill Country Club. The event attracted over 30,000 spectators a day. Many of these spectators (for example, Prince Andrew of Great Britain) were from outside the Rochester area.

A significant number of these visitors wanted to play golf while they were in Rochester. Rochester has several courses that are open to the public. However, many of the courses in the area are private (only members and their guests can play). Due to the dramatic increase in the demand for public golf courses, several of the private courses decided to become public during the week of the Ryder Cup. These courses charged high fees ranging from $100 to $250 per round (normally, their guest fees were around $50). This example highlights that shifts in demand motivate increases in the quantity supplied and the price of a product (in this case, golf tee times).

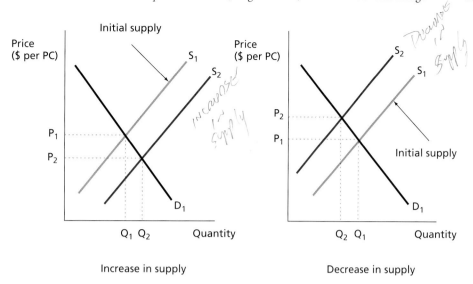

Figure 3.3   The Effects of a Shift in Supply on the Equilibrium Price and Quantity of PCs

The initial equilibrium is where the demand curve, labeled D_1, intersects the supply curve, labeled S_1. The left panel shows the effects of an increase in supply. The result is a lower equilibrium price and an increase in equilibrium quantity. The right panel shows the effects of a decrease in supply. The result is a higher equilibrium price and a lower equilibrium quantity.

These types of changes motivate consumers to purchase more PCs at any given price. At the old equilibrium price, there is a shortage of PCs after the demand shift. This shortage motivates an upward pressure on prices, which in turn stimulates more production. The end result is a higher equilibrium price and quantity. The right panel shows that the opposite effect occurs when demand shifts to the left. This decrease in demand can also be motivated by a variety of factors (for example, a recession that causes businesses to reduce their purchases of PCs, or an increase in personal tax rates that reduces consumers' purchasing power).

Figure 3.3 shows the effects of a shift in supply in the PC market. The left panel displays a shift in supply to the right. A rightward shift implies an increase in supply, since at

---

High Prices and Criminal Activity: Computer Chips Become a Big Black-Market Item

The strong incentives that high prices provide to suppliers to bring products to market can unfortunately be seen in the activites of criminals. Intel 486 chips sold for about $450 to $500 in 1993. These prices motivated increased theft of computer chips. For example, in September 1993, six masked men overwhelmed employees at one of Intel's eight distributors, making off with $739,000 of microprocessors. Many similar robberies have been reported. According to *The Wall Street Journal,* "Forget drugs. Forget arms. If you want to make a black-market killing these days, steal computer chips. Chips are the dope of the 90's." Fortunately, the high prices of computer chips have also motivated legal activity to increase chip supply—other computer companies have developed products to compete with Intel.

Source: E. J. Gonzales (1993), "Chips Become Big Black-Market Item," *The Wall Street Journal* (September 16), B1.

each price producers supply more PCs. Many factors might motivate an increase in supply. For example, a decline in the prices of labor and other inputs used for manufacturing PCs will make PC production more profitable and increase supply. Supply might also increase because of changes in technology that allow for less expensive, more efficient production. At the old equilibrium price, there is a surplus of PCs after the supply shift. This surplus places downward pressure on prices, which in turn stimulates more demand. The end result is a lower equilibrium price and higher equilibrium quantity. The right panel shows that the opposite effect occurs when supply shifts to the left.

Prices as Social Coordinators

The equilibrium of supply and demand highlights the crucial role that prices play in coordinating the consumption and production decisions of individuals. For example, if too few PCs are being produced, prices will rise. High prices signal would-be producers to shift from producing lower-valued products to producing computers. Because property rights are private, individuals reap the reward from redirecting their efforts and therefore have strong incentives to shift production. Higher prices also motivate consumers to reduce the quantity of PCs demanded. The end result is that the quantity demanded equals the quantity supplied.

If everyone trades in the marketplace and all mutually advantageous trades are completed, the price system results in a Pareto-efficient resource allocation.[4] No government intervention or central planning is required. Rather, consumers and producers, acting in their own self-interest, react to price signals in a manner that produces an efficient resource allocation. Prices act to control and coordinate the many individual decisions made in the economy. After trading is completed, the output mix and final distribution of products cannot be changed without making someone worse off. Also, suppliers engage in efficient production.

The basic logic for efficiency in a competitive economy is straightforward. At equilibrium prices, the quantity supplied equals the quantity demanded for all goods and there are no shortages or surpluses. Everyone who wants to make trades has done so, and all gains from trade have been exhausted. In making supply decisions, firms adopt the most efficient production methods and the value-maximizing output mix (these production choices maximize their profits). No changes in either production or distribution can be made without making someone worse off.

Externalities and the Coase Theorem[5]

Externalities exist when the actions of one party affect the utility or production possibilities of another party outside an exchange relationship. Externalities can prevent a free market from being efficient. If a firm emits pollution into the air, it can adversely affect the welfare of the firm's surrounding neighbors. If the firm does not bear these costs, it is likely to select an inefficient level of pollution (that is, to overpollute). In choosing how much to invest in pollution-control equipment, the firm will consider only its own

---

[4]These conditions will be met in a competitive market when trading costs are sufficiently low. Later, we will discuss factors that can motivate inefficiency in a free-market economy.

[5]This section draws on the analysis in R. Coase (1960), "The Problem of Social Cost," *Journal of Law and Economics* 3, 1–44.

personal costs and benefits. Efficient investment would also consider the costs and benefits imposed on the neighbors (the efficient level of investment is where the total marginal costs of additional investment equal the total marginal benefits—not just those incurred privately by the firm).

Prior to 1960, most economists thought that externalities would surely prevent a free-market system from producing an efficient allocation of resources. Government intervention seemed to be needed to enhance efficiency. For example, the traditional recommendation would have been to tax firms based on their levels of pollution. Given this tax, firms would have incentives to reduce pollution.

In 1960, Nobel Prize winner Ronald Coase presented a convincing argument that free-market exchange is much more powerful in producing efficient results than many economists thought. As long as property rights can be traded, there is an incentive to rearrange these rights to enhance economic efficiency. The often-recommended government intervention might be unnecessary and in many cases undesirable. Suppose that a firm has the legal right to pollute as much as it wants. The neighbors can always offer to pay the firm to reduce its pollution level. Thus, the firm faces a cost for polluting (if the firm pollutes, there is an opportunity cost of not receiving compensation from its neighbors). The firm will pollute only if it is more valuable to the firm than the costs to its neighbors. This efficient solution is obtained without a pollution tax. The same degree of pollution can occur even if the neighbors have the legal right to stop the firm from emitting any pollution rather than the firm having the legal right to pollute as much as it wants. In this case, the firm can pay the neighbors for the right to pollute. Regardless of whether the firm or the neighbors have the legal right, the gains from trade are exhausted when the marginal benefit to the firm of polluting is equal to the marginal cost that is imposed on the neighbors.

Coase's argument convinced most economists that externalities were less of a problem than previously thought. It also implied that the distribution of property (legal) rights might have less of an effect on the ultimate use of resources than it has on the distribution of income—so long as these rights can be exchanged. In our example, the firm might emit the same amount of pollution regardless of who has the property right. However, the party with the property right obtains more wealth (since it is the one receiving payments).

Nevertheless, as Coase points out, free-market exchange will not always solve the problem of externalities. The transactions that are necessary to overcome this problem are not free—there are *transaction costs*. These costs include search and information costs, bargaining and decision costs, and policing and enforcement costs.[6] These costs can prevent a preferred outcome from occurring. In our example, the firm might limit its pollution for a payment that is far less than the collective damage imposed on the neighbors. Nevertheless, the costs of bargaining with the firm and the costs of reaching agreement on how the neighbors should split the payment can prevent this mutually beneficial agreement from being reached. Generally, the costs of reaching an agreement increase with the number of bargainers. In our example, the likelihood of reaching an efficient agreement is highest if the firm only has to bargain with one neighbor who owns all the surrounding property.

[6]C. Dahlman (1979), "The Problem of Externality," *The Journal of Law and Economics* 22, 148–162.

Property Rights in Russia

An exchange transaction is an agreement among individuals on property rights to goods. Exchange is significantly limited if property rights are not enforceable. Within well-functioning economies, the legal system is an important institution for enforcing property rights and increases trade in the economy. Former communist countries, such as Russia, have had difficulty converting to a market system because they do not have established legal systems for enforcing property rights. While there are court systems, the inefficiences of these systems significantly limited their usefulness to private companies and individuals (the courts are very slow, expensive, and sometimes corrupt).

The lack of a good legal system offers profit opportunities for firms to create their own mechanisms for enforcing property rights and facilitating trade. Large firms in Russia have their own security forces. If another party does not honor a contract, the security force uses coercive power to force compliance (much like the Mafia). In turn, these large companies have incentives to honor contracts, because it is important for them to maintain good reputations to encourage other parties to deal with them in the future (see Chapter 7). Allegedly, the ability of large firms to enforce contracts in Russia serves as a source of competitive advantage (profits). Small firms have difficulty competing with large firms because they do not have the security forces nor the reputations to ensure contract compliance.

Utilizing legal systems can be expensive, even in developed economies. Managers, throughout the world, have the potential to create value if they can devise more efficient methods for contract enforcement. Many firms invest substantial resource to develop reputations as honest trading partners.

Source: A. Grief and E. Kandel (1995) "Contract Enforcement Institutions: Historical Perspective and Current Status in Russia," in *Economic Transition in Eastern Europe and Russia* (Hoover Institution: Palo Alto, CA), 291–321.

It is also important that property rights be clearly assigned and exchangeable. Suppose that there were no legal system to enforce property rights. Neighbors would be reluctant to pay a firm not to pollute—they do not obtain an enforceable property right to prevent the firm from polluting. After collecting the payment, the firm could renege on its promise to reduce pollution and the neighbors would have no recourse.

This discussion suggests that free-market economies will tend to produce an efficient resource allocation whenever property rights are clearly assigned and the transaction costs of exchanging them are sufficiently low. When these conditions are met, efficiency will occur regardless of the initial distribution of property rights. This general principle is often referred to as the *Coase Theorem.*

THE COASE THEOREM

The ultimate resource allocation will be efficient, regardless of the initial assignment of property rights, as long as the transaction costs are sufficiently low and the property rights are clearly assigned and can be exchanged.

The driving force behind the Coase Theorem is the gain from trade—individuals have incentives to search out and undertake mutually advantageous trades. This principle has important managerial implications. If a manager does not have the property rights to undertake some action, it does not mean that the action cannot be undertaken. If the proposed action creates enough value, the manager can often obtain the necessary property rights from the current owners. Suppose the Watts Construction Company can create substantial value by developing a shopping center on a site that is currently zoned for residential housing. Surrounding property owners might support a change in the zoning requirement, as long as they share in the value creation. Watts might be able to increase this support by agreeing to develop a new public park next to the shopping mall.

The Coase Theorem also suggests that transaction costs are central to the study of organizations. In the absence of transaction costs, efficient outcomes will occur independent of how decision rights are assigned. From an efficiency standpoint, it does not matter whether decision rights are centralized or decentralized. It is transaction costs that make these organizational considerations important. We elaborate on this issue in the section that follows.

The Coase Theorem and the "Fable of the Bees"

A prominently discussed case of externalities is the so-called Fable of the Bees. Beekeepers provide pollination services for the surrounding fruit growers, while the growers, in turn, provide nectar for the bees. Many economists would consider this to be a classic case of externalities. If beekeepers and growers do not receive compensation for the benefits they bestow on other parties, they will underinvest in their activities (from a social standpoint).

The Coase Theorem suggests that beekeepers and growers can privately negotiate to overcome this externality problem. Steven Cheung found that this is exactly what is done. Beekeepers and growers often enter into contracts. Fruit growers hire hives of bees to provide pollination of those trees that give little suitable nectar, while the beekeepers pay growers for the privilege of "grazing" their bees on high nectar–producing trees. Given these payments, beekeepers and growers have incentives to consider the effects on the other party when they make their investment decisions. Through this process, beekeepers and growers can reach efficient levels of investment with no help from the central government.

Source: S. Cheung (1973), "The Fable of the Bees: An Economic Investigation," *Journal of Law and Economics* 16, 11–34.

Free Markets versus Central Planning

History suggests that the price system is more efficient at controlling and coordinating production and consumption decisions in large economies than is central planning. Without the aid of government planners, free-market economies have produced products that are highly valued by consumers and have avoided large shortages and surpluses. In planned economies such as the former Soviet Union, shortages, surpluses, and other production mistakes are common.

There are at least two reasons why markets have been more successful than central planning in large economies. First, the price system motivates better use of knowledge and information in economic decisions. Second, it provides stronger incentives for individuals to make productive decisions.

General and Specific Knowledge[7]

Figure 3.4 shows how the costs of transferring knowledge can be displayed on a continuum. At one end of this continuum is *general knowledge*. General knowledge is essentially free to transfer. Examples of general knowledge are prices and quantities—a store-keeper can easily tell you that the price of sugar is $1 per pound. As the costs of information transfer increase, the information is said to become more *specific*. We use the term *specific knowledge* to denote knowledge that is relatively high on this scale (it is expensive to transfer).

At least three factors influence the costs of transferring information. First are the characteristics of the sender and receiver. Generally, it is less expensive for people of similar training, language, and culture to communicate than for people from different backgrounds. Second is the technology available for communication. For example, the development of

[7]This section draws on the analysis in M. Jensen and W. Meckling (1995), "Specific and General Knowledge, and Organizational Structure," *Journal of Applied Corporate Finance* 8:2, 4–18.

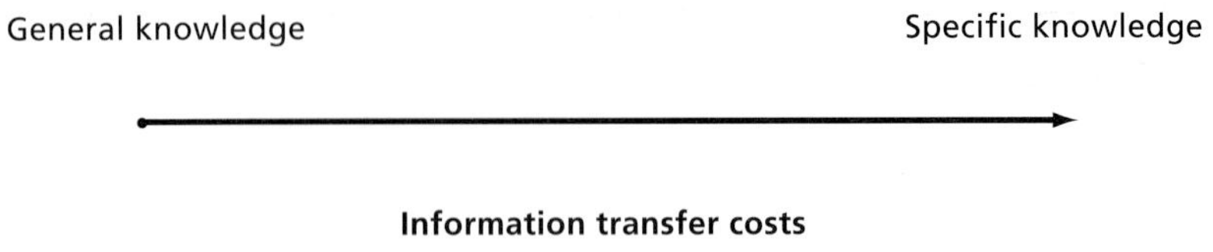

General knowledge   Specific knowledge

Information transfer costs

Figure 3.4   The Costs of Transferring Knowledge

The costs of transferring knowledge can be displayed on a continuum. At one end is *general knowledge,* which is essentially free to transfer. As the costs of information transfer increase, the information is said to become more *specific.* We use the term, *specific knowledge* to denote knowledge that is relatively expensive to transfer.

electronic mail (e-mail) has lowered the costs of transferring information. Third is the nature of the knowledge itself. Some knowledge is difficult to summarize, comprehend, or transfer in a timely fashion. Depending on the exact setting, the following types of knowledge are often specific in nature:

- *Idiosyncratic knowledge of particular circumstances.* The employee on the spot is most likely to know if a particular truck has room for additional cargo or if a certain customer wants to purchase a particular product. If this information is not used immediately, it may become useless. For example, by the time the information about the truck is transferred to another person (such as a central planner), the opportunity to load extra cargo on the truck can be lost (for instance, if the truck has left).
- *Scientific knowledge.* The knowledge of how recombinant DNA works is not easily transferred to nonscientists.
- *Assembled knowledge.* An accountant who has completed a client's tax returns for several years is likely to have assembled important knowledge about the relevant parts of the tax code and the idiosyncrasies of the individual's income and deductions. Another example is learning to operate a complex machine. In neither case is the information easily transferred to others.

Specific knowledge is critical in properly allocating resources. Many economic opportunities are short-lived and must be acted on quickly by the person on the spot (with the

Failure to Use Specific Knowledge at GE

In the late 1970s, aggregate data indicated that houses and families were shrinking. Based on this data, central planners at General Electric concluded that smaller appliances were the wave of the future. Correspondingly, General Electric invested large sums in developing smaller refrigerators and other appliances.

Since the planners had little contact with homebuilders and retailers, they failed to realize that bathrooms and kitchens were not shrinking. Indeed, working couples actually wanted larger refrigerators to reduce the number of trips to the supermarket. Moreover, top management, which also did not have contact with the market, failed to see the planners' mistakes. The result was that General Electric wasted a lot of time and money designing smaller appliances. This loss occurred because the relevant specific knowledge about trends in homebuilding was not incorporated in the decision-making process.

Source: "The New Breed of Strategic Planner," *Business Week* (September 17, 1984) 65.

The Dynamic Nature of Specific Knowledge

Historically, economies of scale have motivated firms in retailing to concentrate on standardized production and distribution. Knowledge about the idiosyncratic demands of people in particular neighborhoods tended to be ignored in the stocking of individual stores in large retail chains—the information was simply too expensive to collect and process.

Due to the development of computers and electronic scanners, information about the idiosyncratic demands of individuals has become less specific. As a result, retail companies have begun to engage in more micromarketing. For instance, the Sears outlet in the North Hollywood section of Los Angeles is tailor-made to suit the neighborhood's Hispanic population. The signs are in Spanish. The store is stocked with ethnic items, such as a broad selection of compact discs and tapes from Central and South American music stars. A few hundred miles to the north, the Sears store in San Jose offers a large number of clothing items in extra-small sizes to attract the area's Asian population. On the other hand, the Sears stores in Florida carry large, roomy clothes that appeal to the large population of elderly residents.

Source: "Customers on Target," *Financial Times* (August 18, 1995).

specific information of the opportunity) or lost. Not incorporating the proper scientific or assembled knowledge into economic decisions can have costly implications. For an economic system to be successful, it must promote the use of the relevant specific knowledge in economic decisions.

Figure 3.4 displays knowledge on a continuum at a *point in time*. It is important to realize that knowledge is dynamic. There are at least two factors that can motivate changes in the costs of transferring knowledge. First is technology—improved communications and computer technology have greatly lowered the costs of transferring certain types of information, making it more general. Second, individuals can take actions to convert specific knowledge to more general knowledge, for example, by drafting an operating manual.

Ikujiro Nonaka and Hirotaka Takeuchi argue that converting hunches, perceptions, mental models, beliefs, experiences, and other types of specific knowledge into a form that can be communicated and transmitted in formal and systematic language is a key aspect of successful new product innovation.[8] As one example, they discuss Matushita's development of an automated fresh bread maker in the 1980s. Specific knowledge of how to knead dough to produce tasty bread was held by master bakers. This knowledge was not easily transferred to others and past attempts to produce fully automated bread makers had failed because they produced poor-quality bread. On the other hand, specific knowledge about how to produce automated bread machines was held by engineers. To produce a successful bread machine, specific knowledge had to be transferred between bakers and engineers. To accomplish this transfer, managers from Matushita took bread-making lessons from a master baker at an Osaka hotel. Eventually, the managers discovered that the key to good bread making is to "twist and stretch" the dough during the kneading process. This concept was general knowledge that could be passed along to design engineers. Matushita's "Home Baker" became the first fully automatic bread-making machine for home use and has been a highly successful product.

[8]I. Nonaka and H. Takeuchi (1995), *The Knowledge-Creating Company* (Oxford University Press: New York).

Use of Specific Knowledge at Apple Computer

Apple's first portable Mac had so many bells and whistles that it weighed 17 pounds. It did not do well in the market. In 1990, Apple began completely reworking the design of the computer from the consumer's viewpoint. The entire product-development team of software designers, industrial engineers, marketing people, and industrial designers were sent into the field to observe potential customers using other products. The team discovered that people used laptops on airplanes, in cars, and at home in bed. People did not want just small computers but mobile computers. In response, Apple designed two distinctive features for its PowerBook computer—the TrackBall pointer and the palm rest in the front of the keyboard. The new product was easy to use and distinctive. Sales improved.

The knowledge of what customers really wanted in a laptop computer was acquired by a team of workers who interacted closely with customers. The team members also had important scientific and assembled knowledge that allowed them to take this new information and use it to design a marketable product. Finally, they had the authority to modify the product based on their findings. It is less likely that this specific knowledge would be incorporated in product design in a large centrally planned economy—where a central office is in charge of making decisions on literally millions of products.

Source: "Hot Products, Smart Design Is the Common Thread," *Business Week* (June 7, 1993) 54–57.

Specific Knowledge and the Economic System[9]

Nobel Prize winner Friedrich Hayek made a convincing argument that free-market economies are more likely to incorporate the relevant specific knowledge in economic decision making than centrally planned economies. He argued that the relevant specific knowledge for economic decision making is not given to any one individual; instead, it is distributed among many people in the economy. This knowledge, by definition, does not lend itself to statistical aggregation, and it is costly to transfer. A central planner does not generally have the mental or computing ability to process large amounts of this type of information. Hayek concluded that central planners will often ignore important specific knowledge in economic decisions.

In contrast, economic decisions in a market system are decentralized to individuals who are likely to have the relevant specific knowledge. Technical and marketing geniuses, like William Gates at Microsoft and Michael Dell at Dell Computer, are free to start new businesses and to market products of their choosing. The information that motivates these decisions does not have to be transferred to some central office in Washington where centralized production decisions are made. Thus, the information is more likely to be used effectively.

The activities of decentralized decision makers are coordinated by prices. For instance, an increase in market-determined wage rates (the price of labor) signals to producers that labor is in short supply and should be conserved. Higher wages, in turn, motivate producers to use less labor. An important advantage of the price system that is stressed by Hayek is that prices economize on the costs of transferring information to coordinate decisions. Companies often do not benefit from knowing all the details of why labor costs have increased. The simple fact that wages have increased tells them most things they need to know to make value-maximizing decisions.[10]

---

[9]This section draws on the analysis in F. A. Hayek (1945), "The Use of Knowledge in Society," *American Economic Review* 35, 1–18.

[10]Producers might also want to know the expected future prices of labor. For instance, if the price increase is expected to be transitory, the company might want to avoid making layoffs.

Fiat—Using Specific Knowledge about Developing Markets

Traditionally, leading car manufacturers have adapted their existing models for sales in developing countries, in spite of the fact that unique conditions prevail in these markets. Fiat, however, has recently invested about $2 billion in developing a new car, the A178, to meet the particular demands of people in developing countries. The car is attractively styled and inexpensive but is built tough to withstand poor road conditions. Specific knowledge about the appropriate design features was obtained from a task force of engineers from Brazil, Italy, Turkey, Poland, Argentina, India, South Africa, and Morocco. Fiat forecasts that it will sell up to 900,000 A178s a year once production goes into full swing. Fiat has the decision rights to produce this product and does not have to convince some central planner of its merits.

Source: "Fiat Steers New Model towards Developing Markets," *Financial Times* (August, 24, 1995).

Incentives in Free Markets

Private property rights are critical for making a free-market economy work because they provide strong incentives for decentralized decision makers to act on their specific information—the wealth effects of economic decisions are borne directly by the resource owners. If Mary Chen owns a piece of property, she has incentives to use the land productively because she gets to keep the profits. If John Dredge can make more productive use of the land, Mary will sell the land to John (there are gains from trade). Property rights are rearranged so that decision rights over resources are linked with the relevant specific knowledge.

In contrast, decision makers in centrally planned economies have limited incentives to make productive use of information (even if they have it) since they do not own the resources under their control. Further, lower-level bureaucrats have limited incentives to

Nobel Prize Winner F. A. Hayek on the "Miracle" of the Price System

"It is worth contemplating for a moment a very simple and commonplace instance of the action of the price system to see what precisely it accomplishes. Assume that somewhere in the world a new opportunity for the use of some raw material, say, tin, has arisen, or that one of the sources of supply of tin has been eliminated. It does not matter for our purpose—and it is significant that it does not matter—which of these two causes has made tin more scarce. All that the users of tin need to know is that some of the tin they used to consume is now more profitably employed elsewhere and that, in consequence, they must economize tin. There is no need for the great majority of them even to know where the more urgent need has arisen, or in favor of what other needs they ought to husband the supply. If only some of them know directly of the new demand and switch resources over to it, and if the people who are aware of the new gap thus created in turn fill it from still other sources, the effect will rapidly spread throughout the entire economic system. This influences not only all the uses of tin but also those of its substitutes and the substitutes of these substitutes, the supply of all things made of tin, and their substitutes, and so on. All this takes place without the great majority of those instrumental in bringing about these substitutions knowing anything at all about the original cause of these changes. The whole acts as one market, not because any of its members surveys the whole field, but because their limited individual fields of vision sufficiently overlap so that through many intermediaries the relevant information is communicated to all. The mere fact that there is one price for any commodity—or rather that local prices are connected in a manner determined by the cost of transport, etc.—brings about the solution which (if conceptually possible) might have been arrived at by one single mind possessing all the information which is in fact dispersed among all the people involved in the process."

Source: F. Hayek (1945), "The Use of Knowledge in Society," *American Economic Review* 35, 1–18.

Japan, Computers, and Industrial Policy

In the early 1990s, a group of prominent policy advocates argued that Japan's output of computers and computer-related products would pass that of the United States during the decade due to the alleged power and success of Japanese government planners. It was argued that the United States was at a competitive disadvantage because it did not rely on central economic planning. The 1990s are now more than half over. "It is not Fujitsu or an NEC or a Hitachi that you stare at every day at the office, but a Compaq or IBM or Apple—all American designed and manufactured." Japanese companies have also been "crushed" in software. In 1994, U.S. computer companies "invaded" the Japanese market for personal computers in a serious manner. In 1994, U.S. companies doubled their share of the Japanese computer market to more than 30 percent.

Source: "Japan, Computers, and Industrial Policy," *The American Enterprise*
(July/August, 1995) 86.

carry out decisons made by the central authority. The best use of a particular automobile might be to transport tourists from a local airport. A central planner, however, might give the car to his brother because he is more concerned about making his brother happy than in making the economy more productive. After all, he does not keep the profits from the taxi enterprise—they go to the state.

Transaction Costs and the Existence of Firms

Coase's Explanation[11]

Hayek's argument suggests that markets are better than central planning. Why, then, is so much activity conducted in firms, where resource allocation decisions are made by managers in a manner that is often akin to central planning?[12] Conceptually, firms do not have to exist. All production and exchange could be carried out by market transactions. In the case of the PC, each consumer could buy all the parts that make up the PC in separate market transactions and then pay someone to assemble them. In reality, of course, most computers are made by firms and only the final products are sold to the consumer.

Ronald Coase provides an answer to the question of why resources are allocated both by markets and firms. His basic argument is that economic transactions involve costs, including search and information costs, bargaining and decision costs, and policing and enforcement costs. There is also a cost if the transaction results in an inefficient resource allocation (we discuss this in detail in Chapter 7). The optimal method of organizing a given economic transaction is the one that minimizes transaction costs.[13] In some cases, the method will be market exchange. In other cases, the method will involve firms.

---

[11]R. Coase, (1937), *Economica.* "The Nature of the Firm," New Series, IV, 386–405.

[12]Within a firm, resources are often transferred from one division to another by an administrative order from management. For example, managers are often transferred among divisions by administrative decisions. Prices are not used to make these decisions—the divisions do not typically bid for the managers.

[13]It is not always possible to separate transaction costs from the basic costs of production. The optimal method of production can depend on the way the transaction is organized. Therefore, it is more precise to say that the optimal method of organizations is the one that minimizes total costs (production and transaction costs). The basic arguments are easier to explain if we focus on transaction costs.

Herbert Simon on Organizations and Markets

The United States is often referred to as a market economy. In reality, much of the economic activity in the United States, as well as in other market economies, is conducted within firms. To quote Herbert Simon, a former Nobel Prize winner:

> Suppose a visitor from Mars approaches the earth from space, equipped with a telescope that reveals social structures. The firms reveal themselves, say, as solid green areas with faint interior contours marking out divisions and departments. Market transaction costs show as red lines connecting firms, forming a network in the spaces between them. Within the firms the approaching visitor also sees pale blue lines, the lines of authority connecting bosses with various levels of workers . . . No matter whether the visitor approached the United States or the Soviet Union, urban China or the European Community, the greater part of the space below would be within the green areas, for almost all the inhabitants would be employees, within firm boundaries. Organizations would be the dominant feature on the landscape. A message sent back home, describing the scene, would speak of "large green areas interconnected by red lines." It would not likely speak of a "network of red lines connecting green spots."

Source: H. Simon (1991), "Organizations and Markets," *Journal of Economic Perspectives* 5, 25–44.

Transaction Costs in Markets

A primary set of costs of using markets for exchange involve the discovery and negotiation of prices.[14] For example, firms have the following two potential advantages:

- *Fewer transactions.* If there are N customers and M factors of production, a firm can hire the M factors and sell to the N customers. The total transactions are N + M. In contrast, if each customer contracts separately with each factor of production, there are N × M transactions. For example, 10 workers might be required to assemble a computer. If there are 1,000 customers and each customer negotiates with each worker, there are a total of 10,000 transactions. If a firm hires the 10 workers and sells computers to the 1,000 customers, there are 1,010 transactions.
- *Informational specialization.* Think of buying a PC. How much do you know about buying each part separately? PC producers, on the other hand, specialize in this knowledge. The consumer buying from a firm only has to be concerned with the quality of the end product.

In Chapter 16, we elaborate on one particularly important set of transaction costs that motivates the existence of firms, those associated with *specific assets*. Assets are specific when they are worth more in their current use than in alternative uses. An example is a machine that is used to produce parts that can only be used by one particular producer. The machine is valuable in producing parts for the particular buyer but is essentially worthless in alternative uses. In this case, independent suppliers will be reluctant to purchase the machine since they do not want to be at the mercy of a single buyer. For instance, suppliers might worry that the buyer will try to force a reduction in future prices, make unreasonable quality or quantity demands, or curtail purchases. It is these

---

[14]Economists generally agree that transaction costs motivate the existence of firms. There is disagreement concerning which transaction costs are most important. Our intent in this chapter is to give the reader a general sampling of the kinds of costs that can be important.

General Motors and Fisher Body

In the 1920s, General Motors and Fisher Body were separate companies. General Motors produced cars with auto bodies supplied by Fisher. To improve efficiency, General Motors asked Fisher to construct a new auto body plant next to a new General Motors assembly plant. Fisher refused, probably in part because it feared investing in such a specific asset (the proposed plant was tailored closely to the General Motors production process). By making this investment, Fisher would have made itself vulnerable to subsequent unreasonable demands from General Motors (for example, to reduce prices). Ultimately, this problem was resolved by General Motors' purchase of Fisher Body to form one large firm.

concerns that make simple market transactions between buyers and sellers unlikely when the relevant assets are highly specific. A potential response to this problem is for the producer to own the machine and make the input parts within the same firm.

Another potential advantage of firms is that in some cases they can reduce transaction costs through established reputations. Individuals are likely to have confidence in trading with parties who are expected to continue to participate in the marketplace for a long time period. They understand that these parties have incentives to be honorable in order to enhance their reputation and future business. Organizations tend to have longer lives than individuals and thus might be expected to be more likely to honor agreements than unknown individuals (some major corporations date back to the 19th century). This increased trust can motivate lower expenditures on negotiating and policing agreements. We discuss this issue in greater detail in Chapters 7 and 18.

Government regulation also helps to explain the existence of some firms. Sometimes firms can produce more cheaply because they avoid taxes at various stages of production compared to market transactions.

Transaction Costs in Firms

We have discussed several transaction costs that can motivate the existence of firms. Given these costs, why isn't the economy one big firm? The answer is that resource allocation by firms also involves transaction costs. For example, as firms become larger, it becomes increasingly difficult for managers to make efficient and timely decisions. They are more likely to make errors and to be less responsive to changing circumstances. As a firm grows larger, decisions must be delegated to nonowners of the firm, and there are costs of motivating these nonowners to work in the interests of the owner. Chapters 7 and 15 contain more detailed discussions of these transaction costs within firms.

Corporate Focus and Stock Returns

Ronald Coase argues that the use of markets involves transaction costs and that sometimes these costs can be reduced by including transactions within firms. However, firms also involve transaction costs. In the 1990s, many companies concluded that they had become too large and diversified. These companies, in turn, decided to focus on core businesses and to shed unrelated activities (for example, through asset sales). Evidence suggests that on average, these firms increased their stock market values by increasing their focus on core activities.

Source: R. Comment and G. Jarrell (1995), "Corporate Focus and Stock Returns," *Journal of Financial Economics* 37, 67–87.

Firms versus Markets: When Markets Ruled

Economic theory argues that economic activities are organized in firms when the cost is lower than using markets, and vice versa. Today, much of the economic activity in the world is conducted within firms. It is hard to envision a world where large firms do not play an important role in the production and distribution of products. The importance of firms, however, is a relatively recent phenomenon. Prior to the middle of the 19th century, there were almost no large firms. Most production was conducted by small, owner-managed operations. The activities of these operations were coordinated almost entirely through market transactions and prices. To quote Alfred Chandler in describing business organization before 1850:

> The traditional American business was a single-unit business enterprise. In such an enterprise an individual or a small number of owners operated a shop, factory, bank or transportation line out of a single office. Normally this type of firm handled only a single economic function, dealt in a single product line, and operated in one geographic area. Before the rise of the modern firm, the activities of one of these small, personally owned and managed enterprises were coordinated and monitored by market and price mechanisms.

The large firm became feasible only with the development of improved energy sources, transportation, and communications. Coal-fired steam power generators provided a source of energy that made it possible for the factory to replace artisans and small mill owners, while railroads enabled firms to ship production in large quantities to newly emerging urban centers. The telegraph allowed firms to coordinate activities of workers over larger geographic areas. These developments tended to make it less expensive to coordinate production and distribution using administrative controls, rather than to rely on numerous market transactions between all the intermediaries in the system.

Source: A. Chandler (1977), *The Visible Hand: The Managerial Revolution in American Business* (Harvard University Press: Cambridge, MA).

Efficient Organization

Individuals involved in trade and production have incentives to implement cost-reducing methods of organization because there are more gains to be shared.[15] For example, at a given price, more profits can be generated if costs are reduced. In competitive markets, individuals will constantly search for new and better ways to reduce costs to improve their competitive advantage and profits. The end result is that economic activities will be organized within firms when the cost is lower than using markets, and vice versa. Also, as we will see, this same process has important implications for the internal design of organizations.

Managerial Objectives

Our discussion to this point has treated decision makers within firms as owners. Owners have a strong interest in increasing the profits of the firm, since they get to keep the proceeds. In public corporations managers are often not the major owners of the firm. Nevertheless, in the next three chapters of the book, we assume that managers strive to maximize single-period firm profits—they make input, output, and pricing decisions with profit maximization as their sole objective. This perspective is a reasonable starting point because if firms fail to make profits over time, they cease to exist. Most managers are under constant pressure to make money. There are also other mechanisms, such as incentive compensation,

---

[15]A firm's profit (Π) is the difference between its total revenues (TR) and total costs (TC): $\Pi = TR - TC$. If a company has sales of \$1,000,000 and costs of \$750,000 it earns a profit of \$250,000.

CEO Turnover and Firm Profits

A standard assumption in microeconomics is that managers strive to maximize profits. One reason why managers are likely to be concerned about profits is that poor profits and stock price performance increase the likelihood that they will be fired. For instance, studies have found that firms in the worst decile of performers were about 1.5 times as likely to have a management change as firms in the best decile of performers.

Source: J. Warner, R. Watts, and K. Wruck (1988), "Stock Prices and Top Management Changes," *Journal of Financial Economics* 20, 461–492; and M. Weisbach (1988), "Outside Directors and CEO Turnover," *Journal of Financial Economics* 20, 431–460.

that work to align the interests of managers and owners. These mechanisms help to make profit maximization a reasonable first approximation of the managers' objective function. Profit maximization is the basic premise used in most economics textbooks. Starting in Chapter 7, however, we present a richer characterization of the firm and analyze management/owner conflicts in greater detail.

Managerial Implications

We began this chapter with an overview of how free-market economies operate. An understanding of this topic is critical if managers are to make productive economic decisions. It is important to understand how a shift in either supply or demand affects product prices. In the next three chapters, we extend this analysis and examine in more detail how managers might make optimal input, output, and pricing decisions.

We also discussed the role of knowledge and incentives in determining the effectiveness of alternative economic systems and the importance of transaction costs in determining whether or not economic transactions are conducted within markets or organizations. While we have focused our discussion at the economic-system level, these issues are directly relevant to understanding firm-level decisions on organizational architecture. If firms are to be productive, they must be structured in ways that promote the use of the relevant specific knowledge and economize on the costs of organization. They must also provide the proper incentives, so that their members behave in a productive manner. Starting in Chapter 7, we extend the concepts introduced in this chapter to questions of organizational architecture.

Summary

There are many different ways to organize economic activities. Economists focus on *Pareto efficiency* in evaluating the effectiveness of alternate economic systems. An allocation is Pareto efficient if there is no alternative that keeps all individuals at least as well off but makes at least one person better off. Pareto-improving changes in a resource allocation are viewed as welfare increasing.

An important feature of a free-market economy is the use of *private property rights*. A property right is a socially enforced right to select the uses of an economic good. A property right is private when it is assigned to a specific person. Private property rights are *alienable* in that they can be transferred (sold or gifted) to other individuals.

In free markets, property rights are frequently exchanged. Trade occurs because it is *mutually advantageous*. The buyer values the good more than the seller, and there are *gains from trade*. Trade is an important form of value creation. Trading produces value that makes individuals better off. Gains from trade also motivate the movement of resources to more productive users.

Prices coordinate the individual actions in a free-market economy. If too little of a good is being produced, prices will rise and producers have incentives to increase output to exploit the profit opportunity. If too much of a good is being produced, prices will fall and producers will have incentives to cut production. The market is in *equilibrium* when the quantity supplied of a product equals the quantity demanded. There are strong pressures in competitive economies that move the market toward equilibrium. In equilibrium, there are no *shortages* or *surpluses*. Equilibrium prices and quantities change with changes in the supply and demand for products.

Externalities exist when the actions of one party affect the consumption or production possibilities of another party outside an exchange relationship. Externalities can cause markets to fail to produce an efficient resource allocation. Competitive markets will produce a Pareto-efficient allocation of resources if the costs of making mutually advantageous trades are sufficiently low. The *Coase Theorem* indicates that the ultimate resource allocation will be efficient, regardless of the initial assignment of property rights, as long as *transaction costs* are sufficiently low and property rights are clearly assigned and exchangeable.

General knowledge is inexpensive to transfer, while *specific knowledge* is expensive to transfer. Specific knowledge is very important in economic decisions. Central planning often fails because important specific knowledge is not incorporated in the planning process. In market systems, economic decisions are decentralized to individuals with the relevant specific knowledge. Prices convey general knowledge that coordinates the decisions of individuals. Private property rights provide important incentives to individuals to act productively, since they bear the wealth effects of their decisions.

All economic activity could be conducted through market transactions. However, even in free-market economies, much economic activity occurs within firms, where administrative decisions rather than market prices are used to allocate resources. Firms exist because of the transaction costs of using markets. However, organizing transactions within firms also involves costs. Individuals have incentives to organize transactions in the most efficient manner—to increase the gains from trade. Economic activities will tend to be organized within firms when the cost is lower than using markets and vice versa.

This chapter provides important background information on both markets and organizations. In Chapters 4 to 6, we extend the analysis of markets and study important managerial decisions such as outputs, inputs, and pricing. In these three chapters, we assume that managers strive to maximize firm profits. In the remainder of the book, we extend the analysis of organizations and cover a variety of important topics about organizational design. A reader interested primarily in organizational design can move directly to Chapter 7 without loss of continuity.

Suggested Readings

R. Coase (1988), *the Firm, the Market, and the Law* (The University of Chicago Press: Chicago, IL).

J. Eatwell, M. Milgate, and P. Newman (1989a), *Allocation, Information, and Markets,* (W. W. Norton: New York).

——— (1989b), *The Invisible Hand* (W. W. Norton: New York).

F. Hayek (1945), "The Use of Knowledge in Society," *American Economic Review* 35, 519–530.

M. Jensen and W. Meckling (1995), "Specific and General Knowledge, and Organizational Structure," *Journal of Applied Corporate Finance* 8:2, 4–18.

O. Williamson (1985), *The Economic Institutions of Capitalism* (Free Press: New York).

Review Questions

3–1. What is Pareto efficiency? Why do economists use this criterion for comparing alternative economic systems?

3–2. What is a property right? What role do property rights play in a free-market economy?

3–3. Twin brothers, Tom and Bill, constantly fight over toys. For instance, Tom will argue it his turn to play with a toy, while Bill argues it is his turn. Their parents frequently have to intervene in these disputes. Their mom has conceived an idea that might reduce these conflicts. In particular, every toy in the house would be "owned" by one of the boys. The owner would have complete authority over the use of the toy. The mom reasons that ownership would cut down on disputes. Any time there is an argument over a toy, the owner gets the final and immediate say. The boys' dad is concerned that this idea will prevent the boys from learning to "share." He envisions that under the new system, Tom will not allow Bill to play with his toys and Bill will not allow Tom to play with his toys. The current system forces them to figure out a way to share the toys. Do you think that their dad's concerns are valid? Explain.

3–4. What do you think will happen to the price and quantity of VCRs if:
  a. The availability of good movies to play on VCRs increases?
  b. Personal income increases?
  c. The price of inputs used to produce VCRs decreases?
  d. The price at local movie theaters declines substantially?

3–5. What is the difference between general and specific knowledge? How can specific knowledge motivate the use of decentralized decision making?

3–6. Evaluate the following statement:

> *Using free markets and the price system always results in a more efficient resource allocation than central planning. Just look at what happened in Eastern Europe.*

3–7. **a.** What are transaction costs?
  b. Give a few examples of transaction costs.
  c. What effect does the existence of transaction costs have on free-market economies?

3–8. If markets are so wonderful, why do firms exist?

3–9. Some people (for example, Hayek) argue that decentralization of economic decisions in the economy leads to an efficient resource allocation. What differences exist within the firm that make the link between decentralization and efficiency less clear?

3–10. In certain professional sports, team owners "own" the players. Owners can sell or trade players to another team. However, players are not free to negotiate with other team owners on their own behalf. The team owners initially obtain the rights to players through an annual process that is used to allocate new players among the teams in the league. They can also obtain the rights to a player by purchasing them from another team. Players do not like this process and often argue that they should be free to negotiate with all teams in the sporting league. In this case, they would be free to play for the team that offers the most desirable contract. Owners argue that this change in rights would have a negative effect on the distribution of talent across teams. In particular, they argue that all the good players would end up on rich, media-center teams such as New York or Los Angeles (because these teams could afford to pay higher salaries). The inequity of players across teams would make the sport less interesting to fans and thus destroy the league. Do you think the owners' argument is correct? Explain.

3–11. The guide at the Washington Monument tells your 10-year-old nephew, "Enjoy the monument. As a citizen you are one of its owners." Your nephew asks you if that is true. What do you say?

3–12. Locust Hill Golf Club is a private country club. It charges an initiation fee of $12,000. When members quit the club, they receive no refund on their initiation fees. They simply lose their membership. Salt Lake Country Club is also a private golf course. At this club, members join by buying a membership certificate from a member who is leaving the club. The price of the membership is determined by supply and demand. Suppose that both clubs are considering installing a watering system. In each case, the watering system is expected to enhance the quality of the golf course significantly. To finance these systems, members would pay a special assessment of $1,500 per year for the next three years. The proposals will be voted on by the memberships. Do you think that the membership is more likely to vote in favor of the proposal at Locust Hill or Salt Lake Country Club? Explain.

chapter 4

Demand

CHAPTER OUTLINE

The Players Theater Company (PTC) is a regional repertory theater in the Midwest. Each year, it produces six plays, ranging from Shakespeare to contemporary musicals. PTC had priced its tickets at $30. On a typical night, about 200 of the theater's 500 seats were filled. The PTC board met recently to discuss a possible price decrease to $25. Advocates of the proposal argued that the decrease in ticket prices would increase the number of tickets sold and the revenue for the theater company.

At the meeting, the PTC board engaged in a heated debate over the proposal. It soon became evident that the board did not have enough information to make a sound decision. For instance, nearby restaurants, which serve PTC customers, had indicated that they were planning to make substantial price increases at the first of the year. Would this increase affect the demand for PTC tickets and thus PTC's optimal pricing policy? While customers might buy more tickets at lower prices, would total revenue or profits necessarily increase? Would it be better to attract additional customers by improving the quality of PTC plays or by lowering price? After much discussion, the proposed decrease in price was tabled for further study.

The discussion at the PTC board meeting highlights the fact that managers require a detailed understanding of product demand to make sound pricing decisions. An understanding of product demand is also important for managerial decisions on advertising, production levels, new product developments, and capital investment projects.

Chapter 3 presented a brief introduction to supply and demand analysis. In that chapter, we introduced the notion of a demand curve and briefly discussed some of the factors that might cause the demand curve to shift. The purpose of this chapter is to provide a more detailed analysis of demand. Important topics include: (1) demand functions, (2) demand curves, (3) factors affecting demand, (4) industry versus firm-level demand, (5) demand for product attributes, (6) product life cycles, and (7) demand estimation. The technical appendix to this chapter shows how to calculate point elasticities, derives the equation for marginal revenue for a linear demand curve, and discusses log-linear demand functions.

Demand Functions

Managers want to know what factors affect the demands for their products. Only by understanding these factors can managers make sound decisions on pricing, output, capital expenditures, and other strategic issues. A *demand function* is a mathematical representation of the relations between the quantity demanded of a product and *all factors* that influence this demand. In its most general form, a demand function can be written as:

$$Q = f(X_1, X_2, \ldots X_n) \tag{4.1}$$

where the X_is are the factors that affect the demand for the product.

The quantity demanded, Q, is the dependent variable in the demand function, since its value depends on the variables on the right-hand side of the equation. These X_is are the independent variables. In this chapter, we focus on three particularly important independent variables: the price of the product, the prices of other products, and the incomes of individuals. The analysis can be extended to include other variables, such as advertising expenditures, tastes and preferences, and consumer expectations (for example, about future prices).

For concreteness, we continue to focus on PTC as an example. We assume that PTC's demand function for tickets on any given night can be expressed by the following linear function:

$$Q = 117 - 6.6P + 1.66P_s - 3.3P_r + 0.0066I \qquad (4.2)$$

where P is the price of PTC tickets, P_s is the price of tickets at a nearby symphony hall, P_r is the average price of meals at nearby restaurants, and I is the average per capita income of area residents.[1]

As our starting point, we assume PTC tickets are currently priced at $30, while symphony tickets and meals are priced at $50 and $40, respectively. Income is $50,000. At these values, PTC is selling 200 tickets per night. We now provide a more in-depth examination of each of the independent variables in the demand function.

Demand Curves

Price and Quantity Demanded

The price of the product is particularly important in demand analysis for two reasons. First, prices are among the most important variables that consumers consider in making purchasing decisions. Second, managers choose the price of their products, while variables such as the price of other companies' products and income levels are largely beyond their control. Given this special importance, economic analysis singles out the effects of price from the other independent variables in the demand function.

A *demand curve* for a product displays how many units will be purchased at each possible price, over some particular length of time, holding all other factors fixed.[2] The Left Panel of Figure 4.1 shows the demand curve for PTC tickets. By convention, price is placed on the vertical axis, while quantity is placed on the horizontal axis. The equation for PTC's demand curve is:

$$P = 60 - 0.15Q \qquad (4.3)$$

This equation is obtained by substituting the current values of the other variables into equation 4.3 and solving for P. The equation indicates that, for example, 200 tickets are purchased at $30 and 133 tickets are purchased at $40.[3]

The demand curve holds other factors fixed. Changes in income and the prices of symphony tickets and restaurant meals will cause shifts in the position of the demand curve (the intercept changes). For instance, the right panel of Figure 4.1 indicates that the demand curve shifts to the right as income increases from $50,000 to $51,000—at each price, consumers buy 6.6 more tickets. Movements along a demand curve are motivated

---

[1]Note that this function assumes that PTC can sell fractional tickets. This assumption does not have a material effect on our analysis. However, it allows us to draw continuous demand curves. One way to think of quantity in this example is as the *average* number of tickets sold in an evening. In this case, fractional tickets are possible.

[2]For the technically inclined: It is possible to derive an individual's demand curve from the indifference curve/budget line analysis presented in Chapter 2. The price of one good—say, food—is varied, holding the price of other goods and money income fixed. The person's optimal choices are recorded. The individual's demand curve simply plots the optimal choices of the good (in this case, food) against the associated prices. The firm-level demand curve, in turn, is the sum of the demands of all individuals at each price.

[3]Rounded to the nearest dollar.

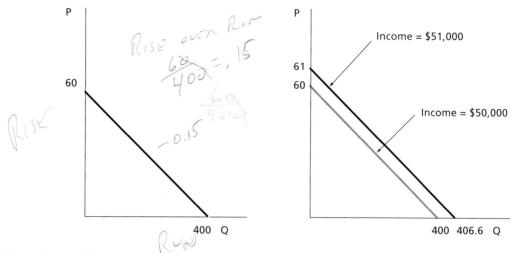

Figure 4.1   Demand Curves

The left panel shows the demand curve for the Players Theater Company (PTC) tickets. By convention, price is placed on the vertical axis, while quantity is placed on the horizontal axis. The equation for PTC's demand curve is: P = 60 − .15Q. The curve indicates that, for example, 200 tickets are purchased at $30 and 133 tickets are purchased at $40. The right panel indicates that the demand curve shifts to the right as income increases from $50,000 to $51,000—at each price, consumers buy more tickets. Movements along a demand curve are motivated by changes in price and are called *changes in the quantity demanded.* Movements of the entire demand curve are motivated by other factors, such as changes in income, and are referred to as *changes in demand.*

by changes in price and are called *changes in the quantity demanded.* Movements of the entire demand curve are motivated by other factors, such as changes in income, and are referred to as *changes in demand.*

Law of Demand

As we discussed in Chapter 3, as a general rule, demand curves slope downward—individuals purchase less (or certainly no more) of a product as the price increases. PTC's demand curve has a slope of −0.15. While it is conceptually possible that individuals might purchase more of a product as the price rises, as a practical consideration, managers are safe to assume that the quantity demanded for their products varies inversely with price. PTC board members would be foolish to think that they would sell more tickets if they raised the price. The negative slope of demand curves has become known as the *law of demand.*

Elasticity of Demand

Demand curves vary in their sensitivity of quantity demanded to price. In some cases, a small change in price leads to a big change in quantity demanded, while in other cases a big change in price leads to a small change in quantity demanded. Information on this sensitivity is critically important for managerial decision making. For instance, PTC would not want to lower its ticket prices to $25 if it could fill the theater by reducing the price to only $28.

Learning the Law of Demand the Hard Way

Mercury One-2-One is a British mobile-phone company. As a promotion to attract new customers, the company offered *free* telephone calls on Christmas to customers who signed on between November 8th and Christmas Eve.

The company "never dreamed its customers would be so generous in spreading the holiday cheer." The promotion generated more than 33,000 hours of calls, jamming the network and prompting hundreds of complaints from people who couldn't get through to place their calls. The volume on Christmas was about 10 times the daily average. Many people placed overseas calls and simply left the phone line open, logging free international calls of up to 12 hours. The average call was about 1½ hours long and the typical caller rang up about $60 in charge—equal to the average *monthly bill* of a cellular company in the United States. The promotion ended up costing the firm millions of dollars. One member of Parliament has vowed to file a complaint with Britain's Board of Trade. To quote one executive of the company, "There's certainly been insatiable demand."

Source: K. Pope (1994), "Phone Company's Gift of Gab Jams Its Lines," *The Wall Street Journal* (December 28), B-1.

One possible measure of the responsiveness of quantity demanded to price is the slope of the demand curve. This measure is not very useful, however, because it depends on the particular dimensions in which the economic quantities are quoted. If the slope of a demand curve is −2 when the quantity is expressed in tons, it is only −0.001 when the quantity is stated in pounds. Thus, the magnitude of the slope coefficient provides limited insights into the sensitivity of quantity demanded to price. Economists have devised a dimensionless measure of this sensitivity known as the *price elasticity* of demand, η. Generally, this elasticity is simply referred to as the *elasticity of demand*.

Price elasticity measures the *percentage change in quantity demanded from a percentage change in price.* Higher price elasticities mean greater price sensitivity. The law of demand indicates that all price elasticities are negative. Convention, however, dictates that we state the elasticity as a positive number. The elasticity of demand, η, is given by:

$$\eta = -(\% \text{ change in Q})/(\% \text{ change in P}) \tag{4.4}$$

Calculating Price Elasticities

The elasticity can be approximated between any two points using the concept of *arc elasticity*.[4] The formula for arc elasticity is:

$$\eta = - [\Delta Q/(Q_1+Q_2)/2] \div [\Delta P/(P_1+P_2)/2] \tag{4.5}$$

where Δ represents the change between the two points.[5] Figure 4.2 displays two points on PTC's demand curve for theater tickets. As shown in the figure, the arc elasticity between these two points is 1.4. Over this region, for every 1 percent change in price, consumers change the quantity of tickets purchased by approximately 1.4 percent.

---

[4]Price elasticity can be measured at a point on the demand curve. The concept of *point elasticity* requires elementary knowledge of calculus and, more importantly, a smooth mathematical demand curve. While our example assumes such a curve, data on demand is often available for only a few price/quantity combinations. We show how to calculate point elasticities in the appendix to this chapter.

[5]Equation 4.4 can be expressed as $\eta = -\Delta Q/Q \div \Delta P/P$. When calculating the elasticity between two points, the question arises as to which Q and P to use in this expression, the starting or ending values. Equation 4.5 uses the average of these two values (the initial plus the ending values divided by 2).

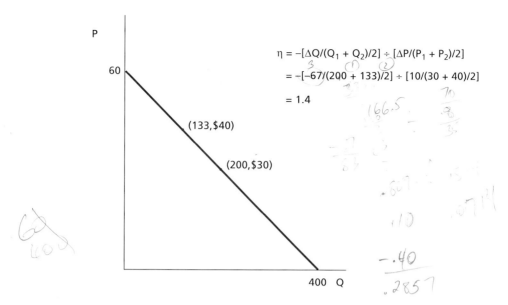

Figure 4.2 Arc Elasticity

This figure displays two points on PTC's demand curve for theater tickets. As shown in the figure, the arc elasticity between these two points is 1.4. Thus, over this range, for every 1 percent change in price there is a 1.4 percent change in the quantity of tickets purchased.

Price elasticities lie between zero and infinity. If the price elasticity is zero, quantity demanded is unaffected by price. In this case, as shown in the left panel of Figure 4.3, the demand curve is vertical. If, as shown in the right panel, the price elasticity is infinite, a small increase in price will cause people to purchase none of the product, and the demand curve is a horizontal line. For instance, a small farmer might not be able to sell any wheat if it is priced above the prevailing market price. When price elasticity equals one, demand is *unitary elastic*. Demand is elastic if the elasticity is greater then one and inelastic if less than one. PTC is interested in how total revenue will change if it lowers ticket prices. As we show below, the relation between revenue and price depends on the demand elasticity.

Increased Foreign Competition and Demand Elasticities

Price elasticities for products usually increase with available substitutes. In recent years, there has been a dramatic increase in the amount of foreign competition facing many American companies. The result has been an increase in the demand elasticities for many American products. One example is film produced by Eastman Kodak. For years, Kodak had a virtual worldwide monopoly in the production of film. Correspondingly, consumers were relatively insensitive to the price of Kodak film—they had no alternative sources. Currently, Kodak faces intense pressure from Japan's Fuji Corporation. Competition also comes from producers of store-brand film, such as the 3-M Corporation in the United States (store-brand film is sold under the store name at large discount drug and grocery stores). As a result, the demand for Kodak film is much more price elastic. This change in price elasticities has motivated Kodak to change its pricing and product development strategies (it can no longer focus exclusively on selling high-quality film at high prices).

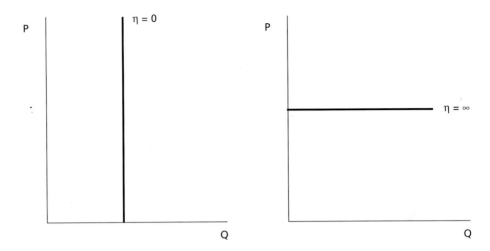

Figure 4.3   Range of Price Elasticities

Price elasticities lie between zero and infinity. If the price elasticity is zero, quantity demanded is unaffected by price. In this case, as shown in the left panel of the figure, the demand curve is vertical. If the price elasticity is infinite, as in the right panel, a small increase in price will cause people to purchase none of the product, and the demand curve is a horizontal line.

Elasticity often varies along a demand curve. For instance, with a linear demand curve, elasticity will be extremely high when the quantities are very low and approach zero as the quantities become large. (Try calculating some arc elasticities along PTC's demand curve.) We discuss this topic in greater detail below. In the appendix to this chapter, we present a demand curve that has constant elasticity (it does not vary along the curve).

Determinants of Price Elasticities

The elasticity of demand tends to be high when there are good substitutes for the product. For instance, the elasticity of demand for PTC tickets is likely to increase with the number of competing events in the city. With many entertainment options, a small increase in the price of PTC tickets might motivate consumers to attend other events. When the alternatives are limited, more customers will decide to pay the higher price for PTC tickets rather than stay at home.

Short-Run versus Long-Run Effects of Increases in Gasoline Prices

In the 1960s, gasoline sold for about 25 cents per gallon in the United States. At this price, Americans tended to purchase large automobiles with poor gas mileage. In the early 1970s, Americans experienced a significant gasoline crisis. Not only did the price rise but for a time there was a shortage of gasoline and people had to wait in line literally for hours to purchase gasoline. The increase in gasoline prices and waiting times resulted in a near-term decline in the quantity demanded of gasoline (people carpooled, drove less frequently, etc.). The longer-term effect was much greater; in response to consumer demand, car companies began designing smaller, more fuel-efficient automobiles. Currently, many cars travel at least 20 miles per gallon (and often much more). In the 1960s, many cars traveled fewer than 10 miles per gallon.

Price Elasticities

Economists have estimated the price elasticities of various products. Some of these estimates are:

(handwritten annotation: LESS THAN 1 PRICE INELASTIC; GREATER THAN 1 PRICE IS ELASTIC)

Sugar	=	0.31
Potatoes	=	0.31
Tires	=	1.20
Electricity	=	1.20
Haddock	=	2.20
Movies	=	3.70

(handwritten annotations: PRICE INSENSITIVE - INELASTIC; PRICE SENSITIVE - ELASTIC - Luxury; small shift in price, big shift in demand)

These estimates indicate that sugar and potatoes have relatively low price elasticities. This might be expected given that these products represent a small portion of most people's budgets. Also, sugar does not have many good substitutes. Haddock and movies have high elasticities. Haddock is a narrowly defined product (as opposed to fish) and has many good substitutes. Movies are a luxury item for many people; at high prices, individuals are motivated to engage in other forms of entertainment.

Source: Summaries of elasticity estimates in E. Mansfield (1988),
Microeconomics (W. W. Norton: New York), 142.

Demand elasticities also can depend on the importance of the good in consumers' budgets. Goods such as salt and pepper that consume a relatively small proportion of a person's income tend to be relatively price insensitive or inelastic. On the other hand, goods such as major appliances and automobiles represent more important purchases and are likely to be more price sensitive.

A third determinant of price elasticity is the length of the period to which the demand curve pertains. Demand tends to be more elastic or responsive to price changes over the long run than over the short run. An increase in PTC ticket prices is likely to result in an immediate decline in tickets sold. The long-run effect will be even larger, as consumers identify other entertainment options or fail to renew season tickets (these effects will cause the demand curve to shift to the left). Similarly, a large increase in the price of heating oil will result in a near-term decline in the quantity of oil demanded. Over time, the effect will be larger as consumers better insulate their homes and shift to gas furnaces.

Price Changes and Total Revenue

How total expenditures on a product change with price depends on the price elasticity. Total revenue is calculated by multiplying the quantity purchased times the price (that is, $P \times Q$). If price elasticity is *inelastic* (less than 1), a 1 percent increase in price results

Demand Elasticities and Airline Pricing

Round-trip airfares are substantially lower if the traveler stays over a Saturday night. Airline companies offer this discount to increase revenues (and profits). The typical traveler who stays over a Saturday night is a tourist. Tourists have relatively high price elasticities for air travel. Lowering the price from the standard fare correspondingly increases revenue—the price decrease is more than offset by the increase in tickets sold. Airline companies do not offer similar discounts to travelers who complete the round-trip midweek. These travelers are primarily business travelers who have relatively inelastic demands. Lowering price would decrease revenue because the decrease in price would not be offset by an increase in tickets sold. Airline companies also do not offer large discounts during peak periods, such as the Christmas season. During these periods, demand is relatively inelastic and they can fill the planes without offering substantial discounts.

Inelastic Demand (η < 1)

⇑ P ⇒ ⇑ Total revenue
⇓ P ⇒ ⇓ Total revenue

Unitary elasticity (η = 1)

ΔP ⇒ No change in total revenue

Elastic demand (η > 1)

⇑ P ⇒ ⇓ Total revenue
⇓ P ⇒ ⇑ Total revenue

Figure 4.4   Price Elasticities, Price Changes, and Total Revenue

How total expenditures on a product change with price depends directly on the price elasticity. This figure shows the relation between price changes, total revenue, and price elasticities.

in less than a 1 percent decrease in quantity and total revenue increases. A price decrease, on the other hand, results in a decrease in revenue. In contrast, if demand is *unitary elastic* (equal to 1), a 1 percent change in price results in an offsetting 1 percent change in quantity and total revenue stays the same. Finally, if demand is *elastic* (value greater than 1) an increase in price results in a decline in revenue, while a decrease in price results in an increase in revenue. These relations are summarized in Figure 4.4. We discuss these relations in greater detail below.

Linear Demand Curves

The PTC decision on whether or not to lower prices depends on the relation between price and total revenue and thus its demand elasticity—it would not make sense for PTC to lower prices if total revenue declined. We now provide a more in-depth analysis of the relation between price and revenue and discuss PTC's optimal pricing policy. Through this analysis, we illustrate the properties of linear demand curves. Knowing these properties is useful for understanding the subsequent analysis in this book.[6]

PTC's total revenue (TR) on any given night is equal to the quantity of tickets sold times the price. Price is given by the demand curve in equation 4.4. Thus, total revenue can be expressed as:

$$TR = P \times Q$$
$$= (60 - 0.15Q)Q$$
$$= 60Q - 0.15Q^2 \tag{4.6}$$

Figure 4.5 graphs PTC's demand and total revenue curves. Total revenue increases as price decreases up to the midpoint of the demand curve. Over this range, the demand curve is elastic—the percentage decline in price is smaller than the percentage increase in quantity demanded. Past the midpoint, price declines result in reduced total revenue; thus, the demand curve is inelastic over this range. The elasticity is unitary at the midpoint. These are general properties of linear demand curves.

[6]There is no reason to believe that most demand curves are linear. We focus on linear demand curves for two reasons. First, linear demand curves are used throughout the economics literature because they simplify the calculations in examples and at the same time illustrate more general principles. Given the widespread use of linear demand curves, it is important to understand their basic properties. Second, even though a demand curve is not linear, it might be reasonably approximated by a line over the relevant image.

An important concept in economics is *marginal revenue,* which is defined as the *change in total revenue given a unitary change in quantity.* Intuitively, the marginal revenue for the first unit is price. Thus, the intercepts of the demand and marginal revenue curves are the same. As quantity continues to expand, marginal revenue is below price— to sell an extra unit, the price charged for all units must decrease. Marginal revenue is positive up to the midpoint of the demand curve (total revenue is increasing over this interval). At the midpoint, marginal revenue is zero and the demand elasticity is 1. Beyond the midpoint, marginal revenue is negative—the increase in revenue from selling another unit is less than the decline in revenue from lowering price. In the appendix, we show that marginal revenue (MR) for a linear demand curve is a line with the same intercept as the demand curve but with twice the negative slope. The equation for PTC's marginal revenue (see Figure 4.5) is:

$$MR = 60 - 0.3Q \tag{4.7}$$

All of PTC's costs are fixed and do not depend on the quantity of tickets sold on a given evening—the actors and utilities have to be paid regardless of how many people are in the audience. Thus, PTC's objective is to maximize its total revenue (for PTC, with costs fixed, maximizing total revenue is the same as maximizing total profit). Figure 4.4 indicates that revenues are maximized at a price of \$30. Under current conditions, PTC should not lower its price to \$25. Currently, it is collecting $\$30 \times 200 = \$6,000$ in revenue per night. If the price is decreased to \$25, total revenue would be $\$25 \times 233 = \$5,825$ per night.[7] The upcoming increase in restaurant prices will change the optimal pricing policy. A practice problem at the end of this chapter examines this change in policy.

Note that, in contrast to this example, most firms do not want to maximize total revenue. PTC, with only fixed costs, is a special case. In most firms, both costs and revenues vary with output. A profit-maximizing firm must consider both effects. We discuss this issue in greater detail in Chapters 5 and 6.

Other Factors that Influence Demand

Prices of Other Products

Complements versus Substitutes

The demand for a product can be affected by the prices of related products. For instance, if the local symphony raises its ticket prices, consumers will be more likely to attend the PTC than the symphony. Thus, there is a positive relation in equation 4.3 between the demand for PTC tickets and the price of symphony tickets. Goods that compete with each other in this manner are referred to as *substitutes*. In contrast, if the local restaurants raise their prices, the demand for PTC tickets falls (note the negative sign in the demand function). For instance, some potential PTC customers will choose to stay home because the price for an "evening on the town" has increased. Products like theater tickets and meals at restaurants, which tend to be consumed together, are *complements*. An example of complements are video recorders (VCRs) and VCR tapes. If the price of VCRs rises, fewer VCRs are purchased; the demand for VCR tapes also falls.

---

[7]From the demand curve: $\$25 = 60 - 0.15Q$. Therefore, Q = 233.

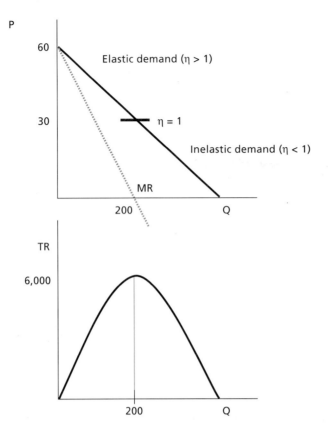

Figure 4.5   Demand, Total Revenue, and Marginal Revenue for Linear Demand Curves

This figure graphs PTC's demand and total revenue curves in the upper and lower panels. Total revenue increases as price decreases up to the midpoint of the demand curve. Thus, over this range, the demand curve is elastic—the percentage decline in price is smaller than the percentage increase in quantity demanded. Past the midpoint, price declines result in reduced total revenue; and thus, the demand curve is inelastic over this range. The elasticity is unitary at the midpoint. An important concept in economics is *marginal revenue,* which is defined as the *change in total revenue given a unitary change in quantity.* In the appendix, we show that marginal revenue (MR) for a linear demand curve is a line with the same intercept as the demand curve but with twice the negative slope. The marginal revenue curve for PTC is pictured in the figure.

Cross Elasticities

One frequently used measure of substitution between two products is the *cross elasticity of demand.* Cross elasticity is defined as the *percentage change in the demand of a good, given a percentage change in the price of some other good.* Cross elasticities between any two goods, X and Y, can be calculated using a formula that is analogous to equation 4.5:

$$\eta_{xy} = [\Delta Q_x/(Q_{x1} + Q_{x2})/2] \div [\Delta P/(P_{y1}+P_{y2})/2] \qquad (4.8)$$

Unlike price elasticities, which are always positive (when you multiply them by −1), cross elasticities can be either positive or negative. Substitutes have positive cross elasticities, while complements have negative cross elasticities.

Estimates of Cross Elasticities

Economists have estimated the cross elasticities for various commodities. Below are a few of these estimates:

Electricity and natural gas	=	0.20
Beef and pork	=	0.20
Natural gas and fuel oil	=	0.44
Margarine and butter	=	0.81

All the pairs of commodities listed above are substitutes. Complements such as VCRs and VCR tapes have negative cross elasticities. Natural gas apparently is not a very strong substitute for electricity. While people can use either gas or electricity for heating, natural gas is not generally used for lighting. On the other hand, natural gas and fuel oil are closer substitutes (both tend to be used for heating). Margarine and butter are strong substitutes.

Source: Mansfield (1988), *Microeconomics* (W. W. Norton: New York), 143.

Whether a commodity has strong substitutes or complements depends, in part, on how finely the commodity is defined. Pepsi and Coke might have relatively large cross elasticities. The cross elasticities between colas, more broadly defined, and other soft drinks are likely to be much smaller.[8]

Cross elasticities are of fundamental importance because managers frequently want to forecast what will happen to their own sales as other companies change their prices. The PTC board is concerned about the effects that a forthcoming increase in restaurant prices would have on its ticket demand. If meals in local restaurants and theater tickets are strong complements, the increase in restaurant prices will cause a significant decline in the demand for PTC tickets. In this case, the PTC board might want to offset this shift in demand by lowering ticket prices or advertising more heavily. In contrast, if meals and tickets are weak complements, the increase in meal prices will have little effect on ticket demand. In this example, a $10 increase in meal prices will result in 33 fewer ticket sales per night. Using the formula in equation 4.8, the corresponding cross elasticity between these

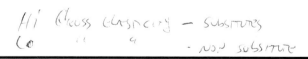

Complementarity between Computer Hardware and Software

Over the past decade, there has been a dramatic decrease in the price of personal computers. Not only has the price of PCs decreased, but their quality and computing power have improved significantly as well. This decrease in the price of personal computers has significantly increased the quantity of PCs demanded. In addition, it has also increased the demand for software products. Today, some of the largest companies in the world (for example, the Microsoft Corporation) specialize in the production of software for PCs. Computer hardware and software are complements and thus have negative cross elasticities.

[8]Below, we extend this discussion to indicate how cross elasticities can be used by managers and regulators to define a firm's industry.

two points [(200, \$40);(167, \$50)] is –0.81—for every 1 percent increase in meal prices over this range there is, on average, a 0.81 percent decline in ticket sales. This elasticity suggests that PTC tickets and restaurant meals are rather strong complements.

Income

Normal versus Inferior Goods

Another factor that can effect the demand for a product is the income of potential buyers. As a person's income increases, more products are purchased, and the combined expenditures for all products rise. The demand for specific products, however, can either rise or fall as income increases. While the demand for *luxury goods,* such as gourmet foods and jewels, would be expected to increase with income, the demand for other goods, such as processed meat and cabbage, might decline. Goods for which demand increases with income are called *normal goods.* PTC tickets are normal goods. Goods for which demand declines with income are called *inferior goods*—for example, bologna or spam.

Income Elasticities

The sensitivity of demand to income is measured by the *income elasticity.* The income elasticity is defined as the *percentage change in the demand of a good, given a percentage change in income (I).* Income elastics can be calculated using the following formula:

$$\eta_I = [\Delta Q/(Q_1 + Q_2)/2] \div [\Delta I/(I_1 + I_2)/2] \tag{4.9}$$

The income elasticity is positive for normal goods and negative for inferior goods.

The income elasticities of a firm's products have important implications. Firms producing products with high income elasticities are subject to cyclical fluctuations. They tend to grow rapidly in expanding economies and contract sharply in depressed economies. Managers must anticipate these fluctuations in managing cash flows and making hiring decisions. The demand for products with low income elasticities are more stable over economic cycles. Studies indicate that goods like domestic servants, medical care, education for children, and restaurant meals tend to have relatively large income elasticities, while goods such as most food products, gasoline, oil, and liquor have relatively small (in absolute value) income elasticities.

Income elasticities also can influence location decisions. For instance, PTC has a relatively high income elasticity (above 1.6). This elasticity was one of the factors that motivated the founders to locate their theater in a community with a high per capita income. They anticipated that they would have fewer customers if they located in a less affluent area.

Other Variables

We have concentrated on three of the most important independent variables in most demand functions—the product's own price, prices of other products, and income. Other variables, such as advertising expenditures, also can be important. In all cases, the analysis is similar. Demand might go up or go down given a movement in some other variable. Sensitivity can be measured by the appropriate elasticity factor—for instance, an advertising elasticity. Obviously, managers do not have the time to consider all conceivable variables that might have small impacts on the demand for their products. Good managerial decision making, requires managers to understand the effects of the most important factors, which usually include the product's own price, the prices of substitutes and complements, and income.

Estimates of Income Elasticities

Economists have estimated the income elasticities for various products. Below are a few of these estimates:

Flour	=	–0.36
Natural gas and fuel oil	=	0.44
Margarine	=	–0.20
Milk and cream	=	0.07
Dentist services	=	1.41
Restaurant consumption	=	1.48

According to these estimates, flour and margarine are inferior goods. People spend less on these goods as their incomes rise. The other goods are normal goods (expenditures on the products rise with income). Dentist services and restaurant consumption are particularly sensitive to income changes.

Source: Mansfield (1988), *Microeconomics* (W. W. Norton: New York), 143.

Industry versus Firm Demand

Industry Demand Curves

While we have concentrated our analysis on firm-level demand, demand functions and demand curves can be defined for entire industries. For instance, a demand function could be specified for the entertainment industry in PTC's market area. Such a function would relate the total ticket sales for all entertainment events to factors that affect this demand. Managers are often interested in total industry demand because it provides important information on the size of their potential markets and trends that will affect them. Moreover, estimates of industry demand sometimes can be obtained inexpensively from outside analysts and business publications.

Firms within an industry compete directly, and their products are likely to be relatively strong substitutes. The overall industry, on the other hand, is less likely to have strong substitutes. A person wanting to go to an entertainment event might choose among several options based on price. Entertainment events, as a whole, have fewer alternatives. Thus, the demands for individual firms within an industry tend to be more price elastic than for the entire industry.

Demand Elasticity for Gasoline

The industry-level demand for gasoline is relatively inelastic—the price of gasoline can change substantially and have little effect on the overall quantity demanded. The demand elasticities facing individual gas stations are much larger. If several gas stations are located at the same intersection, an individual station can lose substantial business to its local competitors by raising its price.

Defining the Industry and Market Area

We have indicated that managers can gain important insights by analyzing industry-level demand. One problem that managers face in conducting this type of analysis is defining the relevant industry and market area. Is PTC competing in the live theater industry or in a more broadly defined entertainment industry? Cross elasticities provide important information to answer these types of questions. The cross elasticity between PTC tickets and symphony tickets is 0.4. This relatively high value (see the box titled Estimates of Cross Elasticities shown earlier in this chapter) suggests that PTC competes against companies in a broader entertainment industry than just live theater.[9] The managers at PTC must also define the relevant geographic area of their marketplace. If PTC raises its prices, will its customers shift to theaters in other nearby cities? If so, these cities should be included in the definition of PTC's market area.

Product Attributes

Thus far, we have taken the *attributes* of the product as given. Our analysis of the demand for PTC tickets is based on the existing quality and selection of plays, the starting times, the quality of seating, and so on. Given these characteristics, we examined how price and other factors affect the demand for PTC tickets.

Consumer demand also plays an important role in the design of the initial product. For instance, do local consumers prefer Shakespeare or contemporary plays? Do they value comfortable seating or seating that is close to the stage? Can the anticipated decrease in demand from increased restaurant prices be offset by changing the starting time of the plays? Delaying the starting time by one hour might give people more time to eat at home before they go to the play.

Answers to these types of questions are important in managerial decision making. Indeed, when managers speak of the importance of understanding consumer demand, they are often referring to understanding the specific product attributes that are important to customers. Marketing managers are responsible for understanding the broad range of product attributes that affect demand. These include price, product design, packaging, promotion and advertising, and distribution channels. This broad focus on demand has played an especially important role in total quality management (TQM) programs that have been adopted by firms throughout the world (see Chapter 17).[10]

An important problem facing most firms is how to incorporate information that may be held by many people throughout a firm—for example, about such matters as consumer demand—into the decision-making process for product design. We defer discussions of this problem until Parts 2 and 3 of the book. These sections provide insights into how to design the firm's organizational architecture to help ensure that the relevant information is incorporated in the decision-making process.

---

[9]Cross elasticities are also used as evidence in antitrust cases. Antitrust cases generally focus on whether or not a company has significant market power in an industry. Thus, the definition of the industry is very important. A company might have a significant market share (and thus apparent power) in a narrowly defined industry, but a small market share in a more broadly defined market. For instance, PTC might be the only live theater company in the region, but be only one of many companies in the entertainment industry.

[10]For a more formal economic analysis of the demand for product attributes, see K. Lancaster (1966), "A New Approach to Consumer Theory," *Journal of Political Economy* 74, 132–157.

Understanding Consumer Demands at The GAP

Companies spend considerable resources trying to determine the specific preferences of their customers. One industry where the knowledge of consumer preferences is particularly important is the apparel industry. Popular fashions frequently change, and successful firms must be "close to the customer." The importance of knowing customer demands is highlighted by the following statement made by the president of The GAP:

> We just keep trying to figure out what people wear on a regular basis. Our business is reading signals from the customer day in and day out.

The GAP's prominence in apparel retailing suggests that this activity can pay off.

Source: S. Caminti (1991), "The GAP Reading the Customer Right," *Fortune* (December 2), 106.

Product Life Cycles

Our discussion of product attributes suggests that managers will constantly seek to develop new and better ways to respond to consumer demands. This activity leads to the introduction of new products. Managers must recognize that the market demand for a new product is unlikely to remain stable over time. Often, the industry demand curve for a new product shifts outward as the product becomes more widely known. Eventually, however, the demand is likely to shift inward as consumers shift toward other new and improved products. This pattern in the demand for new products is known as the *product life cycle.*

As pictured in Figure 4.6, the product-life-cycle hypothesis stylizes the demand for a product into four main phases: introduction, growth, maturity, and decline. In the growth phase, the industry-level demand increases rapidly. In the maturity phase, the demand continues to increase and then begins to decrease. In the decline phase, the demand continues to fall. Eventually, the product is withdrawn from the market. Managers must recognize these trends in new-product planning, as well as in entry, exit, and pricing decisions for given products.

The increase in demand during the growth phase invites new firms into the industry. For instance, the growth in the demand for personal computers (PCs) during the 1990s motivated many firms to produce PCs. Given the entry of new firms, the original firms typically lose market share. If the industry demand grows at a faster rate than the number of new firms, the original firms will obtain sales growth, even though their share of the market falls. If the number of new firms grows faster than the industry demand, the original firms will typically experience an inward shift in their demand curves. These inward shifts will have a depressing effect on prices and firm profits.

This discussion suggests that the first firms to introduce a successful product are likely to have "first-mover advantages." They enjoy high profits until entry occurs. They can also develop a customer base and have a longer time period to learn how to produce the product efficiently. These advantages explain why firms frequently strive to be the first to discover and launch new products. Unfortunately, most new products are not major successes, and the profits from one successful product are often lost on other unsuccessful ventures.

The analysis also suggests that managers should be careful in evaluating whether or not to enter an industry during the growth phase. Competition during this phase can

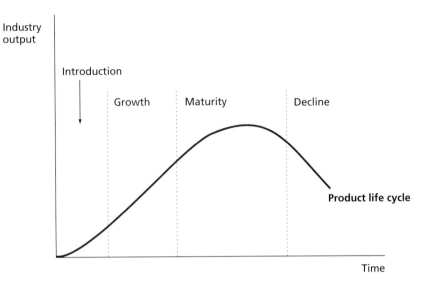

Figure 4.6   Product Life Cycle

The product-life-cycle hypothesis stylizes that the industry demand for a new product goes though four main phases: introduction, growth, maturity, and decline.

be intense, and demand is expected to decline at some point in the future. To prosper in this environment, a new firm must have some type of *competitive advantage* over its rivals (for example, being a low-cost producer). We discuss this issue in more detail in Chapter 6.

Demand Estimation[11]

In the PTC example, we specified the demand function. Managers of companies are not so lucky—they must estimate their own demand functions. Sometimes it is easy to estimate demand, at least for the very near term. Other times it is very difficult. Some companies employ data and statistical techniques to provide numerical estimates of demand functions. Other companies use a more qualitative approach.

Demand estimation is a complex topic that is largely beyond the scope of this book. Here, we simply provide a brief discussion of the three major techniques used in estimating demand: the *interview, direct-market,* and *statistical* approaches. The intent is to provide insights into some of the costs and benefits of each approach. These insights make managers more informed consumers of demand estimates and offer guidance into what type of demand analysis to conduct in a given situation. Although each approach has its limitations, the approaches are not mutually exclusive. Because the limitations differ, many managers employ various methods and pool the estimates to increase their understanding of demand.

[11]This section draws on the analysis in W. Baumol (1977), *Economic Theory and Operations Analysis* (Prentice-Hall: Englewood Cliffs, NJ), 234–236.

Interview Approach

The interview approach attempts to estimate demand through customer surveys, questionnaires, and focus groups. Perhaps the most naive version of this approach is simply to ask consumers what they would purchase if faced with different prices. The answers to these questions can be very unreliable. First, people have incentives to lie since they want the firm to have low prices. Second, even if they try to tell the truth, they can have difficulty forecasting what they would actually purchase in the marketplace.

More sophisticated approaches to consumer interviewing are possible. For example, a consumer might be asked about the difference in price between two substitute products. If the consumer has purchased one of the products and does not know the price of the other, the consumer is likely to be relatively insensitive to price.

Sometimes companies use a *simulated market* where people are given play money and asked to simulate purchase decisions. These experiments can yield useful insights. Again, however, the decisions a person makes with play money need not resemble the decisions the person would make with real money.

Consumer surveys play a particularly important role in providing information about what attributes are valued by customers. Many businesses ask customers to fill out customer service and complaint forms. Businesses often follow up sales or service with telephone calls to customers to ask about product quality and customer satisfaction. Among the most important sources of information about customer preferences are the direct contacts that salespeople and other company representatives have with their customers. All of the interview approaches, however, can produce wildly inaccurate information if the sample is not representative of the population of customers (for instance, if the sample has a disproportionally high number of wealthy individuals).

Direct-Market Approach

A second approach is to use direct-market tests. For instance, PTC might decrease its price to $25 and see how much the quantity demanded changes. An advantage of this approach is the observed reactions are actual purchasing decisions. Companies frequently test market new products in a few "representative" cities.

There are at least two limitations to the direct-market approach. First, direct-market experiments can be risky. Customers lost from a price increase might never be regained, even if the price were lowered. Alternatively, it might be difficult to raise prices once a firm had lowered them (customers might be angry and purchase from other companies). Second, direct-market tests are not controlled experiments, and several changes might be occurring at the same time. For instance, PTC might lower its price at the same time as the symphony. The corresponding change in demand would reflect both effects. Many firms are not like PTC, in that they operate at multiple locations. If a firm has the flexibility to vary prices across multiple locations, it has the potential to gain more information than if it is limited to experimenting at one location.

Statistical Approach

Often, companies use standard statistical techniques such as regression analysis to estimate demand functions. Computers and large databases (on sales, prices, and other relevant factors) have significantly increased the viability of this approach. By using statistical techniques, the effects of specific factors can often be isolated. It is possible to analyze large samples of actual market data to obtain more reliable results.

	1992	1993	1994
Income (I)	3,000	4,000	3,500
Advertising (A)	2	3	2.5
Price (P)	10	10	10
Sales (S)	236	284	260

True demand: S = 120 – 2P + 8A + .04I

Estimated demand: S = 140 + 48A

Figure 4.7   An Example of the Omitted-Variables Problem

The true demand curve of the company in this example is: Sales = 120 –2P + 8A + .04I. The data for 1992 to 1994 are presented in the table. If the analyst omits income and uses statistical techniques to estimate a relation between advertising and sales, the analyst will obtain the following equation: Sales = 140 + 48A. The model predicts sales perfectly (based on the data in the table). The estimated equation, however, significantly overstates the influence of advertising. The omitted-variables problem is present whenever important variables are left out of the analysis that are correlated with the explanatory variables that are included in the analysis.

While the statistical approach has the potential to provide managers with important information on demand, managers should realize that there are potential problems with this approach. Just because a researcher can produce many pages of computer output with corresponding graphs does not mean that the analysis is well done or not subject to question. Below, we briefly discuss three types of problems that analysts encounter in estimating demand.

Omission of Important Variables

The problem of *omitted variables* can be illustrated by an example. Assume that the true demand function for a company is:

$$\text{Sales} = 120 - 2P + 8A + 0.04I \qquad (4.10)$$

where P is the price of the product, A is advertising expenditures, and I is income. Figure 4.7 presents a table with data for 1992, 1993, and 1994. While this data is potentially available to the analyst who wants to estimate demand, the analyst does not necessarily know that both advertising and income are important determinants of demand. Suppose that the analyst ignores income and uses statistical techniques to estimate a relation between sales and advertising.[12] The standard technique of regression analysis would yield the following equation:

$$\text{Sales} = 140 + 48A \qquad (4.11)$$

The model seems to predict sales perfectly (based on the data in the table). The equation, however, significantly overstates the true influence of advertising and can lead to serious mistakes in decision making. Based on this analysis, the company might budget far too much for advertising. The omitted-variables problem is present whenever important variables are left out of the analysis that are correlated with the explanatory variables that are included in the analysis.[13] Including unimportant variables in the analysis does not bias the estimated coefficients for the other variables. However, including irrelevant variables can reduce the precision of the various estimates.

---

[12] The analyst does not have to worry about controlling for price, since it was constant over the period ($10).

[13] The problem does not always result in overstated coefficients on the explanatory variables. Depending on the nature of the correlation among the explanatory variables, the coefficients can either be overstated or understated. The estimated coefficient in this example is overstated because advertising and income are positively correlated.

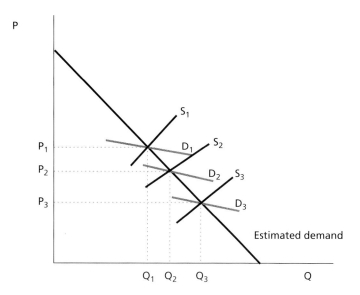

Figure 4.8   An Example of the Identification Problem

An analyst has collected data on past prices and sales in an industry. The demand and supply curves have shifted over the three years. Connecting the three price/quantity points provides a very poor estimate of the current industry demand curve (labeled D_3 in the graph). The three points are *equilibrium* points, given all conditions that affect the demand and supply of the product at each point in time. They are not three points along the same demand curve.

Multicollinearity

If the factors that affect demand are highly correlated (tend to move together), it might be impossible to estimate the individual effects with much precision. For instance, two important variables in the demand function might be income and education. If high income is almost always associated with high education, it might be impossible to separate the two effects.

Identification Problem

Another potentially important problem that can confront the statistical researcher is the *identification problem.* This problem can also be illustrated by example. Suppose an analyst has collected data on past prices and sales for a given industry with the aim of estimating an industry demand curve. In the most recent three years, the following sales and price combinations have been observed: (10, $10), (12, $8), and (14, $6). Is it valid for the analyst to connect these three points as an estimate of the demand curve? Because of the identification problem, the answer is generally no.

Each data combination reflects the intersection of the demand curve and supply curve for the industry for each time period. If the demand curve has shifted over the three years, due to changes in factors such as personal income, the points come from three different demand curves. Connecting the points does not provide an estimate of the current demand curve—in fact, it traces out the industry's supply curve. Suppose in our example that both the demand and supply curves have shifted in each year. As shown in Figure 4.8, the resulting combinations of price and quantity are observed *equilibrium* points, given the conditions during the relevant time periods. Connecting these points provides a poor estimate of the current demand curve, D_3.

Difficulties in Estimating the Demand Curves for Common Stock

There has been a long-running debate over the demand elasticities of common stocks of individual firms. Many economists argue that these demand curves are perfectly elastic, since there are numerous stocks with similar risk-return characteristics available in the market. In this case, the demand curves for individual stocks are horizontal. Other people argue that each stock is unique and has very few substitutes. Here, the individual demand curves would be downward sloping.

Managers care about the slopes of the demand curves for their common stock since these slopes affect the price at which they can sell new securities. If demand curves slope downward, price must be decreased below the current market price to sell new securities. If demand curves are horizontal, new securities can be issued at the current market price. Managers, of course, want to sell new stock at the highest possible price.

The existing empirical evidence suggests that stock prices decline by about 3 percent when firms announce new issues of common stock. This finding seems to suggest that the demand curves for common stocks are downward sloping. This finding, however, is subject to alternative interpretations. If the stock market thinks that firms tend to issue new stock when they are overvalued, an announcement of a new issue will cause the entire demand curve to shift down and price will decline (since the market infers from the new information that the firm is overvalued). The observation that prices decline when new stock is issued is not sufficient to allow us to identify the price elasticity of a firm's common stock—the price decrease might be due to either a shift in demand or a shift in quantity demanded.

This example illustrates that it is not always easy to estimate demand curves, even when prices and quantities are readily available. Indeed, the data on prices and volumes for publicly traded securities are among the best available in the world.

Sometimes, the analyst does not have enough information to solve the identification problem and is better off using consumer surveys or market experiments to estimate demand. Other times, the analyst has enough information to identify the demand function (the analyst needs to be able to identify factors that influence demand, but not supply, and vice versa). One special case in which the analyst does not have to worry about the identification problem is when the *demand curve is stable.* Suppose the demand curve did not shift over the three years and all the sales/price combinations were motivated by changes in supply. In this case, a reasonable estimate of the demand curve can be obtained from the observed sales/price combinations.

Implications

We have discussed some of the difficulties that companies face in trying to estimate the demand for their products. These problems can be difficult to solve. Nevertheless, estimates of demand play a critical role in decision making, especially the pricing decision. Successful managers address these problems the best they can, given imperfect knowledge and limited resources.

Summary

An understanding of product demand is critical for many managerial decisions such as pricing, output levels, capital investment, and advertising. This chapter provides a basic analysis of demand.

A *demand function* is a mathematical representation of the relations among the quantity demanded of a product and the various factors that influence this quantity. We focus on three independent variables in the demand function: the price of the product, the prices of other products, and the money income of individuals.

A *demand curve* for a product displays how many units will be purchased at each price, over some particular length of time, holding all other factors fixed. Movements along a demand curve are motivated by changes in price and are called *changes in the quantity demanded.* Movements of the entire demand curve are motivated by other factors, such as changes in income, and are referred to as *changes in demand.*

Normally, demand curves slope downward to the right—quantity demanded varies inversely with price. This relation is often referred to as the *law of demand.* Demand curves vary in their sensitivity of quantity demanded to price. *Price elasticity* is defined as the percentage change in quantity demanded from a percentage change in price. The price elasticity tends to be high when there are good substitutes for the product and when the good represents a significant expenditure for the consumer. Demand tends to be more elastic over the long run than the short run. How total revenue from a product changes with price depends on the price elasticity. A price increase results in an increase in expenditures when demand is *inelastic* and a decrease in expenditures when demand is *elastic.* Total expenditures remain unchanged when the demand elasticity is *unitary.*

An important concept in economics is *marginal revenue,* which is defined as the *change in total revenue given a one unit change in quantity.* Marginal revenue for a linear demand curve is given by the line with the same intercept as the demand curve but with twice the negative slope. Total revenue increases with quantity when marginal revenue is positive and decreases with quantity when marginal revenue is negative.

The price of related products can affect the demand for a product. Goods that compete with each other are referred to as *substitutes.* Products that tend to be consumed together are *complements.* One frequently used measure of substitution between two products is the *cross elasticity of demand.* The cross elasticity is positive for substitutes and negative for complements.

Another factor that can affect the demand for a product is the income of potential buyers. The sensitivity of demand to income is measured by the *income elasticity.* The income elasticity is positive for *normal goods,* and negative for *inferior goods.*

Demand curves can be defined for individual firms or entire industries. The price elasticities for individual firms within an industry are generally higher than for the industry as a whole. Cross elasticities can be helpful in defining the appropriate industry.

The standard economic analysis of demand takes the *attributes* of the product as given. Information about consumer demand, however, is also important in the initial design of products. Parts 2 and 3 of this book provide important insights into how to design the firm's organizational architecture to help ensure that this type of information is incorporated in the decision-making process.

There are three basic approaches that managers use to estimate demand: the *interview approach,* the *direct-market approach,* and the *statistical approach.* All three approaches can suffer from significant problems. Managers have to do the best they can given imperfect information and limited resources. Knowledge of the potential pitfalls makes managers more intelligent users of demand estimates.

APPENDIX   *Demand*[14]

In the chapter, we presented formulas for arc elasticities (that estimate elasticities between two points on the demand curve). This appendix shows how to calculate elasticities at single points on the demand curve. It also derives the equation for marginal revenue for a linear demand curve and discusses log-linear demand functions.

Point Elasticities

Elasticities measure the percentage change in quantity demanded for a percentage change in some other variable. There are several ways to express the formula for an elasticity. One way, using price elasticity as an example, is:

$$\eta = -(\Delta Q/Q)/(\Delta P/P)$$
$$= -(\Delta Q/\Delta P) \times (P/Q) \qquad (4.12)$$

By definition, as the change in P goes to zero, the limit of the first term $(\Delta/Q/\Delta P)$ is the partial derivative of Q with respect to P. At a particular point on the demand curve, the elasticity of demand for small changes in P is given by:

$$\eta = - (\partial Q/\partial P) \times (P/Q) \qquad (4.13)$$

As an example, consider the demand function for PTC theater tickets:

$$Q = 117 - 6.6P + 1.66P_S - 3.3P_R + 6.6I \qquad (4.14)$$

The point elasticity at the current price/quantity combination of \$30 and 200 tickets is:

$$\eta = -(-6.6) \times (30/200) = 1 \qquad (4.15)$$

Recall that this is the value that we derived graphically in the text (see Figure 4.5).

Other point elasticities for example, point cross elasticities—can be calculated in a similar fashion. Simply substitute the appropriate variable (for example, the price of another product) for P in equation 4.13.

Marginal Revenue for Linear Demand Curves

Marginal revenue (MR) is the change in total revenue for an additional unit of quantity. As the change in quantity becomes very small, the limit of this definition is the partial derivative of total revenue with respect to Q.

Linear demand curves take the following form:

$$P = a - bQ \qquad (4.16)$$

Thus, total revenue, $P \times Q$ can be written:

$$TR = (a - bQ) \times Q$$
$$= aQ - bQ^2 \qquad (4.17)$$

---

[14]This appendix requires elementary knowledge of calculus.

Marginal revenue is:

$$MR = \partial TR/\partial Q = a - 2bQ \tag{4.18}$$

This formula is a line that has the same intercept as the demand curve, but with twice the negative slope.

Log-Linear Demand Functions

The following demand function is frequently used in empirical demand estimation:

$$Q = \lambda P^{\alpha} I^{\gamma} \tag{4.19}$$

where Q is the quantity demanded, P is price, and I is income (other variables such as advertising and the price of other goods are commonly included as other explanatory variables). An important property of this demand function is that the *price and income elasticities are constant* (they do not vary along the demand function) and equal to $-\alpha$ and γ, respectively. In particular:

$$\eta = -(\partial Q/\partial P) \times (P/Q)$$

$$= -(\lambda \alpha P^{\alpha-1} I^{\gamma}) \times (P/\lambda P^{\alpha} I^{\gamma})$$

$$= -\alpha \tag{4.20}$$

Similar calculations can be used to show that γ is the income elasticity.

Taking the natural logarithm of the demand function in equation 4.19 yields:

$$\ln Q = \ln \lambda + \alpha \ln P + \gamma \ln I \tag{4.21}$$

This equation is linear in the logarithms. It can be estimated by standard regression analysis using data on Q, P, and I. The estimated coefficients, α and γ, are estimates of the price and income elasticities. Other types of elasticities—for example cross elasticities—can be estimated by including other variables in the demand equation.

Appendix Problem

The BJC Company has the following demand function:

$$Q = 300 - 30 \text{ Price} + .01 \text{ Income}$$

Currently, price is $5 and income is $20,000.

1. Calculate the point elasticities for price and income.
2. Is the product a normal or inferior good?
3. Is demand elastic or inelastic?
4. What will happen to revenue if the company raises its price?

Suggested Readings

E. Douglas (1987), *Managerial Economics: Analysis and Strategy* (Prentice Hall: Englewood Cliffs, NJ), Part 2.

E. Mansfield (1988), *Microeconomics* (W. W. Norton: New York), Chapter 5.

G. Stigler (1987), *The Theory of Price* (MacMillan: New York), Chapter 3.

Review Questions

4–1. What is the difference between a demand function and a demand curve?

4–2. How will each of the following affect the position of the demand curve for video recorders (VCRs)?

  a. An increase in the price of VCR tapes.

  b. A decrease in the price of VCRs.

  c. An increase in per capita income.

  d. A decrease in the price of movie tickets.

4–3. If the demand for a product is inelastic, what will happen to total revenue if price is increased? Explain.

4–4. What sign are the cross elasticities for substitute products? Explain.

4–5. Distinguish between normal and inferior goods.

4–6. How can cross elasticities be used to help define the relevant firms in an industry?

4–7. Suppose the price of heating oil increases significantly. Discuss the likely short-run and long-run effects.

4–8. The Alexander Machine Tool Company faces a linear demand curve. Currently, it is selling at a price and quantity where its demand elasticity is 1.5. Consultants have suggested that the company expand output because it is facing an elastic demand curve. Do you agree with this recommendation?

4–9. For three years in a row, income among consumers has increased. Alexander Machine Tool has had sales increases in each of these three years. Does Alexander Machine Tool produce inferior or normal goods? Forecasts are that income will continue to rise in the future. Should Alexander Machine Tool anticipate that demand for its products will continue to rise? Explain.

4–10. The cross elasticity between product A and product B is 10. Do you think that product A is likely to face an elastic or inelastic demand curve? Explain.

4–11. John Smith is interested in estimating the industry demand curve for a particular product. He has gathered data on historical prices and quantities sold in the industry. He knows that the industry supply curve has been stable over the entire period. He is considering estimating a regression between price and quantity and using the result as an estimate of the demand curve. Do you think this technique will result in a good estimate of the demand curve? Explain.

4–12. A road engineer uses data on population trends to forecast the use of a particular highway. Her forecasts indicate severe road congestion by the year 2010. She suggests building a new road. Comment on this approach.

4–13. Alexander Machine Tool faces the demand curve: P = $70 − .001Q. What price and quantity maximize total revenue? What is the price elasticity at this point?

4–14. Studies indicate that the income elasticity of demand for servants in the United States exceeds 1. Nevertheless, the number of servants has been decreasing during the last 75 years, while incomes have risen significantly. How can these facts be reconciled?

4–15. Prior to a price increase, the price and quantity demanded for a product were $10 and 100, respectively. After the price increase, they were $12 and 90.

  a. Calculate the arc elasticity of demand.

  b. Is the demand elastic or inelastic over this region?

  c. What happened to total revenue?

4–16. Define marginal revenue. Explain why marginal revenue is less than price when demand curves slope downward.

4–17. In 1991, Rochester, New York, had a serious ice storm. Electric power was out in houses for days. The demand for power generators increased dramatically. Yet the local merchants did not increase their prices, even though they could have sold the units for substantially higher prices. Why do you think the merchants adopted this policy?

chapter 5

Production and Cost

I n 1994, domestic steel prices increased as the U.S. economy recovered from a recession.[1] Indeed, the steel market was the strongest it had been in 20 years. After significant price increases earlier in the year, domestic steel companies were planning to increase sheet-steel prices by another 10 percent at year end. In the tight electrogalvanized markets, price increases as high as 20 percent were expected. U.S. automobile manufacturers were among the companies most affected by these price increases, since they are major users of domestic steel.

To counter the effects of the increase in domestic steel prices, U.S. auto companies began seeking new overseas suppliers. For instance, in July1994, General Motors invited foreign bids for sheet steel from foreign companies such as Sidmar, Solldac, Thyssen, and Klockner. The increases in steel prices also placed pressure on U.S. automakers to use other raw materials in the production process. For example, auto companies were expected to increase their use of aluminum in engines, transmissions, body components, heating and cooling systems, and suspension systems in 1995.[2] Some of these applications were expected to replace cast iron or steel with aluminum. In addition, auto companies increased their research on new ways to use plastics, magnesium, and recyclable materials in their production process. The increases in steel prices were expected to affect the companies' pricing and output decisions.

This example raises a number of questions that are of interest to managers. First, how do firms choose among substitutable inputs in the production process? How does the optimal input mix change with changes in the input prices? How do changes in input prices affect the ultimate cost of production and the output choices of firms? This chapter addresses these and related questions. Major topics include production functions, optimal input choice, costs, profit maximization, cost estimation, and factor demand curves. An appendix derives the factor-balance equation.

Production Functions

A *production function* is a descriptive relation that connects inputs with outputs. It specifies the *maximum* possible output that can be produced for given amounts of inputs. Production functions are determined by the available technology. Production functions can be expressed mathematically. For instance, given existing technology, an automobile supplier is able to transform inputs like steel, aluminum, plastics, and labor into finished auto parts. In its most general form, the production function is expressed as:

$$Q = f(x_1, x_2, \ldots x_n) \tag{5.1}$$

where Q is the quantity produced and $x_1, x_2, \ldots x_n$ are the various inputs used in the production process.

To simplify the exposition, suppose that the auto part in this example is produced from just two inputs—steel and aluminum. A specific example of a production function in this context is:

$$Q = S^{1/2}A^{1/2} \tag{5.2}$$

[1]Details of this example are from "General Motors Eyes Imports to Counter Price Increases," *Metal Bulletin* (July 11, 1994), 21.

[2]A. Wrigley (1994), "Automotive Aluminum Use Climbing in 1995's Models: Automotive Applications Will Use Some 120 Million lbs. in 1995," *American Metal Market* (August 9), 1.

where S is pounds of steel, A is pounds of aluminum, and Q is the number of auto parts produced.[3] With this production function, 100 pounds of steel and 100 pounds of aluminum will produce 100 auto parts over the relevant time period, 400 pounds of steel and 100 pounds of aluminum will produce 200 auto parts, and so on.[4]

Returns to Scale

Returns to scale refers to the relation between output and a *proportional variation of all inputs* taken together. With *constant returns to scale,* a 1 percent change in all inputs results in a 1-percent change in output. For example, equation 5.2 presents a production function with constant returns to scale. If the firm uses 100 pounds of each input, it produces 100 auto parts. If the firm increases both inputs by 1 percent to 101 pounds, it produces 101 auto parts.[5]

With *increasing returns to scale,* a 1 percent change in all inputs results in a greater than 1 percent change in output. An example of such a production function is:

$$Q = SA \tag{5.3}$$

Here, 100 pounds of steel and 100 pounds of aluminum produce 10,000 auto parts, while 101 pounds of steel and aluminum produce 10,201 auto parts (a 2 percent increase in output). Firms often experience increasing returns to scale over at least some region of output. One of the main reasons is that a firm operating on a larger scale can engage in more extensive specialization. For instance, if an automobile company has only three employees and three machines, each employee and machine has to perform a myriad of tasks for the company to produce automobiles. Given the large number of tasks that each worker and machine has to perform, efficiency is likely to be low. In contrast, a large firm employing thousands of workers and machines can engage in much greater specialization. As discussed in Chapter 3, specialization often produces efficiency gains.

With *decreasing returns to scale,* a 1 percent change in all inputs results in a less than 1 percent change in output. An example is:

$$Q = S^{1/3}A^{1/3} \tag{5.4}$$

The likelihood of a firm experiencing decreasing returns to scale is open to debate. Some economists argue that firms should seldom display decreasing returns to scale. If a firm of a given size can produce a given output, why can't it simply replicate itself and produce twice the output with twice the inputs? Indeed, most empirical studies on the subject suggest that the typical firm initially experiences increasing returns to scale, followed by constant returns to scale over a broad range of output. On the other hand, several empirical studies indicate that some firms probably do experience decreasing returns to scale.[6] Also, casual observation suggests that big firms can suffer from inefficiencies (such as perquisite-taking problems) to a greater extent than smaller firms.

---

[3]This production function is an example of a Cobb–Douglas production function, which takes the general form: $Q = \lambda S^{\alpha}A^{\gamma}$. Cobb–Douglas production functions are frequently used in empirical estimation of cost functions. Not all firms, however, have production processes that are well described by this particular type of production function.

[4]$100^{1/2} \times 100^{1/2} = 10 \times 10 = 100$, and $400^{1/2} \times 100^{1/2} = 20 \times 10 = 200$.

[5]$[(100 \times 1.01)^{1/2}] \times [(100 \times 1.01)^{1/2}] = 101$.

[6]For example, E. Berndt, A. Friedlaender, and J. Chiang (1990), "Interdependent Pricing and Markup Behavior: An Empirical Analysis of GM, Ford and Chrysler," working paper, National Bureau of Economic Research, Cambridge, MA.

Units of S	Units of A	Total Product of S	Marginal Product of S	Average Product of S
1	9	3.00	3.00	3.00
2	9	4.24	1.24	2.12
3	9	5.20	0.96	1.73
4	9	6.00	0.80	1.50
5	9	6.70	0.70	1.34

Figure 5.1   Returns to a Factor

This table shows the total, marginal, and average products of S for the production function; $Q = S^{1/2}A^{1/2}$. Input A is held fixed at 9 units. The total product of S is the total output for each level of S; the marginal product of S is the incremental output from one additional unit of S; and the average product of S is output divided by the total units of S.

In our examples, the returns to scale are the same over all ranges of output. For instance, equation 5.2 always displays constant returns to scale, while equation 5.4 always displays decreasing returns. It is possible to have production functions that vary in returns to scale over the range of output. For instance, such a production function might have increasing returns to scale when output is relatively low, followed by constant returns to scale as output continues to increase, and finally decreasing returns to scale when output is high. Other combinations are possible.

Returns to a Factor

Returns to a factor refers to the relation between output and the variation in only one input, *holding other inputs fixed*. Returns to a factor can be expressed as total, marginal, or average quantities. The *total product* of an input is the schedule of output obtained as that input increases, holding other inputs fixed. The *marginal product* of an input is the change in total output associated with a one-unit change in the input, holding other inputs fixed. Finally, the *average product* is the total product divided by the number of units of the input employed.

To illustrate these concepts, consider the production function: $Q = S^{1/2}A^{1/2}$. Figure 5.1 presents the total, marginal, and average product of S, holding A fixed at 9.[7] For this particular production function, total product increases as S increases. Marginal product, however, is declining. This means that while total product increases with S, it does so at a decreasing rate. Average product is also decreasing over the entire range.

More generally, marginal and average products do not have to decline over the entire range of output. Indeed, many production functions display increasing marginal and average products over some ranges. However, most production functions reach a point (S') after which the marginal product of an input declines. This observation is often called the *law of diminishing returns* (or law of diminishing marginal product), which states that the marginal product of a variable factor will eventually decline as the input is increased. To illustrate this principle, consider the classic example of farming a piece of land. Land is fixed at one acre and no output can be produced without any workers. If 10 units of output can be obtained by hiring one worker, the marginal product of the

[7]This production function assumes that production does not have to take place in discrete units. For instance, output might be expressed in tons, where production in fractions of a ton is possible.

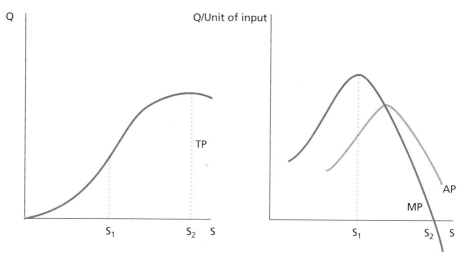

Figure 5.2   Returns to a Factor: A Common Case

This figure illustrates a common pattern for total product, marginal product, and returns to a factor. Marginal product rises, then falls, and eventually becomes negative. When marginal product is rising (between zero and S_1), total product increases at an increasing rate (the curve is convex). When marginal product is falling but positive (between S_1 and S_2), total product continues to increase but does so at a decreasing rate. Beyond S_2, marginal product is negative and total product falls with continued output. Average product is rising when it is below marginal product and is falling when it is above marginal product. Average and marginal products are equal when average product is at a maximum.

first unit of labor is 10. The change in output might be even greater as the firm moves from one to two workers. For instance, two workers might be able to produce 25 units of output by working together and specializing in various tasks. The marginal product of labor is 15 and thus, over this range, marginal product is increasing. Eventually, as the firm continues to add more workers (holding the amount of land fixed), output will grow at a slower rate. At some point, total output might actually decline with additional workers because of coordination or congestion problems. In this case, marginal product is negative.

Figure 5.2 illustrates returns to a factor in this common case. The left panel displays total product, while the right panel displays marginal and average products. As the use of input S goes from zero to S_1, marginal product rises. Over this range total product is

Food Intake and Productivity: An Example of Diminishing Returns

Economist John Strauss analyzed data from a survey of farmers from a small West African country, Sierra Leone. Through this analysis, he was able to estimate the relation between an individual's agricultural output and daily caloric intake. Between zero and 5,200 calories per day, he found a positive association between output and caloric intake. The relation, however, was subject to diminishing marginal returns. For instance, for workers consuming about 1,500 calories per day, a 1 percent increase in caloric consumption increased agricultural output by about 0.5 percent. This impact of caloric consumption on output, declined steadily with increases in caloric consumption. For workers consuming 4,500 calories per day, a 1-percent increase in calories increased output by only 0.12 percent. Beyond 5,200 calories per day, the estimated relation was negative—additional caloric intake *reduced output*. Apparently, beyond that point the marginal product of food intake was negative.

Source: J. Strauss (1986), "Does Better Nutrition Raise Productivity?"
Journal of Political Economy 94, 297–320.

Baseball Averages

Marginal product is above average product when average product is rising and below average product when average product is falling. This relation is a general property of averages and marginals. A useful illustration is a baseball player's batting average. The batting average is defined as the number of hits divided by the number of times at bat. Suppose a player starts a game with an average of .300. If the player gets two hits out of four at bats, the marginal batting average for the day is .500 and the player's batting average must rise. If the player gets one hit out of four at bats, the marginal is .250 and the overall average must drop.

convex—total product increases at an increasing rate.[8] At S_1, diminishing returns set in and the marginal product begins to fall. Between S_1 and S_2, marginal product is positive and so total product continues to increase. However, it does so at a decreasing rate (the curve is concave). Beyond S_2, marginal product is negative and total output falls with increases in S. Average product is rising when marginal product is above average product and is falling when marginal product is below average product. Marginal product and average product are equal when average product is at a maximum. This relation is a general rule.[9] The box on baseball averages illustrates the intuition behind this relation.

Optimal Input Choice

QUANTITY

Production Isoquants

Most production functions allow some substitution of inputs. For example, suppose that a firm with the production function $Q = S^{1/2}A^{1/2}$ wants to produce 100 auto parts. In this case, there are many different combinations of steel and aluminum that will produce the 100 auto parts. For instance, 100 auto parts can be produced using 100 pounds of steel and 100 pounds of aluminum, 25 pounds of steel and 400 pounds of aluminum, or 400 pounds of steel and 25 pounds of aluminum. Figure 5.3 graphs all the possible combinations of inputs that can be used to produce exactly 100 auto parts (assuming efficient production). This curve is called an *isoquant* (*iso,* meaning the same, and *quant* from quantity). An isoquant shows all possible ways to produce the same quantity. There is a different isoquant for each possible level of production. Figure 5.3 shows the isoquants for 100, 200, and 300 auto parts.

Production functions vary in terms of how easily inputs can be substituted for one another. In some cases, no substitution is possible. Suppose that in order to produce 100 auto parts you must have 100 pounds of aluminum and 100 pounds of steel, to produce 200 auto parts you must have 200 pounds of aluminum and 200 pounds of steel, and so on. Having extra steel or aluminum without the other metal does not increase output—they must be used in *fixed proportions.* As shown in Figure 5.4, isoquants from fixed-proportion production functions take the shape of right angles. At the other extreme are *perfect substitutes,* where the inputs can be freely substituted for one another. Suppose that one auto part can always be produced using either a pound of steel or a pound of aluminum. In this case, the firm can produce 100 auto parts by using 100 pounds of

---

[8]For the technically inclined: The marginal product at a point is equal to the slope of the total product curve at that point (MC = $\partial TP/\partial S$). Thus, marginal product is decreasing when the total cost curve is concave and increasing when it is convex.

[9]Averages and marginals also are equal when the average is at a minimum.

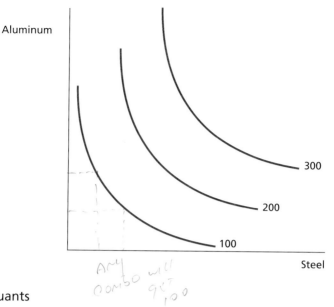

Figure 5.3   Isoquants

An *isoquant* shows all possible ways to produce the same quantity. There is a different isoquant for each possible level of production. This figure shows the isoquants for 100, 200, and 300 auto parts for the production function: $Q = S^{1/2}A^{1/2}$.

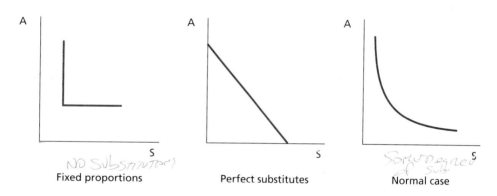

Figure 5.4   Isoquants for Fixed Proportion Production Functions, Perfect Substitutes, and the Normal Case

Production functions vary in terms of how easily inputs can be substituted for one another. In some cases, inputs must be used in *fixed proportions* and no substitution is possible. Here, isoquants take the shape of right angles. At the other extreme are *perfect substitutes,* where the inputs can be freely substituted for one another. Here, isoquants are stright lines. Most produciton functions have isoquants that are between the two extremes. The isoquants in the normal case have curvature but are not right angles.

aluminum or 100 pounds of steel, or any combination in between. As shown in Figure 5.4, the corresponding isoquant is a straight line. Most production systems have isoquants that are between the two extremes. As depicted in Figure 5.4, these isoquants have curvature but are not right angles. The degree of substitutability of the inputs is determined by the curvature—the closer the isoquant is to a right angle (the more convex), the lower the substitutability.

Substitution of Inputs in Home Building

House builders in the Pacific Northwest use large quantities of wood in the construction of residential houses. For instance, wood is used for frames, siding, floors, roofs, and so on. Homebuilders in the Southwest (for example, Arizona) use much more stucco and tile in home construction. An important reason for this difference is that, in contrast to the Pacific Northwest, the Southwest does not have large nearby forests. This example suggests that homebuilders are able to substitute among inputs in building a home. Homebuilders in the Southwest, however, still use wood to frame the house—the substitution of other inputs for wood is not complete.

Generally, it is assumed that isoquants are convex to the origin (as pictured in the right panel in Figure 5.4—the normal case). Convexity implies that the substitutability of one input for another declines as less of the first input is used. In our example, if the firm is using a large quantity of steel and little aluminum, it can substitute a relatively large quantity of steel for a small quantity of aluminum and keep output the same (see Figure 5.3). In this case, aluminum might be much better suited than steel to construct some components of the auto part. As the firm uses more aluminum relative to steel the ability to substitute aluminum for steel declines. Most real-world production processes display this property.

Isocost Lines

Given that there are many ways to produce a given level of output, how does a firm choose its input mix? The answer depends on the costs of the inputs. Suppose that the firm faces competitive input markets and can buy as much of any input as it wants at the going market price. The price of steel is denoted P_S, while the price of aluminum is denoted P_A. Total cost (C) is equal to the sum of the quantities of each input used in the production process times their respective prices. Thus:

$$C = P_S S + P_A A \tag{5.5}$$

Isocost lines depict all combinations of S and A that cost the same amount. Suppose P_S = \$0.50 per pound and P_A = \$1 per pound, and the constant cost level is \$100. In this case:

$$\$100 = \$0.5S + \$A \tag{5.6}$$

or equivalently:

$$A = 100 - 0.5S \tag{5.7}$$

Figure 5.5 graphs this isocost line. Note that the intercept, 100, indicates how many pounds of A could be purchased if the entire \$100 is spent on A. The slope of –0.5 is –1 times the ratio of the two prices (P_S/P_A)—since aluminum is twice as expensive as steel, 0.5 units of A can be given up for one unit of S and the cost remains the same.

Holding the prices of the inputs constant, isocost lines for different cost levels are parallel. Figure 5.5 illustrates this property for the isocost lines for \$100 and \$200. Note that the further away the line is from the origin the higher is the total cost. Holding output constant, the firm would like to be on the lowest possible isocost line. The slope of an isocost line changes with changes in the ratio of the input prices. As depicted in Figure 5.6,

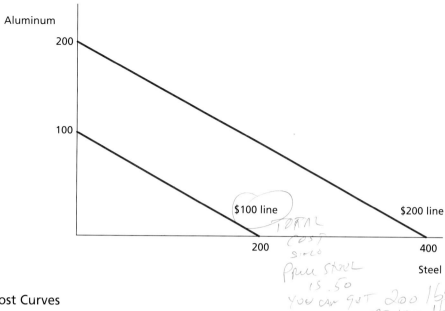

Figure 5.5 Isocost Curves

Isocost lines depict all combinations of inputs that cost the same. In this example, $P_S = 0.50$ per pound and $P_A = \$1$ per pound. The figure shows isocost lines for $100 and $200 of expenditures. The slope of an isocost line is -1 times the ratio of the input prices—in this example, -0.5. Isocost lines for different expenditure levels are parallel.

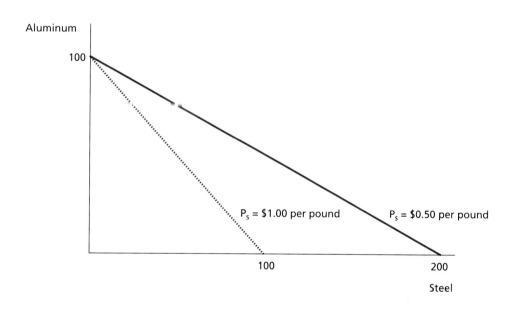

Figure 5.6 Isocost Lines and Changes in Input Prices

This figure shows the effect of changes in input prices on the slopes of isocost lines. The solid line shows the isocost line when the price of aluminum is $1 and the price of steel is $0.50. The dotted line shows the isocost line when the prices of both inputs are $1. Total cost in each case is $100.

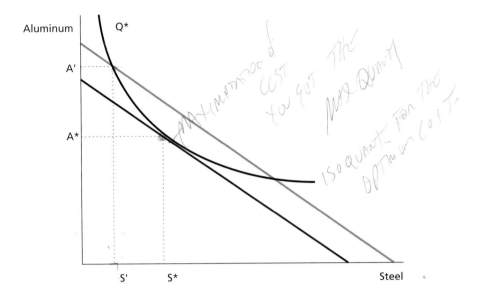

Figure 5.7   Cost Minimization

The input mix that minimizes the cost of producing any given output, Q*, occurs where an isocost line is tangent to the relevant isoquant. In this example, the tangency occurs at (S*, A*). The firm would prefer to be on an isocost line closer to the origin. However, the firm would not have sufficient resources to produce Q*. The firm could produce Q* using other input mixes, such as (S′, A′). However, the cost of production would increase.

---

if the price of steel increases to $1, the line becomes steeper (slope of −1). Here, the firm must give up 1 pound of A to obtain 1 pound of S. Alternatively, if the price of steel falls to $0.25 (not pictured in the figure), the line becomes flatter (slope of −0.25). In this case, the firm only has to give up ¼ pound of aluminum for every pound of steel. Similarly, the slope of the line changes with changes in the price of aluminum. What determines the slope of the line are the *relative prices* (recall the slope is $-P_S/P_A$).

Cost Minimization

For any given level of output, Q*, managers will want to choose the input mix that minimizes the costs. As shown in Figure 5.7, the optimal mix (S*, A*) occurs at the point of tangency between the isoquant for Q* and an isocost line. Managers would like to produce the output less expensively (on an isocost curve closer to the origin). However, lower-cost production is not possible. The firm could select other input mixes to produce Q*.[10] Any other input mix would place the firm on a higher isocost line. Consider the combination (S′, A′) in Figure 5.7. This combination of inputs produces Q* units of output. This output, however, can be produced more cheaply by using less aluminum and more steel.

---

[10]Note the similarity between this cost minimization problem and the consumer's utility maximization problem introduced in Chapter 2. The mathematics are the same. The consumer maximizes utility for a given budget. Cost minimization is equivalent to maximizing output for a given budget (where the budget is that associated with the lowest-cost method of producing the output).

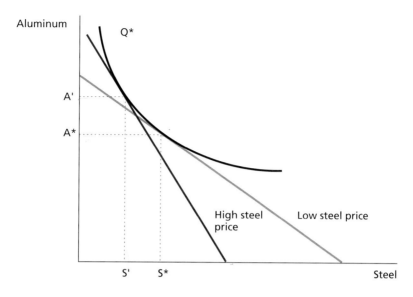

Figure 5.8 Optimal Input Mix and Changes in Input Prices

This figure shows how the optimal input mix for producitng a given output, Q*, changes as the price of an input inceases. In this example, the price of steel increases and the firm uses less steel and more aluminum to produce the output. This effect is called the *substitution effect*. The strength of the substitution effect depends on the curvature of the isoquant. The greater the curvature, the less the firm will substitute between the two inputs.

In the appendix to this chapter, we show that at the optimal input mix, the following condition holds:

$$MP_S/P_S = MP_A/P_A \tag{5.8}$$

where MP_i = the marginal product of input i. (Recall that the marginal product of an input is described in Figure 5.1.) Condition 5.8 has a straightforward interpretation. The marginal-product-to-price ratio indicates how much additional output can be obtained by spending an extra dollar on the input. At the optimal output mix this quantity must be the same for all inputs. Otherwise, it would be possible to increase output without increasing costs by reducing the use of inputs with low ratios and increasing the use of inputs with high ratios. For instance, if the ratio is 10 units per dollar for aluminum and 20 units per dollar for steel, the firm could increase output by 10 units by spending one less dollar on aluminum and one more dollar on steel. Costs would remain constant. The firm is not at an optimal input mix when this type of substitution is possible.

Changes in Input Prices

An increase in the relative price of an input will motivate the firm to use less of that input and more of other inputs. Figure 5.8 shows how the optimal input mix for producing Q* changes in our example as the price of steel increases—the firm uses less steel and more aluminum to produce the output. This effect is called the *substitution effect*. The strength of the substitution effect depends on the curvature of the isoquant. The greater the curvature, the less the firm will substitute between the two inputs for any given change in prices. The substitution effect helps to explain the reactions of automobile companies to increases in domestic steel prices during 1994. These companies increased their use of foreign steel. They also searched for new ways to replace steel with other inputs such as aluminum.

Minimum Wage Laws

In 1994, the minimum wage that an employer could pay a worker in the United States was $4.25 per hour. Since he first took office in 1992, President Clinton has advocated an increase in this minimum wage. He argues that $4.25 per hour was too low and that the poor would be substantially better off by increasing the wage. The analysis in this chapter indicates why many economists and politicians are skeptical about this claim. While it is true that the increase in minimum wage would make some workers better off by increasing their wages, other workers would be made worse off. In particular, the increase in the wage rate is likely to motivate firms to move away from low-skilled workers toward more automation. Thus, the number of workers hired at the minimum wage is likely to decline with an increase in the wage. Estimates suggest that when the minimum wage was increased from $3.35 to $4.25, that employment among teenage men fell by 7.29 percent, and employment among teenage women fell by 11.34 percent; employment among teenage blacks fell by 10 percent. Those obtaining jobs are better off; workers who want a job but can't find one are worse off.

Source: D. Deere, K. Murphy, and F. Welch (1995), "Employment and the 1990–1991 Minimum-Wage Hike," *American Economic Review* 85:2, 232–237.

Costs

We have analyzed how firms should choose their input mix to minimize the costs of production. We now extend this analysis to focus more specifically on the costs of producing different levels of output. Analysis of these costs plays an important role in output and pricing decisions.

Cost Curves

The *total cost curve* depicts the relation between total costs and output. Conceptually, the total cost curve can be derived from the isoquant/isocost analysis discussed above. For each possible level of output, there is a lowest-cost method of production, as depicted by the tangency between the isoquant and the isocost line. The total cost curve simply graphs the cost of production associated with the isocost line and the corresponding output. For instance, if the lowest-cost method of producing 100 auto parts is $1,000, one point on the total cost curve is (100, $1000). If the lowest-cost method of producing 200 parts is $1,500, another point is (200, $1,500). *Marginal cost* is the change in total costs associated with a one-unit change in output. *Average cost* is total cost divided by total output. Managers sometimes refer to marginal cost as incremental cost, while they use the term *unit cost* to refer to average cost.

Figure 5.9 illustrates the total, marginal, and average costs curves for an hypothetical firm. (This figure illustrates a common pattern for cost curves, but not all firms have cost curves with the same shapes.) The left panel indicates that total cost increases with output. Between zero and Q_1, total cost increases but at a decreasing rate (the curve is concave). As shown in the right panel, over this range, marginal cost decreases.[11] Past Q_1, total cost increases at an increasing rate (the total cost curve is convex) and marginal cost increases. Average cost is declining when marginal cost is below average cost and is

[11]For the technically inclined: The marginal cost at a point is equal to the slope of the total cost curve at that point (MC = $\partial TC/\partial Q$). Thus, marginal cost deceases when the total cost curve is concave and increases when it is convex.

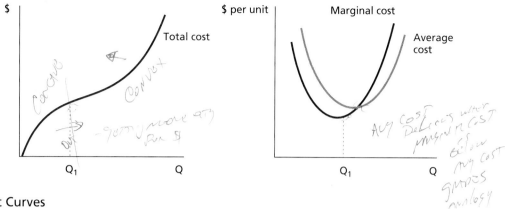

Figure 5.9   Cost Curves

This figure illustrates the total, marginal, and average cost curves of a hypothetical firm. The left panel pictures total cost. Total cost increases with output. Between zero and Q_1, total cost increases but at a decreasing rate (the curve is concave). As shown in the right panel, over this range, marginal cost decreases. Past Q_1, total cost increases at an increasing rate (the curve is convex) and marginal cost increases. Average cost declines when marginal cost is below average cost and rises when marginal cost is above average cost. This relation is a general rule.

rising when marginal cost is above average cost. Average cost equals marginal cost when average cost is at its minimum point. As previously discussed, these relations are general rules—they apply to average costs as well as batting averages.

Production Functions and Cost Curves

With constant input prices, the shapes of cost curves are determined by the underlying production function. For instance, if the production function displays increasing returns to scale over some range of output, long-run average cost must decline over the range. With increasing returns to scale, a 1 percent increase on input expenditures results in a greater than 1 percent increase in output and average cost must fall. In contrast, with decreasing returns to scale, a 1 percent increase in input expenditures results in a less than 1 increase in output and average cost must rise. Finally, constant returns to scale imply constant average cost. U-shaped curves (as pictured in Figure 5.9) are frequently used to illustrate average cost. This slope suggests an initial region of increasing returns to scale, followed by decreasing returns to scale.[12]

There is also a direct link between the marginal cost curve and the underlying production function. Recall from equation 5.8 that cost minimization requires the marginal-product-to-price ratio be the same for all inputs. For illustration, suppose at the optimal input mix to produce 100 units of steel, the marginal-product-to-price ratio for both steel and aluminum is two. By expending $1 more on either input, output increases by two units. The reciprocal of this ratio (1/2) is the marginal cost of producing one additional unit of output—if two units are produced with $1 of additional

---

[12]Some economists argue that the typical long-run average cost curve is L-shaped—once the minimum efficient scale is reached, additional output can be produced at a constant average cost by simply replicating the process (the production function does not experience decreasing returns to scale). But this argument assumes that management costs do not increase disproportionally with firm size. See P. McAfee and J. McMillan (1995), "Organizational Diseconomies of Scale," *Journal of Economics and Management Strategy* 4:3, 399–426.

expenditure on inputs, the marginal cost of producing one extra unit is 50 cents. This example indicates that, holding input prices constant, marginal cost is determined by the marginal productivity of the inputs: The higher the marginal productivity, the lower the marginal cost. If the marginal productivities in our example were doubled, the marginal-product-to-price ratio would be 4 and the marginal cost would be 25 cents. The inverse relation between marginal productivity and marginal cost makes intuitive sense. If substanitally more output can be produced with a small increase in inputs, the marginal cost of producing output is relatively low.

Input prices also can affect the shapes of the cost curves. For instance, a declining average cost can be motivated by discounts on large volume purchases. Similarly, a machine that produces 20,000 units might not be twice as expensive as a machine that produces only 10,000 units. Alternatively, if the firm bids up the price of inputs with large purchases, average cost can rise with increased output. Thus, the long-run average cost curve can slope upward even if the firm does not experience decreasing returns to scale.

Opportunity Costs

Managers must be careful to use the correct set of input prices in constructing cost curves. In Chapter 2, we defined *opportunity cost* as the value of a resource in its next best alternative use. Current market prices for inputs more closely reflect opportunity costs than *historical costs.* For instance, if an auto supplier purchases 1,000 pounds of aluminum for $1,000 and subsequently the market price increases to $2,000, the opportunity cost of using the aluminum is $2,000. If the company uses the aluminum, its replacement cost is $2,000. Alternatively, the current inventory could be sold to another firm for $2,000. In either case, the firm forgoes $2,000 if it uses the aluminum in its production process.

The *relevant costs* for managerial decision making are the opportunity costs. It is important to include the opportunity costs of all inputs whether or not they have actually been purchased in the marketplace. For instance, if an owner spends time working in the firm, the opportunity cost is the value of the owner's time in its next best alternative use.

Short Run versus Long Run

Cost curves can be depicted for both the *short run* and the *long run.* The short run is the operating period during which at least one input (typically capital) is fixed in supply. For instance, in the short run it might be impossible to change the plant size or change the number of machines. In the *long run,* the firm has complete flexibility—no inputs are fixed.

The definitions of short run and long run are not based on calendar time. The length of each period depends on how long it takes the firm to vary all inputs. For a cleaning-services firm operating out of rented office space, the short run is a relatively brief period. For a large manufacturing firm with heavy investments in plant and equipment, the short run might be a relatively long time period.

Short-run cost curves are sometimes called *operating curves* because they are used in making near-term production and pricing decisions. For these decisions, it is often correct to take the plant size and certain other factors as given (since these factors are beyond the control of the managers in the short term). Long-run cost curves are referred to as *planning curves,* since they play a key role in longer-run planning decisions relating to plant size and equipment acquisitions.

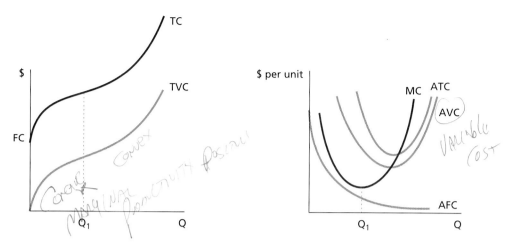

Figure 5.10 Short-Run Cost Curves

This figure displays the short-run cost curves of a hypothetical firm. The left panel pictures total cost (TC) and total variable cost (TVC). Fixed costs simply shift the position of the variable cost curve. The right panel pictures marginal and average costs. Average fixed cost declines with output since the fixed cost is being spread over more units. Marginal cost (MC) declines to Q_1 and then increases beyond that point due to diminishing returns. Marginal cost depends only on the variable input factors and is *completely independent of the fixed cost.* Average total cost (ATC) and AVC decline as long as marginal cost is lower than the average cost and increase beyond that point. Marginal cost is equal to both ATC and AVC at their respective minimum points. Average total cost is always larger than AVC, since ATC = AFC + AVC. However, this difference becomes smaller as output increases and AFC declines.

Fixed and Variable Costs

In the short run, some costs are fixed and do not vary with output. These *fixed costs* are incurred even if the firm produces no output. For instance, the firm has to pay the managers' salaries, interest on borrowed capital, lease payments, and property taxes whether or not it produces any output. *Variable costs* change with the level of output. These costs include items like raw material, fuel, and certain labor costs. In the long run, all costs are variable.

Short-Run Cost Curves

Figure 5.10 displays the short-run cost curves for a hypothetical firm. For this firm, suppose that the basic plant size is fixed and that all other inputs are variable. The left panel pictures total cost. Total cost is the sum of the fixed cost (FC) and total variable cost (TVC). The shape of the total cost curve is completely determined by the shape of the total variable cost curve. Fixed costs simply shift up the position of the curve. Between 0 and Q_1 the total cost curve is concave. Over this range, the marginal productivity of the variable factors is increasing (assuming fixed input prices). Past Q_1, the total cost curve is convex and the marginal productivity of the variable factors is decreasing. This type of pattern is expected given the law of diminishing returns. At low output levels, the fixed inputs are not efficiently utilized. Increasing the variable inputs increases output significantly. Over this range, total cost increases, but does so at a decreasing rate. Eventually, the marginal productivity of the variable inputs declines, and it becomes increasingly expensive to produce extra units of output.

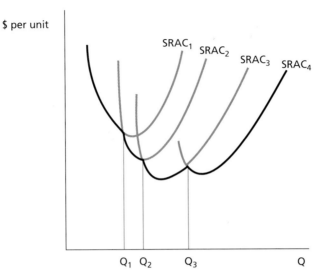

Figure 5.11 Long-Run Average Costs as an Envelope of Short-Run Average Cost Curves

In the long run, the average cost of porduction (LRAC) is less than or equal to the short-run average cost (SRAC) of production. The LRAC curve can be thought of as an *envelope* of the short-run average cost curves. The figure shows four potential plant sizes. Each of the four plants provides the low-cost method of production over some range of output. For instance, the smallest plant provides the lowest-cost method of producing any output from zero to Q_1, while the next largest plant provides the low-cost method of producing output from Q_1 to Q_2, and so on. The heavy portion of each curve indicates the minimum long-run average cost for producing each level of output, assuming that there are only these four possible plant sizes.

The right panel pictures marginal and average costs. Average fixed cost (AFC) is total fixed cost divided by output. Average fixed cost declines with output since the fixed cost is spread over more units. Marginal cost (MC) declines up to Q_1 and then increases beyond that point due to diminishing returns. Note that marginal cost depends only on the variable input factors and is *completely independent of the fixed cost.* Average variable costs (AVC) are total variable costs divided by output. Average total cost (ATC) and AVC decline as long as marginal cost is lower than the average cost and increase beyond that point. Marginal cost is equal to both ATC and AVC at their respective minimum points. Average total cost is always larger than average variable cost, since ATC = AFC + AVC. However, this difference becomes smaller as AFC declines with higher output.

Long-Run Cost Curves

In the short run, firms are unable to adjust their plant sizes. In the long run, however, if a firm wants to produce more output it can build a larger, more efficient plant. In fact, long-run cost curves are referred to as *planning curves,* since they play a key role in longer-run planning decisions relating to plant size and equipment acquisition. In the long run, the average cost of production (LRAC) is less than or equal to the short-run average cost of production. Indeed, the LRAC curve can be thought of as an *envelope* of the short-run average cost curves. Figure 5.11 illustrates this concept. The figure shows four potential plant sizes. Each of the four plants provides the low-cost method of production over some range of output. For instance, the smallest plant provides the lowest-cost method of producing any output from zero to Q_1, while the next largest plant provides the low-cost

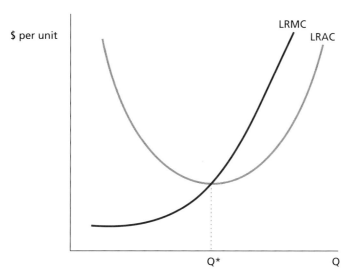

Figure 5.12 Long-Run Average and Marginal Cost Curves

If there are many different plant sizes that vary only slightly in size, the resulting long-run average cost curve (LRAC) is relatively smooth, as pictured in this figure. The long-run marginal cost (LRMC) is below average cost when average cost is falling and above average cost when it is rising. The two are equal at the minimum average cost. The minimum efficient scale is defined as the plant size at which LRAC's are first minimized (Q* in this example).

method of producing outputs from Q_1 to Q_2, and so on. The heavy portion of each curve indicates the minimum long-run average cost for producing each level of output, assuming that there are only these four possible plant sizes.

If we extend this analysis, by assuming there are many different feasible plant sizes that vary only slightly in size, the resulting LRAC curve will be relatively smooth, as pictured in Figure 5.12. This figure also pictures the long-run marginal cost curve (LRMC). As we have discussed, the marginal cost is below average cost when average cost is falling and above average cost when it is rising. The two are equal at the minimum average cost.

Minimum Efficient Scale

The minimum *efficient scale* is defined as that plant size at which long-run average cost first reaches its minimum point. In Figure 5.12, this minimum occurs at Q*. The minimum efficient scale affects both the optimal plant size and the level of potential competition.

Average production cost is minimized at the minimum efficient scale. As we discuss in the next chapter, competition tends to motivate firms to adopt this plant size. If firms build plants that depart significantly from minimum efficient scale, they will be at a competitive disadvantage and typically will either have to change plant size or be forced out of business. One complicating factor is transportation costs. If transportation costs are high, any inefficiencies of smaller regional plants can be overcome by the cost savings for transporting the product to customers. In this case, when total production and distribution costs are considered, firms with plants that are smaller than the minimum efficient scale can survive in a competitive marketplace.

Generally, the number of competitors will be large and the competition more vigorous when the minimum efficient scale is small relative to total industry demand. For instance, suppose that a potential entrant to an industry sees established firms making a

DeLorean Automobiles

The difficulties of competing with plant sizes significantly below the minimum efficient scale is highlighted by the experience of the DeLorean Motor Company. John Z. DeLorean was a high-ranking executive at General Motors. He left GM in 1979 to form his own automobile company, the DeLorean Motor Company. The strategy of the new company was to specialize in high-priced luxury sports cars. The company's first (and only) car was the stainless-steel DMC12 with a list price of $29,000 (a very high price in the early 1980s). Although the minimum efficient scale is relatively large in auto production, DeLorean felt he could compete by designing higher-quality sports cars than the large auto companies. Planned production for 1980 was 3,000 cars. The company soon ran into financial difficulties. In 1982, DeLorean was arrested for conspiring to buy and distribute 220 pounds of cocaine valued at $24 million. Federal officials asserted that DeLorean was entering the drug business to help save his ailing automobile company. Although DeLorean was later acquitted on these charges, the company still faced insurmountable financial difficulties and soon went out of business.

substantial profit. If the firm would have to produce 10 percent of the market's output to be cost efficient, it is likely to drive the price down on entry and is less likely to enter the market than if it would only need to produce 1 percent of the market's output for efficient production.

Industries where average cost declines over a broad range of output are characterized as having *economies of scale.* Significant economies of scale limit the number of firms in the industry. For instance, if the minimum efficient scale is 25 percent of total industry sales, there is only room for four firms to produce at that volume. The level of competition among the existing firms can vary significantly, even if there are only a few firms in the industry. However, threat of entry is less important than in industries where economies of scale are low. The threat of potential new competitors is often an important consideration in a firm's strategic planning. In Chapter 7, we describe in more detail how a firm's market structure affects managerial decision making.

Economies of Scope

Thus far, we have discussed the production of a single product. Many firms, however, produce multiple products. *Economies of scope* exist when the cost of producing a joint set of products in one firm is less than the cost of producing the products separately in independent firms. Joint production can produce cost savings for a variety of reasons. Efficiencies can result from common use of production facilities, marketing programs, and management systems. Also, the production of some products provides unavoidable by-products that are valuable to the firm. For instance, a sheep rancher jointly produces mutton and wool.

Public Utilities

The production of electric power is typically associated with large economies of scale—the average cost of producing electricity decreases with the quantity produced. This production characteristic implies that it is generally more efficient to have one large plant that produces power for an area than several smaller plants. A problem with having one producer of electrical power in an area, however, is that the firm has the potential to overcharge consumers for electricity since there are limited alternative sources of supply. Concerns about this problem provide one motivation for the formation of public utility commissions that regulate the prices that utility companies can charge consumers.

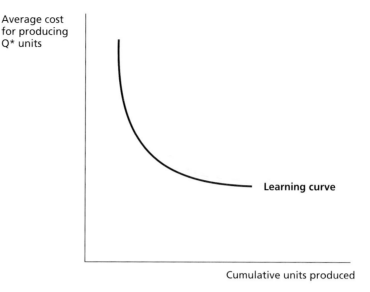

Figure 5.13 Learning Curve

A learning curve pictures the relation between average cost for a given output, Q*, and cumulative past production. In this example, there are significant learning effects in the early stages of production. These effects become minimal as the firm continues to produce the product.

Economies of scope help to explain why many firms produce multiple products. For instance, PepsiCo, Inc., is a major producer of soft drinks. However, it also produces a wide range of snack foods (for example, corn chips and cookies). These multiple products allow PepsiCo to leverage its product development, distribution, and marketing systems.

Economies of scope and economies of scale are different concepts. Economies of scope involve cost savings that result from joint production, while economies of scale involve efficiencies from producing higher volumes of a given product. It is possible to have economies of scope without having economies of scale and vice versa.

Learning Curves

For some firms, the long-run average cost for producing a given level of output declines as the firm gains experience from producing the output. For example, with more output, employees can gain important information on how to improve production processes. They also become more efficient as they gain experience on the job.[13] A *learning curve* pictures the relation between average cost and cumulative volume of production. Cumulative production is the total amount of the product produced by the firm in all previous production periods. Figure 5.13 presents an example where there are significant learning effects in the early stages of production. Eventually, however, these effects are minimal as the firm continues to produce the product.

[13]A. Alchian (1959), "Costs and Outputs," in *The Allocation of Economic Resources,* by M. Abramovitz and others (Stanford University Press: Palo Alto, CA).

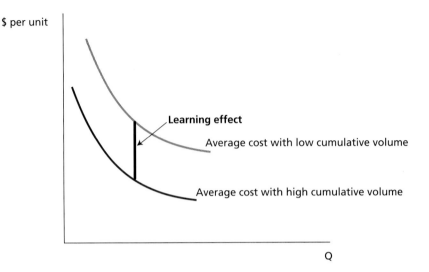

Figure 5.14 Economies of Scale versus Learning Effects

This figure shows the average cost curves for a firm when it has experienced high and low cumulative volume. In both cases, there are economies of scale (average cost declines with output). The average cost for each level of output, however, is lower when the firm has experienced high cumulative volume because of learning effects.

Figure 5.14 shows the difference between economies of scale and learning effects. Economies of scale imply reductions in average cost as the quantity being produced in the production period increases. Learning effects imply a shift in the entire average cost curve—the average cost for producing a given quantity in a production period decreases with cumulative volume. Learning effects can sometimes give existing firms in an industry a competitive advantage over potential entrants. We discuss this issue in more detail in the next chapter.

Profit Maximization

Thus far, we have focused on the costs of producing different levels of output. However, what output level should managers choose to maximize firm profits? To answer this question, we use the concept of *marginal analysis* that we initially introduced in Chapter 2.

Economies of Scale and Learning Effects in the Chemical Processing Industry

Marvin Lieberman studied economies of scale and learning effects in the chemical processing industry. He found that for each doubling in plant size, average production costs fell by about 11 percent. For each doubling of cumulative volume, the average cost of production fell by about 27 percent. Thus, there is evidence of both economies of scale and learning effects of the chemical processing industry. The size of the estimates suggests that learning effects are more important than economies of scale in explaining the observed decline in costs within the industry from the 1950s to the 1907s.

Source: M. Lieberman (1984) "The Learning Curve and Pricing in the Chemical Processing Industries," *Rand Journal* 15, 213–288.

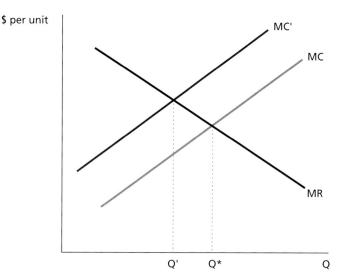

Figure 5.15 Optimal Output and Changes in Marginal Cost

This figure illustrates that an increase in marginal cost (from MC to MC′) lowers the optimal output of the firm (from Q* to Q′).

Marginal costs and benefits are the incremental costs and benefits that are associated with making a decision. It is the marginal costs and benefits that are important in economic decision making. An action should be taken when the marginal benefits of the action exceed its marginal costs. In deciding whether or not to produce one more unit of a product, the marginal benefit is the marginal revenue (see Chapter 4), while the marginal cost is equal to the marginal production cost (including any distribution costs). Fixed costs do not affect the decision. The firm should produce extra units as long as MR is greater than MC; the firm should not produce extra units when MR is less than MC. At the *profit-maximizing level of production,* the following condition holds[14].

$$MR = MC \qquad (5.9)$$

As we saw in Chapter 4, marginal revenue depends on the demand curve for the product. This demand curve will be affected by the degree of competition in the product market. The next chapter presents a detailed analysis of the output decisions of firms in different market settings.

The increase in steel prices in 1994 increased the total cost for automobile manufacturing. Typically, such an increase is accompanied by an increase in the *marginal cost* of production. In this case, the increase in steel prices would not only mean a substitution away from steel to other inputs but also a decline in output. Figure 5.15 shows this effect. Note that this analysis holds other factors constant. If the demand for automobiles is increasing at the same time (thus shifting marginal revenue upward), the net effect can be an increase in output. However, the increase in output will be less than if there were no increase in steel prices.

---

[14]For the technically inclined: Since profits equal total revenues minus total costs, equation 5.9 is the first-order condition for profit maximization. This condition holds at both minimum and maximum profits. At the maximum, the marginal cost curve cuts the marginal revenue curve from below (the second-order condition).

Cost Estimation

Our discussion indicates that a detailed knowledge of costs is important for managerial decision making. Short-run costs play a very important role in operating decisions. For instance, when the marginal revenue from increased output is above the short-run marginal cost of production, profits can be increased by producing more output. Alternatively, if marginal revenue is below the short-run marginal cost, output should be reduced. Long-run costs, in turn, provide important information for decisions on optimal plant sizes and location. For instance, if economies of scale are important, one large plant is more likely optimal with the product transported to regional markets. Alternatively, if economies of scale are small, smaller regional plants that reduce transportation costs are more likely optimal.

If managers are to incorporate costs in their analyses in this manner, they must have good estimates of how short-run and long-run costs are related to various factors, both within and beyond the control of the firm.[15] Among the most commonly used statistical techniques for estimating cost curves is regression analysis. This technique estimates the relation between costs and output (possibly controlling for other factors, such as the product mix and the weather, that affect costs). The data for this analysis can either be time-series data on costs, output, and other variables, or cross-sectional data, which includes observations on variables across firms or plants at a point in time. For instance, in many applications, it is assumed that short-run total costs are approximately linear:

$$VC = bQ \qquad\qquad (5.10)$$

where VC is total variable costs for the period and Q is the quantity of output produced.

A detailed discussion of cost estimation is beyond the scope of this book. Suffice it to say that some of the same types of problems arise in cost estimation as arise in the case of demand estimation (for example, omitted-variables problems). Among the most common problems in cost estimation are difficulties in obtaining data on the relevant costs. Cost estimates are often based on accounting reports, which record historical costs. As we have discussed, these historical costs do not always reflect the opportunity costs of using resources. Also, there is the issue of choosing the appropriate functional form. Equation 5.10 presents a linear model. However, cost curves need not be linear. For instance, it might be appropriate to use a quadratic model, which would include an additional term, Q^2.

One of the most serious problems complicating cost estimation is the fact that most plants produce multiple products. Multiple products are produced in the same plant because there are economies of scope. Instead of producing two different types of cereals in two plants, it is usually cheaper to produce them in one plant. The fixed resources can be used more efficiently. Once a plant is producing multiple products, the total and average cost of a product can only be calculated by allocating the fixed costs to the products. This allocation is often arbitrary and complicated by the existence of joint costs. Cost accountants use the accounting records to track the costs of individual products. Fixed and variable resources used by each product are recorded. These product costs, calculated by the cost accountants, are typically used to estimate short-run and long-run average and marginal costs.

---

[15]In addition, some firms estimate cost curves to obtain insights into their underlying production functions. Recall that the shapes of cost curves depend on the underlying production functions. Thus, it is often possible to infer the characteristics of a production function from the shape of the corresponding cost curves. Typically, the data for estimating cost curves is more readily available than the necessary data for estimating production functions.

Despite these estimation problems, cost curves play an important role in managerial decision making. It is important, however, that managers maintain a healthy cynicism when using these estimates. For instance, in making major decisions, it is generally important for managers to examine whether a tentative decision is still attractive with reasonable variations in the estimated parameters of the cost function—that is, to conduct *sensitivity analysis*.

Factor Demand Curves

In discussing the optimal input mix, we showed that the following condition must hold for efficient production:

$$MP_i/P_i = MP_j/P_j \qquad (5.11)$$

for all inputs i and j. The marginal-product-to-price ratios reflect the incremental output from an input associated with an additional dollar expenditure on that input. The reciprocals of these ratios reflect the dollar cost for incremental output or the marginal cost:

$$P_i/MP_i = P_j/MP_j = MC \qquad (5.12)$$

At the profit-maximizing output level, MR = MC. Therefore, at the optimal output level the following condition must hold:

$$P_i/MP_i = MR \qquad (5.13)$$

or equivalently:

$$P_i = MR \times MP_i \qquad (5.14)$$

Equation 5.14 is the firm's demand curve for input i.[16] It has a straight-forward interpretation. The right-hand side of the equation represents the incremental revenue that the firm obtains from employing one more unit of the input (the incremental output times the incremental revenue). We call this incremental revenue the *marginal revenue product (MRP_i)* of input i. The firm optimally employs additional units of the input up to the point where the marginal cost of the input (its price with constant input prices) is equal to the marginal revenue product of the input. Intuitively, if the marginal revenue product is greater than the input price, the firm increases its profitability by using more of the input. If the marginal revenue product is less than the price of the input, the firm increases profitability by reducing the use of the input. Profits are maximized when the two are equal. Figure 5.16 illustrates the demand curve for an input.[17] At the current input price of P_i, the firm uses Q_i^* units of the input.

Our discussion of the profit-maximizing output level and the optimal use of an input might appear to suggest that these decisions are two distinct choices. The two decisions, however, are directly connected. Once the firm chooses the quantities of inputs, output is determined by the production function. Thus, profit-maximizing firms choose the

---

[16]For the technically inclined: The marginal product of input i can depend on the levels of other inputs used in the production process. Thus, the demand curve for an input must allow other inputs to adjust to their optimal levels as the price of input i changes. This adjustment is not important if the marginal product of input i is not affected by the levels of the other inputs.

[17]For the technically inclined: The second-order condition for maximum profits ensures that the demand curve for the input is the *downward sloping* portion of the marginal revenue product curve. Thus, Figure 5.16 displays only the downward sloping portion of the curve.

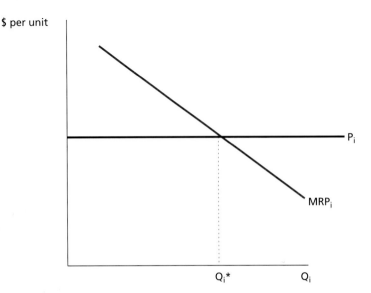

Figure 5.16 Factor Demand Curve

The demand curve for a factor of production is the *marginal revenue product curve* (MRP) for the input. The marginal product is defined as the marginal product of the input times the marginal revenue. It represents the additional revenue that comes from using one more unit of input. The firm maximizes profits when it purchases inputs up to the point where the price of the input equals the value of the marginal product.

output where marginal revenue equals marginal cost and produce that output in a manner where the price of each input is equal to its marginal revenue product. In our initial example, the increase in steel prices would be expected to motivate a *simultaneous* adjustment in the number of automobiles produced and the method used to produce them.

Summary

A *production function* is a descriptive relation that connects inputs with outputs. It specifies the *maximum* possible output that can be produced for a given amount of inputs. *Returns to scale* refers to the relation between output and a proportional variation in *all inputs* taken together. A production function displays *constant returns to scale* when a 1 percent change in all inputs results in a 1 percent change in output. With *increasing returns to scale,* a 1 percent change in all inputs results in a greater than 1 percent change in output. Finally, with *decreasing returns to scale,* a 1 percent change in all inputs results in a less than 1 percent change in output. *Returns to a factor* refers to the relation between output and the variation in only one input, *holding other inputs fixed.* Returns to a factor can be expressed as total, marginal, or average quantities. The *law of diminishing returns* states that the marginal product of a variable factor will eventually decline as the input is increased.

Most production functions allow some substitution of inputs. An *isoquant* pictures all combinations of inputs that produce the same quantity of output. The optimal input mix to produce any given output depends on the costs of the inputs. An *isocost line* pictures all combinations of inputs that cost the same. *Cost minimization* for a given output occurs where the isoquant is tangent to the isocost line. Changes in input prices change the slope of the isocost line and the point of tangency. When the price of an input increases, the firm will partially substitute this input for other inputs (*substitution effect*).

Cost curves can be derived from the isoquant/isocost analysis. The *total cost curve* depicts the relation between total costs and output. *Marginal cost* is the change in total cost associated with a one-unit change in output. *Average cost* is total cost divided by total output. Average cost falls when marginal cost is below average cost; average cost rises when marginal cost is above average cost. Average and marginal costs are equal when average cost is at a minimum. There is a direct link between the production function and cost curves. Holding input prices constant, the slopes of cost curves are determined by the underlying production technology.

Opportunity cost is the value of a resource in its next best alternative use. Current market prices more closely reflect the opportunity costs of inputs than *historical costs.* The *relevant costs* for managerial decision making are the opportunity costs.

Cost curves can be depicted for both the *short run* and the *long run.* The short run is the operating period during which at least one input (typically capital) is fixed in supply. During this period, *fixed costs* can be incurred even if the firm produces no output. In the long run, there are no fixed costs—all inputs and costs are *variable.* Short-run cost curves are sometimes called *operating curves* because they are used in making near-term production and pricing decisions. Fixed costs are irrelevant for these decisions. Long-run cost curves are referred to as *planning curves,* since they play a key role in longer-run planning decisions relating to plant size and equipment acquisitions.

The *minimum efficient scale* is defined as that plant size at which long-run average cost is first minimized. The minimum efficient scale affects both the optimal plant size and the level of potential competition. Industries where the average cost declines over a broad range of output are characterized as having *economies of scale.*

Economies of scope exist when the cost of producing a joint set of products in one firm is less than the cost of producing the products separately in independent firms. Economies of scope help to explain why firms often produce multiple products.

A *learning curve* pictures the relation between average cost and the cumulative volume of production. For some firms, the long-run average cost for producing a given level of output declines as the firm gains experience from producing the output (that is, there are significant learning effects).

The profit-maximizing output level occurs at the point where *marginal revenue equals marginal cost.* At this point, the marginal benefits of increasing output are exactly offset by the marginal costs.

Managers often use estimates of cost curves in decision making. A common statistical tool for estimating these curves is regression analysis. One common problem in statistical estimation is the difficulty of obtaining good information on the opportunity costs of resources. Another problem with estimating cost curves involves allocating fixed costs in a multiproduct plant. Cost accountants track the costs and estimate product costs.

The *marginal revenue product (MRP_i)* of input i is equal to the marginal product of the input times marginal revenue. Profit-maximizing firms use an input up to the point where the MRP of the input equals the price of the input. At this point, the marginal benefit of employing more of the input are exactly offset by the marginal cost.

APPENDIX | *The Factor-Balance Equation*[18]

This appendix derives the factor-balance equation—equation 5.9 in the text:

$$MP_i/P_i = MP_j/P_j \qquad (5.15)$$

This condition must hold if the firm is producing the output in a manner that minimizes costs (assuming an interior solution).

Recall that at the cost-minimizing method of production, the isoquant and isocost line are tangent. Thus, they must have equal slopes. The factor-balance equation is found by setting the slope of the isoquant equal to the slope of the isocost line and rearranging the expression. In the text, we showed that the slope of the isocost line is $-P_j/P_i$. We now derive the slope of an isoquant.

Slope of an Isoquant

The production function in the two-input case takes the following general form:

$$Q = f(x_i, x_j) \qquad (5.16)$$

To find the slope of an isoquant, we totally differentiate equation 5.16. We set this differential equal to zero, since quantity does not change along an isoquant:

$$dQ = [\partial Q/\partial x_i dx_i] + [\partial Q/\partial x_j dx_j] = 0$$

$$(5.17)$$

The slope of the isoquant is defined by dx_i/dx_j. Thus:

$$\text{Slope of an isoquant} = -(\partial Q/\partial x_j)/(\partial Q/\partial x_i) \qquad (5.18)$$

$$= -MP_j/MP_i \qquad (5.19)$$

This expression has a straightforward interpretation. For illustration, assume that at some fixed combination of x_i and x_j the marginal product of i is 1 and the marginal product of j is two. At this point, the slope of the isoquant is 2. This means that two units of i can be given up for one unit of j and output will stay the same. This is true by definition since j has twice the marginal product of i.

Factor-Balance Equation

In the cost-minimizing production method, the slope of the isoquant is the same as the slope of the isocost line:

$$-MP_j/MP_i = -P_j/P_i \qquad (5.20)$$

Rearranging this expression gives us the factor-balance equation:

$$MP_i/P_i = MP_j/P_j \qquad (5.21)$$

This expression generalizes to production functions with more than two inputs.

---

[18]This appendix requires elementary knowledge of calculus.

Suggested Readings

E. Douglas (1987), *Managerial Economics: Analysis and Strategy* (Prentice Hall: Englewood Cliffs, NJ), Part 3.

E. Mansfield (1988), *Microeconomics* (W. W. Norton: New York), Part 3.

G. Stigler (1987), *The Theory of Price* (MacMillan: New York), Chapters 6–10.

Review Questions

5–1. Distinguish between returns to scale and returns to a factor.

5–2. Your company currently uses steel and aluminum in a production process. Steel costs $0.50 per pound, while aluminum costs $1.00 per pound. Suppose the government imposes a tax of $0.25 per pound on all metals. What affect will this have on your optimal input mix? Show using isoquants and isocost lines.

5–3. Your company currently uses steel and aluminum in a production process. Steel costs $0.50 per pound, while aluminum costs $1.00 per pound. Suppose that inflation doubles the price of both inputs. What affect will this have on your optimal input mix? Show using isoquants and isocost lines.

5–4. Is the "long-run" the same calendar time for all firms? Explain.

5–5. You want to estimate the cost of materials used to produce a particular product. According to accounting reports, you initially paid $50 for the materials that are necessary to produce each unit. Is $50 a good estimate of your current production costs? Explain.

5–6. Suppose that average cost is minimized at 50 units and equals $1. What is marginal cost at this output level?

5–7. What is the difference between economies of scale and economies of scope?

5–8. What is the difference between economies of scale and learning effects?

5–9. Suppose that you can sell as much of a product as you want at $100 per unit. Your marginal cost is: MC = 2Q. Your fixed cost is $50. What is the optimal output level? What is the optimal output, if your fixed cost is $60?

5–10. Discuss two problems that arise in estimating cost curves.

5–11. Suppose that the marginal product of labor is: MP = 100 – L, where L is the number of workers hired. You can sell the product in the marketplace for $50 per unit and the wage rate for labor is $100. How many workers should you hire?

5–12. Textbook writers typically receive a simple percentage of total revenue generated from book sales. The publisher bears all the production costs and chooses the output level. Suppose the retail price of a book is fixed at $50. The author receives $10 per copy, while the firm receives $40 per copy. The firm is interested in maximizing its own profits. Will the author be happy with the book company's output choice? Does the selected output maximize the joint profits (for both the author and company) from the book?

5–13. Suppose your company produces one product and that you are currently at an output level where your price elasticity is 0.5. Are you at the optimal output level for profit maximization? How can you tell?

5–14. Semiconductor chips are used to store information in elctronic products, such as personal computers. One of the early leaders in the production of these chips was Texas Instruments (TI). During the early period in the development of this industry, TI made the decision to price its semiconductors substantially below its production costs. This decision increased sales, but resulted in near-term reductions in profits. Explain why TI might have made this decision.

chapter 6

Market Structure

Sealed Air Corporation manufactures a wide variety of protective packaging materials and systems.[1] Among its most famous products are the packing bubbles that "everyone loves to pop." Other products include padded mailing envelopes, pads for absorbing moisture in supermarket meat packages, and equipment and supplies for creating customized foam for packaging fragile or unusually shaped items.

Founded in 1960, Sealed Air initially had strong patent protection on its major products. This protection shielded the company from competition and allowed it to make 45 to 50 percent profit margins. Given the market environment, the company did not face competitive pressures to contain costs or invest wisely. Rather, the company concentrated on developing a sales force and selling products. The company grew and prospered. By the late 1980s, however, Sealed Air faced a much different market environment. Most of its major patents had expired, and senior management anticipated a substantial increase in competition. The management knew that it would have to lower the prices for its products as new firms entered the industry. It also expected the firm to be at a competitive disadvantage, given its inefficient operations and high costs. Historically, the company had faced more competition in Europe, where it did not have strong patent protection, and had fared poorly.

In response to increased competition, the management of Sealed Air initiated several major policy changes to increase the company's efficiency. It launched a manufacturing improvement program to increase the quality of production and reduce costs. It instituted stringent capital budgeting procedures to limit unproductive investment. It substantially increased the leverage of the firm to place pressure on employees to generate enough cash flow to service the debt (and avoid bankruptcy). It also increased financial incentives throughout the firm to focus on efficiency and cash flow. For the most part, these changes appear to have had the desired effect—earnings performance and stock price increased substantially following the policy changes.

The example of Sealed Air illustrates how the policy choices of a firm, such as pricing, leverage, and production techniques, are significantly influenced by the market environment. Policies that work in a protected market environment often have to be changed radically in more competitive environments. It is important that managers understand the firm's market environment and how this environment affects optimal decision making. The purpose of this chapter is to increase that understanding by exploring the implications of alternative market structures. Our primary focus is on the output and pricing decisions in alternative market structures. Subsequent chapters examine in more detail how other policies, such as aspects of the firm's organizational architecture, depend on the market environment.

We begin by discussing markets and market structure in more detail. We then provide an analysis of competitive industries. Perfect competition is at one end of a continuum based on the level of competition within the industry. Perfect competition is an important benchmark and provides significant managerial implications for firms operating in most market settings. Next, we discuss barriers to entry that can limit competition within an industry. This section is followed by an analysis of the market structure at the other end of the continuum: monopoly. In a monopolistic industry, there is only one firm. In contrast to firms in competitive industries, a monopolist has substantial power in setting prices. After a brief discussion of a hybrid structure, monopolistic competition, we examine the pricing policies of firms with market power in more detail. Finally, we consider the case of oligopoly, where a small number of firms constitute the industry.

[1]Details of this example are from K. Wruck (1991), "Sealed Air Corporation's Leveraged Recapitalization," Harvard Business School, Case #9-391-067.

Markets

A *market* consists of all firms and individuals who are willing and able to buy or sell a particular product.[2] These parties include those currently engaged in buying and selling the product, as well as potential entrants. *Potential entrants* are all individuals and firms that pose a sufficiently credible threat of market entry to affect the pricing and output decisions of incumbent firms.

Market structure refers to the basic characteristics of the market environment, including: (1) the number and size of buyers, sellers, and potential entrants, (2) the degree of product differentiation, (3) the amount and cost of information about product price and quality, and (4) the conditions for entry and exit. We begin our discussion of alternative market structures with perfect competition.

Perfect Competition

Competitive markets generally are characterized by four basic conditions:

- A large number of buyers and sellers.
- Product homogeneity.
- Rapid dissemination of accurate information at low cost.
- Free entry and exit into the market.

Most markets are not perfectly competitive. Many markets, however, are close to meeting this description. Also, perfect competition is a *benchmark* that provides insights into other market settings. An example of a market that approximates the conditions for a competitive market is the market for wheat. In this market, there is a relatively large number of farmers who grow wheat, as well as a large number of firms and individuals who buy wheat. Wheat is a relatively homogeneous commodity (the product varies little across producers). There are limited informational disparities, and there is relatively free entry and exit.

In competitive markets, individual buyers and sellers take the market price for the product as given—they have no control over price. If a seller charges more than the market price, buyers will purchase the product from other suppliers. Firms can always sell the product at the market price and have no reason to offer discounts to buyers. In this setting, firms view their demand curves as horizontal—a firm can sell any feasible output at the market price, P_M—but sells no output at a price above P_M. Figure 6.1 illustrates a horizontal demand curve. With a horizontal demand curve, the marginal revenue (MR) and average revenue (AR) are both equal to price.

Firm Supply

Short-Run Supply Decision

In the last chapter, we saw that a firm's profit is maximized at the output where marginal revenue equals marginal cost. The intuition of this result is straightforward—it makes sense to expand output as long as incremental revenue is greater than incremental cost.

---

[2]The specific characteristics of a product often vary across firms. Knowing which firms and individuals to group together as a market, therefore, is not always straightforward. As discussed in Chapter 4, cross elasticities are helpful in defining markets. Products with high cross elasticities can be considered in the same market because they are "close substitutes."

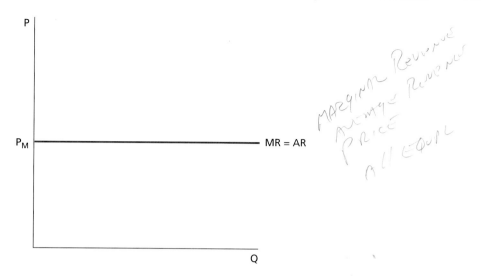

Figure 6.1   Firm Demand Curve in Perfect Competition

In competitive markets, firms take the market price of the product as given. The demand curve is horizontal. Both marginal revenue and average revenue are equal to the market price.

Past this point, profits decline with additional output since incremental revenue is less than incremental cost. In a competitive market, marginal revenue is equal to price (P). In the short run, the firm takes the plant size (and possibly other inputs) as given. The relevant cost is the *short-run marginal cost* (SRMC). The condition for short-run profit maximization in a competitive industry is:

$$P = SRMC \qquad (6.1)$$

This condition, which is one of the most important propositions in economics, indicates that at any price, the firm should choose the output where price equals SRMC. The firm, however, has the additional option of producing no output at all. When the price of the product is not sufficient to cover the *average variable cost* (AVC), the firm is better off producing no output. With no output, the firm loses money since it generates no revenue to cover its fixed cost. However, this loss is less than it would be if the firm produced any other level of output (since the revenue from production would be less than the variable costs of production). The *shut-down condition for the short run* is:

$$P < AVC \qquad (6.2)$$

A firm's supply curve depicts the quantity that the firm will produce at each price. The preceding discussion indicates that the firm's short-run supply curve is the portion of the short-run marginal cost curve that is above average variable cost. Figure 6.2 pictures this supply curve.

Long-Run Supply Decision

Firms can lose money in the short run and still find it optimal to stay in business. In the long run, however, the firm must be profitable or it is better to go out of business. Price must be greater than or equal to *long-run average cost* (LRAC). Thus, the *shut-down condition for the long run* is:

$$P < LRAC \qquad (6.3)$$

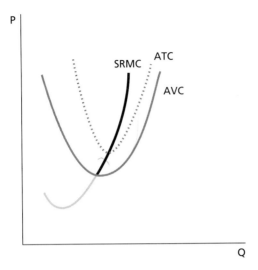

Figure 6.2   The Firm's Short-Run Supply Curve

The firm's short-run supply curve is the portion of the short-run marginal cost curve (SRMC) that is above average variable cost (AVC). At prices below average variable cost, the firm is better off not producing any output.

In the long run, the firm can adjust its plant size. The long-run supply decision of a firm is based on *long-run marginal costs* (LRMC). The long-run supply curve of a firm is the portion of the long-run marginal cost curve that is above long-run average cost. This supply curve is pictured in Figure 6.3.[3]

Competitive Equilibrium

In Chapter 2, we discussed how the market price in a competitive market is determined by the intersection of the industry demand and supply curves. The industry demand curve depicts the total quantities demanded by all buyers in the marketplace at each price. Similarly, the industry supply curve is the sum of all the individual supply decisions (discussed above).

Consider, as an example, the supply and demand curves, labeled S′ and D′ in the right panel of Figure 6.4. Here, the market price is P′. The left panel illustrates the long-run supply decision of a representative firm in the industry (which consists of a number of such firms). At the price, P′, each firm produces Q_i'. Cost curves are defined to include a normal rate of profit (a normal return on capital is included in LRAC). Thus, at the price P′, each firm is earning an *economic profit* (above normal profit). This economic profit is the profit per unit (P′-LRAC) times the total output, Q_i' and is depicted by the abcd rectangle. The existence of economic profits will motivate other firms to enter the industry.[4] This entry will shift the supply curve to the right and lower price. Additional entry will

---

[3]There is no inconsistency between short-run and long-run profit maximization. The LRMC at any given output is equal to the SRMC, given that the firm has the optimal plant size for the output. Hence, the firm can simultaneously choose an output where P = SRMC = LRMC.

[4]Profits reported by firms are based on the accounting definition: sales revenue minus the explicit costs of doing business. The calculation of *accounting profits,* therefore, does not include the opportunity cost of the owner's entrepreneurial effort or equity capital. Economic profits include these costs. Positive economic profits attract entry because the returns are higher than the returns in the alternate activities. Positive accounting profits do not always invite entry—the returns do not always cover the opportunity costs of the owners.

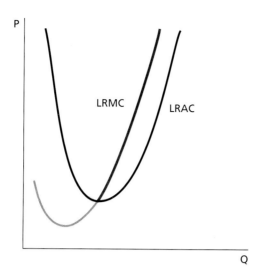

Figure 6.3 The Firm's Long-Run Supply Curve

The long-run supply curve for a firm is the portion of the long-run marginal cost curve (LRMC) that is above long-run average cost (LRAC). If price is below LRAC, the firm should go out of business.

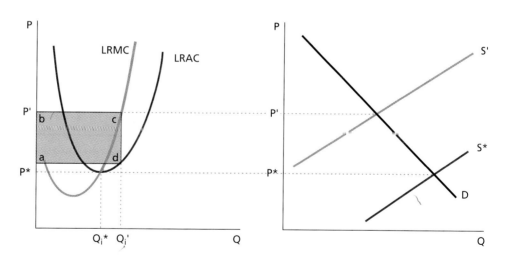

Figure 6.4 Competitive Equilibrium

The left panel illustrates the long-run supply decision of a representative firm in the industry. In the right panel, supply and demand curves (labeled S' and D') determine the market price, P'. At the price, P', the firm produces Q_i'. At the price P', the firm is earning an *economic profit*. This economic profit is the profit per unit (P'-LRAC) times the total output, Q_i', and is depicted by the rectangle abcd. Economic profits will motivate other firms to enter the industry. This entry will shift the supply curve to the right and lower price. Additional entry will occur up to the point where there are no economic profits. This condition occurs at a price of P*. Here, there are no incentives for firms to enter or leave the industry (incumbents are earning a normal rate of profit), and the market is in *equilibrium*. In a competitive equilibrium, firms produce output at the low point on their average cost curves (P=LRMC=LRAC). Thus, the equilibrium is associated with efficient production.

Entry in the Market for Personal Computers

IBM entered the personal computer market in 1981. Its "PC" quickly became a standard for the industry. IBM, however, had almost no patent protection on the PC and it had bought nonexclusive licenses to key elements like the MS-DOS operating system. Profits quickly attracted other firms, such as Dell, Leading Edge, Packard Bell, and Compaq, to produce IBM clones. Within a few years, IBM lost substantial market share in the PC market. Margins (the difference between price and average cost) for PC hardware became razor thin.

occur up to the point where there are no economic profits. This condition is pictured in Figure 6.4 at a price of P^*. Here, there are no incentives for firms to enter or leave the industry (incumbents are earning a normal rate of profit), and the market is in *equilibrium*. In a competitive equilibrium, firms produce output at the low point on their average cost curves ($P=LRMC=LRAC$). Thus, the equilibrium is associated with efficient production.

Strategic Considerations

While few markets are perfectly competitive, many markets approximate this structure. In most industries, there are strong competitive forces that reduce economic profits over time. These forces imply that many strategic advantages (for example, being the first in a new market) are likely to be short-lived. If the conditions in the market resemble the competitive model, it is important to move fast to take advantage of transitory opportunities. In addition, potential entrants should realize that observed economic profits in an industry are likely to be bid away as time passes. This consideration can affect long-range capital spending and entry decisions. For instance, given the threat of increased competition, Sealed Air tightened its scrutiny of internal investment proposals. In a competitive market, firms must also strive for efficiency and cost control. Inefficient firms lose money and are forced out of business. Sealed Air's management understood this when it undertook significant steps to enhance efficiency.

Superior Firms

Even in relatively competitive industries, there are firms that do exceptionally well over long time periods—for example, by being a low-cost producer or having some particular advantage, such as location, relative to competitors. The excess returns, however, often do not go to the owner of the enterprise but rather to the factor input that produces the particular advantage. For example, land close to a highway interchange (and customers) often sells for a higher price than land farther from the interchange. Similarly, the salary of an exceptionally talented manager will be bid up by other firms. In many cases, the firms employing these superior factors of production earn only a normal rate of return ($P = LRAC$).

Phantom Freight

Most of the plywood in the United States comes from the Pacific Northwest. Due to this dominance, plywood prices throughout the country are essentially the Northwest price plus shipping. If this condition did not hold, Northwest suppliers would curtail shipping plywood to cities with low prices and increase shipping to cities with high prices. The changes in supply would affect the prices in the cities until, in equilibrium, the prices across cities would differ only in transportation costs.

In a U.S. court case, Southeast timber producers were sued for charging customers the Northwest price plus shipping and then delivering locally produced plywood. It was ruled that these companies were making unjust profits because they did not actually incur the shipping costs. The jury awarded billions of dollars to the customers. Were these companies really making economic profits? The answer is probably not. The local production in the Southeast had a shipping advantage to Southeast customers. The factor that made this advantage possible was scarce timber land in the Southeast. Presumably, the price of this scarce timber land was bid up to the point where plywood producers were only making a normal profit given the prevailing price for plywood in the Southeast (which was the Northwest price plus shipping).

Source: A. Alchian and W. Allen (1983), *Exchange and Production: Competition, Coordination and Control* (Wadsworth Publishing: Belmont, CA), 228–231.

Barriers to Entry[5]

While the competitive model is a reasonable approximation in many markets, there are other industries where firms have significant market power—prices are affected substantially by the output decisions of individual firms. A necessary condition for market power to exist is that there are *barriers to entry* into the industry.

To understand what constitutes a barrier to entry, it is useful to consider the decisions of individual firms to enter an industry. Firms consider entry into new industries when they observe existing firms making large profits. For instance, if a firm such as Sealed Air is observed making large profits producing packaging materials, other firms are likely to consider entering the industry. The entry decision will depend on at least three important factors. First, a prospective entrant will be concerned about whether its entry will affect the price of the product. This, in turn, depends at least in part on how the existing firms are likely to respond to a new entrant—for example, are they likely to cut price? Second, the potential entrant will be concerned about incumbent advantages—do the existing firms have advantages that make it unlikely that a new firm will enjoy similar profits? Third, the firm will be concerned about the costs of exit. How much will it cost to leave the industry if this incursion fails? We discuss each of these factors in turn.

Incumbent Reactions

Specific Assets
Specific assets are assets that have more value in their current use than in the next best alternative use. Consider the case of the Alaskan Pipeline. It has a high value in its current use. However, what else can it be used for? It can be moved only at great expense, and its alternative uses in its present location are nil. If the existing firms in an industry have invested heavily in specific assets, they are likely to fight harder to maintain position than if the assets are more general and can be shifted at low cost to alternative activities.

---

[5]This section provides a brief summary of the literature in economics on barriers to entry. It draws on the analysis in S. M. Oster (1994), *Modern Competitive Analysis* (Oxford Press: New York).

Excess Capacity at Alcoa

In 1940, Alcoa Aluminum lost an important antitrust case for its production strategy of holding excess capacity. The judge ruled that he could think of no better "effective" deterrent to entry.

Economies of Scale

Industries with large economies of scale have minimum efficient scales that occur at high output levels (see Chapter 5). In these industries, a new entrant must produce a high volume to be cost-effective. Large-scale production is likely to have a significant effect on price. For example, if the minimum efficient scale means producing output equal to 30 percent of the total market demand, price will almost certainly decline if a new entrant tries to capture this share of the market. (There is likely to be substantial price competition from incumbents.) The absolute size of the minimum efficient scale is not as important as is this scale relative to the size of the total market. Minimum efficient scale varies dramatically across industries. In one study, estimates of minimum efficient scale, as a percentage of industry capacity, ranged from 0.5 percent (fruit/vegetable canning) to 33 percent (gypsum products).[6] Globalization of markets increases the effective market size and makes entry more feasible. Consider, for example, the global versus American automobile industries.

Excess Capacity

If firms with excess capacity cut production, they can experience much higher average costs (depending on the slopes of their average cost curves). Also, firms with excess capacity are able to meet the demand from new customers should they lower price to force a new entrant out of business. Potential entrants, therefore, may be less likely to enter when there is excess capacity in the industry because they fear aggressive actions on the part of incumbents.[7] Excess capacity can exist for "innocent reasons." For example, a firm facing cyclical production or growth may have excess capacity over some time intervals. In other cases, the excess capacity may be chosen deliberately to deter entry.

Reputation Effects

Potential entrants can also be influenced by the reputation of the existing firms in the industry in terms of how they react to new entry. At times, it can pay for an existing firm to act against its own short-term interests—for example, by price cutting—to establish a reputation as a tough competitor. Threats by firms to cut prices if new entry occurs are not always credible. If new firms actually enter, the existing firms might not follow through on their threats because they would be harmed by their own price cuts. In this case, it can be reasonable for potential entrants to ignore the threats—if the potential entrants believe that the incumbents are bluffing.

---

[6]K. Lancaster and R. Dulaney (1979), *Modern Economics: Principles and Policy* (Rand McNally: New York), 211.

[7]Excess capacity can occur because of significant declines in industry demand. In this case, profits are likely to be low and entry will not be attractive. Our current discussion focuses on cases where incumbents are making economic profits and have excess capacity. These economic profits might not induce entry because of the fear of price cutting by incumbents.

Incumbent Advantages

Precommitment Contracts

Existing firms often have long-term contracts for raw materials, distribution outlets, shelf space, and delivery of the final product. These contracts can serve as a deterrent to entry, since the customers and suppliers are precommitted to dealing with the incumbent firms rather than new entrants.

Licenses and Patents

Sometimes, entry is limited by government actions, such as licensing requirements and the awarding of patents. For instance, the number of doctors is significantly limited by state licensing requirements. This restriction allows doctors to charge higher prices than if entry were unrestricted. Regulators justify licensing with arguments based on consumer protection. Whether or not consumers benefit from stringent licensing, however, is debatable (given that they pay higher prices). The standard patent life is 17 years. For this period of time, other firms are not allowed to copy the innovation, and the firm with the patent is granted some potential monopoly power. The purpose of patents is to give increased incentives to innovate. From a practical standpoint, the effectiveness of a patent in blocking entry can vary dramatically (patents can be circumvented by clever design, for example). Historically, Sealed Air had derived its market power from strong patent protection. This protection had expired by the late 1980s, leaving the firm vulnerable to increased competition.

Learning-Curve Effects

In Chapter 5, we discussed how average costs are driven down in some industries through production experience. As firms produce more units, they learn how to lower unit costs. Learning-curve effects can result in new firms having a cost disadvantage relative to existing firms. Whether these effects are important depends on whether the new firms can simply copy the techniques learned by the existing firms through their experience. In the case of Sealed Air, costs had not been driven down by learning effects. Indeed, entry was invited by Sealed Air's inefficient production.

Pioneering Brand Advantages

Sometimes, a firm will benefit from being the first in an industry. For instance, in some industries (over-the-counter drugs, for example), a satisfied customer might be reluctant to switch brands even if the price is substantially lower. This tendency is likely to be strongest in *experience goods,* which have to be tried by the customer to ascertain quality; customers might not try a new pain reliever because they are afraid that it might not be as effective as existing brands. Where quality can be judged by inspection prior to purchase, the advantage of the incumbent is likely to be lower. Sometimes the incumbent's advantage with an experience good can be overcome by newcomers through (1) free samples, (2) endorsements, or (3) government certification. However, each of these methods is likely to entail additional costs and deter entry.

Costs of Exit

Another important entry consideration is the cost of exiting an industry. In some industries, it is possible to "hit and run." For instance, forming a new company to replace asphalt on driveways requires little investment in specialized equipment or training. A new

Government Restrictions on Exit

Some regulators want to restrict companies from closing plants. These regulators appear motivated by concerns over people who lose their jobs when a company closes a plant. Restrictions on plant closings, however, are likely to reduce the desirability of entry into an industry—firms will be reluctant to enter an industry if they can't exit easily if they are losing money. Thus, the potential effects of government restrictions on exit are less vigorous competition in the affected industries, higher consumer prices, and lower levels of employment.

firm can enter quickly when the profit potential is high and exit at low cost if profits decline. In other industries, especially those with specific assets, the costs of exit can be high. Here, firms can bear significant costs, such as moving employees to new locations and liquidating plants and other assets when they decide to exit. High exit costs deter initial entry.

Monopoly

Barriers to entry can limit the threat of competition and give incumbent firms market power. While perfect competition is at one end of the spectrum, at the other end is *monopoly*, where there is only one firm in the industry. Here, the industry and firm demand curves are one and the same.

Profit Maximization

Suppose that a monopolist charges the same price to all customers (below, we relax this assumption). As discussed below, such a pricing policy might be motivated by government regulation or the inability to prevent resale among customers. The firm's objective is to choose the price/quantity combination along its demand curve that maximizes profits. This combination occurs where MR = MC.

For illustration, consider the following linear demand curve:

$$P = 200 - Q \tag{6.4}$$

Assume that marginal cost is constant at $10. Recall from Chapter 4 that the MR curve for a linear demand curve is a line with the same intercept and twice the negative slope. Figure 6.5 pictures the demand curve, MR curve, and MC curve in this example. Optimal output occurs at 95 units, where MR = MC. To sell this output, the firm charges a price of $105. The firm makes $95 per unit profit ($105 – $10) for a total profit of $9,025 ($95 × 95), as indicated by the rectangle abcd.

In contrast to pure competition, consumers facing monopolistic suppliers pay more than the marginal cost of production and the firm can earn an economic profit. For instance, up until the time its patents expired, Sealed Air had near monopoly power in some product markets and correspondingly made substantial profits. Monopolies produce lower output than competitive industries. In our example, if the industry were competitive, the market price would be $10 (the marginal cost) and total quantity sold would be 190 units.

Markup Pricing

Additional insights into the monopolist's pricing decision can be developed using the concept of price elasticity developed in Chapter 4. Recall that the price elasticity, η, is a

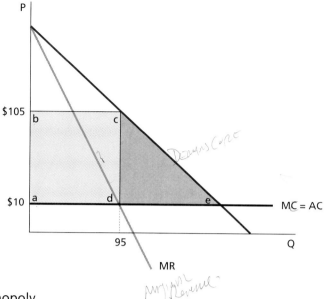

Figure 6.5 Monopoly

This figure illustrates the price and output decisions of a monopolist. In the example, demand is P = 200 − Q. Marginal costs are $10. The profit-maximizing output occurs at 95 units, where MR = MC. To sell this output, the firm charges a price of $105. The firm makes $95 per unit profit ($105 − $10) for a total profit of $9,025 ($95 × 95), as indicated by the rectangle abcd. There are consumers who are willing to pay more than the marginal cost of production who do not receive the product. The associated loss in potential gains from trade is pictured by the triangle cde. The firm does not lower the price to sell to these consumers because it does not want to lower the price for other customers.

measure of price sensitivity. The higher the price elasticity, the more sensitive is the quantity demanded to price changes. With some algebra, it is easy to show that the monopolist's optimal pricing policy of setting marginal revenue equal to marginal cost can be rewritten as:

$$P = MC/[1 - 1/\eta] \qquad (6.5)$$

A monopolist never operates on the inelastic portion of its demand curve ($\eta < 1$). With inelastic demand, total revenue increases with an increase in price. As price is increased, fewer units are sold and production costs fall. With an increase in revenue and a reduction in costs, profits must increase with price. Therefore, we are assured that $\eta > 1$ at the optimal price and the markup over marginal costs is greater than one.

Equation 6.5 indicates that the optimal markup depends on elasticity *at the optimal output level.*[8] If the firm has significant market power, so that the demand elasticity is relatively low, the markup will be high. If the firm has limited market power (for instance, there are many substitute products), the demand elasticity will be high and the markup will be low. In the extreme, when the elasticity is infinite, the market is perfectly competitive and the product sells at marginal cost. Consistent with this analysis, supermarkets typically mark up brand-name products substantially more

---

[8]The markup factor is $[1 - 1/\eta] > 1$. Note that equation 6.5 does not imply that the optimal price can be found by marking up marginal cost by the elasticity factor at any arbitrary output level (for example, current output). The elasticity typically changes with a change in price and the equation will not hold. Equation 6.5 is a condition that holds *at the optimal output level.* If the condition does not hold at the current price/quantity combination, the firm is not maximizing profits.

Monopolistic Competition in Golf Balls

There are many brands of golf balls. Some golfers view the balls as perfect substitutes and will purchase the lowest-priced brand. Other golfers prefer one brand to another. For instance, they might believe one brand of ball flies farther or provides greater control than other competing brands. These golfers are willing to pay a higher price for their favorite ball than competing balls. However, they will often substitute if the price difference is more than a few dollars a dozen. Also, if a company develops some popular feature, like a large number of dimples on the ball, the feature is typically copied by other companies in a short time period. Since a golf equipment company has a *monopoly* in producing its own brand, it has some market power. However, this power is limited given the *competition* in the industry.

than store-brand products (store-brand products are typically sold to consumers with more elastic demand). In our previous example, the demand elasticity at the optimal output level of 95 units is 1.105 (found using the formula in the appendix to Chapter 4). The optimal markup is 10.5, yielding a price of $105.

Inefficient Production

Given the monopolist's output and pricing choice, there are consumers who are willing to pay more than the marginal cost of production who do not receive the product. Thus, not all the gains from trade are exhausted—the outcome is socially inefficient. The associated loss in potential gains from trade is pictured by the triangle cde in Figure 6.5. Consumers, along the corresponding segment of the demand curve, value the product for more than $10 but less than $105 dollars. The firm does not lower the price to sell to these consumers because it does not want to lower the price for other customers (recall that the firm charges the same price to all customers). From the firm's standpoint, the gain from selling to additional customers is more than offset by the loss from having to charge a lower price to all customers.[9]

Monopolistic Competition

As the name implies, *monopolistic competition* is a market structure that is a hybrid between competition and monopoly. In this market structure, there are multiple firms that produce similar products. There is free exit and entry into the industry. Competition is not perfect because the firms sell differentiated products. Examples of industries with these characteristics include toothpaste, golf balls, skis, tennis rackets, shampoo, and deodorant. For instance, Colgate and Crest toothpastes compete directly. Yet many customers do not view them as perfect substitutes, and the companies have some market power. New toothpaste firms are likely to enter the industry if the existing firms are making large profits (there are no significant barriers to entry).

---

[9]The lost gains from trade are sometimes called a *dead-weight loss*. This inefficiency (or *social cost*) is one reason why governments often pass regulations like antitrust laws to restrict the formation of monopolies. These regulations can also be motivated by concerns about the higher prices that consumers pay when they face monopolistic suppliers. While government regulation has the potential to reduce inefficiencies and wealth transfers (from consumers to firms), it is important to keep in mind that government regulation is not costless. (There are salaries for regulators and court costs, for instance.) From a societal viewpoint, the costs of government regulation should be weighed against the benefits.

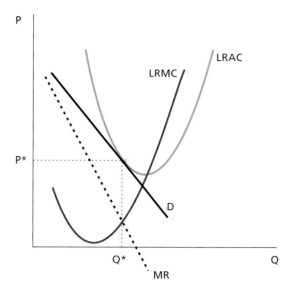

Figure 6.6   Monopolistic Competition

In monopolistic competition, firms sell differentiated products. This figure shows the demand curve for a firm in such an industry. The curve is downward sloping. Similar to monopoly pricing, the firm selects the output where marginal revenue equals marginal cost. Monopolistic competition differs from monopoly in that abnormal profits will invite entry. Entry shifts the demand curve for the firm to the left (as some of the customers buy from the new firms). The firm makes no economic profits when price is equal to average cost. This condition occurs at price P* and quantity Q*.

Monopolistic competition is similar to monopoly in that firms in both market structures face downward sloping demand curves—a toothpaste company can raise its price without losing all sales. Given that the firms face downward sloping demand curves, they strive to select the price/quantity combination that maximizes profits. The output decision is based on the same analysis as for the pure monopolist—choose the output where MC = MR.

The difference between monopoly and monopolistic competition is that in monopolistic competition, economic profits invite entry. If a new dimple pattern on golf balls is a hot seller, other companies will imitate the product. This entry will shift the original firm's demand curve to the left and reduce profits. Zero economic profits exist when the demand curve is shifted to the point where average cost equals price. Figure 6.6 shows this condition.

Entry will tend to force profits to zero. However, some brands will still be more distinctive than others. Also, costs can vary because of differences in production techniques and inputs. It is possible for some firms to make economic profits in monopolistic competition.[10]

---

[10]Monopolistic competition is inefficient for two reasons. First, as in monopoly, there is the loss from not selling to all consumers who value the product at above the marginal cost of production. Second, firms do not operate at the bottom of their average cost curves (see Figure 6.6). Lower average cost would be obtained with fewer firms, each producing more output. Nevertheless, regulation to address these inefficiencies is likely to be undesirable. Consumers value product differentiation and are probably better off with more variety at slightly higher average cost than lower variety produced at lower average cost. Second, because of competition, the monopoly power of firms is likely to be relatively small.

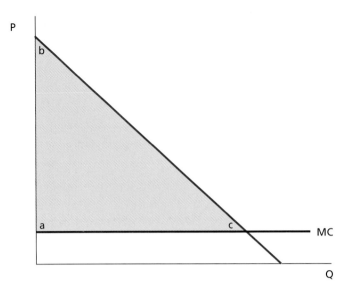

Figure 6.7   Consumer Surplus

Consumer surplus is the difference between what the consumer is willing to pay for a product and what the consumer actually pays when buying it. This figure provides an illustration of consumer surplus. The demand curve reflects what consumers are willing to pay for the product. It is never in the interests of the firm to sell the product at below marginal cost, since it can do better by not producing the product. Thus, the maximum potential gains from trade in this example are given by the triangle abc. The firm's objective is to devise a pricing policy that captures as much of this surplus as possible.

Pricing with Market Power

To this point, we have assumed that the firm sells to all customers at the same price. Firms with market power can potentially increase profits by selling products at different prices to different customers.[11] In this section, we provide a brief introduction to some of the pricing policies that firms use to increase profits.

Consumer Surplus

The concept of *consumer surplus* helps to clarify the objectives of a firm's pricing policy. Consumer surplus is defined as the difference between what the consumer is willing to pay for a product and what the consumer actually pays when buying it. Figure 6.7 provides an illustration of consumer surplus. The demand curve in this figure reflects what consumers are willing to pay for the product. It is never in the interests of the firm to sell the product at below marginal cost, since it can do better by not producing the product. The maximum potential gains from trade in this example are given by triangle abc. Consider a customer who is indifferent between buying and not buying when the price is

---

[11]There are laws that restrict the ability of firms to charge different prices to different customers. Managers contemplating the types of pricing policies discussed in this section should check with legal counsel on the legality of the proposed pricing policy.

P_i > MC. Summing all such consumer's individual surpluses yields the area between the demand curve and MC. If the firm sold the product at marginal cost, all the gains would go to consumers in the form of consumer surplus. Managers, in maximizing profits, try to devise a pricing policy that captures as much of this surplus as possible.[12] We saw that when the firm charges one price to all customers, it captures some, but not all, of this surplus. The firm can potentially do better with a more complex pricing policy.

Price Discrimination

Price discrimination occurs whenever a firm's prices in different markets are not related to differentials in production and distribution costs. With price discrimination, the markup or profit margin realized varies across customers. Two conditions are necessary for profitable price discrimination. First, different price elasticities of demand must exist in various submarkets for the product. Otherwise, there is no point in segmenting the market. When different price elasticities do exist, it is generally optimal to charge higher prices to those customers who are less sensitive to price (if possible). Second, the firm must be able to identify submarkets and restrict transfers among consumers in different submarkets. Otherwise, any attempt to charge differential prices to the submarkets will be undercut by resale across the submarkets. (One group of consumers can buy at the low price and sell to the other groups at a price below the firm's prices to these groups.)

First-degree price discrimination extracts the maximum amount each customer is willing to pay for the product. Each consumer is charged a price that makes him or her indifferent between purchasing and not purchasing the product. In this case, the producer extracts all the potential consumer surplus. This extreme form of price discrimination is rare and is possible only when the number of customers is extremely small. With first-degree price discrimination, the firm sells to all customers who are willing to pay more than the marginal cost of production. All gains from trade are exhausted and the outcome is efficient. All the gains from trade, however, go to the firm.

Second-degree price discrimination involves setting prices based on quantity purchased. Prices are often *blocked,* with a high price charged for the first unit or block of units purchased, and lower prices set for successive units or blocks. Public utilities frequently price in this manner. If the quantity discounts are based solely on costs, then there is no price discrimination. However, large-quantity users are likely to be more price sensitive than low-quantity users, and thus block pricing allows different rates to be charged to the two groups even if per unit costs are similar.

Another type of block pricing can occur in the choice of package size. Suppose you value one hot dog at 40 cents and a second hot dog at 20 cents. If the vendor sells the dogs individually, she has to charge 20 cents or less to get you to buy two. If she sells the dogs in packs of two, she can charge 60 cents for the package, and you will buy the dogs at 30 cents apiece. (The fact that hot dogs tend to come in packs might also be explained by cost arguments: Packaging costs increase less than in proportion to the number of hot dogs.)

Third-degree price discrimination results when a firm separates its customers into several classes and sets a different price for each class. For example, utility companies charge different rates to individual versus commercial users; computer companies give

---

[12]Often, the marginal cost curve is upward sloping. In this case, pricing at the marginal cost of the *last unit* of production will generate both consumer and producer surplus (the producer is selling the inframarginal units at a price above marginal cost). The goal of the manager in this case is the same—to capture as much of the consumer surplus as possible.

educational discounts; and airlines charge different rates based on the amount of notice given for the reservation. As illustrated in the following example, a firm that can segment its market maximizes profits by setting marginal revenue equal to marginal cost in each market segment.

Example of Third-Degree Price Discrimination

Consider the example of the Snowfish Ski Resort, which can separate its demand into local skiers and out-of-town skiers. The marginal cost of servicing a skier of either type is $10. Suppose the resort faces the following demand curves:

Out of town: $Q_0 = 500 - 10P$ (6.6)

Local: $Q_1 = 500 - 20P$ (6.7)

Total demand at any one price is the sum of the demands for the two types of consumers:[13]

$$Q = 1,000 - 30P$$ (6.8)

If the company sells all tickets at one price, profit maximization will occur at (subject to rounding error):[14]

$$P = \$21.66, Q = 350, Q_0 = 283, Q_1 = 67, \text{Profit} = \$4,081$$

The company can make higher profits by charging different prices to the two sets of skiers. The optimal prices are found by setting the marginal revenue equal to the marginal cost in each of the two market segments. Under this pricing policy, the following prices, quantities, and profits are observed:

$$P_o = \$30, Q_0 = 200, P_1 = \$17.50, Q_1 = 150, \text{Profit} = \$5,125$$

where P_0 and P_1 are the prices charged to out-of-town and local skiers, respectively. The resort charges higher prices to the out-of-town skiers, who are less sensitive to ticket prices than local skiers.

Figure 6.8 displays the optimal pricing policy for each market segment. Snowfish treats the two markets as separate and charges the optimal monolistic price to each segment. Consistent with equation 6.5, the optimal markup is lower in the more elastic local market. Using the point-elasticity formula developed in the appendix to Chapter 4, it can be shown that at the optimal prices the elasticities for the local and out-of-town skier markets are 2.33 and 1.5, respectively. The respective markups above marginal cost are 1.75 and 3 (as given by equation 6.5). These markups translate into prices of $17.50 and $30.

[13]This demand curve assumes that price is less than or equal to $25. At higher prices, the local skiers purchase no tickets and the total demand curve is simply the demand curve for out-of-town skiers ($Q = 500 - 10P$).

[14]The reader should know by now that the solution to this problem is found by setting marginal revenue equal to marginal cost and solving for Q. Price can then be found from the equation for the demand curve. For instance, the total demand curve can be obtained by rearranging equation 6.8: $P = 33.33333 - 0.033333Q$. When the tickets are sold at one price to all consumers, the marginal revenue is $MR = 33.33333 - 0.066667Q$. Since marginal cost is $10, the optimal quantity is 350; price is $21.66 (the answers can differ slightly, depending on rounding). The optimal prices and quantities for the individual market segments are found by completing similar calculations using equations 6.6 and 6.7.

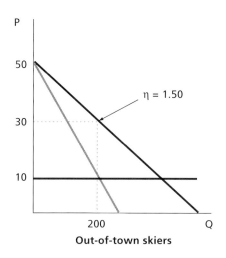
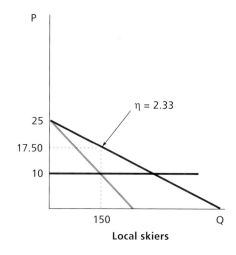

Figure 6.8   Optimal Pricing at Snowfish Ski Resort

Snowfish can segment its customers into two market segments, out-of-town skiers and local skiers. The marginal cost of serving either type of skier is $10. The optimal pricing policy is to set the monopoly price in each market segment. The markup is higher for out-of-town skiers because they have less elastic demands than local skiers. At the optimal prices ($30 and $17.50), the demand elasticities are 1.50 for out-of-town skiers and 2.33 for local skiers.

There are a number of methods that Snowfish might use to charge the two groups different prices. Discount coupons might be sold at supermarkets away from major resort hotels. Presumably, most of the sales at these supermarkets will be to local customers. Alternatively, discount books of tickets (nontransferable) could be sold locally prior to the start of ski season. Ski resorts use both techniques. For either of these policies to work, the resort must prevent local skiers from buying the tickets at $17.50 and reselling them to out-of-town skiers at prices less than $30.

The Little Mermaid: *An Example of Price Discrimination*

Coupons are one method that firms use to charge different prices to different consumers. Presumably, customers that are relatively insensitive to price are less likely to spend time cutting coupons (because of higher opportunity costs of time). An example of a firm using coupons in this manner is the Disney corporation.

When Disney first distributed *The Little Mermaid* videotapes, the tape retailed for around $20. A customer could clip a coupon (available at any store) and mail it in for a $5 rebate. What was going on? Why not simply sell the tapes for $15? Wouldn't costs be avoided? For example, it is expensive to issue and mail checks and print posters and coupons.

To illustrate the potential benefits of the policy, suppose that if the tapes were sold at the same price to all customers, Disney would have priced them at $20. With this policy, Disney would lose the potential profit from selling to consumers who are willing to pay a price above Disney's production cost but less than $20. Disney's apparent objective was to find a way to sell to these consumers at a lower price without having to lower the price to other consumers. One way to partially accomplish this objective was through rebates. Presumably, those willing to purchase at $20 had higher opportunity costs for their time (on average). This made them less likely to fill out and mail in the coupons. Customers not using the rebates paid a price of $20, while the customers using the rebate coupons paid $15.

There are a variety of issues to consider in deciding on such a rebate program. First, there is a tradeoff between the costs of administering the program and the benefits of additional sales. Also, there is the loss of $20 sales to customers who would have purchased at $20 but now use the rebate coupons. Deciding whether or not to implement such a program requires careful analysis.

Examples of Price Discrimination

Business travelers have relatively inelastic demand for air travel compared to vacation travelers. Airline companies attempt to charge business travelers higher prices by setting high prices for seats that are not booked several weeks in advance and when the traveler does not stay over a Saturday night. The airlines correctly anticipate that many business trips are scheduled on the spur of the moment. Also, business travelers are less likely to want to stay over a Saturday night than a person on vacation. Often, airlines charge many different prices for similar seats on the same flight.

Another example of price discrimination is the marketing of generic or store brands. For instance, Mobil Chemical makes garbage bags. It sells them under the brand name Hefty at relatively high prices to customers who are willing to pay higher prices for brand names. Mobil also manufactures similar bags that are sold at lower prices under generic and store-brand names. Some of the bags have labels such as "garbage bags," while others are labeled under the name of the grocery store. These nonbrand names tend to be purchased by people who are more price sensitive. Many manufacturers use similar pricing techniques. For example, television manufacturers often sell the identical model under their brand name and some store name such as JCPenney's. The brand name tends to sell at a higher price and is purchased by the less price-sensitive customer.

Two-Part Tariffs[15]

A two-part tariff is another pricing mechanism that can sometimes be used to increase profits. Here, the consumer pays an up-front fee for the right to buy the product and then pays additional fees for each unit of the product consumed. A classic example is an amusement park, where you pay a fee to get in and then so much a ride. This type of pricing is also used by some golf and tennis clubs, computer information services, telephone companies, and similar service providers.

To illustrate this technique, consider an example where all consumers have identical demands for the product, $P = 10 - Q$. Figure 6.9 displays a demand curve for a representative consumer. The marginal cost of producing the product is $1. The potential consumer surplus that the firm could capture is shown by triangle abc and is equal to $40.50 ($.5 \times 9 \times 9$). Maximum profits can be extracted by charging an up-front fee equal to all the consumer surplus (or slightly less) and then charging a price equal to marginal cost, $1. Under this pricing scheme, the consumer purchases 9 units.

The pricing problem becomes more complicated when consumers vary widely in their demands for the product. Charging a high entry fee allows the firm to extract surplus from consumers who have a high demand for the product. Consumers with lower demand will choose not to purchase. Solving for the optimal entry fee and price in this case is more difficult. If consumers vary widely in demand, it is often best to charge a low entry fee (possibly zero) and then charge a price above marginal cost for use.

Two-Part Pricing at Xerox and IBM

Xerox originally only leased copy machines to customers. The lease contract required customers to purchase the paper from Xerox. Thus, customers had to pay two prices to use the machines, the lease price and the paper price. The price for the paper was set above marginal cost. Thus, high-volume users paid more for using Xerox machines than low-volume users. Similar procedures were used by IBM in their early computer leases (selling computer cards at above cost). One explanation for this practice is price discrimination. So long as the high-volume users had less elastic demands, this was one method of charging them higher prices. The companies earned more than simply selling or leasing the machines to all users at the same price. This practice was the subject of several key court cases. Many of these types of tying arrangements are illegal today.

---

[15]The material in this section draws on the analysis in W. Oi. (1971), "A Disneyland Dilemma: Two-Part Tariffs for a Mickey Mouse Monopoly," *Quaterly Journal of Economics* 85, 77–96.

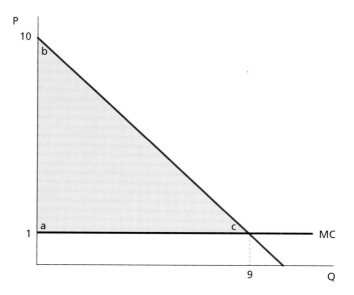

Figure 6.9   Two-Part Tariff

In this example, all potential customers had identical demands. The figure displays a demand curve for a representative consumer, P = 10 − Q. The marginal cost of producing the product is $1. The potential consumer surplus that the firm could capture is $40.50, as shown by triangle abc. Maximum profits can be extracted by charging an up-front fee equal to all the consumer surplus (or slightly less) and then charging a price equal to marginal cost, $1. Under such a scheme, the consumer purchases 9 units.

Other Considerations

To this point, we have not considered the response of rivals or new entrants to pricing decisions. Indeed, the demand curve is formed by assuming that the prices of other goods (for example, competitors' prices) are held constant. The short-run profit-maximizing price (or optimal discrimination policy) is a good point to start the analysis. However, a firm must often consider competitor responses to pricing decisions. For example, a proposed price cut will be more effective if it is not followed by rival firms. Also, potential new entry is important. We have already discussed barriers to entry. In the next section, we will discuss the consideration of rival firms in more detail.

Oligopoly

In *oligopolistic markets,* only a few firms account for most of the production in the market. Products may or may not be differentiated. Firms can earn substantial profits. These profits are not reduced through new entry because of barriers to entry. As we will see economic profits can sometimes be eliminated in oligopolistic industries through competition among the existing firms. Examples of oligopolistic industries include automobiles and steel in the 1950s. These industries had significant economies of scale and other significant barriers to entry. In 1995, the top four cereal makers in the United States produced about 90 percent of the output, while the top eight accounted for almost all the production.

In the analysis of other market structures, we assumed that firms take the prices of their competitors as given. Rival firms were not expected to respond to changes in the prices of any given firm. This assumption was reasonable in the case of competitive markets with many small firms and in the case of monopoly with only one large firm. This assumption, however, is not generally valid in oligopolistic industries. When American Airlines lowers it prices on certain routes, it is obviously concerned about whether United Airlines and other competitors will follow suit. In fact, firms in oligopolistic industries will generally be concerned about how other firms will react to most major policy decisions (for example, advertising campaigns or product decisions). Decision making in these industries requires *strategic thinking*. Decision makers must realize that competitors are rational parties operating in their own self-interest. Thus, it is important for decision makers to place themselves in the shoes of their rivals and consider how they might react.

Nash Equilibrium

To analyze oligopoly, we need an underlying principle to define an equilibrium when firms make decisions that explicitly take each other's behavior into account. Previously, we used the concept that a market is in equilibrium when firms are doing the best they can and have no reason to change price or output. For example, in a competitive equilibrium, there is no reason for new entry or exit (existing firms are making "normal" profits). No existing firm has any reason to change its output level (all are producing where $MC = MR = P$).

We can apply this same basic idea to oligopolistic markets with some modification. In our subsequent analysis, a firm does the best it can, given what its rivals are doing. In doing so, the firm anticipates that other firms will respond to its actions by doing the best they can. The actions are *noncooperative* in that each firm makes decisions that maximize its profits, given the actions of the other firms. The firms do not collude to maximize joint profits. An equilibrium exists when each firm is doing the best it can, given the actions of its rivals. Economists call this a *Nash equilibrium* for Nobel laureate John Nash who first studied these concepts.

To illustrate this concept, assume there are two firms in an industry (*duopoly*). Each independently chooses a price for an identical product. The firms either choose a high price or a low price. The payoffs are given in Figure 6.10 (the entry on the upper right in each cell is for firm A, while the entry on the lower left is for firm B). For example, if both firms charge a high price, firm A's profits are 400 and firm B's profits are 200.[16] The equilibrium is for firm A to charge a high price and firm B to charge a low price. Any other combination is unstable: Given the action of one of the firms, the other firm has the incentive to deviate. For instance, if both firms charge a high price, it is in the interests of firm B to deviate and lower price (its profits go from 200 to 250). The other combinations of firm A charging a low price and firm B a high price and both firms charging a low price are similarly unstable—the firms have an incentive to deviate given the other firm's choice. The Nash equilibrium is self-enforcing. If firm A charges a high price, it is optimal for firm B to charge a low price. Similarly, if firm B charges a low price, it is optimal for firm A to charge a high price. Given the choice of the other firm, there is no reason for the remaining firm to alter its strategy.

The Nash equilibrium in this example is not the outcome that maximizes the joint profits of the two companies. Combined profits would be higher if both firms charged a high price. Conceptually, the combined profits under this pricing policy could be split in

---

[16]The profits differ due to differences in the underlying costs of production.

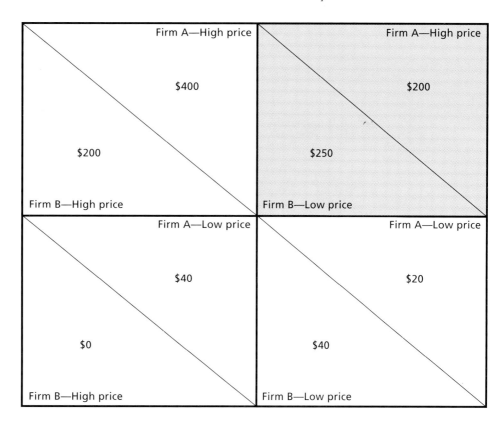

Figure 6.10 Nash Equilibrium

In this example, there are two firms in an industry. Each independently chooses a price for an identical product. The firms either choose a high price or a low price. The payoffs are given in the table (the upper right entry in a cell is the profits for firm A, the lower left is the profits for firm B). The equilibrium is for firm A to charge a high price and firm B to charge a low price—the shaded cell. Any other combination is unstable—that is, given the action of one of the firms, the other firm has the incentive to deviate. The equilibrium is called a *Nash equilibrium.*

a manner that makes both firms better off than under the Nash outcome. For instance, the combined profits of $600 could be split, with each firm receiving $300. As this example illustrates, noncooperative equilibria are not necessarily Pareto efficient. (Often, one or more firms can be made better off, without making other firms worse off, by changing the joint decisions.)

The Cournot Model

The first major economic model of oligopoly was introduced by Augustine Cournot in 1838. To illustrate this model, suppose again that the firms produce identical products and there are two firms in the industry. (This model can easily be extended to more than two firms. The same general results hold. As the number of firms grow, the results approach those of a competitive market.) In the *Cournot model,* each firm treats the *output* level of its competitor as fixed and then decides how much to produce. In equilibrium, neither firm has an incentive to change its output level, given the other firm's choice. (Thus, this is a Nash equilibrium.)

Suppose the duopolists face the following total industry demand:

$$P = 100 - Q \qquad (6.9)$$

where $Q = Q_A + Q_B$. For simplicity, assume that both firms have marginal costs of zero:

$$MC_A = MC_B = 0 \qquad (6.10)$$

Each firm takes the other firm's output as fixed. Thus, the anticipated demand curve for firm i (i = A or B) is:

$$P_i = (100 - Q_j^*) - Q_i \qquad (6.11)$$

where Q_j^* is the anticipated output of the other firm. The marginal revenue for firm i is:[17]

$$MR_i = (100 - Q_j^*) - 2Q_i \qquad (6.12)$$

Firm i's profits are maximized by setting marginal revenue equal to marginal cost (in this case, zero). Doing so, and rearranging the expression, yields the following *reaction curve:*

$$Q_i = 50 - .5Q_j \qquad (6.13)$$

The reaction curve indicates firm i's optimal output given the output choice of firm j. Both firms have the same reaction curve in this example, except that the subscripts are reversed.

The equilibrium is where the two curves cross. At these output levels, each firm is profit maximizing given the other firm's output choice. Neither firm has an incentive to alter its output. The equilibrium is pictured in Figure 6.11. In equilibrium, each firm produces 33⅓ units for a total output of 66⅔ units. The price is $33.34. This output level is less than with pure competition. In pure competition, the total output would be 100 units and the price would be zero (where P = MC). In the Cournot equilibrium, the firms make economic profits. Price is $33.34 and average costs are zero. Each firm makes profits of $1,110.89. This profit is less than the two firms could obtain if they directly colluded and produced the monopolistic output of 50 units (for example, 25 units per firm). Here, the joint profits would be $2,500 rather than $2,221.78. Figure 6.12 shows the three price/quantity outcomes using the original demand curve for the industry.

Price Competition

In the Cournot model, firms focus on choosing output levels. An alternative possibility is that the firms might focus on choosing product price.[18] Here, the Nash equilibrium is for both firms to choose a price equal to marginal cost (the competitive outcome). To see why, suppose one of the firms chooses a price, $P' > MC$. In this case, it is optimal for the other firm to charge a price just below P' to capture all the industry sales. (Customers buy the product from the firm that charges the lowest price.) Given that the second firm charges a price just below P', it is optimal for the first firm to charge a slightly lower price, and so on. Only when the price is equal to marginal cost do both firms have no incentives

---

[17]Recall that marginal revenue for a linear demand curve is a line with the same intercept, but twice the negative slope.

[18]This situation is often referred to as the Bertrand model. Bertrand was a French economist who wrote a short note almost 50 years after Cournot's work was published arguing that in some markets, producers set prices rather than quantities.

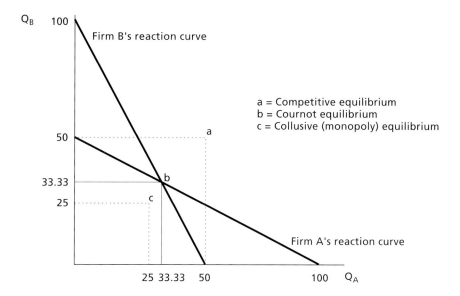

Figure 6.11 Cournot Equilibrium

The duopolists in this example face the total industry demand curve, P = 100 – Q, where Q is the sum of the two outputs. Both firms face a marginal cost of zero. The figure shows the reaction curves for each firm. The reaction curve indicates firm i's optimal output given the output choice of Firm j (i, j = A or B). The Cournot equilibrium is where the two reaction curves cross. Each firm produces 33.33 units. The market price is $33.34. The output for the firms is lower and the profits greater than in the competitive equilibrium. The output for the firms is greater and the profits lower than in the collusive (monopoly) equilibrium.

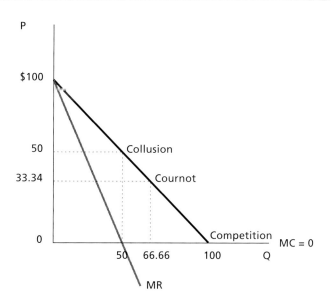

Figure 6.12 Comparison of Prices and Outputs among Collusive, Cournot, and Competitive Equilibria

In this example, the total industry demand curve is P = 100 – Q. Marginal cost is zero. The figure shows the price/quantity outputs for the industry under collusive, Cournot, and competitive equilibria. The output is smallest and the price is highest for the collusive equilibrium. The output is largest and the price is smallest for the competitive equilibrium.

Fare Wars in the Airline Industry

Firms in oligopolistic industries sometimes compete on price, to each other's detriment. An example is the U.S. airline industry in the early 1990s. During this period, the major airlines, including American, United, Delta, and Northwest, repeatedly entered into fare wars that lowered the price of air travel for consumers and lowered the combined profits of the airline industry. For instance, one company would lower its summer fares in the hope of gaining new passengers. Typically, the price reduction was met by other firms within the industry within a matter of days. Outside analysts generally agreed that the firms in the industry lost profits through these price cuts. Indeed, many of these companies reported losses during the period.

to lower price. (Lowering price further would result in selling below cost and a loss.) Of course, both firms would like to devise a way of avoiding competition and earning higher profits. As we discuss below, fostering cooperation can be difficult—if not illegal.

Empirical Evidence

There are many different economic models of oligopoly. We have presented two of them to illustrate that economic theory does not make unambiguous predictions on what to expect in these industries. Some models yield outcomes close to pure competition— firms sell at marginal cost and make no economic profits. Other models yield outcomes closer to pure monopoly. What actually occurs in oligopolistic markets is an empirical issue. The existing evidence supports the hypothesis that oligopolies result in less output than purely competitive industries and that firms earn economic profits (at least in some industries).[19] Firms sometimes compete on price, to each other's detriment, and do not typically earn as much in aggregate as a perfect monopolist.

Cooperation and the Prisoners' Dilemma

As we have discussed, it is in the economic interests of firms in oligopolistic industries to find ways to cooperate and avoid losing profits through competition. Conceptually, the firms are best off if they collude and act as a single monopolist in setting the price and output for the industry. This action maximizes joint profits, which can then be divided among the firms in the industry. The U.S. government understands these incentives and has passed a variety of antitrust laws to prevent firms from fixing prices. These laws are designed to limit the inefficiencies associated with monopoly and to reduce the prices consumers pay for products. Internationally, firms tend to have more latitude in forming cooperative agreements to increase profits (for example, consider the OPEC cartel).[20]

Even when firms are free to cooperate, cooperation is not always easy to achieve. Individual firms have incentives to "cheat" and not follow agreed-on outputs and prices. This incentive can be illustrated by the well-known *Prisoners' Dilemma*. In the Prisoners' Dilemma, there are two suspects who are arrested and charged with a crime. The police do not have sufficient evidence to convict the suspects unless one of them confesses. The

[19]D. Carlton and J. Perloff (1990), *Modern Industrial Organization* (Harper Collins: New York), Chapter 10, discusses some of the relevant empirical literature.

[20]In smaller countries, much of the local production of key products is exported. In this case, it can be in the countries' interests to allow the formation of cartels. Ultimately, consumers pay higher prices and there are inefficiencies. However, many of the costs are borne by people in other countries.

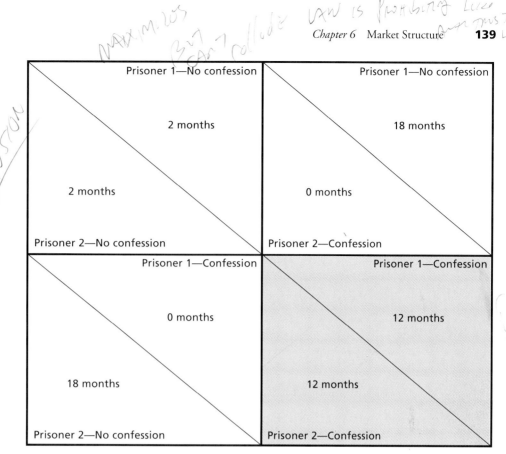

Prisoner 1—No confession; 2 months / 2 months; Prisoner 2—No confession	Prisoner 1—No confession; 18 months / 0 months; Prisoner 2—Confession
Prisoner 1—Confession; 0 months / 18 months; Prisoner 2—No confession	Prisoner 1—Confession; 12 months / 12 months; Prisoner 2—Confession

Figure 6.13 Prisoners' Dilemma

In the Prisoners' Dilemma, there are two suspects, who are arrested and charged with a crime. The police do not have sufficient evidence to convict the suspects unless one of them confesses. The police place the suspects in separate rooms and ask them to confess. If neither confesses, they are convicted of a minor crime (for example, loitering) and are sentenced to two months. If both confess, they spend 12 months in jail. Finally, if one confesses and the other does not, the confessor is released immediately but the other is sentenced to 18 months in jail (12 for the crime and 6 for obstructing justice). The payoffs (in terms of jail time) faced by each individual are pictured. Each entry in the table lists the jail sentences for prisoner A and prisoner B, respectively. The Nash equilibrium is for both suspects to confess—the shaded cell. Given the payoffs, it is always in the *individual interests* of each suspect to confess (taking the action of the other party as given).

police place the suspects in separate rooms and ask them to confess. If neither confesses, they are convicted of a minor crime (for example, loitering) and are sentenced to two months. If both confess, they spend 12 months in jail. Finally, if one confesses and the other does not, the confessor is released immediately but the other is sentenced to 18 months in jail (12 for the crime and 6 for obstructing justice). The payoffs (in terms of jail time) faced by each individual are pictured in Figure 6.13.

The Nash equilibrium is for both suspects to confess. Given the payoffs, it is always in the *individual interests* of each suspect to confess (taking the action of the other party as given). If prisoner A does not confess, prisoner B is set free by confessing. Alternatively, if prisoner A confesses, prisoner B reduces his jail sentence from 18 to 12 months by also confessing. Either way, it is in the interests of prisoner B to confess—confessing is a *dominant strategy.* By symmetric logic, it is also optimal for prisoner A to confess.

Collusion in the Lysine Industry

Mark Whitacre was a high-ranking executive at Archer Daniels Midland Corporation (ADM). He has accused his former employer of engaging in price fixing. Lysine is an amino acid derived from corn used in swine and poultry feed to promote growth. ADM entered the lysine market in 1991. Prior to that time, the market had been dominated by two Japanese companies. ADM quickly gained market share. However, with the competition, the price of lysine fell from about $1.30 per pound to $0.60 per pound. According to Whitacre, ADM executives began discussions in 1992 with their Japanese competitors about how it would be in their mutual self-interest to collude and fix prices. Collectively, the competitors were forgoing millions of dollars of profit per month because of the competition among the three companies. Whitacre indicates that a favorite saying at ADM is:

The competitor is our friend, and the customer is our enemy.

As of 1995, ADM was currently under investigation for price fixing. In addition, it faced numerous lawsuits over the issue.

Source: M. Whitacre, as told to R. Henkoff (1995), "My Life as a Corporate Mole for the FBI," *Fortune Magazine* (September 4), 52–62.

While it is in the individual interests of each party to confess, it is clearly in their *joint interests* not to confess. By not confessing, both parties only serve two months in jail, compared to 12 months when both confess. The Prisoners' Dilemma suggests that any agreement for both to confess is likely to break down when the prisoners make their individual choices unless there is some mechanism to enforce the joint commitment not to confess. One such mechanism is the Mob—both prisoners have incentives not to confess if they expect to be executed by the Mob if they provide evidence to the police.

Cartels consist of formal agreements to cooperate in setting prices and output levels. (These activities are generally illegal in the United States.) Firms trying to maintain cartels can face a Prisoners' Dilemma. Members can agree to restrict output to increase joint profits. However, individual firms have incentives to cheat. If all other firms restrict output, prices will not be affected significantly by the extra output of one firm. However, that firm's profits will increase from selling more. If all firms react to these incentives by increasing output, the cartel breaks down. Actual cartels often unravel because of these incentives. This outcome is pictured in Figure 6.14, which displays the payoffs for two firms attempting to form a cartel. It is in their joint interests to restrict output. Yet, as in the Prisoners' Dilemma, both firms have individual incentives to renege and increase output. The Nash equilibrium is for both firms to increase output.

Cartels can persist if the cartel can impose penalties on cheaters (like the Mob in the Prisoners' Dilemma). For these penalties to be effective, cartel members must be able to observe (or accurately infer) that a firm has cheated. Also, to the extent that cartel members expect to interact on a *repeated basis,* there are increased incentives to cooperate. Repeated interactions also increase the incentives to invest in developing effective enforcement mechanisms to limit cheating. Potentially, these incentives can be strong enough to avoid the Prisoners' Dilemma. In general, cooperation is easier to enforce if the number of firms in the industry is small (it is easier to identify and punish cheaters).

Even when firms are not allowed to form cartels, there may be ways to cooperate to increase profits. For example, over time, a firm might become known as a price leader. Such a firm changes prices in face of new demand or cost conditions in a way that approximates what a cartel would do. Other firms follow the price changes, thus acting like

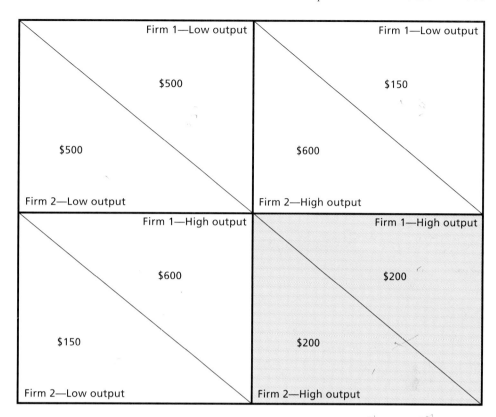

Figure 6.14 Cartel's Dilemma

Two firms attempt to form a cartel. If both firms restrict output, prices are high and each firm's profit is $500. If both cheat on the cartel and increase output, price will be low and each firm's profit is $200. If one firm expands output while the other restricts output, the market price will be at an intermediate level, the firm with the high output will make $600 (because of the increased sales), but the other firm will only make $150 (because of the lower price). These payoffs are pictured. The Nash equilibrium is for both firms to increase output—the shaded cell. Given the payoffs, it is always in the interest of each firm to increase output (taking the output of the other firm as given).

members of a cartel. Individually, firms can still have short-run incentives to cheat (for example, reducing price to get more sales). However, firms might avoid this short-run temptation to foster cooperation in the long run (and hence obtain higher long-run profits).[21]

Other devices that can facilitate cooperation are *most-favored-nation clauses* and *meeting-the-competition clauses* in contracts with buyers. Most-favored-nation clauses provide buyers with guarantees that the seller will not sell to another buyer at a lower price. These clauses reduce the incentive of sellers to lower the price for one buyer because the price concession must be offered to other buyers as well. Meeting-the-competition clauses guarantees that a seller will meet the price of a competitor. Such a clause makes it difficult for firms to cheat on agreements not to lower price since price concessions are likely to be brought to each others' attention by customers.

[21]Indeed, economists have shown that in any long-term relationship, with no specified ending date, cooperation is a *possible equilibrium*—the parties need not succumb to the Prisoners' Dilemma. We discuss this issue in more detail in the appendix to Chapter 7.

Summary

A *market* consists of all firms and individuals who are willing and able to buy or sell a particular product. These parties include those currently engaged in buying and selling the product, as well as *potential entrants. Market structure* refers to the basic characteristics of the market environment, including: (1) the number and size of buyers, sellers, and potential entrants, (2) the degree of product differentiation, (3) the amount and cost of information about product price and quality, and (4) the conditions for entry and exit.

Perfectly competitive markets are characterized by four basic conditions: a large number of buyers and sellers, product homogeneity, rapid dissemination of information at low cost, and free entry into and exit from the market. In competitive markets, individual buyers and sellers take the market price for the product as given—they have no control over price. Firms view their demand curves as horizontal. The firm's short-run supply curve is the portion of the short-run marginal cost curve that is above average variable cost. The long-run supply curve is the portion of the long-run marginal cost curve that is above long-run average cost. In a competitive equilibrium, firms make no economic profits. Production is efficient in that firms produce at the low point on their long-run average cost curves. Firms in competitive industries must move quickly to take advantage of transitory opportunities. They must also strive for efficient production in order to survive. Some firms in the industry can have resources that give them a competitive advantage (for example, a very talented manager). Often the excess returns do not go to the firm owner but rather to the factor of production that is responsible for the particular advantage.

While the competitive model is a reasonable approximation in many industries, there are other industries where firms have substantial market power—prices are affected significantly by the output decisions of individual firms. Market power can exist when there are substantial *barriers to entry* into the industry. Expectations about incumbent reactions, incumbent advantages, and exit costs can all serve as barriers to entry.

The extreme case of market power is *monopoly,* where there is only one firm in the industry. Here, the industry and firm demand curves are one and the same. In contrast to pure competition, consumers pay more than the marginal cost of production and the firm earns economic profits. Output is restricted from competitive levels. The monopolistic outcome is inefficient—not all the potential gains from trade are exhausted. One motive for government regulation of monopoly is to reduce this *social cost.*

As the name implies, *monopolistic competition* is a market structure that is a hybrid between competition and monopoly. Monopolistic competition is like monopoly in that firms in both market structures face downward-sloping demand curves. The market power comes from differentiated products. Examples include the toothpaste, golf ball, tennis racket, and shampoo industries. The analyses of output and pricing policies are similar between the two cases. The difference between monopoly and monopolistic competition is that in monopolistic competition, economic profits invite entry that drives down profits.

Price discrimination occurs whenever a firm's prices in different markets are not related to differentials in production and distribution costs. In maximizing profits, managers strive to capture the maximum amount of *consumer surplus* (subject to the constraint that the product is sold for more than cost). There are three degrees of price discrimination. *Two-part tariffs* are also used by some firms to increase profits.

In *oligopolistic markets,* there are only a few firms that account for most or all of the production in the market. Products may or may not be differentiated. Firms can earn substantial profits. However, these profits can be eliminated through competition among existing firms in the industry. A *Nash equilibrium* exists when each firm is doing the best it can given the actions of its rivals. We use this concept to analyze output and pricing decisions in oligopolistic industries. In the *Cournot model,* each firm treats the *output* level of its competitor as fixed and then decides how much to produce. In equilibrium, firms make economic profits. However, these profits are not as large as could be made if the firms colluded and engaged in monopolistic pricing. Other models of oligopoly yield different equilibria. For instance, one model based on *price competition* yields the competitive solution—price equals marginal cost and there are no economic profits. Overall, economic theory makes no clear-cut prediction about the behavior of firms in oligopolistic industries. The empirical evidence suggests that in at least some oligopolistic industries, firms restrict output from competitive levels and correspondingly make at least some economic profits.

It is in the economic interests of firms in oligopolistic industries to find ways to cooperate and avoid losing profits through competition. Even when firms are free to cooperate, cooperation is not always easy to achieve. Individual firms have incentives to cheat and not follow agreed-on outputs and prices. This incentive is illustrated by the *Prisoners' Dilemma.* This dilemma can cause cartels to be unstable. However, firms can sometimes successfully cooperate when the members can impose penalties or sanctions on defecting firms. Also, cooperation can be sustained through the incentives provided by long-run, *repeated relationships.*

Suggested Readings

A. Dixit and B. Nalebuff (1991), *Thinking Strategically* (Norton: New York).

G. Stigler (1987), *The Theory of Price* (MacMillan: New York), Chapter 3.

R. Pindyck and D. Rubinfeld (1992), *Microeconomics* (Macmillan: New York), Chapters 8–13.

Review Questions

6–1. What four basic conditions characterize a competitive market?

6–2. The short-run marginal cost of the Ohio Bag Company is 2Q. Price is $100. The company operates in a competitive industry. Currently, the company is producing 40 units per period. What is the optimal short-run output? Calculate the profits that Ohio Bag is losing through suboptimal output.

6–3. Should a company ever produce an output if the managers know it will lose money over the period? Explain.

6–4. What are economic profits? Does a firm in a competitive industry earn long-run economic profits? Explain.

6–5. The Johnson Oil Company has just hired the best manager in the industry. Should the owners of the company anticipate economic profits? Explain.

6–6. A Michigan Court ruled in the 1990s that General Motors did not have the right to close a particular Michigan plant and lay people off. Do you think this ruling benefited the people of Michigan? Explain.

6–7. The Suji Corporation has a monopoly in a particular chemical market. The industry demand curve is P = 1,000 – 5Q. Marginal cost is 3Q. What is Suji's profit-maximizing output and price? Calculate the corresponding profits.

6–8. In question 7 on the Suji Corporation, there are unrealized gains from trade. Calculate these lost gains from trade. Discuss policies that Suji might use to capture some of these gains (without lowering the price to all customers).

6–9. Why do companies grant discounts to senior citizens and students?

6–10. You own a theater with 200 seats. The demand for seats is $Q = 300 - 100P$. You are charging $1.25 per ticket and selling tickets to 175 people. Your costs are fixed and do not depend on the number of people attending. Should you cut your price to fill the theater? Explain. What other pricing policies might you use to increase your profits?

6–11. The Snow City Ski Resort caters to both out-of-town skiers and in-town skiers. The demand for ski tickets for each market segment is independent of the other market segment. The marginal cost of servicing a skier of either type is $10. Suppose the demand curves for the two market segments are:

$$\text{Out of town:} \quad Q_0 = 600 - 10P$$
$$\text{Local:} \quad Q_l = 600 - 20P$$

a. If the resort charges one price to all skiers, what is the profit-maximizing price? Calculate how many lift tickets will be sold to each group. What is total profit?

b. Which market segment has the highest price elasticity at this outcome?

c. If the company sells tickets at different prices to the two market segments, what is the optimal price and quantity for each segment? What are the total profits for the resort?

d. What techniques might the resort use to implement such a pricing policy? What must the resort guard against, if the pricing policy is to work effectively?

6–12. Assume the industry demand for a product is: $P = 1,000 - 20Q$. Assume that the marginal cost of product is $10 per unit.

a. What price and output will occur under pure competition? What price and output will occur under pure monopoly (assume one price is charged to all customers)?

b. Draw a graph that shows the lost gains from trade that result from having a monopoly.

c. If the monopolist could perfectly price discriminate (first degree), what are the lost gains from trade? Explain.

6–13. In 1981, the United States negotiated an agreement with the Japanese. The agreement called for Japanese auto firms to limit exports to the United States. The Japanese government was charged with helping make sure the agreement was met by Japanese firms. Were the Japanese firms necessarily hurt by this limited ability to export? Explain.

6–14. All consumers have identical demand for a product. Each person's demand curve is $P = 30 - 2Q$. The marginal cost of production is $2. Devise a two-part tariff that will exhaust all consumer surplus.

6–15. Compare the industry output and price in a Cournot versus a competitive equilibrium. Do firms earn economic profits in the Cournot model? Does economic theory predict that firms always earn economic profits in oligopolistic industries? Explain. What does the empirical evidence indicate?

6–16. What is a Nash equilibrium? Explain why a joint confession is the Nash equilibrium in the Prisoners' Dilemma.

chapter 7

Incentive Conflicts and Contracts

I n 1988, the world witnessed the largest takeover in history—the purchase of RJR-Nabisco by Kohlberg, Kravis, Roberts & Company. The public accounts of this takeover highlight the lavish expenditures and nonproductive decisions of RJR executives prior to the takeover. For example, Burrough and Helyar, in the best-seller, *Barbarians at the Gate,* write:

> *It was no lie. RJR executives lived like kings. The top 31 executives were paid a total of $14.2 million, or an average of $458,000. Some of them became legends at the Waverly for dispensing $100 tips to the shoeshine girl. Johnson's two maids were on the company payroll. No expense was spared decorating the new headquarters, highlighted by the top-floor digs of the top executives. It was literally, the sweet life. A candy cart came around twice a day dropping off bowls of bonbons at each floor's reception areas. Not Baby Ruths but fine French confections. The minimum perks for even lowly middle managers was one club membership and one company car, worth $28,000. The maximum, as nearly as anyone could tell, was Johnson's two dozen club memberships and John Martin's $75,000 Mercedes.*

In addition, it appears that major investment decisions at RJR were often driven by the preferences of managers (for example, pet projects) rather than by value maximization. For example, it is argued that Ross Johnson, chief executive officer of RJR, continued to invest millions of dollars in developing a smokeless cigarette long after it was obvious that the project was not going to be profitable.

The behavior of RJR executives raises at least four interesting issues:

- In previous chapters, we assumed that managers *always* maximize profits. Apparently, they do not. To understand management problems *within the firm,* we need a richer characterization of the firm and managerial decision making.

- RJR suggests that significant conflicts of interest can exist between owners and managers—owners (for example shareholders) are interested in firm value, while the managers are interested in their own utility. What other conflicts of interest exist within firms?

- RJR suggests that owner/manager conflicts can result in reduced productivity and waste. Left unchecked, conflicts of interest can destroy a firm. How do firms limit nonproductive actions to enhance value and avoid destruction?

- If techniques to reduce nonproductive actions exist, why did the owners (shareholders) at RJR allow the managers to engage in such extreme behavior?

In this chapter, we examine these and related issues. We begin by enriching our definition of a firm. We then use this definition to discuss various conflicts of interest that exist within firms. Next, we examine how contracts help to reduce these conflicts. We focus particular attention on the problems created by costly information. Finally, we discuss how reputational concerns can control incentive conflicts within firms. The appendix to this chapter uses the Prisoners' Dilemma (introduced in the last chapter) to illustrate how reputational concerns can motivate cooperation among self-interested individuals.

Firms

In Chapter 3, we characterized the firm by administrative decision making—markets use prices to allocate resources, firms use managers. This led to a discussion of the relative efficiency of firms and markets. Throughout this analysis, and in Chapters 4 to 6, we treated the firm as having one central manager who acts to maximize profits. This characterization is employed frequently in economics and has proven very useful in explaining production and pricing decisions of firms.

The actual decision-making process within firms, however, is extremely complex and differs from this simple characterization in at least three ways. First, there are many decision makers in firms. In large corporations, the board of directors makes major policy decisions such as naming the CEO. The CEO, in turn, retains certain important decision rights while delegating many operating decisions (for instance, pricing and production decisions) to lower-level managers. Even the lowest-paid employee in the firm usually has some decision-making authority. Second, the primary objective of many of these decision makers is not to maximize the profits of the firm. For instance, the investment behavior of the executives at RJR suggests an interest in things other than profit maximization. Third, firms often use internal pricing systems (transfer prices) to allocate internal resources.

Analyzing organizational issues *within the firm* requires a richer concept of the firm. Several useful definitions have been developed by economists.[1] We focus on one definition that is particularly useful for our development.[2] This definition focuses on the fact that the firm is a creation of the legal system. A firm has the legal standing of an individual (it can enter contracts, sue, be sued, and so on). The term *focal point* refers to the firm always being one party to the many contracts that make up the firm. Examples of these contracts are employee contracts, supplier contracts, customer warranties, stock, bonds, loans, leases, franchise agreements, and insurance contracts. The contracts view of the firm is pictured in Figure 7.1.

DEFINITION

The firm is a focal point for a set of contracts.

Some contracts are explicit legal documents, while many others are implicit. An example of an implicit contract is a worker's understanding that if a job is done well, it will result in a promotion. Implicit contracts are often difficult to enforce in a court of law. Later in this chapter, we discuss how reputational concerns can help to ensure that individuals honor implicit contracts.

Incentive Conflicts in Firms[3]

Economic theory argues that individuals are creative maximizers of their *own utility.* Thus, the individuals that contract with the firm are not likely to have objectives that are automatically aligned. The owners of the firm have title to the residual profits (what is left over after other claimants are paid) and are likely to be interested in maximizing the

---

[1]O. Hart (1989), "An Economist's Perspective on the Theory of the Firm,: *Columbia Law Review* 89, 1757–1774.

[2]M. Jensen and W. Meckling (1976), "Theory of the Firm: Managerial Behavior, Agency Costs and Ownership Structure," *Journal of Financial Economics* 3, 305–360.

[3]This section draws on the analysis in M. Jensen and C. Smith (1985) "Stockholder, Manager, and Creditor Interests: Applications of Agency Theory" in *Record Advances in Corporate Finance,* edited by E. Altman and M. Subrahmanyam (Irwin Professional Publishers, Burr Ridge, IL), 95–131.

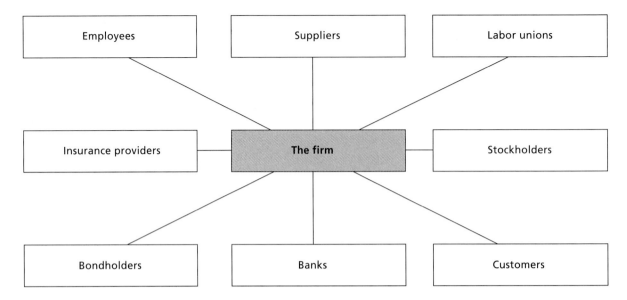

Figure 7.1   The Firm as a Focal Point for a Set of Contracts

The firm is a creation of the legal system that has the standing of an individual in a court of law. The firm serves as one party to the many contracts that make up the firm.

value of these profits. Other individuals within the firm do not necessarily share this goal. We now discuss some of the more important incentive conflicts that arise within firms. We then discuss how contracts can be used to reduce and control these conflicts.

Owner/Manager Conflicts

Owners often delegate the management of firms to professional managers. For instance, in large corporations, the residual profits are owned by shareholders, who delegate significant decision authority to top executives. At least five sources of conflict arise between owners and managers:

- *Choice of effort.* Additional effort by managers generally increases the value of the firm, but additional effort can reduce the utility of managers.
- *Perquisite taking.* It is in the interests of owners to pay sufficient salaries to attract and retain competent managers. However, owners do not want to overpay managers. In contrast, managers are likely to want higher salaries and perquisites such as country club memberships, expensive office furniture, fancy automobiles, day care for children, and French candy.
- *Differential risk exposure.* Managers typically have substantial levels of human capital and personal wealth invested in the firm. This large investment can make managers overly risk averse from the standpoint of the owners, who, at least in the large public corporation, typically hold only a small fraction of their wealth invested in any one firm. For example, the managers might forgo profitable projects because they do not want to bear the risk that a project might fail and bankrupt the firm, leaving them without a job.

The Spectrum of Organizations

The firm can be viewed as a focal point for a set of contracts. One particularly important feature of these contracts is the distribution of the residual profits. Firms vary significantly along this dimension. In a sole proprietorship, the owner/manager is the residual claimant, while in a partnership, the claim is shared by the partners. In the large public corporation, this claim is often held by thousands of shareholders who take little direct interest in managing the company. Management authority is delegated to professional managers, who often have small ownership positions in the firm.

According to Coase (see Chapter 3), individuals have incentives to select the form of organization that minimizes transaction costs. Our discussion of conflicts between owners and managers suggests that problems arise in public corporations because of the significant separation of ownership and control. These problems are costly to resolve. Given these costs, what are the offsetting benefits that promote the prominence of large corporations? One of the largest benefits is that capital is raised from many investors who share in the risk of the company. Shareholders place only a small amount of their wealth in a given company, and thus avoid "placing their eggs all in one basket." This diversification makes risk-averse investors (see Chapter 2) willing to supply capital to corporations at a lower cost. This benefit, however, comes at the cost of having to control the incentive conflicts between managers and owners. Thus, in smaller operations, where raising large amounts of capital is less of an issue, we would expect to find sole proprietorships and small partnerships (where there is less separation of ownership and control). Indeed, this is what is observed.*

---

*Note: There are also tax-related reasons that affect the choice of organizational form. See M. Scholes and M. Wolfson (1992), *Taxes and Business Strategy* (Prentice Hall: Englewood Cliffs, NJ).

- *Differential horizons.* Managers' claims on the corporation are generally limited to their tenure with the firm. Therefore, managers have limited incentives to care about the cash flows of the firm beyond their tenure. Owners, on the other hand, are interested in the value of the entire future stream of cash flows, since it determines the price at which they can sell their claims in the company.
- *Free-cash-flow problems.* Managers can be reluctant to reduce the size of a firm, even if it has no profitable investment projects; they prefer to empire-build. Also, managers often are reluctant to lay off colleagues and friends in divisions that are no longer profitable. Supervisors firing colleagues bear personal costs (disutility), whereas the shareholders receive most of the benefits.

Buyer/Supplier Conflicts

Owners of firms want to acquire high-quality inputs at low prices. Owners of supplying firms want to provide low-cost inputs at high prices. This tension can cause conflicts between buyers and suppliers. Supplying firms worry about the buying firms demanding price concessions, while buying firms worry that suppliers will either shirk on quality (to reduce cost) or raise prices. In Chapter 15, we provide a detailed analysis of buyer/supplier relationships.

Free-Rider Problems

Incentive conflicts also arise with joint ownership. For example, in a large accounting firm, the actions of each partner affect the profits of the organization, which are shared among the partners. This arrangement can motivate partners to *free-ride* on the efforts of

Buyer/Supplier Conflicts in the 1990s

Large firms have become increasingly aggressive at demanding price concessions from suppliers. A survey by the National Association of Purchasing Management of 300 large manufacturers indicates that the average price paid to suppliers decreased by about 1 percent in 1992. This price decline contrasts with price increases ranging from 2 to 5 percent over the previous five years. Large manufacturers have also become more likely to switch suppliers in an attempt to decrease costs.

These activities have increased the strain between buyers and suppliers and have made small suppliers less likely to enter into exclusive contracts with large firms. The co-owner of a small aerospace-industry supplier that derives two-thirds of its sales from Boeing says, "Pressure from Boeing to reduce prices has gotten worse in the past couple of years. They haven't learned to cut costs internally so they are beating up on the vendors. We are looking for new customers wherever we can." In some industries, the conflicts are particularly severe. According to a survey in 1992 by *Ward's Auto World,* a trade publication, more than half of 154 auto-industry suppliers say GM's cost-cutting reorganization was unfavorable to them. GM has been especially aggressive in demanding price cuts from suppliers.

Source: M. Selz (1993), "Some Suppliers Rethink Their Reliance on Big Business," *The Wall Street Journal* (March 29).

---

others. Each partner hopes the other partners will work hard to keep the firm profitable. However, each partner has an incentive to shirk—individuals gain the full benefit of their shirking but only bear part of the costs (their share of the reduced profits). Free-rider problems are common in most group activities and, if left unchecked, can greatly reduce the output of teams. We frequently refer to free-rider problems throughout this book.

Other Conflicts

Similar types of incentive conflicts are likely to arise among most contracting parties in the firm. For example, top managers worry about effort and perquisite-taking problems with lower-level workers. Shareholders and other capital suppliers can have disputes over the optimal dividend and investment policies of the firm. Managers often quarrel with labor unions. Firms can have incentives to default on warranties with customers.

Experimental Evidence on Free-Rider Problems

"More than 50 years ago a German scientist named Ringelmann asked workers to pull as hard as they could on a rope attached to a meter that measured the strength of their efforts. Subjects worked alone and in groups of two, three, and eight.

While the total amount of force on the rope increased as group size rose, the amount of effort by each person seemed to drop. While one person pulling alone exerted an average of 63kg of force, this dropped to about 53kg in groups of three and was reduced to about 31kg in groups of eight. The greater the number of people performing the task, the less effort each one expended.

The impact or effect of any social force directed towards a group from an outside source (for example, a manager) is divided among its members. Thus, the more persons in the group, the less the impact such force will have upon each. Because they are working with others, each group member feels [that others] will take up any slack resulting from reduced effort on their part. And since all members tend to respond in this fashion, average output per person drops sharply."

Source: A. Furnham (1993), "Wasting Time in the Board Room" *Financial Times* (March 10).

Incentive Conflicts throughout the World

Incentive conflicts are not just an American business phenomenon, nor do they only occur in private firms. Rather, these conflicts exist throughout the world in both the private and public sectors. For example, government officials taking bribes is an example of a basic incentive conflict between government officials and the people they represent. In September 1993, Japanese prosecutors arrested the chairman of a leading construction company in a major bribery scandal. The chairman was alleged to have bribed the governor of the Ibaraki prefecture to favor his company's bids for public work projects. The governor was arrested for taking hundreds of thousands of dollars in bribes*

A similar event occurred in China where a bureaucrat confessed to using a safe-deposit box in Hong Kong to stash away more than $1.2 million in cash bribes from companies attempting to get pieces of real-estate deals she controlled. Meanwhile, in the banking sector, the premier of China is attempting to change the common practice by bankers of ignoring credit standards and awarding loans to people "with connections." In one case, eight bankers received stiff sentences, including the death penalty, for accepting bribes in return for loans.†

---

*_The Wall Street Journal,_ September 23, 1993.

†_Business Week,_ July 26, 1993.

Controlling Incentive Problems through Contracts

Why don't incentive conflicts destroy all organizations and cooperative undertakings? For example, shouldn't the fear that managers will use all company resources for their personal benefit prevent owners from delegating operating authority to managers?[4] Fortunately, there are mechanisms that help to reduce incentive conflicts. Among the most important are contracts.[5]

Contracts (implicit and explicit) define the firm's organizational architecture—the decision right, performance evaluation, and reward systems. This architecture provides an important set of constraints and incentives that helps to resolve incentive problems. For instance, if a contract specifies that an executive will receive an annual salary of $200,000, the executive can be placed in jail if she pays herself more—she does not have the decision right to set her own pay.[6] If a manager is evaluated on firm profits and rewarded with a large bonus for good performances, he has incentives to care about firm profits.

Costless Contracting

Under some circumstances, contracts can resolve incentive problems at low cost. As an example, consider Jerry Concannon, the CEO of the Bagby Printing Company. Jerry

---

[4] In fact, some authors suggest that this concern will ultimately cause the collapse of the public corporation. See A. Berle and G. Means (1932), _The Modern Corporation and Private Property_ (MacMillan: New York).

[5] Other important mechanisms are the market for corporate control and the product market. Managers have incentives to increase firm profits because firms with inefficient managers can be taken over by other firms and the management team replaced. Indeed, this is what happened at RJR-Nabisco. Also, inefficient firms eventually go out of business in a competitive market.

[6] Restricting an agent's decision-making authority can reduce incentive problems. However, it can also mean that authority has not been given to the individual with the best knowledge to make the decision. This tension is a fundamental concern in designing the organizational architecture and is the central focus of the next chapter.

gains utility, U, from both his monetary compensation, C, and expenditures on perquisites, P, such as company expenditures on luxury cars, family vacations, and country club memberships:

$$U = f(C,P) \qquad (7.1)$$

If the firm provides no perquisites to Jerry, it must pay him W in cash compensation; otherwise, he will work for another firm. The owners of the firm are willing to pay Jerry W if he consumes no perquisites. However, as CEO, Jerry has numerous opportunities to consume company resources. These opportunities present an incentive problem—Jerry wants to spend company resources on himself, while the owners do not want Jerry to reduce firm value by consuming excess perquisites. Some amount of perquisites actually increase firm value. But beyond this level of perquisite consumption, firm value falls. Excess perquisites are defined as those beyond firm value maximization.

Suppose, for now, that the owners of the firm have precise knowledge of the profit potential of the firm, Π_P. In this case, the realized profits of the firm, Π_R, are:

$$\Pi_R = \Pi_P - P \qquad (7.2)$$

the difference between potential profits and Jerry's perquisite consumption. With this information, the owners can solve the potential incentive problem by offering Jerry the following compensation contract:

$$C = W - (\Pi_P - \Pi_R) \qquad (7.3)$$

This contract, which reduces Jerry's wage by the difference between realized and potential profits, is equivalent to charging Jerry the full price for his perquisites (that is, $C = W - P$).

Figure 7.2 illustrates Jerry's choice of perquisites. His objective is to maximize his utility subject to the constraint that he is paid according to his compensation plan. Jerry chooses the combination (C^*, P^*), which occurs at the tangency point between an indifference curve and the compensation constraint. This combination places Jerry on the highest indifference curve possible given the compensation plan. This choice is Pareto efficient. The owners are indifferent to Jerry's choice—they always pay the equivalent of W (they pay him W–P in cash and P in perquisites). Jerry, however, is better off being able to choose the combination of salary and perquisites that he most prefers. For example, Jerry might prefer a combination of salary and perquisites to a pure salary because he is not taxed on perquisites.[7]

Note how the compensation plan aligns Jerry's and the owners' incentives. Jerry is given the decision right to choose how much the firm spends on his perquisites. The contract, however, charges Jerry the full price for perquisite consumption. In essence, he is rewarded for consuming fewer perquisites. This reward structure gives him private incentives to limit his perquisite consumption.

This example suggests that some perquisite taking by managers is likely to be efficient (from the standpoint of the managers and the firm) because some perquisites increase productivity and because of the differential tax treatment for perquisites and salary. Thus, the perquisite taking by RJR executives was not necessarily inconsistent with the shareholders' objective of profit maximization. Without the perquisites, the shareholders might have had to pay higher salaries to attract and retain the management team. Evidence from

---

[7]This tax effect is reflected in Jerry's indifference curves. Over some range, Jerry is willing to trade more than a dollar of cash for a dollar's worth of perquisites because on an after-tax basis, he is better off. Over this range, the slope of the indifference curve has a slope with an absolute value greater than one. The optimal choice of salary and perquisites occurs at the point where the indifference curve's slope is –1.

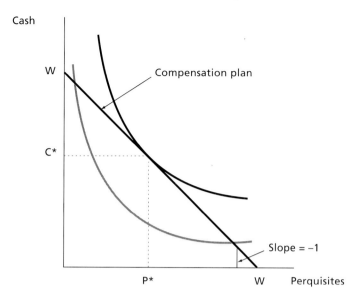

Figure 7.2 Optimal Perquisite Taking

The manager is paid a cash salary, W, as long as the manager maximizes profits. If the manager fails to maximize profits by taking perquisites (for example, too many club memberships, paying excessive salaries to top subordinates, or buying expensive company cars), the owners reduce the compensation by the amount of the lost profits. Given this compensation scheme, the manager chooses the combination (C*, P*). This choice is Pareto efficient.

the stock market, however, suggests that the behavior of RJR executives was excessive. The stock price of RJR went from about $55 per share at the beginning of the takeover contest in October 1988 to about $110 per share when the company was taken over. Furthermore, the management team was subsequently replaced. Thus, the old management team does not appear to have been maximizing the value of the firm.

Costly Contracting and Asymmetric Information

We have shown how, in some cases, contracts can costlessly resolve incentive problems. The example of RJR, however, suggests that contracts are often unsuccessful in accomplishing this objective.

Unlike our hypothetical example, contracts are not costless to negotiate, write, administer, or enforce in practice. For instance, suppose that the owners of Bagby Printing delegate executive compensation decisions to a board of directors. In this case, Jerry might be able to convince board members not to enforce his contract that reduces his salary for perquisite consumption. Indeed, Ross Johnson at RJR tried to keep board members on his side by paying them large retainers. Board members participating in such collusion with senior managers can be replaced, but only at a cost. Legal fees alone can be substantial for writing and enforcing contracts. For example, it is estimated that the legal profession's total receipts were about $91 billion in 1991.[8]

---

[8] *Business Week,* September 6, 1993.

A primary factor that limits the ability of contracts to solve incentive conflicts is costly information. In contrast to our example, it is unlikely that the owners of Bagby Printing would actually know the profit potential of the firm. Information is likely to be *asymmetric*—Jerry knows more than the owners about the profit potential of the firm and his perquisite taking. Given this distribution of information, the owners will not be able to use a compensation contract that requires perfect information about the profit potential of the firm and Jerry's perquisite taking.

There are two general types of information problems that arise in contracting. The first problem is informational asymmetries before the contract is negotiated. The second is the problem of informational asymmetries after the contract is negotiated. Below, we elaborate on each of these problems. We begin with the postcontractual problems because of their importance in this text.

Postcontractual Information Problems

Agency Problems

An *agency relationship* consists of an agreement under which one party, the *principal,* engages another party, the *agent,* to perform some service on the principal's behalf. Many agency relationships exist within firms. Shareholders appoint boards of directors as their agents to manage firms. Boards, in turn, delegate much of the operating authority to top managers, while managers assign tasks to lower-level employees. As we have discussed, there is good reason to believe that the incentives of principals and agents are not naturally aligned. There are *agency problems*—after the contract is set, agents have incentives to take actions that increase their utility at the expense of the principals. For instance, as in the case of RJR, managers might shirk, take perquisites, and choose investment and operating policies that reduce profits but increase the managers' welfare.

Asymmetric information typically precludes costless resolution of agency problems. Since the principal cannot freely observe the actions of the agent, the agent can generally engage in activities such as shirking and perquisite taking without those activities always being detected by the principal. Nevertheless, the principal usually can limit such behavior by establishing appropriate incentives for the agent in the contract and by incurring *monitoring costs.* Also, agents might incur *bonding costs* to help guarantee that they will not take certain actions or to ensure that the principal will be compensated if they do. (For example, agents might buy insurance policies that pay the principal in the case of theft.) The agent is willing to incur these expenses to increase the amount paid to the agent by the principal for the agent's services. Generally it will not pay for either party to incur enough costs to ensure that the agent will completely follow the wishes of the principal (at some point the marginal cost is greater than the marginal benefit for making additional expenditures to increase compliance). The dollar equivalent of the loss in gains from trade that results due to the divergence of interest in the agency relationship is known as the *residual loss.* Total agency costs are the sum of the *out-of-pocket costs* (monitoring and bonding costs) and the residual loss.[9]

---

[9]M. Jensen and W. Meckling (1976), "Theory of the Firm: Managerial Behavior, Agency Costs and Ownership Structure," *Journal of Financial Economics* 3, 305–360.

Example of Agency Costs

To illustrate the concepts of agency costs and asymmetric information, consider Good Tire Company and the law firm Brown & Brown. Good Tire wants outside legal counsel for contracting and litigation, as well as for general legal advice. Brown & Brown is capable of supplying these services.

Good Tire's marginal benefit, MB, for hours of legal services is:

$$MB = \$200 - 2L \qquad (7.4)$$

where L is the hours per week of legal services provided to the firm. Good Tire has some very important legal issues, and so the marginal benefits for legal service are very high for the first hour. As these primary issues are resolved, the company receives advice on less important issues. Thus, the marginal benefit of additional hours of legal services declines with the total number of hours provided.

Brown & Brown's marginal cost, MC, for providing legal services is:

$$MC = \$100 \qquad (7.5)$$

The marginal cost of providing additional hours of legal services is constant at $100 per hour.

Value is maximized—all potential gains from trade between Good Tire and Brown & Brown are realized—at the point where the marginal benefits of legal service equal the marginal costs:

$$MB = MC$$
$$200 - 2L = 100$$
$$L^* = 50 \text{ hours} \qquad (7.6)$$

It is not optimal to provide more than 50 hours of legal services because the marginal benefits are less than the marginal costs. Correspondingly, it is suboptimal to provide less than 50 hours because the marginal costs of providing additional hours are less than the marginal benefits.

Assuming there are no agency problems, the optimal contract would call for 50 hours per week of legal services. For example, Good Tire might agree to pay Brown & Brown $6,250 a week for 50 hours of legal work. This outcome is pictured in the left panel in Figure 7.3. The total gain from the exchange (surplus) is $2,500, as depicted by the triangle labeled S. At a price of $6,250 for legal services, the gains are split evenly between the two companies.[10] The fee covers Brown & Brown's costs of $5,000 (50 × $100) and provides it with a profit of $1,250. Good Tire receives gross benefits of $7,500. However, it pays a fee of $6,250, yielding net benefits of $1,250. If the two firms negotiate other prices for the 50 hours of legal services, the split in gains would be different. If the market for legal services is perfectly competitive, the price would be $5,000 ($100 per hour), and all the gains would go to Good Tire. However, as long as the total hours are 50 the agreement is efficient and the total surplus is $2,500.

There is a potential agency problem that can confound this relationship: It is costly for Good Tire to observe how many hours of legal work Brown & Brown actually provides to the firm (there is asymmetric information). Thus, Brown & Brown might work

---

[10]Recall that total benefits (TB) are equal to the area under the marginal benefit curve, while total costs (TC) are the area under the marginal cost curve. Thus, at 50 hours of legal service, the total surplus is S = TB − TC.

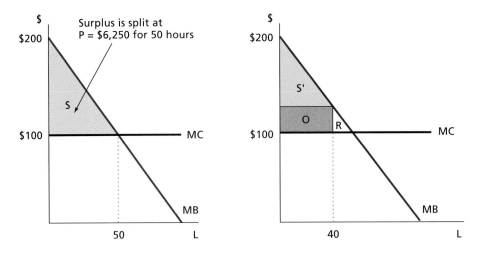

Figure 7.3 Agency Costs in Legal Contracting

The left panel shows the marginal benefit, MB, to Good Tire for hours of legal services, L, and the marginal cost, MC, to Brown & Brown for providing these services. Assuming no agency problems, the optimal number of hours is 50. The total gains from trade, $2,500, are shown by the triangle labeled S. The right panel reflects the agency problem between the two firms—Brown & Brown might bill for more hours than hours worked. The two firms spend $400 each for monitoring and bonding costs. These out-of-pocket costs are shown by the rectangle labeled O. Since it does not pay to solve the agency problem completely, we assume that Brown & Brown ends up providing only 40 hours of legal services. The triangle, R, represents the residual loss of $100. The original surplus S is reduced by the sum of the out-of-pocket costs and the residual loss. The resulting surplus, labeled S', is $1,600. How this surplus is split depends on the price charged for the legal services.

---

less than 50 hours but claim it worked the full amount. Indeed, the problem might be so severe that Good Tire simply does not hire Brown & Brown. In this case, the entire gains from trade are lost. This agency cost is a residual loss—the lost surplus that results because it does not pay to solve the agency problem.

More generally, the two firms might be able to promote a mutually advantageous exchange by controlling the agency problem through expenditures on monitoring and bonding. For example, Good Tire might spend $400 per week to hire an auditor to check Brown & Brown's work, while Brown & Brown might spend $400 per week to document that it is actually conducting legal work for the firm. It is, however, unlikely that it will pay the two parties to spend enough resources to guarantee that Brown & Brown will do no overbilling. For example, the end result might be that, after the $800 expenditures on monitoring and bonding, Brown & Brown provides 40 hours of legal service and bills for 50 hours. Both parties anticipate this outcome and might negotiate a price of $5,200 for the legal service.[11] This price is lower than in the no agency problem case because Good Tire will not pay as much for the anticipated 40 hours as it would for 50 hours.

The right panel in Figure 7.3 illustrates this outcome. The triangle, labeled R, is the residual loss of $100—the lost surplus that results because it does not pay to resolve the

---

[11]Good Tire cannot observe the actual hours worked by Brown & Brown. Nonetheless, it can have *rational expectations* (reasonable expectations given the information that it does have) that Brown & Brown will work 40 hours and bill for 50.

Do Firms Really Have Agency Problems with Their Law Firms?

Our example of agency problems with law firms illustrates a real problem faced by businesses every day—figuring out whether their lawyers are "playing it straight." According to *Business Week*:

> The task is time-consuming and often unpleasant, but for companies battling ever diminishing budgets can be fruitful. General Dynamics, for example, lopped off $186,000, or 42 percent from just one bill when it discovered a law firm charging for what ended up to be useless research. Motorola Inc. saved a pocketful when it confronted counsel for billing it for hours spent preparing documents that, because of a statute passed a year earlier, were no longer required.

Source: "The Verdict: Guilty of Overcharging," *Business Week,* September 6, 1993.

agency problem completely. In addition, the two companies pay $400 each for monitoring and bonding. These payments reduce the surplus by $800, as shown by the rectangle labeled O.[12] The remaining surplus is $1,600. This surplus is equal to the original surplus of $2,500 minus the total agency costs of $900—the sum of the out-of-pocket costs (monitoring and bonding costs) and the residual loss. In the end, Brown & Brown earns a net profit of $800 [$800 = $5,200 – (40 ×100) – 400]. Good Tire obtains net benefits of $800 [$800 = $6,400 – $5,200 – $400].[13] Both firms are $450 per week worse off than in the case where there was no asymmetric information or agency problems.

Incentives to Economize on Agency Costs

It is very important to understand that both the principal and the agent have incentives to resolve agency problems in the least costly manner. By doing so, there are more gains from trade to share between the two parties. In the Good Tire example, there would be an additional $900 of surplus to split between Good Tire and Brown & Brown if the agency problem could be resolved costlessly. (If they didn't have to spend money on auditors and compliance, they could divide the savings between themselves.) For any given scale of activity, it is in the self-interest of individuals to minimize the agency costs in any contracting relationship.[14] Incentives exist to write contracts that provide monitoring and bonding activities to the point where the marginal cost equals the marginal gain from reducing the residual loss. This means that incentives exist within the contracting process to produce an efficient utilization of resources (at least from the standpoint of the contracting parties).

[12]The placement of this rectangle is arbitrary. All that is important is that the area of the original surplus be reduced by the $800 out-of-pocket expenses.

[13]The $6,400 is the gross surplus for Good Tire. It is the area under the marginal benefits curve between zero and 40 hours.

[14]For the technically inclined: For this statement to be strictly true, production costs must be separable from agency costs and there must be no wealth effects. (The choices of the principal and agent are independent of their individual wealth levels.) When these conditions are violated, the individuals might not want to minimize total agency costs. Nevertheless, they still have strong incentives to consider these costs in designing contracts. For our purpose, it is reasonable and convenient to ignore these technical considerations.

**BASIC PRINCIPLE:
VALUE MAXIMIZATION**

Agency problems generate
costs that reduce value. It is in
the interests of all parties to a
contract to develop efficient
solutions to agency problems.
More value is created, which
can be shared among the
contracting parties.

Viewing contracts as efficient responses to the particular contracting problem can be a very powerful tool for explaining observed organizational architectures. As a simple example, consider the difference in the way fruit pickers are paid compared to workers that assemble airplanes. Agricultural workers are usually paid on a piecework basis. The more they pick, the more they get paid. Alternatively, workers that assemble airplanes often are paid straight salary. (The same salary is paid independent of output.) How can we explain this difference in observed contracts? In general, output increases if people are paid on a piecework basis. A person will pick more pieces of fruit per hour if paid by the piece than by the hour. However, piecework payments generate their own set of agency problems. These payments motivate people to focus more on output and less on quality. In fruit picking, a supervisor can monitor the quality of the output cheaply through direct inspection of the picked fruit. In the case of airplanes, quality deficiencies may not be detected until after the employee leaves the job (for example, when the airplane crashes). In this case, the agency costs of piecework payments are larger than the benefits. We use this type of logic throughout the book to explain the design of organizations.

Precontractual Information Problems

Information at the time of contract negotiations is also typically asymmetric. For example, in negotiating a labor contract, the prospective employee typically has superior information on what wage is acceptable, while the employer knows more about what the firm is willing to pay. Precontractual informational asymmetries can cause at least two major problems—bargaining failures and adverse selection.

Bargaining Failures

Asymmetric information can prevent parties from reaching an agreement even when in theory a contract could be constructed that is mutually advantageous. Suppose that Sheri Merriman is willing to accept a job for as little as $2,000 per month and the human resources manager is willing to pay as much as $3,000 per month. In principle, a mutually advantageous contract could be negotiated at any price between $2,000 and $3,000. Neither side, however, is likely to know the other side's reservation price (the highest price that the manager is willing to pay and the lowest price that Sheri is willing to accept). In an attempt to get the best price possible, both parties might overreach, resulting in a bargaining failure. Sheri might claim that she will not work for less than $3,500. The human resources manager, in turn, might discontinue negotiations because he does not think that he can hire Sheri for less than $3,000 (his reservation price). This phenomenon helps to explain the existence of labor strikes that end up hurting both labor and the company. (Strikes result in lower productivity and sales, and thus there are fewer profits to split between labor and the company.)

Adverse Selection

A second problem caused by precontractual informational asymmetries is *adverse selection*. Adverse selection refers to the tendency of individuals, with private information about something that affects a potential trading partner's benefits, to make offers that are detrimental to the trading partner.

	Expected Annual Medical Expenditures
Ann	$100
Bob	$500
Claire	$900
All three individuals	$500 per person

Figure 7.4   Example of Adverse Selection in Insurance Markets

This table shows the expected annual medical expenditures for three individuals. If an insurance company sells insurance to all three at a price above $500 per year, it expects to make a profit. However, if the company prices insurance at $500, Ann is unlikely to purchase the insurance. Bob and Claire have average expected expenditures of $700 per person. Thus, if Bob and Claire are the sole purchasers, the company must sell the insurance at above $700 to break even. In this case, Bob might not buy the insurance. The end result can be a market failure, where the company prices the insurance at $900 and sells only to Claire.

As an example, consider the market for health insurance.[15] Figure 7.4 displays three individuals and their expected medical costs for the year. Ann is very healthy and is expected to spend only $100 on medical expenses, while Claire is quite unhealthy and is expected to spend $900. Bob is in the middle with expected expenditures of $500. The average expected expenditure for all three individuals is $500 per person.

It is likely that each individual knows more about his or her health than an insurance company—individuals know how they have been feeling and their health habits, while an insurance company is likely to have information that is restricted to the typical expenditures for the entire population (by age and sex categories). In this spirit, assume that each individual knows his or her expected expenditure, while the insurance company only knows the expected expenditure for the three individuals as a group—$500 per person. If the company expects to make a profit, it must sell insurance policies at premiums above the expected expenditures of the buyers.

The information structure in this example can cause a market failure. For instance, assume that the insurance company tries to sell insurance at $510. If all three parties buy the insurance, the company expects to make a profit. However, at this price, Ann might not want to purchase insurance. She expects to spend only $100 for medical expenses; from her perspective, the insurance is very expensive.[16] If at a premium of $510 only Bob and Claire buy the insurance, the company on average will lose money. The insurance company might anticipate that healthy individuals will not buy the insurance at $510 and attempt to raise the price. For example, if it sells the insurance policies to both Claire and Bob at $710, it will make a profit. (Their average expected expenditure is $700 per person.) However, at this price Bob is less likely to buy the insurance because the price is substantially above his expected expenditure of $500. In the end, the insurance company might price insurance at above $900 and sell only to Claire, the least healthy of the three.

The company might be able to prevent this market failure and sell insurance to all three parties by becoming better informed about the individual health of its applicants.

---

[15]Managers often are involved in designing or modifying fringe-benefit policies. Understanding the following problem is important in this activity. We discuss this issue in greater detail in Chapter 11.

[16]Since Ann is risk averse, she would be willing to spend more than $100 for insurance (see Chapter 2). However, $510 is too expensive.

Battling Informational Problems in the Automobile Insurance Industry

Robert Plan Corporation specializes in providing automobile insurance to high-risk customers in urban areas. Most insurance companies have stayed away from this market because of high risks from both adverse selection and fraud. Robert Plan has been successful in this market by aggressively addressing both problems.

The company carefully scrutinizes applications to assess the proper premium. It claims that about 70 percent of its applications are "misstated," with applicants fibbing about items like whether they drive to work or where their primary residence is. Robert Plan uses its own private investigators to check out potential fibs. They may visit applicants' homes and follow them as they drive their cars (to determine if they are driving to work).

The company is also concerned about the problem of excessive claims. The company is notorious for being aggressive in ensuring that it does not pay excessive claims. Company investigators say one maneuver that "works well" is letting the air out of a tire to see if someone claiming a back injury "feels well enough to change it." The top management of the company does not "condone this action and says if it is going on it will stop it." However, for the company to survive it must conduct "hand-to-hand combat with fraud."

Source: S. Woolley (1993), "Smile, Cheater, You're on Candid Camera," *Business Week* (October 4).

For example, it might require a medical exam of all applicants, as well as access to all their medical records. In this case, different rates could be charged depending on the health of the individual. Collecting information, however, is costly, and thus there is an incentive to consider these costs in the design of the organization and its policies.[17]

In some cases, adverse-selection problems can be reduced by the clever design of contracts. An insurance company might be able to offer a menu of contracts with different deductibles, coinsurance requirements, and prices that would motivate the individuals to *self-select* based on their private information. For example, Ann might choose a low-priced insurance contract with a high deductible, while Claire might choose a high-priced contract that provides for full insurance. In this case, the company might be able to sell insurance to all three people at a profit.

Sometimes, it is possible for individuals to communicate or *signal* their private information to other parties in a credible fashion. For example, Ann might be able to convince the insurance company that she is very healthy and should be sold insurance at a low rate. (She might document that she participated in 10 marathon races during the year.) Ann's communication to the company will be convincing to the company only if the cost to Bob and Claire for sending the same signal is higher than Ann's. (For example, due to poor health, they are unable to participate in 10 marathons.) Otherwise, they could take the same action to claim they were healthy, and there would be no reason for the company to believe the claim.

Adverse-selection problems are not limited to insurance markets but occur in many settings. Prospective employees are likely to know more about their talents and productivity than prospective employers. Similarly, the seller of a used car knows more about the quality of the car than the buyer. Thus, at a given price, sellers are more likely to offer *"lemons"* than high-quality cars.[18] In these settings, traders often develop mechanisms that

---

[17]The company might also overcome the problem by selling group insurance to a company that employs all three individuals. In this case, the individuals do not select whether or not to be covered. Thus, the insurance company can make a profit at a premium above $500 per person.

[18]G. Akerlof (1970), "The Market for Lemons: Quality Uncertainty and the Market Mechanism," *Quarterly Journal of Economics* 84, 488–500.

help reduce adverse-selection problems. Used-car dealers offer warranties that guarantee that if the car is a lemon, the seller will repair or exchange it at the seller's expense. Also, there are diagnostic mechanics that can provide prospective buyers with additional information about the quality of a car.

Implicit Contracts and Reputational Concerns

Implicit Contracts

Many of the contracts that make up the firm are implicit—they consist of promises and understandings that are not backed up by formal legal documents. Examples include promises of promotions and salary increases for a job done well and informal understandings that suppliers will not shirk on quality. By definition, implicit contracts are difficult to enforce in a court of law and largely depend on the private incentives of individuals to honor the terms of the contract. Given the incentive conflicts that we have discussed in this chapter, how can individuals ever depend on others to honor the terms of implicit contracts? For example, why would an employee ever trust an implicit promise by a manager to give the person a bonus for a job done well? Doesn't the manager always have incentives to default on the contract after the worker's job is complete? Not paying the worker increases profits and the manager's bonus.

Reputational Concerns

The answer to these questions is that reputational concerns can act as a powerful force to motivate contract compliance. In particular, the market can impose substantial costs on institutions and individuals for unethical behavior. Thus, market forces can provide private incentives for honorable behavior. Chapter 18 contains related discussion on promoting ethical behavior in corporations.

As an example, consider a firm that has a long-run contract to provide a metal part to a manufacturing firm each month at a price of $10,000. The cost of producing this product is $9,000, so the profit per unit is $1,000. It is possible for the supplier to produce a low-quality product for $2,000. However, it has agreed to provide a high-quality product. Since the quality of the part is known to the buyer only after the purchase, it would be possible for the supplier to make a profit of $8,000 by producing a low-quality part but claiming it is a high-quality part. The buying firm, however, will detect the quality of the part after purchase and will discontinue future purchases if it is cheated. The supplying firm faces a tradeoff. It can gain $7,000 in the short run by cheating. However, it loses a $1,000 per month future profit stream. The supplier has the incentive to be honest as long as the value of the future profit stream is greater than the short-run gain from cheating.

Typically, the costs of cheating on quality are higher if the information about such activities is more rapidly and widely distributed to potential future customers. In markets like the diamond trade in New York, cheating on quality is quite rare. This market is dominated by a close-knit community of Hasidic Jews who would distribute information about unethical activities rapidly throughout the market. In other broader markets, specialized services that monitor the market help ensure contract performance. *Consumer Reports* evaluates products from toasters to automobiles, the *Investment Dealer's Digest* reports on investment bankers, and *Business Week* ranks MBA programs. By lowering the costs for potential customers to determine quality, these information sources increase the costs of cheating.

Crimes, Lies, and Prudential-Bache

During the 1980s, Prudential-Bache sold partnerships with Clifton S. Harrison to renovate and build commercial properties. Almost all ran into financial troubles. Amid the collapse of the deals, it became public that Harrison, a man presented by Prudential executives as worthy of the highest recommendation, was a convicted criminal who had served 18 months in jail for financial fraud. The brokerage firm apparently knew this all along and decided not to tell. As of October 1993, Prudential was still negotiating with regulators to settle fraud charges. The settlement is expected to cost about $370 million. The firm also faces lawsuits from investors who say the deals destroyed their lives.

   The reputation costs to Prudential have been large. To quote a former Prudential broker, "It's the nearest thing to a disaster I ever encountered . . . our friends have been our clients, and our clients have been our friends. Now we have been deprived of both." Today, Prudential is trying to regain the trust of customers. As its recent campaign slogan says: "The most important thing we earn is your trust."

Source: K. Eichenwald (1993), "Crimes, Lies and Prudential-Bache," *The New York Times* (October 10).

More generally, reputational concerns are most likely to be effective in promoting contract compliance when (1) the gains from cheating are small, (2) the likelihood of detecting cheating is high, and (3) the relationship is long run and repeated (where the returns from maintaining a good reputation are large). When these conditions are not met, reputational concerns are less effective in motivating contract compliance. In many settings reputational concerns are quite important in promoting cooperation and honesty. The ability to enter into self-enforcing agreements can significantly reduce the costs of contracting in an organization. (Fewer resources are used for negotiating and enforcing formal contracts.) The appendix to this chapter uses the Prisoners' Dilemma, introduced in Chapter 6, to provide a more detailed analysis of reputational concerns.

Summary

Treating a firm like an individual decision maker who maximizes profits is a useful abstraction in some contexts. For example, this characterization was used in previous chapters to analyze output and pricing decisions. Analyzing organizational issues within the firm requires a richer definition. A particularly useful definition for our purposes is that the *firm is a focal point for a set of contracts.*

   Since individuals are creative maximizers of their own utility, there are likely to be incentive conflicts among the parties that contract with the firm. Examples include owner/manager, buyer/supplier, and free-rider conflicts. Contracts (explicit and implicit) specify a firm's *organizational architecture* (the decision right, performance evaluation, and reward systems). The architecture provides a set of constraints and incentives that can reduce incentive conflicts. Contracts are not likely to resolve incentive problems completely because they are costly to negotiate, write, and enforce. *Asymmetric information* causes particularly important problems.

   An *agency relationship* consists of an agreement under which one party, the *principal*, engages another party, the *agent*, to perform some service on behalf of the principal. Many agency relationships exist within firms. Agents do not always act in the best interests of principals—there are *agency problems.*

   Asymmetric information usually means that agency problems cannot be costlessly resolved by contracts. The principal can usually limit the divergence of interest by establishing appropriate incentives for the agent in the contract and by incurring *monitoring costs* aimed at limiting the aberrant activities of the agent. Also, agents might incur *bonding costs* to help guarantee that they will not take certain actions or to ensure that the principal will be compensated if they do. Generally, it does not pay to resolve the incentive conflict completely. The dollar equivalent of the loss in the gains from trade that results due to the divergence of interest in the agency relationship is known as the *residual loss*. Total agency costs are the sum of the *out-of-pocket costs* (monitoring and bonding costs) and the residual loss.

Parties to a contract have incentives to resolve agency problems in the least costly manner. By doing so, there are additional gains from trade to share between the parties. Viewing observed contracts as efficient responses to the particular contracting problem can be a very powerful tool for explaining organizational architecture.

Precontractual informational asymmetries can cause breakdowns in bargaining and *adverse selection*. Adverse selection refers to the tendency of individuals, with private information about something that affects a potential trading partner's benefits, to make offers that are detrimental to the trading partner. Adverse selection can cause market failures. Precontractual information problems can be mitigated by information collection, clever contract design, credible communication, and mechanisms such as warranties.

Many of the contracts in firms are *implicit contracts* rather than formal legal documents. Implicit contracts are hard to enforce in a court of law and largely depend on the private incentives of individuals for enforcement. *Reputational concerns* can provide incentives to honor implicit contracts. These concerns are most likely to be effective when (1) the gains from cheating are small, (2) the likelihood of detecting cheating is high, and (3) the relationship is long term and thus the payoffs from maintaining a good reputation are large. It is sometimes possible to structure organizations in ways that increase the likelihood that reputational concerns will promote honorable behavior.

APPENDIX   *Reputational Concerns and the Prisoners' Dilemma*[19]

In this chapter, we have discussed how reputational concerns can promote cooperative behavior, even if individuals are narrowly concerned about their own economic self-interests. Additional insights can be obtained through simple game theoretic examples. In the following example, Jack and Jean work on a production team. They want to agree to a "contract" that both will work hard so that they can earn a bonus. They face a problem in that the contract is not legally binding and the work efforts are not observed until after the work is complete. This problem is similar to the Prisoners' Dilemma introduced in Chapter 6.

Figure 7.5 displays the possible payoffs. If Jack and Jean both shirk, they receive salaries of $1,000. If they both work hard, they receive a bonus. However, they experience disutility from the additional effort. The payoff, net of this disutility, is $2,000. If Jack shirks and Jean works hard, they meet their production target and receive bonus payments. Jack, however, experiences no disutility from working hard and receives a payoff of $3,000. Jean also receives a cash bonus. However, being the only one to exert effort, she incurs a back injury. Her net payoff is $0. The opposite payoffs occur if Jack works and Jean shirks.

The Nash equilibrium in a single-period setting is for both to shirk. Given the payoffs, it is always in their *individual interests* to shirk. If Jean works, Jack is better off shirking

---

[19]This appendix modifies and extends an example in G. Miller (1992), *Managerial Dilemma: The Political Economy of Hierarchy* (Cambridge University Press: Cambridge), 184–186. It requires elementary knowledge of basic statistics and the game-theory concepts introduced in Chapter 6 (Nash equilibrium).

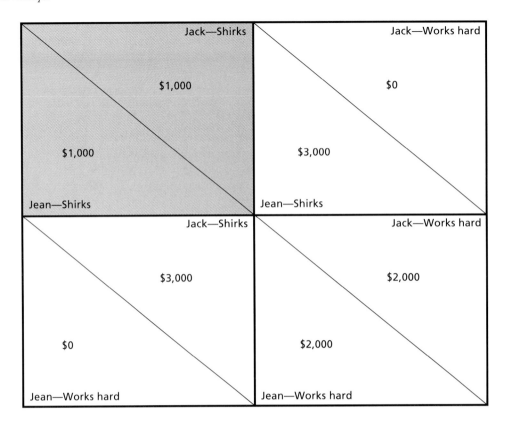

Figure 7.5   Payoffs to Two Team Members in a Single-Period Setting.

The payoff on the lower left in each cell is the payoff for Jean, while the payoff on the upper right is for Jack. If Jack and Jean both shirk, they receive salaries of $1,000. If they both work hard, they receive a bonus. However, they experience disutility from working hard. The payoff, net of this disutility, is $2,000. If Jack shirks and Jean works hard, they meet their production target and receive bonus payments. Jack, however, experiences no disutility from working hard and receives a payoff of $3,000. Jean also receives a cash bonus. However, being the only one to exert effort, she incurs a back injury. Her net payoff is $0. The opposite payoffs occur if Jack works and Jean shirks. The Nash equilibrium in this single-period setting is for both to shirk (shaded cell). Given the payoffs, it is always in their *individual interests* to shirk.

since he receives $3,000 rather than $2,000. Similarly, if Jean shirks, Jack would rather receive the $1,000 from shirking than the $0 payoff from working. This same logic holds for Jean. The equilibrium outcome is not Pareto efficient. Both Jack and Jean would prefer the outcome where they both work—there, payoffs are $2,000, instead of $1,000. The problem is that they can't observe each other's effort until after the work is complete.

Now suppose that Jack and Jean expect to work together in the future. In particular, suppose that in a given work period there is a probability, p, that they will work together in the next period.[20] Thus, the probability that they will work together through n periods is p^{n-1}. Now suppose that Jack and Jean each consider two options

[20]In each period, Jack and Jean choose an effort level, observe output, and receive compensation from the firm.

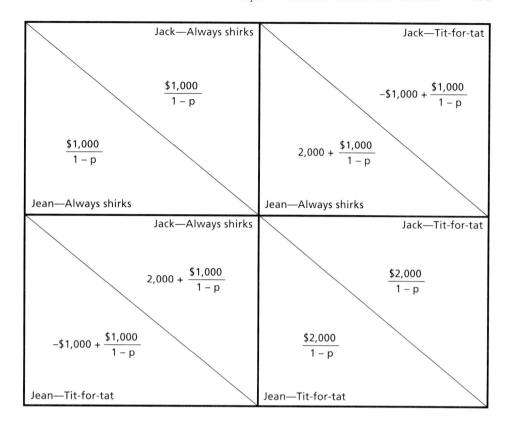

Figure 7.6   Generalized Payoffs for Two Team Members in a Multiperiod Setting

Jack and Jean each consider two options in choosing their effort levels. One is to follow the strategy of *always* shirking every period. The other strategy, known as tit-for-tat, is to work hard for the first period and thereafter mimic the other player's previous choice. For instance, if Jack works hard in the first period and Jean shirks, Jack will shirk in the second period. If one person shirks in the first period, then in all future periods both people shirk (the person who selects to shirk in the first period has chosen the strategy of *always* shirking). The lower-left payoff in each cell is Jean's, while the upper-right payoff is Jack's. In a given work period, there is a probability, p, that they will work together in the next period.

in choosing their effort levels. One is to follow the strategy of *always* shirking every period. If both Jack and Jean select this strategy, the expected sum of each person's future earnings will be:[21]

$$E(\text{future earnings}) = \$1,000 + \$1,000\ p + \$1,000\ p^2 \ldots \qquad (7.7)$$

This expression is an infinite sum with a value of $1,000 [1/(1–p)]. The other strategy, known as *tit-for-tat,* is to work hard the first period and thereafter mimic the other player's previous choice. For instance, if Jack works hard in the first period and Jean shirks, Jack will shirk in the second period. If one person shirks in the first period, then in all future periods both people shirk (the person who selects to shirk in the first period has chosen the strategy of *always shirking).*

Both Jack and Jean want to maximize the expected sum of their individual future earnings from the working relationship. Figure 7.6 shows the generalized payoffs in the setting. Unlike the single-period case, it does not always pay a person to shirk. Clearly, if

---

[21]For simplicity, we ignore discounting future cash flows. Also, the formulation assumes that Jack and Jean have the possibility of living forever. Neither of these simplifications is crucial for our analysis.

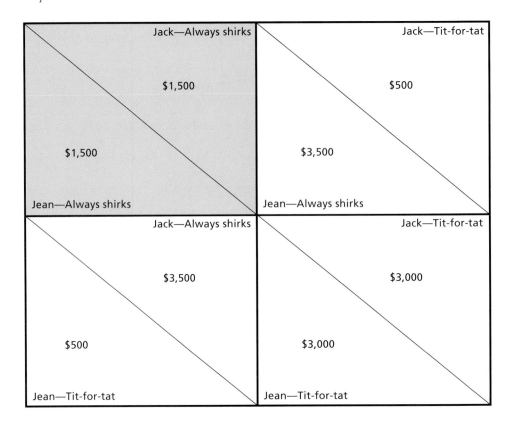

Figure 7.7   Payoffs for Two Team Members of a Production Team When the Likelihood of Working Together in the Future Is Low (p = 1/3)

Jack and Jean each consider two options in choosing their effort levels. One is to follow the strategy of *always* shirking every period. The other strategy, known as tit-for-tat, is to work hard the first period and thereafter mimic the other player's previous choice. For instance, if Jack works hard in the first period and Jean shirks, Jack will shirk in the second period. If one person shirks in the first period, then in all future periods both people shirk (the person who selects to shirk in the first period has chosen the strategy of *always* shirking). The payoff on the lower left in each cell is Jean's payoff, while the payoff of the upper right is Jack's. In a given work period, there is a probability, p, that they will work together in the next period. In this example, the probability of working together in the future is relatively small (1/3). The Nash equilibrium is for both to shirk (shaded cell).

Jean expects Jack to shirk, she will shirk as well, since $\$1,000/(1-p)$ is always greater than $-\$1,000 + \$1,000/(1-p)$.[22] However, if Jean thinks that Jack is going to choose the tit-for-tat strategy, it *can be* in her interest to do so as well. Her expected payoff from selecting tit-for-tat is $\$2,000/(1-p)$. Thus, she will select tit-for-tat whenever p is greater than 1/2—since $\$2,000/(1-p)$ is greater than $\$2,000 + \$1,000/(1-p)$. Symmetric logic holds for Jack's choice.

Figures 7.7 and 7.8 show the payoffs for Jack and Jean for the cases where p = 1/3 and p = 3/4. When p = 1/3, the Nash equilibrium is for both to shirk. The probability of repeated interaction is not large enough to promote cooperation. This example illustrates the general point that reputational concerns are unlikely to promote cooperation when the relationship is expected to be short term. In the second case, two equilibria are possible: mutual shirking or mutual cooperation.

[22]The payoff from tit-for-tat is $[\$0 = (\$1,000p + \$1,000p^2 \ldots)] = [-\$1,000 + \$1,000 + (\$1,000p + \$1,000p^2 \ldots)] = -\$1,000 + \$1,000/(1-p)$.

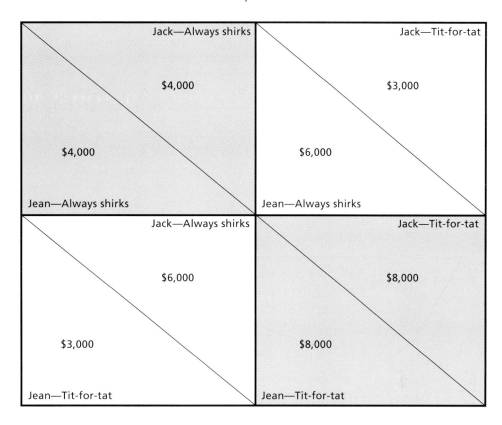

	Jack—Always shirks	Jack—Tit-for-tat
	$4,000	$3,000
	$4,000	$6,000
	Jean—Always shirks	Jean—Always shirks

Figure 7.8   Payoffs for Two Team Members of a Production Team When the Likelihood of Working Together in the Future Is High (p = 3/4)

Jack and Jean each consider two options in choosing their effort levels. One is to follow the strategy of *always* shirking every period. The other strategy, known as tit-for-tat, is to work hard the first period and thereafter mimic the other player's previous choice. For instance, if Jack works hard in the first period and Jean shirks, Jack will shirk in the second period. If one person shirks in the first period, then in all future periods both people shirk (the person who selects to shirk in the first period has chosen the strategy of *always* shirking). The payoff on the lower left in each cell is Jean's payoff, while the payoff on the upper right is Jack's. In a given work period, there is a probability, p, that they will work together in the next period. In this example, the probability of working together in the future is relatively high (3/4). Two Nash equilibria exist. One is mutual shirking; the other is mutual tit-for-tat (both cells are shaded).

The existence of multiple equilibria when p = 3/4 suggests that Jack and Jean's initial expectations are important. For instance, if Jack expects Jean to shirk, he will shirk as well. However, if he expects her to choose tit-for-tat, it makes sense for him to select the same strategy. Jean has similar incentives. Thus, the efficient outcome (for both to work) will occur when there is a mutual expectation that both will work hard. This example suggests that businesses might promote cooperation by fostering particular expectations among employees. For instance, suppose the company publicizes in a credible manner that its employees have a long record of mutual cooperation. Given this "corporate culture," it is reasonable for Jack to expect that Jean will select tit-for-tat. Jean will have similar expectations. Both will select tit-for-tat, and the corporate culture is reinforced.

We have shown that the expected length of the relationship is important in determining the level of cooperation. So are the expected payoffs. For instance, if the payoffs from mutual shirking are increased to $1,500, the probability of working together in the next period must be 2/3 to promote cooperation. Alternatively, if the payoffs from mutual cooperation are $2,500, the probability falls to 1/3. These examples illustrate the general principles, stated in the text, that reputational concerns will work best at resolving incentive problems when the short-term gains from cheating are small and when the gains from continued cooperation are large.

Another factor that is important is the likelihood of being caught shirking. In this example, shirking is observed perfectly before the subsequent period. If Jack and Jean do not know for certain that the other person has shirked, they might continue to cooperate even if the other person has shirked. In this case, the temptation to shirk will be greater.

Managerial Implications

Recently, managers have delegated more work assignments to teams. Free-rider problems can reduce team output and firm value. Managers can limit free-riding and promote cooperation among team members by structuring rewards (for example, bonuses) that are high if the team members cooperate and low if they do not. Also, managers must be careful not to change the composition of teams too frequently—free-riding is a larger problem when team members do not expect to work together in the future.

Appendix Problem

The BQM Company frequently restructures. Employees regularly are transferred among departments and given different job assignments. The management argues that this action promotes a better trained and responsive work force. Do you see any potential problems with this type of frequent restructuring? Does this mean that BQM is making a mistake? Explain.

Suggested Readings

O. Hart (1989), "An Economist's Perspective on the Theory of the Firm," *Columbia Law Review* 89, 1757–1774.

M. Jensen and W. Meckling (1976), "Theory of the Firm: Managerial Behavior, Agency Costs and Ownership Structure," *Journal of Financial Economics* 3, 305–360. Pay particular attention to the first 11 pages.

M. Jensen and C. Smith (1985), "Stockholder, Manager, and Creditor Interests: Applications of Agency Theory," in *Recent Advances in Corporate Finance,* E. Altman and M. Subrahmanyam, eds. (Richard D. Irwin: Burr Ridge, IL), 93–131.

J. McMillian (1992) *Games, Strategies, and Managers* (Oxford University Press: New York).

G. Miller (1992) *Managerial Dilemmas: The Political Economy of Hierachy* (Cambridge University Press: Cambridge).

Review Questions

7–1. What is a firm?

7–2. Give examples of incentive conflicts:

    a. Between shareholders and managers.

    b. Between co-workers on teams.

7–3. What is asymmetric information? How can it limit contracts from solving incentive conflicts?

7–4. Name the two parties involved in an agency relationship.

7–5. What potential problems exist in agency relationships?

7–6. Is it worthwhile for shareholders to seek to completely eliminate agency problems with managers and directors through means such as monitoring? Why or why not?

7–7. What is *adverse selection?* Give an example.

7–8. How do reputational concerns aid in the enforcement of contracts?

7–9. Schmidt Brewing Company is family owned and operated. The family wants to raise some capital by selling 30 percent of the common stock to outside shareholders. The company has been profitable and the family indicates that it expects to pay high dividends to shareholders. The family will maintain 70 percent ownership of the common stock and continue to manage the firm. The rights of shareholders are specified in the company's corporate charter. The charter specifies such items as voting rights (procedures and items subject to a vote), meeting requirements, board size, rights to cash flows, and so on. Once adopted, a charter can only be changed by a vote of the shareholders. What types of provisions in the corporate charter of Schmidt Brewing might motivate minority shareholders to pay higher prices for the stock? Explain.

7–10. Which of the following examples is an adverse-selection problem and which is an agency problem? Explain why. In each case, give one method that the restaurant might use to reduce the problem.

a. A restaurant decides to offer an all-you-can-eat buffet that is sold for a fixed price. The restaurant discovers that the customers for this buffet are not its usual clientele. Instead, the customers tend to have big appetites. The restaurant loses money on the buffet.

b. A restaurant owner hires a manager who promises to work long hours. When the owner is out of town the manager goes home early. This action results in lost profits for the firm.

7–11. Sears Auto Centers recently indicated that they are planning to reinstate commissions for salespeople. They even plan on paying commissions for selling customers brake jobs and wheel alignments. These two products were the core of the 1992 scandal (see Chapter 2). Sears says that it has taken steps to prevent a reoccurrence of past problems. In particular, the decision right to recommend repairs is granted to mechanics who are paid a straight salary. Sales consultants are paid commissions for selling repair services but are not authorized to recommend repairs. Under the old system that caused problems, these individuals diagnosed repair problems and sold the corresponding service to customers. Why do you think Sears wants to reinstall commissions for its salespeople? Do you think that the new safeguard that separates diagnosing problems from selling services will prevent a reoccurrence of past problems? Explain.

7–12. The Sonjan company currently purchases health insurance for all of its 1,000 employees. The company is considering adopting a flexible plan where employees either can have $2,000 in cash or purchase an insurance policy (which currently costs $1,000). Do you see any potential problems with the new plan? Explain.

Part 2

Designing Organizational Architecture

chapter 8

Organizational Architecture

CHAPTER OUTLINE

I n 1984, ITT Corporation was the largest manufacturer of telecommunications equipment in the world, operating in over 80 different countries. It was also broadly diversified, with operations in industrial and consumer products, insurance, automotive parts, telephone service, natural resources, food processing, and utilities. ITT, however, faced a variety of market pressures that made 1984 an especially poor year. To quote *Moody's Handbook of Common Stocks* (Winter 1984–85):

> *ITT's telecommunications operations continued to suffer from soft market conditions in the U.S., a personal computer glut and competitive pricing. European operations are being hurt by the strength of the U.S. dollar.*

In 1984, earnings at ITT were only $2.97 per share, compared to $4.50 a year earlier. Dividends were cut by nearly $1.00 per share. ITT was rumored to be a potential target for a takeover.

Part of ITT's problem was that it had become too large, too diversified, too unfocused. Decision making in the organization was highly formalized and bureaucratic. This system made it difficult for ITT to respond rapidly to changing customer demands and competitive pressures. The inability to act quickly was especially problematic given the dramatic changes occurring in telecommunications and computers.

ITT responded by announcing that it planned to sell over $2 billion in assets in order to focus on its core strengths and major lines of business. As one example of this "asset redeployment program," ITT sold O. M. Scott & Sons Company in a divisional leveraged buyout in December 1986.[1] Scott, the largest producer of lawn care products in the United States, was originally acquired by ITT in 1971.

The buyout was accompanied by organizational changes at Scott that were designed to enhance performance. These changes involved three important aspects of the organization, that we refer to as the firm's *organizational architecture:*[2]

- The assignment of decision rights within the firm.
- The methods of rewarding individuals.
- The structure of systems to evaluate the performance of both individuals and business units.

After the buyout, managers at Scott were given substantial authority to make and implement decisions. As part of ITT, these managers often had to seek approval from executives at a number of levels at ITT headquarters, and approval was frequently denied. To motivate value-enhancing decisions, coverage under the bonus plan was expanded to include additional managers. Payouts for exceeding performance targets were increased substantially from the old plan. For example, average bonuses as a percent of salary for the top 10 managers increased from 13 percent in the two years before the buyout, to 52 percent in the two years after. In addition, employees had substantial financial interests in the firm through

[1]Details of this example are from G. Baker and K. Wruck (1989), "Organizational Changes and Value in Leveraged Buyouts: The Case of the O. M. Scott & Sons Company," *Journal of Financial Economics* 25:2, 163–190.

[2]We thank M. Jensen and W. Meckling for impressing on us the importance of these three features of organizations. See M. Jensen (1983), "Organization Theory and Methodology," *The Accounting Review* 58, 319–339; and M. Jensen and W. Meckling (1995), "Specific and General Knowledge, and Organizational Structure," *Journal of Applied Corporate Finance* 8:2, 4–18. The importance of these three features is also stressed by other authors in economics and management; for instance: P. Milgrom and J. Roberts (1992), *Economics, Organization & Management* (Prentice Hall: Englewood Cliffs, NJ); and D. Robey (1991), *Designing Organizations* (Richard D. Irwin: Burr Ridge, IL).

stock ownership. Before the buyout, employees had owned virtually no stock in the company; after the buyout, employees owned 17 percent of Scott's equity. Correspondingly, the performance-evaluation system was changed to place a heavy emphasis on financial performance, with specific targets for corporate, divisional, and individual performance.

These changes in the organization at Scott were accompanied by a dramatic increase in operating performance. In the two-year period following the buyout, earnings before interest and taxes increased by 56 percent and sales increased by 25 percent. These increases were not caused by a reduction in either R&D expenditures or expenditures on marketing and distribution. Expenditures in both categories increased, as did spending on capital projects. In addition, there were no major layoffs of employees, although employment was reduced from 868 to 792 over the period. One likely explanation for the improved performance is that the changes in Scott's architecture provided managers with decision rights and incentives to implement value-increasing decisions.

The example of O. M. Scott illustrates that organizational architecture is an important determinant of the success or failure of firms. The purpose of this chapter is to introduce the concept of organizational architecture and to provide a broad overview of the factors that are likely to be important in designing the optimal architecture for a particular organization. The next six chapters contain a more in-depth discussion of each of the three components of organizational architecture.

Understanding organizational architecture provides managers with powerful tools for affecting firm performance. As we will see, however, managers must be careful and thoughtful in their use of these tools or the results can be counterproductive. This book presents material designed to help managers be more effective users of these tools.

We begin by discussing the fundamental problem facing firms and markets. We then examine how organizational architecture can help solve this problem.[3]

The Fundamental Problem

The primary goal of any economic system is to produce the output customers want at the lowest cost possible. The challenge of discovering customer demands while reducing costs, both for economic systems and *within* individual firms, is complicated by the fact that important information for economic decision making is generally held by many different individuals. Furthermore, this information is often expensive to transfer (that is, the information is *specific* as opposed to *general*). For example, a scientist is likely to know more about the potential of a specific research project than executives higher up in the firm. Similarly, individual machine operators may know more about how to use their particular machines than their supervisors. In both cases, communicating such information to headquarters for approval is likely to be cumbersome, resulting in many lost opportunities.

A second complication is that decision makers might not have appropriate incentives to make more effective decisions even if they have the relevant information. As discussed in Chapter 7, there are *agency problems*. For example, a scientist might want to complete a research project out of scholarly interest even if convinced the project is unprofitable. Similarly, machine operators might not want to use machines efficiently if this means additional work for them.

---

[3]The material in the first part of this chapter draws on the analysis in M. Jensen and W. Meckling (1992), "Specific and General Knowledge, and Organizational Structure," *Journal of Applied Corporate Finance* 8:2, 4–18.

In sum, the principle challenge in designing both firms and economic systems is to maximize the likelihood that decision makers have (1) the relevant information to make good decisions and (2) the incentives to use the information productively.

There are many alternative ways to organize economic activity to try to achieve these objectives. Economic transactions can occur within markets or firms. Firms can be organized as corporations, partnerships, or sole proprietorships. In each case, there are many different possible organizational architectures. All these alternatives involve costs as well as benefits. As we have discussed in previous chapters, individuals have incentives to select value-maximizing forms of organization. By maximizing the "size of the pie," there is more to share among the parties to the transaction. To achieve this objective, it is important to have a detailed understanding of the architectures of both markets and firms.

Architecture in Markets

The price system helps solve information and incentive problems in markets. In market economies, individuals have private property rights. If Sue Koerner owns a building, she decides how it will be used. If someone else knows how to make better use of the building, Sue can sell it and keep the proceeds. She has strong incentives to use the building productively because she bears the wealth effects.

Hence, the market provides an architecture that promotes efficient resource use. First, through market transactions, decision rights for resources are rearranged so that they tend to be held by individuals with the relevant specific knowledge for using the resources most productively. Individuals with the relevant specific knowledge will profit the most by owning the resources and thus are likely to be willing to pay a higher price to own them. Second, the market provides a mechanism for evaluating and rewarding the performance of resource owners—owners bear the wealth effects of their actions. This mechanism generates important incentives to take efficient actions. A valuable feature of the price system in a market economy is that this architecture is created spontaneously, with little conscious thought or human direction.

Spontaneous Creation of Markets: Evidence from Prisoner-of-War Camps

One interesting feature of markets is how they often arise with limited human direction. As an example, economist R. A. Radford studied economic activity inside prisoner-of-war camps during World War II. In these camps, prisoners obtained rations from the Red Cross consisting of food, cigarettes, and other items. Of course, not all prisoners valued individual items the same. The English preferred drinking tea to coffee, while French prisoners preferred coffee to tea. Some prisoners smoked heavily, while others were nonsmokers. Potential gains from trade quickly motivated exchanging among prisoners. Before long, an organized market developed. Cigarettes became the common currency. Prisoners quoted prices for goods in terms of the number of cigarettes. The price of individual items depended on supply and demand. For example, the price of chocolate would drop dramatically if a new Red Cross shipment substantially increased supply. The markets at the prisoner-of-war camps were quite active and emerged without a central planner saying "let's create a market." The welfare of the prisoners was significantly enhanced by the presence of these markets (although they benefited significantly more when they were set free!).

Source: R. Radford (1945), "The Economic Organization of a P.O.W. Camp," *Economica* 12, 189–201.

Architecture in Firms

Within firms, there are no automatic systems either for assigning decision rights to individuals with information or motivating individuals to use information to promote firm objectives. The organizational architecture is created by executives through the implicit and explicit contracts that comprise the firm (see Chapter 7). For instance, decision rights are granted to employees through formal and informal job descriptions, while performance evaluations and rewards are specified in formal and informal compensation contracts. At both ITT and O. M. Scott, the architectures were designed and implemented by senior management.

Decision Rights

Although transfer prices are used to allocate resources in some firms, most resources are allocated by administrative decisions.[4] For example, the CEO of a company typically transfers a manager from one division of the company to another by a simple command. Similarly, the utilization of a plant can be changed by administrative order. The senior management of a firm must decide how to assign the decision rights among employees.[5] For instance, does the CEO make most major decisions, or are these decisions delegated to lower-level managers? Can machine operators deviate from procedures outlined in company manuals?

Controls

Through the delegation of decision rights, employees are granted authority over the use of company resources. Employees, however, are not owners—they cannot sell company property and keep the proceeds. Therefore, employees have fewer incentives to worry about the efficient use of company resources than the owners. To help control these agency problems, managers must develop a *control system.* That is, managers must structure the other two basic pieces of the organization's architecture, the reward and performance-evaluation systems that help to align the interests of the decision makers with those of the owners. As we discuss below, the optimal control system depends on how decision rights are partitioned in the firm, and vice versa.

Tradeoffs

Once the firm grows beyond a certain size, the CEO is unlikely to have the relevant information for all major decisions. Consequently, the CEO faces three basic alternatives in designing the organizational architecture. First, the CEO can make most major decisions, despite lacking relevant information. In this case, there are limited agency problems and the development of a detailed control system is less critical.[6] However, the

---

[4]In Chapter 14, we discuss the economics of transfer pricing.

[5]In small firms, senior management and owners are often the same. In large firms, owners (the shareholders) delegate most decision rights to the board of directors and the CEO. These parties are charged with developing the architecture for the firm. In this chapter, we treat senior managers and owners as the same. In subsequent chapters, we expand our analysis to discuss potential agency problems between senior management and owners.

[6]The manager still has an agency problem in motivating lower-level employees to follow detailed instructions. However, this agency problem is likely to be less severe than when the manager gives the lower-level employees considerable discretion in making decisions.

Organizational Architecture at Century 21

Century 21 International is the largest real estate firm in the world, accounting for 10 percent of all U.S. residential real estate transactions in 1990. Century 21 operates throughout the United States and in 10 other countries, including Japan, the United Kingdom, and France. In 1990, Century 21 brokers and sales associates assisted over 800,000 families in buying or selling properties, translating into an estimated $80 billion in real estate worldwide and approximately $2.2 billion in commissions.

Given the geographic and cultural diversity facing Century 21, it would not be productive for the U.S. headquarters to make all major decisions. Such centralized decision making would be especially problematic for the international operations, where laws and cultures may be far different than in the United States. To quote Century 21's management:

> We provide the international regions with whatever knowledge we possess on how they can help their franchisees develop better offices. What they use is basically up to them and will reflect their housing market and real estate traditions. We allow our master subfranchisors a great deal of flexibility in running their regions, and internationally we want them to be able to accommodate their services to their culture. We are not going overseas with our system and saying, "This is the way it is, you can't change it." We wouldn't get very far that way. There has to be some flexibility.

Decentralized decision making, however, requires a control system that promotes productive effort. At Century 21, most of the local operators are franchisees. Franchisees are essentially owners of their units and keep a large share of their units' profits. This ownership provides strong incentives to increase sales and value. Also, Century 21 reserves the right to terminate individual franchises that fail to maintain acceptable levels of service.

Source: C. Shook and R. Shook (1993), *Franchising: The Business Strategy that Changed the World* (Prentice Hall: Engelwood Cliffs, NJ).

CEO is likely to make suboptimal decisions. Second, the CEO can attempt to acquire the relevant information to make better decisions. This option can enhance decision making. Yet obtaining and processing the relevant information can be very costly and time-consuming. Third, the CEO can decentralize decision rights to individuals with better information. This choice assigns decision-making authority to employees with the relevant information. But delegating decision rights gives rise to increased agency problems, which means that control systems must be developed. Another potential drawback of decentralization is the cost of transferring information from the CEO to other decision makers in coordinating efforts throughout the firm.

Of course, CEOs can choose a mix of these basic alternatives. For example, senior managers are likely to choose to retain some decisions while delegating others. The optimal choice, as we discuss below, depends primarily on the business environment and strategy of the firm. In some cases—especially in smaller firms in relatively stable industries—senior managers are likely to have most of the relevant information for decision making, and thus decision rights are more likely to be centralized at headquarters. In other cases—especially larger firms experiencing rapid change—senior managers and their corporate staff often will not be in the best position to make many decisions. And, in such cases, decision rights are more likely to be decentralized, with corresponding control systems put in place.

This discussion indicates that the CEO plays a major role in framing the basic architecture for the firm. Organizational decisions, however, are made by managers throughout the firm. For example, when the CEO delegates a set of decision rights to middle-level managers, these managers must decide what decisions to make themselves and what decisions will be delegated to lower-level managers. These lower-level managers are then faced with similar organizational questions. The overall architecture of a firm is determined through this process, ultimately involving managers throughout the firm.

Architectural Determinants

As suggested above, the optimal architecture will be different for different companies. Such structural differences are not random but vary in *systematic* ways with differences in certain underlying characteristics of the companies themselves. To illustrate the point, companies operating in the same industry tend to develop similar architectures. If an important aspect of an industry's environment changes, most companies in that industry will react by readjusting their decision rights and internal control systems.

In Figure 8.1, we summarize those factors that are likely to be most important in designing the optimal architecture for a given firm. At the top of the figure are three aspects of the firm's *external* business environment: *technology, markets, and regulation.* For any firm, these three factors—(1) the technology that affects its products, its methods of production, and its information systems, (2) the structure of its markets (competitors, customers, and suppliers), and (3) the regulatory constraints on its activities—are likely to have the greatest influence on the *business strategy.* By business strategy, we mean the answers to a broad set of questions: What are the firm's primary goals—nonfinancial, as well as financial? What products and services is it providing, and to what customers? And what are the firm's sources of comparative advantage in so doing?

Take the case of AT&T in the early 1980s, before it was broken up into regional operating companies called the Baby Bells. Regulation dictated many aspects of the firm's business strategy—what services it could offer, what customers it could serve, and how much it could charge them. After the breakup of AT&T and the deregulation of the telecommunications industry, both the Baby Bells and the new AT&T were forced to devise new strategies to provide new products, serve new customer bases, and develop new pricing structures.

As shown in Figure 8.1, the ultimate goals of the firm, as reflected in its business strategy, in turn affect its optimal organizational architecture. As the celebrated architect Louis H. Sullivan once observed, "Form ever follows function." Applying the same principle to industry, we see that significant changes in corporate business strategies typically call for major changes in decision-making authority, performance measures for evaluating employees, and incentive-compensation systems.[7]

Returning to our telecommunications example, in the early 1980s, a regulated AT&T faced little competition or pressure for technological innovation. It operated in a reasonably stable environment—one where it made sense for a huge formal bureaucracy to make most important decisions from the top down. Since the breakup of the company, however, the telecommunications industry has experienced almost continuous upheaval, with deregulation, increased competition, and rapid technological change. And, in 1992, after a nearly decade-long series of incremental moves toward decentralization, AT&T established a large number of fairly autonomous profit centers run by managers on pay-for-performance plans tied to their units. In 1995, AT&T broke itself into three separate publicly traded companies and laid off 40,000 employees.

As another example, consider the case of increased foreign competition in the 1980s and 1990s. For years, many large American Companies (for example, ITT, IBM, General Motors, Eastman Kodak, and Xerox) faced limited competition in their product

---

[7]While we emphasize the effects of strategy on architecture, the effects are not all in one direction (note the two-headed arrows). Business strategy also can be influenced by organizational architecture. For instance, a company might decide to enter a new market because its decision and control systems are especially well-suited for this new undertaking.

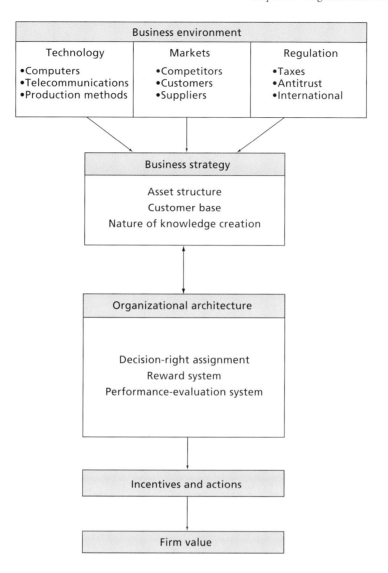

Figure 8.1   The Determinants of Business Strategy, Organizational Architecture, and Firm Value

Market conditions, technology, and government regulation are important determinants of business strategy, which in turn help to determine organizational architecture. Two-way arrows are drawn because there are important feedback effects. Both business strategy and architecture affect the incentives and actions of agents within the firm and thus help to determine firm value.

markets. Many of these companies had substantial market power and had little external impetus to focus on rapid product development, high-quality production, or competitive pricing. Their organizations were highly bureaucratic, with very centralized decision making and limited incentive compensation. Many of these firms experienced a dramatic increase in foreign competition over the past decade (especially from the Japanese). This competition forced these large firms to rethink their basic strategies and increase their emphasis on quality, customer service, and competitive pricing. To accomplish

---

Changing Organizational Architecture at JCPenney

Purchasing decisions at JCPenney used to be relatively centralized. Buyers in New York would decide on the company's clothing lines for the year. Unfortunately, this procedure did not incorporate much of the relevant specific information about what products would sell best at particular stores in different parts of the country. In the 1980s, Penney's invested in satellite communications that provided the firm with closed circuit television. This technology allowed central buyers in New York to display goods to local store managers, who could stock their stores based on their specific knowledge of local tastes and fashions. This type of decentralized decision making was feasible because of the new communications technology.

Source: H. Gilman (1987), "J. C. Penney Decentralizes Its Purchasing:
Individual Stores Can Tailor Buying to Needs," *The Wall Street Journal*
(May 8).

---

these objectives, firms often had to change their architectures. They frequently pushed decision rights lower in the organization, where specific knowledge about customer demands was located (recall the example of O. M. Scott). They also increased their use of incentive compensation and developed performance-evaluation systems that focused on quality and customer service.

In some ways, Figure 8.1 provides an overly simplistic view of the determinants of strategy, architecture, and firm value. The figure admittedly ignores potential feedback effects among the environment, business strategy, and architecture. Consider, for example, how Microsoft invests resources to develop software that, in turn, alters the basic technology facing the firm. Large firms also often have political power that can be used to influence government regulation. While these types of feedback effects can at times be important, in most circumstances managers must take the business environment essentially as given. This environment, in turn, largely determines what the firm can expect to accomplish (its business strategy) and its architecture. Figure 8.1 provides managers with a structured way of thinking about the factors that are likely to affect their firm's architecture. We use this structure throughout the book for analyzing organizational decisions.

Changing Architecture

As we have seen, changes in market conditions, technology, or government regulation can affect appropriate organizational design. But organizational change is by no means a costless process. It is important to assess the costs as well as the benefits in evaluating the merits of an organizational restructuring.

Changing the Organization Too Frequently: Not a New Phenomenon

We trained hard, but it seemed that every time we were beginning to form into teams we would be reorganized. I was to learn later in life that we tend to meet any new situation by reorganizing, and what a wonderful method it can be for creating the illusion of progress while producing confusion, inefficiency, and demoralization.

Petronius Arbiter, 210 B.C.

Changing Organizational Architecture Requires Careful Analysis

At any point in time, there are a set of prominent management techniques that are touted as the key to success. Popular techniques in the 1990s include reengineering, benchmarking, total quality management, broadbanding, worker empowerment, the learning organization, and skill-based pay. Most of these techniques involve fundamental changes in organizational architecture. For example, advocates of total quality management commonly recommend delegating decision rights to teams and not paying incentive compensation based on individual performance.

Adopting the most recent business trend or fad can get a firm in trouble unless the change is warranted by the actual circumstances facing the firm. Unfortunately, many firms appear to adopt changes without careful analysis of the relevant costs and benefits. To quote *The Wall Street Journal,* "Many companies try management fads, only to see them flop."* In fact, surveys indicate that a majority of companies are dissatisfied with the results of organizational changes.

Managers should not change the organization simply because it is the current fad. Certainly, some organizational changes can enhance value. However, managers should carefully consider whether the benefits of a change are larger than the costs, given their particular circumstances.

The Wall Street Journal (July 6, 1993).

First, there are direct costs. The new architecture has to be designed and communicated to employees throughout the company. Moreover, changes in architecture frequently require costly changes in the firm's accounting and information systems. Often, what appears to be a straightforward change in the performance-evaluation system is a major and costly project for the firm's data processing and accounting departments. Literally hundreds of computer programs might have to be changed to alter the accounting and information systems.

Second, and perhaps more important, are indirect costs. Changes in architecture are likely to affect some employees positively (for example, by increasing their responsibility and possibilities for rewards) and other employees negatively. Thus, the attitudes toward change are likely to vary among employees. Dealing with the associated agency problems of implementing change in a firm can be expensive (see Chapter 16). In addition, frequent changes in architecture can have undesirable incentive effects. Increasing the likelihood that workers will change assignments in the near future reduces their incentives to invest in learning new job assignments, devising more efficient production processes, and developing relations with co-workers. Frequent restructuring within a firm causes uncertainty about job assignments and will promote actions that focus more on short-run payoffs and less on long-run investments (see Chapter 7).

Interdependencies in the Organization

It is important to understand that the components of organizational architecture are highly interdependent. The appropriate control system depends on the allocation of decision rights, and vice versa. For example, if decision rights are decentralized, it is important to have a control system that provides incentives for employees to make value-enhancing decisions. Reward and performance-evaluation systems have to be developed that compensate the worker based on performance outcomes. Similarly, if a firm adopts a compensation plan to motivate employees, it is important to grant employees decision rights so that they can act on these incentives. In this sense, the components of organizational architecture are like *three legs of a stool.* It is important that all three legs be designed so that

When the Legs of the Stool Don't Balance

Hammer and Champy give an example of a major airline company where the three legs of the stool did not match. In this example, a plane was grounded for repairs at a given airport. The nearest qualified mechanic was stationed at another airport. The decision right to allow the mechanic to work on the airplane was held by the manager of the second airport. The manager's compensation was tied to meeting his own budget rather than to the profits of the overall organization. The manager refused to send the mechanic to fix the plane immediately because the mechanic would have had to stay overnight at a hotel and the hotel bill would have been charged to the manager's budget. The mechanic was dispatched the next morning so that he could return the same day. A multimillion dollar aircraft was grounded, costing the company thousands of dollars. The manager, however, avoided a $100 hotel bill. Presumably, the mechanic would have been dispatched immediately had the manager been rewarded on the overall profit of the company or, alternatively, if the decision right had been held by someone else with this objective.

Source: M. Hammer and J. Champy (1993), *Reengineering the Corporation*
(Harper Business: New York).

the stool is level. Changing one leg without careful consideration of the other two is typically a mistake. For example, it is unlikely that O. M. Scott would have been as successful after the buyout if managerial decision rights had been changed without accompanying changes in the firm's compensation plan.

Organizational architecture involves a number of interrelated policies and systems within the firm. For example, incentive-compensation schemes for lower-level managers are often based on accounting performance for their particular units. Changing the unit structure and associated compensation schemes can therefore require changes in the firm's accounting system. Similarly, it might be effective to pay the manager of a subsidiary based on the stock market performance of the subsidiary. But, for this policy to be implemented, the subsidiary must be publicly traded. Thus, there can be interdependencies between the organizational architecture and the firm's financing policies. As another example, consider the design of the firm's organizational architecture and its computer/information systems. New computer programs provide expert systems that allow low-skilled workers to complete complicated tax returns, assess the qualifications of mortgage applicants, and perform other tasks that previously required extensive training. These programs have allowed financial-services companies to decentralize additional decision rights to lower-level employees. For example, lower-level employees now have the rights to approve mortgage applications without supervisor approval if the computer program indicates that the applicant is qualified.

Corporate Culture

Corporate culture is one of the more frequently used terms in the literature on organizations. Corporate culture usually encompasses the ways work and authority are organized, the ways people are rewarded and controlled, as well as organizational features such as customs, taboos, company slogans, heroes, and social rituals. Managers are encouraged to develop high-powered, productive cultures. However, little concrete guidance is provided on how to accomplish this goal.

Our focus on organizational architecture is consistent with the concept of a corporate culture. Indeed, our definition of organizational architecture corresponds to key aspects of what is frequently defined as corporate culture. For example, the architecture specifies how authority (decision rights) is distributed among workers and how rewards are determined. The advantage of this approach is that it defines the key components of a firm's corporate culture and analyzes how managers might affect culture by conscious action.

As an example, recall our discussion of Sears Auto Centers in Chapter 2. The old corporate culture at Sears Auto Centers could be characterized as an environment where dishonest salespeople regularly misled customers. After the scandal became public, Sears had to find a way to change this corporate culture. This approach provides direct guidance on how this change might be accomplished—in this case, by changing the compensation scheme.

Some dismiss the "softer" elements of corporate culture (for example, role models, company folklore, and rituals) as being unimportant. Rather, they stress formal architecture as being the primary, if not sole, determinant of firm value.[8] Economics, however, suggests at least two important roles for these elements of corporate culture: communication and helping to set employee expectations.

Corporate Culture and Communication

Most organizations do not write down all the features of their organizations in detailed procedures manuals. Rather, the features are communicated to employees in less formal and potentially less costly ways. Aspects of the corporation such as slogans, role models, and social rituals can be viewed as methods of communicating organizational architecture to workers in a low-cost fashion. A slogan like *At Ford, Quality Is Job 1* emphasizes that workers are expected to focus on quality and customer service, and that this focus will be rewarded by the company. Given this slogan and other reinforcing signals from top management, employees at Ford have a reasonably clear idea of how to respond to situations such as angry customers even without formal policies to follow. Similarly, social rituals, such as training sessions and company parties, can help to disseminate information by increasing the interaction among employees who might not see each other on a frequent basis. Singling out role models or heroes for special awards is another way of communicating what the company values.

Less tangible features of organizations, such as rituals and role models, can be important in reinforcing and communicating organizational architecture. However, they can also increase the costs of changing the culture. Managers can change formal evaluation and compensation schemes and clearly communicate these changes to the relevant employees. Getting employees to change their heroes, customs, and social rituals can be more difficult. These features are often created through informal communication channels; they take time to destroy as well as to create.

Corporate Culture and Employee Expectations

In the appendix to Chapter 7, we illustrate how the decisions of employees to exert effort and to cooperate with other employees can depend on their expectations about how other individuals will behave. In this example, employees work hard only if they think that other employees will work hard as well. Expectations of how other individuals will behave are shaped, in part, by the formal architecture of the firm. If Bruce Scott observes that Chris

---

[8]For instance, managers that subscribe to the teachings of Frederick Taylor believe that the design of work processes and incentive systems are the primary determinants of firm value. F. Taylor (1923), *The Principles of Scientific Management* (Harper & Row: New York).

Corporate Culture at Mary Kay Cosmetics

Total sales at Mary Kay Cosmetics increased from about $198,000 in 1963 to over $613 million in 1993. Mary Kay has built a sales force of 300,000 and has helped to create 74 millionaires (women who have earned commissions of $1 million or more over their careers). A typical sales director earns about $35,000 year, while a national sales director averages about $200,000.

The organizational structure at Mary Kay focuses directly on sales. All sales consultants purchase products directly from Dallas at the same price. Rewards are based solely on sales and recruiting additional sales consultants. There is no cap on what sales consultants earn. As sales and the recruiting of consultants rise, so do commissions. Past resumes and credentials are unimportant—"You say you were a brain surgeon in your last job? Fine. Get a beauty case and start dialing."

What is interesting about Mary Kay is how many features of the firm's culture reinforce each other in a consistent manner. Stories of role models are prevalent throughout the organization. Almost every employee knows the story of Mary Kay Ash, who started out as a young salesperson for Stanley Home Products. She was so poor that she had to borrow $12 to travel from her Houston home to Stanley's 1937 convention in Dallas. Through hard work, she built the Mary Kay Cosmetic Company and amassed a family fortune of over $300 million. Stories of other successful sales consultants permeate the organization. These stories reinforce the architecture and help motivate hard work and increased sales. The company is also famous for lavishly rewarding its successful sales consultants in a very public manner. The annual sales meeting is an extravaganza where individuals are rewarded with complementary pink Cadillacs, jewelry, color-coded suits, badges, emblems, and being crowned as "queens."

The message at Mary Kay is clear. Success is measured by sales and recruiting efforts. Do these things well and you will be rewarded, both financially and through public recognition. This message is consistently communicated through compensation plans, stories of role models, company rituals, and ceremonies.

Source: A. Farnham (1993), "Mary Kay's Lessons in Leadership," *Fortune* (September 20).

Heath is paid a commission on sales, it is reasonable for Bruce to forecast that Chris will exert some effort in trying to increase sales. Expectations, however, are also affected by the less formal aspects of corporate culture. For example, Microsoft has developed a reputation for hiring creative, hard-working individuals. If two Microsoft employees are placed together on a team, it is reasonable for both to expect that the other person is smart and hard working. This analysis suggests that it can be beneficial for managers to use both the formal architecture and other aspects of corporate culture to foster expectations that promote productive choices by employees. For instance, suppose that employees are most likely to focus on quality if they think other employees have the same focus. A manager interested in increasing manufacturing quality might supplement changes in the formal evaluation and reward systems with new slogans, executive speeches, employee relations campaigns, and clever use of the media, all aimed at creating a "quality-centered" culture.

A System of Complements

Features of organizations like rituals and role models can be effective in reinforcing and communicating the goals of the firm, and they have the potential to provide important aspects of a coherent architecture. Their effectiveness in certain cases has led some management experts to claim that a productive corporate culture can be molded without paying *any* attention to formal evaluation and compensation schemes. Some people (for example, quality guru W. Edwards Deming) argue that incentive pay is actually detrimental to a productive organization. Our analysis suggests that it is a mistake to think of these hard and soft aspects of the organization as mutually exclusive or in competition with each other; both can play a valuable role in increasing firm value. The various elements of the organization are more likely to be *complements* than substitutes. In Chapter

16, we present a detailed discussion of Xerox's early efforts to increase product and service quality. The CEO, David Kearns, initially focused on softer elements (slogans, speeches, and media campaigns) to foster a quality culture at Xerox. He soon realized that to be effective, he also had to change the formal evaluation and reward systems.

When an Architecture Fails

Sometimes, managers are either unable or unwilling to design value-increasing architectures or business strategies. Consider the management at RJR-Nabisco in the late 1988s, as highlighted in Chapter 7. In cases such as RJR-Nabisco, value can be created by replacing the existing management with new managers who are willing and able to choose architectures and strategies that increase value.

Firing the Manager

In public corporations, the board of directors has the decision rights to hire, fire, and compensate senior managers. Evidence indicates that boards are most likely to fire managers when firm performance is poor (as measured by stock returns and accounting earnings).[9] Consider Eastman Kodak in 1993. The company was performing poorly, and the senior managers acknowledged that a poorly designed architecture was among the company's most significant problems. The managers, however, were unable to design a better one. The board of directors fired the CEO and hired a new one. The new CEO rapidly changed both the architecture and the strategy of the company. The stock market greeted these actions with a large increase in the stock price of Kodak. At the end of this chapter, we present an expanded case study of this example.

While firing the CEO is a relatively rare event, firings at other management levels are more common. When middle managers perform poorly by selecting bad strategies and architectures for their business units, they can be fired or reassigned by senior managers. Middle managers, in turn, have decision rights to replace lower-level managers.

Market for Corporate Control

Another mechanism for replacing poor management is the market for corporate control (for example, tender offers and mergers). During the last few decades, the wealth of shareholders has increased billions of dollars due to corporate takeovers. Typically, when a poorly performing company is acquired by another company, its management is replaced.[10] The architecture and strategy are also frequently changed. ITT's poor performance in 1988 motivated takeover speculation. However, the existing management took actions to increase firm value and the takeover did not materialize. In contrast, the former management team at RJR-Nabisco did not make the necessary changes to increase

[9]J. Warner, R. Watts, and K. Wruck (1988), "Stock Prices and Top Management Changes," *Journal of Financial Economics* 20, 461–492; and M. Weisbach (1988), "Outside Directors and CEO Turnover, "*Journal of Financial Economics* 20, 431–460.

[10]For a summary of the evidence on corporate takeovers, see G. Jarrell, J. Brickley, and J. Netter (1988), "The Market for Corporate Control: The Empirical Evidence Since 1980," *Journal of Economic Perspectives* 2, 49–68. For evidence on management turnover after takeovers, see K. J. Martin and J. J. McConnell (1991), "Corporate Performance, Corporate Takeovers, and Management Turnover," *Journal of Finance* 46, 671–688.

firm value, and the company was acquired by Kohlberg, Kravis, Roberts & Company (KKR). KKR subsequently replaced the management team and implemented significant changes in RJR's architecture and strategy.

Product Market Competition

When all else fails, inefficient firms eventually go out of business. In Chapter 6, we discuss how competitive pressures tend to drive prices toward marginal cost. If a firm is inefficient and cannot cover its costs at these prices, it eventually has to shut down. As discussed in Chapter 1, this competitive process resembles the natural selection process in biology (*the strong survive*) and is sometimes referred to as economic Darwinism. Barings Bank is a dramatic example of a firm that became insolvent due to a poorly designed architecture.

Managerial Implications

Organizational architecture presents a powerful framework for addressing management problems throughout the organization. In many cases, a problem can be directly traced to defects in organizational architecture (consider O. M. Scott and Sears Auto Centers). By using this framework, managers can respond more quickly to problems and develop more sound solutions. In analyzing business problems and cases, students and managers often find it useful to refer to Figure 8.1 and ask themselves the following set of questions:

- Does the business strategy fit the business environment (technology, market conditions, and regulation) and the capabilities of the firm?
- What are the key features of the current architecture?
- Does the current architecture fit the business environment and strategy? In particular, does the architecture link *specific knowledge* and decision rights in an effective manner and provide *incentives* to use information productively?
- Are the three legs of the stool mutually consistent? Given the decision-right system, does the control system fit, and vice versa?
- If the answers to any of the previous questions suggest a problem, what changes in strategy and architecture should the firm consider?
- What problems will the firm face in implementing these changes?

Evaluating Management Advice

In a competitive marketplace, surviving firms tend to be those firms with the best strategies and architectures, given their business environments. This principle suggests that architectures are not random. There are sound economic explanations for the existing architectures in most industries. Consultants, however, frequently argue that long-standing practices are obviously inefficient and that companies would be better off by following their advice in changing the architecture. For example, many recent books on *empowerment* argue that most firms have made mistakes over a long time period in not delegating more decision rights to lower-level employees. Correspondingly, profits would be improved by increasing

Marmots and Grizzly Bears

Business writers, consultants, and government regulators frequently claim that existing business practices are inefficient, and they propose changes that would allegedly improve productivity. The principle of economic Darwinism, however, suggests that many of these claims are likely to be misguided. In a competitive world, if organizations survive over the long run with a particular architecture, it is unlikely that there is some *obvious change* that could be implemented to increase profits. Sometimes the reasons for survival of a particular practice might not be clear to an outside observer. Existing practices, however, should not be deemed inefficient without careful analysis.

The interaction between marmots and grizzly bears serves to illustrate this point. Marmots are small groundhogs and are a principal food source for certain bears. Zoologists studying the ecology of marmots and bears observed bears digging and moving rocks in the autumn in search of marmots. They estimated that the calories expended searching for marmots exceeded the calories obtained from consuming marmots. Thus, searching for marmots appears to be an inefficient use of the bear's limited resources. Given Darwin's theory of natural selection, bears searching for marmots should become extinct. A well-meaning consultant or government regulator, therefore, might recommend that bears quit searching for marmots.

Fossils of marmot bones near bear remains, however, suggest that bears have been searching for marmots for a long time. An explanation is that searching for marmots provides benefits to bears in addition to calories. For instance, bears sharpen their claws as a by-product of the digging involved in hunting for marmots. Sharp claws are useful in searching for food under the ice after winter's hibernation. Therefore, the benefit of sharpened claws and the calories derived from marmots offset the calories consumed gathering the marmots. The moral is that in biology or business, an outside observer should be very careful in concluding that long-standing practices are inefficient without careful study.

Source: J. McGee (1980), "Predatory Pricing Revisited," *Journal of Law & Economics* 23:2, 289–330.

the empowerment of workers. While this advice clearly makes sense for some firms in some environments (especially if the environment has undergone some fundamental change that favors decentralization of decision rights), our analysis suggests that managers should not be too quick to condemn prevailing organizational forms without careful analysis. The discussion in the subsequent chapters will provide important material to help you conduct this analysis.

Benchmarking

Firms frequently *benchmark* other firms in an attempt to determine value-increasing policies. For example, a firm considering a change in its executive compensation plan is likely to collect information on the compensation plans of other firms. This practice has merit. Firms that survive in the marketplace tend to have strategies and architectures that fit their environment, and studying these firms has the potential to yield important insights. Our analysis has at least three implications for effective benchmarking. First, different architectures are appropriate for different environments. It is important to benchmark firms in similar environments. Second, since it is unusual to find firms in identical environments, it is important to understand any differences in the environments of the benchmarked firms and to take them into account when analyzing the data on firms' policy choices. Third, it is important to view the architecture of other firms as a system of complements. Studying a single feature of another firm's architecture, without considering how it fits with other elements of its architecture, can motivate erroneous conclusions.

Benchmarking the Lincoln Electric Company

Lincoln Electric company has had a long history of earning large profits. Often, this record is attributed to Lincoln's unique reward system, which places a heavy emphasis on incentive compensation (we describe this system in detail in Chapter 13). Managers from all over the world come to the Lincoln Electric headquarters at Cleveland, Ohio, to study the system. Our analysis suggests that these managers should consider Lincoln's business environment, business strategy, and other elements of organizational architecture (for instance, its decision-right system) in their benchmarking. Lincoln's success should not be attributed to its reward system alone but to how well this feature fits with its environment and overall architecture.

Interestingly, Lincoln managers made the costly mistake of ignoring these considerations themselves. During the 1980s, the management at Lincoln decided to export its incentive system internationally through a series of mergers throughout Europe, Asia, and Latin America. Unfortunately, the system did not fit the business environments at many of the new locations. For instance, the influence of unions in Germany and labor laws in Venezuela made it impossible for Lincoln to implement its system successfully. Lincoln ended up losing millions of dollars on these ventures. Lincoln might have avoided these mistakes if it had carefully applied the framework discussed in this book in its decision-making process.

Overview of Part 2

The next six chapters provide a detailed discussion of the three components of organizational architecture—the three legs of the stool. Chapters 9 and 10 analyze the assignment of decision rights. Through the assignment of decision rights, firms create jobs. Two important characteristics of jobs are the variety of the assigned tasks and the authority in making decisions on how to complete these tasks. Chapter 9 examines the issue of decision authority, while Chapter 10 focuses on the assignment of tasks.

Once jobs are created, firms must design reward systems that will attract qualified individuals. Chapter 11 analyzes the level of pay and the components of the compensation package (the mix between salary and fringe benefits). The focus in this chapter is how to design pay packages that allow firms to attract and retain qualified employees at the lowest cost. While the level of pay attracts individuals to jobs, it is generally incentive compensation that provides a primary motivation for employees to complete the assigned tasks. Chapter 12 provides a detailed analysis of incentive compensation.

Incentive plans base their payoffs on measures produced by the performance-evaluation system. Chapter 13 focuses on the performance measurement of individual employees, while Chapter 14 examines the performance measurement of subunits within the firm (for example, divisions and subsidiaries).

Summary

Organizational architecture includes three important components of organizational design that are major determinants of the success or failure of firms:

- The assignment of decision rights.
- The methods of rewarding individuals.
- The structure of systems to evaluate the performance of both individuals and business units.

The fundamental problem facing both firms and economic systems involves trying to ensure that decision makers have the relevant information to make good decisions and

CASE STUDY
Eastman Kodak

For many years, Eastman Kodak had a virtual monopoly in film production. This market power resulted in large profits. It also permitted Kodak to control the timing for introducing new products to the marketplace and responding to changes in consumer demands.

By the 1980s, Kodak's market environment had changed greatly. The Fuji Corporation produced high-quality film that eroded Kodak's market share. Increased competition also came from generic store brands. In addition, the 1980s witnessed a technological explosion. Improved communications, design capabilities, and robotics allowed companies to bring new products to market within months rather than years.

These changes in the market environment placed significant pressure on Kodak. Kodak's stock price dropped from over $85 per share in 1982 to just over $71 in 1984. This 16 percent decline in stock price appears particularly poor when it is compared to the substantial increase in stock prices for the market as a whole. Earnings per share at Kodak also dropped substantially. The company realized it had to change its organization to regain profits and market share. To quote Colby Chandler, former CEO of Kodak, at the 1984 annual meeting:

> Like many companies, we are not used to working in an environment where there is rapid technological transfer from laboratory to the marketplace. But we know that will be important in our future.

During 1984, Kodak undertook a major corporate restructuring. Prior to the restructuring, decision making at Kodak was very centralized. Top-level approval was required for most major decisions. The restructuring created 17 new business units with profit-and-loss responsibility. Business-unit managers were given increased decision-making authority for new products, pricing, and other important policy choices. By decentralizing decision rights, senior management hoped to make the company more responsive to changing customer demands and market conditions. To quote the 1984 annual report:

> In short, Kodak is finding new ways to stimulate the innovative nature of its people. The result: a spirit of independence, new ideas and a quickened pace in the process which turns new ideas into commercial realities.

Unfortunately for Kodak, changing the *assignment of decision rights* did not have a significant impact on the company's performance. In response, Kodak adopted the Management Annual Performance Plan (MAPP) in 1987. Under this plan, the base salary of management employees was reduced by 10 percent and replaced with a variable bonus. The bonus was to average 10 percent, ranging from 0 to 20 percent. Bonus payments were based on individual, unit, and company objectives.

The idea behind MAPP was that changing the *performance-evaluation and reward systems* would motivate managers to be more creative and industrious. The plan, however, did not have a large impact on managerial incentives or corporate profits. In 1993, Kodak officials were quoted as saying that (1) management had not really been held accountable for their failure to deliver results, (2) management had to develop tougher work standards and demote failing employees, and (3) that in the past, managers who advanced at Kodak had excelled in office politics but not necessarily leadership.[*] Frustrated by the continued lack of success, Kodak's board of directors fired its CEO in late 1993.

Discussion Questions

1. What factors motivated Kodak to change its organizational architecture?

2. What mistakes did Kodak make in changing its architecture?

3. What might it have done differently?

4. How does this example relate to the concept of economic Darwinism?

---

[*]*Democrat and Chronicle,* Rochester, NY, June 27, 1993.

that these decision makers have appropriate incentives to use information productively. The price system provides an architecture that helps solve this problem in markets. Through market transactions, decision rights tend to be transferred to individuals with the relevant knowledge to make productive use of the resources. The market also provides a mechanism for evaluating and rewarding the performance of resource owners—owners bear the wealth effects of their actions. A valuable feature of markets is that this architecture is created spontaneously with little conscious thought or human direction.

Markets are not always the efficient method for organizing economic activity—frequently, firms are more efficient. Within firms, there is no automatic system for either assigning decision rights to individuals with information or motivating individuals to use information to promote firm objectives. Organizational architecture has to be created. The appropriate architecture depends on the environment facing the firm. In some firms, senior management will have most of the relevant information for decision making, and relatively centralized decision making is more likely to be adopted. In firms where lower-level workers have the relevant information, decision rights are more likely to be decentralized. In this case, reward and performance-evaluation systems must be developed to control agency problems and to promote better decision making.

Market conditions, technology, and government regulation interact to determine the firm's appropriate business strategy and architecture. The business strategy and architecture, in turn, are major determinants of firm value.

Changes in the external business environment can motivate changes in the firm's organizational architecture. Changing the architecture, however, is costly. In addition to the direct costs of designing and implementing new procedures, there are potentially important indirect costs. Thus, changing architecture should be done only following careful analysis.

The components of organizational architecture are highly interdependent. They are like three legs of a stool. Changing one leg without careful consideration of the other two is usually a mistake. Organizational structure is also related to other policies and systems within a firm, including the accounting and information systems, marketing, and financial policy.

Corporate culture is a frequently used term. Corporate culture is usually meant to encompass the ways work and authority are organized and the ways people are rewarded and controlled, as well as organizational features such as customs, taboos, company slogans, heroes, and social rituals. Our focus on organizational architecture is consistent with the concept of a corporate culture. Indeed, our definition of architecture corresponds to key aspects of what is frequently defined as corporate culture. The advantage of this approach is that it defines the key components of corporate culture and analyzes how managers might affect this culture through conscious action. It also helps to explain why the corporate cultures of firms vary systematically across industries—different environments motivate different architectures. Economics suggests at least two roles for the elements of corporate culture like customs, social rituals, folklore, and heroes: communication and fostering more productive expectations among employees. These elements, however, are likely to be less effective if they are not reinforced by the formal architecture of the firm.

Sometimes, managers are unable or unwilling to adopt value-maximizing architectures or strategies. In this case, value can be created through management replacement. Management replacement occurs through firings and corporate takeovers. If a firm remains inefficient, it will eventually go out of business in a competitive marketplace.

This chapter introduced the concept of organizational architecture and provided a broad overview of the factors that are likely to be important in determining the optimal architecture for a particular organization. The next six chapters contain a more in-depth discussion of each of the three components of organizational architecture: the assignment of decision rights, the reward system, and the performance-evaluation system.

Suggested Readings

M. Jensen (1983), "Organization Theory and Methodology," *The Accounting Review* 58, 319–339.

M. Jensen and W. Meckling (1995), "Specific and General Knowledge, and Organizational Structure," *Journal of Applied Corporate Finance* 8:2, 4–18.

D. Kreps (1990), "Corporate Culture and Economic Theory," *Perspectives on Positive Political Economy,* J. Alt and K. Shepsle, eds. (Cambridge University Press: Cambridge).

P. Milgrom and J. Roberts (1995), "Complementarities and Fit: Strategy, Structure and Organizational Change in Manufacturing," *Journal of Accounting and Economics* 19, 179–208. Focus particular attention on pages 191–208.

Review Questions

8–1. Describe the three aspects of *organizational architecture.*

8–2. What is a major difference between the architectures of markets and firms?

8–3. Suppose that a manager decides that a company's decision making is too centralized. Will simply delegating more decisions to lower-level employees solve the problem? Explain?

8–4. Traditionally, many public utility companies (such as telephone and electric companies) have been highly regulated by the government. Thus, they have been in stable environments, shielded from competition and rapid change. Recently, deregulation has substantially altered the environments of some of these companies. For the first time, they are being exposed to intense competition from other companies. Discuss how this change in the environment is likely to affect the optimal organizational architecture of utility companies.

8–5. In most restaurants, the wait staff receives a large portion of their compensation through tips from customers. Generally, the size of the tip is decided by the customer. However, many restaurants require a 15 percent tip for parties of eight or more. Using the concepts from this chapter, discuss (a) why the practice of tipping has emerged as a major method of compensating the wait staff, (b) why the customer typically decides on the amount of the tip, and (c) why restaurants require tips from large parties.

8–6. How might the softer elements of corporate culture help to increase productivity in an organization? Give some examples of how managers might foster these elements to implement desired change in an organization.

8–7. Prominent management consultants sometimes argue that decision making in teams is usually more productive than decision making by individuals (there are important synergies that arise in teams that are absent when individuals work by themselves). These consultants suggest that most companies have long failed to make proper use of teams. Their advice is that most firms should increase their use of teams significantly. Critique this advice.

8–8. Suppose that you are an executive at ITT in 1984, prior to the leveraged buyout of O. M. Scott. Analyze the problems facing the company.

chapter 9

Decision Rights
The Level of Empowerment

Honda Motor Company was founded in 1948 by Soichiro Honda.[1] Initially, decision making in the company was quite top down. Mr. Honda made virtually all product and design decisions, while finance and marketing decisions were made by his partner, Takeo Fujisawa.

In 1973, Honda retired. Successors adopted a more decentralized decision system. Major decision-making authority was spread among nearly 30 senior executives, who spent much of their time gathered at conference tables hammering out policies in informal sessions called *waigaya,* a Honda word meaning noisy-loud. Engineers in research and development had significant control of the design of new automobiles. Under this so-called Honda System, the company grew and prospered.

By the late 1980s Honda's growth had stalled and profits declined. Honda lost market share in the Japanese auto market, falling from third to fourth behind Mitsubishi. Part of Honda's problem was that it failed to respond to changing tastes in the Japanese auto market. Many Japanese consumers wanted to purchase sporty cars with distinctive styling, yet Honda concentrated on producing four-door family sedans.

In April 1991, the new CEO, Nubuhiko Kawamoto, announced that he was radically changing the decision-making system at Honda by taking direct control of the company's automotive operations in Japan. He reasoned that the company had grown too large for group decision making. To quote Kawamoto:

> *We'd get the people from research, sales, and production together and everyone would say "not this" or "not that." We'd talk but there would be no agreement. Product planning would be on a tight schedule but we would have another discussion, another study and more preparation. Finally, the decision would come months later.*

The centralization of decision rights at Honda was seen as a "cultural revolution." Even after Kawamoto obtained the retired Honda's support for the radical change, Honda employees resisted. In spite of this resistance, the system was changed. As of 1993, powerful "car czars" ran the development of new models, middle managers had clear job responsibilities, and according to some insiders, Kawamoto's power exceeded even that once held by Honda.

The first real test of the new management structure was the unveiling of the 1994 Accord in fall 1993. The vehicle was priced competitively and was widely acclaimed a success. The Accord was named one of the top 10 cars of 1994 by *Car and Driver* magazine and import car of the year by *Motor Trend* magazine.

Honda is just one of many firms that changed the assignment of decision rights within their organizations in the 1990s. In contrast to Honda, many firms decentralized decision rights—for example, through *empowering* employees. An example, again from the automobile industry, is Fiat. In 1992, Fiat announced that it was decentralizing certain decision rights, assigning them to the operating levels and reducing management positions. Other firms decentralizing decision rights in the 1990s include General Electric, Eastman Kodak, Motorola, United Technologies, and Xerox, to name but a few. A common action has been to decentralize decision rights to teams of employees rather than to individuals. The financial press is replete with stories about how companies have improved profits, quality, and customer satisfaction through employee empowerment and other changes in their decision systems.

---

[1]Details of this example are from C. Chandler and P. Ingrassia (1991), "Just as U.S. Firms Try Japanese Management, Honda Is Centralizing," *The Wall Street Journal* (April 11); and M. Williams (1993), "Redesign of Honda's Management Faces First Test with Unveiling of New Accord," *The Wall Street Journal* (September 1).

These examples raise a number of important organizational questions: Can altering the assignment of decision rights really have an important impact on productivity and value? What factors affect the optimal partitioning of decision rights within the firm? When is it optimal to delegate decision rights to a team of employees rather than to specific individuals? The purpose of Chapters 9 and 10 is to address these and related questions. This chapter focuses on a single decision right and asks where that right should be located within the firm. Chapter 10 considers multiple decision rights and examines how combinations of rights are bundled into jobs and subunits (for example, divisions) of the firm.

This chapter begins by providing a more detailed discussion of the problem of assigning tasks and decision rights within the firm. We then present a simple example that illustrates some of the factors that are important in determining the optimal assignment of a decision right (in this case, pricing a product). We use this example to discuss centralization versus decentralization, as well as the placement of a right among employees within the same hierarchical level. We also use this example as a springboard to discuss the tradeoffs between assigning a decision right to an individual versus a team of individuals. Next, we consider the decision process in more detail and define the terms *decision management* and *decision control.* These terms are especially helpful in making the concept of empowerment more precise. Finally, we examine how the incentives of employees trying to influence decision makers can affect the optimal assignment of a decision right within the firm. The appendix provides a more detailed analysis of some of the problems that can arise in group (team) decision making.

Assigning Tasks and Decision Rights

Firms transform inputs into outputs, which are sold to customers. This *process* typically involves many *tasks.* For example, at Honda Motor Company, vehicles have to be designed, assembled, painted, sold, and delivered. An important element of organizational architecture is partitioning of the totality of tasks within the organization into smaller blocks and assigning them to specific individuals and/or groups.

Through the process of designing the organization, specific *jobs* are created. For example, if a set of clerical tasks is bundled together and assigned to an individual, a secretarial job is created. Jobs have at least two important dimensions: (1) the *variety of tasks* that the employee is asked to complete and (2) the *decision authority* to determine when and how best to complete those tasks.

Jobs vary substantially in terms of the variety of tasks and decision authority. Figure 9.1 pictures four possibilities. Point 1 displays a combination of few tasks and limited decision authority. An example is a typist in a typing pool who concentrates on a single task and has limited discretion on what to do or how to do it. Point 2 shows a combination of many tasks and limited decision authority. For instance, clerical jobs typically involve numerous tasks (filing, typing, answering the phone, and scheduling meetings, for example) but limited decision authority. Point 3 pictures a narrow set of tasks with broad decision authority. As an example, consider a salesperson who has broad decision rights concerning which customers to call, what sales pitch to make, what prices to charge, and so on. Yet the person concentrates on one principal task—selling products to customers. Recently, there has been a trend towards creating jobs like Point 4 that are less specialized and where employees have broader decision authority. The reasons for this trend will become evident as we proceed through the next two chapters.

As a manager moves up in the corporation, design issues consume larger amounts of the person's time. For example, the manager of a purchasing department plays an important

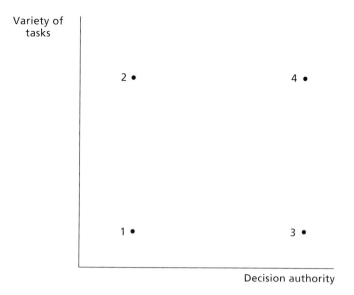

Figure 9.1   Dimensions of Job Design

Two important dimensions of job design are the *variety of tasks* and *decision authority.* This figure illustrates four possible combinations. Traditionally, many firms have created jobs like Point 1, which involve few tasks and limited decision authority. Lately, there has been a trend toward jobs like Point 4, which involve many tasks and broad decision authority. However, it is easy to give examples of jobs like Point 2 that involve many tasks and limited decision authority—for instance, certain clerical jobs. Similarly, it is easy to point to examples of jobs like Point 3 that involve few tasks and broad authority—for instance, certain sales jobs.

role in defining the tasks each employee in the department performs. Unfortunately, the problem of partitioning tasks into jobs is extremely complex. It involves the assignment of literally thousands of tasks and decision rights. It also involves simultaneous consideration of other corporate policies such as performance evaluation and compensation policy—the other two legs of the organizational architecture stool. Although current theory is not sufficiently well developed to provide a detailed solution to this general problem, through some relatively simple examples we can derive important insights. In this chapter, we present such an example to study the issue of decision authority. The next chapter considers the problems of *bundling* tasks into jobs and jobs into subunits of the firm. Thus, this chapter concentrates on the horizontal axis in Figure 9.1 (breadth of decision authority), while Chapter 10 concentrates on the vertical axis (variety of tasks).

Our primary example in this chapter involves Bob's Auto Company, a firm selling automobiles in two cities. As pictured in Figure 9.2, the management of the firm consists of Bob Morris, the CEO, and two local managers, Michele Cox and Jeri Coles. The local managers oversee the operations in the two cities. We concentrate on one specific task/decision right, pricing. Assigning an individual the right to set prices at a local unit increases that person's decision authority. If Bob grants the local managers the right to set prices, he reduces his decision authority and correspondingly increases the decision authority of the local managers. Initially, we assume that either Bob sets the prices at the local units or he grants the right to set prices to the local managers. In reality, Bob can grant the local managers some decision authority without giving them full pricing rights—for example, Bob might allow the managers to set prices within a given range. We consider these additional possibilities later in the chapter.

The issue of *centralization versus decentralization* focuses on which level of the firm's hierarchy to place the decision right. The firm is said to have centralized decision making if

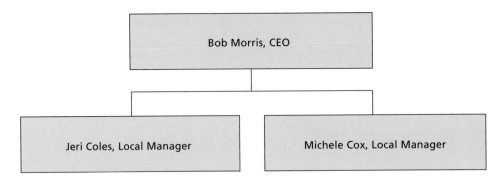

Figure 9.2   Organizational Structure of Bob's Auto Company

Bob's Auto Company markets automobiles in two cities. Robert (Bob) Morris is the CEO. The two local managers oversee the operations in the two cities. The one important decision right in this example is the pricing decision. The first question involves centralization versus decentralization. Should Bob make the pricing decisions or should they be decentralized to Jeri and Michele? The second question involves horizontal placement of decentralized decision rights. If pricing decisions are decentralized, should Bob: (1) grant each manager the pricing right for her own location, (2) grant both decision rights to one manager who makes all pricing decisions, or (3) grant the decision rights for the two locations to both managers and ask them to work as a team?

---

the right is assigned to Bob and decentralized decision making if the right is assigned to the local managers. A second issue is *choosing where in a given hierarchical level a decision should be made.* The decision authority of both local managers is increased if both are given decision rights for pricing. Alternatively, Bob might decide to increase the decision authority of only one of the local managers—for example, by letting Jeri make all pricing decisions. We begin by discussing centralization versus decentralization. We subsequently consider the lateral issue of where across a hierarchy to place the right.

Centralization versus Decentralization

Most of the analysis of assigning decision rights has focused on the question of whether to centralize or decentralize decision rights.[2] We utilize Bob's Auto to illustrate the major implications of this analysis. The basic question is should Bob set the prices at the two locations or should the pricing decisions be decentralized to the local managers? The answer to this question depends on the benefits and costs of decentralized decision making (relative to centralized decision making).

[2]As an example of the standard treatment of this topic, see R. Kaplan and A. Atkinson (1989), *Advanced Management Accounting* (Prentice Hall: Englewood Cliffs, NJ). Also see M. Jensen and W. Meckling (1995), "Specific and General Knowledge, and Organizational Structure," *Journal of Applied Corporate Finance* 8:2, 4–18, and A. Christie, M. Joye, and R. Watts (1996), "Decentralization of the Firm: Theory and Evidence," working paper (University of Rochester: Rochester, NY). For a more technical discussion of these issues, see. S. Athey, J. Gans, S. Schaefer, and S. Stern (1994), "The Allocation of Decisions in Organizations," working paper, Stanford University, Palo Alto, CA: M. Aoki (1986), "Horizontal vs Vertical Information Structure of the Firm," *American Economic Review* 76, 971–983; J. Cramer (1980), "A Partial Theory of the Optimal Organization of Bureaucracy," *Bell Journal of Economics* 11, 683–693; J. Marshak and R. Radner (1972), *The Economic Theory of Teams* (Yale University Press: New Haven, CT); and R. Sah and J. Stiglitz (1988), *"Committees, Hierarchies and Polyarchies,"* Economic Journal 98, 451–470.

Improving Performance through Decentralization: The Zebra Team

Eastman Kodak manufactures about 7,000 black-and-white film products that are used for a variety of purposes such as printing, X rays, and even spy satellites. Annual sales of these products are about $2 billion. Prior to 1989, Kodak used a very centralized decision-making process for manufacturing film. Manufacturing was divided into functions such as emulsion mixing (used for coating film), film coating, and film finishing. People in each of these functions reported up the line to functional managers.

In the late 1980s, poor performance motivated Kodak to reorganize the manufacturing of black-and-white film. Primary responsibility for the entire flow of the process was decentralized to a team of managers. A key feature of the new organization was the use of self-directed work teams.

The results of this reorganization were impressive. The "Zebra Team" cut production costs by some $40 million and inventory by about $50 million. In film finishing, what had taken four to six weeks was accomplished routinely in two days. In film coating, what had taken 42 days was done in less than 20. New products were brought to market in half the time.

A good example of how the Zebra Team made effective use of local specific knowledge is the development of Cholach's Chariot. *Accumax* is a film product used in the manufacturing of circuit boards. Any dust on the film translates into a broken wire on a circuit board and thus makes the film worthless. Accumax is finished and slit into final products in a high-tech, ultraclean room. Unfortunately, the old supply cart used to transport the film to storage was not dust-free and thus much film was wasted. Bob Cholach was a slitter operator with specific knowledge about how the problem could be fixed—an airtight transport cab. Through his efforts, such a cab was designed and built, resulting in significant benefits to the company. Comparing the new empowered work environment with the old system, Cholach noted:

> In the old days I'd have been told, "That's not your job—don't worry about it." But here I was given the power and finances to design and build something that would help my teammates. It wasn't like dropping a piece of paper into a suggestion box, either. They let me run with it from start to finish.

Source: S. Frangos with S. Bennett (1993), *Team Zebra* (Oliver Wight Publications: Essex Junction, VT).

Benefits of Decentralization

More Effective Use of Local Knowledge

The local managers are likely to have important information about the local markets. For example, they are likely to have better information than Bob about the demands and price sensitivities of particular customers. They are also likely to know more about the quality and condition of their used cars. This information is potentially costly to transfer. If Bob makes all pricing decisions, either the firm incurs information transfer costs or bears the cost of making decisions without the relevant knowledge. Decentralizing decision rights links decision-making authority with local specific knowledge and thus can reduce the costs of information transfer and processing. The improved use of local knowledge is thus one of the major benefits of decentralized decision making.

Centralized decisions require local managers to seek permission to change prices. Local information has to be transferred to Bob or be ignored. Subsequently, Bob has to deliberate and convey his decisions back down to local managers for implementation. This process takes time, and decision making is slower as a result. Such delays can lead to lost sales. Granting decision rights to the local managers promotes more rapid decision making and quicker responses to changing market conditions.[3]

[3]In the Honda example, decentralized decision making was slower than centralized decision making. However, in Honda's case, decision rights were decentralized to a team of employees rather than to an individual. Thus, the bottleneck was in the centralized coordination of the inputs from a number of team members. Later in this chapter we discuss how team decision making can be time-consuming.

Conservation of Management Time

If Bob makes local pricing decisions, substantial opportunity costs can be incurred—using top-management time for pricing decisions means the time cannot be used for other decisions. Often, it is better to decentralize operating decisions to local managers and focus the senior managers' attention on strategic decisions (for example, what car lines to sell and how to promote them). As Alfred Sloan, former CEO of General Motors and an early proponent of decentralization, described:

> *My office force is small. That means we do not do much routine work with details. They never get up to us. I work fairly hard, but it is on the exceptions . . . not on routine or petty details.*[4]

Training and Motivation for Local Managers

It is important for firms to attract talented employees and to train them as eventual replacements for senior management. Decentralizing decision rights promotes both objectives. Granting responsibility helps to attract and retain talented, ambitious local managers (who are likely to value this aspect of the job). It also provides experience in decision making that is important training for more senior positions.

Costs of Decentralization

Agency Costs

Decentralizing decision rights marries authority with local specific knowledge. However, the local managers do not necessarily have strong incentives to act to maximize the value of the firm. For example, the managers might sell cars to their friends at low prices or obtain kickbacks from customers in return for selling at low prices. Developing an effective control system to motivate desired actions is not always easy or inexpensive. Also, there are residual losses because it generally does not pay to resolve agency problems completely. Usually, agency problems are larger the further down in the organization decision rights are placed.[5]

Ideally, Bob would like to measure the effect of the local managers' decisions on the value of the firm. If Bob could, it would be relatively easy to use compensation schemes to motivate value-maximizing behavior. Unfortunately, observing the effect of individual decisions within the firm on firm value is usually impossible. Compensation schemes can be based on performance measures such as internal accounting numbers. For example, the local managers might be paid based on total profits for their units. However, as we will discuss in Chapters 11 through 14, developing effective compensation schemes and performance measures is difficult. The firm can use other mechanisms—for example, direct monitoring—to reduce agency problems, but none of these techniques is costless.

Coordination Costs and Failures

If the two local managers set prices independently, they can ignore important interaction effects. For instance, lowering the price in one city might divert sales from the other city (if they are nearby). It can also be wasteful for both managers to conduct the same type

---

[4] A. Sloan (1924), "The Most Important Thing I Ever Learned about Management," *System*, 124.

[5] There are agency problems even with centralized decision making—the decision maker is concerned that employees might not follow orders. These agency problems are usually less severe than the agency problems from decentralized decision making.

of market analysis to decide on their pricing policies if their markets are similar. For instance, most of the information might be obtained by conducting only one survey, or more precise estimates might be derived by pooling the observations.

Less Effective Use of Central Information

Local managers do not necessarily have all the relevant information to make good pricing decisions. Bob might have important information about product costs, upcoming promotions, and new products from the automobile manufacturer. Bob also might have important knowledge and expertise for solving pricing problems. Often, central managers obtain important information from observing the effects of various policies implemented through time and across multiple locations. In contrast, local managers generally have more limited experience and obtain direct information from only one location. There can also be economies of scale in having Bob make pricing decisions for all units within the firm (some decisions only have to be made once, rather than multiple times). And if industry conditions are such that rapid decision making is important, the benefits of centralization of decision rights where central information is important are even greater.

This discussion implies that an important role of central management in a decentralized decision system is to promote information flows and coordination among decision makers in the firm. These activities are likely to be costly. For instance, transferring information to local decision makers can be expensive. Coordination and central information costs will be lowest when the product demands and costs for the local units are independent (for example, the locations are far apart) and the relevant knowledge for decisions is held by the local managers.

The Benefits and Costs of Decentralized Decision Making

Benefits	Costs
More effective use of local knowledge	Agency costs
Conservation of the time of senior management	Coordination costs and failures
Training and motivation for local managers	Less effective use of central information

Graphical Illustration of the Tradeoffs

To illustrate the basic tradeoffs in this example, assume that the pricing decision can be decentralized to the local managers in varying degrees. We use D to represent the degree of decentralization of the pricing decision. When $D = 0$, all pricing decisions are made by Bob; as D increases, the local managers are granted more decision rights. For example, at a low level of D, the managers might have the authority to alter centrally determined prices within a 5 percent band. At a sufficiently high D, the local managers have full authority to set prices. For simplicity, assume that D is continuous. Also, suppose that the benefits of decentralization can be written:

$$\text{Benefits} = B \times D \tag{9.1}$$

where B is a positive constant. The benefits include better use of local knowledge, conservation of senior management time, and training/motivation for local managers.

There are, however, costs associated with decentralization. For instance, there are increased agency problems, and the decisions of the local managers have to be coordinated. Also, there are the increased costs of having to transfer central information to local decision makers. Assume the costs of decentralization are:

$$\text{Costs} = (A \times D) + (C \times D^2) \tag{9.2}$$

where A and C are positive constants. The first term, AD, represents the agency costs from decentralization; the second term, CD^2, represents the coordination/central information costs. This formulation assumes that coordination/information costs increase at an increasing rate with decentralization.[6] For example, it becomes more and more difficult to coordinate decisions as decision rights become more decentralized.

The objective of the firm is to choose D to maximize the net benefits, where:

$$\text{Net benefits} = \text{Benefits} - \text{Costs} = BD - AD - CD^2 \tag{9.3}$$

Figure 9.3 graphs the benefits and costs of decentralization. Net benefits are maximized where the vertical distance between the benefits and the costs is greatest. This condition occurs at:

$$D^* = (B - A)/2C \tag{9.4}$$

As is standard in problems of this type, D^* is the point at which the marginal benefits of decentralization equal the marginal costs.[7] At this point, the additional benefits from more decentralized decision making are just offset by the additional costs. (The slopes of the cost and benefit curves are equal.)

Over time, it is likely that the costs and benefits of decentralization will change. For example, the importance of local knowledge can change with changes in competition in the industry or shifts in consumer demand. Also, the costs of transferring information and controlling agency problems can fall due to new technologies (for example, consider fax machines and network computers). Changes in the benefits of decentralization can be represented by changes in B, the coefficient in the benefits equation. For example, if the importance of local knowledge increases with more global competition, B increases. Equation 9.4 and Figure 9.3 indicate that increases in B are associated with increases in the optimal amounts of decentralization. Changes in the agency and coordination information costs of decentralization can be represented by changes in A and C, respectively. Both equation 9.4 and Figure 9.3 indicate that an increase in these costs is associated with a decrease in the optimal level of decentralization.

Our analysis of centralization versus decentralization can help us to understand the changes in the assignment of decision rights at Honda Motor Company in 1991. Recall that after Soichiro Honda retired in 1973, the relevant specific knowledge for decision making was spread among many executives, making the benefits of decentralization high. In the context of our example, Honda could be viewed during this period as operating with an appropriately high level of decentralization. By 1991, however, Honda had grown tremendously and consensus decision making was no longer effective. Also, Nubuhiko Kawamoto, the new CEO, had been a Honda engineer and had detailed specific knowledge about designing automobiles—thus, the benefits of decentralization were lower than in the past (when senior management had less of the relevant knowledge). In response to

[6]Coordination and central information costs do not have to be quadratic, and the other benefits and costs do not have to be linear. We have used these functional forms to produce convenient solutions in our example. The basic principles of our analysis do not depend on these assumptions.

[7]The solution to this maximization process can be obtained through elementary calculus. Alternatively, equation (9.3) is quadratic, and thus you can use the quadratic formula to solve for the roots of the equation. The two roots, 0 and $(B - A)/C$, are where net benefits equal zero. The parabola is at a maximum midway between the two roots: $(B - A)/2C$. Note that the optimal point, D^*, is where the vertical distance between the benefits and costs is greatest. This point occurs where the slope of the benefit curve is equal to the slope of the cost curve. The slope of the benefit curve is the marginal benefit, while the slope of the cost curve is the marginal cost. Thus, the optimal point is where the marginal benefit of decentralization equals the marginal cost.

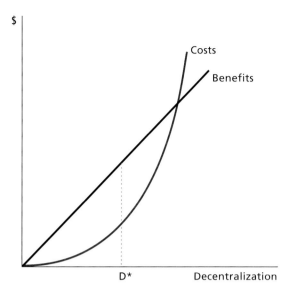

Figure 9.3   A Graphical Illustration of the Tradeoffs between Centralization and Decentralization of Decision Making at Bob's Auto Company

In this example, the local managers have important specific knowledge that is valuable for decision making, and timeliness of response is important. The benefits of decentralization are given by Benefits = BD, where D is the level of decentralization of pricing decisions and B is a positive constant. These benefits include better use of local knowledge, increased response times, conservation of the time of senior management, and training/motivation for local managers. The costs are given by Costs = AD + CD^2, where the first term, AD, represents the increased agency costs from decentralization and the second term, CD^2, represents the increased coordination costs (A and C are positive constants). The optimal level of decentralization is D* = (B − A)/2C. At this point, the marginal benefits and the marginal costs of decentralization are equal. (The slopes of the total benefit and cost curves are the same.)

---

these changing conditions, Kawamoto increased the level of centralization. In the context of our example, there had been a reduction in the benefits of decentralization, B, and an increase in the costs, resulting in a lower D*, the optimal level of decentralization.

Our graphical illustration simplifies the centralization/decentralization decision in many ways. For example, the analysis is much more complicated if the assignment of more than one decision right is considered. Also, the example takes the divisional structure of the firm as given (two operating divisions and a headquarters). More generally, the unit structure is determined along with the assignment of decision rights. (We discuss this issue in the next chapter.) It is particularly important to emphasize that when a firm changes its decision system, it is necessarily optimal to make simultaneous changes in other organizational features, such as the performance-evaluation and reward systems. (As we noted in Chapter 8, these aspects of organizational architecture are like three legs of a stool, and it is important to keep them in balance.) It is often desirable to accompany decentralization with an increased emphasis on performance and incentive compensation (in order to motivate the empowered decision makers). Our illustration is incomplete in that it does not incorporate simultaneous changes in these other organizational variables. (We discuss these issues in Chapters 11 through 14). Despite these limitations, the example highlights some of the important tradeoffs in deciding on the degree of decentralization.

Implications

Our analysis indicates that there are costs and benefits of decentralization. These costs and benefits are likely to vary across firms and time. In this section, we begin by discussing how the optimal level of decentralization is likely to vary across firms. We then discuss factors motivating the recent trends toward decentralization in many firms.

Across Firms

In Chapter 8, we discussed how the firm's business environment and strategy are major determinants of organizational architecture. We focused particular attention on three factors in the environment: technology, market conditions, and regulation. We expect that the net benefits of decentralization will be highest in rapidly changing environments. In unregulated industries in which market conditions and production technologies frequently change, the timely use of local knowledge is likely to be particularly important. In more stable environments, companies can use centralized decision making and concentrate on gaining economies of scale through large-scale standardized production.

Corporate strategy focuses primarily on the scope of the firm, such as the number of different products that the firm sells. We expect that the benefits of decentralization are likely to increase as the firm enters more markets. If a firm is highly diversified, it is less likely that senior managers have the specific knowledge to make good operating decisions across its various businesses. *Business strategy* focuses largely on whether to be a cost leader in an industry or to develop differentiated products for which customers are willing to pay a price premium. While not always true, it seems likely that decentralization will be more important for firms following a differentiation strategy. Such a strategy requires effective use of information on customer demands and competitor offerings. Often, this information is held by people lower in the organization. Cost strategies often focus on low-cost production of standardized products, where local knowledge is often less important.

Another element of business strategy is the degree of vertical integration (for instance, whether a manufacturing firm should make its own inputs or provide its own retail distribution and service network—see Chapter 15). In general, we expect as the firm becomes larger, either through vertical integration or through geographic expansion, that the appropriate level of decentralization will increase. As firm size increases, more decisions have to be made. Time and mental-processing constraints will preclude central managers from making all major decisions.

Centralized decision making has particular advantages when coordination of activities within the firm are important. For instance, hub-and-spoke airlines schedule short-haul flights from the spokes to arrive at roughly the same time at a central hub. Passengers connect to their next flights that leave later. Airlines using centralized scheduling are able to coordinate the flights schedules and arrange baggage connections at lower cost, offering greater convenience to customers, than if schedules were determined by multiple decentralized decision makers (for example, the pilots). Similarly, it is important for large banks to coordinate the development of automatic teller machines centrally, so that all branches use the same system.

Empirical evidence on some of these arguments is provided by A. Christie, M. Joye, and R. Watts, who examine decentralization of decision making between the CEO and the next layer of senior management (general managers) for a sample of 121 firms.[8] They find that larger firms with more local specific knowledge, higher diversification, and less-regulation are more likely to have a greater degree of decentralization.

---

[8]A. Christie, M. Joye, and R. Watts (1996), "Decentralization of the Firm: Theory and Evidence, working paper (University of Rochester: Rochester, NY).

Computers and Information Transmission: The Rapid Response Team at McKinsey & Company

Decentralized decision making takes advantage of local specific knowledge. However, local decisions need to be coordinated. Also, these decisions can often be enhanced by providing local decision makers with useful information from other parts of the organization. An example of the importance of computers in transferring information to local decision makers involves McKinsey & Company.

McKinsey & Company is one of the most prominent management-consulting firms in the world. In 1989, it had over 2,000 professionals working at over 50 offices spread across five continents. It is important for McKinsey to have relatively decentralized decision making because of the vast amounts of local specific knowledge held by on-site professionals. Nevertheless, for McKinsey to deliver consistent and state-of-the-art products, it is important to communicate throughout the organization.

In 1989, McKinsey formed the Rapid Response Team. The purpose of this team was to respond to requests about the best current thinking and practice by providing ready access to both documents and experienced consultants. This activity requires a computerized database that catalogs printed material and the experience profiles of consultants throughout the organization. In 1991, the Rapid Response Team responded to over 1,000 requests for information and assisted nearly a quarter of the firm's consultants and clients throughout the world.

Source: J. Katzenbach and D. Smith (1993), *The Wisdom of Teams* (Harvard Business School: Boston).

Recent Trends

In contrast to Honda Motor Company, the general trend over the last decade has been toward greater decentralization. In Chapter 8, we discussed how changes in organizational architecture are motivated by changes in the basic economic environment. We now discuss those factors that have changed in the environment to motivate decentralization.

In the past decade, global competition has increased tremendously in many industries. Consider, for example, the automobile, film, and computer industries. This competition has placed pressure on firms to cut costs, produce higher-quality products, and meet the demands of customers in a more timely fashion.[9] The information for improving quality, customer service, and efficiency is often located lower in the organization. Thus, these competitive pressures have increased the benefits of decentralization for many firms.[10]

Technology has motivated changes in the level of decentralization for two reasons. First, the rate of technological innovation has increased dramatically. Firms must either respond quickly to the resulting changes in market conditions and production technologies or lose profits. This innovation can motivate firms to decentralize decision rights when important aspects of the knowledge of new technologies is not held by the central corporate office. Second, new technologies have significantly altered the costs of information transfer (for instance, cellular phones and fax machines). In some cases, these changes have worked to promote decentralization. For example, computers and telecommunications systems (satellites and fiber optics) have reduced the costs and time of transferring central information to local decision makers to coordinate and enhance decentralized decisions. Computers also have made it less expensive to track the sales and production costs of individual products. This reduction in costs has increased the feasibility of developing more precise performance standards for local decision makers to use in incentive compensation plans.

[9]See Chapter 16 for a detailed discussion of how increased competition from the Japanese placed pressure on Xerox Corporation to improve quality and cut costs.

[10]Foreign competition has also weakened the power of labor unions in the United States to enforce inefficient work rules (for example, contract restrictions limiting the tasks that specific employees can perform). When competition was largely restricted to domestic, heavily unionized firms, there was limited pressure to change work assignments and decision rights in American firms. Competition from more efficient foreign and nonunion competitors changed this environment.

Computer Technology and Busting the Bureaucracy: Cypress Semiconductors

Computer technology has allowed senior managers to communicate more directly with lower-level employees. As a result, this technology makes it less expensive for senior managers to control and coordinate the actions of individuals. Thus, it has reduced the demand for middle managers, who traditionally have played an important role in transmitting information from the top of the organization to lower levels. An example of the use of computer technology in this context is Cypress Semiconductors. T. J. Rodgers, CEO of Cypress, uses a computer system to track the daily objectives of every company employee. The company essentially has no middle management. To quote an article from *Fortune*:

> The computer system allows the CEO to stay abreast of every employee and team in his fast-moving organization. Each employee maintains a list of 10 to 15 goals like "Meet with marketing for new product launch," or "Make sure to check with Customer X." Noted next to each goal is when it was agreed upon, when it's due to be finished and whether it's finished yet or not.
>
> This way, it doesn't take layers of expensive bureaucracy to check who's doing what, whether someone has got a light enough workload to be put on a new team, and who's having trouble. Rodgers says he can review the goals of all 1,500 employees in about four hours, which he does each week.

Source: B. Dumaine (1991), "The Bureaucracy Busters," *Fortune* (June 17), 46.

In other cases, the effect has been in the opposite direction—local information has become less expensive to transfer to central headquarters, thus favoring more centralized decision making. For example, computerized cash registers allow central tracking of inventory and can increase the benefits of centralized purchasing. Many of the restocking decisions within the Wal-Mart chain are now handled by an automated system through which suppliers restock items at individual stores whenever the computer system indicates that inventories have fallen to a specified level. Managers at individual stores have few decision rights over inventory levels.

Technological advances have also allowed many firms to flatten their management structures. Traditionally, firms have relied on *middle managers* to transmit information and instructions from senior management to lower-level employees. Middle managers have also played an important role in coordinating and monitoring the actions of these lower-level employees. Newer computer technology, by facilitating communication between senior management and lower-level employees, has reduced demands for middle managers. Technology also has motivated changes in the roles of middle managers. In many firms middle management's role has shifted from being a conduit in the information flow to one that more closely resembles the coach of a sports team—assembling the optimal set of players, helping them to design winning strategies, providing motivation, and so on.

Assigning Decision Rights across a Hierarchical Level

While discussion of decision rights often focuses on centralization versus decentralization, lateral issues also can be important. In our auto dealership example, if Bob decentralizes decision rights, he can either (1) grant the two managers the pricing decisions for their own locations, (2) grant both decision rights to one manager who makes all pricing decisions, or (3) grant the decision rights for pricing at the two locations to both managers and ask them to work as a team in deciding on the pricing policy. As in the centralization versus decentralization problem, the relevant factors in making this choice include the distribution of knowledge and the costs of coordination and control. For example, granting decision rights to the managers separately takes greater advantage of local specific knowledge. However, pricing at the two locations will not necessarily be well coordinated. Alternatively, granting all decision rights to one manager promotes coordinated decision making and takes advantage of any economies of scale in having one person make both decisions. But it comes at the potential expense of less effective utilization of the other manager's local knowledge. There might also be differences in agency costs between these two alternatives. For example, it might be less expensive to monitor the decisions of one person than two. The value of the third option, granting decision rights to a team of managers, depends on a number of factors, which we discuss in the next section. Which of the three options is best depends on the specific circumstances facing the firm. For instance, having the two managers make independent decisions is likely to dominate when the two markets are more independent and more of the relevant knowledge for pricing is at the individual unit level.

Questions relating to the lateral placement of decision rights frequently arise within organizations. For example, should personnel decisions be made within each individual division, or should these rights be granted to a separate human resources department? Should a divisional manager be in charge of R&D, or should this function be performed elsewhere in the organization? Can a college of business operate its own placement center, or must it rely on centralized placement services of the university?

Assigning Decision Rights to Teams

Team Decision Making

Our analysis of Bob's Auto suggests that a firm might want to assign a decision right to a team of employees rather than to one individual. In this discussion, we use the term *team* to refer broadly to the many different types of work groups that have decision-making authority (teams, committees, task forces, and so on); for our purposes, more refined definitions are unnecessary. Firms grant decision rights to teams of employees for at least three basic purposes:[11] (1) to manage activities, (2) to make products, and (3) to recommend actions. Teams that manage activities are often comprised of several individuals from different functional areas (for example, marketing and finance). Teams that make products are often at the plant level. For example, some firms have granted to teams of production employees the decision rights to set their own work schedules and assignments and to organize the basic production process. Both types of teams tend to be relatively permanent. The assignment is to manage some particular business or subprocess. Teams that recommend actions focus on specific projects and normally disband when the task is complete. An example is the Silver Bullet Team formed at Eastman Kodak to reduce the use of silver, the most expensive ingredient in making film; Kodak is the world's largest user of silver. Below, we discuss the benefits and costs of group decision making relative to assigning the decision right to one individual.

Benefits of Team Decision Making

Improved Use of Dispersed Specific Knowledge
The relevant specific knowledge for decision making is often dispersed among multiple people in an organization. For instance, the relevant knowledge for designing new products

[11]Katzenbach and Smith (1993).

is often held by a variety of employees, including scientists, engineers, and sales personnel. By definition, specific knowledge is expensive to assemble and transfer to a single decision maker. Also, it can be important for the individuals with the relevant knowledge to share information among themselves. By sharing information in a group setting, new ideas might be generated that would not occur in bilateral communications between each individual and a central decision maker. By sharing information, employees also become better informed for future decisions and actions. Granting decision rights to a team encourages the members to communicate and to brainstorm. Final decisions are made through consensus or some type of voting mechanism. Multiple individuals with specific knowledge are involved in the decision-making process.

Employee Buy-In

Employees often suspect that management-initiated decisions benefit managers at the expense of other employees often claim that they grant decision rights to groups of employees to increase employee "buy-in." It is asserted that employees who take part in a decision process are more likely to support the final decision and be more active in its implementation. This occurs for at least three reasons: First, asymmetric information and uncertainty, in turn, prevent employees from knowing the full consequences of a decision. Second, a group of employees has less to fear if they make the decision themselves or if the decision is made by employees with similar interests (see Chapter 16 for a related discussion). Reduced concerns about the effects of the decision increase employee buy-in, even when the same decision would have been made by the central manager. Third, employees have stronger incentives to invest in implementing decisions that they recommend because their reputations depend on the ultimate outcomes of the decisions.

Costs of Team Decision Making

Collective-Action Problems

Collective decision making is often slow. Recall how it took months for senior executives at Honda Motor Company to reach a consensus on policy decisions. Also, group decisions are not always efficient or rational (consider the old saying about the committee that set out to design a horse—but in the process designed a camel).[12] Group decision making can also be subject to manipulation and political influence. In the appendix to this chapter, we illustrate how the common decision rule of majority voting can be subject to manipulation. Management implications of this analysis are stressed.

Free-Rider Problems

Team members bear the full costs of their individual efforts but share the gains that accrue to the team. This arrangement encourages team members to free-ride on the efforts of others (see Chapter 7). As we discuss in subsequent chapters, free-rider problems can be reduced through appropriate performance-evaluation and reward schemes. However, these schemes are costly to administer.

---

[12]K. Arrow (1963), *Social Choice and Individual Values* (John Wiley & Sons: New York).

Team-Based Organization: Hallmark Greeting Cards

It used to take about two years for Hallmark to bring a new card to market. A new card had to move through the various functional areas (for example, art, design, production, and marketing). Some of these functions were located in separate buildings. All this took time. Now Hallmark uses teams and organizes around specific holidays. For example, one team might work on cards for Mother's Day and another for Valentine's Day. Teams are given most of the decision rights for the design and marketing of particular cards. Through this process, Hallmark has cut its time to market new cards in half. For Hallmark, team decision making has proven more productive than centralized decision making.

Source: T. Stewart (1992), "The Search for the Organization of Tomorrow,"
Fortune (September 22), 92–98.

When Will Team Decision Making Work Best?

Some managers and consultants suggest that team decision making is almost always better than individual decision making.[13] Our discussion indicates that this suggestion is not correct. Team decision making is optimal only if the benefits are larger than the costs. Team decision making is most likely to be productive in environments where the relevant specific knowledge for the decision is dispersed among individuals and where the costs of collective decision making and controlling free-rider problems are low.

Team decision making is a common component of total quality management programs (TQM). Many firms have increased their use of team decision making in the last few years through the implementation of TQM programs. As we discuss in Chapter 17, experience indicates that the *indiscriminate use* of teams in TQM programs can be counterproductive—in such cases, the costs exceed the benefits.

Optimal Team Size

Increasing the size of the team enhances the knowledge base of the team. However, it also increases the incentives to free-ride, as well as other costs associated with collective decision making. For instance, as team size grows, it can become difficult to make decisions and work in a coordinated fashion. The optimal team size is at the point where the marginal costs of adding a new member equal the marginal benefits. Katzenbach and Smith argue that their research indicates virtually all effective teams that they observed had no more than 25 members and many were much smaller (ranging from 2 to 25).

Decision Management and Control[14]

Thus far, our characterization of decision making has been rather simplified. In particular, we have generally assumed that either an agent has a decision right or does not. In reality, some aspects of a decision can be decentralized while other aspects can be maintained at a higher level. For example, at Bob's Auto, the managers might be granted the

---

[13]For example, Katzenbach and Smith (1993).

[14]The material in this section draws on the analysis in E. Fama and M. Jensen (1983), "Separation of Ownership and Control," *Journal of Law & Economics* 26, 301–326.

right to set prices within some range but have to obtain approval from Bob for larger price changes. Thus, the decision authority of an employee can be increased (see Figure 9.1) without granting the employee all rights to a particular decision.

A useful characterization of the decision process is provided by Fama and Jensen. In particular, they divide the decision-making process into four steps:

- *Initiation.* Generation of proposals for resource utilization and structuring of contracts.

- *Ratification.* Choice of the decision initiatives to be implemented.

- *Implementation.* Execution of ratified decisions.

- *Monitoring.* Measurement of the performance of decision agents and implementation of rewards.

DEFINITION

Decision management: The initiation and implementation of decisions.

Decision control: The ratification and monitoring of decisions.

BASIC PRINCIPLE

Allocating Decision Rights: If decision makers do not bear the major wealth effects of their decisions, decision management and decision control will be held by seperate decision makers.

Often, firms assign initiation and implementation rights to the same agents. Fama and Jensen refer to these functions as *decision management.* They use the term *decision control* to refer to the ratification and monitoring functions.

Employees do not normally bear the full wealth effects of their actions—there are agency problems. Granting an agent rights in both decision management and decision control will typically lead to suboptimal behavior. In the case of Bob's Auto, if the local managers make pricing decisions and there is no monitoring or other control, the managers are more likely to use the decision rights for their own benefit. For instance, the managers might sell cars to family and friends below cost. Based on this logic, Fama and Jensen argue that whenever decision makers are not owners, decision management and decision control will be separated. Only when the decision maker is also the major residual claimant—the person with the legal rights to the profits of the enterprise once all the other claimants of the firm (for example, bondholders and employees) are paid—does it make sense to combine decision management and control.

A prominent example of separating decision management and decision control is the presence of a board of directors at the top of all corporations. In large corporations, the residual claimants are shareholders. The management of the firm is largely the responsibility of the CEO, who typically owns less than 1 percent of the firm's stock. To mitigate potential agency problems, shareholders grant major decision-control rights to the board of directors. The board ratifies major decisions initiated by the CEO. The board also has monitoring authority and the rights to fire and compensate the CEO. However, since board members are often not major shareholders, there is still a role for other parties to "monitor the monitor." This role is performed by large blockholders (such as public pension funds) and takeover specialists. If board members do a poor job, they can be replaced through election or corporate takeover.

The principle of separation of decision management and control helps to explain the frequent use of hierarchies in organizations. In hierarchies, decision management is formally separate from decision control; that is, decisions of individuals are monitored and ratified by individuals who are above them in the hierarchy. The same agent may have decision-control and decision-management functions—for example, divisional managers might have approval rights over certain initiatives of lower-level employees and at the same time have to request authorization for the division's capital-expenditure plan. The important thing is that one agent not have the rights in both decision management and decision control for the *same decision.* In smaller organizations, where one person (or a small number) has the relevant knowledge to make decisions, it is expensive to separate decision management from decision control. In this case, the two functions are often

Should the Positions of CEO and Chairman of the Board Be Separated?

Many commentators complain that boards of directors of U.S. companies fail to provide adequate discipline of senior managers. Of particular concern is the common practice of combining the titles of CEO and chairman of the board. On the surface, this practice seems to violate the principle of separating decision management and decision control. Benjamin Rosen, chairman of Compaq Computer, voiced this concern succinctly:

> When the CEO is also Chairman, management has *de facto* control. Yet the board is supposed to be in charge of management. Checks and balances have been thrown to the wind.*

Large shareholder associations and pension funds have in recent years sponsored proposals at Sears Roebuck and other large firms calling for separation of the titles. Government officials have considered regulations to force this change.

Contrary to the allegations of reformers, combining the CEO and chairman titles does not necessarily violate the principle of separation of decision management and decision control. The extreme case of no separation exists only when the board has the CEO as its only member. Indeed, the boards of several large U.S. companies, including American Express, Eastman Kodak, General Motors, IBM, and Westinghouse, have fired their CEOs/chairmen in recent years.

Estimates indicate that the titles are combined in over 80 percent of U.S. firms. In the vast majority of the remaining cases, the chairman is the former CEO. Proponents of regulations to force firms to appoint outsiders as chairman essentially argue that almost all major firms in the U.S. are inefficiently organized. While this assumption may be correct, reformers have presented no cogent argument for how such an important corporate-control practice can be wealth-decreasing and still survive in the competitive marketplace for so long across so many companies.

*USA Today, April 22, 1993.
Source: J. Brickley, J. Coles, and G. Jarrell (1996), "Corporate Leadership Structure: On the Separation of the Positions of CEO and Chairman of the Board," working paper (University of Rochester: Rochester, NY).

combined. In such cases the decision maker also tends to be the major residual claimant to avoid agency problems. (For example, the company is organized as a sole proprietorship, partnership, or corporation where a few people own all the stock.)

While management and control rights for a decision are often granted to individuals at different levels in the organization, they are sometimes granted to separate individuals at the same level of the corporate hierarchy. For example, the quality of the output of a manufacturing division is sometimes monitored by a quality unit with equal status in the organization. Similarly, internal auditors often monitor units on the same hierarchical level.

The concepts of decision management and decision control are also useful in making the term *empowerment* more precise. Managers sometimes are unclear about what rights are being granted when they say they are empowering employees. This ambiguity can lead to disputes and conflicts between management and employees—for example, when management reverses the decisions of employees who thought they were empowered. The principle of separation of decision management and control suggests that empowerment should not mean that an employee has all rights to a particular decision. An empowered employee might have explicit rights to initiate and implement decisions; however, there is still an important role for managers to ratify and monitor decisions. Ratification does not necessarily mean that an employee must seek approval for every decision. In some cases, managers might want to preratify decisions within a particular range (*boundary setting*). For instance, we discussed how the managers at Bob's Auto might be given authority to set prices within some range. In any case, Bob would want to maintain monitoring rights over the decision. Often, conflicts over empowerment can be avoided by a careful discussion about what rights are actually being delegated to the employee.

Separation of Decision Management and Decision Control: Not a New Concept

The English merchant guilds were formed during the 12th century. These precursors to the modern corporation were chartered by the crown and given a monopoly to conduct trade within their own towns, usually in return for a payment to the crown. Each guild would specialize in a particular trade (carpenters, stone cutters, pewterers, etc.). The guilds held property and elected officials to manage the trade and property. Incorporation by the crown created a legal entity that could conduct business.

In order to protect the members of the guild from embezzlement and mismanagement by their elected officers, the charters of the guilds contained provisions for the election of auditors from the general membership to audit the financial records of the guild. For example, The Worshipful Company of Pewterers of the City of London was audited by the members. The Book of Ordinances of 1564 contains the following "order for ye audytors":

> Also it is agreed that there shalbe foure Awdytours Chosen euery yeare to awdit the Craft accompte and they to parvese it and search it that it shall be perfect. And also to accompt it Correct it and allowe it So that they make an ende of the awdet therof between Mighelmas and Christmas yearely and if defaute made of ffenishings thereof before Christmas yearly euery one of the saide Awdytours shall paye to the Craft box vj s. viij d. pece.

Audits by members of the guild are early examples of separating decision management from control. The guild officers had decision management rights, but decision control rights in the form of annual monitoring of financial transactions were vested in member auditors.

Source: E. Boyd (1968), "History of Auditing," in *History of Accounting and Accountants,* R. Brown, ed. (A.M. Kelley: New York), 79. Also, R. Watts and J. Zimmerman (1983), "Agency Problems, Auditing, and the Theory of the Firm: Some Evidence," *Journal of Law & Economics* 26, 613–633.

Influence Costs[15]

To this point, we have assumed that decision-making authority is either granted to an individual or a team within the firm. Once the right is granted, the agent or team is actively involved in decision making (subject to ratification and monitoring from others). Sometimes, firms use bureaucratic rules that purposely limit active decision making. For example, airlines allocate routes to flight attendants based on seniority—there is no supervisor who decides who gets which route. Similarly, some firms base promotions solely on years worked with the firm. Some universities do not permit grade changes once the grade is recorded.

One potential benefit of limiting discretion in making decisions is that it reduces the resources consumed by individuals trying to influence decisions. Employees are often quite concerned about the personal effects of decisions made within the firm. For example, flight attendants care about which routes they fly. Employees are not indifferent to which colleagues are laid off in an economic downturn. These concerns motivate politicking and other potentially nonproductive *influence activities.* For instance, employees might waste valuable time trying to influence decision makers. In vying for promotions, employees might take dysfunctional actions to make other employees look bad.

Not assigning the decision right to a specific individual lowers *influence costs*—there is no one to lobby. But such a policy can impose costs on an organization. Consider individuals who are competing for a promotion. These individuals have incentives to provide

[15]The material in this section draws on the analysis in P. Milgrom (1988), "Employment Contracts, Influence Activities and Efficient Organization Design," *Journal of Political Economy* 96, 42–60.

Influence Costs at Reynolds Tobacco

After a century of "one-for-all," the Sticht [the CEO] succession scramble split Reynolds into warring camps. No longer did people pull together for the company. Now they looked after the interests of the executive they hitched their star to: Wilson, Horrigan, or Abely. Preparing for a financial analysts' meeting, Wilson and Abely quarreled over who would speak first, a squabble Sticht finally had to settle. At a rehearsal for presentations to a companywide conference, Abely had run over his allotted time when Horrigan stomped into the room. "What's that . . . doing up there?" he stormed. "It's my time." Abely ordered a feasibility study on spinning off Sea-Land. Wilson, to whom Sea-Land reported, got wind of it and confronted John Dowdle, the treasurer, who was doing the study. "I'm sorry, I can't tell you about that," Dowdle said. "Abely will fire me if I tell you." Horrigan hired a public relations firm to get him nominated for the right kinds of business and humanitarian awards to enhance his resume. Horrigan's big score: a Horatio Alger award.

Source: B. Burrough and J. Helyar (1990), *Barbarians at the Gate* (Harper Perennial: New York), 58.

evidence to their supervisor that they are the most qualified for the promotion. This information is often useful in making better promotion decisions. However, the information comes at a cost—employees spend time trying to convince the supervisor that they are the most qualified rather than on other activities such as selling products. It makes sense to run a "horse race" as long as the marginal benefits from better information are larger than the marginal costs of the influence activity. But the race should be stopped at the point where the marginal value of additional information about individual qualifications is equal to the marginal cost of additional influencing activity.

In some cases, the firm's profits are largely unaffected by decisions that greatly impact individual employee welfare. For example, firm profits might be unaffected by which flight attendant gets the Hawaii route versus the Sioux Falls route. It is in this setting that bureaucratic rules for decision making are most likely. The firm benefits from a reduction in influence costs but is little affected by the particular outcome of the decision process.

Summary

Firms engage in the *process* of transforming inputs into outputs, which are sold to customers. An important element of organizations is partitioning the totality of *tasks* of the organization into smaller blocks and assigning them to individuals and/or groups within the firm. Through the design process, jobs are created. Jobs have at least two important dimensions, *variety of tasks* and *decision authority*. This chapter focuses on decision authority. The next chapter focuses on the bundling of tasks.

In *centralized decision systems,* most major decisions are made by individuals at the top of the organization. In *decentralized systems,* many decisions are made by lower-level employees. Decentralized decision making has both benefits and costs. Potential benefits include more effective use of local knowledge, conservation of management time, and training/motivation for lower-level managers. Potential costs include agency and coordination costs and less effective use of central information. The optimal degree of decentralization depends on the marginal benefits and the marginal costs. These costs and benefits vary across firms and over time. There has been a recent trend toward greater decentralization, motivated in part by increased global competition and changes in technology.

Decision rights are not just assigned to a hierarchical level but to particular positions within the hierarchical level. Similar to the centralization versus decentralization problem, relevant factors in making this horizontal choice include the distribution of knowledge and the costs of coordination and control.

CASE STUDY
Medford University

Medford University is a research university with about 10,000 students. It has a good liberal arts undergraduate program, a top-rated medical school, and a fine law school. It employees about 12,000 people. A majority of these employees work at the university hospital. Lately, the university has faced significant financial pressures. It is in intense competition for quality students with other colleges. Recent financial donations have been small. The hospital is under intense pressure to reduce costs because of changing health care regulations and insurance coverage.

The university currently spends about $100 million annually on fringe benefits (health insurance, retirement plans, and so on). It also faces large future payments of promised medical benefits to current and future retirees. The president of the university has appointed a task force to design a new fringe benefit package. The task force consists of faculty and staff from departments throughout the university. The task force has been asked to consider the university's tenuous financial condition. The president wants to reduce expenditures on fringe benefits (while maintaining the quality of the faculty and staff). The president has appointed the chief administrator of the hospital as the chairman of the task force. The president also has

appointed one of his key assistants, the vice provost, to serve as secretary of the task force (to take minutes and coordinate meeting schedules).*

Discussion Questions

1. Why did the president appoint a task force to consider the issue of fringe benefits? He could have asked the university's human resources department to design a plan.
2. Should the president anticipate that all members of the task force will strive to cut university expenses? What actions can the president take to increase the likelihood that the task force members have this objective as a major priority?
3. Why did the president appoint the administrator of the hospital as the chairman of the task force? The chairman of the task force, in turn, has delegated much of the work to subcommittees (a health insurance committee, a retirement committee, and so on). What advice would you offer the chairman in appointing subcommittee chairs? Explain.
4. Does the president want to commit to accepting the committee report or does he want to reserve the right to make modifications? Explain.
5. Why did the president appoint a key assistant as secretary of the task force?

* More complete answers to these questions can be developed by incorporating the material in the appendix to this chapter.

Sometimes, firms assign decision rights to *teams* of employees rather than to specific individuals. Firms assign decision rights to teams for at least three basic purposes: managing activities, recommending actions, and making products. The use of team decision making can sometimes increase productivity; however, this is not always the case. Team decision making is most likely to be productive when the relevant information is dispersed and the costs of collective decision making and controlling free-rider problems are low.

Decision management refers to the initiation and implementation of decisions, while *decision control* refers to the ratification and monitoring of decisions. When agents do not bear the major wealth effects of their decisions, it is generally important to separate decision management from decision control. A prominent example of this principle is the presence of a board of directors at the top of corporations. This principle also helps to explain the presence of *hierarchies* in most organizations. It can also help to make the concept of empowerment more precise.

Sometimes, firms adopt rules that limit the discretion of decision makers. For example, airlines assign routes to flight attendants based solely on seniority. One benefit of limiting discretion is that it reduces the incentives of individuals to engage in costly *influencing activity* (for example, politicking). Some influencing activity is valuable in that it produces information that improves decision making. Firms are, therefore, most likely to limit discretion when firm profits do not depend heavily on the decisions but where the decisions are of significant concern to employees (as in the case of assigning routes to flight attendants).

APPENDIX   *Problems in Collective Decision Making*[16]

Managers commonly delegate decisions to groups of employees through the use of teams, committees, and task forces. The presumption is that team members have important specific knowledge to make the decisions and that they are more likely to buy in to decisions when they take part in the decision-making process. Managers should realize that team members are not always aligned in their personal interests, nor do they necessarily share the interests of the overall company. Also, group decision processes can sometimes be manipulated by team members. It is important for managers to understand these potential problems with teams. These problems are the subject of this appendix.

The Example of Majority Voting

Suppose that senior management appoints a team of three managers to recommend a new marketing strategy. Julio is from the finance department, while Stacey and Glenn are from the marketing and sales departments, respectively. Senior management wants the three managers to consider the interests of the overall company. However, given their current compensation schemes and positions in the company, they are more closely aligned with the interests of their particular departments than with the firm as a whole. For instance, Glenn is evaluated by the vice president of sales. Glenn knows that the vice president will be unhappy with any recommendation that reduces the size or influence of the sales department. Glenn thus has incentives to represent the views of the vice president on the task force.

The managers are considering three options, labeled Plans A, B, and C. The top panel of Figure 9.4 shows the preferences of the three managers. Each prefers a different plan. The managers decide to select a plan through a majority vote. When all three plans are considered together, each receives one vote and there is no winner. The managers, therefore, decide to conduct pairwise votes. The middle panel of Figure 9.4 displays the outcomes of all possible pairwise votes. The bottom panel shows the ultimate outcomes from the three possible sequences of pairwise votes. Any one of the three plans can win

---

[16]The material in this appendix draws on the analysis in K. Arrow (1963), *Social Choice and Individual Values* (John Wiley & Sons: New York).

depending on the order in the election! This example suggests that agenda control can be very important. If Stacy has the right to select the order of voting (for instance, she is a team leader), she can manipulate the voting outcome in her favor.[17]

Majority voting is commonly used in group decision making, especially when the group is large. For instance, task forces of 20 or more people commonly vote on issues. Sometimes, other voting rules are used. For instance, some groups require unanimity for passage (each person has a veto). Others require a supermajority (for example, two-thirds of the votes). Small groups often do not vote on issues formally. Rather, they make decisions by consensus. Nevertheless, the basic points of our analysis continue to hold—the outcome need not be efficient, can be subject to manipulation, and can depend on the order in which proposals are considered. Indeed, Nobel prize–winner Kenneth Arrow has demonstrated that any collective decision-making mechanism, other than granting the decision right to an individual, is subject to the types of problems illustrated in this example (depending on the preferences of the individuals in the group).

The analysis in this appendix has several important implications for managers who delegate decisions to groups of employees:

- Managers cannot assume that members of a team will always have the interests of the company as their primary objective—there are agency problems. These problems must be considered in forming a team. Sometimes, people with important information should be left off a team if the agency costs of including them on the team are large.
- Managers can reduce the agency problems on teams through incentive compensation plans. In our example, the existing compensation scheme motivated the managers to focus on their own departments rather than the firm as a whole. Compensating the managers based on the firmwide valuation effects of the team's recommendation would alter these incentives. If all three managers were concerned about the overall value of the firm, there would be no problem.[18]
- Agenda control can be a powerful device in group decision making. Not only can the outcome be affected by the order of the voting (as in Figure 9.4) but it can also be affected by the timing of the election. For instance, the vote might be set when it is known that a particular manager cannot attend. Senior managers, therefore, have an interest in who is appointed to positions such as team leaders and committee chairs. In this example, the senior manager would favor a team leader who cares about firm-value maximization (the agenda control would be used to benefit the overall firm).

---

[17]Our example assumes that the managers vote their preferences in each round of the voting. Managers might choose to vote *strategically*—they might vote in a manner that is inconsistent with their preferences in the first round to achieve a preferred outcome in the final round of voting. While strategic voting is a strong possibility in this setting, the basic point of our analysis remains—managers can influence the outcome if they have agenda control. See appendix problem 3.

   Note also that majority voting does not always result in this type of order-dependence outcome. It depends on the preferences of the individual team members.

[18]It is difficult to develop incentives schemes that completely resolve agency problems within teams. As we discuss in the text, it is difficult to design schemes that hold individuals fully responsible for their own actions. Thus, there are often incentive to free-ride in teams. We discuss this issue in greater detail in subsequent chapters.

Preferences

	Most Favored	Second Favored	Least Favored
Julio	A	C	B
Stacey	B	A	C
Glenn	C	B	A

Pairwise Votes

	A versus B	A versus C	B versus C
Julio	A	A	C
Stacey	B	A	B
Glenn	B	C	C
Winner*	B	A	C

Sequence of Pairwise Votes

Round 1	Round 2	Ultimate Winner
A versus B	B† versus C	C
A versus C	A† versus B	B
B versus C	C† versus A	A

*Majority-voting rule.
†Winner of the first round.

Figure 9.4   Majority Voting and the Order of Consideration

This figure presents an example of how the outcome of a series of pairwise votes can depend on the order that the votes are taken. The top section shows the preferences of the three managers who are voting on the proposals, A, B, and C. The middle section shows the outcomes of all possible pairwise votes. The example assumes that the managers vote their preferences in each election. A majority-voting rule is used. The bottom section displays the ultimate outcome of a sequence of pairwise votes (the winner of the first vote is run against the remaining proposal). Any outcome is possible, depending on the order of consideration. In contrast to this example, the order of consideration does not always matter in majority voting—it depends on the individual preferences of the voters.

Appendix Problems

1. What factors should a manager consider when deciding on the composition of a team charged with making an important decision?

2. Suppose the managers in the example in this appendix do not necessarily vote according to their preferences in each round of the voting. Rather, they might vote for a less preferred option in the first round to obtain a preferred outcome in the final round. Suppose that Julio has agenda control. How should he manipulate the agenda to achieve his preferred outcome?

Suggested Readings

E. Fama and M. Jensen (1983), "Separation of Ownership and Control," *Journal of Law & Economics* 26, 301–326.

M. Jensen and W. Meckling (1995), "Specific and General Knowledge, and Organizational Structure," *Journal of Applied Corporate Finance* 8:2, 4–18.

R. Kaplan and A. Atkinson (1989), *Advanced Management Accounting* (Prentice Hall: Englewood Cliffs, NJ), Chapter 13.

G. Miller (1993), *Managerial Dilemmas: The Political Economy of Hierarchy* (Cambridge University Press: Cambridge).

Review Questions

9–1. Discuss the costs and benefits of decentralized decision making relative to centralized decision making.

9–2. Rusty Laird, chief of personnel, has been instructed to increase female hiring at the Morton Cement Company. Laird will be evaluated by the company president Larry Smith on his success or failure in meeting this goal. Smith does not evaluate the performance of any of the division chiefs and each chief must approve all new division employees.

Do you expect Laird to succeed in this endeavor? Why or why not? Explain your reasoning.

9–3. Define the terms *decision management* and *decision control*. Under what circumstances might it be optimal to make one individual responsible for both decision management and decision control? What do you expect the ownership of common stock to look like in such a firm? Explain.

9–4. Jan Vanderschmidt was the founder of a successful chain of restaurants located throughout Europe. He died unexpectedly at the age of 55. Jan was sole owner of the company's common stock and was known for being quite authoritarian. He personally made most of the company's personnel decisions. He also made most of the decisions on menu selection, food suppliers, and advertising programs. Employees throughout the firm are paid fixed salaries and were heavily monitored by Vanderschmidt. Jan's son, Joop, spent his youth driving BMWs around Holland and Germany at high speeds. He spent little time working with his father in the restaurant business. Nevertheless, Joop is smart and just received his MBA degree from a leading business school. Joop has decided to follow his father as the chief operating officer of the restaurant chain. What advice about organizational architecture for the company would you offer Joop now that he has taken over?

9–5. Discuss the positive and negative effects of a university rule that would not allow professors to change a grade once recorded.

9–6. United Airlines assigns flight attendants to routes using the following procedure: Once a month, the attendants request the routes they prefer, with conflicts resolved strictly on the basis of seniority. Why does United use this procedure rather than simply having the supervisor of the attendants assign the flights?

9–7. Many companies have been experimenting with organizing their manufacturing around teams of employees. The employees are given decision rights on such things as how to organize the work and employee schedules. Often the employees are paid based on team output. Sometimes, this organizational arrangement has worked well. In other cases, it has not. Discuss the conditions under which you think that this type of team organization is most likely to succeed.

9–8. A leading business school currently uses study teams in the MBA program. Each team has five members. Some of the work in the first year is assigned to study teams and graded on a group basis. Discuss the tradeoffs involved with enlarging student study groups in the MBA program from five to six people.

9–9. It is frequently argued that for empowerment to work, managers must "let go of control" and learn to live with decisions that are made by their subordinates. Evaluate this argument.

9–10. It is sometimes argued that empowerment can be successful only if managers learn to live with decisions made by lower-level employees. Managers are to set clear boundaries within which employees can make decisions (for example, allowing a salesperson to set prices between $15,000 and $20,000). Managers should never overturn a decision if it is within the boundaries. Rather, good decision making should be encouraged through proper incentives and training. Do you agree that for empowerment to work, managers should always set clear boundaries and live with decisions within these boundaries? Explain.

9–11. Several Fortune 100 companies have nominated members of the clergy to be members of their boards of directors. Discuss the advantages and disadvantages of such a proposal.

9–12. An organizational consultant evaluates your division. She indicates that she does not like the divisional manager's top-down management style. She recommends setting up a board that consists of the divisional manager and his top 10 department managers. The consultant suggests that all major policy decisions be made by the board by a majority voting rule. She argues that this process will make for better use of information within the organization. She also argues that our political system is a democracy and works well and that the same concept could be applied beneficially within the corporation. Evaluate the recommendation.

9–13. The Colorado Symphony Orchestra (CSO) was formed after the Denver Symphony was no longer financially viable. CSO's corporate charter requires that it cannot have an operating deficit in any year. Revenues plus donations plus grants plus other income must equal or exceed operating expenses. CSO balances its budget each year by adjusting the musicians' salaries. For example, in 1995 the musicians were not paid the last two weeks of the year.

CSO's board of directors and executive management committees are composed of one-third each of musicians, full-time CSO staff, and community supporters of the CSO.

In most organizations, it is unusual for labor to have representation on the board of directors and management committees. Explain why you would expect musicians to have seats on the CSO board and management committees.

chapter 10

Decision Rights

Bundling Tasks into Jobs and Subunits

IBM Credit Corporation is a wholly owned subsidiary of IBM. Its major business is the financing of installment-payment agreements for IBM products. If IBM Credit were a stand-alone company, it would rank in the Fortune 100 finance companies with assets valued at over $10 billion. In 1993, IBM Credit was touted in the financial press for decreasing the time required to process a credit application from six days to four hours.[1] This decrease in cycle time was achieved through a substantial rebundling of the tasks performed by individual employees. Prior to *reengineering,* individuals performed narrowly assigned tasks. For example, one employee would check the applicant's credit while another would price the loan. Employees were grouped based on functional specialties to form the basic subunits of the firm (for example, the credit and pricing departments). After reengineering, applications were handled by "case workers" who were assigned most of the tasks involved in processing the application. The basic subunit structure of the company was correspondingly altered.

The results at IBM Credit suggest that the bundling of tasks into jobs and subunits of the firm can dramatically affect a firm's productivity. This chapter examines these important managerial decisions. We begin by analyzing the problem of how to bundle tasks into jobs. We then consider the problem of combining jobs into subunits of the firm. We conclude the chapter by discussing recent trends in the assignment of decision authority (the topic of Chapter 9) and the bundling of tasks (the topic of this chapter). We expand on the example of IBM Credit to illustrate these trends. Later in the book, in Chapter 17, we discuss the topic of process reengineering in more detail. The appendix to this chapter uses a simple game-theoretic example to illustrate some of the basic principles from this chapter.

Bundling Tasks into Jobs

In Chapter 9, we discussed how jobs have at least two important dimensions—decision authority and variety of tasks. We then analyzed the topic of decision authority in greater detail. We now turn to the second dimension, the bundling of tasks. The problem of how to bundle tasks is obviously quite complex; unfortunately, limited formal analysis of the topic exists. Nevertheless, the problem is economic in nature— managers face a set of *economic tradeoffs* when they bundle tasks. As in the case of decision authority, important insights into the nature of these tradeoffs can be gained through simple examples.

Specialized versus Broad Task Assignment

Financial Software Inc. (FSI) is a distributer of financial software. Its customers include individual consumers and businesses. Within FSI, there are two primary activities or *functions,* selling software and after-sales service (helping customers install the software on their systems and managing its interface with other programs). Thus, as displayed in Figure 10.1, FSI must perform four basic tasks—sales and service for each of the two customer groups. Of course, these four basic tasks could be subdivided into a much larger number of smaller tasks. To keep the analysis tractable we ignore this finer partitioning and assume that the firm has but four tasks. Our analysis readily extends to more general cases.

---

[1]Details of this example are from M. Hammer and J. Champy (1993), "The Promise of Reengineering," *Fortune* (May 3), 94–97.

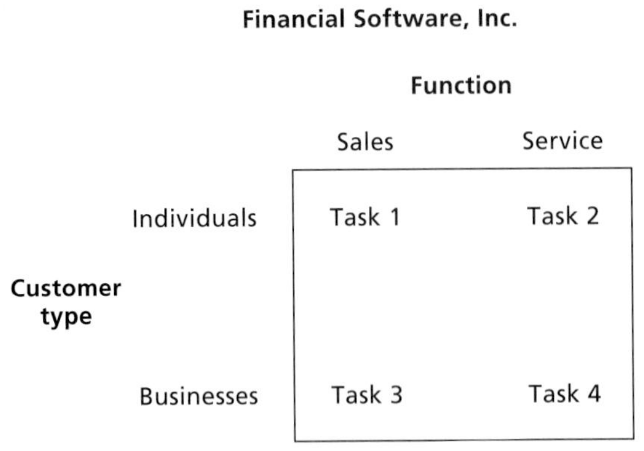

Financial Software, Inc.

Function

	Sales	Service
Individuals	Task 1	Task 2
Businesses	Task 3	Task 4

Customer type

Figure 10.1 Tasks at Financial Software Incorporated

Financial Software Inc. (FSI) is a distributor of financial software. Its customers include individual consumers and businesses. Within FSI, there are two primary activities or *functions,* selling software and after-sales service (helping customers install the software on their systems and interfacing it with other programs, for instance). As displayed in the figure, FSI must perform four basic tasks—sales and service for each of the two customer groups.

FSI operates at multiple locations throughout the country. At its planned new Greensboro office, each of the four tasks is expected to take four hours per day to complete. Thus, the firm must hire two full-time employees in this office. In structuring the two jobs, the most obvious alternatives are to (1) have each employee specialize in one function (either selling or service) that is performed for both customer groups or (2) have one employee provide both sales and service to individual consumers and the other employee perform both functions for business customers. We refer to the first alternative as *specialized task assignment* and the second as *broad task assignment.* We now discuss the relative benefits and costs of these two groupings.

Benefits of Specialized Task Assignment

There are at least two important benefits that can arise from using specialized rather than broad task assignment:

- *Exploiting comparative advantage.* Specialized task assignment allows the firm to match people with jobs based on skills and training and correspondingly has employees concentrate on their particular specialties. For example, FSI can hire salespeople to sell and technicians to provide service. The principle of comparative advantage suggests that this specialization will often produce higher output than having individuals perform a broad set of tasks—there are potential economies of scale in concentrating on a smaller number of tasks.
- *Lower cross-training expenses.* With specialized task assignment, each employee is trained to complete one basic function. With broad task assignment, employees are trained to complete more than one function, which can be expensive. For instance, suppose at FSI the service function requires a skilled technician with an advanced college degree, while the sales function requires an individual with only a high school diploma. Specialized task assignment allows FSI to hire one person with an advanced degree and one person without an advanced degree. With broad task assignment, the level of education required is usually the highest level across the assigned tasks. Thus,

Adam Smith on the Economies of Specialization

With specialized task assignment, employees concentrate on performing a narrow set of tasks. Adam Smith, an important 18th-century economist and philosopher, was among the first to recognize the potential gains from this type of specialization. In his classic book, *The Wealth of Nations,* he argued how a number of specialized employees, each performing a single step in the manufacturing of pins, could produce far more output than the same number of generalists making whole pins. Smith presents the following description of a pin factory using specialized employees:

> One man draws the wire, another straightens it, a third cuts it, a fourth points it, a fifth grinds it at the top for receiving the head; to make the head requires two or three distinct operations; to put it on is a peculiar business, to whiten the pins is another; it is even a trade by itself to put them into the paper.

Smith notes that a small factory with 10 specialized employees could produce about 48,000 pins a day, while 10 employees working independently could not have produced 20 pins per day.

Source: A. Smith (1776), *The Wealth of Nations* (Modern Library: New York, 1937), 4.

broad task assignment requires FSI to hire two people with advanced degrees and train them to perform both functions. If it costs more for FSI to hire a person with an advanced degree than a person with only a high school diploma, broad task assignment is more expensive than specialized task assignment.

Costs of Specialized Task Assignment

While specialized task assignment has advantages relative to broad task assignment, it also has drawbacks. Some of the costs of specialized task assignment are:

- *Foregone complementarities across tasks.* Sometimes, performing one task can lower the cost of having the same person perform another task. For example, important information about a customer's service requirements might be gained through the sales effort. This information is less likely to be utilized if sales and service are conducted by separate people; it can be costly to transfer the information to the other individual. As another example, consider the case of two employees on an automobile assembly line. The first attaches the door to the car frame and the second attaches the latching mechanism and makes sure the door latches to the frame. If the first does not align the door properly, the second will have more difficulty getting the door to latch properly. Combining both tasks into one job increases the care with which the person attaching the door checks for proper alignment before the latch is attached.
- *Coordination costs.* The activities of specialized employees have to be coordinated. For instance, FSI would have to establish procedures for transferring sales orders to service technicians. Also, it might have to appoint a manager to handle exceptions to these procedures (for instance, before committing to the purchase of the software, a customer might demand authorization for specialized installation). Developing and coordinating activities can be expensive.
- *Functional myopia.* With specialized task assignment, employees tend to concentrate on their individual functions rather than on the overall process of providing good sales and service to customers. For example, a salesperson who is compensated primarily through commissions will have incentives to sell software to customers even if the sale imposes large service costs on the company, as when the software is not well matched with the customer's existing computer system.

- *Reduced flexibility.* Failure to cross-train employees has costs as well as benefits. For example, if only one person is trained to perform a particular function, what happens if the person is sick or on vacation? Also, having only one person trained to do a job in a firm can place the firm at a disadvantage when bargaining with the employee over salary and other benefits.[2] These problems are likely to be greatest in small companies, since large companies are more likely to have several people trained to perform any given task.

Incentive Issues

Our discussion of the costs and benefits of specialized versus broad task assignment has focused on informational and technological considerations. Incentive issues can also be important. From an incentive standpoint, it is sometimes better to have employees concentrate on a narrow set of tasks, while in other circumstances, a broad set of tasks is preferred.

With broad task assignment, the firm is not only concerned with how hard employees work but also with how they allocate effort among the tasks.[3] For instance, senior managers at FSI would be concerned with how the employees balance their efforts between sales and service. Designing an evaluation and compensation scheme that motivates an appropriate balance of effort is complicated by the fact that the effort exerted on some tasks is often more easily measured than for other tasks. At FSI, the sales effort might be easily estimated by sales volume, while it might be quite difficult to measure the quality of after-sales service—there are no good direct indicators of service quality, and poor quality might reveal itself very slowly over time (only as customers fail to make repeat purchases). If FSI pays a sales commission, employees will concentrate on sales at the expense of providing good after-sales service to customers—selling increases their incomes, while providing better service has a small impact (it affects income only through its effect on repeat purchases). FSI can reduce this incentive to misallocate effort by not paying a sales commission. However, the employees might have relatively low incentives to exert effort on either task. One potential response to this problem is to use specialized task assignment. The salesperson could be provided high-powered incentives to concentrate on sales. The service person would not be evaluated on quantifiable output measures. Service could be evaluated on more subjective measures, such as customer-satisfaction surveys. We discuss these issues in greater detail in Chapter 13.

In some cases, producing output requires the coordinated execution of several separate tasks that individually are hard to assess. Here, it can make sense to assign all the tasks to one individual who is accountable for the final product. For instance, in the example of attaching doors and latches to automobiles, assigning both tasks to one employee makes it easy to identify who is to blame if the door does not latch properly. Similarly, at FSI the failure of a customer to make a repeat purchase might be due to either poor sales effort or service. Having one employee conduct both sales and service facilitates identification of the employee responsible for the unhappy customer.

---

[2]L. Stole and J. Zwiebel (1993), "Organizational Design and Technology Choice with Nonbinding Contracts," working paper (University of Chicago: Chicago).

[3]B. Holmstrom and P. Milgrom (1991), "Multitask Principal-Agent Analyses: Incentive Contract, Asset Ownership and Job Design," *Journal Of Law Economics and Organization* 7, 24–52.

Costs and Benefits of Specialized Task Assignment

Benefits	Costs
Comparative advantage/economies of scale	Foregone complementarities across tasks
Lower cross-training expenses	Coordination costs
	Functional myopia
	Reduced flexibility

Incentive issues can favor either specialized or broad task assignment, depending on the nature of the production technology and information flows.

Productive Bundling of Tasks

The choice between specialized and broad task assignment depends on the technological, informational, and incentive issues discussed above. One variable that is likely to be of particular importance in making this decision is the relative degree of complementarity among tasks within versus across functional areas. At FSI, the magnitude of the benefits of specialized task assignment depends largely on how related are the selling efforts between the two customer groups. If there are only minor differences between selling to individuals and businesses, training employees to do one makes them well suited to do the other. In contrast, if the selling tasks are very different between individuals and businesses, little is gained by training one employee to perform the two selling tasks compared to training separate employees. In addition, any economies of scale that result from specializing in sales are likely to be small. Similarly, the costs of specialized task assignment at FSI depend on the importance of complementarities across functional areas. When these complementarities are low (for instance, little valuable information is gained about service through the selling effort), little is lost by having employees concentrate on a single function. It is also relatively easy to coordinate the individual specialists through the use of routine procedures. Ultimately, the degree of complementarity among tasks depends on how specialized knowledge is created and the costs of transferring knowledge. It also depends on the technology used in the production process.

Our example of FSI is quite simplified, and in most settings, more complicated task divisions are feasible. For instance, the selling function might have two phases—the initial contact and closing the deal. The initial contact requires less specialized product and service knowledge than closing the deal but is potentially more time-consuming. Here, it might be better for a salesperson to handle the initial contact and have a joint call by both the salesperson and service person to close the deal. As another example, at some locations, more complete specialization might be feasible. For instance, an employee at an office with a larger sales volume could concentrate solely on selling to individuals or to businesses. While our basic example of FSI abstracts from these more complicated considerations, it nevertheless isolates some of the key considerations in deciding on how to divide tasks into jobs.

Bundling of Jobs into Subunits

Our discussion of specialized versus broad task assignment highlights the economic tradeoffs of bundling tasks into jobs. Managers are confronted with a similar set of tradeoffs when they bundle jobs into subunits (for example, departments, divisions, and subsidiaries).

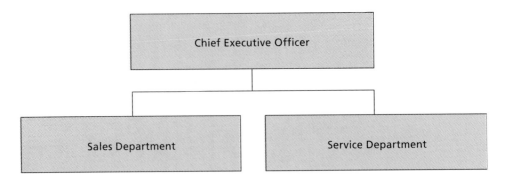

Figure 10.2 Financial Software Incorporated (FSI) as a Functional Organization

This figure displays an organizational chart for FSI when jobs are grouped by functional specialty. These jobs are characterized by specialized task assignment. All the sales jobs in the organization are grouped together to form a sales department, while the service jobs are grouped together to form a service department. These departments are charged with managing their particular functions across the firm's entire product line. The CEO's office plays an important role in defining organizational architecture, coordinating activities across departments, and making key operating decisions.

Grouping people together within a subunit lowers the communication and coordination costs among the people *within the subunit.* For instance, they often report to the same manager, who facilitates information flows and coordination. Employees are also more likely to form closer working relationships if they share the same work space (especially if they are evaluated and compensated on subunit performance). Managers, however, must devise methods of coordinating activities *across the subunits.* For instance, rules and procedures must be developed for coordinating activities among interdependent subunits; managers must be appointed and granted the authority to rule on exceptions to these procedures; and liaison staff and coordinating committees must often be appointed to address interunit issues. In summary, there is a tradeoff between the benefits that come from grouping people together and the costs of coordinating their activities with other subunits. In addition, it is also important to consider incentive issues— some groupings make it easier to devise productive performance-evaluation and reward systems than other groupings (we elaborate on such incentive issues in Chapter 14).

In what follows, we begin by describing two classic methods of grouping jobs into subunits—by function and by product and/or geography. We then discuss the economic tradeoffs between these two subunit designs. This discussion is followed by an examination of other methods that firms use to group jobs into subunits.

Grouping Jobs by Function

One common method of grouping jobs is by functional specialty (engineering, design, sales, finance, and so on). This organizational arrangement is sometimes referred to as the *unitary* or *U-form* of organization because it places each primary function in one major subunit (rather than in multiple subunits). Figure 10.2 displays an organizational chart for FSI under this type of functional grouping. Individual jobs are characterized by

Financial Software, Inc.

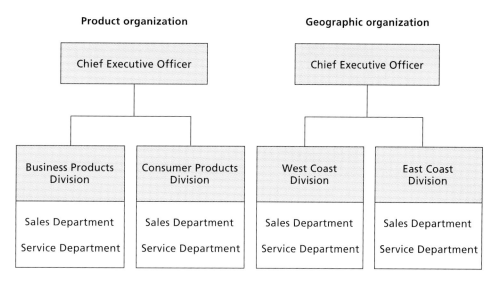

Figure 10.3 Financial Software Incorporated (FSI) as a Product and Geographic Organization

This figure shows how FSI would look organized around product or geography. In the first case, the company is divided into a business products division and a consumer products division. Each of these divisions has its own sales and service departments that focus on the particular products of the division. (Often, jobs within the business units are grouped by functional area.) Organized geographically, the company is divided into a west coast division and an east coast division. In this case, the sales and service departments within each business unit serve both individual and business customers within their geographic areas.

specialized task assignment. All the sales jobs in the organization are grouped together to form a sales department, while the service jobs are grouped together to form a service department. These departments are charged with managing their particular functions across the firm's entire product line. Senior management plays an important role in defining the architecture, coordinating activities across departments, making key operating decisions, and setting corporate strategy. Rules and procedures are established for coordinating the activities across the functions. For example, detailed procedures are established to transfer sales orders to the service department. Exceptions and special cases are handled by the senior management and/or coordinating committees (which often include senior division managers and corporate staff).

Grouping Jobs by Product or Geography

Another prominent subunit design is the *multidivisional form (M-form)* of organization, which groups jobs into a collection of business units based on product or geographic area. Operating decisions such as product offerings and pricing are decentralized to the business-unit level. Senior management of the firm is responsible for major strategic decisions, including organizational architecture and the allocation of capital among the business units. Figure 10.3 shows how FSI would look organized around product or geography. In the first case, the company is divided into a business products division and a consumer products division. Each of these divisions has its own sales and service departments that focus

Concentrating on Functions at Cadillac

Some of the coordination problems that can arise within a functional organization are highlighted by the process that Cadillac formerly used for developing new products. Under this process, engineers were grouped by narrow functional specialty and charged with completing a related set of tasks:

> The designer of the car's body would leave a hole for the engine, then the power-train designer would try to fit the engine into the cavity, then the manufacturing engineer would try to figure out how to build the design, and finally the service engineer would struggle to invent ways of repairing the car. The results were predictable. On one model, the exhaust manifold blocked access to the air-conditioning compressor, so seasonal maintenance meant removing the exhaust system. On another model, the connection between the spark plugs and the spark plug wires was so tight that mechanics tended to break the wires when they pulled them off to check the spark plugs.

Automobile companies have been able to reduce problems of this type by moving to a system of "concurrent engineering" where everyone affected by design participates in the process as early as possible. Often, companies use development teams that are charged with the entire process. Development teams group jobs by product rather than by function.

Source: W. Davidow and M. Malone (1993), *The Virtual Corporation*
(Harper Business: New York).

on the particular products of the division (often, jobs within the business units are grouped by functional area). Organized geographically, the company is divided into a west coast division and an east coast division. In this case, the sales and service departments within each business unit serve both individual and business customers within their geographic areas.

Tradeoffs between Functional and Product/Geographic Subunits

Benefits of Functional Subunits

There are at least three major benefits from grouping jobs by function. First, this grouping helps to promote effective coordination within the functional areas. For instance, a supervisor in service can assign employees to specific projects based on current work load and expertise. It is also generally easier for functional specialists to share information if they are in the same department. For example, if a service technician develops a new solution to a problem, that employee's supervisor can help promote its use by training other technicians in the department. Second, this grouping helps to promote functional expertise. Individuals focus on developing specific functional skills and are directly supervised by knowledgeable individuals who can help with this development. Third, there is a well-defined promotion path for employees. Employees will tend to work their way up within a functional department (for example, from salesperson to local sales manager to district sales manager). Having a well-defined promotion path can reduce employee uncertainty about career paths and thus can make it less expensive to attract and retain qualified employees (recall the Chapter 2 discussion of risk aversion).

Problems with Functional Subunits

While functional grouping has advantages, it also has disadvantages. First, there is the opportunity cost of using senior management's valuable time coordinating functions and making operating decisions. This time might better be spent on activities such as long-range planning (deciding in which businesses the company should compete, planning strategies to be successful in these businesses, and implementing the firm's organizational architecture). Second, there can be significant, time-consuming coordination problems across departments. At FSI, when a sale is made by the sales department, the order has to be communicated to the service department, which in turn must schedule the required customer service.

The Formation of Multidivisional Firms in the Oil Industry

In the 1950s, most of the Fortune 500 oil companies were organized into functional departments. These companies were not performing well in competition with smaller corporations. Oil companies began experimenting with their organizational architectures. The design that appeared to work best was the multidivisional form of organization. Some of the firms organized around geographic areas, while other firms organized around product lines. Companies that switched to the M-form early outperformed other companies that did not switch as soon. By the middle 1970s, most large oil companies had switched to the multidivisional form of organization. Those that did not switch tended to be smaller companies that performed well under the old structure.

Source: H. Armour and D. Teece (1978), "Organizational Structure and Economic Performance," *Bell Journal of Economics* 9, 106–22.

This process can cause lengthy delays in serving the customer. Moreover, important information can be lost in these transfers between departments. Third, employees sometimes concentrate on their functional specialties rather than on the process of satisfying customers. For instance, the sales department might focus on achieving department goals, even if it imposes costs on other departments in the firm. A salesperson might promise rapid installation to a customer even though the work load of the service department is high.

Benefits of Product/Geographic Subunits

An advantage of the M-form of organizing for large corporations (especially in dynamic environments) is that decision rights for operations are assigned to individuals lower in the organization, where in many cases the relevant specific knowledge is located. Managers of business units are compensated based on the performance of their units; this provides incentives to use this specific knowledge more productively. Decentralizing decision rights to business-unit managers also frees senior management to concentrate on other, more strategic issues. The separation of the corporate office from operations focuses senior executives' attention on the overall performance of the corporation rather than on specific aspects of the functional components. A product/geographic focus promotes coordination among the functions that must be completed to produce and market a particular product or to serve a given geographic area.

Problems with Product/Geographic Subunits

Business-unit managers tend to focus on the performance of their own units. This focus is consistent with the maximization of firm value so long as product demands and costs are independent across business units. In this case, firm value is simply the sum of the values of the individual units. Frequently, there are important interdependencies among units that must be taken into account if firm value is to be maximized. For example, there is likely to be some overlap in customers, intermediate products are often transferred between subunits, and the units share common resources. If managers focus on their own units and do not consider these interdependencies, overall firm value is reduced. For example, the west and east coast divisions of FSI might compete against each other for a national customer and reduce overall firm profits by selling products at a lower price than if they coordinated their marketing. This problem can be mitigated by forming *groups* of interrelated business units and paying unit managers based on overall group performance. However, as we discuss in subsequent chapters, developing a compensation scheme that appropriately motivates unit managers is not easy. Splitting functional personnel among business units also forgoes potential economies that might result from combining similar specialists within one subunit.

Benefits and Costs of Functional Organization Relative to Product/Geographic Organization

Benefits	Costs
Improved coordination among functional specialists Promotes functional expertise Well-defined promotion path	Less effective use of local product/geographic information Opportunity cost of senior management time Coordination problems among subunits Functional focus—it is difficult to design compensation plans that promote a focus on profits and customers

Where Functional Subunits Work Best

Functional grouping works best in small firms with a limited number of products. In these firms, it is relatively easy for senior managers to coordinate operating decisions across departments in a timely and informed fashion. For large firms with more diverse product offerings, senior executives are less likely to have the specific knowledge for making operational decisions for the company. In addition, the opportunity cost of having senior management concentrate on operating and coordination issues rather than major strategic issues for the firm can be large.[4] Here, grouping by product or geography will often be the preferred alternative.

Another variable that is likely to affect the desirability of functional subunits is the rate of technological change in the industry. Here, it is important to think of technological change broadly to include new products, new production techniques, and organizational innovations. Functional subunits are more effective in environments with a more stable technology, since frequent communication across functional departments and specialists is less important and interactions can be handled through routine rules and procedures. In addition, senior management is likely to possess more of the relevant specific knowledge to coordinate the functional areas.

In less stable environments, direct communication across functional areas is more important and new situations are more likely to arise that will challenge established coordination procedures. In turn, senior managers are less likely to have all the relevant specific knowledge to address these challenges. Rather, the specific knowledge is more likely to be spread across employees throughout the firm. For example, the frequent introduction of new products increases the benefits of communication among salespeople and design engineers about customer demands and preferences. Similarly, it is important for development and manufacturing personnel to share information when production techniques and technologies are changing more frequently.

Finally, in a rapidly changing environment, there is likely to be more uncertainty about the optimal organizational architecture. With divisions organized around products or geography, different divisions can experiment with different architectures. For example, when Citibank began making a market in swaps, it opened trading desks in New York, Toronto, London, and Tokyo. The different operations competed with each other as well as with other financial institutions for business. By encouraging experimentation with the architecture of these businesses, Citibank exploited the benefits of economic Darwinism within the firm. As experience mounted, the best procedures were made standard across the bank. Thus, when an environment is more dynamic, the desirability of a product/geographic organization increases.

---

[4]O. Williamson (1975), *Markets and Hierarchies* (Free Press: New York).

Environment, Strategy, and Architecture

In Chapter 8, we discussed how the optimal organizational architecture is influenced by the firm's business environment and strategy. Our discussion of the optimal subunit configuration highlights this influence. Both environmental factors (such as the rate of technological change) and the firm's business strategy (whether the firm produces multiple products, chooses to operate in multiple locations, and so on) affect the desirability of functional versus product/geographic organization.

An important illustration of the influence of the environment and strategy on subunit design is the experience of large U.S. firms at the beginning of the 20th century. The first large firms in the United States were the railroad companies, which emerged around 1850.[5] These firms initially organized around basic functions such as finance, pricing, traffic, and maintenance. As the incidence of large firms increased in other industries in the late 1800s (such as steel, tobacco, oil, and meatpacking), most followed the lead of the railroads and organized around basic functions. As companies like Du Pont, General Motors, and General Electric continued to expand (both geographically and in the number of product lines) in the early 1900s, they began faring poorly in product markets where they faced smaller competitors—their organizational architectures did not fit their changing environments or strategies. In response, these companies began experimenting with different organizational forms. After significant experimentation, many large companies adopted the M-form of organization. Economic historian, Alfred Chandler concludes:[6]

> *The inherent weakness in the centralized, functionally departmentalized operating company . . . became critical only when the administrative load of the senior executives increased to such an extent that they were unable to handle their entrepreneurial responsibilities efficiently. This situation arose when the operations of the enterprise became too complex and the problems of coordination, appraisal, and policy formulation too intricate for a small number of top officers to handle both long-run, entrepreneurial, and short-run, operational administrative activities.*

Matrix Organization

Some firms attempt to capture the benefits of both functional and product/geographic organization by using overlapping subunit structures.[7] In these *matrix organizations,* there are functional departments such as finance, manufacturing, and development. Employees from these functional departments are also assigned to subunits organized around product, geography, or some special project. Matrix organizations are characterized by intersecting lines of authority—the term *matrix* refers to the intersecting lines resulting from such an organizational arrangement. Individuals report to both a functional manager and a product manager. Functional departments usually serve as the primary mechanism for personnel functions and professional development. The functional managers typically have the primary responsibility for performance reviews (since they have

---

[5]A. Chandler, Jr. (1977), *The Visible Hand: The Managerial Revolution in American Business* (Belknap Press: Cambridge, MA).

[6]A. Chandler, Jr. (1966), *Strategy and Structure* (Doubleday: Garden City, NY) 382–383.

[7]For a more detailed discussion of matrix organizations, see W. Baber (1983), *Organizing for the Future* (The University of Alabama Press: Tuscaloosa, AL).

Intel Corporation: A Matrix Organization

Intel Corporation's organizational structure in 1992 provides an example of a matrix organization. The company organized around five major product groups, including entry-level products, Intel products, microprocessor products, multimedia and supercomputing components, and semiconductor products. Intel staffed these groups with people from the basic functional groups of corporate business development, finance and administration, marketing, sales, software technology, and technology and manufacturing. Thus, individual workers were members of both product and functional groups.

Source: A. Dhebar (1993), "Intel Corporation: Going into OverDrive,"
Harvard Business School Case 9-593-096.

better technical knowledge for evaluating an employee's performance). Product managers provide input into these reviews. For example, in hospitals, nurses work with physicians and medical technicians in the delivery of health care in "product line" hospital units such as pediatrics or orthopedics. Much of the nurses' specific directions in caring for a particular patient comes from physicians. Yet in many hospitals, nurses are hired, supervised, and evaluated by other nurses who ultimately report to the director of nursing. Physicians have only advisory authority in this process.

Matrix organization is often used in industries such as defense, construction, and management consulting. These industries are characterized by a sequence of new products or projects (for example, building a new airplane or a new shopping mall). Individuals are assigned to work in teams on particular projects and are reassigned to new project teams after the initial projects are completed. Given the nature of the projects in these industries, it is important for individuals across functional areas to communicate and to work together closely. For example, a successful airplane design must meet the demands of the customer; thus, there are benefits from the use of product-oriented teams. However, it is critical that the plane be aerodynamically sound. Thus, these projects also benefit from a high level of functional expertise, which is promoted by maintaining functional areas.

Figure 10.4 shows how FSI might look if it were organized as a matrix organization. The firm maintains functional departments for sales and service. Employees from these departments are simultaneously assigned to either the business-product or consumer-product subunits ("teams"). Functional managers focus on managing their particular function across both products, while product managers focus on managing particular products across functions.

A potential advantage of a matrix organization, relative to a functional organization, is that employees are more likely to focus on the overall business process rather than on their own narrow functional specialty. However, in contrast to a pure product/geographic organization, functional supervision is maintained; there is a mechanism for helping to ensure functional excellence and for providing opportunities for advancement and development.

Potential problems with the matrix form of organization arise from the intersecting lines of authority. Employees who are assigned to product teams do not automatically have strong incentives to cooperate or be concerned about the success of the team. Rather, individuals might be more concerned about how their functional supervisors view their work (since functional supervisors do the primary performance reviews). Moreover, employees often see their roles as being representatives for their functional areas. Employees can be overly concerned about how the decisions of a product team impact their particular area. These problems can be reduced by appropriate design of

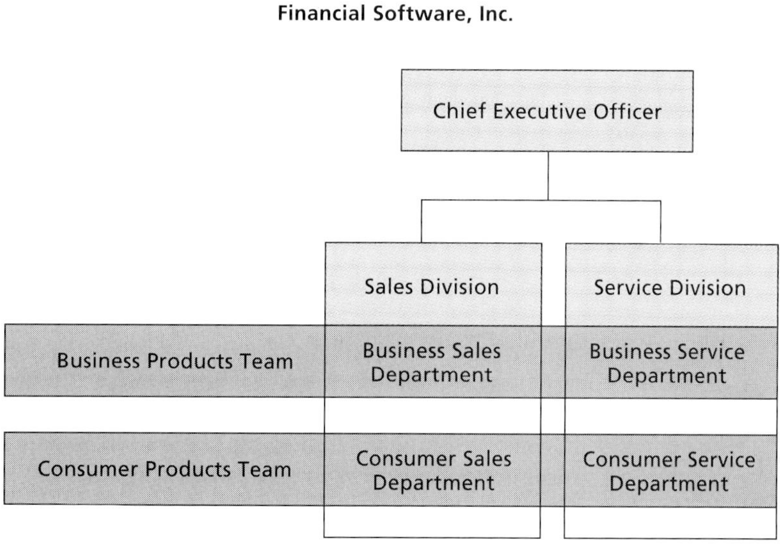

Financial Software, Inc.

Figure 10.4 Financial Software Incorporated (FSI) as a Matrix Organization

This figure shows how FSI might look organized as a matrix organization. The firm maintains functional divisions of sales and service. Individuals from these divisions are simultaneously assigned to either the business-products or consumer-products subunits (teams). These teams are indicated by the shaded rectangles. The functional managers focus on managing the particular function across both products, while the product managers focus on managing particular products across functions.

the performance-evaluation and reward systems (discussed in subsequent chapters). Individuals will be more concerned about the output of a product team if their compensation depends on team output. A related problem with matrix organizations is the potential for disputes between functional and product managers and the cost of resolving such disputes.

Mixed Designs

Often, firms use more than one method to organize subunits. Chase Manhattan Bank uses three types of subunits for different activities within the bank. Chase Delaware handles all the bank's credit-card business. The business for individuals and middle-market firms is organized geographically. Large business customers are served by specific teams that generally operate out of New York City. Frequently, these teams are set up by industry. As another example, large corporations often organize their international divisions around the matrix concept (with overlapping country and product managers), while their domestic subunits are organized around function, product, or geography.

Network Organization

Firms (and groups of firms) have experimented with other methods of organizing subunits. One example is the so-called network organization. *Network organizations* are divided into work groups based on function, geography, or some other dimension. The relationships among these work groups are determined by the demands of specific projects and work activities rather than by formal lines of authority. These relationships are fluid and frequently change with changes in the business environment.[8] The Japanese *keiretsu,* which is an affiliation of quasi-independent firms with ongoing, fluid relationships, is another example of a network organization. Networks can facilitate information flows and cooperative undertakings among work groups. However, their heavy reliance on implicit understandings and informal relationships can lead to misunderstandings or opportunism.

Organizing within Subunits

We have examined the topic of partitioning the firm into major subunits. The same analysis applies to grouping jobs within subunits (for example, departments). Grouping jobs into functional departments at a business-unit level is most likely to be effective when the unit is small and has a limited range of products. In contrast, in large business units with diverse product offerings, organizing by product or geography can be the preferred alternative. Product/geographic organization is also likely to be more desirable in rapidly changing business environments, since senior management is less likely to have the relevant specific knowledge to make operating and coordination decisions.

Recent Trends in the Assignment of Decision Rights

Traditionally, many firms have created jobs that specify limited decision authority (the topic of Chapter 9) and narrow task assignments. In turn, these jobs have tended to be grouped by functional specialty (either at the overall firm level or at the business-unit level). During the 1990s, there has been a significant shift toward granting employees broader decision authority and less specialized task assignments. Many companies have also shifted from functional subunits toward more product-oriented organizations. As we discuss below, these changes have been motivated by increased global competition and various technological changes.

To illustrate some of the factors that have motivated such organizational changes, we examine IBM Credit Corporation in more detail. Figure 10.5 lists the basic functions that IBM Credit must perform to process a credit application.[9] The credit of the applicant has to be checked; the deal must be priced (an interest rate must be chosen); formal contracts have to be written; and final documents must be compiled and sent to the applicant.

Prior to reengineering, IBM Credit was organized around these four basic functions. Figure 10.6 shows an organizational chart for IBM Credit under this functional structure. The firm was divided into functional departments, including credit, pricing, contracts, and documents. Employees, were typically assigned a specialized set of tasks within their functional areas and given limited decision authority on how to complete

---

[8]W. Baker (1992), "The Network Organization in Theory and Practice," in *Networks and Organizations,* N. Nohria and R. Eccles, eds. (Harvard Business School: Boston), 397–429.

[9]Details of this example are from M. Hammer and J. Champy (1993), *Reengineering the Corporation* (Harper Business: New York). Our discussion of IBM Credit abstracts from many of the details of the actual operation of the company. For example, we do not consider the company's credit-collection activities, and the organizational chart is highly simplified. This simplification allows us to illustrate the main points of our analysis without becoming bogged down in less relevant detail.

IBM Credit Functions

- Credit checking
- Contract preparation
- Pricing
- Document preparation

Figure 10.5   Functions at IBM Credit

This figure lists the basic functions that IBM Credit must perform in order to complete the process of transforming credit applications into formal credit offers.

them. For example, a clerk in the credit department might have the simple task of logging applications using prescribed procedures. Coordination across functional departments was accomplished by senior management, often through formal rules and procedures. For example, IBM Credit had procedures for transferring credit applications among the various functional departments. Department heads served together on committees to assist in the coordination process. With this architecture, customers received relatively poor service. IBM Credit took about six days to process a credit application, and it was difficult to provide timely information to the customer about the status of an application. However, each application was subject to a careful credit check and each stage of the process was conducted by functional experts.

When IBM Credit was the only major producer of mainframe computers, few customers were lost due to delays in processing finance applications. Rather, it could focus on careful and deliberate application procedures. The emergence of Japanese competitors (for example, Hitachi) increased pressure on IBM to change its business strategy to focus more on customer service and to shorten the time required to process a credit application. Otherwise, it faced a significant decrease in sales.

New information and computer technologies enabled IBM Credit to develop internal systems to support an organizational change. For instance, some of the necessary information for processing a credit application was stored previously in a manual filing system.

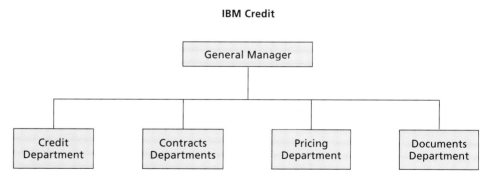

Figure 10.6   IBM Credit with Functional Organization

Under a functional organization, the firm is divided into functional departments, including credit, contracts, pricing, and documents. Employees are typically assigned a specialized set of tasks within their functional areas.

David Kearns on Increased Foreign Competition

Over the past few decades, competition has increased in many industries. This increased competition has been motivated by such things as lost patent protection, reduced transportation costs, deregulation, and improved technology throughout the world. David Kearns was CEO of Xerox during the 1980s. During his tenure, Xerox faced a substantial increase in foreign competition. This increased competition motivated Xerox to improve customer service and the quality of its products. To achieve this objective, Xerox substantially reassigned decision rights by empowering workers and moving away from functional organization. In Kearn's words:

> About the only consoling factor was that I knew we weren't the only ones in the soup. Global competition had set upon this country, and everyone was vulnerable. American business was threatened not only by Japan and Korea. Europe was mobilizing into a potent force that demanded serious consideration. And yet, as I looked around me, I saw that so many great and admired companies were doing nothing but sitting on their hands. Like us, they were kissing away their businesses and laying the groundwork for their own destruction.
>
> After my string of trips to Japan and after deep introspection about Xerox's strengths and flaws, the solution began to point in one direction. Our only hope for survival was to urgently commit ourselves to vastly improving the quality of our products and service. This was something a lot of corporations talked about, but it was extraordinarily difficult to do. It meant changing the very culture of Xerox from the ground up. Everyone from the cleaning people to the chairman would have to think differently.

Source: D. Kearns (1992), *Prophets in the Dark* (Harper Business: New York), xv–xvi.

Given this system, it made sense to assign certain tasks to individuals who had familiarity with and proximity to this data. Computerizing this database allowed employees throughout the firm to access this information directly, which permitted the firm to more easily reassign tasks. Similarly, IBM Credit was able to develop computer programs to assist less-skilled personnel in pricing loans. Such expert systems make functional expertise less important (thereby diminishing the importance of one of the advantages of their old organizational architecture).

Given these competitive pressures and new technologies, IBM Credit completely changed its assignment of decision rights. Under the new structure, pictured in Figure 10.7, individual *case workers* have the primary decision rights and responsibility for

---

Recent Trends in Organization: GTE

During the 1990s, there has been a trend toward more product-oriented organizations. An example of a firm that reorganized along these lines is GTE, the telephone company. Traditionally, GTE had been organized into functional departments such as repair, billing, and marketing. This structure often frustrated customers, who had difficulty locating which person in the company was responsible for addressing particular problems. Due to increased competitive pressures, GTE decided that it had to offer dramatically better customer service to its telephone customers. Rather than making incremental improvements in each of its functional departments, GTE decided to reorganize around the basic process of providing customer service. In particular, customers wanted one-stop shopping—for example, one number to fix an erratic dial tone, question a bill, sign up for call waiting, or all three, at any time of the day. GTE began meeting this demand when it set up its first pilot "customer care center" in Garland Texas in 1992. GTE management states that preliminary data from these pilot projects indicates a 20 to 30 percent increase in productivity. Customers also obtain better service.

Source: T. Stewart (1993), "Reengineering: The Hot New Management Tool," *Fortune* (August 23), 41–48.

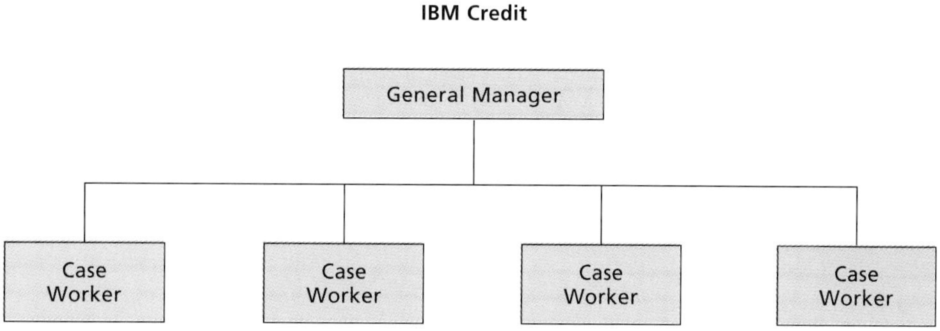

IBM Credit

Figure 10.7 IBM Credit's Revised Organization

Under the revised structure, individual case workers have the primary decision rights and responsibility for completing all the steps in the credit-granting process. Each financing request is assigned to a case worker, who checks the applicant's credit, prices the deal, completes the contracts, and so on. There are some functional specialists in the firm (not shown on the chart) who help the case workers when difficult or unusual circumstances arise.

completing all the steps in the credit-granting process. Each financing request is assigned to one case worker, who checks the applicant's credit, prices the deal, and draws the contracts. Employees have significant decision authority in completing these tasks, and the functional subunits of the firm have largely been abandoned.[10] Performance-evaluation and reward systems were correspondingly changed to focus more specifically on processing times and customer service. With this new organizational architecture, IBM Credit is able to process a credit application in about four hours. Customer satisfaction has increased correspondingly.

IBM Credit and GTE are but two examples of the many firms that have undertaken similar restructurings in the 1990s. The success stories from these restructurings have led some management consultants to advocate widespread change for all firms throughout the world. The analysis in Chapters 9 and 10, however, indicates that a firm should not restructure without carefully considering whether a reassignment of decision rights is warranted given its particular business environment and strategy.

While changes in technology and competition have shifted the optimal assignment of decision rights in many firms, these shifts have not occurred in all industries. The benefits of narrow task assignment and functional specialization are still likely to be high for many firms in relatively stable industries. Consider, for example, a small coal-mining operation. Here, it is likely to continue to make sense to have some employees concentrate on mining the coal, while other employees sell it, and still other employees deliver it.

---

[10]Some functional specialists remain in the organization to help the case workers with difficult or unusual circumstances.

F. W. Taylor on Iron Workers

Frederick Winslow Taylor, an industrial engineer at the beginning of the 20th century, is known as the father of scientific management. His views were quite influential in affecting the assignment of decision rights in many firms. In particular, he argued that the attributes of lower-level employees dictated that they be granted limited decision authority and a narrow set of tasks. In his words:

> Now one of the very first requirements for a man who is fit to handle pig iron as a regular occupation is that he shall be so stupid and so phlegmatic that he more nearly resembles in his mental make-up the ox than any other type. The man who is mentally alert and intelligent is for this very reason entirely unsuited to what would, for him, be the grinding monotony or work of this character. Therefore the workman who is best suited to handling pig iron is unable to understand the real science of doing this class of work. He is so stupid that the word "percentage" has no meaning to him, and he must consequently be trained by a man more intelligent than himself into the habit of working in the accordance with the laws of this science before he can be successful.

Many modern managers do not think that this view of lower-level employees is accurate in today's environment. The work force of today is better educated than in Taylor's time, and modern production technologies often call for increased education and less brawn. Correspondingly, many managers have empowered lower-level employees by giving them broader decision authority and a less specialized set of tasks.

Source: F. Taylor (1923), *The Principles of Scientific Management* (Harper & Row: New York), 59.

Summary

The bundling of tasks into jobs and subunits of the firm is an important policy choice that can dramatically affect a firm's productivity. The primary purpose of this chapter is to examine this bundling decision.

We distinguish between two types of jobs, those with *specialized task assignment* and those with *broad task assignment*. With specialized task assignment, the employee is assigned a narrow set of tasks related to one functional specialty—for example, sales. With broad task assignment, the employee is assigned a broader variety of tasks. The benefits of specialized task assignment relative to broad assignment include exploiting comparative advantage and lower cross-training expenses. The costs of specialized task assignment include foregone complementarities from not performing multiple functions, coordination costs, functional myopia, and reduced flexibility. Incentive issues can favor either specialized or broad task assignment, depending on the production technology and information flows. The appropriate bundling of tasks depends on the magnitude of the costs and benefits of each alternative. One variable that is likely to be of particular importance is the relative degree of complementarity among tasks within versus across functional areas. Specialized task assignment is favored when the complementarity of tasks within a functional area is relatively high.

Firms can group jobs into subunits based on functional specialty, geography, product, or some combination of the three. *Functional subunits* group all jobs performing the same function within one department (for example, a sales department). The CEO's office plays a major role in coordinating these departments and in making operating decisions. Benefits of functional organization are the promotion of coordination and expertise within functional areas and provision of a well-defined promotion path for employees. Problems with functional organization are: the high opportunity cost of employing senior management time to coordinate departments and make operating decisions; handoffs across departments that can take significant time; coordination failures across departments; and employees concentrating on their own functional specialties rather than the customer. Functional subunits are likely to work best in small firms with a limited number of products operating in relatively stable environments.

CASE STUDY
Bagby Copy Company

Bagby Copy Company is a hypothetical worldwide producer of copy machines. It manufactures 10 different copiers, ranging from low-end desktop copiers that sell for a few hundred dollars to high-volume document machines that retail for over $200,000.

Each copy machine requires a wiring bundle. Each bundle contains several hundred wires and connectors that provide circuits connecting the paper-flow units, scanner, and photo receptor to the internal computer logic. The wire harness is plugged into various components during the assembly process. It is possible to assign each major task in this process to different employees. For example, a given employee might focus on one of the many connectors or on testing the completed wire harness. Alternatively, one individual can be assigned the task of producing and testing a completed harness.

In either case, there are a group of employees that are assigned individual tasks to produce a wire harness for a particular copier. In total, there are 10 subgroups of wire harness makers. One alternative is to place all 10 groups in one wire harness department. Another alternative is that each of these 10 subgroups can be assigned to and report to a manager responsible for a particular copier.

Bagby operates in five European countries. Currently, it has separate subunits in each country, where a country manager manages the manufacturing and marketing of all 10 copiers. The company is considering two alternatives. One would be to organize its foreign operations around products. In this case, there would be 10 international product managers with decision rights for managing the manufacturing and sale of a particular copier throughout Europe. The company is also considering a matrix organization, organized around product and country.

Discussion Questions

1. Discuss the tradeoffs that Bagby faces in choosing between specialized and broad task assignment.
2. Discuss the tradeoffs between these two methods of grouping wire-harness makers into subgroups.
3. Discuss the tradeoffs Bagby faces in choosing among the country, product, and matrix forms of organizing its international operations.

Larger, more diverse firms often find it desirable to form subunits based on product or geography. In the *multidivisional (M-form) firm,* operating decisions are decentralized to the business-unit level. Senior management of the firm is responsible for major strategic decisions, including finding the optimal organizational architecture and allocating capital among business units. A primary benefit of the M-form corporation is that decision rights for operations are assigned to individuals lower in the organization where the relevant specific knowledge is located. Managers of business units are compensated based on the performance of their units so as to provide incentives to use this specific knowledge productively. Decentralizing decision rights to business-unit managers also frees senior executives to concentrate on other issues. Problems with the M-form of organization arise because business-unit managers often have incentives to take actions that increase the performance of their business units at the expense of other units in the firm. These problems can be mitigated through careful design of business units and by paying business-unit managers based on *group performance* (where the group consists of profit centers with interrelated costs and demands). It is usually difficult, however, to control this problem completely. Multidivisional firms also forgo potential economies that might result from combining similar functional specialists within one unit.

Some firms maintain an overlapping structure of functional and product/geographic subunits. These *matrix organizations* have functional departments such as finance and marketing. Members of these departments are assigned to cross-functional product teams (subunits). Team members report to both a product manager and a functional supervisor. Generally, performance evaluation is conducted by the functional supervisor. Matrix organization is common in project-oriented industries such as defense, construction, and consulting. An advantage of a matrix organization, in contrast to a pure functional organization, is that individuals are more likely to focus on the overall business process rather than just on their own narrow functional specialty. Potential advantages over a pure product organization are that the functional departments help to ensure functional excellence and provide additional opportunities for advancement and development. Potential problems with the matrix organization arise from the intersecting lines of authority. An employee is likely to have loyalties divided between the goals of the project team and the goals of the functional department. This problem can be mitigated by appropriate design of the performance-evaluation and reward systems. However, as we will see in subsequent chapters, accomplishing this objective can be difficult.

Firms often use more than one method for organizing subunits. They also use other less standard ways of organizing subunits. One example is a *network organization.*

Decisions on how to group jobs must be made at many levels in the organization. Our analysis of the costs and benefits of alternative groupings of jobs focuses on the overall firm level (how to form major subunits). The same basic analysis applies to the grouping of jobs at lower levels within the firm.

Historically, many firms have created jobs that are low in decision authority and narrow in task assignment. Recently, there has been a trend toward granting employees more decision authority and broader task assignments. Many companies have also shifted away from functional subunits toward more product-oriented organizations. These trends can be explained by certain technological changes and increases in global competition, along with accompanying changes in business strategies.

APPENDIX   *Battle of the Functional Managers*[11]

This appendix uses a simple game-theoretic example to illustrate some of the tradeoffs that firms face in grouping jobs into subunits. Currently, the Quick Motorcycle Company is functionally organized. Two of its main departments are design and marketing. Chris Heath is the manager of the design department, while Jane Phillips manages marketing.

Chris has two options for designing a new product. One design focuses on speed, while the other design focuses on safety. Jane has two options for the corresponding marketing campaign. One option focuses on young consumers and concentrates on magazine advertising, while the other option focuses on older people and a more active television campaign. Figure 10.8 displays the payoffs that Chris and Jane face for each combination of design and marketing programs (for example, from their respective bonus plans or personal preferences). The payoffs indicate that coordinating the design and marketing is important. If Chris chooses design option 1, while Jane undertakes marketing plan 2, both Chris and Jane receive low payoffs ($100 each). A similar outcome exists if Chris chooses design option 2 and Jane chooses marketing plan 1. In this setting, two Nash equilibria

---

[11]This example is based on the "battle of the sexes" game. For example, see R. Gibbons (1992), *Game Theory for Applied Economists* (Princeton University Press: Princeton, NJ).

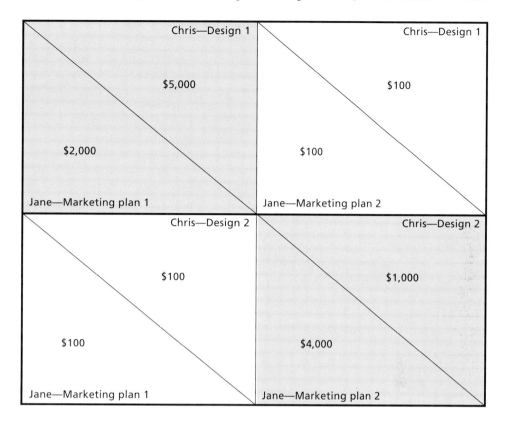

Figure 10.8 Battle of the Functional Managers

Quick Motorcycle Company is functionally organized. Chris Heath, the manager of the design department, selects from two designs for a new product. Jane Phillips, the market manager, selects from two marketing plans. There are two Nash equilibria: Design option 1 and marketing plan 1; design option 2 and marketing plan 2. Both Chris and Jane prefer to coordinate their actions rather than not coordinate (and end up in the off diagonal). However, they disagree on the preferred equilibrium.

are possible. One is design option 1 and marketing plan 1; the other is design option 2 and marketing plan 2. Chris and Jane have a conflict over which equilibrium each prefers. Chris receives a higher payoff in the first case, while Jane receives a higher payoff in the second case. Nonetheless, both Jane and Chris prefer either equilibrium to cases where they fail to coordinate.

Suppose that total firm profits are correlated with the combined payoffs for both Chris and Jane. In this case, the CEO of the firm prefers the combination of design option 1 and marketing plan 1. With complete information about the payoff structure, the CEO selects this option and then allows design and marketing departments to focus on their specialties in implementing the program. This focus on specialization would allow each department to take advantage of its relative strengths. It also allows Chris and Jane to coordinate the new program with other design and marketing projects in their respective departments. Thus, this example illustrates that functional organization can work well if the CEO has the specific knowledge to coordinate the activities of the functional managers at low cost. This specific knowledge, in turn, is most likely to be held by the CEO in small firms in relatively stable environments.

In a rapidly changing environment it is unlikely that the CEO will know the payoffs facing the managers for each of the options (or even know all the available options). In this case, the CEO does not have the knowledge to order the profit-maximizing alternative. Both Chris and Jane prefer coordination to noncoordination. However, they do not agree on the preferred alternative. There is no guarantee that they will choose the value-maximizing equilibrium. Indeed, they might fail to reach either equilibrium. Chris and Jane have to make concurrent decisions.[12] In an attempt to achieve their preferred equilibrium, they might fail to coordinate and both will suffer. In any case, they will consume resources bargaining ("battling") over which options to choose. In this environment, the CEO might want to reconfigure the subunits around products (the firm produces multiple products). The decisions on the design and marketing of each product would be made within one subunit. Profit-maximizing choices could be motivated through profit-based bonus plans. In choosing this organizational option, the CEO forgoes any efficiencies that come from combining a given functional activity (across all products) within one unit. If the benefits of functional grouping are high, rather than changing the subunit structure, the CEO might want to foster coordination through the formation of coordinating committees and changes in performance-evaluation and reward systems that promote profit-maximizing choices.

Appendix Problem

In the early 1900s, General Motors (GM) had separate divisions that manufactured Buicks, Cadillacs, Chevrolets, Oaklands, and Oldsmobiles. Decision rights were highly decentralized and there was little direction or coordination from the central corporate office. As a result, the divisions often failed to coordinate decisions on design standards, which prevented them from taking advantage of economies of scale in buying or making common components (for example, spark plugs). Discuss potential organizational changes that GM might have adopted to reduce this coordination problem.

Suggested Readings

A. Chandler, Jr. (1977), *The Visible Hand: The Managerial Revolution in American Business* (Belknap Press: Cambridge, MA).

A. Chandler, Jr. (1966), *Strategy and Structure* (Doubleday: Garden City, NY).

M. Hammer and J. Champy (1993), *Reengineering the Corporation* (Harper Business: New York).

O. Williamson (1975), *Markets and Hierarchies* (Free Press: New York).

Review Questions

10–1. Discuss the costs and benefits of specialized task assignment relative to broad task assignment. What variables are likely to be particularly important in determining the optimal choice between these two alternatives?

10–2. Define the following: functional organizations, product organization, geographic organization, matrix organization, and network organization.

---

[12]Both design and marketing require long lead times before a final product is brought to market. It obviously takes time to design and test a product. Similarly, in marketing, an advertising agency must be chosen, a marketing/advertising campaign must be developed, contracts with the media have to be negotiated, and so forth. In Jane's and Chris's case, both must commit to a specific option at about the same time.

10–3. Discuss the circumstances under which you think functional organizations will work best.

10–4. Discuss the pluses and minuses of matrix organizations.

10–5. Why do you think many U.S. firms have reorganized their international divisions from a country focus to matrix organizations focusing on both country and product?

10–6. In the early 1990s, Chrysler Corporation placed nearly all decisions about the development of a new vehicle in the hands of a single, cross-functional product team. In contrast, General Motors used an approach that placed a stronger emphasis on functional specialties. Small teams were established that consisted of experts from the same functional field. Each team was charged with a particular assignment that related to its area of specialization. For example, one team might have had the primary responsibility for the design of the body of the vehicle, while another team might have been charged with developing the drive train. The teams worked simultaneously on their specific tasks. Some individuals on these teams also served on additional cross-functional teams that were charged with coordinating the development process across the functional areas. Discuss the relative advantages and disadvantages of these two approaches to product development.

10–7. For many years, your firm has been protected by patents. Technological change and the introduction of new products have been slow. Soon, these conditions will change. Your patent protection is expiring, and the rate of technological change and innovation has increased substantially. Discuss how these changes are likely to affect your firm's optimal bundling of tasks into jobs and subunits.

10–8. Johnson & Johnson (J&J) is one of the largest medical products companies in the world. In 1994, it had 33 major lines of business, with 168 operating companies in 53 countries. Decision rights in J&J were quite decentralized. For instance, in 1993, the baby oil manager in Italy ran his own factory and got to decide such things as package size, pricing, and advertising. Similarly, other country managers had considerable discretionary authority for similar products sold in their countries. This type of decentralized decision making has served J&J well—its returns to shareholders have been very good. Significant changes, however, are occurring in J&J's environment. In particular, trade barriers have been significantly reduced in Europe.

    a. Describe the advantages of J&J's decentralized decision making that have helped to explain the success of the company.

    b. What organizational changes do you think J&J should consider given the change in the environment? Explain. Draw a new organizational chart for J&J's international operations (based on your suggestions).

10–9. Bob's Auto Repair Shop is currently organized as follows: a repair manager meets with the customer to discuss the problems with the car. A repair order is completed. The mechanics specialize in particular types of repairs (for example, air conditioning, body work, etc.). Typically, a car in the shop requires work by several specialists. The manager plans the sequence of service among the specialists. The car is then serviced by each of the necessary specialists in turn. Discuss how Bob's Auto might look if it reorganized around the process of fixing an automobile. Discuss the pluses and minuses of the current structure compared to the more product-oriented structure.

10–10. Many companies are making increased use of telecommuting, which consists of employees working out of their homes, linked to the central office by telephone, computer, and fax machine. Discuss the benefits and costs of telecommuting. What types of occupations are likely to be best suited telecommuting? Explain why.

chapter 11

Attracting and Retaining Qualified Employees

CHAPTER OUTLINE

RKO Warner Video sells and rents prerecorded video tapes.[1] It is one of the largest video chains in the New York City area with about 40 stores. It has an enormous inventory and specializes in high-quality service and attractive decor.

In 1988, RKO owned and operated 24 video stores. While the company had been reasonably successful, senior management was concerned about two human resource problems. First, turnover of employees was "unacceptably high." Second, "the quality and consistency of performance by store managers varied considerably across the chain." In structuring the store manager positions, RKO's senior management had bundled specific tasks and decision rights into jobs (see Chapters 9 and 10). For instance, store managers had key responsibility for making sure the racks were alphabetized, keeping the store clean, opening on time, returning the tapes to the racks promptly, ordering product from the warehouse, and keeping checkout times short. RKO, however, had not designed a complementary reward system to motivate appropriate effort on these tasks—RKO's *organizational architecture* was poorly designed.

To address these concerns, RKO adopted a new bonus plan for store managers. The aims of the plan were twofold. First, the company wanted to raise the level of compensation to "attract and keep qualified store managers." Second, RKO wanted to structure the compensation package in a manner that would motivate managers to "be more conscientious and take pride in their work."

While the plan suffered from some design flaws, it accomplished the two objectives, at least in part. The plan had a substantial impact on the level of pay and made RKO more competitive in the local labor market. In early 1988, RKO store managers received annual salaries ranging from $21,000 to $28,000. The new bonus plan was targeted at increasing these base salaries by about 15 percent, depending on performance. In fact, during the first quarter under the bonus plan, two store managers received substantially more in bonus pay than in base pay. While the incentive effects of the plan are harder to document, there is some evidence that the plan also had a positive impact on managerial performance.

The example of RKO highlights two important objectives of compensation policy: (1) *to attract and retain qualified employees,* and (2) *to motivate employees to be more productive.* This chapter concentrates on the first of these objectives—attraction/retention. We postpone a detailed discussion of incentive compensation until the next chapter. Since the two topics are interrelated, we also discuss some incentive-related issues in this chapter. In particular, we examine how the level of pay can be used not only to attract and retain employees but also to motivate them.

We begin by providing a more detailed discussion of the objectives of compensation contracting. We then present a benchmark economic model of employment and wages. Subsequently, we extend the basic model and examine the implications of costly information about market wage rates, compensating differentials, investments in human capital, internal labor markets, and the choice between salary and fringe benefits.

Contracting Objectives

In Chapter 7, we emphasized that it is in the joint interests of contracting parties to maximize the value created by their relationships. By maximizing value, the size of the overall "pie" is maximized and all parties can be made better off. This general principle

---

[1]Details of this example are from S. Shimer, under the supervision of G. Baker (1993), "RKO Video, Inc.: Incentive Compensation Plan," Harvard Business School Case 9–190–067.

holds for labor contracts. By designing compensation contracts that maximize the value of employees' output net of costs, firm value is maximized and both the owners of the firm and their employees can be made better off.

Individuals will not participate in an employment relationship unless they receive at least their opportunity cost. If they do not receive their *reservation utilities*—the utility they could obtain in their next best alternative—they will quit and go to work for another firm (or withdraw from the labor force). Since individuals gain utility from compensation, the level of compensation is a key factor in attracting and retaining qualified employees. Owners must also receive an adequate return on investment, or they will close the business and reinvest elsewhere. In a competitive market, paying employees more than the competitive rate results in a cost disadvantage that in the long run could drive the company out of business. Owners have incentives to design compensation packages that allow them to attract and retain employees with the required skills at the lowest possible cost.

The Level of Pay: The Basic Competitive Model

In this section, we present a benchmark model of employment and compensation (patterned after the standard competitive model). This model is a useful starting point for analyzing issues related to the level of pay. Subsequently, we extend the analysis to consider other important issues.

Suppose the labor market is characterized by the following conditions:

- The labor market is *competitive.* Firms have no discretion over the wages they pay to employees; rather, wages are determined by supply and demand in the marketplace.
- Market wage rates are costlessly observable.
- Individuals are identical in their training and skills.
- All jobs are identical. They do not vary in their risk, location, level of intellectual challenge, travel opportunities, and so on.
- There are no long-term contracts. Rather, all labor is hired in the "spot" market for a single day.
- All compensation comes from monetary compensation. The firm does not provide any fringe benefits such as vacation pay or health insurance.

Setting the Wrong Level of Pay at Salomon Brothers

In the first year out of the training program, 1983, Howie Rubin made $25 million for Salomon Brothers in the new activity of mortgage-backed securities. The several-hundred million dollar question was first raised by Howie Rubin: Who really made the money, Howie Rubin or Salomon Brothers? Salomon Brothers decided it was the company and refused to pay Rubin more than the normal pay scale. In his first year, Rubin was paid $90,000, the most permitted a first-year trader. In 1984, his second year, Rubin made $30 million trading. He was then paid $175,000, the most permitted a second-year trader. In the beginning of 1985 he quit Salomon Brothers and moved to Merrill Lynch for a three year guarantee: a minimum of $1 million a year, plus a percentage of his trading profits.

After 1985, Salomon Brothers lost much of its market share in mortgage-backed securities to other firms such as Merrill Lynch.

Source: M. Lewis (1989), *Liar's Poker* (Norton Press: New York), 126.

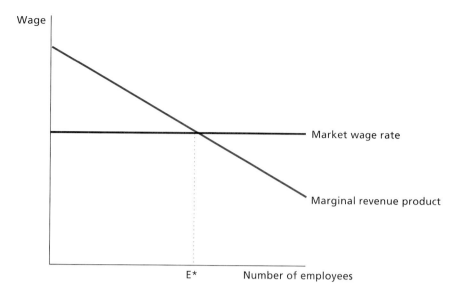

Figure 11.1 How Firms Choose Employment and Wages: The Basic Competitive Model

In our basic model, firms have no discretion over the wages they pay to employees; rather, the wages are determined by supply and demand in the marketplace. As shown in the figure, individual firms continue to hire employees up to the point E*, where the marginal revenue product equals the market-determined wage rate. Until this point, hiring additional employees brings more revenue into the firm than it costs to hire the employee. Past this point, the costs of hiring additional individuals are larger than the benefits.

Figure 11.1 shows the hiring decisions of individual firms in this market setting. Each firm continues to hire employees to the point where the marginal revenue product equals the market-determined wage rate (see Chapter 5 for an extended analysis of this problem). Until this point, hiring additional employees produces more revenue than it costs to hire the individuals. Past this point, the costs of hiring additional individuals are larger than the benefits. The hiring decisions of all firms in the market determine the demand curve for labor. The supply curve is determined by the decisions of individuals on whether to accept the given wage rate or stay out of the labor force. The market wage rate equates supply and demand.

The implications of this analysis are that if a firm pays too little (below the market wage rate), it will not be able to attract qualified employees or it will have high turnover. This principle motivated RKO to raise its level of pay. On the other hand, a firm that pays too much will have long queues for job openings and low turnover. However, the firm will do poorly in the marketplace for its products relative to firms that do not overpay and hence have lower total costs. Facing a competitive market for its products, it will eventually go out of business.

Costly Information about Market Wage Rates

In contrast to the benchmark model, compensation in many labor markets is not readily observable. Individuals vary in characteristics and are not typically perfect substitutes. Thus, observing the wage for one individual does not provide full information on what it takes to hire another. In addition, firms do not share complete information about their levels of compensation. The difficulty in observing the market price for labor means that it is not always easy to tell if a firm is underpaying or overpaying its employees.

Paying Too Much at Nucor?

When Nucor's mill in Darlington, South Carolina, advertised to fill eight openings last fall, over 1,300 applicants showed up, creating such a traffic jam that state police had to be called out. Unfortunately, the force was a bit thin—three officers were already at Nucor applying for jobs.

It is possible that the number of applications at Nucor included many unqualified candidates. But the size of the applicant pool certainly motivates the questions of whether Nucor is paying too much and whether it wants to pay more than the market wage rate for particular jobs.

Source: N. Perry (1988), "Here Come Richer, Riskier Pay Plans," *Fortune* (December 19), 58.

Our discussion to this point suggests that two important indicators of whether a firm is paying the market wage rate are: (1) the number of applications it receives for job openings and (2) the quit rate for existing employees. If a firm is inundated by *qualified applicants* when it advertises a job opening, and the turnover rate among existing employees is low, it is likely that the firm is paying above the market wage rate.[2] In contrast, if the applicant rate is low and turnover is high, the firm is probably paying below the market rate.

In choosing the rate of pay, it is important to consider the tradeoffs between incremental compensation and turnover costs. Turnover costs include the costs of recruiting employees, training expenses, and reduced productivity from employing inexperienced employees. In addition, if employees expect that they will work for the firm for only a short time, they are less likely to be concerned about how their actions affect the long-run cashflows of the firm. For instance, a salesperson might push to make a sale to collect a commission, knowing that the customer will be unhappy with the product and will reduce future purchases. Sometimes, employees who leave a firm take customers and trade secrets to competing firms. Nonetheless, turnover also has beneficial effects on the firm—for example, it adds "new blood" and fresh ideas to the organization.

Outside job offers made to existing employees are also indicative of market rates. While these offers provide important information about the market value of existing employees, firms must be careful in deciding whether to match these offers. Failure to match can result in losing valued employees. A policy of matching all outside offers, however, encourages employees to invest in generating offers. This activity takes time away from work and also increases the likelihood that employees will obtain offers that entice them to leave the firm.

Compensating Differentials[3]

Our benchmark model does not consider differences in working conditions across jobs. In reality, jobs vary in many dimensions, among them are: the quality of the work environment, the geographic location, the length of the commute, the exposure to danger, the

[2]Paying above the market wage rate will typically place the firm at a competitive disadvantage. As we discuss below, however, there are several reasons for why some profit-maximizing firms might want to pay above the market wage rate.

[3]In this section, we discuss the key points of the theory of compensating differentials as they relate to managerial decision making. For an expanded discussion of compensating differentials, see R. Ehrenberg and R. Smith (1988), *Modern Labor Economics,* 3rd ed. (Scott Foresman: Glenview, IL), Chapter 8.

Compensating Differentials for Working at Night

Many production employees in the United States work night shifts. Since most employees prefer to work during the day, firms have to pay compensating differentials to attract enough employees to staff their night shifts. Research suggests that in 1984, night employees in manufacturing plants received about 30 cents more per hour than day employees. The average manufacturing wage in 1984 was $9.18.

Source: S. King and H. Williams (1985), "Shift Work Pay Differentials and Practices in Manufacturing," *Monthly Labor Review* 108 (December), 26–33.

characteristics of co-workers, and the degree of monotony on the job. Holding the salary level constant across job offers, an individual will choose the job with the most desirable characteristics (such as low risk of injury and a nice location). To attract employees to less desirable jobs, firms must increase the level of pay.[4] The *extra* wage that is paid to attract an individual to a less desirable job is called a *compensating wage differential*. For instance, RKO probably has to pay more to attract a manager to work at night at a dangerous location than it does to attract a manager to work during the day at a safe location.

The prediction that unpleasant jobs pay more than pleasant jobs *holds other factors constant.* Variation in job requirements for education, skills, and training also account for differences in pay. For example, an office job in a pleasant work environment might pay more than the relatively unpleasant job of garbage collector because the skills required for the office job are higher. Garbage collectors, however, will be paid more than similar unskilled labor in more pleasant jobs.

Some of the best evidence of the existence of compensating wage differentials is provided by studies that relate wages to the risk of fatal injury on the job.[5] Using data from around the world, wages were found to be positively associated with the risk of being killed on the job, holding other factors constant. The estimates of the magnitude of the compensating differential are relatively imprecise and vary across studies, but they indicate that employees receive between $20 and $300 more per year for every 1 in 10,000 increase in the risk of being killed on the job. These estimates imply that a firm with 1,000 employees could save between $20,000 and $300,000 in wage costs per year by increasing the level of safety enough to save one life every 10 years.

Compensating wage differentials have two important effects. First, all societies have unpleasant tasks that must be completed (for instance, most have morticians and garbage collectors). Compensating differentials attract people to these jobs and reward them for their efforts. Individuals who accept unpleasant tasks tend to be the ones who bear the lowest cost for performing them. For example, if a wage premium is offered for working in a noisy factory, the people most likely to apply are those least bothered by noise. Individuals who are significantly averse to noise would choose to work in a quiet environment at a lower wage. Second, the existence of compensating differentials causes employers who offer unpleasant work environments to have higher labor costs. Employers can reduce

[4]This prediction assumes that employees can obtain relatively good information about important characteristics of the job either before or shortly after employment. This assumption is likely to be valid in many cases. For instance, an applicant for a firefighter position in an arid location is likely to know that the job is hazardous. The applicant can also observe the quality of the fire station and equipment. The applicant can collect other information about the work environment from current or past employees.

[5]For a more detailed summary of this empirical work, see Ehrenberg and Smith (1988), 266–270.

Labor Secretary's Bid for Plant Safety Runs into Skepticism

In the summer of 1994, Labor Secretary Robert Reich charged a Bridgestone Tire subsidiary with 107 safety violations. He also levied a fine of $7.5 million. The labor secretary ostensibly took this action on behalf of the employees at the tire plant. To quote the secretary, "American workers are not going to be sacrificed at the alter of profits." The secretary, however, was "amazed" when the employees and local community did not support his action. Indeed, employees were generally skeptical and nonsupportive of his claims. For example, one employee indicated that the secretary "didn't know what the hell he was doing."

The lack of employee support for this action can be explained by the theory of compensating differentials. Dangerous jobs pay a premium over jobs in safer environments. Employees who accept dangerous jobs consider themselves better off than if they were working at lower wages in safer environments. Thus, regulations that force firms to provide safer work environments and lower wages (wages have to be reduced to remain competitive) can make employees worse off. In addition, the company might lay off employees if it is too expensive to comply with the regulations.

While employees can be harmed by this type of regulatory action, there are at least two arguments that might justify government intervention. First, the employees might not have good information about the level of danger. For example, they might think that a plant is safer than it really is. (Why the government, however, would be better informed about the level of safety at a plant than the employees is not obvious.) Second, there are other parties that have to be considered. For example, employees who get hurt on the job can impose costs on society through subsidized medical care and disability payments. While the overall costs and benefits of this type of regulation are hard to estimate, it is clear that employees do not always believe that they benefit.

Source: A. Nomani (1994), "Muffed Mission: Labor Secretary's Bid to Push Safety Runs into Skepticism," *The Wall Street Journal* (August 19), 1.

their labor costs by enhancing their work environments. This possibility implies that the firms providing better work environments will be those firms that can do so at low cost (since the marginal cost of providing a pleasant environment is low relative to the marginal benefit of reducing the penalty).

This discussion suggests there is a job-matching process in labor markets where firms offer and individuals accept jobs in a manner that makes the most of their strengths and preferences. Organizations have incentives to reduce the risk of injury in order to reduce wage premiums. In turn, the people who take risky jobs are likely to be the most tolerant toward risk (individuals *self-select* based on their risk preferences). For example, fishing companies often find it too expensive to reduce the risk of injury beyond some standard, and thus they must offer wage premiums to crews of fishing boats. Individuals applying to work on these boats are likely to be among those most willing to place their lives at risk on the job. Because of this self-selection, the compensating differential is less than if the firm had to hire an average person from the population. A firm that can provide a safe environment at a low cost will offer low-risk jobs and lower wages; these positions will be filled by more risk-averse employees.

Human Capital[6]

In our benchmark model, all individuals are alike. Yet, employees often vary in their abilities, skills, and training. *Human capital* is a term that characterizes individuals as having a set of skills that can be "rented" to employers. The value of human capital is determined

[6]Material in this section draws on the analysis in G. Becker (1983), *Human Capital* (University of Chicago Press: Chicago).

by supply and demand in the marketplace. Individuals invest in their human capital through education and training, migration, and search for new jobs. The return on this investment consists of higher wage rates that come from having more valuable human capital (college graduates typically earn more than high school graduates).

It is useful to distinguish between *general* and *specific* human capital. General human capital consists of training and education that is equally useful to a wide variety of different firms. Investments in general human capital include obtaining an MBA degree, learning general principles of engineering, or learning popular word-processing programs. Specific human capital, on the other hand, is more valuable to the current employer than alternative employers. Investments in specific capital include such things as learning the details of a particular firm's accounting system or product information.

In the benchmark model extended to allow for differences in training, firms would not invest in general training. The gains from general training go to the employees, not firms—if a firm does not pay the employee the market price for the new skills, the individual moves to another firm that is willing to pay. Thus, employees pay for their own general training. Correspondingly, employees are reluctant to invest in specific training, since it does not increase their market values. Thus, in the benchmark model, firms must pay for specific training.

Internal Labor Markets

While our benchmark model provides a relatively good description of some labor markets, such as the market for unskilled agricultural workers, it does a poor job describing employment and wages in many other cases. In contrast to the model, many firms rarely reduce employee compensation and frequently invest in general training (such as paying tuition for an employee to obtain an MBA). Also, employees often invest their time and effort in developing firm-specific skills.

Many firms are better characterized as having *internal labor markets,* wherein outside hiring is done primarily at entry-level jobs and most other jobs are filled from within the firm. Firms with internal labor markets establish *long-term relationships* with employees. It has been estimated that in 1991, the typical employee between 45 and 54 had been with his or her current employer for 10 years. Another study found that over half of all men and one-fourth of all women in the United States work for the same employer for at least 20 years.[7]

Established career paths and the prospect for promotions play important roles in firms with internal labor markets. These firms interact with outside labor markets only on a limited basis. Rather than simply reflecting outside market conditions, the rates of pay (discussed in more detail below) and job assignments in internal labor markets are often determined by administrative rules and implicit understandings. Firms can have more than one internal labor market. For example, the internal market for white-collar employees might have little interaction with the internal market for blue-collar employees. In addition, firms with internal labor markets typically offer some jobs that are well described by the basic model—for instance, certain low-skilled positions.

Agreements between employers and employees concerning compensation and responsibilities are contracts. Firms generally do not enter into formal written agreements (*explicit contracts*) with nonunion employees. Rather, most employees work under *implicit*

---

[7]J. Aley (1994), "The Myth of the Job Hopper," *Fortune* (September 19), 32; and R. Hall (1982), "The Importance of Lifetime Jobs in the U.S. Economy," *American Economic Review* 72, 716–24.

Internal Labor Markets in Japan

Large companies in Japan make extensive use of internal labor markets. Many Japanese executives spend their entire careers with the same firm. Senior executives virtually never move from one major firm to another. Firms rarely go outside to hire for any position other than entry-level jobs. Turnover is extremely low. Pay is tied largely to seniority, and the differences in pay among employees are small relative to the differences in American companies.

Small pay differentials would be difficult to maintain if there were an active outside labor market in Japan. Market pressures would tend to bid up the salaries of the strong performers. Recently, poor performance has placed pressures on Japanese firms to reconsider their policies of lifetime employment guarantees. If many firms abandon this policy, the outside labor market is likely to become more active.

Source: M. Aoki and R. Dore, eds. (1994), *The Japanese Firm* (Oxford University Press: Oxford, UK).

---

contracts (a set of shared, informal understandings about how firms and employees will respond to contingencies).[8] Implicit contracts differ from explicit contracts in that they are typically unwritten and less enforceable in a court of law. Firms and employees, however, often have strong economic incentives to honor implicit contracts to protect their reputations (see Chapter 7). A primary reason for the frequent use of implicit contracts is that it would be quite costly to detail all possible contingencies and associated responses in a formal document.

Reasons for Long-Term Employment Relationships

In Chapter 3, we discussed how all methods of organizing economic activity involve transaction costs. Firms have incentives to consider these costs and to organize economic exchanges in an efficient manner.[9] Spot-market exchange is not always the most efficient way to organize firm/employee relationships. There are at least three factors that help to promote the widespread use of the long-term employment relationships found in internal labor markets. These factors include specific human capital, employee motivation, and information about employee attributes.

Firm-Specific Human Capital

Long-term relationships provide incentives for employers and employees to invest in specific training. If employers and employees expect that their relationships will be of short duration, limited incentives exist to make this investment. Correspondingly, long-term relationships allow firms and employees to capture the benefits of accumulated specific human capital.

Employee Motivation

The prospect of a long-term relationship with a firm provides powerful incentives for employees to work on behalf of their employers. Employees considering shirking, stealing, and other dysfunctional activities must weigh the benefits of these actions against the costs of losing future benefits should they be caught and fired. Since there is more to

---

[8]S. Rosen (1985), "Implicit Contracts," *Journal of Economic Literature* 23, 1144–75.

[9]R. Coase (1988), *The Firm, the Market, and the Law* (University of Chicago Press: Chicago).

lose in long-term relationships than in short-term relationships, the incentives to engage in productive activities are higher in long-term relationships.[10] Also, as we discuss below, long-term relationships increase the flexibility that a firm has in designing compensation packages to motivate employee effort.

Learning Employee Attributes

Over time, managers receive much information about the skills, work habits, and intelligence of individual employees. Employers then can use this information in matching employees and jobs within the firm. For example, firms with internal labor markets have fewer surprises in filling higher-level jobs than firms that rely on outside labor markets.

Costs of Internal Labor Markets

Not all firms have internal labor markets. Some firms rely heavily on outside markets to fill positions at all levels. The observation that some firms do not have internal labor markets suggests that the costs of these markets can be larger than the benefits. One potentially important problem with internal labor markets is the restricted competition for higher-level jobs in the organization. If a firm only considers internal candidates for higher-level jobs, it will not always hire the most qualified person (who may be from outside the firm). The likelihood of finding a desirable candidate in the outside labor market is highest when the job does not require specific training (since experience with the firm does not create an advantage in the job). Thus, theory suggests firms are more likely to use internal labor markets where specific training is important. Indeed, firms in the steel, petroleum, and chemical industries, where complicated production technologies take significant time to learn, tend to rely on internal labor markets, while firms in the shoe and garment industries do not.[11] Firm-specific skills are arguably less important in garment and shoe manufacturing than in steel, petroleum, or chemicals.

Pay in Internal Labor Markets

Careers and Lifetime Pay

Employees who take jobs at firms with internal labor markets often have expectations that they will spend much of their *careers* at the same firm. Thus, in considering an entry-level job, a prospective employee will generally focus on the entire stream of earnings over the anticipated career path. For example, an individual might accept a job at Firm A that pays less than another job offered at Firm B because the individual anticipates faster compensation growth at Firm A.

The fact that individuals tend to base employment decisions on career earnings gives firms with internal labor markets flexibility over setting the level and sequence of pay. In contrast to the basic model, firms do not need to pay the market wage rate (or equivalently,

---

[10]This statement assumes that an employee cannot costlessly replicate the same stream of benefits by changing to a new employer. For example, the new job might pay lower compensation, the individual might incur moving costs, there might be a period of unemployment, and so on.

[11]P. Doeringer and M. Piore (1971), *Internal Labor Markets and Manpower Analysis* (D. C. Heath: Lexington, MA).

Hiring an Outside CEO at Kodak

Eastman Kodak had a long history of filling senior positions exclusively with long-time employees. An advantage of this policy is that senior executives have significant experience with the firm and detailed specific knowledge of the company. The prospect of promotion and long-term employment also provides important motivational effects. A disadvantage, however, is that sometimes the best people for senior jobs are outsiders.

During the late 1980s and early 1990s, shareholders placed intense pressure on Kodak's board to appoint outsiders to senior positions. Many shareholders thought that hiring outsiders was necessary to bring new skills and vision into the firm. In late October 1993, Kodak announced that it had hired George Fisher, CEO of Motorola, as the new CEO. The stock market greeted this announcement with an 8 percent increase in Kodak's stock price (from the close of the market on October 26th to the close on the 28th). This reaction represented a $1.6 billion increase in the overall value of the company.

---

in equilibrium, the marginal revenue product) at each point in time. Rather, firms can vary compensation over a career path, as long as the overall value of the remaining stream is competitive at each point in time (valued as highly by employees as streams offered by competing firms in the labor market).

Economists have identified at least three ways that firms can use their flexibility in setting the level and sequencing of pay to enhance employee motivation. These methods include the payment of efficiency wages, upward sloping earnings profiles, and tying major pay increases to promotions. As we will discuss, however, influence costs can affect the desirability of taking full advantage of this flexibility.

Efficiency Wages

In many jobs, it is difficult to monitor employee actions. It is also difficult to devise incentive compensation schemes that motivate desired behavior. For example, manufacturing companies want production employees to work hard. In most cases, it is difficult to measure employee effort with much precision. In addition, the payment of piece rates or other output-based compensation can motivate employees to shirk on quality.

One potential way to motivate employees in these cases is to pay compensation *above* the market rate. Paying a premium for employees obviously increases labor costs. However, it can have the desirable effect of motivating them not to shirk. Individuals who are paid a wage premium are likely to reduce their shirking because they are afraid that if they are caught and fired, they will lose the premium. (They will be unemployed or have to accept a lower-paying job.) This effect will be greatest for employees who have long time horizons with the firm, since they have more to lose. Wage premiums of this type are often referred to as *efficiency wages*. Efficiency wages also provide incentives for employees to stay with the firm. These incentives can be particularly important when the employee has specific human capital (the firm does not want to replace the employee with a less trained person).[12]

Economists debate whether the use of efficiency wages is widespread. While the empirical evidence is inconclusive, some studies suggest that firms in particular industries use efficiency wages with relatively high frequency. The authors of one study find systematic wage differences across industries after controlling for many job and employee

---

[12]For a more detailed analysis of efficiency wages, see G. Akerlof (1984), "Gift Exchange and Efficiency Wages: Four Views," *American Economic Review* 74, 78–83; C. Shapiro and J. Stiglitz (1984), "Equilibrium Unemployment as a Worker Discipline Device," *American Economic Review* 74, 433–44; and J. Yellen (1984), "Efficiency Wages Models and Unemployment," *American Economic Review* 74, 200–208. If all firms in an industry pay efficiency wages, there will be unemployment. (The supply of labor will exceed demand.) The threat of unemployment can provide incentives for employees not to shirk. Note that in the basic model, marginal revenue product and the wage rate are independent. The efficiency-wage concept, however, suggests that they can be related—employees' marginal products can be affected by their wage rates due to incentive effects.

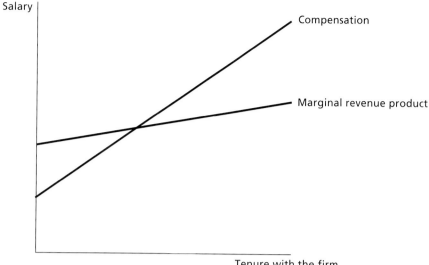

Figure 11.2 **An Example of an Upward Sloping Earnings Profile**

This figure displays possible growth patterns of both marginal revenue product and compensation for a representative employee in a given firm. Within this particular firm, both marginal revenue product and compensation increase as the employee becomes more experienced. Compensation, however, increases at a faster rate. In the early years, the employee is paid below the marginal revenue product, while in later years the employee is paid more. The employee is underpaid in early years but is willing to work for the firm because of the expectation of being overpaid in subsequent years. Under this compensation scheme, a young employee has incentives to work hard to avoid being fired and losing future wage premiums. An older employee, in turn, does not want to get fired because of being paid more than can be earned at other firms.

characteristics. In addition, they find a negative relation between turnover and industry wage differentials, suggesting that employees in high-wage industries receive wage premiums. The authors interpret this evidence as consistent with the hypothesis that efficiency wages are paid in certain industries.[13]

Job Seniority and Pay[14]

Compensation typically increases with seniority within the firm. Part of this increase is explained by increases in productivity that come from experience. In many firms, however, compensation increases faster than productivity as the employee ages. Firms frequently offer attractive retirement packages to encourage older employees to retire and (unless precluded by law) often have mandatory retirement. For example, the employee must retire at age 65.[15]

One explanation for these age-related policies is that they provide incentives to employees to work in the interests of the firm. To see how, consider the example pictured in Figure 11.2. This figure displays the growth patterns of the marginal revenue product and compensation for a representative employee within a particular firm. Both the marginal

---

[13]A. Krueger and L. Summers (1988), "Efficiency Wages and the Inter-Industry Wage Structure," *Econometrica* 56, 259–293. Another empirical paper that supports the notion of efficiency wages is P. Osterman (1994), "Supervision, Discretion, and Work Organization," *American Economic Review* 84, 380–384.

[14]Material in this section draws on the analysis in E. Lazear (1979), "Why Is There Mandatory Retirement?" *Journal of Political Economy* 87, 1261–84.

[15]Amendments made to the Age Discrimination Employment Act in 1978 and 1986 have precluded mandatory retirement for most workers in the United States.

Motivating Honesty in the Local Police Force

Economists Gary Becker and George Stigler were asked to consider ways to reduce the corruption in the Chicago police force. The recommendation of these Nobel laureates was to pay the police more than the market wage rate. With sufficiently high premiums, the police would have incentives not to take bribes from criminals. For this condition to hold, the immediate gains from taking bribes must be offset by the expected loss in wage premiums given the possibility of being caught and fired. Thus, the required premium to prevent cheating depends on the size of the bribes and the likelihood of getting caught. Higher bribes and lower likelihood of getting caught translate into higher required premiums.

Paying wage premiums will entice a large number of people to apply for job openings. To reduce the surplus of applicants, Becker and Stigler suggested that the jobs be sold to officers. The price of jobs would reflect the expected premiums. Under this scenario, the payment for a job can be considered as a bond posted by an officer not to cheat. If the officer is honest, the officer gets the bond back in the form of the premium wage. If the officer cheats and gets caught, the bond is lost.

The suggested wage premiums are very similar to the concept of efficiency wages. In more modern theories of efficiency wages, however, employees do not purchase jobs. The concept of buying jobs may seem unusual. However, many people essentially do this when they purchase the right to manage an outlet of a franchise company.

Source: G. Becker and G. Stigler (1974), "Law Enforcement, Malfeasance, and Compensation," *Journal of Legal Studies* 3, 1–18.

---

revenue product and compensation increase as the employee becomes more experienced. (The analysis does not change if we allow for declines in productivity in later years.) Compensation, however, increases at a faster rate. In the early years, the employee is paid below the marginal revenue product, while in later years the employee is paid more. The employee is underpaid in early years but is willing to work for the firm because of the expectation of being overpaid in subsequent years. Under this compensation scheme, a young employee has incentives to make firm-specific human capital investments and to work hard to avoid being fired and losing future wage premiums. An older employee does not want to get fired because of being paid more than can be earned at other firms.

Firms that employ this type of compensation policy have short-run incentives to fire older employees, since older employees are paid more than they are worth. Unjustified firings of older employees, however, are not in the long-run interests of firms because they reduce the incentive effects of the compensation plan—employees will not believe that hard work will lead to wage premiums when they get older. Most firms cannot continue to pay premiums to all older employees and stay in business. Thus, these firms will adopt policies that help to ensure that older employees will retire when they reach a particular age. For example, a mandatory retirement age could be chosen where the present value of the underpayments in the early years offsets the overpayments in the later years. Thus, over their entire careers, employees are still paid their marginal revenue products (as in the basic model). Such a condition helps the firm survive in a competitive marketplace.

Promotions[16]

Firms are typically partitioned into hierarchical levels, where the jobs at a given level pay more than positions at lower levels. Employees move up the hierarchy through promotions. Since employees compete for promotions, promotions can be viewed as contests or tournaments among employees. Employees' productivity is higher trying to win these contests.

---

[16]Material in this section draws on the analysis in E. Lazear and S. Rosen (1981), "Rank Order Tournaments as Optimal Labor Contracts," *Journal of Political Economy* 89, 841–64.

A Horse Race at General Electric

Sometimes, firms "run horse races" among internal candidates. Under this procedure, the candidates are notified that they are competing for a job with higher pay and prestige. The contest provides significant incentives for the candidates to perform since the prize for winning can be very large. General Electric ran such a horse race to fill the CEO position when Reginald Jones retired in 1981. The winner was Jack Welch. In 1993, Welch was paid $4 million in salary and bonuses. The next highest paid person in the firm received $1.7 million.

Source: R. Vancil (1987), *Passing the Baton* (Harvard Business School: Boston).

Promotions obviously play an important role in providing incentives in many organizations.[17] One benefit of using a promotion-based incentive scheme is that it commits the firm to serious performance reviews of its employees. Promoting the wrong person to a job can impose significant costs. Employers have incentives to conduct in-depth performance reviews to reduce the likelihood of making such mistakes. Another primary benefit is that promotion contests help to filter out random shocks in evaluating performance. Typically, the employee with the best *relative performance* is chosen for promotion. As we discuss in Chapter 13, there are potential risk-sharing benefits that come from using relative performance measures rather than absolute performance measures.[18] In particular, employees are less likely to be rewarded or penalized for factors beyond their control—common shocks that affect all the contestants in the promotion contest are filtered out of the decision.

Promotion-based schemes can have several significant drawbacks.[19] First, judging people on relative performance can undermine employee cooperation, and employees might even sabotage the work of others. Second, promotions can be a rather crude tool for providing incentives. Promotions only occur at discrete intervals, and either the employee is promoted or not. Monetary incentives, such as bonus payments, are more flexible. Third, there can be serious conflicts between matching people for jobs and providing incentives. The so-called Peter Principle argues that employees keep getting promoted until they reach jobs that they cannot handle. Fourth, employees do not always value promotions. For example, research scientists and professors often do not want administrative positions. Fifth, promotion contests can subject decision makers to significant influencing activities.[20]

Despite these drawbacks, promotions are a widely employed method for motivating employees throughout the world. Lately the prospect for promotion in many firms has fallen due to an overall reduction in middle-management positions and a slowing in growth rates. This development reduced the incentives for many employees, who think that the chances for promotion are low even if they do a good job. In response, many

[17]Promotions also play an important role in matching people with jobs based on skills and ability.

[18]Relative performance measures are based on how a worker performs compared to a peer group. Absolute performance measures compare the worker's performance to some predetermined standard.

[19]G. Baker, K. Murphy, and M. Jensen (1988), "Compensation and Incentives: Practice and Theory," *Journal of Finance* 43, 593–616.

[20]Promotions are typically based on the subjective judgments of people rather than objective output measures (such as pieces produced). As we discuss in more detail in Chapter 13, subjective performance evaluation can motivate nonproductive actions to influence the supervisor's rating.

firms have tried to restore employee incentives by adopting more explicit pay-for-performance plans. The American Productivity and Quality Center reports that 75 percent of employers in the United States have an incentive plan (such as a profit or gain-sharing plan) for rank-and-file employees, and that roughly 80 percent of these plans have been adopted since 1983.[21]

Influence Costs

Co-workers frequently compare compensation levels. Differences in pay among co-workers motivate employees to seek explanations for compensation decisions. Employees also use information about the pay of other employees to lobby for pay increases. It is frequently conjectured that firms reduce the differentials in pay to cut down on this type of influence activity. This policy, however, comes at a cost; underperforming employees are likely to be paid too much, while more productive employees are likely to be under-compensated and leave the firm. Influence costs also help to explain why many firms try to keep their compensation decisions confidential. In many cases, however, it is difficult to prevent co-workers from sharing information on compensation.

Firms often expend significant resources on evaluating and comparing jobs within the organization. One popular method is the Hay System.[22] Under this system, each job within the organization is evaluated on factors, such as required know-how, problem-solving skills, the number of people supervised, and accountability. Based on this evaluation, each job is assigned a total number of points and placed in a position within the firm's hierarchy. Jobs at a given level in the hierarchy have similar ranges in compensation. For example, jobs included in the same level might pay from $20,000 to $25,000, depending on experience and qualifications. While salaries reflect external market rates to some extent, a major emphasis is placed on internal consistency among jobs (equal pay for equal work). Internal consistency appears to reduce employee complaints about compensation policies and helps to protect the firm against liability in discrimination suits. However, if pay is related to the number of employees supervised, such a plan can lead to empire building by managers.

The Salary/Fringe-Benefit Mix[23]

In our benchmark model, individuals receive their compensation in the form of cash payments. Most employees, however, receive a significant amount of their compensation in the form of *fringe benefits*—compensation that is either in kind or deferred.

Examples of in-kind payments are health insurance and membership in a company recreation center, where the employee receives an insurance policy or a service rather than cash. Payments to pension plans and Social Security are examples of deferred compensation. For the typical American employee, about 75 percent of the total compensation package is pay for time worked, while about 25 percent is fringe benefits. Based on the cost to the employer, the most important fringe benefits are pensions and insurance, pay

---

[21]N. Perry (1988), "Here Come Richer, Riskier Pay Plans," *Fortune* (December 19), 50–58.

[22]For a more detailed discussion, see G. Milkovich and J. Newman (1993), *Compensation* (Richard D. Irwin: Burr Ridge, IL), Chapter 4.

[23]Material in this section draws on the analysis in Ehrenberg and Smith (1988), Chapter 11.

Influence Costs and Pay in Universities

The potential for influence activity is especially high in firms where employees have common knowledge about each other's pay. Our discussion suggests that these firms might limit the differences in pay to reduce influence costs. One study provides empirical evidence on this issue by examining compensation levels in academic departments at about 2,000 colleges. Common knowledge about pay is more likely in small departments, in departments where the members frequently interact on a social basis, and in public institutions (where public disclosure of pay is often required). Consistent with the influence-cost arguments, the study found that all three factors were associated with reductions in the dispersion of pay.

Source: J. Pfeffer and N. Langton (1988), "Wage Inequality and the Organization of Work: The Case of Academic Departments," *Administrative Sciences Quarterly* 33, 588–606.

for leave time (vacations and sick or other leave), and mandated contributions to Social Security and Workers Compensation. Many employees also receive benefits such as company-paid education, dental care, discounted meals, and subsidized recreation programs.

Employee Preferences

Salary and fringe benefits are typically not perfect substitutes from an employee's viewpoint. One reason is taxes—certain fringe benefits (such as health insurance) are not subject to income taxes when received by the employees. For example, an employee who wants to purchase an insurance policy that costs $5,000 would prefer the firm to provide the policy rather than $5,000 in cash. Since insurance policies are purchased with after-tax dollars, an employee in a 33.33 percent tax bracket would have to receive $7,500 in salary to purchase the policy. The employee might also want the firm to purchase fringe benefits because the benefits can be purchased by the firm at lower prices. For example, a firm might be able to provide group insurance at a lower cost per employee than if employees individually purchased the insurance. On the other hand, employees often prefer $5,000 in cash to $5,000 in fringe benefits, since the cash gives them more flexibility in selecting their purchases.[24]

In our initial analysis, we do not break fringe benefits into finer categories. Rather, we consider the choice between salary and overall fringe benefits. Later, we discuss the mix of fringe benefits. Figure 11.3 pictures an employee's preferences for salary and fringe benefits using indifference curves. The convexity of the curves implies that the employee is willing to substitute a relatively large amount of salary for additional expenditures on fringe benefits when the employee is paid primarily cash (possibly due to tax considerations). However, this willingness to substitute declines as the employee receives more fringe benefits (the employee prefers cash for other purposes).

The employee, of course, would like to be on as high an indifference curve as possible. A firm, however, will be able to hire the individual as long as the compensation package meets the individual's reservation level of utility. If the compensation package provides this level of utility, this person is better off working at the firm than working for alternative employers or not working at all. For example, the reservation utility of the individual

[24]D. Mayers and C. Smith (1981), "Contractual Provisions, Organizational Structure, and Conflict Control in Insurance Markets," *Journal of Business* 54, 407–434.

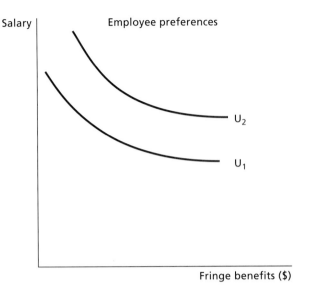

Figure 11.3   Employee Preferences for Salary and Fringe Benefits

This figure pictures an employee's preferences for salary and fringe benefits using indifference curves. The convexity of the curves implies that the employee is willing to substitute a relatively large amount of money for additional fringe benefits when the employee is paid primarily cash (possibly due to tax considerations). However, this willingness to substitute declines as the employee receives more fringe benefits (the employee wants cash for other purposes).

---

in Figure 11.3 might be pictured by the indifference curve labeled U_2. The reservation utility of the individual would increase if the compensation packages offered by other employers become more attractive.

Employer Considerations

Initially, suppose that the firm's managers do not care whether they pay an employee cash or use the same amount of cash to provide fringe benefits. For instance, both expenditures might be deductible for corporate tax purposes, and so it costs the firm the same amount in either case. Figure 11.4 displays isocost curves for a representative firm under this assumption. Each curve is a straight line with a slope of -1; firm value is unaffected by the split between salary and fringe benefits. Along any isocost curve, the expenditures for labor are the same. Firm value would be highest with the lowest isocost curve possible (since lower isocost curves imply lower labor expenses and higher profits).

The Salary/Fringe-Benefit Choice

Suppose that all individuals that the firm might hire have similar preferences for wages and fringe benefits. Figure 11.5 pictures an indifference curve for the reservation utility of a representative employee. The firm can hire this individual using any compensation package along this curve. The figure also shows selected isocost curves for the firm. Management's objective is to choose the compensation package that meets the reservation utility of the employee at the lowest cost. The optimal choice is (S^*, F^*), where the indifference curve is tangent to the isocost curve. Management could choose other combinations

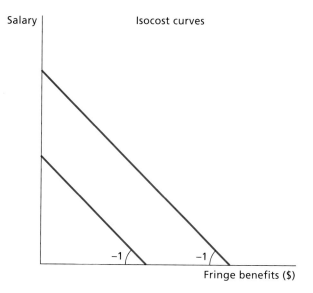

Figure 11.4 Employer Preferences for Paying Salary or Fringe Benefits

This figure displays isocost curves for a representative firm, under the assumption that firm value is unaffected by whether it pays the employee cash or uses the same amount of cash to provide fringe benefits. Each curve is a straight line with a slope of −1; firm value is unaffected by the split between paying a dollar for salary or a dollar for fringe benefits. Along any isocost curve, the labor expenses for the firm are the same. Firm value is highest on the lowest isocost curve possible (since lower isocost curves mean lower labor expenses and higher profits).

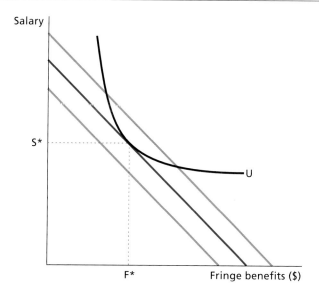

Figure 11.5 The Optimal Mix between Salary and Fringe Benefits

The figure pictures an indifference curve, U, for the reservation utility of a representative individual that the firm is trying to hire. The firm can hire the individual using any compensation package along this curve. The figure also shows selected isocost curves for the firm. To maximize firm value, choose the compensation package that meets the reservation utility of the individual at the lowest cost. This optimal choice is (S*,F*), where the indifference curve is tangent to the isocost curve. Management could choose other combinations along the indifference curve. However, these combinations are more expensive. While the firm could offer combinations that are less expensive than (S*,F*), these combinations would not meet the individual's reservation utility.

Paying for Fringe Benefits at Lincoln Electric

The willingness of firms to listen to the preferences of employees suggests that employees pay for their own fringe benefits. For instance, most companies would be willing to pay higher salaries if employees did not want health insurance. Employees, therefore, face an opportunity cost of lost salary when they receive fringe benefits. Lincoln Electric, a manufacturing company in Cleveland, makes this tradeoff very clear to employees. Employees at Lincoln receive about half their compensation in the form of annual bonus payments. Fringe-benefit costs are taken out of this bonus payment and are shown on the employees' pay stubs. On several occasions, Lincoln employees have voted against dental plans because the majority of employees prefer cash.

along the indifference curve. However, these combinations are more expensive. While management could offer combinations that are less expensive than (S^*, F^*), these combinations would not meet the individual's reservation utility.

This analysis suggests that it is in management's interest to listen to employee preferences about fringe benefits. If employees prefer that the company buy a dental policy over paying them the same amount in cash, the firm should offer the dental policy. Offering the dental policy makes the employees better off and firm value no lower. Indeed, if the change results in paying employees more than their reservation utilities, the firm can lower cash wages further and share in the gains. (The firm might do this by giving lower raises in the following year.) Designing more efficient contracts allows the firm to attract and retain employees at a lower cost.

We have assumed that firm value is unaffected by the split between paying a given amount of cash to employees and spending the same amount on fringe benefits. While this assumption is likely to be valid in many cases, there are at least two complicating factors. First, taxes at the firm level can be important. For example, the firm might have to pay Social Security taxes on wages but not fringe benefits. This tax changes the slope of the firm's isocost curves. For example, assuming a tax rate of 6 percent, managers would be indifferent between paying $1.00 for salary or $1.06 for fringe benefits. The slope of the isocost curve is $-.943$. As pictured in Figure 11.6, it is better to offer higher fringe benefits and lower salary than without the tax. Note that personal taxes are incorporated in the employee's indifference curves, while firm taxes are incorporated in the isocost curves of the firm. Thus, our analysis suggests that in designing compensation packages, management should consider the *total* tax bill for the employee and the firm.[25] Reducing overall taxes means that there is more money to split between the firm and the employee. It is generally inappropriate to focus only on the taxes of one party (for example, firm taxes).

The second complication is that fringe benefits can affect employee behavior in ways that affect firm profits. For example, sick leave can motivate absenteeism. Similarly, liberal insurance coverage can reduce employee incentives to worry about prices for medical care. These types of incentive effects can affect the appropriate compensation package. For example, some firms have reduced insurance coverage to employees for the express purpose of providing employees with incentives to negotiate with doctors over price. Presumably, employees do not like to bargain with doctors and must be offered higher wages to offset this increased cost in addition to the higher wages to offset the reduced insurance coverage in

[25]M. Scholes and M. Wolfson (1992), *Taxes and Business Strategy* (Prentice Hall: Englewood Cliffs, NJ).

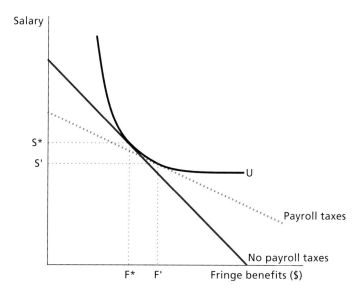

Figure 11.6 Optimal Choice of Salary and Fringe Benefits with Payroll Taxes

This figure illustrates how payroll taxes can affect the optimal choice of salary and fringe benefits. In the first case, the firm does not pay payroll taxes (such as Social Security) on wages or fringe benefits. The optimal choice is (S*,F*). In the second case, the firm pays payroll taxes on wages, but not fringe benefits. This tax flattens the isocost curves for the firm, and the optimal choice is (S′,F′). In the second case, the firm pays lower salaries and higher fringe benefits.

the fringe benefit package. However, the cost to the firm will be reduced if the increase in wages is less than the reduction in insurance costs. These considerations can shift the slope of the isocost curves in either direction and thus can either increase or decrease the optimal amount of fringe benefits.

Using Fringe Benefits to Attract Particular Types of Employees
Employers often care about the personal characteristics of the individuals that they hire. For example, firms facing higher costs of turnover might favor hiring people with families since they are less likely to quit. Alternatively, firms with intense work environments, such as investment banks in New York City, might favor hiring single people because they are likely to work longer hours. Firms are constrained in using salary offers to attract a particular type of labor force. For example, firms are likely to violate discrimination laws if they offer people with families more money than people without. Firms, however, can sometimes use the mix between fringe benefits and salary to attract particular types of employees.[26] Figure 11.7 pictures an example. The figure displays an isocost curve for the firm and indifference curves representing the reservation utilities of people who are single and people who have families. In this example, people with families have a higher preference for fringe benefits (for example, health insurance) than single people. If management wants to attract individuals with families, it will offer high fringe benefits

[26]Our objective in this section is to describe how firms use the salary and fringe benefit mix to attract particular types of individuals. We are not arguing that such a policy is ethical, just, or legal in all cases.

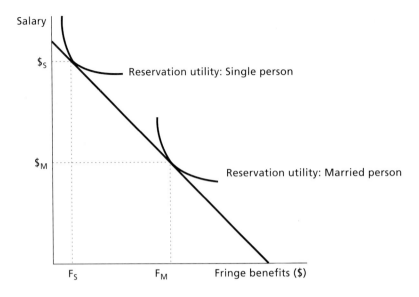

Figure 11.7   Using the Mix between Salary and Fringe Benefits to Attract Particular Types of Employees

The figure displays an isocost curve for the firm and indifference curves representing the reservation utilities of people who are single and people who have families. In this example, people with families have a higher preference for fringe benefits (for example, health insurance) than single people who prefer cash. If management wants to attract individuals with families, it will offer high fringe benefits and low wages, ($_M,F_M). In this case, only people with families will apply for the job. Single individuals will not apply because the package does not meet their reservation utilities. If, instead, management wants to hire single people, it will offer high salary and low fringe benefits, ($_S,F_S).

---

and low wages, ($_M,F_M). In this case, people with families are more likely to apply for the job. Single individuals are less likely to apply because the package does not meet their reservation utilities. If, instead, management wants to hire single people, it will offer high salary and low fringe benefits, ($_S,F_S).

The Mix of Fringe Benefits

Our basic analysis of the choice between fringe benefits and salary also applies to the choice of the mix of fringe benefits. For example, it typically makes sense to provide employees with disability insurance, rather than dental insurance, whenever the employees prefer the disability insurance (assuming the same cost to the company). In this spirit, some companies have adopted menu or *cafeteria-style* benefit plans, where individual employees allocate a fixed fringe-benefit allowance among a variety of choices. The potential benefit of these plans is that not all employees value benefits the same. By allowing them to choose, they will work for the firm at a lower overall cost.

Cafeteria plans entail costs that can limit their desirability. First, they are more expensive to administer. For example, employees must be informed of all their options and an administrative system has to be established to record choices, make the appropriate payments to suppliers, allow for changes in choices, and complete the appropriate tax forms.

Second, cafeteria plans can generate adverse-selection problems that increase the cost of benefits. Adverse selection is likely to be a particular problem in the case of health, life, and disability insurance. As discussed in Chapter 7, individuals know more about their likelihood of getting sick than an insurance company. This asymmetric information is less a problem if the insurance company provides the benefits to all employees as a group. However, when free to choose, the people who are most likely to buy insurance are those who find it a good deal at the quoted price. Thus, at any given price, the insurance company is likely to attract a clientele that causes it to lose money. To reduce the likelihood of losing money, the insurance company can do things like demand physical examinations and investigate past medical records before agreeing to insure an applicant. However, these actions increase the costs of providing the benefit. To reduce the adverse-selection problem, companies often allow employees to opt out of health insurance only if they can document that their spouse has coverage at another firm. This policy limits the amount of discretion that employees have on whether to buy health insurance, and helps to ensure that the insurance company will have both high and low health risks in the pool. Also, a cafeteria plan is more likely to be valued by two-career families since, for example, one spouse can acquire dental insurance while the other obtains health insurance.

Summary

Chapters 9 and 10 discussed how firms assign decision rights. A second important component of organizational architecture is the reward system—productive firms design compensation plans that *attract and retain* qualified employees and *motivate* them to exert effort and make productive decisions on behalf of the firm. This chapter focuses primarily on how firms attract and retain qualified employees and how the level of pay can be used to motivate employees. The next chapter focuses on incentive compensation.

In our benchmark model of wages and employment (patterned after the standard competitive model), firms have no discretion over the wages paid to employees; rather, wages are determined by supply and demand in the marketplace. If a firm pays too little, it will have difficulty attracting employees to job openings and will experience high turnover. A firm that pays too much will have numerous job applicants and low turnover. In addition, the firm will have high costs and will compete poorly in the product market. In some settings, however, it is not obvious whether a firm is paying the market wage rate to employees. Important indicators are the application and quit rates and the nature of outside job offers made to existing employees.

This benchmark model does not consider differences in the working conditions across jobs. Actual jobs vary in many dimensions, such as geographic location and the risk of danger. Holding other factors constant, unpleasant jobs must pay a *compensating differential* to attract employees. Compensating differentials attract employees to unpleasant tasks and give companies incentives to enhance the work environment whenever it is cost-effective.

Human capital is a term that characterizes individuals as having a set of skills that can be "rented" to employers. A useful distinction exists between *general* and *specific* human capital. General human capital consists of training and education that is equally useful to many different firms. Specific human capital, on the other hand, is more valuable to the current employer than alternative employers. In our benchmark model, employees pay for their own general training, while employers pay for specific training.

The benchmark model provides a good description of some labor markets, such as the market for unskilled agricultural workers. It is less useful in describing employment and wages in many other cases. Many firms are better characterized as having *internal labor markets,* where outside hiring is done only at entry-level jobs and most other jobs are filled from within the firm. Internal labor markets are characterized by *long-term relationships* between the employee and the firm. Long-term relationships can be beneficial because they give employers and employees incentives to invest in specific training, provide incentives for employees to work in the interests of the firm, and allow firms to take advantage of information about employee attributes. One cost of using internal labor markets is that it is not always desirable to hire people from within the firm for higher-level positions.

Employees taking jobs in internal labor markets evaluate *career earnings.* Thus, firms with internal labor markets have flexibility in setting the level and sequencing of pay. Firms can vary compensation over the career path, as long as the overall remaining stream of earnings is competitive at each point in time relative to the streams offered by other firms in the same labor market. Economists have identified at least three ways that firms can use their flexibility in setting the level and sequencing of pay to enhance employee motivation. These methods include the payment of *efficiency wages, upward sloping earnings profiles,* and tying major pay increases to *promotions. Influence costs,* however, can affect the desirability of taking full advantage of this flexibility. Firms potentially reduce the dispersion of pay among co-workers to limit influence costs.

The typical American employee receives about 25 percent of total compensation in the form of *fringe benefits* such as vacation time, insurance coverage, and contributions to retirement plans. Salary and fringe benefits are not perfect substitutes for most employees. Tax benefits and the fact that the company can often purchase fringe benefits more cheaply favor fringe benefits. The desire for flexibility in making purchases can favor cash payments. Employers have incentives to listen to the preferences of employees when it comes to the choice between salary and fringe benefits. By listening to these preferences, firms can design compensation packages that attract and retain qualified employees at the lowest cost. Firms can sometimes use the salary/fringe-benefit mix to attract particular types of employees. For example, offering liberal insurance coverage is more likely to attract people with families than single individuals, who likely prefer cash payments. Firms also have incentives to listen to employee preferences when it comes to choosing the mix of fringe benefits. This incentive has motivated many firms to consider *cafeteria-style* benefits. Widespread use of these plans is limited due to administrative costs and *adverse-selection problems.*

Suggested Readings

M. Aoki (1988), *Information, Incentives, and Bargaining in the Japanese Economy* (Cambridge University Press: Cambridge).

G. Becker (1983), *Human Capital* (University of Chicago Press: Chicago).

P. Doeringer and M. Piore (1971), *Internal Labor Markets and Manpower Analysis* (D. C. Heath: Lexington, MA).

R. Ehrenberg and R. Smith (1988), *Modern Labor Economics,* 3rd ed. (Scott Foresman: Glenview, IL), Chapters 8, 9, and 11.

Review Questions

11–1. Explain the following quotation: "My employer doesn't determine my salary, he determines where I work."

11–2. In the basic competitive model, why do employees pay for general training and firms pay for specific training?

11–3. Why do firms form internal labor markets?

11–4. Evaluate the following statement: "Firms are free to set salaries in any manner they want in an internal labor market."

11–5. Present an economic argument for why firms often have mandatory retirement (where allowed by law).

11–6. How do influence costs affect pay within internal labor markets?

11–7. The U.S. Congress is considering proposals that would limit the level of top executive pay to some multiple of the lowest-paid employee in the company (for example, executive pay must be less than 10 times the lowest-paid employee). Do you think this proposal is a good idea? Explain what effect the proposal would have on the involved companies.

11–8. President Clinton proposed eliminating the tax deduction for all compensation for CEOs over $1 million unless the pay is tied to company performance. Proponents argue that this proposal will benefit shareholders. "Everyone knows that CEOs are overpaid and that their pay is not appropriately tied to performance. This legislation helps to solve both problems." Present an argument against this proposal.

11–9. The Brown Tool Company is a multidivisional firm with offices throughout the country. The company sets the salaries of most of its positions at the central level. For example, secretaries are paid $8 per hour throughout the company. Discuss two important reasons why the firm might adopt such a policy. Discuss two important problems that the policy might cause.

11–10. A recent study concluded that many employees fake sickness to avoid going to work. The authors argue that through unwarranted sick leave employees "steal" about $150 billion a year from firms. This amount is three times larger than the estimated loss from shoplifting. One proposal is for Congress to outlaw the granting of sick leave to employees. The argument is that companies would be much better off because they would not incur the giant losses associated with sick leave. Further, the costs of taking sick leave would be internalized with the employees. Comment on this proposal.

11–11. The University of Rochester used to pay all faculty a 10 percent bonus as a substitute for a retirement plan. Individuals could either place this money in a retirement fund or keep the cash. Placing money in the fund deferred taxes on the income until the point of withdrawal. Changes in the U.S. tax code forced the university to change this policy. In particular, employees cannot be given options of this type but must either be covered or not covered as a group. The university now has the following policy: All new faculty members without prior service at another university are given a 10 percent bonus in cash. This payment is treated as ordinary income for tax purposes. Most new faculty are young people fresh out of graduate school. All faculty members with more than two years of service must place the bonus in a retirement account. Taxes are deferred until withdrawal from the account. Explain why it might make economic sense for the university to have such a two-group plan, rather than treat all employees (old and new) the same.

11–12. The University of Medford pays the full tuition for the children of faculty members at any university in the world. Recently, this policy has received bad publicity. The argument has been made that people in other occupations have to pay the tuition costs for their children and so should college professors. According to this argument, it is not fair to have these relatively well-paid people get subsidized in this manner. The board of trustees of the University of Medford has been asked to reconsider this policy. Provide an economic argument for why the board of trustees might want to continue this policy.

11–13. Payments under some retirement plans are based on the average earnings in the last few years of employment. Discuss the potential incentive effects of this policy.

chapter 12

Incentive Compensation

CHAPTER OUTLINE

The fibers division is the largest of Du Pont's chemical businesses, with 1989 sales of nearly $6 billion. It has departments ranging from automobile seat covers to apparel. In October 1988, this division announced "one of the most ambitious pay-incentive programs in America."[1] The plan covered nearly all of the division's 20,000 employees, including both management and rank-and-file employees.

Under the plan, a portion of employees' pay would be placed into an "at-risk pool." If the business exceeded its profit goals for the year, the employees would get a multiple of the at-risk monies as a bonus. If not, the employees stood to lose the money in the pool. The intent was to eventually have as much as 6 percent of the annual pay at risk. Initially, the plan was adopted for a three-year trial period. Many other companies indicated that they were watching this experiment carefully to see what they could learn about incentive pay. To quote Robert C. Gore, a vice president at Towers Perrin Company (a major compensation consulting firm), "The attention that the American business community has given to the Du Pont program is tremendous."

In 1990, the division had to achieve a target of 4 percent real-earnings growth for the employees to recover their at-risk pay. Profits for the first nine months, however, were off 26 percent, due largely to a bad economy and unexpectedly high input prices. Demand for the division's products had declined significantly due to weak housing and automobile markets, and oil prices had risen significantly because of the Gulf War. By fall 1990, it was obvious that the employees were likely to lose this money. Employee discontent was very high—employees were facing significant financial losses, due largely to factors beyond their control. In October 1990, Du Pont suddenly canceled the incentive program with more than a full year to go in the trial period. In the words of the fibers division chief, "I have to conclude it was an experiment that didn't work."

Given the widespread interest in this experiment, it is important to understand why the Du Pont plan failed. Is incentive pay, as some critics claim, simply a bad idea? If so, any firm adopting a large-scale incentive plan is making a mistake and likely to experience the same fate as Du Pont. Alternatively, can the failure of this scheme be traced to basic design problems that could have been avoided by more careful planning? This chapter analyzes the economics of incentive compensation. The analysis suggests that Du Pont's failure was largely due to problems with the structure of the plan. Correspondingly, the analysis provides insights into how companies might design better compensation plans.

We begin this chapter by providing a more detailed discussion of incentive problems. We then examine how ownership can solve some of these problems by providing strong incentives to individuals to take efficient actions. Next, we consider one important limitation of ownership in controlling incentive problems—inefficient risk bearing. The implications of risk bearing for the design of compensation contracts are emphasized. Next, we review some of the key insights about incentive compensation contained in the economics literature. We begin by discussing the standard principal/agent model. We then extend this basic analysis by considering the informativeness principle, group incentive pay, multitask principal/agent problems, alternative forms of incentive pay, and the role of incentive pay in self-selection. Toward the end of the chapter, we discuss the debate on whether incentive pay works, and we provide a case study on CEO compensation to allow the reader to apply some of the concepts we have developed on compensation policy. The appendix examines multitask principal/agent problems in more detail.

---

[1]Details of this example come from two articles: L. Hays (1988), "All Eyes on Du Pont's Incentive Program," *The Wall Street Journal* (December 5), B-1, and R. Koening (1990), "Du Pont Plan Linking Pay to Fibers Profit Unravels," *The Wall Street Journal* (October 25), B-1.

The Incentive Problem

As described in Chapter 7, incentive problems exist in firms because owners and employees have different objectives. For example, an insurance company wants its salespeople to sell products to customers, but the salespeople might prefer to play golf. Similarly, a research company wants its scientists to develop marketable products, while the scientists might prefer to work on more interesting but less marketable ideas. Presumably, the employees at Du Pont's fibers division have other interests than simply making and selling fibers products.

Consider the example of the American Assembly Corporation (AAC), a small company that assembles parts for several large manufacturing firms. As in many companies, there is a basic conflict between the aims of the owners and the aims of the employees. The owners would like employees to work hard, while the employees would prefer longer coffee breaks and working at a slower pace.

To add concreteness to the discussion, consider the problem of motivating one representative employee at AAC, George Smith. For simplicity, focus on a single time period (for example, motivating George over a single week or month). George's preferences with respect to income and work are portrayed by the following utility function:[2]

$$U = I - e^2 \qquad (12.1)$$

where I is his income for the period and e is the number of units of effort exerted (for example, hours spent actually assembling parts). This utility function, which measures utility in dollar equivalents, indicates that he becomes better off as his total income increases, but becomes worse off as he exerts more effort on behalf of the firm. As George exerts effort, he suffers decreased utility because he would rather engage in other activities. His reservation utility is $1,000. The firm must provide George with this level of utility or he will not work for the firm.

The firm benefits from George's effort, since more parts are assembled. The benefits to AAC from his effort are:

$$B = \$100e \qquad (12.2)$$

Suppose that his effort is costlessly observable. In this case, the firm can offer George a compensation contract that pays him a sum of money if, and only if, he provides a specified level of effort. He will accept this contract, as long as he is paid his reservation utility. To meet this condition, the firm must pay him a wage of $1,000 + e^2$. If he is paid $1,000 + e^2$, then his utility is $U = (\$1,000 + e^2) - e^2 = \$1,000$ and he receives his reservation utility. The profits to the firm, P, from his efforts are:

$$P = \$100e - (\$1,000 + e^2) \qquad (12.3)$$

The firm then chooses the e that maximizes profits.

Figure 12.1 provides a graphic illustration of this problem. The figure pictures both the benefits to the firm ($100e) and the costs ($1,000 + e^2$). Profits are the difference between the two. As the figure indicates, maximum profits occur at $e = 50$. At this effort level, George is paid $3,500 and the profits for AAC are $1,500. This outcome is the efficient bargaining solution for the two parties. George is indifferent among the possible

---

[2]We chose this particular utility function (as well as the firm's benefit function, discussed below) to simplify the calculations. Our basic results, however, are quite general and are not specialized to this particular example.

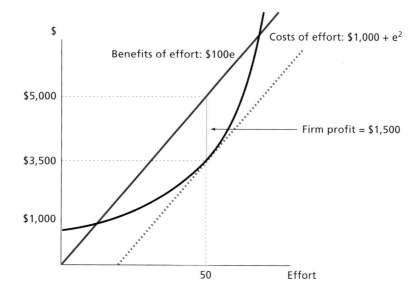

Figure 12.1 The Optimal Effort Choice at AAC

This figure pictures both the benefits and the costs to the American Assembly Corporation (AAC) from the efforts of a given employee. Profits are the difference between the two. Maximum profits occur at e = 50. This example assumes that the employee will exert the agreed-upon effort as long as he is paid his reservation utility. To meet this constraint, the firm must pay a wage of $1,000 + e^2$. This payment meets the reservation wage of $1,000 and reimburses the employee for his disutility of effort. Benefits to the firm are $100e. At the optimal effort level, e = 50, $5,000 in gross benefits are generated. The employee is paid $3,500 and firm profits are $1,500. The firm can get the employee to exert more effort by paying him more. However, the costs are larger than the benefits. The effort choice of 50 is efficient—the employee is indifferent among the possible choices (since he is paid his reservation utility in each case), and the profits for the firm are maximized at this level.

effort choices (he is paid his reservation wage in all cases), while firm profits are maximized at 50. The firm could get him to provide additional effort by paying him more. However, the marginal costs to the firm are higher than the marginal benefits. At the optimal effort level of e = 50, the marginal costs of effort are equal to the marginal benefits; all the benefits and costs to both parties thus are considered.[3]

Thus far, we have assumed that George's effort is costlessly observable. In many cases, however, e will not be observable by either the firm or a court of law. In addition, the firm might not be able to tell whether George worked hard by simply observing his output. Often, output is difficult to measure and is affected by factors beyond the employee's control.[4] In this case, there is a standard agency problem. If George promises to provide 50 units of effort and is paid a fixed salary of $3,500, he has the incentive to renege on his promise and provide less effort. He gets paid anyway and is better off by not working as

---

[3] Recall that the marginal benefit at a point is equal to the slope of the total benefit at that point. The same relation holds between marginal cost and total cost. Using elementary calculus, the slope of the total cost curve is 2e, while the slope of the total benefit curve is 100. The optimal effort level is 2e = 100; thus e = 50.

[4] In our example, the firm can infer e from observing B, George's output. More generally, B would be affected by factors that are beyond the control of the employee. For example, the following relation might hold: B = $100e + \mu$, where μ is a random error. Random factors that might affect his output include the quality of raw materials and equipment failures. With the random error term, the firm cannot infer e simply from observing B.

hard. The firm might suspect that George did not work hard. However, it would not know for sure. In this case, a straight salary of $3,500 does not provide George with appropriate incentives. Rather, AAC must devise some other type of contract that motivates him to provide additional effort.

This simple example illustrates three important points about incentive problems:

- Incentive problems exist because of conflicts of interest between employers and employees. If the interests of employees and employers were perfectly aligned, there would be no reason to worry about incentives.
- Incentive conflicts do not cause problems when actions are observable. Firms can identify the most efficient actions and pay employees only if these actions are taken. For instance, if the actions of employees at Du Pont were costlessly observable, there would be no reason for the firm to have a profit-based plan for employees. Rather the employees could be appropriately motivated by contracts based directly on employee productivity.
- In a competitive labor market, employees must be compensated for undertaking undesirable actions. (There are compensating differentials.) It is not usually sensible to have employees work as hard as physically possible. In choosing the optimal action, there is a tradeoff between the benefits of the action for the firm and the personal costs to the employees.

Incentives from Ownership

In some cases, there is a simple way to solve incentive problems even when the actions of employees are unobservable. The solution is to sell each employee the rights to his or her total output. The agency problem is caused by the fact that most of the costs of exerting effort are borne by employees, while most of the gains go to the employer. By selling employees their output, both the benefits and costs of exerting effort are internalized by employees and thus employees will make more productive choices. For instance, in the AAC example, the firm could sell George the rights to the value of his output ($100e) for a price of $1,500. AAC makes the same profits as when effort was costlessly observable. George's objective, in turn, is to maximize his personal utility given by:

$$U = (\$100e - \$1,500) - e^2 \tag{12.4}$$

where the first term represents the income from exerting effort (the value of the output minus the $1,500 payment to the company) and the second term represents the disutility of effort. Given this problem, George will choose to exert 50 units of effort and will have utility of $1,000.[5] This outcome is the same as in the perfect information case. It is achieved even though the employer cannot observe George's effort.

This discussion highlights the strong incentive effects that come from ownership. Ownership is often used in practice as an incentive mechanism. For example, about one-third of all retail sales in the United States are made through franchised outlets. In franchising, the future profits of each unit are sold to franchisees, who as owners have strong

---

[5]This solution can be found using elementary calculus (see footnote 3) or a graphical analysis, as in Figure 12.1. We will present a more detailed analysis of the employee's effort choice later in this chapter.

incentives to maximize value.[6] As another example, in the 1980s there were a large number of managerial buyouts of firms and divisions of firms, where the managers went from the status of employees to owners. While some aspects of these buyouts might be controversial, the evidence indicates that the managers operated the units more efficiently when they became owners.[7]

There are at least three important factors that limit the use of ownership in solving incentive problems:

- *Wealth constraints.* Limited wealth can make ownership infeasible. For instance, while the senior managers at Du Pont might have stronger incentives if they owned the company, few management groups in the world would have access to enough funds to make the purchase.
- *Risk aversion.* Typically, employees do not have full control over their outputs. Rather, outputs usually depend on random outside events, as well as employee efforts. For example, Du Pont's profits are affected by changes in the oil, housing, and automobile markets. Ownership, in making employees fully accountable for their actions, also makes them vulnerable to random events beyond their control that affect their output. Given that employees do not like to bear risk, employee ownership entails a risk-bearing cost (see Chapter 2). As we discuss below, this cost must be considered in designing incentive contracts.
- *Team production.* It is often impossible to measure the profit contribution of a given employee. In most firms, there are production synergies, where the total output is greater than the sum of what each employee could produce individually. Identifying the separate contributions when there is this type of "team production" is problematic. The firm could be owned jointly by the employees. However, this solution does not solve the agency problem—there would be the standard free-rider problem discussed in Chapter 7.

Optimal Risk Sharing

To illustrate some of the basic principles of efficient risk sharing, consider the example of David McKoy and Cindy Callaway. David receives a monthly income from a trust fund. Depending on the performance of the fund, this income can either be $0 or $10,000, each with a probability of .5. David's expected income is $5,000.[8] However, the income stream is risky—half the time, David gets $0. Cindy also has a trust fund with the same income possibilities. Half the time she gets $0; the other half $10,000. The income flows for David and Cindy are *independent.* (That is, regardless of the outcome for David, the

[6]P. Rubin (1978), "The Theory of the Firm and Structure of the Franchise Contract," *Journal of Law & Economics* 28, 223–233; and J. Brickley and F. Dark (1987), "The Choice of Organizational Form: The Case of Franchising," *Journal of Financial Economics* 18, 401–420. In most franchise agreements, the central company receives an ongoing sales royalty from the franchisee. This royalty provides incentives to the central company to honor commitments on training and promoting the brand name. The franchisee's claim on future profits is typically limited to some time period—for example, 20 years. The contract is often renewable.

[7]S. Kaplan (1989), "The Effects of Management Buyouts on Operating Performance and Value," *Journal of Financial Economics* 24, 217–254.

[8]The expected income is the *average* amount that David will receive in a month. It is calculated by adding together each possible income multiplied by the respective probability: $(10,000 \times .5) + (\$0 \times .5) = \$5,000$.

Joint Outcomes	Probability	Individual Payoffs from Splitting
($0;$0)	.25	$ 0
($0;$10,000)	.25	5,000
($10,000;$0)	.25	5,000
($10,000;$10,000)	.25	10,000
		E(Income) = $5,000

Figure 12.2 Example of Risk Sharing

In this example, two people receive incomes from different trust funds. Each fund pays either $0 of $10,000, each with a probability of .5. The two funds have independent payoffs. The left column displays the possible joint payoff outcomes, while the middle column shows the probability of each outcome occurring. For instance, ($0;$0) is the outcome where both funds pay $0 for the period. The probability of this outcome is .25. The right column shows the individual incomes if the two people agree to split the payoffs from the two funds. Splitting the payoffs makes both people better off, compared to relying solely on the payoffs from their own individual funds. The expected income in either case is $5,000. However, risk is reduced by the pooling of the funds. For instance, each person has a .5 chance of receiving no income when keeping all the income from his or her own fund. The two people only have a .25 chance of receiving no income when they pool the funds.

probability is still .5 that Cindy will get $0.)[9] The left column of Figure 12.2 displays the joint distribution of outcomes for David and Cindy.[10] The probability of each outcome is given in the middle column.

Assuming that David and Cindy are *risk averse* (holding the expected income constant, the person prefers less risk), they can both be made better off by agreeing to split the combined income. The possible payoffs for each individual are given in the right column of Figure 12.2. The expected income per individual is still $5,000. By sharing the risks, however, the variability of their individual incomes has been reduced. The variability is reduced because the likelihood that both Cindy and David will be lucky or unlucky is less than the likelihood that only one of them is lucky or unlucky. For example, by sharing the risks, the probability of getting nothing is only .25, compared to .5 with no risk sharing. Being risk averse, they prefer the less volatile income stream. (Ideally, they would like income streams that are certain.) It is this reduction in volatility from pooling risks that drives the purchase of insurance, as well as the purchase of diversified portfolios (for example, mutual funds).

People often differ in their attitudes toward risk. Some people are relatively willing to take huge financial gambles, while others are not. An efficient allocation of risk takes these differences in preferences into account. For example, suppose that Cindy is *risk neutral,* while David is risk averse. (A risk-neutral person cares only about the expected payoff and does not care about the risk.) Cindy will value each of the two random income flows at $5,000 (the expected value), while David will not. For example, David might be willing to accept a certain payment of $4,000 for his risky income flow. Here,

[9]We assume that the flows are independent to simplify the calculations in the example. The basic insights of this analysis hold as long as the two flows are not perfectly positively correlated.

[10]A joint outcome ($X,$Y) refers to David receiving X dollars while Cindy receives Y dollars. Since the events are independent, the probability of any joint outcome is the probability of the first event (that David receives $X) multiplied by the probability of the second event (that Cindy receives $Y). For example, the probability that both will receive $0 is .5 × .5 = .25.

there are gains from trade by having Cindy buy David's income. A payment of $4,500 would split the potential gains of trade between the two parties. Each party would be better off by $500.

The common stock of large corporations is typically held by many investors with well-diversified portfolios. Because of this diversification, investors are not overly concerned about the fortunes of any one company. (Things tend to balance out over their entire portfolios; that is, one firm is lucky while another firm is unlucky.)[11] Employees, in contrast, receive large fractions of their incomes from individual companies and care greatly about the fortunes of individual firms. This difference in outlook implies that employees of a firm can often be viewed as being more risk averse than the owners of the firm. Note that we are not saying that employees necessarily have fundamentally different preferences than owners. Rather, it is the differential ability to diversify firm-specific risk that makes shareholders in large corporations less concerned about risk.

Assuming that the owners of the firm are essentially risk neutral, it is better from a risk-sharing standpoint to pay employees fixed salaries and let the total risk of random income flows be borne by the shareholders. By paying fixed salaries, the firm avoids having to pay a compensating differential for risk (a *risk premium*) to attract and retain the desired work force.

Effective Incentive Contracts

Our discussion to this point suggests that compensation contracts serve at least two important functions. First, they are used to motivate employees. Second, they are used to share risk more efficiently. Unfortunately, there is a tradeoff between these two objectives. Efficient risk sharing suggests that it is better to pay employees fixed salaries, while incentive considerations suggest that it is better to tie pay to performance. A compensation contract strikes an appropriate balance between these two considerations.

BASIC PRINCIPLE

Tradeoffs between Incentives and Risk Sharing

- When the owners of a firm are essentially risk neutral, it is better from a *risk-sharing standpoint* to pay employees fixed salaries and let the risk of random income flows be borne by owners (for example, shareholders in large corporations).

- Fixed salaries do not provide strong incentives. Incentives are provided by basing pay on performance.

- The first two points indicate that there is a trade-off between paying incentive compensation to increase effort and the associated costs of inefficient risk bearing. Often, an effective contract consists of a fixed salary and some variable component based on performance.

Economists have devoted significant resources to studying how to design effective compensation contracts. In this section, we summarize some of the more important findings from this research. We begin with the most basic model in the economics literature, the standard principal/agent model. This model considers a contracting situation that closely resembles our example of George Smith of the AAC Company. The model,

---

[11]For example, H. Markowitz (1959), *Portfolio Selection* (John Wiley & Sons: New York), and W. Sharpe (1964), "Capital Asset Prices: A Theory of Market Equilibrium under Conditions of Risk," *Journal of Finance* 19, 179–211.

however, generalizes this example and focuses on choosing the optimal contract when the employer cannot observe the employee's effort. Following the introduction of the basic model, we extend the analysis by considering the informativeness principle, group incentive pay, multitask principal/agent problems, types of incentive pay, and the role of incentive pay in self-selection.

Principal/Agent Model

The Basic Model

Economic analysis of incentive compensation begins with the basic principal/agent model.[12] This model presents a relatively simple characterization of the contracting process. However, it illustrates the tradeoffs between risk sharing and incentives and provides a number of useful insights for designing more effective compensation plans. In this single-period model, there is an employer (the principal) who wants the employee (the agent) to work on the employer's behalf. The employer is risk neutral, while the employee is risk averse. The most basic analysis focuses on one employee. Concerns about teamwork do not arise in the basic model.

Consider the example of Ellen Sleeter of the Roseburg Fax Company. Ellen's output, Q, is a function of her effort, plus some random effect, μ (with expected value 0 and variance, σ^2):

$$Q = \alpha e + \mu \qquad (12.5)$$

where output is defined as the market value of the production. The model does not consider the possibility that Ellen might manipulate the observed output level (for example, by "cooking the books"). Both Ellen and her supervisor can observe the output.

If Ellen increases effort by one unit, output goes up by α units. Thus, α is Ellen's marginal productivity—the higher the α, the higher her marginal productivity. The random effect, μ, reflects factors that can affect output but are beyond Ellen's control (for example, equipment failures). The higher σ^2, the more likely it is that the output will experience larger random shocks.

Optimal risk sharing suggests that there are benefits from having the owners of the Roseburg Fax Company bear the output risk and pay Ellen a fixed salary. For example, Ellen might agree to put forth effort level e^* and be paid a fixed salary, W, for this effort. The owners of Roseburg Fax receive the difference between the value of the output and W.

$$\text{Owner's profits} = (\alpha e + \mu) - W \qquad (12.6)$$

There is, however, an agency problem with this arrangement if Ellen's supervisor cannot observe her effort level or μ, the random shock. Ellen has the incentive to agree to e^* as an effort level but then exert less effort. Her supervisor will tend to observe lower output when she shirks. However, Ellen can claim the result is due to bad luck (that is, μ was negative).

---

[12]One of the first presentations of this model is B. Holmstrom (1979), "Moral Hazard and Observability," *Bell Journal of Economics* 10, 74–91.

Employee's Effort Problem

Incentives can be provided to Ellen by basing part of her compensation on realized output. For example, consider Ellen's incentives under the following contract:

$$\text{Compensation} = W_o + \beta Q \qquad (12.7)$$

where $0 \leq \beta \leq 1$. This contract pays Ellen a fixed wage, W_o, plus a proportion, β, of the output, Q.[13] To illustrate Ellen's effort choice, suppose $W_o = \$400$, $\beta = .2$, $Q = \$100e + \mu$, and $C(e) = e^2$, where $C(e)$ is Ellen's cost of effort in dollar equivalents. Given these values, the compensation contract is:

$$\text{Compensation} = \$400 + .2(\$100e + \mu) \qquad (12.8)$$

The benefit to Ellen from exerting effort is that it increases compensation—each unit of effort increases her compensation by \$20 (.2 × \$100). Random shocks, μ, affect total compensation but do not affect the benefits of exerting effort. For any realization of μ, compensation is always \$20 higher for every extra unit of effort provided. Thus, in choosing the optimal effort level, Ellen can ignore μ. (It does not affect the costs or benefits of her effort.)[14] Ellen's cost from exerting effort is e^2. Her objective is to choose the effort level that maximizes the net benefits.

Figure 12.3 displays how Ellen's compensation and personal costs increase as she exerts more effort. As shown in the figure, the optimal effort choice is 10. Note that the figure shows total costs and benefits. The marginal benefits and marginal costs at any effort level are equal to the slopes of the total curves at that point. The difference between total costs and benefits is greatest when the slopes of the total curves are equal. Thus, at the optimal choice ($e = 10$), the marginal costs of effort are equal to the marginal benefits, and net benefits are maximized. If Ellen exerts more than 10 units of effort, the extra income is not sufficient to compensate her for the extra disutility she experiences from exerting more effort. When e is less than 10, Ellen is made better off by exerting more effort, since the additional compensation is more than sufficient to cover the added costs of the additional effort.

Figure 12.4 shows how Ellen's effort choice changes with changes in the fixed wage, W_o, and the incentive coefficient, β. Changing the fixed wage from \$400 to \$800 results in a parallel shift in compensation, but Ellen still chooses $e = 10$. The fixed wage *provides no incentives* for Ellen to work harder since it does not affect the *marginal benefits* of effort. Marginal benefits are \$20, regardless of the fixed wage. In contrast, when the incentive coefficient is increased, Ellen selects a higher effort level. For instance, with $\beta = .3$, Ellen selects 15 units of effort. In this case, marginal benefits increase to \$30 and Ellen exerts more effort.

The implications of this analysis should be contrasted with the common argument that well-paid employees work harder because they are happier on the job. In our analysis, higher pay does not provide incentives unless it is tied to good performance. It is important to

---

[13]For simplicity, we restrict our attention to linear compensation contracts. One justification for focusing on linear contracts is that they are commonly observed in practice. For instance, salespeople and real estate agents often are paid commissions, while factory workers are frequently paid piece rates. Linear contracts have the advantage of providing consistent incentives to the worker that do not depend on past output (the marginal payoff for increasing output by one unit is constant). In contrast, lump-sum bonuses that are paid once some threshold is reached lose their incentive effects once the target is met. For a technical justification for linear contracts, see B. Holmstrom and P. Milgrom (1987), "Aggregation and Linearity in the Provision of Intertemporal Incentives," *Econometrica* 55, 303–28.

[14]For the technically inclined: Throughout our analysis, we assume that Ellen's attitude toward risk does not change with her level of wealth. Relaxing this assumption means that she will consider an additional effect in choosing the effort level. In particular, the effort choice will affect her utility by altering the costs imposed on her from bearing risk. We ignore this potential effect because it complicates the analysis without providing substantially more insights.

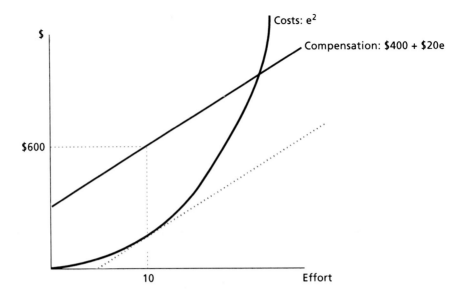

Figure 12.3 The Employee's Effort Choice

This figure shows how the compensation and personal costs increase as the employee exerts more effort. The compensation function is $400 + $20e. The employee's cost function is e^2. The objective of the employee is to choose the effort level that maximizes the net benefits. This maximization occurs at e = 10. At this point, the marginal benefits of effort ($20) are equal to the marginal costs. The employee's expected compensation is $600.

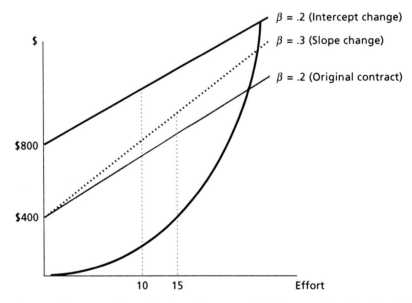

Figure 12.4 How the Employee's Effort Choice Changes with Changes in the Fixed Wage and Incentive Coefficient

The initial contract is Compensation = $400 + .2($100e). The picture shows that increasing the fixed wage from $400 to $800 causes a parallel shift in the compensation function but does not alter the effort choice (it stays at 10). Changing the incentive coefficient (β) from .2 to .3 changes the slope of the line and increases the amount of effort to 15.

Motivating Employees at Allen-Edmonds Shoe Company

Agency theory argues that tying pay to performance motivates employees more than fixed salaries. Allen-Edmonds Shoe Company learned this principle the hard way. Allen-Edmonds is a manufacturer of high-priced shoes. For years, it paid its factory employees based on individual output through a piece-rate system. In 1990, acting on the advice of quality experts, the company abandoned the piece-rate system and started paying employees fixed hourly wages. The intent was to encourage employees to focus on quality and teamwork. Productivity plummeted as employees were observed taking more breaks and "fooling around." After the company lost $1 million in 1990, it reinstated piecework payments. Productivity and profits immediately "shot back up." An executive of the company stated, "Our people needed the discipline that the piecework system gives to them."

Source: B. Marsh (1993) "Allen-Edmonds Shoe Tries 'Just-In-Time' Production," *The Wall Street Journal* (March 4), B-2.

note that our analysis focuses on a single time period. In a multi-period setting, a high level of pay can motivate employees if the *likelihood of being fired is contingent on performance.* (See the discussion in the last chapter on efficiency wages.) In this case, the threat of layoff is a method of tying pay to performance. High pay and guaranteed tenure with the firm, however, provide no incentive effects.

The Optimal Contract

We have shown how Ellen will choose effort under different compensation contracts. The firm's problem is to choose the specific compensation contract that maximizes expected profits, given Ellen's anticipated effort choice. The primary choice variable is β. Given this choice, W_0 can be adjusted up or down to meet Ellen's reservation utility. Selecting a contract with a high β benefits the owners of the firm because it increases Ellen's effort. However, choosing a high β also involves costs for the firm. The expected compensation that the firm must pay to Ellen increases with β for two reasons. First, as discussed above, Ellen must be compensated for exerting more effort. Second, increasing β imposes additional risk on her—the variable portion of compensation increases. As risk increases, so does the compensating differential that must be paid to induce Ellen to remain with the firm. The optimal contract involves an appropriate balancing of these costs and benefits.

Incentive Pay and Expected Compensation

A study of earnings of employees in 500 U.S. firms in the footwear and clothing industries found that piece-rate employees on average were paid 14 percent more than employees paid straight salaries. This premium was found after controlling for union status, sex, and other variables that might affect compensation. Economic theory suggests at least three reasons for this wage premium. First, people work harder under piece rates than under fixed salaries and must be compensated for the extra effort. Second, piece rates impose risk on employees; output is affected by random factors such as equipment failures. Thus firms using piece rates must pay a compensating differential for risk. A third reason—which we have not discussed in this chapter—is that piece rates are likely to attract more highly skilled and productive employees (since they will earn more under piece rates than under fixed salaries). Firms have to pay more for skilled employees than for unskilled employees.

Source: E. Seiler (1984), "Piece Rate vs Time Rate: The Effect of Incentives on Earnings," *Review of Economics and Statistics* 66, 363–376.

Factors that Favor High Incentive Pay

1. Output is sensitive to the employee's effort.
2. The employee is not very risk averse.
3. The level of risk that is beyond the employee's control is low.
4. The employee's response to increased incentives is high (the employee exerts a lot more effort).

Figure 12.5 Implications of the Principal/Agent Model

The model suggests that the four factors listed in this figure are likely to be particularly important in determining how strongly to base pay on performance.

Implications

Typically, the employee is offered an incentive contract that implies less effort than would be required if the employer could costlessly observe the effort choice. When effort is observable, the optimal effort level, e^*, can be elicited without imposing risk on the employee. When effort is unobservable, the employer could elicit e^* by paying sufficiently high incentive pay. However, the costs of inefficient risk bearing make this an undesirable choice.[15]

The formal analysis suggests four factors that are likely to be important in selecting how strongly pay should be tied to performance. These factors are summarized in Figure 12.5. The first factor is the sensitivity of output to additional effort from the employee. In our example, this factor is captured by α (Ellen's marginal productivity). A high α implies that incentive pay (holding other factors constant) is effective because the benefits of motivating effort are high. A second factor is the risk aversion of the employee. Higher risk aversion implies a higher cost from inefficient risk bearing and thus a lowering of the use of incentive pay. The third factor is the level of risk that is beyond the employee's control (σ^2). When the level of risk is low, output is determined primarily by the employee's effort and it makes sense to pay higher levels of incentive compensation. When the risk is high, incentive compensation imposes high costs for inefficient risk bearing. The fourth factor is how much additional effort the employee exerts as incentives are increased. If the employee is unresponsive to increased incentives, high incentive compensation imposes risk on the employee without inducing additional effort. Thus, there is no reason to pay high incentive pay. The responsiveness to incentive pay depends on the personal costs to the employee for exerting additional effort. For instance, changing the cost function in Figure 12.4 from e^2 to e^3, makes Ellen less responsive to changes in incentives. With the original cost function, Ellen increases effort by 5 units as β is increased from .2 to .3. But the increase is only .58 under the second cost function.[16]

---

[15]The basic model assumes that the employer has the relevant knowledge to solve this problem, including knowledge of the production function, the worker's utility function, and the variance of the random error term. For a mathematical derivation of the results in this section, see Chapter 7 of P. Milgrom and J. Roberts (1992), *Economics, Organization, and Management* (Prentice Hall: Englewood Cliffs, NJ).

[16]For the technically inclined: It is the second derivative of the cost function that is important in determining the response rate: Larger second derivatives (or equivalently steeper marginal cost curves) translate into lower response rates.

Du Pont Revisited

The principal/agent model points to at least two problems with the Du Pont plan. Both problems stem from using divisional profits as an output measure. First, while these profits are affected by the collective efforts of all divisional employees, *individually* employees have little effect on the measure. For example, a given employee out of 20,000 can increase his or her work effort substantially and have almost no effect on divisional profits. Thus, the individual αs are low and the plan provides limited incentives for employees to exert effort. (They bear costs from exerting effort but gain few personal benefits.) The limited incentives are due to the classic *free-rider problem* discussed in Chapter 7. Du Pont would have provided stronger incentives if it had paid the employees based on output measures over which they had greater control (for example, their own output). We discuss this issue in greater detail below under the topic of group incentives. The second problem is that divisional profits are affected by many random factors (σ^2 is high), and thus the compensation plan imposes significant uncontrollable risk on the employees. In the next section, we discuss methods that Du Pont could have used to reduce this inefficient risk bearing.

Informativeness Principle[17]

BASIC PRINCIPLE

Informativeness Principle

In designing compensation contracts, theory suggests that it is productive to include all performance indicators that provide additional information about the employee's effort (assuming the measures are available at low cost). Measuring the employee's effort with more precision reduces the costs of inefficient risk bearing and leads to a more efficient effort choice.

As we have seen, incentive problems exist because of imperfect information. If the actions of employees were observable at zero cost, it would be easy to write contracts to motivate appropriate behavior. It follows that the inefficiencies that result from incentive problems can be reduced by improvements in information. The standard principal/agent model assumes that there is only one indicator of an employee's effort, the employee's output. In many cases there are other sources of information that can be used to determine whether or not the employee worked hard. For instance, Du Pont was able to tell that the decline in profits in 1990 was not due to a lack of effort on the part of divisional employees by observing the performance of other companies and gathering information such as government reports on unemployment. Appropriate use of this type of information increases the precision by which employee effort is measured, and when included in the compensation contract (with the appropriate weights) reduces the costs of inefficient risk bearing. In theory, it is optimal to include all indicators that provide additional information about the employee's effort in the compensation contract (assuming the measures are available at low cost). This basic idea is called the *informativeness principle.*

One important source of information about an employee's effort level is the output of co-workers performing similar tasks. For instance, if a salesperson's performance is bad in a given year, was the person unlucky or lazy? If average sales in the company declined substantially over the same time period, it is likely that the employee was simply unlucky. If other salespeople had great years, the salesperson is more likely to have been lazy. The informativeness principle indicates that information about other employees' sales should be included in the compensation contract as a benchmark (that is, to use a *relative performance contract*). Chapter 13 provides an extended discussion of relative performance evaluation and highlights several potential problems that can make relative performance evaluation undesirable.

---

[17]Material in this section draws on B. Holmstrom (1982), "Moral Hazard in Teams," *Bell Journal of Economics* 13, 324–40.

The informativeness principle indicates that it is typically beneficial to include low-cost indicators in the compensation contract that improve the employee's performance measure. It can also be desirable for the firm to expend additional resources on developing even more precise measures of performance. Here, there is a tradeoff between the costs of developing better performance measures and the benefits of improved risk sharing and effort motivation.

The informativeness principle suggests that Du Pont could have reduced the risk imposed on the employees by including other indicators in the contract. For instance, rather than using an absolute performance standard (such as 4 percent of real earnings growth), the target could have been set relative to the growth of other firms in the same industry. This type of contract might have avoided the problems that the company faced in 1990, when employees were likely to lose money under the plan due to no fault of their own.

The informativeness principle also suggests that Du Pont could have reduced the uncontrollable risk imposed on its employees by adjusting earnings to reflect external changes in market conditions. For example, the company could have adjusted division profits for the change in oil prices from the Gulf War. In fact, the firm might want to enter financial contracts (for example, futures, forwards, swaps, or options) to transfer this risk from the fibers division to external markets to reduce the risk imposed on the division's employees and the compensating differentials required in their compensation packages.[18]

Group Incentive Pay

In the basic principal/agent model, employees are motivated by being paid based on their *own output*. Many firms, however, base incentive pay on *group performance*. (Du Pont is an example.) For example, of 425 companies responding to a 1987 survey by the Hay group, 87 percent offered some type of incentive pay in addition to base salary. The most common forms of incentive pay were profit-sharing plans and other types of group incentive plans (for instance, plans based on productivity improvements).[19]

There are at least three reasons why firms might favor group incentive plans over individual plans:

- Individual performance is often difficult to measure, while the performance of a group of employees often can be measured at reasonably low cost. For example, the owner of a small grocery store can tell whether the overall business is doing well from the store's profits. Measuring the performance of each of the employees is much more difficult.
- Group pay emphasizes cooperation and teamwork, while some individual incentive plans (depending on design) motivate more self-centered actions.
- Group plans can motivate employees to monitor each other for bad performance. Mutual monitoring is beneficial because the specific knowledge about individual performance is often held by co-workers.

Standard free-rider arguments, however, provide a strong reason to question whether group plans provide powerful incentives—particularly when the group is quite large. In Du Pont's fibers division, with 20,000 employees, the contributions of individual employees have virtually no effect on the overall bottom line. In this case, profit-sharing plans would appear to have limited incentive effects. Yet this is not surprising. Do you

---

[18]C. Smith (1995), "Corporate Risk Management: Theory and Practice," *Journal of Derivatives* 2, 21–30.

[19]L. Hays (1988), "All Eyes on Du Pont's Incentive Program," *The Wall Street Journal* (December 5), B-1.

really expect that paying a janitor on overall company performance would really motivate the person to push the broom harder or to complain when other janitors shirk on their jobs?[20] These arguments suggest that large-group incentive plans (like Du Pont's) impose risk on employees but have limited benefits.

While many economists find the free-rider arguments to be quite compelling, there are some offsetting considerations that potentially help to explain the widespread popularity of group plans (even if free-riding is a potential problem). First, it might be beneficial to increase the awareness of employees about the stock-price performance and profitability of the company. By focusing on these measures, employees learn how managerial and employee actions affect the bottom line. For instance, employees might be less likely to complain about a corporate restructuring when they see that it increases stock price. Indeed, it probably does not take much stock ownership to motivate most employees to monitor the stock price on a frequent basis. Hence, these benefits can be obtained while shifting little risk to the employees. Second, employees might experience disutility from taking actions that harm other members of a group that they closely identify with. Thus, when the group receives incentive pay, employees might not want to harm co-workers by shirking on the job. In this case, feelings like guilt and shame might motivate employees, even if they do not face direct financial consequences from shirking.[21] Third, paying employees on stock-price performance and profits sends signals to employees about what is valued in the company. These signals serve to reinforce a performance-based corporate culture (see Chapter 8). To be most effective, however, they must be complemented by other features in the organizational architecture that provide more direct incentives.

Multitask Principal/Agent Problems[22]

In the standard principal/agent model, effort is one-dimensional—the firm only cares about how hard the employee works. Most jobs involve a variety of tasks. For instance, employees on an assembly line can spend time increasing output, improving quality, performing preventative maintenance, or helping co-workers. Similarly, professors at universities allocate their time among teaching, research, consulting, and administrative duties. Thus, managers usually have to be concerned not only with how hard employees work but also with how they allocate their time among assigned tasks; university officials are not indifferent about how professors allocate their time.

Motivating an employee to strike the appropriate balance among tasks is not easy. A complicating factor is that in some tasks, effort is more easily monitored and output more easily measured than in others. For example, university officials can observe teaching ratings, while the quality of administrative service is harder to measure. Compensating the employee based on what is measurable will encourage the employee to exert effort on the compensated tasks but shirk on other tasks. For example, paying professors based solely on teaching ratings will encourage effort on teaching at the expense of administrative service and research. Similarly, paying an assembly employee based on output will encourage the employee to produce more units but to ignore quality or helping

---

[20]This example was suggested by K. Murphy.

[21]E. Kandel and E. Lazear (1992), "Peer Pressure and Partnership," *Journal of Political Economy* 100, 801–817.

[22]Material in this section draws on B. Holmstrom and P. Milgrom (1991), "Multitask Principal-Agent Analysis: Incentive Contracts, Asset Ownership, and Job Design," *Journal of Law, Economics and Organization* 7, 24–52.

co-workers. These multitask considerations suggest that firms often might want to avoid paying employees based solely on measurable outputs. The appendix to this chapter provides a more detailed analysis of these considerations.

Given enough time, however, managers are likely to obtain information about the overall performance of employees. For example, deans have the opportunity to observe the service of professors on committees; they hear comments on faculty research from colleagues; they talk to students about teaching quality. Incentives can be provided to employees by basing promotions, terminations, and periodic pay adjustments on this type of information. Indeed, universities rely heavily on these mechanisms to motivate faculty. Evaluating this information usually requires *subjective judgments* on the part of managers. To provide proper incentives to employees, managers must develop reputations of being impartial and objective. To be most effective, firms must establish performance measures and rewards that motivate managers to develop these reputations. Chapter 13 provides an expanded discussion of subjective performance evaluation.

Forms of Incentive Pay

Typically, the term *incentive pay* conjures up images of piece rates, commissions, and cash bonus plans, where the employee is paid based on measurable output. This image is not surprising given that more than a quarter of the employees in the U.S. manufacturing sector receive at least part of their income through these types of incentive plans.[23] Our discussion in this chapter suggests that mechanisms like tying promotions and salary adjustments to performance are also forms of incentive pay. Broadly speaking, any compensation contract (explicit or implicit) that rewards employees for good performance or punishes employees for bad performance can be considered incentive pay. (Recall the Mary Kay Cosmetic Company's innovative use of incentives, as discussed in Chapter 8.) Under this definition, all of the following are forms of incentive compensation:[24]

- Bonuses for good performance.
- Salary revisions based on performance.
- Piece rates and commissions.
- Stock ownership and profit-sharing plans.
- Prizes for winning contests (for example, vacations).
- Promotions and titles for good performance.
- Firings and other penalties for bad performance.
- Unvested pensions that are forfeited on dismissal.
- Preferred office assignments for good performance.

It is important to note that rewards *do not have to be monetary.* Rewards can consist of anything that employees value. For example, managers in some organizations have little flexibility in what they pay employees. Nevertheless, incentives can be provided by rewarding good-performing employees with better offices, trips to training sessions at nice locations, preferred parking spaces, special honors, and desirable job assignments.

[23]J. McMillan (1992), *Games, Strategies, and Managers* (Oxford University Press: New York), 93.
[24]G. Baker, M. Jensen, and K. Murphy (1988), "Compensation and Incentives: Practice versus Theory," *Journal of Finance* 43, 593–616.

Imaginative Incentives to Reduce Absenteeism

During the 1940s, one company successfully reduced absenteeism by holding a daily raffle. The prizes were various products that were especially hard for employees to obtain during the shortage-prone war years. Employees had to be present to win.

In a second scheme, adopted by an automobile company, employees were awarded points for each day that they were present at the factory. The points could be redeemed for prizes, such as tickets to popular vacation attractions. The interesting feature of the plan was that the points were not given to the employee but to the employee's spouse! Reports indicate that with the spouse helping to monitor employee attendance, the absenteeism rate declined significantly.

Source: R. Ehrenberg and R. Smith (1988), *Modern Labor Economics* (Scott Foresman: Glenview, IL), 417.

Incentive Compensation and Information Revelation

The basic principal/agent model assumes that the employer and employee have the same information at the time of initial contract negotiations. In some contracting situations this precontractual information is asymmetric.[25] For example, a prospective employee is likely to know more about the likelihood of quitting over the next year than the prospective employer. Similarly, sales representatives are more likely to know about the sales potential of their territories than are higher-level managers.

Sometimes it is possible for the firm to induce employees to reveal their private information by clever design of the compensation contract. Consider the example of Onex Copy Company. This company uses sales representatives throughout the country to sell copy machines to customers. Each salesperson is assigned a specific territory. Some territories have greater sales potential than others. For simplicity, suppose that there are only two types of territories, good and bad. Good territories have the potential to generate $2 million in sales, while bad territories have the potential to generate only $1 million in sales. The sales representatives know the quality of their own territories. Central managers do not have the information to distinguish which territories are good and bad.

The firm would like to use information about whether specific territories are good or bad to evaluate the performance of the sales representatives. The company also wants accurate forecasts to plan production cycles. The company could simply ask the sales representatives to state the quality of their territories. The sales representatives with good territories, however, are likely to lie—if the firm thinks that a good territory is bad, the representative will look good when sales are high. (Alternatively, the representative can generate the expected bad sales with limited effort.)

In this example, the firm can induce the representatives to tell the truth by offering the following menu of contracts. Sales representatives who state that their territories are good receive compensation contracts that pay 2.6 percent of sales. Sales representatives who state that their territories are bad receive a flat wage of $50,000. Given this choice, it is in the interests of all sales representatives to tell the truth—representatives with bad territories would prefer the $50,000 wage contract (2.6 percent of $1 million = $26,000), while people with

[25]In Chapter 7, we divided asymmetric information into two categories—precontractual and postcontractual. Thus far, in this chapter, we have focused on postcontractual information problems (also called *moral-hazard* problems). In this section, we discuss precontractual information problems (also called *adverse-selection* problems).

Providing Incentives to Work and Tell the Truth at IBM Brazil

There is no systematic evidence on how frequently firms design compensation contracts to provide incentives for truthful information revelation and hard work. We are aware of one example, IBM Brazil. During the 1970s, this company experimented with a compensation scheme that rewarded its salespeople for accurate sales forecasts and actual sales performance. At the start of each period, headquarters would provide salespeople with forecasts of future sales in their territories. Each salesperson would then indicate what proportion of this forecast he thought he could meet. For instance, a value of 1 would indicate that the salesperson expected to meet the forecast, while a value of 1.5 would indicate that he thought he could beat it by 50 percent. The bonus payments under the plan rewarded salespeople for actual sales, relative to the company forecasts, and sales relative to their own forecasts. The payments were set in a manner that encouraged both hard work and accurate forecasts.

   According to IBM's management, the plan seemed to work relatively well. The company did encounter some unanticipated problems in implementation. For instance, salespeople quickly learned how the plan could be "gamed" by shifting sales between sales periods. For example, a salesperson might delay a sale in one period in order to promote higher sales and improve personal sales forecasts in the future. IBM, however, implemented penalties that discouraged this type of behavior. The difficulties that IBM encountered in implementation might help to explain why these types of plans are not used more frequently by other companies.

Source: G. Jacob (1978), "Tie Salesmen's Bonuses to Their Forecasts,"
Harvard Business Review 56 (May–June), 116–23.

good territories would prefer the contract that pays 2.6 percent of sales (for them, a $52,000 payout). The key to making the scheme work is that the compensation for each type of employee is higher when the information is correctly reported than when it is not.

   In this example, there are many potential compensation schemes that can induce truth telling. The problem for the firm is to choose the most profitable contract. Onex is likely to want the compensation contract to provide strong performance incentives, as well as to induce truth telling. Thus, it might choose to pay commissions to both types of employees but structure alternative commission rates to induce truth telling.

Does Incentive Pay Work?

Throughout this chapter, we have argued that compensation plans motivate employees. While this argument is readily accepted by many people, it is not without controversy. Quality guru W. Edwards Deming has gone so far as to assert that "pay is not a motivator." In the same spirit, psychologist Alfie Kohn, in a controversial article on the merits of incentive pay states, "Bribes in the workplace simply can't work."[26]

   Critics of incentive pay generally rely on two basic arguments. The first is that money does not motivate employees. As support for this view, it is pointed out that employees usually rank money relatively low when it comes to factors that make a job attractive. Factors such as the nature of work and quality of colleagues appear more important. The second, more prominent, criticism is that it is difficult (if not impossible) to design an effective incentive compensation scheme. Support for this argument is provided by the many examples of flawed compensation schemes that have produced unwanted behavior

[26]A. Kohn (1993), "Why Incentive Plans Cannot Work," *Harvard Business Review,* September–October, 54–63.

The Power of Incentives: Evidence from Chinese Agriculture

One especially interesting piece of evidence on the effectiveness of incentive pay comes from one of the largest economic experiments in history—reforms in Chinese agriculture in the early 1980s. Between 1952 and 1978, the Maoist period, Chinese agriculture revolved around the commune system. Under this system, employees were divided into production teams. There were some attempts to tie pay to performance. However, these incentives were relatively weak, and there was a tendency to base pay on family size, independent of effort. From 1980 to 1984, under the rule of Deng Xiaoping, the commune system was gradually replaced by the "household-responsibility system." Under this system, each peasant family was given a long-term lease on a plot of land. The family had to deliver a quota of agricultural products to the government each year, but it could keep any production in excess of the quota. This additional output could be consumed by the family or sold to others.

Economic theory argues that the ownership of residual claims on output provides strong incentives. Thus, this theory predicts higher productivity under the household-responsibility system than the commune system. Empirical studies support this prediction. For instance, one study estimated that productivity in Chinese agriculture increased by nearly 50 percent over the period of the Dengist reforms.

Source: J. McMillan (1992), *Games, Strategies, and Managers* (Oxford University Press: New York), 96–98.

(for example, the case of Sears Automotive Centers discussed in Chapter 2). Interestingly, the two lines of criticism are somewhat at odds with one another. If money did not motivate people, incentives schemes would not produce the dramatic changes in behavior that proponents of the second argument cite. In making a similar point, economist George Baker notes, "The problem is not that incentives can't work but that they work all too well."[27]

Certainly, it is easy to point to many examples of compensation schemes that have caused dysfunctional behavior among employees. We have done so throughout this book. Incentive schemes also involve administrative costs, such as keeping track of output and explaining the system to employees. The important question is not whether incentive plans entail costs (which they certainly do) but whether it is possible to design incentive plans where the benefits are larger than the costs. Examples like the Lincoln Electric Company (discussed in Chapter 13) suggest the answer is yes. Also, the fact that incentive plans (commissions, piece rates, and bonus plans) have survived so long in a competitive marketplace suggests that the net benefits of incentive pay are often positive.

Unfortunately, the scientific evidence on this debate is limited.[28] There are numerous studies indicating that tying pay to performance has a positive impact on employee performance. Other studies reach the opposite conclusion. Since many of the studies on this topic have serious flaws, it is difficult to draw strong conclusions from the evidence. Our overall reading of this literature indicates that incentive compensation can be value-enhancing if properly designed and implemented. Our intent is to provide insights into how managers might accomplish this task.

[27]G. Baker (1993), "Rethinking Rewards," *Harvard Business Review,* November–December, 44–45.

[28]G. Milkovich and J. Newman (1993), *Compensation* (Richard D. Irwin: Burr Ridge, IL), Chapter 8.

CASE STUDY
The Debate over CEO Compensation

The most visible and highly paid person in most corporations is the chief executive officer (CEO). CEO compensation is particularly important to firms for three reasons. First, the compensation package is likely to be important in attracting and retaining good CEOs. Second, the form of the pay contract is likely to help determine whether the CEO focuses on value maximization or some other objective. Third, employees throughout the organization carefully watch CEO pay. Important morale problems can occur when employees think that the CEO is overpaid. For instance, employees complain bitterly when they are asked to take pay cuts because the company is in trouble yet the CEO at the same time gets a big raise.

Controversy over CEO pay has increased significantly in recent years. One charge is that the *level* of CEO pay is too high. It is easy to point to many CEOs who report compensation in the millions of dollars (reported compensation figures typically include salary and bonus payments, as well as gains from exercised stock options). For example, in 1991, Stephen Wolf was paid over $18 million as CEO of UAL. To quote Edward Lawler, "CEO pay just seems to get more absurd each year. What is outrageous one year becomes a standard for the next."

The second major criticism of CEO pay concerns *how* CEOs are paid. Critics argue that CEOs are agents of stockholders and that CEO pay should be based heavily on stock-price performance. Michael Jensen and Kevin Murphy provide the most detailed evidence on this topic. They estimate that for the typical CEO, a $1,000 change in the value of the company stock results in about a $3.25 change in CEO wealth. They argue that this relation (which is equivalent to the CEO owning .325 percent of the common stock) is too small and that most companies would be better off if they increased incentive pay for CEOs. Some support for this view seems to come from studies that document an increase in stock price when companies announce that they are increasing incentive pay for CEOs.

Discussion Questions

1. Do you think the fact that most American CEOs are paid so much more than rank-and-file employees suggests CEOs are overpaid? Explain.
2. Is it obvious that $3.25 per thousand is too low incentive pay for CEOs? Explain.
3. Does the observation that the stock price increases when firms increase incentive pay for CEOs suggest that most CEOs do not receive enough incentive compensation? Explain.

Sources: J. Byrne (1991), "The Flap Over Executive Pay," *Business Week* (May 6), 90–112; M. Jensen and K. Murphy (1990), "CEO Incentives—It's Not How Much You Pay, But How," *Harvard Business Review* (May–June), 138–153; J. Haubrich (1994), "Risk Aversion, Performance Pay, and the Principal-Agent Problem," *Journal of Political Economy* 102, 258–276; and J. Brickley, S. Bhagat, and R. Lease (1985), "The Impact of Long-Range Compensation Plans on Shareholder Wealth," *Journal of Accounting and Economics* 7, 115–29.

Summary

Incentive problems exist because of conflicts of interest between employers and employees. These problems are easily resolved when actions are costlessly observable. Firms can identify the most efficient actions by employees and pay employees only if these actions are taken. In most situations employee actions are not observable at low cost. Here, firms can motivate employees through incentive compensation.

In a competitive labor market, employees must be compensated for undertaking undesirable actions. (There are compensating differentials.) Thus, it is not sensible to have employees work as hard as possible. In eliciting particular actions, there is a tradeoff between the benefits of the action for the firm and the personal costs to the employees.

Sometimes, there is a simple way to solve incentive problems even when the actions of employees are unobservable. The solution is to sell each employee the rights to his or her total output. The agency problem is caused by the fact that most of the costs of exerting effort are borne by employees, while most of the gains go to the employer. By selling employees their output, both the benefits and costs of exerting effort are internalized by employees and thus employees will make more productive choices. We observe this solution being approximated in franchising and managerial buyouts. There are at least three important factors that limit the use of ownership in solving incentive problems: wealth constraints, team production, and costs of inefficient risk bearing.

Risk-averse individuals do not like to bear financial risks and thus prefer income flows with less volatility. Risk-averse individuals can benefit from sharing risks because it lowers the volatility of the individual cash flows. People often vary in their attitudes toward risk. For instance, some people are more willing to take financial gambles than others. An efficient allocation of risk takes these differences in preferences into account. If one party is risk neutral while another party is risk averse, it is better to have the risk neutral party bear all the risk and the other party to receive a fixed payment.

Stockholders of firms often hold diversified portfolios and can be considered essentially risk neutral when it comes to the fortunes of a given firm. (Good luck by some firms tends to be offset by the bad luck of other firms within a diversified portfolio.) Employees, in contrast, have much of their human capital invested in a single firm and can be viewed as risk averse. Thus, from a risk-sharing standpoint, it is better to pay employees fixed salaries and to let the total risk of random income flows be borne by the shareholders. Fixed salaries, however, provide limited incentives for employees to exert effort—*there is a tradeoff between optimal risk sharing and optimal incentives.*

Economic analysis of incentive compensation begins with the basic principal/agent model. This model presents a relatively simple characterization of the contracting process. However, it illustrates the tradeoffs between risk sharing and incentives and provides a number of useful insights for designing better compensation plans. In particular, the model suggests that firms should pay more performance-based pay when: (1) the sensitivity of output to additional effort by the employee is higher, (2) the employee is less risk averse, (3) the level of risk that is beyond the employee's control is lower, and (4) the employee responds to increased incentives by exerting substantially more effort.

According to the *informativeness principle,* it is useful to include all indicators that provide additional information about employee effort into the compensation contract (assuming these indicators are available at low cost). Including these indicators in the contract reduces the randomness of payouts and thus the costs of inefficient risk bearing. One important source of information about an employee's effort is the output of co-workers performing similar tasks. The informativeness principle suggests that it is useful to employ *relative performance evaluation.* In Chapter 13, however, we discuss several factors that can limit the desirability of relative performance evaluations.

In the basic principal/agent model, employees are motivated by being paid based on their own output. Many firms base incentive pay on *group performance.* Common reasons for the group incentive pay are that group performance can be less expensive to monitor than individual performance; group performance emphasizes teamwork; and group plans motivate employees to monitor each other's performance. Standard free-rider arguments provide a strong reason to question whether group plans provide powerful incentives—particularly when the group is large. There are at least three factors that might help to explain the widespread popularity of these plans (even if free-riding is a potential problem). First, it can be beneficial to increase the awareness of employees about stock-price performance and profitability (assuming employees can be motivated to monitor these measures by relatively small plans that do not shift much risk onto the employees). Second, employees might feel guilty from shirking and imposing costs on co-workers who are compensated on group performance. These feelings might motivate employees, even if the direct financial consequences are small. Third, paying employees on firm performance sends a strong signal to employees about what is valued in the company. To be most effective, however, these signals must be reinforced by other parts of the organizational architecture that provide more direct incentives.

Most jobs involve a variety of tasks. Motivating an employee to strike the appropriate balance among tasks is not easy. A complicating factor is that some tasks are more easily measured than others. Compensating the employee based on what is measurable will encourage the employee to exert more effort on the compensated tasks but shirk on other tasks. These *multitask considerations* suggest that firms might often want to avoid paying employees based solely on measurable outputs. Given enough time, managers are likely to obtain information about the overall performance of employees. Incentives can be provided by basing promotions, terminations, and periodic pay adjustments on this information. Often, this information is not easily quantifiable but is based on the subjective opinions of supervisors.

The term *incentive pay* conjures up images of piece rates, commissions, and cash bonus plans, where the employee is paid based on measurable output. Broadly speaking, however, any compensation contract (explicit or implicit) that rewards employees for good performance or punishes employees for bad performance can be considered incentive pay. *Rewards do not have to be monetary.* Rather, rewards consist of anything that the employee values.

The basic principal/agent model assumes employers and employees have the same information at the time of initial contract negotiations. In some contracting situations precontractual information is asymmetric. Sometimes it is possible for the firm to induce employees to reveal their private information by clever design of the compensation contract. For such a scheme to work, the payoffs to employees must be higher when they are honest than when they misreport information.

Throughout this chapter, we have argued that compensation plans motivate employees. While this argument is accepted by many, it is not without controversy. Critics of incentive pay rely on two basic arguments. The first is that money does not motivate people. The second, more prominent criticism is that it is difficult (if not impossible) to design an effective incentive compensation scheme. The first argument seems inconsistent with the many examples where monetary incentives have dramatically affected employee behavior. The second argument is correct—developing an appropriate incentive scheme is not always easy. The important question is whether plans can be designed where the benefits exceed the costs. Examples such as Lincoln Electric suggest it can be done. Our intent is to provide insights into how managers might design value-maximizing contracts.

APPENDIX | *Multitask Principal/Agent Theory*[29]

This appendix provides a more detailed example of the multitask principal/agent model. It also uses this framework to analyze the corporate practice of *telecommuting*—employees working out of their homes and communicating with the central office via fax, computer, or telephone. This application illustrates how principal/agent theory can provide insights into specific managerial policy decisions.

---

[29]This appendix requires knowledge of elementary calculus. The material in this appendix draws on the analysis in Milgrom and Holmstrom (1991).

Multitask Model

Steve McKinley is a production employee at the Ohio Dye Company. He works 10 hours per day. His job consists of two tasks, assembling parts and checking the quality of his output. He is paid a piece rate for each part that he assembles. He also receives a bonus that is based on the quality of his output. Denote t_1 and t_2 as the hours per day he devotes to producing output and checking quality, respectively. Steve's incentives are high enough so that he will not shirk—he works the full 10 hours. Therefore, $t_2 = (10 - t_1)$.

Suppose that Steve's compensation translates into the following relation between compensation and the time allocated to each activity:

$$\text{Compensation} = \alpha_1 (6t_1^{1/2}) + \alpha_2 t_2$$

$$= \alpha_1 (6t_1^{1/2}) + \alpha_2 (10 - t_1) \qquad (12.9)$$

where the αs are the weights that the compensation plan places on quantity and quality (the *incentive coefficients*).[30] Steve's objective is to maximize his compensation. He chooses t_1 to meet the following first-order condition:

$$\alpha_1 (3t_1^{-1/2}) = \alpha_2 \qquad (12.10)$$

This condition has a straightforward interpretation. The left-hand term is the marginal benefit for allocating time to producing higher quantity, while the right-hand term is the marginal benefit for allocating time to producing higher quality. At an interior solution, these marginal returns must be equal. If the marginal benefits are not equal, Steve is better off devoting more time to the activity with the higher value and less time to the activity with the lower value. The left panel of Figure 12.6 provides an illustration. When t_1 is small, the returns for devoting extra time to quantity are high relative to the returns from allocating time to quality. Here, it makes sense to increase the time devoted to quantity and correspondingly reduce the time spent on quality. As Steve continues to increase the amount of time he spends on quantity, the marginal benefit declines.[31] At the optimum, t_1^*, the marginal returns are equal. Beyond t_1^*, the marginal returns from allocating time to quantity are less than for allocating time to quality.

If Steve's supervisor chooses α_1 and α_2 so that the marginal return for one of the activities is always higher over the relevant range, $0 \leq t_1 \leq 10$, Steve will devote all 10 hours to the activity with the higher marginal return (there is a corner solution). The right panel of Figure 12.6 provides an illustration where Steve spends all his time on quantity.

Solving equation 12.10 for t_1 yields:

$$t_1 = 9 (\alpha_1/\alpha_2)^2 \qquad (12.11)$$

This equation shows that when $\alpha_1 = \alpha_2$, Steve will spend nine hours producing output and one hour checking its quality. Observing how t_1 and t_2 change with changes in the αs provides two important insights:

- There are two ways that a manager can motivate an employee to devote more time to a task. First, the manager can increase the incentive coefficient for that task. Second, the manager can reduce the incentive coefficient for the alternative task. In our example, Steve will devote more time to quantity if either α_1 is increased or α_2

---

[30]The terms in this equation are chosen to simplify the calculations and yield reasonable values for the time allocated to the two activities. Our basic results, however, are quite general and are not specialized to this particular example.

[31]For simplicity, we assume that time devoted to producing quantity is more strenuous than that devoted to quality. Thus, with more time devoted to quantity, he becomes tired and less productive. We have assumed that the marginal benefit from allocating time to quality is constant. This assumption is not necessary.

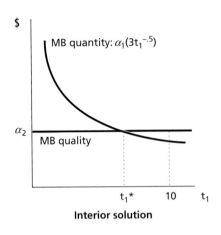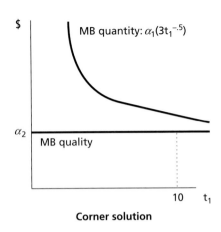

Figure 12.6 Optimal Allocation of Effort

In this example, Steve must allocate his time between two activities, producing quantity and checking its quality. The number of hours devoted to quantity is t_1. Since he works 10-hour workdays, he devotes $t_2 = (10 - t_1)$ hours to quality. The left panel shows the case where there is an interior optimum. At this optimum, the marginal benefit, MB, from allocating additional time to either activity is the same. Steve spends t_1^* hours on quantity and $(10 - t_1^*)$ hours on quality. The right panel shows a corner solution. In this case, the marginal benefits for quantity are higher than the marginal benefits from quality over the relevant range ($0 \leq t_1 \leq 10$) and Steve allocates all his time to producing output.

is decreased. Increasing α_1 increases the direct return from investing in quantity, while decreasing α_2 reduces the opportunity cost (the compensation that is lost from not investing in quality).

- If an incentive coefficient for a given task is sufficiently small, relative to the other incentive coefficient, an employee will devote no time to the task. In our example, if $(\alpha_1/\alpha_2)^2 > 1.12$, Steve will devote no time to quality ($1.12 \times 9 > 10$ hours). This result indicates that if a manager wants an employee to devote time to multiple tasks, the manager must be careful to provide balanced incentives. Setting too strong an incentive for one task can undermine effort on other tasks.

An Application: Telecommuting

Recently, there has been an increase in the use of telecommuting by large firms. The asserted benefits of this practice are (1) companies can reduce office expenses (it can be less expensive to reimburse an employee for a home office than provide office space in an urban center), (2) employees avoid wasteful commutes to work, (3) firms can hire quality employees at lower wages by offering them the flexibility to work out of their homes (for instance, employees can balance child care and work more easily), and (4) employees can be closer to customers (for example, salespeople who have homes in their sales territories).

One potential drawback with telecommuting is the lost synergy that results from having employees work at separate locations. For instance, there is likely to be less information sharing, team production, and so on. While computer technologies (such as e-mail) reduce these concerns, they can still be important and limit the viability of telecommuting in many occupations. For instance, it would not be feasible for a dental assistant to telecommute. Our focus is on a second potential concern with telecommuting—the problem of motivating employees to exert effort on their jobs.

In analyzing telecommuting, it is useful to envision the employee being at home and choosing how to allocate time between two activities, home and work. The incentive coefficient for home activities (α_1) is the personal benefit the employee obtains from spending extra time playing with children, watching television, working in the garden, and so on. The incentive coefficient for working on company activities (α_2) depends on the compensation plan.

Viewed in this context, the multitask model has at least two important points relating to telecommuting. First, it is usually important to provide incentive compensation to telecommuters.[32] Without sufficient incentives, employees tend to shirk and devote most of their time to home activities rather than working on the job. Second, the most viable jobs for telecommuting are those where output is easily measured, and thus incentive compensation can be used most readily. For instance, sales jobs are often good candidates for telecommuting, since incentives can be provided by sales commissions. (Synergies from having salespeople work out of a central location are also likely to be relatively low.) If it is difficult to measure employee output, it can be better to *require the employee to come to work* at a central location. This requirement has two effects. First, it makes it easier to monitor the employee's efforts. Second, it is equivalent to reducing the incentive coefficient on home activities to zero (the employee is unable to devote time to home activities and thus cannot gain from these activities). Since there are fewer activities that compete for their time, employees spend more time on work-related activities.

Appendix Problem

Life insurance agents focus on selling policies. The company expects little follow-up in terms of providing ongoing customer service. In contrast, auto insurance agents are often expected to provide ongoing customer assistance after a policy is sold (answering questions about the policy, providing assistance in filing claims, and so on).

Some insurance companies use independent agents to sell their policies. These agents are paid solely on commission and are often allowed to sell the products of other companies (the agent presents the customer with a choice of plans across multiple companies). Other insurance companies hire their own agents. These employees are restricted from selling other companies' products and are sometimes paid a salary in addition to any commission they might receive.

1. Which type of insurance company, life or auto, is more likely to use the in-house agent? Explain. (Be sure to discuss why the in-house agent faces product restrictions and is not always paid on a pure commission basis.)
2. Some auto insurance companies separate the tasks of selling and customer service and assign them to different people. Why do you think they do this?

Suggested Readings

G. Baker, M. Jensen, and K. Murphy (1988), "Compensation and Incentives: Practice versus Theory," *Journal of Finance* 43, 593–616.

J. McMillan (1992), *Games, Strategies, and Managers* (Oxford University Press: New York), 91–129.

P. Milgrom and J. Roberts (1992), *Economics, Organization, and Management* (Prentice Hall: Englewood Cliffs, NJ), 206–247.

[32]As discussed in the text, this incentive pay need not take the form of a commission or a piece rate. Rather, it can be a bonus plan, a promotion based on performance, and so on.

Review Questions

12–1. Evaluate the statement: "Employers want employees to work as hard as possible."

12–2. Two employees are assigned to work overseas for a two-year period. One person sells his house in the United States, while the other leases it for two years to another family. Which house do you think will be in better condition after the two years? Explain.

12–3. Explain why an investor is usually better off if she holds a diversified portfolio rather than investing all her resources in the stock of one company.

12–4. Discuss tradeoffs between efficient risk bearing and incentives in compensation plans.

12–5. Some companies reward salespeople based on their performance relative to other salespeople in the company. Why would a company want to do this?

12–6. Evaluate the statement: "Profit-sharing plans are good; they encourage teamwork."

12–7. Some school districts have compensated teachers based on the performance of students on standardized tests. Do you think this is a good idea? Explain.

12–8. Evaluate the following statement: "John is paid a straight salary with no bonus pay. Obviously, he has no incentives to do a good job."

12–9. Bobby Joe's Cookie Company sells freshly baked cookies to customers in shopping malls. The company has expanded and opened outlets in many cities such as San Francisco and London. Bobby Joe has been on the cover of several business magazines. The articles stress that he works very long hours and is often at the stores monitoring the quality of the product and making sure the cookies are produced with "tender loving care." Bobby has indicated that he will never franchise units. To quote Bobby Joe, "We do not want to turn into just another fast-food franchise company. Our success is based on high-quality products produced with great care and love. We do not want to lose this quality by expanding through franchises. Rather, we prefer to maintain ownership of all units to ensure continued good service and quality." Evaluate Bobby Joe's policy of not franchising units.

12–10. The Roman Empire taxed many faraway provinces. Rome would auction the rights to tax collection to the highest bidder. The winning bidder was given the right to set the tax rate for the province and the right to collect (and keep) the taxes. In turn, the winner would pay the bid amount to the Roman government. Assume: (1) the Emperor is a young man interested in maximizing the present value of all future revenues to Rome from auctioning off the tax rights, and (2) the auction for the rights to each province is conducted annually.

   a. Give two reasons why Rome would auction off the rights to tax collection rather than simply sending a Roman soldier to collect the taxes.

   b. Discuss two problems this system might generate for the Emperor.

12–11. There has been an increased emphasis on compensating employees through incentive pay. High incentive pay, however, is not likely to be productive in all settings. Discuss the factors that are likely to favor paying high incentive pay to employees.

12–12. In 1995, Philip Morris Company ratified a new labor pact that gave employees stock in lieu of pay increases. The agreement covered 7,800 employees, with each employee being given 94 shares (1994 value of about $60 per share). Employees cannot sell the stock for at least a year and forfeit the stock if they quit or are fired before the year expires. *Business Week*[33] argued that the "deal was good for Philip Morris" because the employees' base pay and fringe benefits did not rise. Also "current shareholders' shares won't be diluted, since employees probably will get less than 500,000 shares out of 850 million outstanding." Discuss the pros and cons of this policy compared to a policy of simply giving a cash bonus to employees of a similar dollar value.

12–13. Two successful firms are observed with quite different compensation plans for its salespeople. One firm pays its salespeople on a commission basis, while the other firm pays its salespeople fixed salaries. Do you think that one of the two companies is making a mistake? Explain.

---

[33]A. Bernstein, "At Philip Morris, Blue Chips for Blue Collars," *Business Week,* March 27, 1995.

chapter 13

Individual Performance Evaluation

CHAPTER OUTLINE

Lincoln Electric Company, headquartered in Cleveland, Ohio, was founded in 1895 to manufacture electric motors and generators.[1] In the early part of the 20th century, the firm became the premier supplier of electric arc welding machines and welding disposables (electrodes). In 1993, it had 22 plants in 15 countries. Prior to expanding manufacturing operations outside of the United States, Lincoln Electric had an almost unbroken string of profitable operations and was often cited as the model of productivity gains and cost savings.

At the heart of Lincoln Electric's success is a strategy of building quality products at a lower cost than its competitors and passing the savings on to customers by continuously lowering prices. Lincoln has been able to implement this strategy, in part, through an employee incentive system that fosters labor productivity increases arising from a pay-for-performance compensation plan. For production employees, wages are based entirely on piecework. In addition, a year-end bonus averages approximately 100 percent of regular compensation.

A key element of Lincoln's organizational architecture, and the topic of this chapter, is the performance-evaluation system. There are two components of Lincoln's performance evaluation: pieces produced and merit rating. The first component is an objective, readily quantifiable performance measure for each production employee—the number of good units produced. The employee's wage is equal to the piece rate times the number of good units produced. (Employees are not paid for defects.) The piece rates, set by the time study department, allow employees producing at a standard rate to earn a wage comparable to those for similar jobs in the local labor market. However, by working hard—in some cases even through meal and coffee breaks—employees can double and sometimes triple their pay. Moreover, Lincoln's policies prohibit piece-rate changes simply because an employee is making "too much" money. Finally, any employee who has been at Lincoln for at least two years is guaranteed employment for at least 75 percent of the standard 40-hour week.

The second component of Lincoln's evaluation scheme is the employee's merit rating. These ratings are used to determine the employee's share of the bonus pool. The size of the bonus pool approximately equals wages and is about twice Lincoln's net income after taxes, although there is substantial annual variation in the size of the pool. Each employee's merit evaluation is based on employee dependability, quality, output, and ideas and cooperation, assessed primarily by the employee's immediate supervisor.

Two important observations emerge from Lincoln Electric. First, the performance-reward system uses as an input, the output from the performance-evaluation system—the two systems are linked. Second, firms use both highly objective, explicit measures of performance (piecework) and subjective measures (ideas and cooperation).

Employee performance is evaluated for at least two reasons. First, performance evaluation provides employees with feedback on job achievement that provides important information on how to improve performance. Second, performance evaluation is used in determining rewards and sanctions (raises, bonuses, promotions, reassignments, and firings). The issues that arise in studying performance evaluation generally differ for the two purposes. For example, if evaluations are used solely to provide feedback, employees are unlikely to try to distort their evaluations to make themselves look better. But distortions to improve reported performance are likely if employees are compensated based on performance.

---

[1]Details of this example are from N. Fast and N. Berg (1975), "The Lincoln Electric Company," Harvard Business School Case 376-028.

Japanese Car Makers Adopt Performance Evaluations

The large Japanese automobile companies are beginning to adopt traditional Western performance-evaluation systems and to link compensation and promotion more closely to individual performance.

Honda and Toyota have been examples of lifetime employment in Japan's auto industry. But in 1993 and 1994, both companies announced plans to change this practice. In 1993, Honda became the first Japanese car company to adopt a merit-pay plan that ties the manager's pay to achieving performance goals. In 1994, Toyota announced that it would depart from its seniority-based pay and promotion system. Mazda and Nissan announced they were adopting merit-pay systems for their managers in the summer of 1994.

Source: R. Johnson (1994), "Advance or Perish, Honda Tells Managers," *Automotive News* (March 18).

In this chapter, we focus primarily on the second reason for performance evaluation—as input for setting rewards and sanctions for employees. This chapter and the next describe the performance-evaluation system, the third leg of our three-legged stool that comprises the firm's organizational architecture. Performance evaluation involves evaluating both individuals and subunits of the firm. This chapter focuses on individual performance evaluation. The next chapter examines various issues in evaluating subunits within the firm.

To organize our discussion of individual performance evaluation, we return to the principal/agent model presented in Chapter 12. In that model, the employee's output, Q, depends on effort, e, and random factors, μ:

$$Q = \alpha e + \mu \tag{13.1}$$

where α is the employee's marginal productivity. For every unit of effort, α units of output are expected. In this model, e and μ are unobservable by management, but α is known to both management and the employee. If the employee is paid a fixed wage, independent of output, Q, the employee has incentives to shirk because low Q can be blamed on negative μ, which is not observable. (Remember, effort is costly to the employee.) To limit such shirking, the firm bases employee compensation on output:

$$\text{Employee compensation} = W_o + \beta Q \tag{13.2}$$

where β represents the sensitivity of pay to performance. Compensation contracts such as these create incentives for employees to reduce their shirking on effort. But these contracts also impose risk on employees because pay is now a function of μ, the random variable. Since the employee is risk averse, the firm must compensate the employee for bearing this risk or else the employee will work someplace else. This additional compensation for bearing such risk is called a *compensating differential.*

In this simple principal/agent model, output was assumed observable and hence contractible; Q is an *objective performance measure.* The employee and the firm can write compensation contracts based on Q at relatively low cost. Compensation and performance evaluation (two legs of the stool) are explicitly linked.

The simple model in equation 13.2 and equation 13.3 (which follows) implicitly includes the following assumptions:

- The principal knows the employee's production function ($Q = \alpha e + \mu$) and α, but not the actual values for e and μ.
- There is a single, quantitative measure of performance—output.

- Output can be observed at zero cost.
- The employee cannot game the performance measure.
- The employee produces a single output; there are no multiple tasks.
- Any mutually beneficial contract is feasible; labor markets are unregulated.
- The employee works independently; there is no team production.

Clearly, managers in practice must implement performance-evaluation systems in situations that do not conform to some or all of these assumptions. The remaining sections of this chapter describe the various issues that arise when these assumptions are relaxed.

Estimating the Performance Benchmark

Solving for the optimal β in equation 13.2 requires management to know α in equation 13.1. Since the employee's marginal productivity is not readily observable, management must estimate it. To illustrate the issues involved in estimating the employee's marginal productivity, consider the following simplified example. Craig Cook can assemble a particular model of welder at the following daily rate:

$$\text{Units assembled} = 5\,e_c + \mu_c \qquad\qquad (13.3)$$

where e_c is the number of hours of normal effort worked, and μ_c is a random error term. If Craig works 8 hours at a normal effort level, $e_c=8$; then on average he can assemble 40 welders (5×8). On average the error, μ_c, is zero. If Craig works 8 hours but at a faster, more strenuous pace ($e_c>8$)—the equivalent of, say, 12 hours at a normal effort level ($e_c=12$)—then 60 units per day are assembled on average. If he slacks off and takes numerous short breaks, e_c might only be 5, and 25 units on average are assembled.

While the average error, μ_c, is zero, the number of units assembled is subject to potentially large shocks, which means that the variance of μ_c is not zero. For example, if Craig receives low-quality parts or subassemblies, the number of units assembled will be down even though Craig expended normal amounts of effort ($e_c \geq 8$) because more time is required to fit together each slightly out-of-specification part. Or perhaps Craig is idled for a few minutes each hour waiting for parts delivery. In these cases, μ_c is negative. Alternatively, he might get lucky and assemble more than $5e_c$ units because of an unusually good set of parts, ample parts inventory, good tools, or few distractions.

The assembly department in the preceding example could establish the benchmark of 40 welders assembled per employee per day. Production above 40 is considered good performance and less than 40 is considered poor performance. The standard of 40 is absolute in the sense that it is fixed and known before the employee exerts effort. Management, however, might not know exactly the relation between effort and production (welders assembled = $5e + \mu$) or that the average employee exerts 8 units of effort a day. Thus, the output of the average assembler must be estimated. There are at least two ways to do this: motion and time studies and historical production data analysis.

Motion and Time Studies

In motion and time studies, industrial engineers estimate how much time a particular task or work activity requires, with the goal of determining the preferable work method. Motion studies involve the systematic analysis of work methods, considering the raw materials, the design of the product or process, the process or order of work, the tools, and the activity of each step. Besides estimating how long a particular activity should take, industrial engineers are often able to redesign the product or process to reduce the required time. Time studies employ a wide variety of techniques for determining the duration a particular activity requires under certain standard conditions. Work sampling (one type of time study) involves selecting a large number of observations taken at random intervals and observing how long employees take performing various components of the job. Motion and time studies are often expensive in terms of engineering time used in the studies. They also suffer from potential bias because of employees' incentives to underperform during the study period to set lower quotas.

Past Performance and the Ratchet Effect

Using historical data on past performance is a common mechanism for setting performance goals. Unfortunately, it often leads to a perverse incentive called the *ratchet effect*. The ratchet effect refers to basing next year's standard of performance on this year's actual performance. However, performance targets usually are adjusted in only one direction: upward. A bad year usually does not cause subsequent years' targets to fall. This "ratcheting up" of standards causes employees to avoid substantially exceeding the quota so as not to raise the standard for future periods by too much.[2] Many illustrations of dysfunctional behaviors induced by the ratchet effect exist:

- In the old Soviet Union, central planners would set a plant's production quota based on past experience. Plant managers meeting their targets received various rewards, and those missing the target were punished. This created incentives for managers to just barely exceed the quota.
- Companies often base a salesperson's bonus on meeting target sales where the target is based on last year's sales. If salespeople expect an unusually good year, they will try to defer some sales into the next fiscal year. They may take the customer's order but delay processing it until the next fiscal year.
- In one automobile engine assembly plant, a labor productivity performance goal was mandated each year. Each department's target was based in part on last year's performance plus an increase. This created incentives for managers to defer making big productivity improvements in any one year, preferring instead to spread them over several years.[3]

Lincoln Electric avoids the dysfunctional problems of the ratchet effect by its policy that the piecework rate cannot be changed even if the employee is making too much money. Once a piecework rate is set by the time study department, it is never changed until production methods or processes are changed, or unless the employee challenges the rate and a new time study is conducted.

Another way to reduce the problems caused by ratcheting up each year's performance targets is more frequent job rotation. If you know that next year someone else has to meet the sales figures you achieve this year, you will sell more now. However, job rotation destroys job-specific human capital such as customer-specific relationships.

---

[2]If the employee's bonus is a function of how much output exceeds the target, then some of the incentive not to exceed the target by a large amount is reduced. The actual dysfunctional incentives created by the ratchet effect depend on the exact form of the incentive compensation contract. For example, if past performance is used to set β in equation 13.2, very different incentives are created than if past performance is used to set a target performance and a fixed bonus is paid if actual output exceeds the target.

[3]R. Kaplan and A. Sweeney (1993), "Peoria Engine Plant (A)," Harvard Business School Case 9-193-082.

Multiple Performance Measures[4]

The simple principal/agent model assumes a single employee. Often, there are multiple employees performing the same task (for example, several salespeople). Multiple employees performing the same task allow the firm to take advantage of the informativeness principle described in Chapter 12.

The Informativeness Principle

The informativeness principle states that management should use any (low cost) information about the employee's effort in the compensation contract. These additional indicators reduce the risk from uncontrollable factors the employee bears by more accurately estimating the random, uncontrollable common shock. Reducing this risk from uncontrollable factors reduces the compensating differentials the firm must pay employees to entice them to bear risk. For example, in assigning course grades, many instructors "curve" the grades. Instead of awarding a grade of A for scores of 94 to 100, the top 15 percent of the class receives A's. Curving the grades controls for unusually easy or hard exams and is a way of removing some of the risk from students.

Multiple employees performing the same task can provide additional signals about the random errors affecting any one employee. For example, if, in assembling welders, Craig exerts average effort of e = 8, he expects to produce 40 units. In addition to Craig, Debbie Lane also assembles welders, and her output is:

$$\text{Units assembled by Debbie} = 5\,e_d + \mu_d \qquad (13.4)$$

where e_d is the number of hours of normal effort worked by Debbie, and μ_d is her random error term. If Craig's and Debbie's error terms, μ_c and μ_d, are positively correlated because they depend on many of the same conditions (raw material quality and working conditions), then in evaluating Craig's performance, management can look at Debbie's output for information about uncontrollable factors affecting Craig's production.

Relative Performance Evaluation

Besides Craig and Debbie, suppose a number of employees are assembling the same welders. To reduce the risk of noncontrollable factors, management takes the average number of welders assembled by all the employees. Forty welders per employee per day is the expected number of welders, given normal quality and no unusual events. Suppose the average number of welders across all the employees on a given day is 43. Then average $\mu = 3$ (40–37). And if Craig produced 41 welders that day, his compensation is adjusted downward by some part of the three units. Using the output of other employees to adjust the employee's output in the compensation contract is called *relative performance evaluation*. (The appendix to this chapter discusses methods to estimate the adjustment.)

---

[4]Material in this section draws on the analysis in B. Holmstrom (1982); "Moral Hazard in Teams," *Bell Journal of Economics,* 324–40, and R. Gibbons and K. Murphy (1990), "Relative Performance Evaluation for Chief Executive Officers," *Industrial and Labor Relations Review,* 30S–51S.

Relative Performance Evaluation in Banking

Research suggests that firms use relative performance evaluation. One study focuses on subsidiary bank managers in multibank holding companies. Turnover of these managers is greater when their own bank's performance is poor and when the median bank's performance in the same holding company is high. This study's findings are consistent with market and industry risk being filtered out in making compensation and retention decisions.

Source: D. Blackwell, J. Brickley, and M. Weisbach (1994), "Accounting Information and Internal Performance Evaluation: Evidence from Texas Banks," *Journal of Accounting and Economics* 17, 331–358.

Within-Firm Performance

Using other employees' output in the same firm to estimate the average error can have the benefit that the reference group is subject to similar shocks if they all sell the same products and face the same competitors and economywide factors. However, forming a reference group from employees inside the same firm can have drawbacks. In most cases, employees' jobs are not identical. Some salespeople have large established territories, others small developing ones. Customer types can vary dramatically across sales territories.

If an internal reference group is formed and its group average is used to assess normal performance, the group has incentives to punish "rate busters"—high-producing employees who raise the average. In a classic research study known as the Hawthorne experiments, employees were observed hitting colleagues who exceeded the commonly accepted output rate.[5] Thus, employee collusion to hold down the benchmark can occur. Also, instances of sabotage are observed in relative performance evaluations. Instead of working hard and increasing their own performance, co-workers sabotage their peers in the reference group. Alternatively, employees might try to get themselves classified into a reference group that has weak performance so they will appear above average.

Relative performance evaluation also affects recruiting incentives. Employees often are involved in interviewing and selecting potential colleagues. If paid based on relative performance, such employees have incentive to sabotage recruiting by hiring less competent new employees. This improves the relative performance of the current employees.

Across-Firm Performance

To overcome a lack of an internal reference group or to avoid the pernicious actions of sabotage and collusion, some firms employ external benchmarking. Firms either exchange information directly or do so through a trade association that aggregates information across several firms to mask individual firm data. Thus, average performance in other firms is used as the reference group. For example, the Securities and Exchange Commission requires publicly traded firms to select a benchmark reference group of other firms and report how their firm has performed relative to that benchmark when describing their executive compensation. This is an example of selecting a reference group outside the firm.

There are several disadvantages of external benchmarking. This method is often precluded by data availability; other firms view their performance data as proprietary and thus are unwilling to share it. Even if firms are willing to share data, for firms in the same industry such cooperation potentially is illegal under the antitrust laws. Moreover,

---

[5]H. Parsons (1974), "What Happened at Hawthorne?" *Science* 183 (March 8), 927.

Potential Costs of Relative Performance Evaluations

Individuals gaming performance-evaluation systems are not uncommon. This example illustrates the lengths to which some people will go sabotaging others when their advancement is based on relative performance evaluations.

> I was recently talking to a friend of mine who works at a big bank. When I asked him about his new promotion, he told me how he got it. He managed to crack the network messaging system so that he could monitor all the memos. He also sabotaged the work group software and set back careers of a few company-naive souls who didn't realize that someone was manipulating their appointment calendars. They would miss important meetings and be sent on wild-goose chases, only to look like complete buffoons when they showed up for appointments that were never made. By the time any of these bumpkins knew what hit them, they had a new vice president.

Source: J. Dvorak (1988), "New Age of Villainy," *PC Magazine* (September 27).

the employees in outside firms may not be subject to the same common shocks as the employees in the reference group. Thus, the risk to the employees in the benchmarking firm may be increased, not decreased.

Opportunism

Employees can behave opportunistically in other ways that affect their performance evaluation. This section describes two examples of such opportunism: gaming and the horizon problem.

Gaming

Our principal/agent model assumes the employee only shirks in the amount of effort exerted this period. If reported output is not perfectly correlated with firm value, employees endeavoring to increase reported output might cause firm value to decline. Thus, objective measures of output can motivate employees to engage in nonproductive efforts to improve their evaluations. Recall the costs Sears incurred when its mechanics overcharged customers for unneeded car repairs. Doing so increased their income but was extremely damaging to the firm. Other examples include the following: a salesperson might offer

Relative Performance Evaluation for CEOs

CEO compensation (salary plus bonus) and turnover likelihoods depend on relative performance evaluation. Gibbons and Murphy examine 2,214 CEOs serving in 1,295 large, publicly traded, U.S. corporations from 1974 to 1986. They find that CEOs' compensation is positively related to their own stock return performance and negatively related to the stock return in the market and industry. That is, compensation is higher when the CEO's own firm's stock return is higher and when the market or industry stock return is down. Finally, they study the likelihood that the CEO is replaced. Executive turnover is lower the larger the firm's own stock price return and the lower the industry return. If the industry is performing poorly, the CEO is more likely retained, holding everything else constant.

Source: R. Gibbons and K. Murphy (1990), "Relative Performance Evaluation for Chief Executive Officers," *Industrial and Labor Relations Review* 43, 30S–51S.

Gaming Objective Performance-Evaluation Schemes

This example illustrates how one manager successfully gamed the performance-evaluation system used in deciding when to close unprofitable mines.

> In this particular company, mines were shut down after the yield per ton of ore dropped below a certain level. One old marginal mine managed to stay open for several years because of the strategic behavior of its management. It happened that the mine contained one very rich pocket of ore. Instead of mining this all at once, the management used it as its reserve. Every time the yield of the ore it was mining fell below an acceptable level, it would mix in a little high grade ore so the mine would remain open.

Source: E. Lawler and J. Rhode (1976), *Information and Control in Organizations* (Goodyear Publishing: Santa Monica, CA), 87–88.

customer discounts to shift sales from one evaluation period to another; an employee paid based on output might reduce quality to increase output; and a divisional manager compensated on weight of output might substitute heavier inputs (lead instead of aluminum). At Lincoln Electric, typewriters had counters to record the number of characters typed, and secretaries were paid on this basis. Piecework for secretaries was abandoned when one secretary who earned much more than the others was found staying at her desk during lunch and coffee breaks typing the same character as fast as she could. Thus, seemingly objective measures of performance such as sales or output can often create incentives for employees to take firm-value reducing actions (such as lowering product quality) if such actions increase their measured performance.

Horizon Problem

Objective output measures tend to focus on the short run because of the difficulty of objectively measuring consequences that might occur in the future. Short-run, objective performance measures can cause employees—especially those about to change jobs or leave the firm—to concentrate their efforts on producing results that will favorably influence their appraisals. For example, consider a 64-year-old salesperson paid on commission and facing mandatory retirement at age 65. This person has little incentive to develop long-term customer relationships.

Measurement Costs

When it is costly to observe the employee's output, performance evaluation becomes much more complicated (and interesting). For example, your waiter may seem to have performed well at the restaurant. But you do not know for sure he served you caffeinated instead of decaffeinated coffee until 2 A.M. when you cannot sleep. The quality of a patent attorney's work is not known until others challenge the patent. Measuring an elementary teacher's output is complex. Relying on standardized test scores does not adequately capture student learning. Or, a research scientist's output is difficult to quantify and observe. "Observability" is really a question of cost. Almost everything is observable—even effort—at some cost. How hard an employee works can be measured by attaching heart-rate monitors, videotaping the person, and observing how many rest breaks are taken. But such measurements can be extremely costly.

Measuring What Counts

(D)etermining the weight of an orange may be a low cost, accurate operation. Yet what is weighed is seldom what is truly valued. The skin of the orange hides its pulp, making a direct measurement of the desired attributes costly. Thus the taste and amount of juice it contains are always a bit surprising.

Source: Y. Barzel (1982), "Measurement Cost and the Organization of Markets," *Journal of Law & Economics* XXV, 27–48.

Costs are incurred in generating performance measures. For example, accounting systems must be developed and maintained to keep track of sales, costs, quality, or divisional profits. Computer systems and software that can produce detailed reports are more complicated. Since the measures are used for performance evaluation, management and clerical time must be spent ensuring the accuracy of the performance measures.

In our simple principal/agent model, the employee's output is used in setting compensation. However, output depends on random factors, μ. To the extent the firm can reduce the variance of these random factors via more accurate performance measures, the lower the compensating differential the firm must pay the employee to bear this risk. A value-maximizing firm will trade off an extra dollar of reducing the variance of μ (by more accurate accounting and clerical systems, for instance) for a dollar reduction in the risk premium that must be paid to the employee.

In general, the more incentive pay in the employee's compensation package, the more risk the employee bears and the more the firm should spend on measurement systems to reduce the variance of these random factors. Thus, the choice of the optimum β in equation (13.2) and the choice of how much to spend measuring performance are jointly determined. These two legs of the stool are complements. Increasing the employee's incentive compensation (β) should be accompanied by increasing the precision with which output is measured.[6]

In some cases, observing and measuring the employee's output becomes so expensive that the firm begins to look for alternative proxy variables that capture the employee's performance. Often, the firm abandons the use of objective, explicit measures of output and uses more subjective yet comprehensive measures of performance. For example, suppose you hire an individual to paint your house. You value how long the paint stays on the house. The longevity of the paint job is determined by how well the surface is scraped and prepared and the quality of the paint used. After the house is painted, you could hire an engineer to test the surface or wait and see how long it lasts. Instead, a subjective performance evaluation of the painter's reliability in completing the job on time, keeping the work site clean and tidy, removing excess paint from the windows, and so forth can be used in lieu of an objective measure. These other attributes presumably are correlated with the more difficult to observe attribute—effort expended on surface preparation. Yet, these subjective measures are more easily observed.

[6]For a more formal treatment of this principle, see P. Milgrom and J. Roberts (1992), *Economics, Organizations, and Management* (Prentice Hall: Englewood Cliffs, NJ), 226.

Subjective Performance Evaluation

Subjective performance reviews are conducted because it is expensive to accurately measure the employee's output that is valued by the firm. In fact, most employees are not evaluated exclusively by objective measures. Rather, their performance evaluations tend to include subjective elements. For example, most employees receive annual performance reviews from supervisors. These reviews often form the basis for setting salaries and promotions. Even when compensation is based entirely on objective measures (piece rate in agriculture), the firm reserves the right to fire employees for low-quality production, tardiness, the inability to get along with co-workers, or other undesirable behavior. Lincoln Electric bases factory employees' wages entirely on piecework, which is an objective measure. But in addition to this objective measure, Lincoln also uses a subjective merit evaluation to set the employee bonus, which is approximately the same magnitude as wages.

We first describe one reason firms use subjective performance measures—namely, assigning multiple tasks to employees. Then various subjective evaluation schemes are described. Finally, problems with subjective evaluations are summarized.

Multiple Tasks and Unbalanced Effort

As discussed in Chapter 10, multiple tasks are often assigned to one employee because there is an efficiency gain due to bundling the tasks. For example, secretaries answer phones, word process, file, and make appointments and travel plans. Or, an employee might be expected to sell products to existing customers, contact potential new customers, and fill out reports. All of these tasks are complementary to selling the product.

Suppose Craig Cook performs two tasks, assembling welders and training new employees to assemble welders. Some activities are more easily measured, such as counting the number of welders Craig assembles; others, like training new assemblers, are more difficult to assess. If Craig's evaluation is based primarily on the easily measured tasks (welders assembled), he has incentives to concentrate his efforts on these activities. Craig will not allocate the optimal amount of time to the other unmeasured tasks (see Chapter 12).

Recall that this problem can affect optimal job design. For example, a firm might want to have certain employees concentrate only on assembling welders when complementarities among tasks are low. These employees could then be evaluated on their output of assembled welders. Other employees would concentrate on training new assemblers and correspondingly be evaluated on their training. By separating the tasks, each employee can be given stronger incentives to focus on the single task.

Subjective reviews evaluate an employee's performance on a more comprehensive basis. All aspects of the job that are less easily measured can be considered along with more easily measured activities. For example, the supervisor can consider the employee's efforts at being cooperative, being part of a team, being responsive to potential customers, or filling out reports accurately. Craig's supervisor can observe how Craig instructs the new hires, how patient he is, and how they ultimately perform as assemblers in assessing Craig's performance as a trainer. Moreover, if the employee games the performance measure—takes firm-value-reducing actions that increase the objective performance measure—the supervisor (if aware of these dysfunctional actions) can penalize the employee in the subjective performance evaluation.

Subjective Evaluation Methods

There are two widely used subjective performance-appraisal systems: standard-rating-scale systems and goal-based systems. Goal-based systems tend to be more explicit and less subjective than standard-rating-scale systems.

Standard-Rating-Scale Systems

Standard rating scales require the evaluator to rank the employee on a number of different performance factors using, for example, a five-point scale: far exceeds requirements, exceeds requirements, meets all requirements, partially meets requirements, does not meet requirements. The different performance factors judged vary across firms and positions within firms but often include the following:

- Achieves forecasts, budgets, objectives.
- Sets and attains high performance goals for self and group.
- Organizes effective performance through oral and written communications.
- Emphasizes teamwork among subordinates.
- Updates knowledge of job-related skills.
- Identifies and resolves problems.
- Evaluates subordinates objectively.
- Ensures equal opportunities for all subordinates.

After ranking the subordinate on each of these narrow criteria, the evaluator then assigns a rating for the overall job: excellent, better than satisfactory, satisfactory, needs further improvement, and unsatisfactory. Most subjective performance appraisals contain a section where the supervisor provides detailed comments on the employee's strengths and weaknesses and offers specific recommendations for improvement and further employee development.

Goal-Based Systems

In a goal-based system, each employee is given a set of goals for the year. For example, goals might be: hold training sessions for all employees in the department by November 1, or hire four additional qualified members of minority groups. These goals tend to be more objective and easier to measure than the more vague performance factors used in the standard rating scales such as "emphasizes teamwork." Nevertheless, these goals are still more subjective than standard piecework measures. At the end of the year, the supervisor writes a memo detailing the extent to which each goal is met. An overall evaluation of the employee is based on the extent to which the goals are achieved.

After evaluators have rated the employee using either standard rating scales or a goal-based system, evaluators usually then review the evaluations with their supervisors. This helps ensure the accuracy of the review and promotes consistency of criteria across employees. Next, supervisors give copies of the evaluations to the employees and meet with them to review the evaluations. The employee can respond in writing to the evaluation, including the expression of formal disagreement with any of the specifics in the appraisal. Finally, the evaluators and their supervisor review the feedback provided by the evaluator and the employee's response.

In the vast majority of cases, the employee's immediate supervisor does the performance evaluation. In a few cases, firms have experimented with peer evaluations—especially in situations where teams are important. The benefit of peer evaluations is that peers have more information about typical performance in group assignments and the actual contribution of the individual to the team. Offsetting the better specific knowledge of

360-Degree Performance Reviews

Boeing Co., the aircraft manufacturer headquartered in Seattle, Washington, began using 360-degree reviews in 1992. Such review systems are not new. What is new is the jargon invented to make these performance-evaluation systems appear to be a recent innovation.

Privately held W. L. Gore & Associates employs 5,600 employees and manufactures Gore-Tex waterproof fabric. All employees are called associates. There are no "bosses," but each employee is assigned a "sponsor" who acts as a mentor. Gore has been using 360-degree evaluation as part of its performance feedback since 1958. Under this system, annual evaluations are gathered on all associates from the individual's peers, subordinates, and superiors. The evaluations are anonymous and rate employees on their contributions to the success of the business during the past year. All ratings on each employee receive equal weight. Compensation committees composed of sponsors with specialized knowledge of the area use the rankings to award pay increases or performance warnings.

Source: J. Lopez (1994), "A Better Way?" *The Wall Street Journal Supplement* (April 13), R6.

---

peers is the added costs of training everyone in the team to do evaluations. Moreover, peer evaluation can increase the tensions within the team. For example, some team members might systematically lower everyone else's ratings to make themselves look better. Or, friends may be rated highly to increase their chance of being promoted to supervise their former colleagues. Finally, the team might decide to collude to give everyone a high performance rating.

Frequency of Evaluation

Most subjective performance evaluations are conducted yearly. Because salary adjustments are made annually, firms require annual evaluations. The benefits of more frequent evaluations (say monthly) unlikely offset the higher costs. However, there are some examples of more frequent review. Often new hires are evaluated at the end of three months. During this probationary period the firm must decide whether to keep the employee. Also during this period, frequent feedback helps the worker learn and improve performance. For new hires, more frequent evaluations can be valuable. Consultants and lawyers are evaluated after each professional assignment by the partner-in-charge of the engagement. The person's performance is known, and there is no reason to wait until the end of the year to evaluate performance.

Problems with Subjective Performance Evaluations

There are several potential problems with subjective performance evaluation.

Reneging

There is the potential that the firm will renege on promises to employees to reward good performance.[7] For example, management might promise to give raises to those who perform well. Afterward, management might unjustifiably say that work is poor to avoid higher payments. It is less likely that an employee will be successful in a lawsuit involving subjective performance measurement than when the employee can document that a firm reneged on an explicit contract.

[7]G. Baker, R. Gibbons, and K. Murphy (1994), "Subjective Performance Measures in Optimal Incentive Contracts," *Quarterly Journal of Economics* CIX, 1125–1156.

The incentive to renege on implicit contracts will be largest for firms in financial difficulty (near bankruptcy). Reneging also can occur when a supervisor has a short horizon with the firm and is compensated on business-unit profits. (Unit profits might be increased in the short run by not granting raises to employees.) However, as discussed in Chapter 7, managers in healthy firms generally have incentives to maintain good reputations for honoring implicit contracts. We discuss these issues further in Chapter 18.

Shirking among Supervisors[8]

Disciplining employees and informing them of their shortcomings are often unpleasant tasks. Supervisors do not bear the full wealth effects of their decisions. Therefore, there is the potential agency problem that supervisors will not provide accurate performance evaluations. For example, a supervisor might tend to rate all performance highly to avoid conflict with subordinates. Alternatively, a supervisor might rank employees based on personal likes and dislikes rather than on job performance. Bias adds noise to the performance-evaluation system, typically reduces morale and the employees' incentives to work hard, and thereby lowers overall firm output.

Indirect empirical evidence suggests managers tend to assign relatively uniform performance ratings to employees. In a study of 7,000 performance ratings of managers and professionals in two firms, the researchers report that 95 percent of all appraisals were in just two categories: Good and Superior (Outstanding).[9] A survey of employee attitudes at Merck & Co., a large U.S. pharmaceutical firm, reported the following attitudes:[10]

- Managers are afraid to give experienced people a 1, 2, or 3 rating. It's easier to give everyone a 4 and give new people a 3.
- Charlie's been in that job for 20 years. He hasn't done anything creative for the last 15 years. Do you think my manager would give him a 3 rating? No way! Then he'd have to spend 12 months listening to Charlie complain.
- What's the use of killing yourself? You still get the same rating as everyone else, and you still get the same 5 percent increase. It's demoralizing and demotivating.

This evidence suggests that low-rated, disgruntled employees can impose costs on supervisors. In response, supervisors bias their evaluations. Hence, performance ratings are inaccurate appraisals of the employee's true performance. Biased, inaccurate appraisals reduce the incentive of employees to improve their performance by working harder and can lead to the promotion of less-qualified people. Here, the problem does not lie in the evaluation system per se but rather in the incentives for the evaluators.

To overcome the tendency to rate all employees above average, some firms impose a forced distribution where a fixed fraction of employees are assigned to each category (that is, the supervisor must rank a certain percentage of the employees as poor). However, forced distributions may not accurately reflect the true distribution of performance in each work group. Forced ranking systems can cause problems, especially when the size of the group being evaluated is small. For example, having to rank one of four employees as

---

[8]C. Prendergast and R. Topel (1993), "Discretion and Bias in Performance Evaluations," working paper (University of Chicago: Chicago), and C. Prendergast (1992), "An Agency Approach to Bias in Organizations," working paper (University of Chicago: Chicago).

[9]J. Medoff and K. Abraham (1980), "Experience, Performance, and Earnings," *Quarterly Journal of Economics* 95, 703–736.

[10]Quotes excerpted from a 1985 Merck report by K. Murphy (1992), "Performance Measurement and Appraisal: Motivating Managers to Identify and Reward Performance," in *Performance Measurement, Evaluation, and Incentives,* W. Bruns, ed. (Harvard Business School: Boston), 37–62.

poor might force the supervisor to rate a good-performing employee as poor; inaccuracies from the forced distribution might be larger than those from a biased supervisor. Moreover, forced distributions do not necessarily reduce the costs imposed on the supervisor. Under a forced distribution, supervisors might assign ratings based on the potential costs employees will impose on them—not based on the employees' true performances.

At Lincoln Electric, supervisors have incentives to do a good job because they are evaluated and compensated on the job they do in evaluating lower-level employees. Also, employees can discuss their ratings with senior management. Problems of bias are likely to be lower if the supervisor is held accountable for the future performance of individuals that are promoted based on the supervisor's recommendation.

Influence Costs

Influence costs (discussed in Chapter 9) include those non-productive activities employees engage in to influence outcomes—in this case, politicking for higher ratings by their supervisor. One potential method of reducing these costs is to rotate supervisors or employees more frequently (getting on the good side of one supervisor is of limited benefit). Rotation of employees, however, can limit potential synergies and cost reductions that arise with repeated interaction between a given manager and employee. New supervisors have limited knowledge of employees' specialized skills. Also, more frequent rotation potentially increases total influence costs, since the employee has more lobbying opportunities.

Government Regulation of Labor Markets

The principal/agent model assumes that both parties are free to arrive at whatever mutually agreeable contract they want and that the markets for labor are unregulated. However, government regulates labor markets and hence constrains the contracts employees and principals would otherwise write. Since the 1960s, federal laws in the United States dealing with affirmative action and equal employment opportunity (EEO) have had a major effect on both the performance-evaluation systems and the reward systems. Federal and state legislation and court actions have forced companies to document their compensation and promotion decisions to demonstrate their actions are related to performance and are not influenced by the employee's race, color, religion, sex, age, or national origin.

Labor laws and court decisions have had a significant effect on the performance-appraisal systems. In deciding cases involving alleged discriminatory employment practices, the courts look more favorably at companies with the following characteristics:[11]

- Similar individuals in the firm are treated equally and consistently.
- The firm's job descriptions are clearly written and well defined.
- The appraisal system has clear criteria for evaluating performance such as written objective scales and dimensions.
- There are specific written instructions on how to complete the performance appraisal.
- Employees are provided feedback about their performance appraisal.
- Higher-level supervisors' evaluations are incorporated into the appraisal system.

---

[11]Major federal legislation includes the Equal Pay Act of 1963, Title VII, and the Civil Rights Act of 1964. A. Barnes, T. Dworkin, and E. Richards (1994), *Law for Business* (Richard D. Irwin: Burr Ridge, IL), Ch. 23; G. Milkovich and J. Newman (1993), *Compensation* (Richard D. Irwin: Burr Ridge, IL), 316–318.

While these characteristics appear sensible and even worthwhile, government regulation has negative side effects. The presence of possible legal scrutiny of the firm's performance-evaluation systems pushes these systems to become more formal, more objective, with less reliance on subjective appraisal. Every action and appraisal must be documented. The firm's human resources department typically assumes the role of ensuring the firm is complying with the labor laws.

The performance-appraisal system that meets regulatory criteria does not necessarily maximize firm value absent the regulation. For example, many Japanese managers try "to make everybody feel that he is slated for the top position in the firm"[12] by delaying differentiating among cohorts and performance appraisals for 12 to 15 years after joining the firm. Such limitations on annual feedback to employees would potentially run afoul of the affirmative-action laws in the United States and thus would be strenuously opposed by the human resources departments at most large corporations. Hence, U.S. firms find it more difficult to use less-formal, more-subjective performance-evaluation systems than their foreign competitors, even though such systems might be firm-value enhancing in a less regulated setting.

Government regulations cause U.S. firms to spend more money than they would otherwise on appraisal systems that document to a court's satisfaction the firm's compliance with affirmative-action regulations. Thus, regulations likely cause some U.S. firms to adopt different performance-appraisal systems. This is another example of how regulation affects the firm's optimal choice of organizational architecture.

Combining Objective and Subjective Performance Measures

Performance-evaluation systems generally fall on a continuum between the two extremes, objective and subjective evaluation systems. Objective measures consist of items like output and sales that can be easily quantified and thus explicitly measured. Objective measures can be used in formal contracts between the employee and the firm. Subjective measures consist of noncontractible judgments about employee performance (the year-end evaluation from a supervisor). Subjective measures are used in implicit contracts. Few jobs' performance measures are purely objective or purely subjective, most measures involve mixtures of both. In many cases, organizations that use objective measures also use subjective measures to evaluate the same employee (as does Lincoln Electric, for example). Investment bankers pay bonuses based on fees generated by the employee and also use subjective measures such as the "quality of the deals."[13]

Both objective and subjective performance measures can be inaccurate measures of the employee's contribution to firm value. As the accuracy of either measure decreases, more weight will be placed on the other in determining performance (holding its accuracy constant). As the accuracy of each measure decreases, the risk the employee bears increases, as does the compensating differential the employee must be paid.

Besides being inaccurate, both objective and subjective measures can induce various dysfunctional behaviors. We pointed out earlier that objective measures can create incentives for gaming, which reduces firm value, as in the case of the Sears auto repair business. If supervisors shirk when writing subjective performance reviews, employees' incentives to

---

[12]N. Hatvany and V. Pucik (1981), "Japanese Managerial Practices and Productivity," *Organizational Dynamics* 13. Also, M. Aoki (1988), *Information, Incentives and Bargaining in the Japanese Economy* (Cambridge University Press: Cambridge).

[13]Baker, Gibbons, and Murphy (1994).

Objective and Subjective Performance Evaluation at Fiat

This example illustrates how one very large company, Fiat, combines both objective and subjective performance reviews into a single, integrated system.

The Italian firm, Fiat, is one of the world's largest corporations, with over 250,000 employees in 16 operating sectors. While automobiles are its largest product, Fiat also has operating units in railway systems, aviation, publishing and communications, and financial and real estate services.

In the 1980s, Fiat introduced a formal management by objectives (MBO) evaluation program for its 500 highest-level managers. Under the MBO program, annual bonuses of up to about 30 percent of their base salary are awarded for meeting objectives.

Managers have a set of objectives tailored to the specific situations. Managers in charge of profit centers have profit and debt objectives. Profit targets are defined in terms of net profit before taxes. Because Fiat had a dangerously high level of debt in the 1980s, profit center managers also were given objectives to lower their group's borrowings. Besides these specific financial objectives, managers have other performance indicators such as increasing sales in particular markets, completing an acquisition, improving quality or customer service, and introducing new products or processes.

Even though managers meet the particular objectives, unless the larger group achieves its goals, no bonus would be paid. For example, the Fiat Group has 16 sectors headed by a manager. If the entire Fiat Group fails to meet its objectives, none of the 16 sector managers receive their bonuses, even though some of them achieved their goals.

Each manager has a set of weightings attached to each objective. Unless the manager achieves a minimum level of profits before taxes, no bonus is paid. Once this threshold profit level is achieved, then the weights attached are 20 percent to 40 percent profits, 10 percent to 20 percent reducing debt, and 10 percent to 15 percent for each of three or four other performance targets. Each objective is scored on a five-point scale, with 3 being the minimum acceptable score. Superiors set the targets for each objective. In setting the performance targets, the following probabilities of achieving each target are supposed to be used:

Performance Level	Ideal Probability of Achievement
3 (threshold)	90–99%
4 (good)	50–60%
5 (excellent)	10–20%

For example, suppose "install new production-control system" is an objective that has a weighting of 20 percent. If the system is installed by November, it is judged as a 3 threshold. To achieve a 4, installation must be completed by October. And a 5 is earned if completed by September. If actual completion is October, a 4 is earned with a weighting of 20 percent and 0.80 (4 × 20%) is added to the manager's other performance objectives to compute an overall grade—say, 3.69.

A performance rating of 3 receives a bonus of 12 percent of salary. Ratings below 3 receive no bonus. A rating of 4 receives an 18 percent bonus, and a 5 receives a 30 percent bonus. Fractional ratings are scaled (e.g., a 3.69 receives 12% + 0.69 × [18% − 12%] or 16.14%). The median manager's rating is between 4.1 and 4.4. In any given year about 10 percent of the managers are rated below 3.0 and about 15 percent are rated 4.9 or better.

The performance-evaluation system at Fiat is similar to those used by large U.S. corporations.

Source: K. Merchant and A. Riccaboni (1992), "Evolution of Performance-Based Management Incentives at the Fiat Group," in *Performance Measurement, Evaluation, and Incentives,* W. Bruns, ed. (Harvard Business School: Boston), 63–96.

work hard are reduced. Also, employees will generate influence costs lobbying for higher subjective ratings. Finally, implicit contracts using subjective measures are more easily abrogated by the firm than formal contracts based on objective measures. The employee must trust that the firm will not renege on the implicit contract. An important constraint on the firm from reneging is its reputation. Thus, firms facing a greater likelihood of financial distress will find subjective evaluations more costly to use.

Because the costs and benefits of objective and subjective measures vary across jobs, in some situations only objective measures are observed, others are mixtures of both, and in other cases, only subjective performance measures are observed. Each firm will face specific costs and benefits of objective and subjective measures and will tailor its performance measures to its circumstances. Moreover, the costs and benefits are likely to vary over various divisions of the firm and jobs. However, employees performing similar tasks in similar industries tend to have similar performance-evaluation systems because the costs and benefits of the alternative evaluation schemes will be similar.

Both objective and subjective performance measures are costly. When these costs are large, firms tend not to rely on performance evaluations for setting rewards and punishments. Paying employees straight salary and giving simple cost-of-living raises to all employees will lead to predictable shirking and other agency problems. However, these costs might be lower than the costs of implementing a performance-based incentive plan.

Team Performance

As discussed in Chapter 9, teams are often used at all levels of the organization. Teams are formed because they are more successful at assembling specialized knowledge for decision making than at trying to pass the knowledge through the traditional hierarchy. As discussed below, teams can also prove useful when one employee's productivity affects the productivity of other employees. For instance, one complaint by employees at Lincoln Electric is that their pay suffers when employees ahead of them on an assembly line are unable to keep them supplied with work.

Team Production

To illustrate the performance problems of teams, consider the following example. Craig and Debbie assemble welders. To simplify the notation, assume Craig and Debbie exert a common effort level, e, whether in a team or not. If they work independently, their individual output is:

$$\text{Individual output} = 5e + \mu \tag{13.5}$$

where e represents the individual effort of either Craig or Debbie and μ is a random error term with zero mean and positive variance. If Craig and Debbie work as a team, they produce:

$$\text{Team output} = 4e^2 + \mu \tag{13.6}$$

For e > 2.50, the expected output working as a team is higher than the output of working independently:

$$\text{Expected team output} = 4e^2 > \text{Expected individual output} = 5e + 5e \tag{13.7}$$

This is illustrated in Figure 13.1. Craig and Debbie's team output is always larger than the sum of their individual output whenever they each exert 2.50 units of effort.

In this example, there are team-production effects—output is potentially higher when Debbie and Craig work as a team. Team output can be larger because Debbie and Craig help each other. Large, awkward pieces can be attached in less than half the time by two people assisting each other than if Craig and Debbie worked independently. In other cases, team output is larger than individuals working separately because the team makes better use of the knowledge of its members.

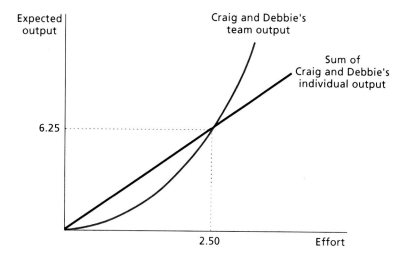

Figure 13.1 Comparing Individual and Team Output

When Craig and Debbie each exert at least 2.50 units of effort, their team output is greater than their output working independently.

Evaluating Teams

Teams are formed because of team-production effects.[14] Evaluating the performance of individual team members, however, is complicated by the fact that there is no measure of individual output; only team output is observed. Typically, it is optimal to evaluate team members, at least in part, on team output. Using team output focuses team members on a common objective and helps to promote cooperation. However, paying team members on group output provides individuals with incentives to free-ride. These incentives are relatively low in two-person teams. But as the team size continues to grow, these free-rider problems can become substantial.

Free-rider problems can be reduced by evaluating team members not only on team output but on other measures as well. For instance, the following factors might be used to assess the performance of Craig and Debbie: the number of hours worked, a supervisor's subjective evaluation of how hard they are working, the condition of their tools, and peer evaluations. Peer evaluations consist of Debbie's evaluation of Craig's work and Craig's evaluation of Debbie's work. Peer reviews are often important in evaluating the individual performance of team members because it is the peers that have the specific information about how each team member has performed.

Sometimes the costs of controlling free-rider problems in teams are larger than the benefits that come from team production. In this case, it is better to work individually rather than as a team. For instance, if evaluating Debbie and Craig on team output provides low incentives to exert effort and the costs of monitoring individual performance (for example, through supervisor or peer reviews) are high, the net value of their combined output might be higher with individual production and performance evaluation.

---

[14]A. Alchian and H. Demsetz (1972), "Production, Information Costs and Economic Organization," *American Economic Review* 62, 777–795.

Peer Review Performance Ratings of Teams

This example describes the specific areas and skills evaluated for individuals working on teams. One small company is organized around nine management teams. Each team member rates all other team members on a five-point scale on each of the following topics:

- Expresses opinions freely.
- Comes to meetings prepared.
- Takes initiative.
- Accepts criticism.
- Listens to others.
- Delegates authority.
- Shares information freely.
- Bases decisions on sound data.
- Values all customers.
- Recognizes others' contributions.

These individual peer ratings are then averaged across team members and items to arrive at an overall peer evaluation for each team member. Pay and promotion decisions as well as future team assignments are based on these evaluations, along with the team's overall performance.

As another example of evaluating team output, consider the case of student project teams in college courses. Such projects build leadership skills and teach students how to work more effectively in teams. Such projects also enhance learning by allowing students to share their understanding and helping all students on the team to learn more than if they each did the project individually. Instructors assigning projects to study teams generally give the same grade to all members of the team. Thus, the team is evaluated based on the team's joint output.

One of the key tasks for new teams is to develop the internal architecture for the team. Decision rights (task assignments) must be partitioned among the team members. Accordingly, members must decide how to evaluate the work efforts of team members. Finally, members must decide on the rewards and punishments for members of the group. Sometimes the rewards and punishments are social; for example, a shirking member may be ostracized.

Peer Pressure in Teams

Levi Strauss, maker of Levi jeans, installed 39 multitask teams in one of its sewing plants. Each team has 20 to 30 employees responsible for completing individual orders by assembling full pairs of pants, instead of each employee specializing as zipper sewers or belt-loop attachers. In essence, at this plant, jobs were redesigned from being functional to being more multitask and process-oriented (recall Chapter 10's discussion).

Employee incentive compensation is based on team output, which creates free-rider problems, which in turn have led to absenteeism and shirking, which causes tempers to flare. Supervisors on the plant floor spend more time intervening to prevent "big fights." The plant manager reports, "Peer pressure can be vicious and brutal." Before installing the multitask teams, each employee received two weeks of training in group dynamics and an additional one-day seminar in "let's-get-along sessions" with private consultants. These training sessions have not resolved the conflicts.

Source: R. Mitchell (1994), "Managing by Values," *Business Week*
(August 1), 50.

Returning to the student case project, rather than assigning all the members of the team the same project grade, the total project grade can be apportioned among the team members based on their peer reviews where unequal team grades are possible. Thus, while the overall project's grade might be a B+, some team members might receive an A– and others a B as long as the average across the team is a B+. Providing the team with the decision rights to evaluate each other reduces the free-rider problem and increases team production. But it can also reduce morale and lead to increased influence costs as team members lobby each other for better evaluations. These dysfunctional incentives are likely to be greater if the team is formed for a single project. As described in Chapter 7, free-rider problems are smaller if the team spans several courses and students have more incentives to invest in their reputations.

Summary

The last four chapters examined the first two components of organizational architecture: the assignment of decision rights and the reward systems. This chapter began examining the third component: the performance-evaluation system.

Performance evaluation is conducted for both individuals within the firm and sub-units of the firm. How did Taylor perform and how did Morgan's team perform? Such questions require individual and team performance evaluations. Also, Morgan and Taylor are in the automotive-products division. How did this division perform? Answering this last question requires divisional performance measures. Individual performance-evaluation systems are the focus of this chapter, and divisional performance evaluation is discussed in Chapter 14.

The simple agency model in Chapter 12 suggests that part of the employee's compensation be based on performance (output). But basing pay on output requires that output be observable at low cost and not subject to manipulation by the firm. Moreover, the model assumes the firm and employee are free to contract in an unregulated labor market. This chapter explores how individual performance evaluation is affected when these assumptions are violated.

To set the optimum compensation package, management must know the employee's marginal productivity of effort. One way for management to estimate the employee's marginal productivity is to use motion and time studies or data on past performance. If past performance is used, dysfunctional incentives due to the *ratchet effect* can result. Employees will limit output if they expect next period's target benchmark will be raised. To reduce the dysfunctional consequences of the ratchet effect, performance estimates are set at the beginning of the period and rarely adjusted for random, unusual events.

Often a manager has available multiple signals regarding the employee's output. The informativeness principle from Chapter 12 suggests that the manager ought to use all these signals (if available at low cost) because they allow the firm to reduce the risk the employee bears and thus lower the compensating differential the employee must be paid. Applying the informativeness principle suggests that when multiple employees are performing similar tasks, their combined output provides a signal about the common random shocks affecting all their outputs. Thus, the employee's compensation should be adjusted relative to peers. This is called *relative performance evaluation.* Relative performance evaluation requires the firm to establish a reference group of employees to use as the benchmark. But relative performance evaluations can lead employees to collude or sabotage co-workers to improve their evaluations. Moreover, establishing the appropriate reference group and measuring its performance is costly.

Another assumption of the model is that the employee only shirks on effort. If output is not perfectly correlated with firm value, employees attempting to increase output might cause firm value to decline. Such dysfunctional results can occur when employees game the system—as in the Sears auto mechanics case of overcharging customers.

Measuring output can be very costly in some cases. For example, measuring the output of a teacher is likely very costly. Firms will select performance evaluations based on the direct cost of the measure, the cost of employee opportunism induced by the performance measure, and the indirect cost incurred by imposing more risk on the employee. In some cases, the measurement costs or the costs from employees' dysfunctional attempts to maximize explicit performance measures become so great that alternative measures of performance are sought. *Subjective performance evaluations* are periodic reviews by supervisors that usually incorporate a comprehensive examination of all the employee's outputs. Subjective evaluations can be based on either standard rating scales for a number of different areas or goal-based systems. Standard rating scales have the appearance of objectivity but entail subjective judgments by the evaluator. Goal-based systems set performance targets at the beginning of the year that the evaluator uses at the end of the year to determine an overall, subjective evaluation.

Subjective performance measures also involve costs. It becomes easier for a manager or the firm to renege on the promise to reward good performance because it is harder to define what is "good." There is more latitude to exercise favoritism and introduce bias in subjective measures. Finally, subjective systems often generate more influence costs as employees try to lobby for better ratings.

While the agency model assumes the parties are free to contract, in reality labor laws constrain their choices. The equal employment opportunity laws in the United States have had a pronounced effect on performance-evaluation systems. Defending oneself against affirmative-action lawsuits has caused firms to adopt more explicit, objective appraisal systems than they otherwise would have chosen voluntarily.

Subjective and objective performance evaluations usually complement each other. Subjective evaluations often are used to reduce the incentives of employees to engage in opportunistic behaviors that increase the costs of objective measures. For example, the Lincoln Electric secretary who typed meaningless characters during lunch can be penalized by the subjective system: the supervisor could fire the secretary or give the secretary a poor subjective evaluation.

Finally, when employees work in teams, each individual's marginal contribution to the team's output depends on others' effort. We say there are synergies or interdependencies among employees. Measuring individual output is difficult, and it is costly to disentangle individual shirking from others' effort. Evaluating teams of employees usually requires a measure of team performance while still recognizing individual contributions to the team. Individual performance is rewarded to overcome free-rider problems. In some cases, each team member's bonus is based on individual performance, but the bonus is only paid if the entire team meets or exceeds its goals.

APPENDIX   *Optimal Weights in a Relative Performance Contract*[15]

In this chapter, we argued that it can be optimal to base an employee's pay on performance *relative* to some benchmark group such as employees within the same organization who perform similar tasks. The advantage of this type of system is that it filters out

---

[15]This appendix requires elementary knowledge of statistics, decision theory, and calculus. Material in this appendix draws on the analysis in Milgrom and Roberts (1992) Chapter 7.

common shocks in the evaluation of employees and thus reduces the costs of inefficient risk bearing. In this appendix, we consider how a risk-neutral firm might optimally weight the performance of such a benchmark group in a compensation contract.

For simplicity, we restrict our attention to simple linear compensation contracts of the following form:

$$\text{Compensation} = W_0 + \beta(Q - \lambda \bar{Q}), \tag{13.8}$$

where W_o and β are fixed parameters, Q is the employee's own output, and $\bar{Q}$ is the average output of the benchmark group (for example, similar employees in the firm). W_o is the employee's fixed wage under a relative performance contract. We are interested in how to choose the optimal λ. Note that if $\lambda = 0$, average output receives no weight and thus is left out of the contract. In contrast, if $\lambda = 1$, then compensation is based on a simple difference between own output and average output.

In the discussion that follows, we will show that expected compensation can be held the same by just adjusting W_0. Second, under certain assumptions, the employee's effort choice is independent of λ. Third, we will show how to choose λ to minimize the risk the employee bears. Since expected compensation can be the same for any λ and if the effort choice isn't affected by λ, then the efficient contract is the one that minimizes the risk borne by the employee.

Expected Compensation
Rewriting equation 13.8 yields:

$$\text{Compensation} = W_o + \beta Q - \beta \lambda \bar{Q} \tag{13.9}$$

Expected compensation in equation 13.9 is $W_o + \beta E(Q) - \beta \lambda E(\bar{Q})$. Expected compensation can be held constant at any level of λ by adjusting W_o by $+ \beta \lambda E(\bar{Q})$

Effort Choice
Under certain assumptions, the employee's effort choice is independent of λ. In this case, the firm can choose λ without being concerned about how it might affect employee productivity. In particular, suppose that the employee's cost of exerting effort is given by the function $C(e)$, which expresses the disutility of effort in dollar equivalents. The employee's certainty equivalent can be approximated by the following formula:[16]

$$\text{Certainty equivalent} = E[W_o + \beta(Q - \lambda \bar{Q})] - .5rs^2 - C(e) \tag{13.10}$$

where E denotes the expectation operator, r is the coefficient of absolute risk aversion, and s^2 is the variance of compensation. In this expression, the first term on the right-hand side represents expected compensation, the second term is the risk premium (employees discount the expected value because they are risk averse), and the last term is the cost of effort. We make two additional assumptions: (1) the effort of the employee does not affect the average output of other employees of the benchmark group and (2) r is a constant. Employees want to maximize their certainty equivalent with respect to the effort choice, e

---

[16]A certainty equivalent is the amount of cash that employees would require with certainty to make them indifferent between this certain sum and the uncertain income stream. The approximation of the certainty equivalent in equation 13.9 is a basic result in decision theory. It holds when the risk is small and the utility function is sufficiently smooth. J. Ingersoll (1987), *Theory of Financial Decision Making* (Rowman & Littlefield: Totowa, NJ), 38.

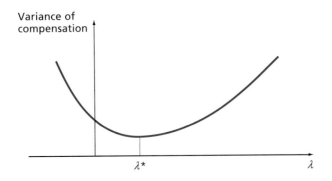

Figure 13.2 Choosing the Optimal Weight in a Relative Performance Contract

This figure reflects a simple linear contract of the form Compensation = $W_0 + \beta(Q - \lambda \bar{Q})$, where W_0 and β are fixed parameters. Q is the employee's own output, and $\bar{Q}$ is the average output of the benchmark group (for example, similar employees in the firm). Pictured is the variance of compensation as a function of λ. Given the assumptions in the analysis, the optimal weight, $\lambda^* = Cov(Q, \bar{Q})/Var(\bar{Q})$. This is the value that minimizes the variance of compensation.

(which is equivalent to maximizing their utility). Conceptually, the maximizing effort level is found by taking the partial derivative of the certainty equivalent with respect to effort, e, and setting it equal to zero. The first-order condition is therefore:

$$\beta Q' = C'(e) \qquad (13.11)$$

where Q' and $C'(e)$ are partial derivatives with respect to e. This expression indicates that the employee chooses the effort level that equates marginal benefits and marginal costs. The marginal benefit is the extra compensation that the employee receives from exerting more effort, and the marginal cost is the extra disutility that he experiences from working harder. Note that λ does not enter into this equation, since the average output of other employees does not depend on his effort. Thus, in this case, the firm can choose any value for λ without affecting the employee's effort level.

Minimizing Employee Risk
Note from equation 13.10 that the employee is made better off by reducing the variance of compensation (it lowers the discount for risk). The firm, on the other hand, is not harmed by this choice because the employee exerts the same effort level under any λ and W_0 can be adjusted to keep expected compensation the same. Indeed, the firm can potentially share in the gains from the risk reduction to the employee by paying a lower expected value of compensation (since the firm can meet the reservation wage of the employee with a lower expected value of payout).

Basic statistics allows us to express the variance of compensation (equation 13.8) as:

$$Var(Compensation) = \beta^2[Var(Q) + \lambda^2 Var(\bar{Q}) - 2\lambda Cov(Q, \bar{Q})] \qquad (13.12)$$

Figure 13.2 shows a picture of this quadratic function. The optimal weight is λ^* at the bottom of the parabola. Using basic calculus, we can show that:

$$\lambda^* = Cov(Q, \bar{Q})/Var(\bar{Q}). \qquad (13.13)$$

Equation 13.13 has a very intuitive interpretation. The numerator of the expression, $Cov(Q, \bar{Q})$, is a measure of the association between his own output and the average output of other employees. The higher this association, the more information average output contains about random shocks that affect the employee's output (the better is the "signal"). For example, if this covariance is zero, average output contains no information about these shocks and should not be included in the compensation contract. The denominator of the expression is the variance of average output. The higher this variance, the more noise there is in average output and the less information it contains about the employee's effort. The optimal weight, λ^*, can be estimated using a time series of observations on own output and average output.[17]

Firms sometimes base compensation on the simple difference between the employee's output and average output. This measure is equivalent to choosing $\lambda = 1$. Our analysis indicates that this choice is not always optimal and in some cases can be worse than excluding average output in the contract (for example, when the covariance between the two variables is small). Indeed, the optimal weight could be negative if the two variables were negatively correlated.

Appendix Problem

Assume a salesperson has the following annual compensation package:

$$C = \$15,000 + .2(\text{Own sales})$$

This compensation plan induces the employee to exert a given level of effort in selling. Given this effort level, expected sales are $30,000 per year.

Below are 10 years' worth of data for the individual's sales and the average sales for other employees in the company (the salesperson's own sales are not included in calculating this average). The expected value of average sales is also $30,000. However, in any given year, average sales might rise or fall depending on general economic conditions, and so on. Some of these same conditions affect the sales of the individual. The salesperson has no impact on the average sales for other employees.

Year	Own Sales	Average Sales
1	30,000	30,000
2	24,000	27,000
3	36,000	28,500
4	27,000	27,000
5	33,000	36,000
6	30,000	33,000
7	25,500	27,000
8	24,000	24,000
9	34,500	30,000
10	36,000	36,000

1. Based on the 10 years of data, calculate the average annual pay and standard deviation for the salesperson under the existing compensation scheme.
2. Calculate the average pay and standard deviation for the salesperson under the alternative plan:

$$\$21,000 + .2(\text{Own sales–Average sales})$$

---

[17]Those readers familiar with linear regression analysis should note that the right-hand side of equation 13.12 is the formula for the slope coefficient in a simple linear regression, where the employee's output is the dependent variable and average output of other employees is the explanatory variable. Thus, this formula can be estimated through a simple regression.

Note: We adjust the intercept of the pay plan by $6,000 to reflect the average loss imposed on the employee by subtracting .2(Average sales) from the compensation. This adjustment keeps the expected pay the same as before. Also, the sample mean of average sales over a 10-year period need not equal the expected value of $30,000.

3. Does including the average sales in the pay package alter the incentives of the employee to work hard? Explain. (Assume the employee cannot affect the average by collusion, sabotage, etc.)
4. Is this pay plan superior to the original plan from a risk-sharing standpoint?
5. Devise an even better plan using the more general form:

$$C = a + .2(\text{Own sales} - \lambda\text{Average sales})$$

(Remember to adjust the intercept to keep expected compensation the same.)
6. Calculate the average pay and standard deviation for this plan.

Suggested Readings

A. Alchian and H. Demsetz (1972), "Production, Information Costs and Economic Organization," *American Economic Review* 62, 777–795.

G. Baker, R. Gibbons, and K. Murphy (1994), "Subjective Performance Measures in Optimal Incentive Contracts," *Quarterly Journal of Economics* CIX, 1125–1156.

Y. Barzel (1982), "Measurement Cost and the Organization of Markets," *Journal of Law & Economics* XXV, 27–48.

E. Lazear and S. Rosen (1981), "Rank Order Tournaments as Optimal Labor Contracts," *Journal of Political Economy,* 89, 841–864.

G. Milkovich and J. Newman (1993), *Compensation* (Richard D. Irwin: Burr Ridge, IL).

G. Milkovich, and A. Wigdor (1991), *Pay for Performance* (National Academy Press: Washington, D.C.).

Review Questions

13–1. Discuss some of the costs and benefits of 360-degree evaluation systems.

13–2. Semco S.A. in Sao Paulo, Brazil, has 500 employees and manufactures capital goods. The employees elect their managers and evaluate them every six months. Managers rated poorly are transferred or fired. There are 100 nonunion employees who set their own performance standards and arrange their own work schedules. Twice a year, the nonunion employees receive a market salary survey and are asked to set their own pay for the next six months. Employees setting their pay too low receive that amount, as do employees requesting too high a salary. If management decides after one year that the employees' salaries were above what they were worth to the company, these employees are fired. The 400 unionized employees' pay is set by union contract. Critically evaluate Semco's performance-evaluation system.[18]

13–3. In 360-degree performance review programs, personnel evaluations are collected anonymously from employees knowing the manager being evaluated (superiors, subordinates, and co-workers). These are tabulated and a consensus summary is provided to the manager. Each manager being evaluated also does a self-evaluation, and this is used to benchmark how closely the manager and the co-workers' assessments match. About one-third of the managers match their co-workers, one-third have an inflated view, and one-

[18]J. Lopez (1994), "A Better Way?" *The Wall Street Journal Supplement* (April 13), R6.

third rate themselves lower. Those who overrate themselves tend to be judged "least effective" as perceived by their coemployees. However, these overraters are more common higher up in the organization.[19]

    a. What does the breakdown of three one-thirds indicate?

    b. Offer some plausible explanation of why overraters are higher up in the organization.

13–4.   The following quote is based on statements made by quality expert W. Edwards Deming:

> *If by bad management the components of a company become competitive, the system is destroyed . . . A common example lies in the practice of ranking people, divisions, teams, comparing them, with reward at the top and punishment at the bottom. Jobs and salaries are based on comparisons. Teams naturally become competitive; divisions become competitive. Each tries to outdo the other in some competitive measure. The result is higher costs, battle of market share. Everybody loses.[20]*

Do you agree with Deming that performance evaluations based on comparative rankings always reduce company value? Explain.

13–5.   The U.S. Navy is revamping its officer fitness report system.[21] Under the old system, officers were ranked into one of four categories, where 4.0 was the highest grade. This old system had been used for 20 years and grade inflation had become rampant. Eighty percent of all sailors routinely were ranked a perfect 4.0. One officer remarked, "Let's face it, 85 percent of the people are 4.0 and 80 percent [of those] have every mark in 4.0." A retired admiral commented, "The old system wasn't entirely broke, it was just deteriorating over time and became less and less useful."

The Navy decided to change the evaluation system because of the natural tendency for senior officers to promote their own subordinates over unknown sailors. Not everyone deserved a 4.0, but to get their own people promoted, senior officers had to play along because that's what everyone else was doing.

The new system requires each officer to be rated on a 1–5 scale in seven areas: professional expertise, leadership, support for equal opportunity programs, military bearing and appearance, teamwork, mission accomplishment, and interpersonal skills. The total points out of 35 possible are then used to provide an overall promotion recommendation:

- Clearly promote.

- Must promote.

- Promotable.

- Progressing.

- Don't promote.

The number of ratings in the top two categories—"clearly promote" and "must promote"—will be severely restricted to at most 20 percent of the evaluations. If an officer is evaluating 10 junior officers, at the most only two can receive the top two ratings.

What will be the predictable consequences of the new system? What are the likely outcomes? What are the pros and cons of the new system?

13–6.   Evaluate the following statement:

> *The overarching purpose of a measurement system should be to help a team, rather than senior managers, gauge its progress. A team's measurement system should primarily be a tool for telling the team when it must take corrective action.[22]*

---

[19]B. O'Reilly (1994), "360 Feedback Can Change Your Life," *Fortune* (October 17), 93–100.

[20]R. Aguayo (1990), *Dr. Deming: The American Who Taught the Japanese about Quality* (Fireside Simon & Schuster: New York), vii–viii.

[21]E. Blazar (1995), "The New Standard of Excellence," *Navy Times* (March 20), 12–14.

[22]C. Meyer (1994), "How the Right Measures Help Teams Excel," *Harvard Business Review* (May–June), 96.

13–7.   The Green Shoe Company is considering going to a piece rate system, where manufacturing employees are paid based on their level of output. Discuss what factors the firm should consider in deciding whether or not this idea should be implemented. How should the initial piece rate be set? Under what circumstances should the company alter the piece rate once it is adopted?

13–8.   Your company currently has a bonus plan for its sales managers. If annual sales for a manager's unit exceed $1 million, the manager receives a $10,000 bonus. In a typical year, about 5 of the 10 managers in the firm meet the target and receive the bonus. However, the number receiving the bonus varies from year to year due to the state of the economy, which in turn has an effect on sales. The company is considering replacing the bonus plan with a plan that rewards the top-five-selling managers each year with a $10,000 bonus. Discuss the potential benefits and costs of the new plan relative to the old plan.

13–9.   Communities are frequently concerned about whether or not police are vigilant in carrying out their responsibilities. Several communities have experimented with incentive compensation for police. In particular, some cities have paid members of the police force based on the number of arrests that they personally make. Discuss the likely effects of this compensation policy.

13–10.   A consultant does not like the fact that you use subjective performance measures in your firm. He argues that they are arbitrary and should be replaced with objective measures. He stresses that objective measures provide a clear target for employees, but mentions none of the potential costs. What are the potential problems associated with using objective performance measures?

13–11.   Some firms have recently adopted 360-degree performance evaluations. Under this evaluation scheme, the employee is evaluated not only by supervisors and peers but also by employees who report to the employee being evaluated. Discuss why a firm might want to adopt 360-degree reviews. What are the likely problems with this type of performance evaluation?

13–12.   Evaluate the following quote:

> *Teams do not spring up by magic. Nor does personal chemistry matter as much as most people believe. Rather, we believe that . . . most people can significantly enhance team performance. And focusing on performance—not chemistry or togetherness or good communications or good feelings—shapes teams more than anything else.*[23]

13–13.   A basic principle in accounting is that of "responsibility accounting." Under this principle, it is inappropriate to base performance evaluation on measures that are beyond the control of the employee. Do you think that you should ever include variables in a worker's compensation plan that are not under at least partial control of the employee? Explain.

---

[23]J. Katzenbach, and D. Smith (1993), *The Wisdom of Teams* (Harvard Business School: Boston), 61.

chapter 14

Divisional Performance Evaluation*

CHAPTER OUTLINE

*Parts of this chapter were previously published as J. Brickley, C. Smith, and J. Zimmerman (1995), "Transfer Pricing and the Control of Internal Corporate Transactions," *Journal of Applied Corporate Finance* 8, 60–67.

C SX is a large freight railroad with a fleet of locomotives, containers, and railcars.[1] Its total revenues in 1995 were $10.5 billion. CSX transports freight in containers connecting trucks and cargo ships. In 1988, CSX changed the way it evaluated internal divisions. It adopted economic value added (EVA). EVA is the after-tax operating profit of the division minus the total annual opportunity cost of the capital invested in the division. The total annual cost of capital is the product of the division's cost of capital times the amount of capital invested in the division. The EVA of one of CSX's major division's was a negative $70 million. This means that in this division, the opportunity cost of the capital invested in the division exceeded its operating profits by $70 million. The CEO of CSX informed the managers of this division that if they could not raise their EVA to break even by 1993, their division would be sold.

By 1993, after reorganizing and measuring these managers' performance using EVA, freight volume increased by 25 percent, the number of freight trailers was reduced from 18,000 to 14,000, and the locomotive fleet fell from 150 to 100. Instead of allowing the trailers and containers to sit idle, managers now had incentives to use them or reduce their numbers. Under the old performance-evaluation system, managers were not charged for the opportunity cost of the capital employed by their investments, and they treated the existing stock of containers and trailers as "free." By 1993, containers and trailers were loaded and back on the tracks in five days rather than sitting idle for two weeks. This division's 1993 EVA was about $30 million. CSX's stock price rose from $28 in 1988 when EVA was adopted to $75 in 1993.

Chapter 13 described individual performance-evaluation systems. This discussion is extended in this chapter to evaluating the performance of subunits or divisions of the firm, as in the CSX example. As described in Chapter 10, firms are organized in a variety of ways: by function, by product line, or by geography. In essence, all organizations partition decision rights to subunits within the firm. This chapter describes various ways organizations measure the performance of these subunits. The next section describes the commonly used cost centers, expense centers, revenue centers, profit centers, and investment centers. These subunits are assigned different sets of decision rights and accordingly use different performance-evaluation metrics (costs, revenues, profits, EVA). Because subunits of the organization interact with each other and often exchange goods or services among themselves, the reported performance of each center involved in the exchange depends on the rules used to value the exchange. Divisional performance evaluation of subunits exchanging goods or services requires establishing an internal transfer price for these exchanges. The following section discusses these transfer-pricing issues. Finally, because most firms rely on their accounting systems to measure some of the performance of the subunits, the subsequent section discusses some general issues involving use of the accounting system in measuring performance.

Measuring Divisional Performance[2]

Organizations are divided into subunits, each given some decision rights and then each evaluated based on performance objectives for that subunit. Rewards are often based on performance evaluations. The performance-evaluation and reward systems should be

---

[1]Details of this example are from S. Tully (1993), "The Real Key to Creating Wealth," *Fortune* (September 20), 38–50. EVA is a registered trademark of Stern Stewart.

[2]Material in this section draws on the analysis in M. Jensen and W. Meckling (1986), "Divisional Performance Measurement," working paper (Harvard Business School: Boston).

consistent with the decision rights allocated to the subunit manager. (The three legs of the stool should be matched.) Chapter 10 described alternative organizational structures: U-form, M-form, and matrix organizations. In the U-form, one unit might be responsible for manufacturing, another unit for R&D, another marketing, and so forth. These basic building blocks of the organization are the work groups that define and characterize what each part of the firm does. Senior management attempts to evaluate the performance of these various subunits both for setting rewards for lower-level managers as well as for making business decisions—for instance, which units to expand.

Chapter 9 pointed out that teams often can produce more than individuals working independently. The subunits of the organization are, in effect, production teams. For example, the maintenance department maintains the facilities; marketing structures and implements the marketing plans; research and development undertakes R&D; and the Pizza Hut division of PepsiCo sells pizzas. Each subunit can generally be characterized as one of five categories based on the decision rights it has and the way its performance is evaluated: (1) cost centers, (2) expense centers, (3) revenue centers, (4) profit centers, and (5) investment centers. At CSX, the railroad moved from evaluating some of its divisions as profit centers to evaluating them as investment centers.

Cost Centers

Cost centers are established whenever a subunit is assigned the decision rights to produce some output and the unit's efficiency in achieving this objective is to be measured and rewarded. Cost center managers are granted decision rights for determining the mix of inputs (labor, outside services, and materials) used to produce the output. Managers of cost centers are evaluated based on their efficiency in applying inputs to produce outputs. Since they are not responsible for selling the products, they are not judged on revenues or profits.

To evaluate the performance of a cost center, its output must be measurable. Moreover, central management in the organization must have the specialized knowledge and decision rights to specify the department's output or budget. Manufacturing departments like the welder assembly department at Lincoln Electric are usually cost centers The output of the welder assembly department is measured by counting the number of welders completed. Besides manufacturing settings, cost centers are also used in service organizations such as CSX's railcar maintenance department (where output is measured as the number of railcars maintained), check processing by a bank (number of checks processed), or food services in a hospital (number of meals). In addition to measuring output, its quality must be easily observable. If not, cost center managers evaluated on costs have incentives to meet their targets by cutting quality. Lincoln Electric must have mechanisms to ensure that the assembled welders meet quality standards, which implies that quality must be reasonably easily observed.

There are various objectives used for evaluating cost center performance. Two are:

- Minimize costs for a given output.
- Maximize output for a given budget.

In Chapter 5, we indicated that to maximize profit, managers must (1) select the optimal output, Q^*, and (2) produce this output at minimum cost. Cost center managers focus primarily on the second of these activities—cost minimization. Their task is to choose the efficient input mix. For example, the manager of the railcar maintenance department at CSX is told to service 100 railcars per day of a fixed specification and quality. The manager is evaluated on meeting the production schedule and reducing the cost of servicing the 100 railcars. The quantity decision tends to be made by central management. The first potential evaluation criterion directly focuses on cost minimization. Minimizing costs given a prespecified quantity is consistent with profit maximization if Q^* is selected as the target output.

The second potential evaluation criterion, maximizing output for a given budget, provides incentives equivalent to the first criterion, as long as the specified budget is the minimal budget that is necessary for producing Q^*. For example, the manager has a fixed budget ($27,500 per week) and is evaluated based on the number of railcars serviced that meet quality specifications within the fixed budget. In either the first or second case, the manager has incentives to select the cost-minimizing input mix for producing Q^*.

For both objectives, the manager is constrained by either total output or budget. Effective implementation requires that central management chooses either the profit-maximizing output level or the correct budget for efficient production of this output level. But under both cost center arrangements, the cost center manager has incentives to reduce costs (or increase output) by lowering quality. Therefore, the quality of products manufactured in cost centers must be monitored.

Sometimes, cost center managers are evaluated based on minimizing average cost. In this case, the manager has the incentive to choose the output at which average costs are minimized and to produce this output efficiently. It is important to emphasize that profit maximization need not occur at the point where average costs are minimized. For example, suppose a cost center has some fixed costs and constant marginal costs. Then average unit costs continue to fall with increases in output. To illustrate, assume total costs are:

$$TC = \$300,000 + \$6\,Q \qquad (14.1)$$

Fixed costs are $300,000, and marginal costs are a constant $6 per unit. Given the equation for total costs, average costs are derived by dividing both sides of the equation by Q to get:

$$AC = \frac{TC}{Q} = \frac{\$300,000}{Q} + \$6 \qquad (14.2)$$

With constant marginal cost, as quantity produced increases, AC falls. In this situation, a cost center manager who is evaluated based on minimizing average unit costs will push to increase output even as inventories mount. Focusing on average costs can provide incentives for cost center managers to either overproduce or underproduce (depending on how the profit-maximizing output level compares to the quantity where average costs are minimized). In general, minimizing average unit cost is not the same as maximizing profits. Maximum profits occur where marginal costs and marginal revenues are equal, which need not be where average unit costs are lowest. In the simple example in Figure 14.1, profits are maximized by selling 6 units. However, minimum average cost occurs by producing 9 units.

Cost centers work most effectively if (1) the central managers have a good idea of the cost functions, can measure quantity, and can set the profit-maximizing output level and appropriate rewards; (2) the central managers can observe the quality of the cost center's output; and (3) the cost center manager has specific knowledge of the optimal input mix. Figure 14.2 (at the end of this section) summarizes the decision rights and measures used to evaluate performance of the various centers and when the particular center is used.

Quantity	Price	Revenue	Total Cost	Total Profits	Average Cost
1	$35	$ 35	$ 78	$–43	$78.0
2	33	66	83	–17	41.5
3	31	93	90	3	30.0
4	29	116	99	17	24.8
5	27	135	110	25	22.0
6	25	150	123	27	20.5
7	23	161	138	23	19.7
8	21	168	155	13	19.4
9	19	171	174	–3	19.3
10	17	170	195	–25	19.5

Figure 14.1   Example Demonstrating that Minimizing Average Cost Does Not Yield the Profit-Maximizing Level of Sales.

Minimizing average unit cost is not the same as maximizing profits. Maximum profits occur where marginal costs and marginal revenues are equal, which need not be where average unit costs are lowest. This simple example shows that profits are maximized by selling 6 units. However, minimum average cost occurs by producing 9 units.

Expense Centers

Cost centers are a common way of organizing manufacturing units. Activities such as personnel, accounting, patenting, public relations, and research and development, however, are often organized as expense centers. Like cost centers, expense centers are given fixed budgets and asked to maximize service/output. A major difference between expense centers and standard cost centers is that output is measured more subjectively than objectively. Thus, an expense center is a cost center that does not produce an easily measurable output.

The difficulty in observing the output of an expense center has several implications. The expense center is given a total budget and told to provide as much service as possible. Because the cost per unit of output is difficult to measure, the users of the center often are not charged for the center's services. Users tend to overconsume the services and expense centers are virtually always requesting larger budgets. The central corporate budget-granting organization has difficulty determining the budget that maximizes firm value, again because the output is not easily observed. Expense center managers usually derive larger benefits from managing larger staffs (empire building), which reinforces the tendency of these centers to grow faster than the firm as a whole. If the central budget office tries to cut the expense center's budget, the expense center manager might threaten to reduce those services that are most highly valued by users to enlist their help lobbying the budget-granting managers not to cut the budget.

There are a number of devices used to control the size of expense centers. One is to benchmark their budgets against those of similar-sized firms. Another is to reorganize the firm and place the expense center under the control of the largest user, who then has specialized knowledge of the expense center's value and the decision rights to set the expense center's budget. But this reorganized structure can have the disadvantage of causing other units to get too little of the service to the extent that the other users of the expense center are charged more than marginal cost. Without a charge-back system for the expense center's services, then outside users may be allocated none of its services.

Revenue Centers

Revenue centers are used to organize the marketing activities of selling, distributing, and sometimes servicing finished products received from manufacturing. The idea behind a revenue center is to compensate the manager for selling a set of products. For example, a regional sales office might be evaluated as a revenue center. The regional sales manager, Sue Koerner, is given a budget for personnel and expenses and has decision rights as to how to deploy the budget to maximize revenue. Sue has limited discretion in setting the selling price; typically, she must keep the price within a prescribed range.

Similar to a cost center, there are various objectives that can be used in evaluating revenue center performance. One objective is to maximize revenue for a given price (or quantity) and budget for personnel and expenses. That is, the revenue center is told the price of each product it sells and is given a fixed operating budget. This objective is consistent with profit maximization if central management chooses the correct price–quantity combination for each product sold by the revenue center.

Giving Sue decision rights over product pricing or quantity and then evaluating her based on maximizing total revenue is usually inconsistent with profit maximization. To maximize revenue, Sue goes to the point where marginal revenue equals zero—not to where it equals marginal cost. Since marginal cost usually is greater than zero, Sue's firm loses money on units sold at prices below marginal cost.

Revenue centers work best if (1) the central managers have the knowledge to select the correct price–quantity combination, (2) the central managers have the knowledge to select the optimal product mix (otherwise, the salesperson shifts effort toward selling higher-revenue-generating products rather than selling products that generate higher profits), and (3) the sales managers have specialized knowledge of the demand curves of the customers in their sales district.

Profit Centers

Profit centers are often composed of several cost, and possibly expense and revenue, centers. Profit center managers are given decision rights for input mix, product mix, and selling prices (or output quantities) given a fixed capital budget. Profit centers are set up when the knowledge required to make the product mix, quantity, pricing, and quality decisions is specific to the division and costly to transfer.

Managers rely on their internal accounting systems to provide performance measures for profit centers. Profit centers usually are evaluated on the difference between actual and budgeted accounting profits for the division. While measuring the profits of profit centers is seemingly straightforward, two complications often consume managers' attention: how to price transfers of goods and services between business units (transfer pricing) and which (if any) corporate overhead costs to allocate to business units. Managers in every firm are constantly debating these two issues. We examine the transfer-pricing problem in the next section.

Motivating individual profit centers to maximize profits will not generally maximize profits for the firm as a whole when there are interdependencies among business units. For example, individual units focusing on their own profits generally ignore how their actions affect the sales and costs of other units.[3] One division can free-ride on another

---

[3]Conceptually, other units could offer money to take these effects into account. However, in the presence of transaction costs, these offers are likely to be limited.

division's quality reputation, thereby reaping short-run gains at the expense of the other division. For example, Chevrolet and Buick are two profit centers in General Motors. Suppose Chevrolet, in pursuit of maximizing its profits, decides to raise the quality of its cars. This can affect consumers' perceptions of the average quality of all General Motor cars—including Buick's perceived quality. An enhanced reputation for all General Motors cars helps Buick. But if Chevrolet does not receive any credit for Buick profits, it will tend to ignore the positive externality it generates for Buick and will tend to underinvest in quality enhancements. To help managers internalize both the positive and the negative externalities their actions impose on other profit center managers, firms often base incentive compensation not just on the manager's own profit center profits but also on a group of related profit centers' profits and/or firmwide profits. Unless the entire firm makes a certain profit target, no individual profit center manager earns a bonus.

Investment Centers

Investment centers are similar to profit centers. However, they have additional decision rights for capital expenditures and are evaluated on measures such as return on investment. Investment centers are most useful where the manager of the unit has specific knowledge about investment opportunities as well as information relevant to making operating decisions for the unit.

Investment centers are often composed of several profit centers. They have all the decision rights of cost and profit centers, as well as the decision rights over the amount of capital to be invested. For example, suppose the consumer electronics group of an electronics firm is comprised of three profit centers: the television division, the VCR division, and the stereo division. Consumer electronics has decision rights over the amount of capital invested in the group and is evaluated based on the return on the capital invested. There are two commonly used measures of performance for investment centers: return on investment and residual income.

Accounting ROI

Return on investment (ROI) is the most commonly used investment center performance measure. ROI is the ratio of accounting net income generated by the investment center divided by total assets invested in the investment center. It has intuitive appeal because ROI can be compared to external market-based yields to provide a benchmark for a division's performance. However, using ROI creates problems. ROI is not a measure of the division's economic rate of return because accounting income (the numerator) is not a measure of economic profit and "investment" (the denominator) is not the market value of the division's investment. Economic profit is the change in value over the period. Accounting rules dictate that accounting net income excludes some value increases and includes some value declines. For example, accounting net income excludes land value appreciation until the land is sold but includes market value declines even though the land has not been sold. Accounting net income tends to be conservative—recognize all losses and defer all gains. Also, accounting depreciation, which is deducted from accounting profits, does not necessarily reflect the change in the value of fixed assets.

Managers have incentives to reject profitable projects with ROIs below the mean ROI for the division because accepting these projects lowers the division's ROI. For example, suppose the division has an average ROI of 19 percent, which is above its 15 percent cost of capital.[4] A new investment project that is 10 percent the size of the existing division investment is available. Its ROI is 16 percent, which also is above its cost of capital of 15 percent; thus, taking this project would increase firm value. But if this project is accepted, the division's ROI falls to 18.7 percent ($.90 \times 19\% + .10 \times 16\%$). If the division is evaluated based on increasing ROI, management will reject the project, even though its returns exceed the opportunity cost of capital.

Riskier projects require a higher cost of capital to compensate investors for bearing additional risk. If managers are rewarded solely for increasing their ROI without being charged for any additional risk imposed on the firm, they can have incentives to plunge the firm into risky projects. Finally, a manager with a short time horizon who is evaluated based on ROI would prefer projects that boost ROI in immediate years even if they are unprofitable projects (the horizon problem).

Accounting Residual Income

To overcome some of the incentive deficiencies of ROI, such as divesting projects with ROIs above their cost of capital but below the division's average ROI, some firms use *residual income* to evaluate performance.[5] Residual income measures divisional performance by subtracting the opportunity cost of capital employed from division profits. For example, suppose a division has profits of $20 million and investment (total assets) of $100 million. Furthermore, this division has a required cost of capital of 15 percent. Its ROI is 20 percent, which is in excess of its opportunity cost of capital (15 percent). Residual income is $5 million ($20M − 15% × 100M). Under the residual income approach, divesting a project with an ROI of less than 20 percent but above 15 percent lowers residual income, although it raises average ROI.

Nonetheless, residual income has its own problems. Residual income is an absolute number; thus, larger divisions typically have larger residual incomes than smaller divisions. This makes relative performance-evaluation comparisons across investment centers of different sizes more difficult. To implement residual income measures requires that senior managers estimate the opportunity cost of capital for each division. Each division will have a different required cost of capital to allow more precise performance evaluations by controlling for risk differences. However, the risk adjustments also potentially lead to greater influence costs as divisional managers lobby to lower their required capital costs.

Like ROI, residual income measures performance over a single year. It does not measure the impact of actions taken today on firm value in the future. For example, by cutting maintenance, current period residual income (and ROI) is increased, but future cash flow and hence firm value can be jeopardized.

Figure 14.2 summarizes our discussion of the various types of subunits of the firm. Notice that the performance-evaluation measure and decision-right assignment are in balance. The decision rights assigned to the center and the performance measures are matched. Although not explicit in this figure, to ensure that our three-legged stool remains balanced, we assume that performance rewards are tied to the performance evaluations. Also note the linkage between decision rights assigned to each center and the location of the knowledge. For example, if a center does not have knowledge of customer demand curves, it does not have decision rights for pricing and hence is evaluated as a cost center.

---

[4]Cost of capital is the rate of return the firm must pay the market to raise capital. If the firm can raise money at 15 percent and invest in projects earning 16 percent, the value of the firm increases.

[5]For a more detailed discussion of residual income, see D. Solomons (1968), *Divisional Performance: Measurement and Control* (Richard D. Irwin: Burr Ridge, IL).

	Decision Rights	Performance Measures	Typically Used When
Cost Center	Input mix (labor, material, supplies)	Minimize total cost for a fixed output Maximize output for a fixed budget	Central manager can measure output, knows the cost functions, and can set the optimal quantity and appropriate rewards. Central manager can observe the quality of the cost center's output. Cost center manager has knowledge of the optimal input mix.
Expense Center	Input mix (labor, material, supplies)	Minimize total cost for a fixed level of services Maximize service for a fixed budget	Output is difficult to observe and measure.
Revenue Center	Input mix (labor, material, supplies)	Maximize revenues for a given price (or quantity) and operating budget	Central manager has the knowledge to select the optimal product mix. Central manager has the knowledge to select the correct price or quantity. Revenue center managers have knowledge of the demand curves of the customers in their sales district.
Profit Center	Input mix Product mix Selling prices (or output quantities)	Actual profits Actual profits compared to budgeted profits	Profit center manager has the knowledge to select the correct price/quantity. Profit center manager has the knowledge to select the optimal product mix.
Investment Center	Input mix Product mix Selling prices (or output quantities) Capital invested in center	Return on investment Residual income EVA	Investment center manager has the knowledge to select the correct price/quantity. Investment center manager has the knowledge to select the optimal product mix. Investment center manager has knowledge about investment opportunities.

Figure 14.2   Summary of Cost, Expense, Revenue, Profit, and Investment Centers

Decision rights and performance measures are balanced across the various subunits of the organization.

EVA Is Often Linked to a Change in the Compensation Scheme

At the beginning of this chapter, CSX's use of EVA (economic value added) was described as a performance measurement scheme that is being widely heralded and adopted by such companies as AT&T, Briggs & Stratton, Coca-Cola, Equifax, and Quaker Oats. EVA is a variant of residual income. The formula for EVA is:

$$\text{EVA} = \text{Adjusted accounting earnings} - (\text{Weighted average cost of capital} \times \text{Total capital})$$

This is the same formula as residual income. The only difference is that the variables used in computing EVA are more carefully measured than normally was done in the past. Instead of using the same accounting procedures that are used in reporting to shareholders, different accounting procedures are used to arrive at "adjusted accounting earnings." For example, standard U.S. accounting rules require that the entire amount spent on research and development each year be deducted from earnings. This creates incentives for managers with a short time horizon to cut R&D spending. One adjustment to accounting earnings is to add back R&D spending and treat it as an asset to be depreciated, usually over five years. Total capital, in the above formula, consists of all the firm's assets, including the amount invested in R&D and other adjustments made to earnings.

Another variable used in calculating EVA is the weighted average cost of capital, which includes the cost of equity and the cost of debt. The cost of equity is the price appreciation and dividends the shareholders could have earned in a portfolio of companies of similar risk. This is the opportunity cost the shareholders bear by buying the company's stock. The cost of debt is the current market yield on debt of similar risk. The costs of debt and equity are weighted by the relative amounts of debt and equity. Suppose the cost of equity is 18 percent, the cost of debt is 10 percent, and the firm's capital structure is 40 percent debt and 60 percent equity. Then, the weighted average cost of capital is 14.8% ($0.60 \times 18\% + 0.40 \times 10\%$).*

EVA, like residual income, measures the total return after deducting the cost of all capital employed by the firm. It estimates the economic profits of the firm in the period (usually a year). Many of the firms adopting EVA to measure divisional performance did so as part of a corporate reorganization. AT&T was organized as a huge corporate monolith only providing balance sheets for a few large groups such as long-distance services. In 1992, AT&T reorganized into investment centers, each resembling an independent company. The long-distance service function now has 40 units selling 800 service, telemarketing, and public telephones. Each is measured using EVA. Besides decentralizing decision rights and adopting EVA as the performance measure, firms also change the third leg of the three-legged stool, the reward system. Manager bonuses are based on EVA.

Besides introducing EVA in 1988, CSX also changed its management compensation plan. In 1991, CSX introduced a stock incentive program whereby 160 managers accepted a plan to purchase CSX stock at the market price of $48. They paid 5 percent in cash, and CSX loaned them the balance at 7.9 percent interest. If the stock price is above $69 per share in July 1994, CSX forgives the loan's interest and 25 percent of the principal. If the stock is below $69, the managers must pay all the interest and principal. With the stock selling at about $77 at the end of July 1994, the managers made a substantial profit—but so did the shareholders.

Notice that besides linking pay to the performance measure, EVA, CSX also changed the performance reward system.

---

* EVA is calculated on an after-tax basis. In particular, adjusted accounting earnings are net of income taxes and the weighted average cost of capital is computed as follows. The after-tax cost of debt is computed using 1 minus the marginal corporate tax rate times the market yield on debt of similar risk. For example, suppose the market yield on equivalent debt is 15 percent and the marginal corporate tax rate is 38 percent. The after-tax cost of debt is 9.3 percent ($15\% \times [1-0.38]$). If the cost of equity is 20 percent and the proportions of debt and equity are the same, the after-tax weighted average cost of capital is 14.65 percent ($0.50 \times 9.3\% + 0.50 \times 20\%$).

Sources: B. Stewart (1991), *The Quest for Value* (Harper Business); and S. Tully (1993), "The Real Key to Creating Wealth," *Fortune* (September 20), 38–50.

Transfer Pricing

As discussed above, firms organize into business units. Whenever business units transfer goods or services among themselves, measuring their performance requires that a *transfer price* be established for the goods and services exchanged. For example, suppose a large chemical company is organized into profit centers. Besides producing for and selling to outside customers, these profit centers also sell intermediate products to other profit centers within the company. In order to measure the performance of these profit centers, each of these internal transactions requires a transfer price. The purchasing division pays the transfer price, and the producing division receives the transfer price.

Some executives do not view the transfer-pricing problem as important from the overall firm's perspective. They think that changing transfer-pricing methods merely shifts income among divisions and that, except for relative performance evaluation, little else is affected. But this is a mistake: *The choice of transfer-pricing method does not merely reallocate total company profits among business units—it affects the firm's total profits.* Think of the firm's total profit as a pie. Choice among transfer-pricing methods not only changes how the pie is divided among the business units but also the size of the pie to be divided.

Managers make investment, purchasing, and production decisions based on the transfer prices they face. If these transfer prices do not accurately reflect the value of the resources from the firm's perspective, the managers will make inappropriate decisions and the value of the firm will be reduced. For example, if the opportunity cost to the firm of producing an intermediate chemical is $20 per kilogram but the transfer price is $30, the purchasing division will consume too little of the chemical and total firm profits will be reduced. Purchasing-unit managers will have the incentive to shift away from using the chemical to other inputs that in reality are more expensive for the firm. Also, because transfer prices affect the performance evaluations of unit managers, incorrect transfer prices can result in inappropriate promotion and retention decisions.

Transfer prices are much more prevalent in organizations than many managers realize. Firms often have extensive charge-back schemes for internal service departments. Consider the charges that the advertising department receives from the maintenance department for janitorial service, or the monthly charge for telephones, security services, data processing, and legal and personnel services. Most firms charge inside users for these internally provided services. These charge-back schemes are internal transfer prices. Such charge-back systems also exist in hospitals, universities, and other non-profit organizations.

Because the use of transfer prices (including charge-back systems) is widespread in many firms and because transfer pricing affects performance evaluation and hence the rewards managers receive, fighting over the transfer price between divisions is inevitable. Transfer pricing is a continuing source of tension within firms. It is not uncommon for managers in many multidivisional firms to be involved in a succession of transfer-pricing disputes over the course of their careers.

An additional factor in determining an optimal transfer price is taxes. If the producing and purchasing divisions are in different countries with different tax rates, then taxes affect the opportunity cost of the product and thus the optimal transfer price. The producing division pays income taxes on the difference between its costs and what it receives for each unit, which is determined by the transfer price. In general, to minimize the sum of the two taxes, the firm should set the transfer price so as to allocate as much of the profit as possible to the division in the country with the lower tax rate.[6] To simplify the analysis, this section focuses on the organizational economics of transfer pricing and ignores these important tax issues.

Economics of Transfer Pricing

The transfer-pricing rule is quite simple to state: The optimal transfer price for a product or service is its opportunity cost; that is, it is the value forgone by not using the product transferred in its next best alternative use. Unfortunately, as we will see, this simple-to-state rule is often difficult to implement in practice.

Transfer Pricing with Costless Information

To illustrate the concept of opportunity cost, suppose the firm has two profit centers, manufacturing and distribution, and senior management is considering making a product in manufacturing and transferring it to distribution. Assume also that manufacturing's marginal cost of production is $3 per unit, and that it has excess capacity. If the product is transferred to distribution, distribution can sell it and receive $5 for each unit, net of its own marginal cost. Also, everyone knows each division's cost and revenue data.

If the unit is not manufactured, the firm saves $3 in manufacturing costs but forgoes $5 in revenue, for a net loss of $2. If the unit is manufactured and transferred, the firm forgoes $3 (marginal cost to produce) and receives $5, for a net receipt of $2. The better alternative is to transfer the unit. The resources forgone by transferring it from manufacturing to distribution—and hence the opportunity cost of such a transfer—are $3 per unit, the same as manufacturing's marginal cost of production.

As this example is meant to suggest, the marginal cost of producing the unit is often its opportunity cost. But this is not always the case. Sometimes, the opportunity cost is the marginal revenue of selling the intermediate good externally. For example, suppose manufacturing can produce one unit for $3, and can either transfer that unit to distribution or sell it for $4 outside the firm—but, because of limited capacity, it cannot do both. In this case, by having manufacturing transfer the unit to distribution, the firm forgoes selling the intermediate good in the market. And thus, even though the marginal cost of producing the unit is $3, the opportunity cost of making the transfer is $4.

Manufacturing will produce to the point where the marginal cost of the last unit equals the transfer price. Likewise, distribution will buy units from manufacturing as long as distribution's net receipts just cover the transfer price. When opportunity cost is used to set the transfer price, and both manufacturing and distribution are maximizing their respective profits, total firm profits are maximized—assuming there are no interdependencies between the business units (a case we consider later). Thus, in this simple example, the transfer price represents the marginal cost to distribution. If the transfer price is too high or too low relative to opportunity cost, distribution purchases too few or too many units and firm profits are not maximized.

---

[6]International tax treaties and local regulation constrain the transfer-pricing methods firms can use for tax purposes. M. Scholes and M. Wolfson (1992), *Taxes and Business Strategy* (Prentice Hall: Englewood Cliffs, NJ).

Transfer Pricing with Asymmetric Information

The preceding discussion assumes that everyone knows manufacturing's marginal production cost is $3, the intermediate product has an external price of $4, distribution's marginal revenue is $5, and whether manufacturing has excess capacity or not. If all this knowledge is readily available, there would be no reason to decentralize decision making in the organization. Central management has the knowledge to make the decision and could retain the decision rights or, if the decision rights were delegated, monitor the process at low cost. In reality, much of the information is not readily available to central management. Especially in large, multidivisional firms, such knowledge generally resides at lower levels of the firm where it is private knowledge, costly to either transfer or verify by senior management. In some circumstances, lower-level managers have incentives to distort the information they pass up to senior managers. To illustrate these incentives, we consider a firm with market power (see Chapter 6).

Consider the situation where Burt Brown, the manager of manufacturing, is the only person with knowledge of his division's marginal costs, and assume that Burt seeks to maximize the profits of his division. Even if distribution is allowed to purchase the product on the outside, if manufacturing has market power in setting the transfer price, it will attempt to set the price above marginal cost to increase its *measured* profits. When this happens, the firm manufactures and sells too few units of the product. This is analogous to the social loss from monopoly described in Chapter 6. The manufacturing division, possessing what amounts to monopoly rights in information, behaves like a monopolist. And just as monopolists earn "monopoly profits" by raising prices and restricting output below the socially optimal level, manufacturing's higher profits lead to lower-than-optimal production levels and reduced total firm profits.

This problem can be illustrated by example. For simplicity, consider a firm that produces one product with the following demand:

$$P = 110 - 5Q \tag{14.3}$$

Assume the product is produced at a constant marginal cost of $10. Profit maximization occurs by setting marginal revenue = marginal cost. At this condition, $Q^* = 10$ and $P^* = 60$. Firm profits are $500 ($60 \times 10 - 10×10). Figure 14.3 depicts this situation.

Assume manufacturing produces the good at MC = 10 and transfers it to distribution at a transfer price, P_t. Suppose the only cost to the distribution division is the transfer price. (For simplicity, additional distribution costs are equal to zero.)

Distribution's demand curve for the product is the firm's demand curve. How many units of the good will the manager of this unit want to buy at each possible transfer price? Note that distribution's marginal cost is the transfer price $MC_d = P_t$. Distribution maximizes division profit by setting $MC_d = MR_d$. Hence, in this case, the firm's marginal revenue curve represents distribution's demand for the good and thus is the derived demand curve facing manufacturing: $P_t = 110 - 10Q$ (the marginal revenue curve in Figure 14.3).

Next, assume that manufacturing sets the transfer price. It has monopoly power, and because of costly information, senior management cannot monitor the decision. What price will manufacturing set and what quantity of the good will be produced? The manager of manufacturing sets marginal cost equal to marginal revenue: $MC_m = MR_m$. The marginal cost = 10. As discussed above, manufacturing faces a *derived demand curve* equal to the marginal revenue curve for the firm: $P_t = 110 - 10Q$. The marginal revenue for the manufacturing division is, therefore, $P_t = 110 - 20Q$. Profit maximization for manufacturing will involve setting the transfer price at $60 and selling five units of the good. (See the left panel in Figure 14.4.) Facing a transfer price of $60, distribution will

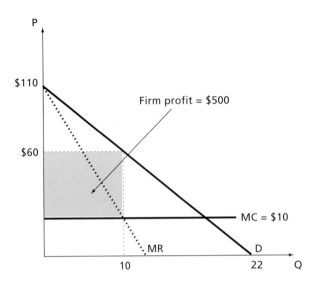

Figure 14.3   Profit-Maximizing Price

A firm faces the following demand curve: $P = 110 - 5Q$. The product is produced at a constant marginal cost of $10. Profit maximization occurs by setting marginal revenue = marginal cost. At this condition, $Q^* = 10$ and $P^* = 60$. Firm profits are $500 ($60 × 10 - $10 × 10).

in turn sell the five units to the external market at a price of $85 (right panel in Figure 14.4). Total firm profits are $375 (5 × $85 − 5 × $10), which are lower than at the profit-maximizing output of 10 units ($500). Manufacturing has profits of $250, while distribution has profits of $125. Both divisions are making profits, but total firm profits are lower in Figure 14.4 than in Figure 14.3.

The basic problem is that distribution, facing a transfer price of $60, is over-estimating the *opportunity* cost to the firm of producing extra units of the good ($10). Hence, from the firm's standpoint, distribution stops short of the optimal quantity to be sold to the external market. The transfer price that ensures firm profit maximization in this example is the marginal production cost of the unit. Note, however, that manufacturing does not want to transfer at that price because it makes a lower profit ($0 in this example).

The above discussion thus illustrates the basic incentive problems associated with internal transfers when information is privately held by divisional managers. Opportunity cost is the transfer price that maximizes firm value. But because business-unit managers tend to have better knowledge of opportunity costs than senior management, and because transfer prices are typically used in performance evaluation and in setting managerial rewards, divisional managers have incentives to distort information to influence the transfer price.

Complicating matters further, getting the information necessary to calculate opportunity costs is especially difficult for senior management because opportunity costs depend on the firm's next best alternative use of the good or service. Central management is likely to know less about the next best use of a product, and the resources used to make the product, than the manager of the division that produces it. Moreover, the next best alternative will change as the firm's business opportunities change. For example, sometimes the firm has excess capacity and manufacturing can sell the good both internally

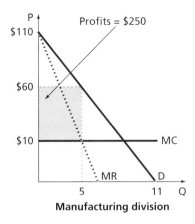

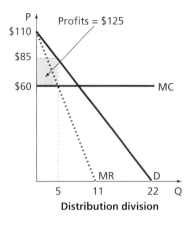

Figure 14.4 Decentralized Firm

In the decentralized firm, manufacturing produces the good at MC = 10 and transfers it to distribution at a transfer price, P_t. Distribution's demand curve for the product is the firm's demand curve. Distribution's marginal cost is the transfer price $MC_d = P_t$. Distribution maximizes profit (for the unit) by setting $MC_d = MR_d$. The firm's marginal revenue curve represents distribution's demand for the good and is, therefore, the demand curve facing manufacturing: $P_t =$ 110 − 10Q. The manager of manufacturing sets marginal cost equal to marginal revenue: $MC_m = MR_m$. The marginal cost = 10. The marginal revenue for the manufacturing division is $P_t =$ 110 − 20Q. Profit maximization for manufacturing will involve setting the transfer price at $60 and selling five units of the good (see the left panel). Facing a transfer price of $60, distribution will in turn sell the five units to the external market at a price of $85 (right panel). Total firm profits are $375 (5 × $85 − 5 × $10), which are lower than at the firm profit-maximizing output of 10 units ($500). Manufacturing has profits of $250, while distribution has profits of $125.

and externally. At other times, the firm has only enough current capacity to produce for either the inside or outside user. This specialized knowledge of the alternatives is known primarily by the division managers.

Problems arise if either distribution or manufacturing has the decision rights to set the price of the goods or services transferred and the other division cannot purchase or sell outside. Manufacturing will set a price above opportunity cost to capture some monopoly profits, and distribution will purchase fewer units than if the correct (lower) transfer price is set. But, if given the decision rights to determine the price, distribution will set a transfer price below the opportunity cost and manufacturing will supply too few units. Again, the number of units transferred is below the profit-maximizing level. If central management knows the opportunity cost, it doesn't have to decentralize decision making to the profit centers and can dictate both price and quantity decisions.

The economics of transfer pricing is best summarized by the following:

The economist's first instinct is to set the transfer price equal to marginal cost. But it may be difficult to find out marginal cost. As a practical matter, marginal cost information is rarely known to anybody in the firm, because it depends on opportunity costs that vary with capacity use. And even if marginal cost information were available, there is no guarantee that it would be revealed in a truthful fashion for the purpose of determining an optimal transfer price.[7]

---

[7]B. Holmstrom and J. Tirole (1991), "Transfer Pricing and Organizational Form," *Journal of Law, Economics, and Organizations* 7, 201–228.

The Successive Monopoly Case

A basic principle in economics says that to maximize the value of the firm, a monopoly price should be charged only once while all other transfers are charged at marginal cost. To illustrate, suppose a paper box company has both a patented technology for making boxes and a patented box design. The production technology belongs to the manufacturing division and the unique box design is sold by the distribution division. Distribution buys the boxes from manufacturing, and both divisions are run as profit centers. Further assume that manufacturing has enough capacity to sell both internally and externally. Thus, the opportunity cost of manufacturing's transfer is its marginal production cost.

Transfer-pricing theory implies that the profit-maximizing solution in this case is to set the price to external customers at the price where the firm's marginal revenue is equal to the combined marginal costs of manufacturing and distribution. This result obtains if distribution buys the boxes from manufacturing at marginal cost. In this case, to maximize its own profits, distribution will set the external price at the point where the marginal revenue from customers equals the sum of distribution's own marginal cost and the transfer price, which is manufacturing's marginal cost.

In this case, however, if the transfer price is marginal cost (and assuming marginal cost is less than or equal to average cost), manufacturing reports no profit. If manufacturing tries to report a profit by charging distribution a transfer price above marginal cost, firm profits are lower than in the original case. For, if manufacturing is able to set the transfer price above marginal cost, then when distribution sets the final price to the customer, it will equate marginal revenue to a now higher marginal cost—that is, its own marginal cost plus the transfer price. To maximize its own profits, distribution will thus set the price "too high," buy fewer units from manufacturing, and hence fewer units will be sold than under the profit-maximizing case above.

The transfer-pricing rule thus holds that when two divisions inside the same firm have market power (that is, they are able to charge prices above long-run marginal cost), both divisions should not be allowed to charge prices above their own costs. When there are such successive monopolies within firms, only one division should be permitted to charge a price above cost. If monopoly prices are charged at both stages of the production process, firm profits will not be maximized.

Common Transfer-Pricing Methods

The correct transfer price, then, is opportunity cost. But, we also have noted, determining opportunity costs is expensive, in part because the information necessary to calculate such costs resides with operating managers who have incentives to distort it. To address this problem, companies sometimes commission special studies of the firm's cost structure by outside experts. Such studies, however, are not only costly, but their findings become outdated whenever the firm's business opportunities change. On the other hand, if senior management simply vests the right to set the transfer price with either manufacturing or distribution, prices are likely to be set too high or too low, resulting in too few units transferred and firm profits lower than they could be.

Because determining opportunity costs is itself an expensive undertaking, managers resort to various lower-cost approximations. There are at least four different ways that firms can approximate the opportunity cost of the units transferred: market price, marginal production cost, full cost, and negotiated pricing. As discussed below, each of these four methods is better than the others in some situations but not in others. For example, if the divisions operate in different countries with different tax rates, then the choice of method will be driven in part by tax considerations. If manufacturing faces lower tax rates than distribution, full-cost prices will allocate more of the profit to the lower-taxed division than marginal-cost prices. Our aim in the rest of this section is to set forth the advantages and disadvantages of each so that managers can select the best transfer-pricing method for their particular situation.

Market-Based Transfer Prices

The standard transfer-pricing rule offered by most textbooks is this: Given a competitive external market for the good, the product should be transferred at the external market price. If manufacturing cannot make a long-run profit at the external price, then the company is better off not producing internally and instead should purchase in the external market. If the purchasing division cannot make a long-run profit at the external price, then the company is better off not processing the intermediate product and instead should sell in the external market.

In short, the use of market-based transfer prices is often assumed to produce the correct make-versus-buy decisions. In many situations, however, market price will not provide an accurate reflection of opportunity cost. If both the firm and the market are making the intermediate good, the question arises, *Can both survive in the long run?* If one can produce the good at a lower, long-run average cost than the other, the high-cost producer should not be producing the intermediate product.

It is important to keep in mind, however, that transactions generally take place inside rather than outside firms whenever the cost of repetitive internal contracting is cheaper than outsourcing.[8] For example, production of different kinds of goods tends to take place inside the same firm when there are important interdependencies or synergies among those products. And, of course, the more valuable are such synergies, the more likely is the firm to continue producing internally.[9]

At the same time, however—and this is what makes the issue of transfer pricing so difficult—in circumstances where the firm is more likely to produce a good internally, the external market price is less likely to provide an accurate reflection of the opportunity cost of internal production. For example, it is often the case that an intermediate good is either not being produced by other firms or that the good produced externally is not identical to the good produced internally. In one case, there is no market price; in the other, the market price will often be an unreliable guide to opportunity cost. And, even when there are virtually identical "cheaper" external products, producing internally can still make sense insofar as it provides greater quality control, timeliness of supply, or protection of proprietary information. When these factors are included in the analysis, the external market may no longer be "cheaper."

In such cases, use of the market price as the transfer price may understate the profitability of the product and its contribution to the value of the firm.[10] Suppose, for example, an intermediate product can be purchased (but not sold) externally for $3 per unit. Synergies such as high transaction costs of using the market make it beneficial to

[8]Advantages to internal transactions include the elimination of credit risk, lower marketing costs, and learning from production. Chapter 3 and R. Coase (1937), "The Nature of the Firm," *Economica* 4, 386–405. For a summary of the arguments for the types of costs that are lowered by firms, see R. Watts (1992), "Accounting Choice Theory and Market-Based Research in Accounting," *British Accounting Journal* 24, 242–246. These arguments include economies of scale in contracting, team production and monitoring, postcontractual opportunism, and knowledge costs. Chapter 15 deals with these topics.

[9]Interdependence or synergies that cause production to occur inside the firm are classic economic externalities. If interdependencies in production or demand functions exist, the market price does not capture these interdependencies. The same occurs inside the firm and causes the external price to mismeasure the opportunity cost of one more unit being transferrred.

[10]This point has been recognized by others. As one notes, "observed market prices cannot directly guide the owner of the input to perform in the same manner as if every activity he performs were measured and priced." In S. Cheung (1983), "The Contractual Nature of the Firm," *Journal of Law & Economics* 26 (April), 5. R. Ball (1989), "The Firm as a Specialist Contracting Intermediary: Applications to Accounting and Auditing," working paper (University of Rochester: Rochester, NY).

produce the item internally. Internal production avoids the costs of writing and enforcing contracts. Suppose there are $.50 worth of synergies, so that the correct transfer price is $2.50 in the sense that $2.50 is the opportunity cost to the firm. But, if the market price of $3.00 is used as the transfer price, distribution will purchase fewer units than if $2.50 was used, and the value of the firm will not be maximized.

Marginal-Cost Transfer Prices

If there is no external market for the intermediate good or if large synergies among business units cause the market price to be an inaccurate measure of opportunity cost, then marginal production cost may be the most effective alternative transfer price. As we saw earlier, marginal cost represents the value of the resources forgone to produce the last unit.

As with other transfer-pricing methods, however, there are problems with marginal production cost as a measure of opportunity cost. One is that manufacturing does not necessarily recover its fixed costs. If all manufacturing's output is transferred internally and marginal cost is below its average total cost, manufacturing's fixed costs are not recovered. Thus, manufacturing appears to be losing money.[11]

One variation of marginal-cost transfer pricing is to price all transfers at marginal cost while also charging distribution a fixed fee for these services. Distribution pays marginal cost for the additional units and buys the number of units that maximize firm profits. Unlike straight marginal-cost pricing, this variation allows manufacturing to cover its full cost and earn a profit. The fixed fee represents the rights by distribution to acquire the product at marginal cost, and it is set to cover manufacturing's fixed cost plus a return on equity.

Another problem with marginal-cost transfer pricing occurs in situations where the marginal cost per unit is not constant as volume changes. Suppose the marginal cost per unit increases as volume expands (say, a night shift at higher wages per hour is added). If marginal cost is greater than average cost and all users are charged the higher marginal cost, the total paid by all the users is greater than the total cost of the firm. Users who did not expand their volume will still see their costs increase. In such cases, conflicts are likely within the firm over the appropriate measure of marginal cost and whether all users should pay marginal cost or just those users who expanded output, thereby prompting the addition of the night shift.

A similar problem arises when manufacturing approaches capacity. To illustrate the problem, let's assume manufacturing is considering a $2.5 million outlay to add more capacity. These capacity additions costs of $2.5 million are variable in the long run but become short-run fixed costs (depreciation and higher utilities and maintenance). Thus, conflicts arise between manufacturing and distribution as to whether these additional capacity costs should be included in the transfer price or not. What makes such conflicts so difficult to resolve is that there is no indisputably objective method for calculating marginal costs. They are not reported in *The Wall Street Journal*. Instead, they have to be estimated, generally as "variable costs," from accounting records. While most of the components of marginal cost are easily observed, such as the cost of direct labor and direct material, some components are difficult to estimate. For example, it is not easy to estimate the additional costs the purchasing department bears when additional units are manufactured.

---

[11]Of course, if central management knows the magnitude of the fixed costs, they can budget for this loss. But, once again, if central management knows the magnitude of the fixed costs, then it knows marginal cost, and thus there is little reason to have a separate business unit and transfer-pricing system in the first place.

Marginal-cost transfer pricing also creates incentives for manufacturing to distort marginal cost upward, perhaps by misstating some fixed costs as variable. For example, how much of the electricity bill is fixed and how much is variable? Since these classifications are to some extent arbitrary, resources are wasted as managers in manufacturing and distribution debate various cost terms and their applications—and as senior managers are forced to spend time arbitrating such disputes.

Moreover, under marginal-cost transfer pricing, manufacturing even has the incentive to convert a dollar of fixed costs into more than a dollar of marginal costs—for example, by using high-priced outsourcing of parts instead of cheaper internal manufacturing—even though this clearly reduces the value of the firm. For manufacturing, the use of outsourcing can remove the burden of any fixed costs while distribution, as well as the firm as a whole, bears the extra cost for such decisions.

Full-Cost Transfer Prices

Because of the information-and-incentive problem described above, simple, objective, hard-to-change transfer-price rules can lead to higher firm value than transfer-pricing rules that give one manager discretion over the transfer price. Objective transfer-pricing rules such as those based on full accounting cost are often adopted primarily to avoid wasteful disputes over measuring marginal costs. Since full cost is the sum of fixed and variable cost, full cost cannot be changed simply by reclassifying a fixed cost as a variable cost.

The problem, however, is that full-cost transfer pricing causes distribution to purchase too few units. Full-cost accounting generally overstates the opportunity cost to the firm of producing and transferring one more unit internally. And so distribution will usually buy too few units internally. Full cost also allows manufacturing to transfer all of its inefficiencies to distribution. Thus, manufacturing has little incentive to be efficient under a full-cost transfer-price rule.[12]

Despite all these problems, however, full-cost transfer pricing is quite common. In various surveys of corporate practice, full-cost transfer prices are used 40 to 50 percent of the time.[13] In most cases, moreover, the definition of full cost includes both direct materials and labor as well as a charge for overhead.

One likely reason for the popularity of full-cost transfer prices is their ability to deal with the problem of changes in capacity. As a plant begins to reach capacity, opportunity cost is likely to rise because of congestion and the cost of alternative uses of now-scarce capacity. Hence, opportunity cost is likely to be higher than direct materials and labor costs. In this case, full cost might be a closer approximation to opportunity cost than just the cost of materials and labor.

Perhaps the most important benefit of full-cost transfer pricing, however, is its simplicity and hence its low cost of implementation. Because of its simplicity and objectivity, full-cost transfer pricing reduces influence costs. That is, because operating managers have much less ability to manipulate full-cost than marginal-cost calculations,

---

[12]To be sure, marginal-cost transfer prices also allow the selling division to export some of its inefficiencies to the purchasing division, but the problem is not as pronounced as under full cost. Nevertheless, the problem of exporting inefficiencies to the buying division through cost-based transfer prices is reduced if the purchasing division can purchase externally as well as from the selling division. This forces the selling division to remain competitive.

[13]J. Zimmerman (1995), *Accounting for Decision Making and Control* (Richard D. Irwin: Burr Ridge, IL), Chapter 4.

senior management does not have to arbitrate disputes over what costs are to be included in calculating the transfer price. Nevertheless, managers should consider carefully whether full-cost pricing is optimal for their particular situation. If the opportunity cost is substantially different than full cost, the firm's forgone profits can be significant.

Negotiated Transfer Prices

Transfer prices can be set by negotiation between manufacturing and distribution. This method can result in transfer prices that approximate opportunity cost because manufacturing will not agree to a price that is below its opportunity cost and distribution will not pay a price that is above what it can buy the product for elsewhere.

In this case, the two divisions have the incentive to set the number of units so as to maximize the combined profits of the two divisions. Once the value-maximizing number of units is agreed on, the transfer price determines how the total profits are divided between the two divisions. In terms of Figure 14.3, if the two divisions negotiate over both price and quantity, they have the joint incentive to set Q=10 because this maximizes the total profit to be split, $500. If the two divisions just negotiate over price, there is no guarantee they will arrive at the transfer price that maximizes firm value.

But while negotiation is a fairly common method, it too has drawbacks. It is time-consuming and can produce conflicts among divisions. Divisional performance measurement becomes sensitive to the relative negotiating skills of the two division managers. Moreover, if the two divisions negotiate a transfer price without at the same time agreeing on the quantity to be transferred at that price, there is no guarantee that they will arrive at the transfer price that maximizes firm value.

Reorganization: The Solution If All Else Fails

In some cases, transfer-pricing conflicts among profit centers can become sufficiently divisive to impose large costs on the firm. These costs take the form of both influence costs and the opportunity costs that arise when other than firm-value-maximizing transfer prices are chosen. Costly transfer-pricing disputes usually occur when the relative volume of transactions among divisions is large. In such cases, a small change in the transfer price can have a large effect on the division's reported profits. Hence, the potential for (and destructive effects of) opportunistic transfer-pricing actions by operating managers is substantial.

If transfer pricing becomes sufficiently dysfunctional, reorganize the firm. For example, senior management could combine two profit centers with a large quantity of transfers into a single division. Alternatively, it might make more sense to convert manufacturing into a cost center rather than a profit center and compensate the operating head based on efficiency in production. Or, it might even organize both divisions as cost centers and keep the pricing and quantity decisions at the central office.

A final possibility is to give distribution the right to produce the input. That is, change the decision rights allocation and allow both manufacturing and distribution the rights to make the transferred good. However, this alternative can be expensive (due to duplication of effort).

Internal Accounting System and Performance Evaluation[14]

Accounting costs, revenues, profits, return on investment, and residual income usually are used as performance measures of cost, expense, revenue, profit, and investment centers. Accounting costs are frequently used as transfer prices. The accounting system is an important component of the firm's performance-evaluation system and thus is an integral part of the firm's control system (performance-evaluation and reward systems). This section elaborates on accounting's role within the firm.

Uses of the Accounting System

We usually think of the firm's accounting system as its external financial reports (balance sheets and income statements) to the shareholders, taxing authorities, regulators, and lenders. The external financial reports (both quarterly and annual) are a vastly aggregated view of the enormous amount of data provided internally. Internally, managers rely on detailed, often computer-accessible, operating reports of expenses, product costs, and customer account balances from the accounting system.

The internal reports are used by management for two general purposes: decision management and decision control. As discussed in Chapter 9, the decision-making process is divided into decision management (initiation and implementation) and decision control (ratification and monitoring). Managers frequently have both decision-management and control rights, but normally not for the same decisions. More senior managers in the firm tend to hold more decision-control rights, while decision-management rights tend to be delegated to managers lower in the firm. To exercise either decision-management or decision-control rights, managers require knowledge. Some of that knowledge is provided by the accounting system. Therefore, the accounting system is used for both decision management and decision control—but as we will discuss, its primary function in most firms is decision control.

Decision management requires estimates of future costs and benefits. Initiating an investment decision to build a new plant requires that the manager forecast future alternate uses of this plant. Designing a marketing campaign requires judgments of likely future sales and competitors' responses. Managers frequently use accounting-based data as inputs to their decisions. Accounting numbers provide a starting point for forecasting future consequences of proposed actions. Most firms have accounting-based budget systems. Managers forecast costs and revenues for the next year in preparing their budgets. This process forces managers to be forward looking, to coordinate their operations with those managers most directly affected by their decisions, and to share specialized knowledge of their markets and production technologies. Accounting-based budgets provide the framework for such coordination and knowledge sharing.

While helpful for decision management, accounting systems are generally more useful for decision control (ratification and monitoring). In fact, this is the primary reason they evolved. Accounting systems are based on historical costs and historical revenues. Historical costs record what the firm paid for its current resource base and are backward looking. Internal accounting systems protect against theft of company assets, fraud, embezzlement.

---

[14]Material in this section draws on the analysis in Zimmerman (1995).

They also provide a scorecard for how a business unit did historically by measuring costs, profits, or residual income. Monitoring is by definition an historical function, one well served by the accounting system. Since accounting systems are primarily used for decision control—to prevent malfeasance and to measure past performance—when it comes to providing managers with information for decision management, accounting systems are often found wanting.

Tradeoffs between Decision Management and Control

Considering how the accounting system is used for both decision management and decision control leads to a number of important insights. First, accounting measures, to the extent they are used for monitoring purposes, are not under the complete control of the people being monitored (the operating managers).

Second, managers with decision-management rights tend to be dissatisfied with financial measures for making operating decisions. The data often are at too aggregate a level and hence do not provide sufficient detail for the decision. In response, operating managers develop their own, often nonfinancial, information systems to provide more of the knowledge required for decision management. But at the same time, they rely on accounting-system output to monitor the managers who report to them.

Third, nonaccounting measures frequently are more timely than accounting measures. Not every decision requires ratification or monitoring. Decision monitoring can be based on aggregate data to average out random fluctuations. Instead of monitoring every machine setup, it is usually more effective to aggregate all setups occurring over the week or month together and make sure the average setup cost is within acceptable levels.

One survey reports that managers rely on nonfinancial data (labor counts, units of output, units in inventory, units scrapped) to run their day-to-day operations. But when asked about their "most valuable report in general," they said it was the monthly income or expense statement because this was one of the measures used to judge their performance.[15]

In choosing among alternative accounting systems, managers often must make tradeoffs between decision management and decision control. Consider the transfer-pricing decision. The transfer-pricing method that most accurately measures the opportunity cost to the firm of transferring one more unit inside the firm might not be the transfer-pricing method that gives internal managers incentive to maximize firm value. For example, if the transfer-pricing method that most accurately measures the opportunity cost of units transferred (decision management) also requires manufacturing to reveal privately held and hard-to-verify knowledge of costs, then manufacturing has much discretion over the transfer prices. If these prices are important in rewarding managers (decision control), manufacturing can distort the system to its benefit. Given the reward system, a transfer-pricing scheme that is less subject to managerial discretion might in the end be a more accurate measure of opportunity costs than one that requires managers to disclose private, hard-to-verify knowledge.

All accounting (and nonaccounting) performance measures are prone to managerial opportunism in the form of accounting manipulations and dysfunctional decisions. Managers can choose depreciation methods that reduce expenses and increase reported earnings (straight-line depreciation). These accounting choices artificially raise ROI. Investment center managers can increase ROI by rejecting (or divesting) profitable projects with ROIs below the average ROI of the division. Most accounting measures are short-term measures of performance. They all suffer from the horizon problem, whereby managers

---

[15]S. McKinnon and W. Bruns (1992), *The Information Mosaic* (Harvard Business School: Boston).

Activity-Based Costing

In the late 1980s and early 1990s, discussions of a new accounting system, activity-based costing (ABC), appeared in every popular professional magazine. *Fortune* declared, "Trim waste! Improve service! Increase productivity! But it does all that—and more." Under traditional accounting systems, overhead costs of common resources are allocated to products or lines of business using very simple formulas such as percent of direct labor or percent of total revenue. For example, both riding and walk-behind lawn motors are produced in the same plant and both models use common resources. In calculating the accounting cost of the mowers, the plant's overhead costs are allocated to mowers based on the direct labor charged to each mower. The old system miscosts complex products requiring more specialized overhead resources. Managers claimed to be misled and to underprice products they thought were profitable when they were not.

Under ABC, different categories of overhead (purchasing, engineering, inspection) are assigned to products based on the underlying cost-drivers of that overhead department. Purchasing department costs are allocated based on the quantity of purchase orders issued or the number of different parts purchased. ABC is claimed to give a more accurate estimate of a product's true costs.

ABC proponents argue their product costs are more useful for decision making than the traditional numbers. While numerous firms have investigated ABC systems and have conducted pilot studies, few firms have abandoned their old, simpler cost-allocation schemes. These firms use the ABC-based numbers for special studies but still base performance evaluation on their traditional accounting systems. Why?

The ABC systems are designed by the operating managers. These are the people with the specialized knowledge of the overhead cost-drivers. Yet these are the people whose performance is being judged. One reason ABC is not replacing traditional accounting systems is the dictum against giving control of the accounting system to the people being monitored by the accounting system.

There is a second reason why ABC is not replacing traditional systems. The accounting measures are used for performance evaluation as well as decision making (product pricing decisions). Altering the way the purchasing department costs are allocated to products causes some product costs to increase and others to decrease, causing some product managers to appear less profitable and other product managers to appear more profitable. Changes in the accounting system are changes in the performance-evaluation systems. And without corresponding modifications in the compensation schemes, accounting system changes create windfall gains for some managers and windfall losses for others. Altering accounting cost allocations creates "winners" and "losers" who impose influence costs on the organization.

Source: T. Paré (1993), "A New Tool for Managing Costs," *Fortune* (June 14), 124–129.

emphasize short-term performance at the expense of long-term returns. Therefore, each accounting-based performance-measurement scheme requires careful monitoring by senior managers to reduce dysfunctional behavior by lower-level managers.

In the United States, accounting methods are regulated and managers must choose accounting methods from *generally accepted accounting procedures* (GAAP). However, managers still have considerable discretion. External, third-party auditors ensure the accuracy and consistency of the accounting reports. Most firms employ a single accounting system for multiple purposes: reporting to shareholders, taxes, internal decision management and control, and often regulation.[16] Debt agreements, management compensation plans, and financial reports utilize these accounting-based numbers. Using the same numbers for many purposes controls the incentives to distort the numbers for any single purpose.

Finally, no performance-measurement and reward system works perfectly. There always remains some managerial decisions that enhance the manager's welfare at the expense of

---

[16]While the firm has "one" accounting system, the accounting numbers are often adjusted for special purposes. For example, the system may use straight-line depreciation for shareholders but adjust these numbers to accelerated depreciation for taxes.

CASE STUDY
Celtex

Celtex is a large, very successful, decentralized specialty chemical producer organized into five independent investment centers. Each of the five investment centers is free to buy products either inside or outside the firm and is judged based on residual income. Most of each division's sales are to external customers. Celtex has the general reputation of being one of the top two or three companies in each of its markets.

Don Horigan, president of the synthetic chemicals (synchem) division, and Paul Juris, president of the consumer products division, are embroiled in a dispute. It all began two years ago when Juris asked Horigan to modify a synthetic chemical for a new household cleaner. In return, synthetic chemicals would be reimbursed for out-of-pocket costs. After spending considerable time perfecting the chemical, Juris solicited competitive bids from Horigan and some outside firms and awarded the contract to an outside firm who was the low bidder. This angered Horigan, who expected his bid to receive special consideration because he developed the new chemical at cost and the outside vendors took advantage of his R&D.

The current conflict has to do with synchem producing chemical Q47, a standard product, for consumer products. Because of an economic slowdown, all synthetic chemical producers have excess capacity. Synchem was asked to bid on supplying Q47 for consumer products. Consumer products is moving into a new, experimental product line and Q47 is one of the key ingredients. While the magnitude of the order is small relative to synchem's total business, the price of Q47 is quite important in determining the profitability of the experimental line. Horigan bid $3.20 per gallon. Meas Chemicals, an outside firm, bid $3. Juris is mad because he knows that Horigan's bid contains a substantial amount of fixed overhead and profit.

Synchem buys the base raw material, Q4, from the organic chemicals division of Celtex for $1 per gallon. Organic chemical's out-of-pocket costs (i.e., variable costs) are 80 percent of the selling price. Synchem then further processes Q4 into Q47 and incurs additional variable costs of $1.75 per gallon. Allocated fixed overhead adds another $.30 per gallon.

Horigan argues that he has $3.05 of cost in each gallon of Q47. If he turned around and sold the product for anything less than $3.20, he would be undermining his recent attempts to get his salespeople to stop cutting their bids and start quoting full-cost prices. Horigan has been trying to enhance the quality of the business he is getting, and he fears that if he is forced to make Q47 for consumer products, all of his effort the last few months would be for naught. He argues that he already gave away the store once to consumer products and he won't do it again. He questions, "How can senior managers expect me to return a positive residual income if I am forced to put in bids that don't recover full cost?"

Juris, in a chance meeting at the airport with Debra Donak, senior vice president of Celtex, described the situation and asked Donak to intervene. Juris believed Horigan was trying to get even after their earlier clash. Juris argued that the success of his new product venture depended on being able to secure a stable, high-quality source of supply of Q47 at low cost.

Donak has hired you as a consultant and has asked you to do the following:

Discussion Questions
1. Prepare a statement outlining the cash flows to Celtex of the two alternative sources of supply for Q47.
2. Offer advice regarding how Donak should handle the issues raised by Juris.

the shareholders. The key question is: Does the system outperform the next best alternative after all the costs and benefits are included? One should avoid the "nirvana fallacy," which advocates discarding a system because it allows some remaining managerial opportunism. The nirvana fallacy arises when one compares a real system to an assumed but unachievable "perfect" system.[17]

[17]H. Demsetz (1969), "Information and Efficiency: Another Viewpoint," *Journal of Law & Economics* XII, 1–22.

Summary

Chapter 13 described individual performance-evaluation systems; this chapter extends the discussion to evaluating divisional performance.

Decision rights are allocated to cost, expense, revenue, investment, and profit centers. These centers often are then evaluated and rewarded based on accounting-based performance measures. Cost centers are delegated decision rights over how to produce the output but not over price or quantity. Cost centers are evaluated either on minimizing total cost for a fixed output, or maximizing output for a fixed total cost. Expense centers such as personnel departments are like cost centers except that their output is not easily quantifiable. This difficulty in quantifying output means users often are not charged for the expense center's output; hence the demand for expense center services tends to grow faster than the firm's output.

Revenue centers also are similar to cost centers, with the difference that they are responsible for marketing the products. They have decision rights over how to sell or distribute the product, but not over the price-quantity decision. Revenue centers are evaluated on maximizing revenue for a given price or quantity and a fixed budget for operating expenses.

Profit centers have all the decision rights of cost centers plus the product mix and pricing decisions. They do not have decision rights over the level of investment in their profit center. Profit centers are evaluated based on total profits. Finally, investment centers are like profit centers except they also have decision rights over the amount of capital invested in their division. Evaluating performance of investment centers involves adjusting profits for the amount of capital invested. Two commonly used investment center measures are return on investment (ROI) and residual income (or economic value added, EVA). Both measures create incentives for managers to eliminate assets that are not covering their opportunity cost of capital. However, ROI gives incentives to eliminate profitable projects with returns below the average ROI for the division. Residual income does not have this incentive problem, but as a performance measure it makes comparing divisions of different sizes difficult.

Large companies, particularly those operating in multiple lines of business, are typically organized into multiple business units or divisions. Such an organizational architecture is generally intended to furnish senior managers with information about the profitability (or efficiency) of different businesses and to provide accountability and incentives for the operating managers charged with running those businesses.

Nevertheless, when there are significant interdependencies or synergies among different business units, often involving internal transfers, motivating individual profit centers to maximize their own profits will not generally maximize profits for the firm as a whole. Individual units focusing on their own profits often will ignore how their actions affect the sales and costs of other units.

One valuable role of a transfer-pricing scheme, then, is to lead managers to allocate resources internally in ways that take account of such interdependencies among divisions. But transfer pricing is a very complicated undertaking. The likelihood of getting the wrong answer is high, and the consequences of so doing—primarily in the form of mistaken pricing and output decisions—can be material. Thus, the transfer price not only changes how total profits are divided among business units, it affects total firm profits.

The challenges posed by the transfer-pricing problem stem primarily from information asymmetries. The opportunity cost of a transferred resource is the correct transfer price. But accurate information about opportunity cost is usually the private knowledge of local divisional managers. If either the buying or selling division can set the transfer price unilaterally, it has incentives to behave opportunistically. The selling division will set too high a price trying to capture monopoly profits, and too few units will be transferred. If the buying division is allowed to set the transfer price, a price below the true opportunity cost is likely to be chosen; again too few units will be transferred.

Because accurate information about opportunity costs is so expensive to obtain (or at least to verify), managers generally rely on approximations such as market values, marginal costs, full costs, and negotiated prices. Each of these approximations work better than others in certain circumstances.

Market-based transfer prices are most useful when competitive external markets exist. But if an external market is employed, why is the firm producing the good or service? If there are important synergies favoring internal production, the external market price is unlikely to capture them. For example, if there are transaction costs of using the market, such as writing and enforcing contracts, then the transfer price is the market price less the transaction costs.

Marginal cost is another popular transfer-pricing method. But marginal cost is expensive to estimate and can generate influence costs as managers debate whether certain expenditures are "marginal" or not.

Full-cost transfer prices are objective, simple-to-compute transfer prices. They are also widely used in practice. However, full-cost transfer prices likely suffer from setting the transfer price above opportunity cost.

Negotiated transfer prices, although time-consuming to establish, give both parties to the contract the incentive first to negotiate the quantity that maximizes firm profits and then negotiate the transfer price that determines how the total profits will be divided.

No matter what transfer-pricing method is used, it is normally important to allow both the buying and selling divisions access to the external market. In this case, the external market acts as a check on opportunistic managerial behavior. But again, if the external market is employed, one must examine whether the firm should be producing the intermediate product at all.

Finally, most divisional performance-evaluation systems rely on internally generated accounting-based numbers. These accounting-based performance metrics are for decision control (decision ratification and decision monitoring). Besides exercising decision-control rights, employees also exercise decision-management rights (decision initiation and implementation). Exercising decision-management rights requires knowledge; often managers turn to their accounting systems for the information. But the accounting systems of most firms are designed for decision control, not necessarily for decision management. This leads to a tradeoff between these two uses and to the general conclusion that most managers find their accounting systems wanting when it comes to providing information for decision management.

Suggested Readings

R. Eccles (1985), *The Transfer Pricing Problem: A Theory for Practice* (Lexington Books: Lexington, MA).

J. Gould (1964), "Internal Pricing in Firms When There Are Costs of Using an Outside Market" *Journal of Business* 37, 61–67.

J. Hirshleifer (1964), "Internal Pricing and Decentralized Decisions," in *Management Controls: New Directions in Basic Research,* Bonini, Jaediecke, and Wagner, eds. (McGraw-Hill: New York).

B. Holmstrom and J. Tirole (1991), "Transfer Pricing and Organizational Form," *Journal of Law, Economics, and Organizations* 7, 201–228.

D. Solomons (1968), *Divisional Performance: Measurement and Control* (Richard D. Irwin: Burr Ridge, IL).

B. Stewart (1991), *The Quest for Value* (Harper Business, New York).

J. Zimmerman (1995), *Accounting for Decision Making and Control* (Richard D. Irwin: Burr Ridge, IL), Chapters 4 and 8.

Review Questions

14–1. Auto-fit is a multidivisional firm that produces auto parts. It has the capacity for annual production of 100 units of a particular part. The marginal cost of producing each unit is $10. These units can either be sold internally to other divisions or to external customers. The external market price is $20. The allocated share of corporate overhead for each part produced is $5. Total corporate overhead expenditures do not vary with the production of the part. How many units of the part should the company produce? What is the theoretically correct transfer price (should the company decide to transfer the part internally)? Explain.

14–2. High Tech, Inc., has strong patent protection on a particular type of computer chip. High Tech uses the chip for the internal production of PCs. It also sells the chip to other manufacturers on the open market. Does High Tech necessarily want to charge the same price to both external and internal customers? Explain.

14–3. A firm has a demand curve: P = 50 – Q. Its total costs are:

$$TC = 110 + Q + 3Q^2$$

Prepare a table that computes the profit-maximizing quantity. What quantity minimizes average cost? (Hint: Prepare a figure like 14.1 for Q=1, 2, . . . , 10.)

14–4. Assume a firm faces a demand curve: P = 6,600 –10Q. The total cost of production is TC = Q^2 and marginal cost is MC = 2Q. What are the optimal output, price, and profits for the firm?

Now assume that the firm is divided into two profit centers. One division manufactures the product at a total cost of TC = Q^2 and then transfers it to a selling division that faces the firm's demand curve. The selling division has no costs other than the transfer price for the product. Assume that the manufacturing division has the power to set the transfer price and that the selling division can only buy internally. The selling division, however, can select the quantity to purchase. What transfer price will the manufacturing unit select? What are the resulting profits for the two units? From the firm's standpoint, what is the optimal transfer price?

14–5. Chips Computer Company assembles personal computers and sells them in the retail marketplace. The company is organized into two profit centers: the assembly division and the distribution division. The demand curve facing the company (and the distribution division) is P = 3,000 – 10Q. The marginal cost for assembly (which includes purchasing the parts) is constant at $500. The distribution division faces constant marginal distribution costs of $50 per unit. What is the profit-maximizing retail price and output for the firm as a whole? If the assembly division has monopoly power to set the transfer price, what transfer price will it select (assuming it knows all the information above)? Calculate the profits for the two divisions in this case.

14–6. The Xtrac Computer Company is organized into regional sales offices and a manufacturing division. The sales offices forecast sales for the upcoming year in their territories. These figures are then used to set the manufacturing schedules for the year. Prices of the computers are determined by corporate headquarters, and the salespeople are paid a fixed wage and a commission on sales. The regional sales offices are evaluated as revenue centers. The regional sales manager is paid a small wage (about 30 percent of total pay) and a commission on all sales in her territory (about 70 percent of total pay) that exceeds the budget.

Xtrac has a notoriously bad track record for forecasting computer sales. Its budgets always underforecast sales, and then, during the year, manufacturing scrambles to produce more units, authorizes labor overtime, and buys parts on rush orders. This drives up manufacturing costs. At first, management thought the underforecasting problem was due to high unexpected growth in the computer industry. But Xtrac even underforecasts sales when the economy is slow and the industry growth is below its long-run average.

    a. What is the likely reason Xtrac persistently underforecasts sales?

    b. What are some likely explanations for the reason in part (a)?

    c. Propose three likely solutions, and critically evaluate each of them.

14–7. Scoff Division of World-Wide Paint is currently losing money, and senior management is considering selling or closing Scoff. Scoff's only product, an intermediate chemical called Binder, is used principally by the latex division of the firm. If Scoff is sold, latex division can purchase ample quantities of Binder in the market at sufficiently high quality levels to meet its requirements. World-Wide requires all of its divisions to supply product to other World-Wide divisions before servicing the external market.

    Scoff's statement of operations for the latest quarter is:

Scoff Division Profit/Loss
Last Quarter
($ thousands)

Revenues:		
Inside	$200	
Outside	75	$275
Operating expenses:		
Variable costs	$260	
Fixed costs	15	
Allocated corporate overhead	40	315
Net income (loss) before taxes		$ (40)

Notes:

    1. World-Wide Paint has the policy of transferring all products internally at variable cost. In Scoff's case, variable cost is 80 percent of the market price.

    2. All of Scoff's fixed costs are avoidable cash flows if Scoff is closed or sold.

    3. Ten percent of the allocated corporate overhead is caused by the presence of Scoff and will be avoided if Scoff is closed or sold.

Calculate the annual net cash flows to World-Wide Paint of closing or selling Scoff.

14–8. Suppose a firm has two different accounting systems. For example, suppose it uses EVA to measure and reward management performance. To calculate EVA, annual spending on research and development is recorded as an asset and then depreciated in calculating earnings. In reporting earnings to shareholders, R&D spending in any given year is expensed against earnings.

    Describe some of the likely consequences that can arise if the firm tries to maintain two different accounting systems.

Part 3

Applications of Organizational Architecture

chapter 15

Vertical Integration and Outsourcing

I n 1989, Eastman Kodak sold its mainframe computers to IBM and contracted with IBM to do much of Kodak's data processing for the next 10 years.[1] This *outsourcing* of computer services was newsworthy specifically because no company of Kodak's size or prominence had turned over its computers to outsiders before. Other large companies began considering similar moves. In 1990, U.S. businesses spent $7.2 billion on outsourced computer operations. According to some estimates, these expenditures were expected to double by 1995.

Under the contract with Kodak, IBM is responsible for operating Kodak's data center. IBM provides the operating software and hardware and is responsible for backups and file protection. Kodak retained its own staff for developing applications software and is responsible for most data entry. For example, Kodak provides IBM with the basic data for running its sales-forecasting models and has developed much of the specific software for this application. IBM is responsible for running Kodak's programs on its operating system.

Outsourcing has not been limited to information systems. Chrysler Motors now buys about 70 percent of its parts from external suppliers. Reebok, one of the leading athletic shoe companies in the world, owns no plants. Rather, it contracts out all footwear production to suppliers in various Asian countries. In 1992, Du Pont sold its copy machines to Lanier and contracted with the company to provide copying services. Kodak used to operate its own kitchens to provide meals for the 40,000 employees at its headquarters in Rochester, New York. In 1992, Kodak sold this operation to the Marriott Corporation. Among the services most often outsourced are trucking, catering, data processing, copying, and accounting.

Outsourcing involves a fundamental change in organizational architecture. First, it reassigns decision rights relating to certain assets and employees from one firm to another. For instance, to staff its new data center IBM hired about 300 people who formerly had worked for Kodak. IBM now owns the mainframes that serve Kodak and has the decision rights on the utilization, maintenance, and replacement of these machines. Second, performance-evaluation and reward systems also generally change with outsourcing. Kodak previously evaluated its data processing units as cost centers. By contrast, the senior managers at the new IBM-run data center are evaluated on business growth, operational efficiency, and satisfaction of Kodak users. Overall, the IBM unit more closely resembles a profit center than a cost center. Since Kodak pays scheduled fees for computer services, IBM directly benefits if it can improve efficiency and cut costs.

This discussion of outsourcing raises a number of important questions:

- What are the costs and benefits in choosing between the alternate architectures that are implied by within-firm production versus outsourcing?
- What activities make the most sense to outsource? Why are data processing, catering, copying, and trucking among the most frequently outsourced services? Why did Kodak outsource the operation of its data center to IBM but maintain the responsibility for developing applications software?
- When a company outsources, what are the determinants of the specific contract provisions? Why did Kodak and IBM negotiate a 10-year contract instead of a one-year contract? Why do some firms grant distributors exclusive rights to particular territories?
- What has motivated the recent trend in increased outsourcing?

[1]Details of this example are from W. Richmond, A. Seidmann, and A. Whinston (1992), "Incomplete Contracting Issues in Information Systems Development Outsourcing," *Decision Support Systems* 8, 459–477; D. Kirkpatrick (1991), "Why Not Farm Out Your Computing," *Fortune* (September 23), 103–112; and S. Tully (1993), "The Modular Corporation," *Fortune* (February 8), 106–114.

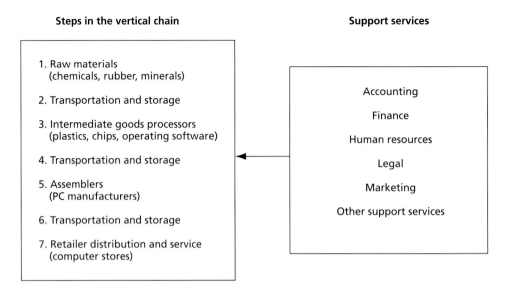

Figure 15.1 The Vertical Chain of Production for Personal Computers

At the top of the chain are the raw materials such as chemicals, metals, and rubber that are used as inputs to produce PCs. These inputs are transported to intermediate goods processors. These processors (for instance, plastics manufacturers, chip makers, and operating software producers) make the intermediate products that are used in the final construction of the PCs. These intermediate goods must be transported to the companies that assemble them into the final consumer products. Finally, these products are transported to retail stores, which sell them to consumers. Each step of the vertical chain is supported by administrative services such as accounting, finance, and marketing.

We begin by discussing the process of producing and marketing products. We then discuss tradeoffs among alternative ways of organizing the steps in this process (market transactions, long-term contracts, and vertical integration). Other topics include the appropriate length of a contract, contracting with independent distributors, and reasons for the recent increases in outsourcing. The appendix to this chapter provides a more detailed example that highlights some of the tradeoffs between company ownership and outsourcing.

Vertical Chain of Production

Consumer goods are produced through a series of steps described by the *vertical chain of production.*[2] Figure 15.1 pictures the vertical chain for personal computers (PCs). At the top of the chain are the raw materials such as chemicals, metals, and plastics that are used as inputs to produce PCs. These inputs are transported to processors that make the intermediate products that are used in the final construction of PCs (for instance, plastics manufacturers, chip makers, and operating software producers). The intermediate goods are transported to companies that assemble them into PCs. Finally, the PCs are transported to retail stores, which sell them to consumers and provide after-sales servicing. Each step of the vertical chain is supported by administrative services such as accounting, finance, and

[2]D. Besanko, D. Dranove, and M. Shanley (1995), *The Economics of Strategy* (John Wiley & Sons: New York), 71.

Outsourcing: Choosing along a continuum

Spot markets   Long-term contracts   Vertical integration

Figure 15.2   Input Production—Choosing along a Continuum

It is often useful to think of the outsourcing decision as a choice along a continuum of possibilities. At one extreme, a product or service can be purchased from any one of a large number of potential suppliers in the spot market. At the other extreme, the company can produce the product or service internally within a division of the firm through vertical integration. Between these extremes are long-term contracts. Contracts take a variety of forms, including standard supply and distribution contracts, joint ventures, lease contracts, franchise contracts, and strategic alliances.

marketing. Firms can locate at different positions along the vertical chain. Intel is an intermediate-goods processor that manufacturers computer chips; Dell Computers, which sells IBM-compatible PCs, concentrates on final assembly and distribution. Firms can also specialize in providing support services (for instance, legal and accounting firms).

When a firm participates in more than one successive stage in the vertical chain, it is said to be *vertically integrated.* Firms vary significantly in their degree of vertical integration. Dell Computers owns no plants and manufactures virtually none of its component parts. It does not make or even stock the over 650 software products that it sells. Dell simply leases two small factories to assemble computers from parts acquired from other companies and orders software products from Merisel, a large distribution company. IBM is much more vertically integrated, producing many of its component parts and software in-house. IBM also maintains its own sales force for mainframe computers.

Firms change their degree of integration over time. An organization that begins to produce its own inputs is engaging in *backward* or *upstream* integration, while an organization that begins to market its own goods or to conduct additional finishing work is engaging in *forward* or *downstream* integration. Lincoln Electric integrated backward recently when it began manufacturing certain inputs for its welding machines that previously were supplied by outside companies. Pepsico, on the other hand, integrated forward when it acquired Pizza Hut and Taco Bell, which sell Pepsico's soft drinks.

The term *outsourcing* is frequently used to describe a movement away from vertical integration—moving an activity outside the firm that formerly was done within the firm. An example of this usage is "Kodak recently outsourced its computer operations to IBM." The term *outsourcing* is also used to describe an ongoing arrangement whereby a firm obtains a part or service from an external firm. An example of this usage is "Reebok has always outsourced much of its footwear production to foreign companies."

It is often useful to think of the outsourcing decision as a choice along a continuum of possibilities. As pictured in Figure 15.2, at one extreme the part or service can be purchased from any one of a large number of potential suppliers in the *spot market* (where the exchange is made immediately at the current market price with no long-term commitment between the buyer and the seller). At the other extreme, a company can vertically integrate and produce the part or service internally.[3] In the middle are long-term contracts between

---

[3]See chapter 14 for a discussion of how firms organize internal production into divisions. That chapter also examines the corresponding transfer-pricing issues.

Long-Term Contracts

In this chapter, we do not differentiate among the various types of long-term contracts. Rather, we focus on how firms choose among spot markets, contracts, and vertical integration. Long-term contracts, however, can take a variety of forms. First, there are *standard supply and distribution contracts* between independent firms. For instance, IBM and Kodak have a 10-year supply contract, where IBM agrees to provide specific computer services to Kodak for a given price. The contract contains many provisions specifying the nature of the service and the duties and obligations of each of the contracting parties. Second, there are *joint ventures.* In the typical joint venture, a new firm is formed that is jointly owned by two or more independent firms. The new firm might be responsible for conducting research, supplying inputs for a subset of the firms, or for downstream activities such as marketing or distributing a product. Drug companies form research joint ventures to conduct basic research on new drugs. The output of this research is shared by the partners in the venture. Similarly, an American company and European company might form a joint venture to market the American company's products in Europe. Third are *lease contracts,* where a firm acquires an asset such as a machine or building through a lease agreement with another firm. Fourth are *franchise agreements,* which grant an independent businessperson the rights to use the parent's proven name, reputation, and business format in a given market area. Fifth are *strategic alliances.* This term is used to describe a variety of agreements between independent firms to cooperate in the development and/or marketing of products. For instance, an airline company and a car rental company might agree to promote each others' products and to participate in joint promotional schemes.

independent or quasi-independent firms. Long-term contracts take many forms, including long-term supply and distribution contracts, franchise contracts, leasing contracts, joint ventures, and strategic alliances. Many of the recent outsourcing decisions move the firm from vertical integration to long-term contracting (Kodak and IBM for computer services, Kodak and Marriott for food service, Du Pont and Lanier for copying services). We begin our analysis of outsourcing by considering some of the advantages of acquiring parts and services in spot markets. We use the term *market transactions* to refer to sales and purchases in the spot market; the term *nonmarket transactions* refers to either vertical integration or long-term contracts.

Benefits of Buying in Competitive Markets

Figure 15.3 presents the standard diagram of a competitive equilibrium (as discussed in Chapter 6). The figure illustrates that competitive markets result in efficient production—production occurs at the lowest possible average cost per unit. Price is equal to average cost, implying that buyers acquire the product at cost (which includes a normal rate of return on investment).[4] Over time, suppliers adopt technological advances that lower the costs of production and/or enhance the quality of the product. Lower costs are passed along to buyers in the form of lower prices. This analysis suggests that when competitive outside markets are available to purchase goods and services, firms should use them. In most cases, a firm cannot acquire the product more cheaply through a nonmarket transaction, and in many cases it will cost more.

One concern with internal production is producing a high-enough volume to take advantage of scale economies in production. In Figure 15.3, the minimum point on the

---

[4]Recall that if price is above long-run average cost, firms are making economic profits and new firms enter the industry. The increase in supply drives down the price. Alternatively, if price is below long-run average cost, firms are losing money and exit occurs.

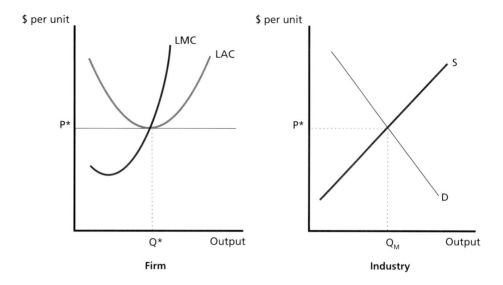

Figure 15.3 Competitive Equilibrium

This figure illustrates that competitive markets result in efficient production. The right panel displays the supply and demand curves for the industry. Their intersection determines the market price. The left panel pictures the output decision of a representative firm in the industry. Production occurs at the lowest possible long-run average cost (LAC). Buyers acquire the product at cost (P* = LAC = LMC, where LMC = Long-run marginal cost). The analysis suggests that when competitive outside markets are available for inputs, firms should use them. In most cases, the firm cannot produce more cheaply itself, and in many cases it will cost more.

average cost curve is at a volume of Q* units. Individual firms in the marketplace produce this volume. If a firm requires less than Q* units and produces the amount internally, it will have a higher average cost. The firm could produce Q* and sell the surplus in the open market. However, this choice requires the firm to enter a new market — one that is not its primary line of business. As we discuss below, diversifying into unrelated fields can reduce value. Empirical studies suggest that diversified firms frequently perform poorly relative to firms that are more focused.[5]

Another concern with nonmarket procurement is the cost of motivating efficient production. Divisions within large firms can be inefficient, yet continue to survive, if they are subsidized by more profitable units within the firm. Firms must adopt costly incentive and control systems to motivate internal managers to engage in efficient production. Similarly, parties to a long-term supply contract must be motivated to carry out their parts of the agreement. Independent firms, on the other hand, face more direct market pressures. If they are inefficient in their main line of business, they lose money and eventually are forced to liquidate.

Due to such concerns, most firms use markets to acquire many, if not most, of their inputs. Few companies produce their own automobiles, trucks, fuel, copy machines, pencils, staples, telephones, office furniture, or bathroom fixtures. Most of these products are

[5]P. Berger and E. Ofek (1995), "Diversification's Effect on Firm Value," *Journal of Financial Economics* 37, 39–65; R. Comment (1995), "Corporate Focus and Stock Returns," *Journal of Financial Economics* 37, 67–87; and K. John and E. Ofek (1995), "Asset Sales and Increase in Focus," *Journal of Financial Economics* 37, 105–126.

Made in the USA

Companies sometimes label their products "Made in the USA." This statement apparently appeals to the sentiment among some consumers that Americans should purchase only American-made products to protect domestic jobs. The claim also helps companies gain contracts from the U.S. government. The common practice of acquiring many inputs from outside suppliers, however, makes it difficult to define what really is made in the USA. In early September 1994, the FTC charged two small athletic shoe companies, New Balance and Hyde Athletic Industries Inc., with deceptive advertising for saying that their products were "Made in the USA." While the companies sew and glue the bulk of their shoes in the United States, they import many of the component parts, such as soles and uppers, from Asia. Hyde Athletic agreed to change its label to "Made in the USA from domestic and imported components." New Balance disputed the claim. This issue could affect many companies, ranging from Dell Computers to General Motors, who emphasize domestic production but rely on foreign companies for various inputs and services.

Source: M. Oneal (1994), "Does New Balance Have an American Soul?"
Business Week (December 12), 86–90.

acquired through market transactions. Firms also often rely on external markets for many of their downstream activities, such as product distribution. For instance, Procter & Gamble sells many of its products (such as soap and toothpaste) through independent grocery stores and drugstores. The key point is that well-functioning markets provide powerful incentives for efficient production and low prices. It is value maximizing to acquire many goods and services through market transactions.

Reasons for Nonmarket Transactions

Our analysis appears to argue against nonmarket transactions—firms should concentrate on a particular stage of the production/distribution process and acquire other inputs and services through market transactions with outside suppliers and distributors. There are, however, at least three primary reasons why firms often use nonmarket transactions to acquire inputs and downstream services: transaction costs, taxes/regulation, and monopoly power.

Transaction Costs

In Chapter 3, we discussed the architecture of markets. We argued that markets effectively link specific knowledge and decision rights; moreover, they provide incentives for decision makers to use this information effectively. We posed the question: *Why aren't all economic transactions conducted through markets?* Ronald Coase answered this question by arguing that market transactions are not costless.[6] For instance, they involve the costs of searching for trading partners and negotiating the relevant prices. Parties to a transaction have incentives to use other mechanisms, such as internal production, when the transaction can be completed at a lower cost. There are at least four factors that can make the costs of nonmarket transactions lower than the costs of market exchanges. These factors include firm-specific assets, costs of measuring quality, coordination problems, and externalities.

[6]For a collection of Coase's work on this topic, see R. Coase (1988), *The Firm, the Market, and the Law* (University of Chicago Press: Chicago, IL).

Firm-Specific Assets[7]

Production typically requires investment in assets. As examples, IBM requires mainframe computers to provide computer services to Kodak and suppliers require machines to make parts. Sometimes these assets can be transferred easily among alternative uses. Mainframe computers can be used to serve Kodak or another company. These are general-purpose computers that can be used to serve a variety of customers. Other assets are significantly more valuable in their current use than in their next best alternative. For example, the Alaskan Pipeline is materially more valuable for transporting oil than for any other conceivable use. If IBM writes a specialized computer program to run Kodak's payroll, the program is more valuable for Kodak's payroll than for some other firm's payroll (which offers different fringe benefits, for instance). While the program could be adapted for use by other firms, changing the program is costly. Assets that are significantly more valuable in their current use than in their next best alternative use are referred to as *firm-specific assets.* There are four particular instances in which asset specificity is most likely to occur:[8]

- *Site specificity.* The asset is located in a particular area that makes it useful only to a small number of buyers or suppliers and it cannot be moved easily. An example is the Alaskan Pipeline, which can be used only by oil producers in Alaska.
- *Physical-asset specificity.* The product design makes it especially useful to a small number of buyers. An example is a specialized machine tool that is used to make parts for one particular type of automobile.
- *Human-asset specificity.* The transaction requires specialized knowledge on the part of the parties to the transaction. An example is the knowledge that IBM employees must acquire about Kodak's unique processes in order to provide computer services to the company.
- *Dedicated assets.* The expansion in facilities is necessitated only by the requirements of one or several buyers. An example is a chip producer who adds extra capacity to serve one particular computer company.

If a supplier invests in a specific asset to serve a particular customer, the supplier places itself in a tenuous position for future negotiations. For example, consider a supplier who invests $50,000 for a machine tool (such as a metal punch-press die) to produce a particular part. The part is used only by one manufacturer, and the machine tool has no other uses or salvage value—it is very specific. The variable cost of production is $1 per unit and the useful life of the machine tool is 50,000 units. The supplier must be able to sell the parts for at least $2 per unit to break even. The buyer, however, is in a strong position to argue for a price concession after the investment is made. At this point, the investment is a *sunk cost,* and the supplier will continue to operate as long as it can cover its variable costs of $1 per unit. Thus, the buyer can potentially force the supplier to accept a price as low as $1, even though the supplier loses on its initial investment. Anticipating this *hold-up problem,* the supplier will not invest in the machine tool in the first place unless it receives a guarantee that the buyer will continue to pay $2 per unit and will buy at least 50,000 units.

---

[7]Material in this section draws on the analysis in B. Klein, R. Crawford, and A. Alchian (1978), "Vertical Integration, Appropriable Rents, and the Competitive Contracting Process," *Journal of Law & Economics* 24, 297–326.

[8]O. Williamson (1985), *The Economic Institutions of Capitalism* (Free Press: New York).

Buyers also face potential hold-up problems if they purchase key inputs from a single supplier that has invested in the relevant firm-specific assets. For instance, a specialized chip supplier might demand a large price increase when it knows that a computer company has a large backlog of orders and that there are no alternative sources of supply.

These potential hold-up problems can be controlled by vertical integration. If the buying firm invests in the machine and produces the part internally, it does not have to worry about subsequently arguing with another firm over prices. An alternative to integration is for the buyer and supplier to enter into a long-term supply contract. The buyer might agree to purchase 50,000 units from the supplier over the next five years at a cost of $2 per unit. Contracts are not costless to write or to enforce, and so the preferred alternative depends on the relative costs of vertical integration versus contracting. This tradeoff is considered in greater detail below.

Measuring Quality

It is difficult to monitor the quality of some inputs and services. The buyer might not learn that a part is defective until long after purchase. In this case, the seller can have the incentive to cheat the buying firm—once a price is set, the supplier can increase its profits by supplying a lower-quality, lower-cost product. Buyers can sometimes avoid these problems by transacting with companies that have established reputations for quality and/or who can offer credible warranties for their products. Otherwise, buyers should produce the products in-house. Alternatively, buyers can negotiate a long-term supply contract that provides appropriate incentives for quality production. Internal production and long-term contracts are especially useful when maintaining the quality of the part is critical for the overall success of the product. (We discuss this issue further in Chapter 18.) These nonmarket forms of organization do not necessarily change the distribution of information among the parties. However, they allow the company to develop contractual incentives that motivate quality production.

Extensive Coordination

Some activities require extensive coordination. For example, railroads rely on extensive feeder traffic for their routes. In principle, it would be possible to use the price system for each link in the network. Rail companies could pay each other to use their lines, with prices adjusting to changes in supply and demand. Such a system would be complicated and expensive to operate. An alternative is for the railroad companies in the network to merge and to address the various coordination problems internally. Railroad companies were among the first large firms in the United States. These large firms were motivated, at least in part, by the benefits of using internal managers to coordinate rail activity.[9]

A related reason for vertical integration is to coordinate pricing among retail units. The pricing decisions of individual retailers can have effects on other units in the system. For instance, it might be optimal from a companywide standpoint to set prices where some units sustain losses. (When McDonald's stays open, customers are less likely to try Burger King.) Independent retailers cannot always be expected to set optimal systemwide prices since they care only about the profits from their own units. In principle, the central company could set the retail prices; however, antitrust law does not allow it. Prices can be coordinated if the company owns its own retail outlets.

---

[9]A. Chandler (1977), *The Visible Hand—The Managerial Revolution in American Business* (Belknap Press: Cambridge, MA). Also, D. Carlton and M. Klamer (1983), "The Need for Coordination Among Firms with Special Reference to Network Industries," *University of Chicago Law Review* 50, 446–65.

Reducing Externalities

Firms often invest in developing reputations and customer loyalty. This investment can increase the demand for a company's products. Firms, however, can have problems motivating independently owned distributors to invest sufficient resources to maintain a brand name—there is a free-rider problem. Independent retailers in a distribution system have incentives to shirk on advertising and depend on the efforts of other units in the system to attract customers. These retailers also might want to cut costs by hiring less-skilled, lower-priced labor. A given owner of a retail unit receives all the benefits from reducing the unit's labor costs but bears only part of the costs from providing poor service to customers—any decline in future sales is likely to be shared with other units. The incentives to free-ride are particularly large when the retailer deals with customers who are not likely to make repeat purchases at the particular unit.

The free-rider problem can be reduced through vertical integration, where managers of stores are compensated in ways that do not promote free-riding, or through long-term contracts with terms that motivate increased sales efforts. We provide a detailed discussion of distribution contracts later in this chapter.

Taxes and Regulation

Taxes and regulation also can motivate vertical integration. If one stage of production is heavily taxed while another is not, taxes might be reduced by shifting profits to the low-tax activity. A firm can potentially capture these gains by integrating vertically and having the low-tax unit charge inflated transfer prices to the high-tax unit. Tax authorities are aware of this incentive and limit this type of activity.[10]

Similarly, a regulated company might want to integrate vertically to shift profits from a regulated segment of the business, where profits are restricted, to an unregulated segment of the business. In 1984, AT&T settled an antitrust suit with the Department of Justice by splitting into several firms. One of the concerns of the Justice Department was that it was difficult to monitor cost-shifting among AT&T's regulated business (for example, telephone service) and other less regulated businesses (for example, telephone equipment). The breakup of AT&T reduced these concerns.[11]

Monopoly Power

There are several ways that a firm might use vertical integration to increase monopoly profits. The following example illustrates one of these methods—using vertical integration to price discriminate.[12] Consider a firm, DrugCo, that has a patent on a particular chemical compound used as an input in the production of two different pharmaceutical products. One of the products is a pain reliever that competes with many other pain relievers. The other helps to cure a particular type of cancer, and faces no good substitute. The industry demand for the two retail products (pain reliever and cancer drug) is given by:

$$\text{Pain relief:} \quad P = 100 - 5Q \tag{15.1}$$

$$\text{Cancer cure: } P = 200 - 10Q \tag{15.2}$$

---

[10]M. Scholes and M. Wolfson (1992), *Taxes and Business Strategy: A Planning Approach* (Prentice Hall: Englewood Cliffs, NJ), Chapter 2.

[11]D. Carlton and J. Perloff (1990), *Modern Industrial Organization* (Harper Collins: New York).

[12]For additional methods, see Carlton and Perloff (1990), Chapter 16.

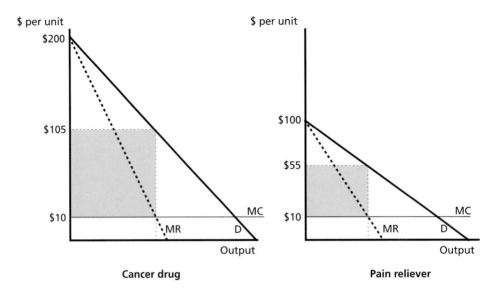

Figure 15.4 Using Vertical Integration to Price Discriminate

DrugCo has a patent on a chemical compound used as an input in the production of two different pharmaceutical products: a pain reliever that competes with many other products and a cancer drug. The marginal cost to DrugCo for producing the chemical compound is $10 per unit. The industry-level demand curves for the two products are the same demand curves facing DrugCo for the chemical compound. The optimal price to charge manufacturers who produce the pain reliever is $55. The optimal price for those who produce the cancer drug is $105. However, if DrugCo tries to sell to some companies at $55 and other companies at $105, potential arbitrage is available. One way to effectively price discriminate is for DrugCo to integrate forward into the retail market for pain relievers. It would sell the pain reliever to consumers at $55 and the chemical compound to the manufacturers of the cancer drug at $105.

The marginal cost to DrugCo for producing the chemical compound is $10 per unit. For simplicity, suppose that a drug manufacturer can take the chemical compound and transform it into one unit of either retail product (pain reliever or cancer drug) at zero marginal cost incurring no additional distribution or marketing costs. Many manufacturers can produce and distribute the retail drugs. Competition among these retail manufacturers will drive the retail prices of the pain reliever and cancer drug down to the retail manufacturers' marginal costs, which in this example is the wholesale price (see Chapter 6) of DrugCo's chemical compound. Thus, the demand curves facing DrugCo at the wholesale level are the same as the retail demand curves given in equations 15.1 and 15.2.

To maximize total profits, DrugCo would like to set marginal revenue equal to marginal cost in each market. As shown in Figure 15.4, the optimal price to charge retail drug manufacturers who produce the pain reliever is $55. The optimal price for those who produce the cancer drug is $105.[13] Since both retail markets are competitive and there are no other costs, the price to consumers in the two markets would be $55 and $105. However, if DrugCo tries to sell to some manufacturers at $55 and other manufacturers at $105, potential *arbitrage* is available—manufacturers who buy at $55 can sell the chemical compound to other manufacturers at less than $105 and make a profit. They will undercut any attempt by DrugCo to sell to manufacturers at $105.

[13]Recall from Chapter 6 that these prices are easily found by setting the marginal revenue in each market (implied by the two demand curves) equal to the marginal cost of $10.

Price Discrimination and Antitrust Law

Firms that integrate vertically to engage in price discrimination can sometimes be held accountable under antitrust law. Alcoa had monopoly power in the production of virgin aluminum ingots, an intermediate good. It integrated into the lower-priced markets (for example, rolled sheet) and "squeezed" competitors in these markets. The judge who wrote the opinion in the antitrust case proposed a "transfer-price test" to assess whether a firm is engaged in a price squeeze. The test considers whether the integrated firm could sell the final output profitably at prevailing prices, assuming it had to pay the same price for the input as it charges downstream competitors. The court determined Alcoa could not. In our example, DrugCo would operate at a loss if it paid $105 for the input and sold the pain reliever to consumers at $55.

Source: *United States* v. *Aluminum Company of America* (1945), 148 F. 2d 416.

One way that DrugCo can prevent arbitrage is to integrate forward and manufacture the pain reliever. The company would price the pain reliever at $55 in the retail market and sell the base drug at $105 in the wholesale market. Arbitrage is no longer possible (assuming that the pain reliever cannot be transformed back into the chemical compound at low cost). Integrating forward into the retail market for the cancer drug will not solve the problem. If DrugCo tried to price the cancer drug at $105 and sell the chemical compound at a wholesale price of $55, other retail manufacturers would begin to produce and market the cancer drug (after buying the chemical compound at $55). DrugCo would not be able to maintain a price of $105. It must integrate forward into the lower-priced (more *elastic*) pain-reliever market.

Other Reasons

Another potential reason for nonmarket procurement is to ensure the supply of an important input. In contrast to the standard economic model, shortages sometimes occur in actual markets. For example, theaters do not always raise their prices for popular movies. Rather, tickets are allocated on a first-come, first-served basis when demand exceeds supply. Similarly, companies sometimes face rationing or short supply of particular inputs. Companies might integrate vertically or enter long-term contracts to increase the likelihood of reliably receiving an input.

Firms also use nonmarket procurement to avoid sharing proprietary information with other firms. For instance, a firm might be reluctant to provide an independent supplier with detailed information about its production processes because it fears that the supplier will share the information with other firms. It is potentially easier to control the leakage of sensitive information when dealing with internal employees or long-term suppliers.

Another common explanation for nonmarket transactions relies on technological factors. For example, some people explain the common ownership of steel milling and steel production by the close technological links of the two processes. This argument is flawed. While it is true that there are benefits from having these operations at one location, technology does not dictate ownership. Steel mills could buy hot steel ingots from other companies located in the same building. The reasons they do not are not due to technological factors but rather result from contracting problems—independent companies do not want to expose themselves to the hold-up problems that arise from this type of firm-specific investment.

Vertical Integration versus Long-Term Contracts[14]

We have discussed reasons why a firm might acquire a good or service through a non-market transaction. This section considers the tradeoffs between the two general types of nonmarket transactions, vertical integration and long-term contracts. We examine these tradeoffs using the example of Universal Motors, a hypothetical producer of new automobiles. Universal is considering whether to produce its own auto bodies or to obtain them from an independent supplier through a long-term contract. In either case, a new auto body plant must be constructed. There will be ongoing production, maintenance, and capital-replacement costs. Universal wants to choose the organizational arrangement that maximizes value.

Incomplete Contracting

If contracts were costless to plan, negotiate, write, and enforce, it would not matter if Universal made its own auto bodies or bought them from an outside supplier. In either case, a *complete contract* would be negotiated, which specified exactly what was expected of each party under all possible future contingencies. Severe penalties would ensure compliance. The actions of each party would be chosen to maximize value (the level of investment, ongoing expenditures, production quantities, designs, and so on). With vertical integration, the contracts would be between the firm and employees, while a long-term supply contract would be between two independent firms.

Contracting, however, can be expensive. First, it is difficult to foresee and plan for all possible contingencies. Universal might want to make future changes in the design of its auto bodies should customer tastes change or if a competitor develops a superior body design. However, Universal's managers are unlikely to know the optimal response until the situation confronts them. Second, it is expensive to negotiate contracts. Self-interested parties often find it difficult to agree on contracts—consider the strikes in professional sports. Third, it is costly to enforce contracts. When contractual disputes arise, the contracting parties are likely to incur legal expenses and spend valuable time either preparing for court or renegotiating contracts. Contract costs necessitate *incomplete contracts*—many contingencies will be omitted and open for future negotiation. For example, the Kodak–IBM outsourcing contract states that IBM must maintain a state-of-the-art data center. The exact technology, software, and communications system are not specified.[15]

The prospect of future negotiations can motivate suboptimal investment. Parties to the contract realize that part of the gains from their investments (in capital or effort) are likely to go to other parties—they are not protected by a complete contract. For example, as we discuss below, a supplier will be reluctant to invest effort or capital to reduce production costs if the buyer is likely to capture most of the gains by renegotiating a lower purchase price for the input.

---

[14]Material in this section draws on the analysis in Williamson (1985). Important references on this topic include Klein, Crawford, and Alchian (1978); S. Grossman and O. Hart (1986), "The Costs and Benefits of Ownership: A Theory of Vertical and Lateral Integration," *Journal of Political Economy* 94, 691–719; O. Hart (1995), *Firms, Contracts, and Financial Structure* (Oxford Press: Oxford, UK).

[15]Richmond, Seidmann, and Whinston (1972), 463.

Contracting Problems and Investment Incentives: Evidence from China

The early 1990s witnessed a substantial growth in American investment in China. American financial institutions loaned substantial amounts of money to Chinese businesses, while other American companies invested in a variety of Chinese business ventures. By 1995, many of these American companies experienced problems in collecting debts from Chinese businesses. One problem in enforcing contracts with Chinese businesses is that the legal system in China is "primitive." In addition, "China's corporate managers are accustomed to the old socialist system, where they could simply ignore their debts"—there is little market-based enforcement of contracts.

Leasing companies that have financed specific assets have been "particularly vulnerable because the collateral—usually heavy equipment or production lines—is difficult to seize once installed. And even if it can be repossessed, China lacks a good secondary market for equipment." The inability to write enforceable contracts has made American companies question whether it is a good idea to make specific investments in China.

Source: P. Engardio (1994), "Why Sweet Deals Are Going Sour in China,"
Business Week (December 19), 50–51.

Ownership and Investment Incentives[16]

The owner has the right to determine the *residual use* of an asset—any use that does not conflict with prior contract, custom, or law. Residual rights give an individual increased *power* to capture the gains from an investment and can affect investment incentives. For instance, house owners have the residual rights for their properties. As long as their actions are consistent with the law and existing contracts (for example, zoning requirements and restrictive covenants in the deed), they are free to sell or rent their houses. The ability of owners to capture the gains from investing in house repairs through higher selling prices makes it more likely that owners will take care of houses than renters. Renters are reluctant to invest in repairs if most of the gains go to owners.[17]

Vertical integration and long-term contracts differ in their assignment of ownership rights. Vertical integration keeps the ownership rights for the relevant assets within one firm, while long-term contracting apportions them between firms. As we discuss below,

Renting and Asset Abuse

Renters do not bear the total costs from abusing an asset, since it is owned by the rental company; thus, rental assets frequently are abused. "In one case, a fellow rented a sports car with 12 miles on it. He took out the high-powered engine and installed it in a "stock car," to run a high-speed 500-mile race. After crossing the finish line, he reinstalled the engine in the rental car and returned it. The rental company could not successfully prosecute because it failed to establish the number of miles that had been put on the engine. The rental car still showed low mileage, and the rental fee to the customer/car racer was only $24."

Source: D. McIntyre (1988), "Rent a Reck," *Financial World* (September 20), 72.

[16]Material in this section draws on the analysis in Hart (1995).

[17]C. Smith and L. Wakeman (1985), "Determinants of Corporate Leasing Policy," *Journal of Finance* 40, 896–908.

the optimal choice between vertical integration and long-term contracts depends, at least in part, on which ownership structure motivates the most productive investment decisions. The appendix to this chapter provides a more detailed example of this basic idea.

Specific Assets and Vertical Integration

Specific assets can cause substantial investment distortions among independent contractors. Consider the investment incentives of Hunter Body Company, a potential supplier to Universal. Hunter Body would have to construct a plant next to one of Universal's major production facilities. Transportation costs and special designs make this plant quite specific—its value is much less to other car companies that are farther away and use different body designs. Asset specificity places Hunter in a tenuous position. Without the guarantee of a complete contract, Hunter will be concerned that Universal will try to lower the price for auto bodies once the investment is made (recall from Chapter 5 that Hunter has incentives to operate as long as price is greater than *average variable cost*). Universal might claim that Hunter is supplying low-quality products and demand a price concession. Given litigation costs, Hunter might be forced to accept the lower price. This concern reduces Hunter's incentives to invest in the plant. Similarly, Universal might be reluctant to tailor-make their cars to fit Hunter products because it fears that Hunter will be opportunistic and increase the price for its auto bodies. In this example, investment incentives can be improved through vertical integration. If Universal constructs its own auto body plant (or buys Hunter), it is in a position to capture the gains from its investment. It does not have to worry that some outside firm will try to extract part of the returns by demanding a different price for auto bodies.[18] Other transaction costs might decline as well, since the companies do not have to negotiate a complicated legal contract.

These arguments help to explain why vertical integration can be preferred to long-term contracting. Why is this not always the case? What limits the entire economy from being served by one gigantic firm that produces all products? The answer lies again in investment incentives. Consider Universal's purchase of lightbulbs. Universal purchases lightbulbs from the General Electric Company (GE). Since lightbulbs are not a specialized product, the purchasing arrangement harms neither GE's nor Universal's investment incentives. GE is willing to make investments that reduce the costs of making lightbulbs because it benefits from these investments. If Universal tries to capture some of the benefits from GE's investment by offering a lower price for lightbulbs, GE will simply sell the bulbs to another customer. If GE tries to raise the price of its bulbs to extract profits from Universal, Universal will buy bulbs from another company, such as Phillips Electronics. In contrast, if Universal purchases GE and operates it as an internal division, investment incentives can be distorted. As divisional managers, GE's management might have reduced incentives to invest in innovative activities, since part of the credit for value-enhancing ideas will go to Universal's senior management. In addition, GE's management might invest in nonproductive activities, such as trying to *influence* senior management's decisions (salaries, allocating capital to the divisions, and so on).[19]

---

[18]With costless contracting, the hold-up problem could be solved in the following way: The contract could specify optimal investments by Hunter and Universal, and anticipated holdups could be compensated for in advance by appropriate side payments between Hunter and Universal.

[19]P. Milgrom and J. Roberts (1994), "Bargaining Costs, Influence Costs, and the Organization of Economic Activity," in *Perspectives on Positive Political Economy,* J. Alt and K. Shepsle, eds. (Cambridge University Press: Cambridge), 57–89.

Lease versus Buy

Firms frequently decide between leasing and buying an asset. Economic theory suggests that firms are most likely to own assets that are highly firm-specific. For example, Le Roy Industries leases some of its forklifts and other vehicles but buys outright the very specialized machinery it needs to make suspension parts for Ford, General Motors, and Chrysler cars. To quote Charles Teets, vice president and chief financial officer of the company:

> It takes about a year to make the machinery we need. It would be very hard to find a lessor interested in our type of equipment because of the long lead-time. After the lease expired, no lessor would want the equipment back.

Source: "The New Attraction in Leasing" (1987), *Nation's Business* (March).

These arguments suggest that *the likelihood of vertical integration increases with the specificity of the asset.* With less specialized assets, market transactions or long-term contracts are more likely to produce efficient investment incentives. This proposition is one of the most important ideas in the economic literature on organizations. Empirical tests support its validity. As an example, J. Stuckey examined aluminum refineries that are located near bauxite mines.[20] Not only are the refineries specific to particular mines due to transportation costs, the refineries also invest in specialized equipment. Stuckey found that in virtually all cases, there is vertical integration.

Research indicates that specific assets are especially likely to motivate integration in *uncertain environments.* In uncertain environments, the contracting problems with specific assets are particularly severe—it is nearly impossible to specify what actions each party should perform under all future contingencies. In more predictable environments, relatively complete contracts can be negotiated that mitigate hold-up problems.

The arguments in this section are summarized in Figure 15.5. When asset specificity is low, it is generally best to rely on market exchange, regardless of the level of uncertainty. As the degree of asset specificity increases, the desirability of nonmarket transactions increases. Uncertainty increases the desirability of vertically integrating firm-specific assets; when asset specificity and uncertainty are both high, vertical integration is likely to be the preferred alternative.

This analysis of firm-specific assets helps to explain why catering, trucking, copying, and mainframe computing are among the most frequently outsourced services. These activities are sufficiently specialized that spot-market transactions are not viable. Nonetheless, these activities involve assets that are not highly firm-specific. Food-service equipment, trucks, copy machines, and computers can be used by many different companies—therefore, the potential for hold-up actions is relatively low. Furthermore, for activities like copying, it is easy to write a relatively complete contract (uncertainty is reasonably low). There are also potential benefits from using independent firms that specialize in large-volume production. Moreover, the transactions are quite *repetitive;* thus, it makes sense to contract with a single supplier on a long-term basis. (The supplier makes customer-specific investments in learning how to serve the customer; hence, it is expensive to change suppliers.) These factors imply that it is often optimal to contract for these services.

[20]J. Stuckey (1983), *Vertical Integration and Joint Ventures in the Aluminum Industry* (Harvard University Press: Cambridge, Mass). See also E. Anderson (1985), "The Salesperson as Outside Agent or Employee: A Transaction Cost Analysis," *Marketing Science* 4, 234–54; E. Anderson and D. Schmittlein (1984), "Integration of the Sales Force: An Empirical Examination," *Rand Journal of Economics* 15, 385–95; and W. Kim, D. Mayers, and C. Smith (1996), "On the Choice of Insurance Distribution Systems," *Journal of Risk and Insurance* (forthcoming).

Uncertainty

	Low	Medium	High
Low	Market Transaction	Market Transaction	Market Transaction
Medium	Contract	Contract or Vertical Integration	Contract or Vertical Integration
High	Contract	Contract or Vertical Integration	Vertical Integration

Asset Specificity (vertical axis label)

Figure 15.5 Asset Specificity, Uncertainty, and the Procurement Decision

When asset specificity is low, it is generally optimal to use simple market transactions for procurement. As the degree of asset specificity increases, nonmarket transactions (contracts and vertical integration) become more desirable. When uncertainty is low, relatively complete contracts can be written. Thus, contracts can be used to resolve incentive conflicts motivated by firm-specific assets. As uncertainty increases, contracting becomes more expensive. Vertical integration of firm-specific assets becomes more likely as uncertainty increases.

One advantage of having IBM provide computer services to Kodak is that IBM provides similar services to other companies. This higher volume can lower the cost for Kodak. The costs of training technical specialists can be spread across more users; software can be written that is used by more than one company. Also, IBM is able to attract higher-quality computer specialists than Kodak, since IBM's scale of operation provides a much richer set of career opportunities. Conceptually, Kodak could capture some of these gains by purchasing IBM and operating the two companies as one large enterprise. However, the costs of managing such a large enterprise would be likely to outweigh the benefits.

Vertical Integration in the Aerospace Industry

Scott Masten studied the make-versus-buy policies of a major aerospace contractor. The firm made many products for the U.S. government. The company had to choose between making each product or subcontracting it to another firm for production. Economic theory suggests that internal production is more likely when the assets are specific and the uncertainties in contracting are large.

Masten used two measures of asset specificity for each product. The first measured design (physical-asset) specificity, while the second measured site specificity. He also measured the complexity of the product design, which was intended to proxy for uncertainties in contracting. Consistent with the theory, he found that products that were highly design-specific and highly complex were more likely to be produced internally. When the product was both design-specific and complex, there was a 92 percent probability of internal production. If the product was design-specific but not complex, the probability of internal production was 31 percent. The probability of internal production was only 2 percent when the product was neither design-specific nor complex. For this particular company, site specificity was unimportant.

Source: S. Masten (1984), "The Organization of Production: Evidence from the Aerospace Industry," *Journal of Law & Economics* 27, 403–17.

Other Reasons

Unions are another factor that can affect the choice between vertical integration and contracting. For instance, some of the major airlines have threatened labor unions that they will outsource their kitchen operations to other companies to avoid paying union wages. The major automobile companies have made similar statements with respect to the manufacturing of component parts. Some firms are reluctant to integrate into a unionized activity because they fear that the move might motivate their employees to organize.

There are sometimes issues of controlling sensitive, proprietary information that affect decisions of outsourcing versus vertical integration. For example, in the specific case of Kodak outsourcing computing services to IBM, there is a potential problem with Kodak-specific knowledge about electronic imaging. Kodak invests heavily in electronic-imaging R&D. To exploit this investment fully, Kodak must carefully guard this information. Since IBM is an obvious competitor in the electronic-imaging market, outsourcing Kodak's computing services presents a potential problem—one that demands the design of careful controls to keep IBM personnel from accessing Kodak's proprietary information. Note that the costs of designing and administering these controls affects the optimal policy choice. If they are high, Kodak might reject IBM as an outsourcing partner in favor of another vendor with less overlap in the electronic-imaging market (perhaps Electronic Data Systems), or Kodak might reject outsourcing altogether. Along these lines, Prahalad and Hamel argue that it is often unwise for a company to outsource its "core competencies" (those capabilities that are fundamental to a firm's performance and strategy).[21] Rather, according to this argument, firms should keep core competencies within the firm to enhance their development and to prevent other firms from developing similar capabilities.

The financial press often argues that obtaining inputs through contracts with other firms "frees companies to use scarce capital for other purposes." This claim is questionable given the existence of well-developed capital markets. Having another firm produce a product does not reduce investment, it simply shifts the capital expenditures to another firm. Buyers still pay for this investment through the price of the product. The important question is whether more value is created by producing the product internally or externally. If internal production is more valuable, the firm can raise money in the capital market for financing the relevant assets. (Capital is not "scarce" for good projects.) If external production is more valuable, funds can be raised by the supplier.

Continuum of Choice

While we have discussed long-term contracting versus vertical integration as a choice between two policies, it is important to keep in mind that the outsourcing decision falls on a continuum. For example, sometimes it is desirable for a firm to maintain ownership of a firm-specific asset and contract with another firm to operate it. This ownership pattern reduces potential hold-up problems because if there is a contract dispute, the owner can simply take the asset and contract with an alternate firm to provide the service (neither side faces large losses). This ownership pattern is most viable if the asset can be moved at low cost and the value of the asset is insensitive to asset maintenance or abuse. Alternatively, the owner must be able to provide the service operator with sufficient incentives to maintain and not to abuse the asset.

---

[21]C. Prahalad and G. Hamel (1990), "The Core Competence of the Corporation," *Harvard Business Review* (May–June), 79–91.

A related example is Kodak's decision to contract with IBM for providing operating software and hardware but to maintain responsibility for applications software. Development of applications software is likely to be more specific to Kodak than development of operating software that can be used for many different applications and firms. IBM, therefore, has greater incentives to focus on the development of the operating software, while Kodak has greater incentives to focus on the applications software. The location of specific knowledge reinforces these incentives—Kodak knows more about its specific applications, while IBM knows more about general computing. The observed organizational arrangement reflects these incentive and information effects.

Contract Length

A major advantage of long-term contracts over short-term contracts is that they increase the incentives of the contracting parties to make firm-specific investments. For example, IBM would have limited incentives to invest in learning Kodak's special computing demands if it anticipated only a short-term relationship between the two companies.[22] On the other hand, it is costly to write and litigate long-term contracts in uncertain environments, where it is difficult to plan for potential changes in technology, input prices, product demands, and the like. Thus, firms might be expected to enter long-term contracts when the desired investment is relatively firm-specific and where the environment is relatively stable. Alternatively, if the firm faces a highly uncertain environment and large investments in firm-specific assets, vertical integration is more likely to be the preferred alternative. Finally, if the investment in firm-specific assets is relatively low or the lives of the assets relatively short, the firm can more easily enter into short-term contracts with suppliers or rely on spot market transactions.

Contracting with Distributors

While our examples have focused on supply contracts, the same analysis applies to distribution contracts. As assets become more specific, vertical integration becomes more desirable. A number of other interesting issues, however, arise in distribution contracts. These issues are the subject of this section.

Free-Rider Problems

Earlier in this chapter, we discussed the incentives of independent distributors to free-ride on the reputation of a brand name, and how these incentives can motivate suboptimal sales efforts (for example, insufficient expenditures on advertising and other inputs).

---

[22]Long-term contracts provide the greatest incentives when they have uncertain expiration dates (the parties expect the contracts might be renewed). There are strong incentives to cheat in the last period when a contract has a known ending date, since maintaining the reputation as a good partner has no benefit (ignoring third-party effects). The parties, knowing that they will not cooperate in the last period, have incentives to cheat in the next-to-last period. (There are no reputational concerns since they know that the other party will not cooperate in the last period.) The incentives to cheat in the next-to-last period affect the incentives in the previous period, and so on. In this case, the contract can *unravel,* so that the parties have the incentive to cheat in the first period. L. Telser (1980), "A Theory of Self-Enforcing Agreements," *Journal of Business* 53, 27–44.

Divorce between Outsourcing Partners

Not all outsourcing ventures work—some end in divorce. Hibernia National Bank and Capital Bank used to outsource their computer operations to IBM. To cut its costs, IBM pooled the software support staff for the two banks. Both banks used software from Hogan Systems, a business partner with IBM from 1987. In 1993, Hibernia estimated it could save $40 million over eight years by switching to a new outsourcing partner, Systematics Financial Services Inc. Capital followed Hibernia and also shifted to Systematics. Subsequently, Hogan and IBM parted ways. This example and others like it suggests that prospective outsourcing partners should anticipate the possibility that the venture will not work out and plan accordingly (for example, by negotiating the equivalent of a prenuptial agreement—what to do with assets, severance payments, and so on).

Source: "ISSC: A Tale of Marriage and Divorce" (1994), *Information Week*
(July 18), 13.

One method to reduce this problem is vertical integration.[23] The other method is to use contracts with specific provisions to control free-rider problems. Two contract terms that specifically address this concern are advertising provisions and exclusive territories.

Advertising Provisions

There are several related methods that firms use to increase advertising at the local level. First, the company can charge its retail subcontractors an advertising fee and have the central company be responsible for advertising. For instance, most franchise contracts require that, in addition to the base royalty payment, individual units pay a percentage of sales to the central company to provide advertising. One potential problem with this approach is that the local unit, not the central company, might have the specific knowledge relevant for effective local advertising. A second alternative that addresses this concern is for the central company to share in the local advertising costs. (For example, it might pay half of any advertising expenditures.) The decisions on local advertising are made by the local managers. A third alternative is to require distributors to contribute to regional advertising funds. The distributors have the primary decision rights to decide how to spend the monies in the funds.

Exclusive Territories

One of the most common methods for reducing free-riding is to grant individual distributors the exclusive rights to operate in a given market area. For example, a Toyota dealership might have a contract that prevents Toyota from opening another dealership within 30 miles. By giving distributors monopoly rights for specific market areas, there are fewer incentives to free-ride, since the distributors internalize more of the benefits from their sales efforts. (Fewer benefits go to other units not owned by the given distributor.) Exclusive territories can also create extra profits for local distributors. These profits can provide additional incentives not to free-ride—if the manufacturer catches the distributor free-riding and terminates the contract, future profits are lost.[24]

[23]H. Marvel (1982), "Exclusive Dealing," *Journal of Law & Economics* 25, 1–25.

[24]B. Klein and K. Murphy (1988), "Vertical Restraints as Contract Enforcement Mechanisms," *Journal of Law & Economics* 31, 265–97.

Company Ownership versus Franchising

We have discussed how a central company can reduce the incentives of an independent distributor to free-ride on the brand name through contracts with terms that motivate increased sales efforts. When the free-rider problem is severe, it can be less expensive to simply own the distribution units centrally. Managers of a company-owned unit have fewer incentives than an independent distributor to free-ride on the reputation, since they do not get to keep the profits from the unit—the reduction in costs (for example, from decreased advertising) flow through to the central company, not the managers.

Most franchise companies do not franchise all their retail outlets. The typical company franchises about 80 percent of the units and owns the other 20 percent. Our argument suggests that central companies are most likely to own the units that receive a significant amount of business from customers who are unlikely to make repeat purchases at the particular units (the incentives to free-ride in this case are large). On average, fast-food restaurants are more likely to serve transient customers than auto-service companies. (Customers tend to use the same unit repeatedly for oil changes and tune-ups.) Consistent with the theory, the typical restaurant franchise company owns about 30 percent of its units, while the typical auto service franchise company owns about 13 percent of its units.

Source: IFA Educational Foundation and Horwath International, *Franchising in the Economy 1991.*

Double Markups

While granting distributors monopoly power over specific market areas reduces free-rider problems, it can create another problem—*double markups.* Since both the manufacturer and the distributor face downward sloping demand curves, each has the incentive to mark up the product's price above marginal cost. The result is that the customer faces two markups rather than one. The quantity of the product demanded is lower than optimal, and the combined profits for the manufacturer and distributor are not maximized. The following is a numerical example illustrating this problem, as well as the contract terms that might be used to reduce it.

Example

Suppose that the Toyota Motor Company faces the following demand for its automobiles in the Medford, Oregon, market area:

$$P = 55{,}000 - 100Q \tag{15.3}$$

Toyota can produce the automobiles at a constant marginal cost of \$5,000. To simplify the computations, assume there are no fixed costs in producing or selling cars. To maximize profits, Toyota must select the quantity and price where marginal revenue equals marginal cost. As pictured in Figure 15.6, the optimal quantity and price are $Q^* = 250$ and $P^* = \$30{,}000$. Firm profits are \$6.25 million.

Now suppose that Toyota sells its vehicles through Medford Motors, an independent distributor that has the exclusive right to sell Toyotas in the Medford market area. Under the contract, Toyota sets the wholesale price, while Medford Motors selects the quantity to purchase and the retail price. For simplicity, suppose that the only marginal cost facing Medford Motors for automobiles is the price charged by Toyota. (There are no variable distribution costs.) The owners of Medford Motors care only about their own profits, while the managers of Toyota care only about Toyota's profits. The problem facing Toyota is to choose the wholesale price, P_w, that maximizes its profits.

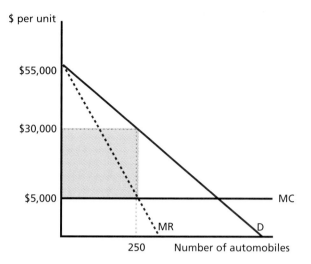

Figure 15.6 Optimal Output in an Example of the Double Markup Problem

Toyota can produce automobiles at a constant marginal cost of $5,000. To maximize profits, Toyota must select the quantity and price where marginal revenue equals marginal cost. The optimal quantity and price are Q* = 250 and P* = $30,000. Firm profits are $6.25 million (assuming no fixed costs).

To solve this problem, Toyota's management would like to know the quantity that Medford Motors would purchase at each possible wholesale price. Toyota can infer this demand curve by analyzing the problem from the perspective of Medford Motors. Medford Motors faces the retail demand curve for autos given in equation 15.3. Medford Motors maximizes its profits by setting its marginal revenue, implied by this retail demand curve, equal to P_w, its marginal cost. Thus, Medford Motors' marginal revenue curve is the effective demand curve Toyota faces. (At any wholesale price, Medford buys the quantity indicated by its marginal revenue curve.) As pictured in Figure 15.6, this curve is:

$$P_w = 55,000 - 200Q \qquad (15.4)$$

Given Medford Motors' demand for automobiles, what wholesale price will Toyota choose? Toyota maximizes its profits by setting its marginal revenue equal to its marginal cost of $5,000. Since Toyota faces a demand curve of $P_w = 55,000 - 200Q$, its marginal revenue is MR = 55,000 − 400Q. Toyota's profits are maximized by selecting a wholesale price of P_w = $30,000. At this price, Medford Motors will buy 125 automobiles and set a retail price of $42,500. Toyota will have profits of $3.125 million, and Medford Motors will have profits of $1.563 million, for combined profits of $4.688 million.

This outcome, which is pictured in Figure 15.7, is inefficient. Toyota and Medford Motors fail to maximize their joint profits. Both parties could be made better off by coordinating their prices and volume choices—we already have shown that they could earn up to $6.25 million (versus $4.688 million). In addition, with the double mark ups, consumers pay $42,500 for 125 Toyota automobiles rather than $30,000 for 250 automobiles.

This problem does not automatically disappear if Toyota merges with Medford Motors. We saw in Chapter 14 that exactly the same problem can arise within firms, when products are sold between two profits centers through internal transfer prices. As we discussed, the

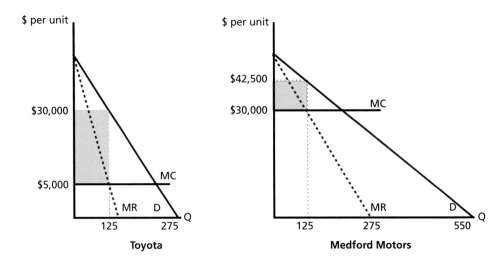

Figure 15.7 Example of Double Markups

Toyota sets the wholesale price for its automobiles, while Medford Motors selects the quantity to purchase and the retail price. Medford Motors maximizes profit by setting the wholesale price equal to its marginal revenue. Thus, Medford Motors' marginal revenue curve is Toyota's demand curve. Toyota maximizes profit by setting its marginal cost of $5,000 equal to its marginal revenue. Toyota selects a wholesale price of $30,000, a $25,000 markup above its marginal cost, while Medford Motors selects a retail price of $42,500, a $12,500 markup above its marginal cost. Medford Motors sells 125 cars at this price. The combined profits are $4.688 million. The two companies could earn combined profits of $6.25 million if they cooperate and sell 250 automobiles to consumers at a price of $30,000.

transfer-pricing problem can be reduced by appropriate organizational design. Our current focus is on how this problem might be reduced between two independent firms through specific contractual terms.

Two-Part Pricing

Medford Motors will purchase 250 automobiles if Toyota sets a wholesale price of $5,000. This quantity maximizes the joint profits of the two firms and results in a retail price of $30,000. The entire profits, however, go to Medford Motors, since Toyota is selling the automobiles at cost. One solution is for Toyota to charge Medford Motors an up-front franchise fee—thereby obtaining its share of the profits through this fee—and then to sell automobiles to Medford Motors at $5,000 each. Since Medford Motors' purchasing decision is based on marginal cost, not total cost, it will still purchase 250 automobiles and set a retail price of $30,000. If Toyota charges Medford Motors an up-front fee of $3.125 million for the exclusive rights to the Medford market area, the combined profits of $6.25 million are split evenly between the two companies. Once the fee is collected, Toyota might try to increase the wholesale price of the automobiles to increase its profits. Thus, for such a solution to work, Toyota must be able to commit credibly to sell automobiles to Medford Motors at marginal cost.

Quotas

An alternative method for maximizing the combined profits is for the two companies to agree on a minimum purchase requirement. Medford Motors could agree to purchase at least 250 automobiles at a prespecified wholesale price (above $5,000). Given the details in this example, Medford Motors will purchase exactly 250 automobiles and sell them at $30,000 to retail customers. The level of the prespecified wholesale price determines the split of the profits between the two companies. A wholesale price of $7,500 splits the profits evenly. Toyota must be able to commit credibly to the wholesale price, while Medford Motors must purchase the agreed-upon quota.

Regulatory Issues

Some regulators and scholars are suspicious of contract terms such as exclusive territories that potentially limit competition. Nevertheless, most nonprice contract terms are not *per se* illegal (always illegal) under federal antitrust law. They are judged on a *rule of reason,* where the court attempts to consider the benefits of the terms (such as increased sales efforts) against potential anticompetitive effects. In some states, automobile dealers and franchisees have successfully lobbied their legislators to limit the control that central companies impose (for example, in setting quotas and terminating contracts). In addition, federal law restricts central companies from directly controlling the pricing of distributors at the retail level. A detailed treatment of these regulatory issues is beyond the scope of this book.[25] Suffice it to say that it usually is important for firms to engage expert legal counsel in designing supply and distribution contracts.

Recent Trends in Outsourcing

The 1990s have witnessed an increase in outsourcing by major companies. At least four factors have contributed to this trend. First, there has been a dramatic increase in worldwide competition. This competition has placed pressure on firms to reduce costs and become more efficient. Some scholars argue that many American firms were "flush with cash" in the 1960s and 1970s and tended to waste this cash through such actions as overly integrating.[26] Some of the recent outsourcing decisions might be corrections for poor investment decisions of the past. Second, new flexible production technologies allow suppliers to adapt more easily to customer demands. Thus, in some cases, assets are becoming less firm-specific, which favors contracting over vertical integration. Third, improvements in information and communications technology make it easier to identify potential partners and to communicate with them after an agreement is reached. Electronic data interchange (EDI) allows firms to connect their computers to one another. These computers can automatically order inventory directly from a supplier with little human intervention. Fourth, during the early 1990s, there was a worldwide recession, which caused excess capacity in many industries. Firms could often obtain large discounts from external vendors. (This effect is potentially more cyclical than permanent.)

Many of the recent outsourcing decisions do not move firms from internal production to the other end of the spectrum—spot market transactions. Rather, the movement has been to an intermediate arrangement—long-term contracting. Many firms have also moved away from acquiring inputs in the spot market. To improve quality and lower unit costs, firms such as General Motors and Xerox have cut their number of suppliers

---

[25]For a more detailed treatment of these issues, see R. Posner (1976), *Antitrust law* (University of Chicago Press: Chicago); and D. Carlton and J. Perloff (1990).

[26]M. Jensen (1986), "Agency Costs of Free Cash Flow, Corporate Finance and Takeovers," *American Economic Review* 76, 323–329.

CASE STUDY
Universal Motors

Universal Motors produces automobiles. It has asked the American Fabric Company to consider a proposal to become a supplier of automobile seats. Under the proposal, American Fabric would construct a $20 million plant near one of Universal's production facilities. Universal would purchase 100,000 car seats per year at a price is $280 per seat for 15 years—the useful life of the plant. (The actual proposal contains an adjustment for inflation. Ignore this complication in the analysis).

American Fabric's financial analysts have examined the proposal. It appears to be a profitable opportunity. The amortized cost of the plant is $2.6 million per year (at a discount rate of 10%). The annual costs are $25.4 million per year. Therefore, the average total cost is $280 per seat—ATC = ($25.4 million + $2.6 million) / 100,000 = $280. The financial analysts have examined Universal's financial outlook. While it has not been highly profitable in all years, there is essentially no probability of bankruptcy over the next 15 years. Since the proposed price covers the cost, the financial analysts think that the proposal should be accepted. (It breaks even with a fair rate of return on invested capital of 10%.)

You have been asked to analyze the contract proposal. You have seen the financial analysis and think the cost estimates are correct. You are aware that, due to its location, the proposed plant has no

alternative use other than supplying seats to Universal. The salvage value of the plant, in the event of liquidation, is $2 million.

Discussion Questions

1. One concern you have is that Universal might try to lower the effective purchase price of the seats after the plant is built (by reneging on the contract or demanding higher quality seats for the same price). Once the plant is built, how much can the purchase price fall before American Fabric liquidates the plant?
2. What factors would you consider to determine if opportunistic behavior by Universal is a likely possibility?
3. Does Universal have to worry about any opportunistic actions by American Fabric?
4. Discuss factors that might make it difficult to write a contract that would limit opportunistic behavior by both companies.
5. Discuss the costs and benefits of Universal vertically integrating and supplying its own automobile seats.
6. Discuss the costs and benefits of having Universal construct the plant and having American Fabric operate it on a contractual basis.

dramatically and correspondingly have increased the number of long-term partnerships with independent firms. Thus, the current trend can be viewed as a movement from both ends of the spectrum toward the middle.

Recent technological changes, such as just-in-time production methods, electronic data interchanges, and total quality manufacturing, require close links between manufacturers, suppliers, and distributors. Rather than inspecting parts and materials from numerous suppliers on delivery, a few suppliers are selected and their production processes are certified as meeting high quality standards. Thus, although the various activities in the manufacturing/distribution process are conducted by different firms, it is important that these firms remain closely linked. In such cases, these factors make spot market transactions undesirable.

Summary

When a firm participates in more than one successive stage of the production or distribution of a product or service, it is said to be *vertically integrated.* Firms change their degree of integration over time. An organization that begins to produce its own inputs is engaging in *backward* or *upstream* integration, while an organization that begins to market its own goods or to conduct additional finishing work is engaging in *forward* or *downstream* integration. The term *outsourcing* is frequently used to describe a movement away from vertical integration—moving an activity outside the firm that was formerly done within the firm. The term *outsourcing* also is used to describe an ongoing arrangement where a firm obtains a part or service from an external firm. It often is useful to think of the outsourcing decision as a choice along a continuum of possibilities, ranging from spot market transactions to vertical integration with an array of long-term contracts in between.

Well-functioning markets provide powerful incentives for efficient production and low prices. It is value maximizing for firms to acquire many goods and services through market transactions. Economists have identified at least three primary reasons why a firm might want to engage in nonmarket procurement: *transaction costs, taxes/regulation,* and *monopoly power.* At least four factors can make the transactions costs of nonmarket procurement lower than the costs of market exchange. These factors include firm-specific assets, costs of measuring quality, coordination problems, and externalities.

Firm-specific assets are assets that are significantly more valuable in their current use than in their next best alternative use. Investment in firm-specific assets can cause material problems between suppliers and buyers and is a primary reason for nonmarket transactions. Once the investment in firm-specific assets is made, there is a *sunk cost*—the supplier has incentives to continue the relationship as long as the variable costs are covered (even if the total costs are not). This incentive subjects the supplier to a potential *hold-up problem.* The buyer can also be held up by the supplier. One way to reduce these problems is to integrate vertically. The other method is to negotiate a detailed contract that spells out what is expected of each party.

Due to contracting costs, most contracts are *incomplete*—many contingencies are unspecified and subject to future negotiation. The prospect of future negotiations can motivate suboptimal investment (in capital and effort). Parties to the contract realize that part of the gains from their investments are likely to go to other parties—they are not protected by a complete contract.

The owner has the right to determine the *residual use* of an asset—any use that does not conflict with prior contract, custom, or law. Residual rights give an individual increased *power* to capture the gains from an investment and thus can provide investment incentives. Vertical integration and long-term contracts differ in their assignment of ownership rights. Vertical integration keeps the ownership rights for the relevant assets within one firm, while long-term contracting apportions them between firms. The choice between vertical integration and long-term contracts depends, at least in part, on which ownership structure creates more productive investment decisions. A primary prediction of the economics literature is that as an asset becomes more firm-specific, the firm is more likely to choose vertical integration over long-term contracting. Better investment incentives are expected, and overall contracting costs are reduced.

The analysis suggests that firms will enter long-term contracts when the desired investment is relatively firm-specific and where the environment is relatively stable and predictable (in stable environments, negotiating more complete contracts is easier). Alternatively, if the firm faces a more uncertain environment and large investments in firm-specific assets, vertical integration is more likely to be the preferred alternative. Finally, if the investment in firm-specific assets is relatively low (the assets are unspecialized) or the lives of the assets relatively short, the firm can either enter into short-term contracts with suppliers or rely on spot market transactions.

Independent distributors can have incentives to *free-ride* on a brand name. One method to reduce this problem is vertical integration. The other method is to use contracts with specific provisions that reduce free-rider problems. Two types of contract terms that specifically address this concern are *advertising provisions* and *exclusive territories*. While exclusive territories help to reduce free-rider problems, they create another problem—*double markups*. This problem, which is analogous to the transfer-pricing problem studied in Chapter 14, can be reduced through *two-part pricing* or *quotas*.

There are at least four factors that have contributed to the recent trend in outsourcing—increased worldwide competition, the development of less firm-specific production technologies, improvements in information and communication technologies, and excess capacity from a worldwide recession. The recent trend, however, is not from vertical integration to spot market transactions. It is a movement from both ends of the spectrum toward the intermediate arrangement of long-term contracting. Recent technological changes, such as just-in-time production methods, electronic data interchanges, and total quality management, require closer links between manufacturers, suppliers, and distributors. These changes reduce the desirability of spot market transactions in many cases.

APPENDIX | *Ownership Rights and Investment Incentives*[27]

This appendix provides a more detailed example of how ownership rights can affect investment incentives (in this case, investments in effort). Through this example, some of the important tradeoffs between vertical integration and long-term contracts become more evident.

Basic Problem

The AGT Company manufactures computer modems. The company is owned by Roxanne Rock. The Custom Circuit Company makes circuit boards for AGT. AGT is Custom's only customer, while Custom is AGT's sole supplier of circuit boards. The boards are tailor-made for AGT and cannot be used by other manufacturers (the boards are firm-specific). The owner of Custom Circuit is Jim Gail.

AGT might want to make future design changes in its circuit boards. For simplicity, suppose that the future benefit of a design change to AGT can take on two values, 20 or 40, while the costs to Custom of making the change can either be 10 or 30. The likelihood of a high benefit and a low cost is influenced by both Roxanne's and Jim's efforts. Let x equal the probability that the benefit is 40. Roxanne can affect this probability through her efforts—in fact, we assume that Roxanne's efforts completely determine x. For instance, by working with customers, she can determine the best design change to make. She can also spend time marketing the revised product. These types of activities increase the probability that the benefits from the design change will be large. However,

---

[27]This appendix utilizes elementary probability theory and calculus. Material in this section draws on the analysis in B. Holmstrom and J. Tirole (1989), "Theory of the Firm," in *Handbook of Industrial Organization*, vol. 1, R. Schmalensee, ed. (North Holland: Amsterdam, the Netherlands), 69–72.

the personal cost to Roxanne of exerting effort is $10x^2$. As an example, if Roxanne exerts enough effort so that x is .5, she incurs a personal cost of $10(.5)^2 = 2.5$. Similarly, Jim's actions completely determine y, the probability that the cost equals 10, at a personal cost of $10y^2$. For instance, Jim can exert effort on developing more cost-effective ways to manufacture the new circuit boards.

Neither Roxanne's nor Jim's effort choices are observable by the other party. Roxanne does not know y and Jim does not know x. While both Roxanne and Jim can ultimately observe the realized costs and benefits of the design change, they cannot be verified by a third party. It is not possible to provide either party with incentives through a contract tied to realized costs or benefits of the design change.

Ideal Effort Choices

Value is created by a design change whenever the benefits of the change exceed the costs. The only time where the design change does not create value is when the benefits are 20 and the costs are 30. Both Roxanne and Jim are risk neutral. It is in their joint interests to choose effort levels that maximize the expected surplus. By maximizing the size of the pie, there is more value to share and both parties can be made better off. Ideally, the total expected surplus, S_T, for the two companies is:

$$S_T = (40 - 10)xy + (40 - 30)x(1 - y) + (20 - 10)(1 - x)y - 10x^2 - 10y^2$$
$$= 30xy + 10x(1 - y) + 10(1 - x)y - 10x^2 - 10y^2$$
$$= 10xy + 10x + 10y - 10x^2 - 10y^2 \tag{15.5}$$

This equation is maximized by choosing effort levels of $y = x = 1$.[28] The total expected surplus net of effort costs is 10.

Actual Effort Choices under the Contract

The specific contract between AGT and Custom requires that a design change be approved by both companies. Since Roxanne and Jim have equal bargaining power, they anticipate that they will split the surplus that is available from any future design change. For instance, if the benefits are 40 and the costs are 10, the total surplus is 30. A price for the circuit boards of 25 splits the gains—Roxanne gains $40 - 25 = 15$ and Jim gains $25 - 10 = 15$.

Roxanne and Jim *choose their effort levels privately* (the effort choices cannot be observed by the other person). Each person chooses an effort level that maximizes his or her own surplus, given the anticipated effort choice of the other party. As we shall see, both parties choose effort levels below the values that maximize the joint surplus. The low effort choices result from the standard free-rider problem. Roxanne and Jim bear the total costs of their personal efforts but receive only half the benefits.

Consider Roxanne's problem. Her expected surplus, S_R, is:

$$S_R = .5(40 - 10)xy^* + .5(40 - 30)x(1 - y^*) + .5(20 - 10)(1 - x)y^* - 10x^2$$
$$= 15xy^* + 5x(1 - y^*) + 5(1 - x)y^* - 10x^2$$
$$= 5xy^* + 5x + 5 - 10x^2 \tag{15.6}$$

---

[28]The first three terms in equation 15.5 are the three possible outcomes of positive surplus multiplied by the probability of the outcome. The last two terms are the effort costs. Note: If the benefits are 20 and the costs are 30, the design change is not implemented; the term $(0)(1 - x)(1 - y)$ drops out of equation 15.5. The first-order conditions are: $10 + 10y - 20x = 0$ and $10 + 10x - 20y = 0$. The solution is $x = y = 1$.

where y* is the effort level that she expects Jim to exert.[29] Taking the partial derivative with respect to x and setting it equal to zero:

$$\partial S_R / \partial x = 5y^* + 5 - 20x = 0 \tag{15.7}$$

Jim's first-order condition is similarly:

$$\partial S_J / \partial y = 5x^* + 5 - 20y = 0 \tag{15.8}$$

In a Nash equilibrium, both Jim's and Roxanne's first-order condition will be met and the effort choices will be x = one-third and y = one-third (at these values, neither party has the incentive to alter his, or her choice). The total surplus, net of effort costs, is 5.6 (substitute y = x = one-third into equation 15.5).

Vertical Integration

One way to change effort incentives is for the two firms to integrate vertically—either by having AGT buy Custom or by having Custom buy AGT. Consider the case where Roxanne purchases Custom from Jim and hires him as an employee to manage AGT's "Custom Circuit Division." Ownership gives Roxanne the decision rights to implement the design change without Jim's approval (she has the *residual use rights*). Since Jim has no bargaining power, all the surplus goes to Roxanne. Jim has no incentives to exert effort on increasing the likelihood of a low production cost—he bears all of the costs for his personal effort and reaps none of the benefits. (Recall that we have ruled out incentive contracts tied to realized costs or benefits of design changes.) Given y = 0, the cost of implementing the design change is 30 for certain. Roxanne's benefits from investing are:

$$(40 - 30)x - 10x^2 \tag{15.9}$$

Roxanne will choose x = ½. The total surplus, net of investment costs, is 2.5.[30] The case where Custom buys AGT is symmetric, Jim invests y = ½, and total net surplus is 2.5.[31] Clearly, vertical integration is not superior to a long-term contract.

Optimal Organizational Choice

When Roxanne and Jim are negotiating the sale of either company, they can share the expected surplus in any manner by negotiating the appropriate purchase price. They have incentives to choose the ownership structure that maximizes the expected net surplus. Given the numbers in this example, they will choose not to combine the two companies. Nonintegration creates more value than integration.

This example illustrates that ownership structure can matter because it affects investment incentives. (In this case, investments in effort.) Ownership gives individuals increased power to capture the fruits of their efforts (see Chapter 7) and thus can provide

[29]She bears the full cost of her effort, $10x^2$, but only receives half the benefits.

[30]Roxanne's first-order condition is: $10 - 20x = 0$. The solution is x = one-half. The total surplus is found by substituting x = one-half and y = 0 into equation 15.6.

[31]This symmetry is a result of the cost and benefit functions in our example. More generally, it can matter who buys whom.

important incentives. In this example, nonintegration is better than integration because both parties' investments are important. It is better to provide moderate incentives to both Jim and Roxanne than strong incentives to only one party. It is easy to envision cases where integration will be the preferred alternative. For instance, suppose that Roxanne can exert effort to affect the benefits of the design change, but Jim has little control over the costs. Here, it would make sense for AGT to own Custom. This ownership structure provides strong incentives for Roxanne to exert effort and weak incentives for Jim. These incentives are optimal, since only Roxanne's effort matters. Conversely, it makes sense for Custom to own AGT when Jim's effort is substantially more important than Roxanne's.

In this example, we have ruled out the possibility that effort can be motivated by incentive compensation (making payments based on the realized costs and benefits). We made this extreme assumption specifically to isolate the important incentive effects of ownership. More generally, owners can motivate internal employees through incentive compensation. For instance, if AGT purchased Custom, Roxanne might be able to pay Jim in a manner that would encourage him to exert some effort to reduce costs. Similarly, in the nonintegration case, AGT and Custom might be able to include incentive clauses in the contract that would encourage investment (for instance, Custom might receive extra revenue from AGT if it can produce the new design at low cost). As we discussed in Chapters 12 to 14, incentive schemes and performance evaluation are not costless activities. In a more detailed analysis, AGT and Custom would have to compare the value that could be created under nonintegration with an optimal supply contract to the value that could be created under integration with optimal incentive compensation contracts. The basic point of our analysis continues to hold—*ownership structure matters because it can affect investment incentives.*

Appendix Problems

1. Insurance companies contract with independent agents to sell policies and provide ongoing services to customers. Ongoing client services tend to be more important in auto insurance companies than life insurance companies. In some insurance companies, the agents "own" the client list. If they quit representing the firm, they can take the clients with them to a new company. In other cases, the insurance company owns the list. The agent is not allowed to take clients to another company. (There is a formal contract with this provision.) Do you think life insurance companies or auto insurance companies are more likely to employ independent agents who own their client lists? Explain.

2. In explaining a decision to purchase an independent R & D laboratory, an executive of the acquiring company said:

    We felt we had to purchase the company to give us patent rights on any important discoveries. Without these rights, we would have few incentives to invest in the marketing and distribution systems that are necessary to support the discoveries.

    Evaluate this logic.

Suggested Readings

D. Carlton and J. Perloff (1990), *Modern Industrial Organization* (Harper Collins: New York), Chapter 16.

O. Hart (1995), *Firms, Contracts, and Financial Structure* (Oxford Press: Oxford, UK).

B. Klein, R. Crawford, and A. Alchian (1978), "Vertical Integration, Appropriable Rents, and the Competitive Contracting Process," *Journal of Law & Economics* 24, 297–326.

P. Rubin (1990), *Managing Business Transactions* (Free Press: New York).

O. Williamson (1985), *The Economic Institutions of Capitalism* (Free Press: New York).

Review Questions

15–1. What is the difference between upstream and downstream integration?

15–2. What are the advantages of buying goods and services in a competitive market?

15–3. Why don't firms obtain all their inputs through simple market transactions?

15–4. What is a specific asset? What problems do they cause in contracting?

15–5. What is an incomplete contract? Why is the idea of an incomplete contract important in explaining the choice between vertical integration and long-term contracting?

15–6. What does it mean to own an asset? How can ownership affect investment incentives?

15–7. Quick Type Inc. is a typing service. It consists of a pool of typists that type manuscripts and papers for other companies. Get Slim, Inc., is a health spa with whirlpools, gyms, and specially mirrored walls. Both companies utilize the same amount of space. Which company is more likely to own its building and why?

15–8. Discuss the pros and cons of the policy described in the following quote from *Fortune:*[32]

> *According to the new thinking, any kind of work to which a company can't bring a special set of skills should be spun off, outsourced or eliminated. Thus AT&T, GE, IBM, and Shell Oil are in the process of spinning off legal, public relations, billing, payroll, and other services. What's left, whether it's a $100 million corporation or a $100 billion corporation, is the ideal size . . . For example, if marketing is a competitive advantage in an industry, then it should build up its marketing muscle and employ outside suppliers and service firms to do everything else.*

15–9. Your company has a patent for a particular electronic component. This component is used as an input in the manufacturing of two different consumer appliances. In one case, the appliance can only be produced using your part, and so demand is relatively inelastic in this market segment. In contrast, the other consumer appliance can be produced with substitute inputs. Hence, your demand is relatively more elastic in this market segment. Assume that business law does not allow you to market the input at different prices to different customers. Discuss how the law restricts you from implementing your optimal pricing policy. Discuss how vertical integration might be used to maximize your firm's profits. Be specific, indicating which consumer market you would choose to enter. Explain.

15–10. The Black Diamond Company specializes in mining coal. It would like to build a processing plant right next to its major mine. The location of this mine is relatively remote and is not near other coal mines. Tax considerations, as well as government regulations, dictate that the processing plant be owned and operated by some independent company (other than Black Diamond). Your company, the Greg Norman Coal Company, is considering building and operating the plant for Black Diamond on a contract basis. Your job is to negotiate the contract with Black Diamond. Discuss the terms that you will try to get Black Diamond to agree to in the contract. Explain why these terms are important to you.

---

[32]B. Dumaine and J. Labate, April 20, 1992, "Is Big Still Good?" *Fortune,* 50.

15–11. Two parts in a taillight for an automobile are the exterior cover of the light (the red part viewed by other drivers) and the lightbulbs. Which of these parts is an automobile manufacturing company most likely to produce in-house? Explain.

15–12. Evaluate the following quote:

> *The major advantage to outsourcing is that it reduces a company's capital costs, freeing the company to use scarce capital for other purposes.*

15–13. Many firms have recently outsourced activities to other firms. Two of the most common activities that have been outsourced are trucking and food catering. Discuss several reasons why these activities are likely to be relatively good candidates for outsourcing.

15–14. Assume that Ford Motor Company can produce an automobile at a constant marginal cost of $4,000. The demand for the car in the Rochester area is: $P = 60,000 - 100Q$.

    a. What is the profit-maximizing price and quantity? What are the profits from this activity?

    b. Now suppose that Ford sells its cars through an independent distributor, Rochester Autos, which has the exclusive right to sell new Fords in the Rochester area. Under the contract, Ford sets the wholesale price, while Rochester Motors selects the quantity to purchase and the retail price. The only cost facing Rochester Motors is the wholesale price of the car. Ford and Rochester Autos both strive to maximize their own profits. What are (1) the wholesale price, (2) the retail price, (3) the quantity sold, and (4) the combined profits of Ford and Rochester Autos?

    c. Describe how Ford might use a two-part pricing scheme to eliminate this successive monopoly problem with Rochester Motors. (No calculations are necessary.)

15–15. Discuss the free-rider problem that occurs among independent distributors of a product. Discuss how exclusive territories can be used to reduce this problem. What is a major drawback of granting exclusive territories?

15–16. Grow-Fast Inc. has a patent on a chemical product that is used as a key input in producing farm and home agricultural fertilizer. Currently, Grow-Fast produces the product and sells it to companies who manufacture the final products for the farm and home users. Grow-Fast faces the following demand curves from the farm and home market segments:

$$\text{Farm:} \quad P = 300 - 10Q$$
$$\text{Home:} \quad P = 100 - 5Q$$

Grow-Fast can produce the product at a constant marginal cost of $1. Calculate the optimal prices that Grow-Fast would like to charge in each market segment to maximize profits. Discuss how vertical integration might be used to accomplish this pricing policy. Be sure to indicate which market Grow-Fast should vertically integrate in (assume they can only integrate in one). Explain why you chose this market.

15–17. In explaining the recent acquisition of a supplier, an executive made the following argument: "We purchased the supplier so that we could keep the profit rather than pay it to some other firm." Evaluate this argument.

chapter 16

Leadership: Motivating Change within Organizations

CHAPTER OUTLINE

In 1982, David Kearns was appointed CEO of Xerox Corporation, the leading producer of copy machines in the world.[1] At that time, the company faced significant problems. Between 1976 and 1982, Xerox's share of installations of copiers in the United States dropped from about 80 percent to 13 percent. Japanese companies such as Canon, Minolta, Ricoh, and Sharp had become major players in this market. These companies were selling copiers at prices that were lower than Xerox's costs for producing competing machines.

A primary reason for Xerox's decline in market share was poor product quality. As Kearns put it:

> *Our customer cancellations were rapidly on the rise, our response to the problem was to try to outrun them by pushing hard to get enough new orders to offset the customers we had lost. Customers were fed up with our copiers breaking down and our service response.*

Kearns reasoned that if something was not done, "Xerox was destined to have a fire sale and close down by 1990." The "only hope for survival was to urgently commit the company to vastly improving the quality of its products and services."

According to Kearns, most Xerox employees understood neither how bad the problem was nor the importance of enhancing product quality. He realized that even as CEO, he could not implement his vision of improving product quality by simply ordering 100,000 employees to focus on quality. First, the employees were not trained to produce quality products. Second, unless employees were convinced that it was in their interests to focus on quality, it would be difficult to motivate them to alter their behavior. Certainly, Kearns did not have the time to monitor each employee to see if his vision was carried out. Third, Kearns feared that painting too dismal a picture would induce some key people to leave the company.

In response to these concerns, Kearns initiated a strategy to shift corporate direction. He realized that many Xerox employees would oppose the kind of dramatic change he envisioned. They would fear for their jobs, worry about changes in job assignments, be concerned about having to move to new locations, and so on. Kearns began by convincing a select group of key executives that focusing on quality was essential. These individuals helped to refine the quality vision and to convince other employees of the potential benefits of this change in focus. Employees throughout the company received substantial training in quality techniques. The importance of quality was stressed at every opportunity (media releases, management speeches, signs on bulletin boards, and so forth). The potential crisis posed by the Japanese successes was emphasized.

After much training and promotion, the desired change in culture simply was not occurring. It was then that Kearns realized that to affect employee behavior, senior management had to do more than just cajole and plead—the performance-evaluation and incentive systems also had to change. As Kearns says:

> *Unless people get rewarded and punished for how they behave, no one will really believe that this is anything more than lip service. A widespread problem [with implementing change] that was singled out was that people said we were still promoting and rewarding employees who weren't true believers and users of the quality process. This was creating noise in the system and sending mixed signals. It had to stop.*

[1] Details of this example are from D. Kearns and D. Nadler (1992), *Prophets in the Dark* (Harper Business Press: New York).

Kearns accordingly initiated changes in the criteria for promotions and salary decisions, placing major emphasis on customer satisfaction and quality. Eventually, the culture at Xerox did change. In 1989, Xerox won the Malcolm Baldrige National Quality Award.

This example suggests that effective leadership is much more than developing an appropriate vision for the company. It is critical to motivate people to follow that vision. Changes in a firm's organizational architecture (the assignment of decision rights, reward system, and performance-evaluation system) can play an important role in motivating significant organizational change. "Selling" the proposal to other employees is also important.

In this chapter, we use the framework developed in this book to provide insights for more effective leadership. The analysis presents an important example of how this framework can be used to provide a structured discussion of this popular (but not necessarily well-understood) topic. The insights in this chapter are useful not only for people at the top of the organization but also for employees throughout the firm who have the opportunity to perform various leadership roles. Indeed, the analysis is helpful for all individuals who want to have their ideas implemented within any organization.

We begin by discussing the concept of leadership in more detail. Next, we discuss decision making within firms and present a framework for understanding attitudes toward change within organizations. This framework is used to analyze various strategies for motivating employees to endorse proposals for change. These strategies include changing the organizational architecture, strategic design of the proposal, and selling the proposal. The final sections of the chapter contain an analysis of the sources of individual power within an organization and a brief discussion of the use of symbols (role modeling, formal creeds, stories, and legends) in leadership. An appendix presents a simple example of the strategic value of commitment and crisis.

Leadership

Webster's defines *leadership* as "leading others along a way, guiding." This definition suggests that there are at least two important characteristics of good leadership. First, the leader must help the organization to choose the right path (vision, goal, or plan). Second, the leader must help motivate people to follow it. Much of the popular literature on leadership stresses these two characteristics. To quote John Gardner, "The two tasks at the heart of the popular notion of leadership are goal setting and motivating."[2] Since these tasks are performed by people throughout the organization, leadership is in no sense the exclusive domain of senior management. Many employees in the firm play important leadership roles.

Vision Setting

By vision, we simply mean a course of action for the firm.[3] Sometimes leaders conceive a corporate vision by themselves. According to Kearns, he was among the first people to envision Xerox as a quality-based organization. Senior managers usually do not have all

---

[2]J. Gardner (1990), *On Leadership* (Free Press, New York), 11.

[3]The management literature differentiates among the terms *vision, strategies, and plans.* Visions represent goals and objectives, while strategies and plans relate to how to achieve them. For our purpose, this differentiation is unimportant. We are interested in any type of proposal that implies change for the organization. We use the term *vision* as a catchall for these proposals.

Vision Setting: Lessons from the Enterprise

In my experience, the best-run companies have a basic philosophy that the people in the company know and understand. Sometimes this philosophy is formalized in a mission statement. Here is the best mission statement I have ever heard.

> These are the voyages of the Starship Enterprise. Her five-year mission: To explore strange new worlds, to seek out new life and new civilizations, to boldly go where no man has gone before.

Crew members of the Starship *Enterprise* know exactly what they are supposed to do. Suppose you are the dumbest person on the ship. And suppose you encountered a strange new world. What should you do? Explore it, perhaps. There is even an emotion telling you how you should go about exploring it. Boldly.

What if your company encounters a strange new opportunity? Without a basic philosophy, even a business's smartest employees have to improvise when they meet a new or challenging situation. We could do worse than rewriting the Star Trek mission statement for whatever venture we are on. Make the language exact, the goal specific, and even your worst employee will make you proud.

Source: D. Marinaccio (1994), *All I Really Need to Know I Learned from Watching Star Trek* (Crown Publishers: New York).

---

the relevant specific knowledge and cannot be expected to devise important visions entirely by themselves. In many cases, visions emanate from lower-level employees or even from people outside the firm (for example, consultants). Often, the information for formulating a vision has to be assembled by combining the knowledge of numerous individuals. Firms typically involve many employees in developing mission statements. One aspect of effective leadership involves structuring organizational architecture in a manner that motivates employees with the relevant specific knowledge to initiate value-enhancing proposals—to take part in vision setting. It is this view that has motivated much of the current literature on the role of managers in empowering employees to "unleash their untapped creativity."

Motivation

While an appropriate vision is important, it cannot create firm value unless it is implemented. The task of motivation is at least as important as the task of goal setting. It is often better to implement a "second best" plan than to identify the best plan but fail to implement it. The literature on leadership often emphasizes motivation skills:[4]

- "Leadership is the *process of persuasion* or example by which an individual induces a group to pursue objectives held by the leader or his or her followers."
- "I define leadership as leaders *inducing* followers to act for certain goals that represent the values and the motivations—the wants and needs, the aspirations and expectations—of both leaders and followers."
- "The one who knows the right thing but cannot achieve it fails because he is ineffectual. The great leader *needs . . . the capacity to achieve.*"

---

[4]Italics in the following quotes are ours. The quotes are taken, respectively, from Gardner (1990), 1; J. Burns (1978), *Leadership* (Harper & Row: New York), 19; and R. Nixon (1982), *Leaders* (Warner Books: New York), 5.

Some people argue that leaders motivate people to follow visions through personal charisma, style, and inspiration. Under this view, the bonds between leader and follower are more emotional than rational. Strong emotional ties motivate individuals to follow the leader's call to action. Leaders often cited as charismatic include Gandhi, John F. Kennedy, and Martin Luther King, Jr. Charisma probably explains much of the behavior of individuals in some settings (for example, in certain religious cults). While business managers might glean some valuable lessons from studying the styles of inspirational leaders, for most people, charisma is difficult to acquire.

The economic framework suggests that other attributes of effective leadership can be learned. Economics stresses that people make choices that are in their own self-interest. They are more concerned about their own welfare (which can include concerns about family, community, and so on) than they are about the welfare of the owners of the company. Under this view, the problem of motivating employees to follow a proposed direction or course of action is just the standard agency problem. Below, we discuss techniques that managers can use to address this problem.

Decision Making in Firms

Agency Problems and Organizational Politics

Academic discussions often treat decision making as a purely intellectual exercise: the relevant alternatives are identified, analysis is conducted, and the best alternative is chosen. (Consider the standard treatment of capital budgeting in finance courses.) Implementation problems are often ignored. In this context, good leadership is equivalent to *initiating* good proposals and conducting careful analysis. In most firms, the decision process is much more complicated than this simple characterization. While developing good proposals and conducting careful analysis are important, they are far from sufficient for effective leadership. Just because a proposal would enhance the value of the firm is no guarantee that it will either be *ratified* or *implemented*.[5] Due to agency problems, decision making within firms often resembles decision making in *political settings* such as government. There are self-interested people involved in group decision making.[6] To quote Jeffrey Pfeffer:

> *Organizations, particularly large ones, are like governments in that they are fundamentally political entities. To understand them, one needs to understand organizational politics, just as to understand governments, one needs to understand government politics.*[7]

---

[5]Recall that four important steps in the decision-making process are initiation, ratification, implementation, and monitoring (see Chapter 9).

[6]As we have discussed in previous chapters, if there were no transaction costs, individuals in the group would agree unanimously on a course of action to maximize value. By maximizing the size of the pie all of the individuals are made better off—every individual's piece of the pie can be enlarged by the appropriate side payments. Transaction costs limit the likelihood of this outcome in large organizations. For example, suppose that laying off a group of workers will create value and the labor union has the power to stop the layoff. With no transaction costs, the owners and labor will agree on the layoff. The owners share the increase in value by making appropriate severance payments to the workers. Both parties are better off. Bargaining costs often prevent this result from occurring (asymmetric information is a particular problem). In this case, the parties do not have a shared common interest in maximizing value. Similar to other political settings, conflicts arise as all parties try to maximize their own share of the pie.

[7]J. Pfeffer (1992), *Managing with Power* (Harvard Business School: Boston), 8.

Henry Kissinger on Decision Making

Former Secretary of State Henry Kissinger offers the following observation about decision making:

> Before I served as a consultant to Kennedy, I had believed, like most academics, that the process of decision-making was largely intellectual and all one had to do was to walk into the President's office and convince him of the correctness of one's view. This perspective I soon realized is as dangerously immature as it is widely held.

Source: H. Kissinger (1979), *The White House Years* (Little, Brown: Boston), 39.

Framework for Understanding Attitudes toward Change

To provide deeper insights into the decision-making process within firms, consider the hypothetical example of Glenn Westwood, a general manager at the BCT Corporation. Like David Kearns at Xerox, Glenn is convinced that his division must adopt a quality-improvement program to remain competitive. Glenn needs support from the CEO for ratification of the program and support from employees in his division for implementation. Glenn does not think that the quality program will be a success unless he has the full support of his department managers. He also depends on these managers for advice, because they have important specific knowledge about whether his proposal is a good idea. If the managers strongly oppose his proposal, Glenn would consider withdrawing it. For illustration, we focus on Linda Hilderbrandt, a department manager who reports to Glenn.

Consider the proposal from Linda's perspective. Linda is risk averse and interested in maximizing her own utility, which increases with the expected payoffs that she receives from BCT, P_L, and falls with the standard deviation of these payoffs, σ_L (see Chapter 2):

$$U_L = f(\overset{+}{P_L}, \overset{-}{\sigma_L}). \tag{16.1}$$

The expected payoffs include both monetary and nonmonetary compensation from the company. For instance, Linda gains utility from her salary, supervising a large number of employees, working in California, and administering a large budget. Linda will not support Glenn's proposal simply because it increases firm value. It must increase her personal utility.

Figure 16.1 shows Linda's expected payoff and standard deviation under the *status quo* (assuming the company does not adopt the proposed program). Also displayed is the indifference curve, which contains all combinations of expected payoffs and standard deviations that provide Linda with the same utility as the status quo. (Recall that northwest movements in the graph are utility increasing.) For Linda to favor Glenn's proposal over the status quo, she must view the proposal as placing her in the region of the graph labeled "favor proposal."

Linda will oppose the proposal if it reduces her utility. For instance, if she thinks that the proposal will increase the likelihood that she will be laid off, she is likely to be against the change. Now Linda is unlikely to come right out and say that she does not like the proposal because she fears for her job. She is more likely to question Glenn's underlying analysis—even if she thinks it is right. She might waste time developing spurious evidence to convince people that the proposed program is unworkable. She might try to block the program by failing to do her part during implementation. If many employees in the firm take similar actions, the proposal will fail.

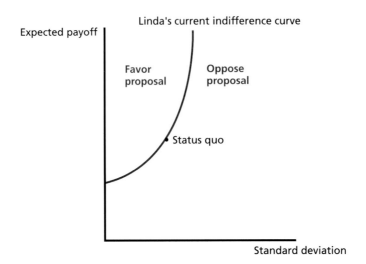

Figure 16.1 Framework for Understanding Attitudes toward Change

In this example, Linda is a department manager at the BCT Corporation. Linda is risk averse. Her utility increases with her expected payoffs from the company and falls with the standard deviation of these payoffs. This figure displays the indifference curve associated with the *status quo* (assuming the company does not change its course of direction). Linda will support proposals for change in the favor proposal region of the figure and be against proposals in the oppose proposal region.

Glenn cannot observe Linda's personal preferences. But he can analyze how the proposal is likely to affect her and make an educated guess of how she will react. One important factor to consider is the existing organizational architecture. What decision rights does she currently have and how will she be affected by the proposal? How is she rewarded? If Linda is paid a bonus based on divisional sales and the proposal is likely to reduce those sales, it is reasonable for Glenn to assume that Linda will oppose the proposal.

Suppose that Glenn forecasts that Linda will oppose the proposal. He might be able to gain her support by taking three general types of actions. First, he can change the organizational architecture so that it is in Linda's interest to support the proposal. Second, he can change the proposal so that she is more likely to support it. Third, he might be able to sell the proposal to Linda by convincing her that it is actually in her self-interest to support the proposal. We discuss each of these general actions below.

Changing the Organizational Architecture

Glenn can make two general changes in his division's architecture that will help him gain support for his proposal. First, he can identify individuals who are likely to support the proposal and give them increased decision rights (and correspondingly reduce the decision rights of individuals who are likely to oppose the proposal). Second, he can change the performance-evaluation and reward systems so that it is in the self-interest of more employees to support the new program. Kearns made both types of changes in architecture at Xerox.

Mismanaging Organizational Politics at Xerox

Good analysis is not enough to motivate the implementation of new ideas in an organization. Often, a concerted effort to gain the support of other employees is necessary. Xerox's Palo Alto Research Center (PARC) invented the first personal computer, the first graphics-oriented monitor, one of the first hand-held computer mouses, the first word processing program for nonexpert users, the first local area communications network, the first object-oriented programming language, and the first laser printer. Xerox failed to capitalize commercially on this inventive technology. One reason was that PARC was physically removed from the rest of Xerox and apparently did not understand the importance of motivating other units in the firm (such as marketing) to support its technological visions. Employees at PARC were characterized as being arrogant and suffering from a "we/they attitude toward the rest of Xerox." In the words of Jeffrey Pfeffer:

> By not appreciating the interdependence involved in a new product launch and the skills required to manage that interdependence, PARC researchers lost out on their ambition to change the world of computing, and Xerox missed some important economic opportunities.

Source: J. Pfeffer (1992), *Managing with Power* (Harvard Business School: Boston), 38–39.

To illustrate the effect of changes in the performance-evaluation and reward systems, suppose that Linda is currently paid a salary plus an additional bonus, based on the sales for her department. Denote Linda's expected payoff and standard deviation, given this compensation scheme and *not implementing* Glenn's proposal, as the status quo (SQ). The indifference curve associated with SQ is pictured in Figure 16.2 (labeled "original indifference curve"). Glenn's proposal makes Linda worse off relative to the status quo—the expected payoff is lower and the standard deviation is higher. Linda will try to convince Glenn that the proposal is a bad idea and will not work hard at implementing it, should it be adopted. Now suppose that before suggesting the proposal, Glenn changes the performance-evaluation and reward systems. Linda is now evaluated on product quality. If the quality in her department is poor, she has an increased likelihood of job loss. This change in the reward system produces a new status quo (SQ'). Without adopting a quality program, chances are that Linda's quality will suffer and she may be fired. The change in the architecture places her on a lower indifference curve (labeled "after changes in the architecture"). Now when Glenn proposes his quality program, he receives Linda's support. She wants to take actions to improve quality in her department because she is made better off. She will want to attend quality workshops, provide instruction to her employees in quality techniques, and so on—she now supports the implementation of Glenn's proposal.[8]

Obtaining the approval of the CEO for the program and the support of department managers will not ensure that Glenn's proposal will be implemented successfully. There are potential agency problems with other employees within the division (for example, production workers). Glenn can anticipate some of these problems by carefully analyzing these employees' incentives. For instance, will these employees fear for their jobs or have less challenging work assignments? Through this analysis, he can identify the employees who are most likely to resist implementation. Glenn can make changes in the architecture

---

[8]In this illustration, the change in the reward system affects Linda's assessment of the status quo. Glenn's changes in the reward system might also affect Linda's expected payoffs and risk under the proposed change. The basic point continues to hold—Glenn can influence Linda's attitude about the proposal by making changes in the architecture.

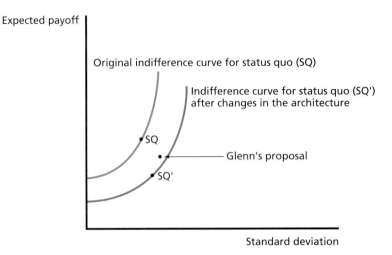

Figure 16.2 Changing the Architecture to Gain Support for a Proposal

In this example, Linda will not support Glenn's proposal, given her current compensation scheme. The status quo provides her with higher utility. Glenn changes the architecture so that the status quo is worse—if Linda does not improve quality, she is likely to be fired. Now, when Glenn introduces the proposal, Linda will support it and will do her part during the implementation phase.

to reduce the anticipated problems. He can make sure that certain groups of employees are monitored closely in the implementation phase (recall that monitoring is the fourth step in the decision-making process). He also might make additional changes in the performance-evaluation and reward systems. For example, he can reward employees (for example, through promotions) for successfully implementing the quality concept. Or he can promise employees that they will not lose their jobs due to quality improvements. This promise increases support for these programs (see Chapter 17).

David Kearns wanted to make dramatic changes in the culture at Xerox. To motivate employees to support these changes, he altered the firm's performance-evaluation and reward systems. But most employees *must exercise leadership within the existing architecture*—they do not have the authority to make changes in either the performance-evaluation or reward systems. Even CEOs often have to work within the existing organizational architecture, since changing architecture can be expensive. (For instance, frequent changes in the evaluation and reward systems can discourage employees from making long-run investments and developing relationships with co-workers—see Chapter 8.) The following discussion suggests methods that managers can use to get their proposals implemented within the existing organizational architecture. These techniques also can be used in conjunction with changes in the architecture.

Proposal Design

Managers can analyze the incentives of key decision makers and design proposals that are likely to be supported. We discuss three issues relating to proposal design: flexibility, commitment, and distributional consequences.

Leverage and Commitment

Firms obtain financing through combinations of equity and debt. Common stock is the most frequently used source of equity capital for large firms. Dividend payments to holders of common stock are discretionary. The board of directors can reduce dividend payments without placing the firm in bankruptcy. Payments to debt holders must be made in a timely fashion to avoid bankruptcy. During the 1980s, many firms increased their amount of debt substantially through activities such as selling bonds and repurchasing common stock.

High leverage can serve as a commitment that management intends to make changes in the firm to increase cash flows to meet the higher debt payments (for example, through cutting costs), since failure to increase cash flows can result in bankruptcy. Managers have their "feet to the fire," since they do not want to lose their jobs. Managers in firms financed primarily by equity can be under less pressure to make changes to increase cash flows, since they have more flexibility to decrease cash payouts to security holders. There are many determinants of the optimal amount of debt in a firm's capital structure. This discussion suggests that one determinant can be the desire of senior managers to commit to employees and outside stakeholders that they will take actions to increase or maintain high cash flows.

Source: M. Jensen (1986), "Agency Costs of Free Cash Flow, Corporate Finance, and Takeovers," *American Economic Review* 76, 323–29.

Maintaining Flexibility

Holding the expected payoffs of a proposal constant, employees are more likely to support new proposals if they entail lower risk. One way to convince people that the risk of a proposal is low is to design the proposal so that it can be modified easily once it is under way. A manager might suggest starting with a limited pilot program, involving only one region or a single product. If the pilot is successful, the program can be expanded. If not, it can be discontinued at low cost. Experiments of this type provide more precise estimates of the costs and benefits of proposed actions while committing only limited resources. A small-scale test does not commit the firm to adopt the program throughout the company—it provides an "option" to do so.

Commitment

While maintaining flexibility has benefits, it also can have costs. If employees think that senior management is not committed to the change, they have less reason to take the change seriously. In addition, employees who are against the change have increased incentives to take actions to convince senior management that the change is a bad idea. David Kearns made it quite clear that he was committed to the quality program at Xerox and that employees should take the change seriously. The appendix presents a more detailed example of the strategic value of commitment.

Distributional Consequences

Most proposals for change have distributional consequences—some employees gain and others lose. For instance, a plan to reduce the power of middle managers will harm middle mangers but benefit certain line workers. Managers can design proposals so that the distributional effects promote support among key decision makers. Returning to our example, Figure 16.3 considers the case of Linda and another department manager, John

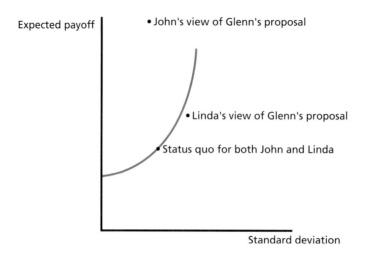

Figure 16.3 Analyzing the Distributional Consequences of a Proposal

In this example, Glenn's initial design of a proposal would be highly favored by John and slightly opposed by Linda (both have the same initial indifference curve under the status quo). Glenn can obtain both people's support by redesigning the proposal. For instance, he can reassign some employees that would have reported to John under the original proposal to Linda. Assuming that both John and Linda gain utility from supervising larger departments, Linda gains and John loses utility. The objective is to make changes so that both Linda and John view the proposal as being better than the status quo.

Both John and Linda have the same utility function. They also view the status quo exactly the same (so they are on the same initial indifference curve). Glenn's proposal greatly benefits John but harms Linda slightly. Glenn can obtain support from both John and Linda by modifying the proposal so that John is less well off and Linda is slightly better off. For instance, some of the employees that would have reported to John under the initial proposal might be reassigned to report to Linda. If Linda values supervising a larger number of employees, she is more likely to support the proposal.

Selling a Proposal

Employees' attitudes toward a proposed change depend on their assessment of the expected payoffs and risk under the new proposal, relative to the status quo. The sponsor of the proposal will often have information that can affect this assessment. The sponsor might be able to convince the employee to support the proposal by credibly conveying this information to the employee.

Careful Analysis and Groundwork

Glenn can anticipate initial opposition to his quality proposal because people are risk averse. Individuals who are confronted with a new idea are likely to be unsure of the personal consequences of the action relative to the status quo—and thus are likely to oppose it. Glenn correspondingly should take time to explain his analysis to key employees and to convince them that his analysis is correct. He might meet with these employees to discuss the proposal and

Reputation and Influence

Decision makers often rely on the advice of people with established reputations. This tendency is emphasized by H. Mintzberg:

> I found that chief executives faced complex choices. They had to consider the impact of each decision on other decisions and on the organization's strategy. They had to ensure that the decision would be acceptable to those who influence the organization as well as ensuring that resources would not be overextended. They had to understand the various costs and benefits as well as the feasibility of the proposal. They also had to consider questions of timing. All this was necessary for the simple approval of someone else's proposal. At the same time, however, delay could cost time, while quick approval could be ill considered and quick rejection might discourage the subordinate who had spent months developing a pet project. One common solution to approving projects is to pick the man instead of the proposal. That is, the manager authorizes those projects presented to him by people whose judgment he trusts.

Source: H. Mintzberg (1975), "The Manager's Job: Folklore and Fact,"
Harvard Business Review (July–August), 49–61.

answer questions. He can give speeches on the topic, write an article for the company paper, and so on. By carefully communicating the reasons he supports the plan, uncertainty is reduced. Correspondingly, there is increased support for the proposal—more people view the proposal as being in the "favor proposal" region of Figure 16.1.

As a general rule, it is unwise to introduce important proposals at meetings and then request on-the-spot decisions. Without laying the proper groundwork, such proposals are likely to be tabled for further study or simply rejected. Since people are risk averse, they tend to favor the status quo until they are convinced otherwise.

Relying on Reputation

People have reasons to listen to a person with an established reputation for offering sound proposals. First, past success is an indicator of analytical and organizational skills as well as the likelihood of future success. Second, a successful person has strong incentives to conduct a careful analysis to avoid damaging that established reputation. If other employees are confident that a manager usually makes good decisions, they will attach lower standard deviations to that manager's proposals and hence are more likely to support them. A manager with an established reputation can garner support for a proposal by strongly asserting that it is beneficial. It is important for managers not to misuse their reputations by forcefully arguing for marginal proposals. A manager's reputation will be diminished if proposals turn out to be unsuccessful. Also, it is important not to fight too many losing battles—to avoid a reputation of always being on the wrong side of issues.

A sponsor also can increase support for a proposal by obtaining the endorsement of other managers with good reputations. Therefore, it is often useful to conduct detailed discussions with these managers. If they agree with the analysis, it is more likely that it is correct. Moreover, their endorsement will generate additional support throughout the organization.

Emphasizing a Crisis

A complementary strategy to overcome the normal preference for the status quo is to argue that the current situation is worse than people think. The popular literature frequently argues that employees are most likely to favor change when an organization is in a *crisis* (if change doesn't occur, the organization is going to fail). Managers can promote a willingness to change if they can convince employees that the firm does face a crisis. Kearns gained support for his program at Xerox by repeatedly highlighting the threat from Japanese competition. Of course, this strategy works best if the firm faces an actual crisis. Individuals understand the incentives that proponents of proposals have to state that the organization faces a crisis and correspondingly are unlikely to accept this argument unless it is credible. In the case of Xerox, it was easy to document the lost business. Also, it was easy to point to other industries, such as steel and automobiles, which were having similar experiences. The effect of this action is to shift employee assessments of the utility associated with the status quo downward. This shift enlarges the support region, similar to the analysis in Figure 16.2. Thus, Glenn can gain Linda's support if he provides her with new information that causes her to be less optimistic about the status quo. The appendix illustrates how an employee's attitude toward change can depend on whether the firm faces a crisis.

Organizational Power

Economics suggests that an employee's attitude toward change will depend on the personal effects of the proposal. These effects are likely to depend on the identity of the sponsor. Some proposal sponsors have more personal *power* than others to affect the payoffs received by other employees. To be effective, it is important for managers to understand the sources of this power and how to acquire it.

Sources of Power [9]

Where does power in organizations come from? There are no laws that require people to obey or support the wishes of others within the firm. Corporate power does not come from the ability to force others to follow commands. It comes from other people who *voluntarily agree* to comply with a leader's wishes or proposals. For this voluntary action to occur, it must be in the interests of these people to cooperate with the leader. This section discusses potential sources of power and influence.

Formal Authority

Some power comes from the formal position within the organization. If a manager has the right to fire, promote, and compensate an employee, the employee obviously has an economic incentive to comply with the manager's wishes.[10] In our example, Glenn can count on some support from his employees even if the employees think that the proposal will harm them because not supporting it might harm them even more (Glenn might fire them). For instance, these employees are likely to speak in favor of the proposal at public meetings. In addition, Glenn's formal authority gives him the right to make certain decisions without consulting others. The power that is attached to a formal position is not without limits. There is the usual agency problem that employees might ignore their manager's wishes. Also, employees can take actions to get the manager replaced (a "palace revolt"). Disgruntled employees might form a coalition to complain to the CEO that Glenn is incompetent. Finally, some companies conduct 360-degree performance reviews where employees provide formal input into the performance evaluations of the managers.

---

[9]Material in this section draws on the analysis in Pfeffer (1992).

[10]Assuming the employee cannot costlessly obtain a comparable position at another firm.

Power and Resource Control—Voting on Antitakeover Amendments

Economic theory suggests that the control of important resources provides a person with power. Other people are afraid not to support the person's proposals because they fear that they will lose access to the important resource.

An illustration of the importance of this argument is provided by studies of corporate voting on antitakeover amendments. These amendments make it more difficult for outsiders to take control of a company through a corporate takeover. The existing evidence suggests that some of these amendments reduce the wealth of shareholders but benefit incumbent managers who become more secure in their jobs. The decision on whether or not to adopt these management-sponsored amendments is held by the shareholders, who would appear to have the incentives to vote against the amendments. Management, however, has power over certain institutional investors, such as banks and insurance companies, because they derive business from the firm that is under management control—if they don't vote in favor of management-sponsored amendments, they risk losing important business. Empirical evidence indicates that these types of institutional investors are more likely to support management-sponsored antitakeover amendments than other, more independent, investors. The evidence also suggests that management groups who do not have enough power to get amendments passed tend not to propose amendments because they do not want to bear the reputation costs of proposing an amendment that fails.

Source: J. Brickley, R. Lease, and C. Smith (1994), "Corporate Voting: Evidence from Charter Amendment Proposals," *Journal of Corporate Finance* 1, 5–31.

Control of Physical and Monetary Resources

People are granted rights to control resources within organizations. Some individuals have budget authority, while others decide on the allocation of office space or the priority for using copy machines. Control over these resources is a source of power. Individuals are reluctant to challenge a person who controls an important resource because they fear that it will affect their access to the resource. For example, department managers might support Glenn because he controls the budget from which they receive funds.

This discussion suggests that individuals can increase their organizational power by gaining control over key resources. This concept can be important in deciding whether to apply for a particular job or task within the firm—jobs and tasks are more attractive if they contain decision rights over resources others value. Also, a person can sometimes create power by developing a service or product that is important to other people in the organization. For example, the data processing manager in a company might increase personal power by offering a repair service for computers within the organization. This action will create greater power if the firm prohibits the use of external vendors, requiring employees to use this internal service for computer repair.

Throughout this book, we have argued that it is important to link decision rights and specific knowledge. The present discussion suggests a secondary factor that executives might consider in assigning decision rights over key resources—it can be important to grant power to managers who have the most potential to increase firm value.[11] For example, suppose that an executive can assign decision rights over corporate computing to one of two divisional managers, Sanjai Kumar or Maria Lopez. Both managers have the specific knowledge to manage the computer resources effectively. Sanjai, however, has a greater potential to affect firm value through his proposals than Maria (Sanjai manages a division with greater opportunities to create value). Further, Sanjai's proposals require the support

[11]This point relates to Hart's argument that the allocation of power and control of resources can affect investment decisions and thus value. O. Hart (1995), *Firms, Contracts, and Financial Structure* (Oxford Press: Oxford, UK).

Ford Motor Company and the $5 Dollar Day

In 1914, Ford Motor Company paid a wage rate of $2.20 per day to factory workers. This rate was very close to the prevailing market rate in the Detroit area. Annual turnover at Ford was over 300 percent, as employees would take jobs at different companies for slightly higher wages. Management had little power over its employees. If a supervisor was too demanding or difficult, employees would simply quit and go to work for a different firm. To combat this problem, Henry Ford increased the daily wage to $5 per day. This wage rate gave Ford tremendous power over his employees since they did not want to lose their jobs and work for someone else at $2.20 per day. To quote Henry Ford:

> I have a thousand men who if I say "Be at the northeast corner of the building at four a.m." will be there at four a.m. That is what we want: Obedience.

Sources: D. Halberstam (1986), *The Reckoning* (Avon Books: New York), and S. Meyer (1981), *The Five Dollar Day: Labor, Management, and Social Control in the Ford Motor Company, 1908–1921* (State University of New York Press: Albany, NY).

and cooperation of employees in other divisions of the firm. In this case, the executive will want to assign the decision rights over computing to Sanjai, since they will give him increased power to persuade other employees to support his proposals.

Control of Information

A particularly important resource in most organizations is information. The information held by any particular employee depends on things like the employee's position, office location, social network, and special skills. Not all employees have equal access to information. Since most employees require various types of information to be effective in their jobs, people with information have power—they can trade information for support. Some employees at BCT might support Glenn because they depend on him to keep them informed about what is going on in the company. Individuals can attempt to increase their access to information (and power) by lobbying for centrally located office space (for example, at the corporate headquarters), developing a social network within the organization, applying for jobs that are "in the information loop," or volunteering for key committee assignments.

Viewing the firm as the focal point for a set of contracts (see Chapter 7) provides a useful way to think about the control of information in a firm. Under this view, the firm is characterized as a network of contracts between the firm and other parties such as suppliers, customers, and employees. Many of these contracts are informal, and important information is held by people at the contracting nodes. Controlling access to this information can vest a person with substantial power. It would be quite difficult for a firm to fire an employee who has been the primary contact with a key customer for 20 years. The employee possesses specific information on items from company promises to customer requirements, and turnover in this position would be costly for the firm. Andre Shleifer and Robert Vishny argue that managers sometimes choose investment projects that give them an informational advantage and thus make it more costly for shareholders to replace them.[12]

[12]A. Shleifer and R. Vishny (1989), "Management Entrenchment: The Case of Manager-Specific Investments, *Journal of Financial Economics* 25, 123–139.

The Power of Information: Evidence from a French Tobacco Factory

An interesting example of the power of information comes from a French cigarette plant in the 1960s. The equipment in this plant was highly automated and subject to mechanical failures. The manuals that explained how to repair this equipment had been destroyed in a fire, and the only people with the knowledge to fix the machines were the maintenance engineers at the factory. This monopolistic access to important information gave the engineers enormous power. Without them, the plant could not run, and it was impossible to replace them. Indeed, the engineers had sufficient power to have a managing director of the company removed from his job. When new engineers were trained in the plant, they were instructed verbally and asked to destroy any notes once they mastered the material. These actions helped the engineers to maintain their power over time.

Source: M. Crozier (1964), *The Bureaucratic Phenomenon* (University of Chicago Press: Chicago).

Friends and Allies

Having close personal ties with decision makers increases the likelihood that the decision makers will act on your behalf. Managers sometimes hire or promote their friends to key positions over more-qualified candidates. One reason for this action is that the managers believe they can trust their friends for support. Some employees make a point of doing favors for other individuals in the firm (for example, providing assistance on difficult projects or filling in for other people when they are on vacation) to increase the likelihood that these individuals will help or support them in the future. Glenn is more likely to obtain support for his proposal if he has developed allies within the company.[13]

Tying the Proposal to a Popular Initiative

Sometimes it is possible to free-ride on the power of other people in the firm to gain support for a proposal. Perhaps, in our example, BCT's CEO has stressed the importance of product quality to the media and to customers through a program entitled "Quality 2000." Glenn can claim that his proposal is an integral part of the CEO's vision for the company and fits nicely within the Quality 2000 program. Casting up the proposal in this manner makes it less likely that other employees will raise objections because they will not want to argue against an important initiative sponsored by the CEO.

Coalitions and Logrolling[14]

A manager can sometimes increase power through *logrolling*. A logroll consists of a coalition of individuals who are largely indifferent to each other's demands but agree to support each other's requests so that each can get what he or she wants. A classic example is the coalition that forms each year in the U.S. Congress to pass the Rivers and Harbors Act. This act contains many local projects that individually would receive support from only a few legislators. The act passes by a majority vote because certain legislators band

---

[13]For an economic analysis of gift giving and exchange, see G. Akerlof (1982), "Labor Contracts as Partial Gift Exchange," *Quarterly Journal of Economics* 97, 543–569, and J. Rotemberg (1994), "Human Relations in the Workplace," *Journal of Political Economy* 102, 684–718.

[14]Material in this section draws on the analysis in W. Riker (1962), *The Theory of Political Coalitions* (Yale University Press: New Haven, CT).

Logrolling in Government and Business

Many of the classic examples of logrolling come from government. For example, one stylized example involves big business, unions, and farmers, where a winning coalition consists of any of the two groups. Farmers have an advantage in this setting because their demands are more likely to be consistent with the demands of unions and big business than are the demands of big business and unions likely to be consistent with each other. Indeed, farmers often want things that are relatively unimportant to the other two groups. Farmers, in turn, often don't care much about the demands of the other groups. This mutual indifference makes farmers good partners in a coalition. In contrast, big business and labor unions are likely to make a poor coalition. This helps explain why farmers have been unusually successful in getting favorable regulation established by the government.

While many of the examples of logrolling come from government, it is also prevalent in most types of organizations. For example, a marketing executive and a manufacturing manager might form a logroll to provide mutual support for each other's funding requests. In contrast, two manufacturing executives who are interested in mutually exclusive projects would not enter into a coalition. To quote Professor James March:

> Logrolls are found not only in the United States Congress, but also in business firms, military organizations and universities.

Source: J. March (1994), *A Primer on Decision Making* (Free Press: New York), 157–159.

together to provide mutual support for each other's proposals. In our example, Glenn might form a logroll with other general managers in the company to support his proposal before the CEO. He can agree to support the proposals of these managers to expand their divisions in front of the CEO if they back his quality proposal. In business firms (as in many other settings), these types of agreements virtually always take the form of implicit promises or understandings rather than formal contracts.

Coalition Obstacles

In trying to form a logroll, Glenn should anticipate at least three potential problems. First, identifying potential candidates for the logroll is not always easy. Second, there is the issue of credible promises. Decisions in firms do not all occur at the same time. Glenn might need immediate support from the other managers, while the proposals from these managers might not be considered until next year. The other managers might be reluctant to support Glenn because they do not believe that he will follow through on his part of the bargain. Third, there is likely to be asymmetric information about how the proposal affects other people's welfare. Glenn does not know for certain who is indifferent about his proposal. Individuals who are truly indifferent might claim that they would be harmed by the proposal and are unwilling to support Glenn unless he makes many concessions to their wishes. As discussed in Chapter 7, this type of strategic misrepresentation can result in bargaining failures—in this case, the logroll might fail to materialize. Despite these problems, however, effective coalitions are often formed. Indeed, this type of deal making or "horse trading" is common in organizations.

Proposal Detail and Logrolling

As we discussed, Glenn is not only concerned about getting his proposal adopted, he also is concerned about agency problems that can occur after the program is under way. Glenn can reduce these agency problems by being very specific about what is expected of each key employee (so he leaves little discretionary decision authority). This strategy, however, entails two potentially significant costs: First, it limits the ability of employees

Political Skills and Organizational Productivity

The development and exercise of power in organizations is about getting things accomplished. The very nature of organizations—interdependent, complex systems with many actors and many points of view—means that taking actions is often problematic. Failures in implementations are almost invariably failures to build successful coalitions. Although networks of allies can obviously be misused, they are nevertheless essential in order to get things done.

Source: J. Pfeffer (1992), *Managing with Power* (Harvard Business School: Boston), 108.

to act on their specific knowledge in the implementation phase. In this sense, Glenn faces the basic tradeoff in project design that we have emphasized throughout this book—the tradeoff between the effective use of specific information and agency problems. Second, being overly specific in the ratification phase can make it more difficult for Glenn to assemble an effective coalition. Logrolling often requires that the terms of the proposal be somewhat vague to limit potential conflicts. Specific proposals provide employees with greater opportunities to argue about details.[15]

Is Organizational Power Bad?

We have argued that leaders often use personal power and political skills for motivating change within organizations. Yet words like *power* and *politics* frequently connote negative images to many people. It is easy to conjure up images of Machiavelli offering insidious advice to the prince on how to increase his power. Similarly, one can envision managers becoming overly absorbed in office politics and favoritism.

Obviously, attempts to gain power involve costs. For instance, having key employees spend time on logrolling can be expensive. In Chapter 9, we discussed how these influence costs can affect the appropriate architecture of the organization. Firms that survive in the marketplace are likely to be those firms that limit unproductive uses of employee time. It is also important to recognize that power and political skills can have important benefits. Organizations involve people working together. Without political skills and power, leaders often would fail to implement value-increasing plans and the organization would suffer immensely.

In summary, power and political skills are, in and of themselves, neither good nor bad. They are important attributes that can be used either for productive or unproductive purposes. Managers are naive if they think that they can be effective without them.

The Use of Symbols

Our analysis thus far in this chapter has focused on the formal organizational architecture and strategies for gaining support for proposals. The popular literature often stresses that effective leadership requires clever use of symbols such as role modeling, formal creeds, stories, and legends. For example, an executive interested in increasing customer

[15]J. March (1994), *A Primer on Decision Making* (Free Press: New York), 170–171.

The Use of Symbols at Nordstrom's

Nordstrom's is a department store chain that is famous for stressing customer service and satisfaction. The vision of the Nordstrom family (who manage the firm) is to offer the customer the best in service, selection, quality, and value.

The importance of customer service is stressed to employees by the frequent telling of stories about sales clerks who performed such heroics as changing a customer's flat tire in a store parking lot, paying a customer's parking ticket, and lending money to a customer who was short on cash to make a purchase. One particularly interesting story is the one about the sales clerk who refunded money to a customer irate about some newly purchased tires. The clerk cheerfully refunded the money even though the customer did not have a receipt. The fascinating part of the story is that Nordstrom's does not sell tires!

Nordstrom's does not rely on these types of stories alone to motivate employees to provide customer service. It has an extensive incentive system that stresses sales and customer service.

Source: H. Weston (1991), *Nordstrom: Dissension in the Ranks,* Harvard
Business School Case, N9-191-002.

service might take the time to talk to customers directly—ensuring these actions are visible to other employees through media releases and video tapes. The executive might retell stories about employees who have gone out of their way to serve customers. The company also might adopt formal creeds and statements to emphasize the manager's basic vision for the company.

We view these types of symbols as an aspect of corporate culture that performs a potentially important communication function; the symbols inform employees about what is valued in the company (see Chapters 8 and 18). But again, symbols are unlikely to be effective in motivating employees to take particular actions unless reinforced by the firm's performance-evaluation and reward systems. David Kearns came to realize this and ultimately had to change the reward system at Xerox before he could successfully implement his quality program.

Summary

This chapter uses the framework developed in Part 2 of this book to provide insights into more effective *leadership*. The analysis presents an important example of how this framework can be used to provide a structured discussion of this popular but not necessarily well-understood topic.

The leadership literature stresses two important tasks that all leaders must perform—setting goals and motivating employees. To accomplish these tasks, management must design decision right, performance-evaluation, and reward systems that effectively link relevant specific knowledge with decision-making authority and provide appropriate incentives for decision makers to act on their information. In this sense, much of this book has focused on key components of leadership.

Academic discussions often treat the process of decision ratification as a purely intellectual exercise. In most firms, however, the decision process involves significant agency problems. As a result, decision making in firms often resembles decision making in political settings.

Effective leadership is facilitated by carefully considering other employees' perspectives on proposals for change. It is important to recognize that people are typically risk averse and interested in their own well-being. An important factor to consider is the existing organizational architecture. How will the proposed change affect specific employees in terms of their decision rights and payoffs from the organization?

CASE STUDY
Global Insurance

Global Insurance is a disability insurance company. Traditionally, it has organized its corporate headquarters around functional specialties. After an application for an insurance policy arrives at headquarters from a field agent, it is processed through a series of functional departments. One department checks to see if the application is filled out correctly, another department checks the medical history of the applicant, and so on. Among the final steps is the underwriting decision, where the company agrees to accept the policy. This task is handled by trained underwriters.

One of the most important departments at Global is human resources. This department administers the personnel system. Currently, the system has nearly 2,000 discrete jobs titles. Human Resources administers this system (for instance, screening job applicants, reviewing promotion decisions, having key decision rights on salary levels and job classifications, and providing training throughout the organization). The director of human resources is viewed by most employees as a key person in the organization.

A major problem with Global's organizational structure is that it takes nearly a month to process an insurance application. Applications can sit for days in inboxes, as they move from department to department. Global's CEO, Ahmad Rajiv, has decided that the company must reorganize to remain competitive. He has a vision to do away with most of the functional departments. Insurance applications would be handled by *case workers,* who would do all the steps from initial inspection of the application through underwriting. These case workers would be supported by a computer system that would allow access to medical record data bases and other information necessary for processing an application. The management information system manager would be charged with developing the information system. Case workers would receive training in underwriting from the existing underwriters in the firm. Entry-level case workers would be required to have at least a two-year degree from a community college. The number of job titles would be reduced significantly. Most of the people would have titles like associate or partner. Training, promotion, and hiring rights, currently held by human resources, would be decentralized to senior case managers (partners). The human resources department would play an important role in transitioning to the new system (dismantling existing training programs and turning them over to case managers, reducing the size of its staff, and so on). Through similar programs, other insurance companies have been able to reduce their application processing times dramatically. They also have reduced their work forces significantly.

Discussion Questions
1. Which employees in the organization do you think will be opposed to Ahmad's proposal? Who will support it?
2. What problems can the opponents cause in implementing the plan?
3. What actions should Ahmad take to increase the likelihood that his plan will be successfully implemented?

Managers can make two general types of changes in architecture that will help them gain support for their proposals. First, they can identify individuals who are likely to support their proposals and give them increased decision rights. Second, they can change the performance-evaluation and reward systems so that it is in the self-interest of more employees to support their suggestions.

Developing proposals that can be discontinued at low cost can increase support. Flexibility, however, has costs as well as benefits. Sometimes it is better for managers to demonstrate a greater commitment to a change so that employees take the change more seriously. Managers can analyze the incentives of key decision makers and design proposals that are more likely to be supported.

The sponsor will often have information that can affect other employees' assessments of a proposal. The sponsor might be able to convince other employees of the merits of the proposal through careful analysis and groundwork, relying on a reputation for good decision making, and/or emphasizing a crisis.

Some managers have more personal *power* than others to affect the payoffs to other employees. Power in organizations generally does not come from the ability to force others to follow commands. Rather, power comes from other people who *voluntarily agree* to comply with a leader's proposals. For this voluntary action to occur, it must be in the interests of these other people to cooperate with the leader. Sources of power include formal authority derived from the position in the firm, control over important physical or monetary resources, control over information, and friends/allies. Sometimes it is possible to use the power of another employee by tying the proposal to a program backed by the powerful employee.

Employees can gain support for proposals by *logrolling*. A logroll consists of a coalition of individuals who are largely indifferent to each other's demands but agree to support each other's requests so that each can get what he or she wants.

Words like *power* and *politics* often conjure up negative images. Our view is that power and political skills are neither universally good nor bad. Rather, they are important attributes that can be used for either productive or unproductive purposes. Managers are naive if they think that they can be effective without them.

Symbols such as role modeling, formal creeds, stories, and legends can play an important role in communicating the leader's vision to employees. However, they are unlikely to be effective in motivating employees to take particular actions unless they are reinforced by the firm's performance-evaluation and reward systems.

APPENDIX   *Strategic Value of Commitment and Crisis*

In this chapter we discussed how a crisis and a leader's demonstrated commitment to change sometimes helps to motivate change within an organization. In this appendix we use a simple game-theoretic example to illustrate these ideas.

Tammy Conte is chief financial officer of the GSA Company, while Bruce Kelly is the general manager of the company's largest division. A major meeting of the board of directors is scheduled for next week. Tammy will recommend the firm's leverage ratio for the next year. She will either recommend high leverage, where the firm will borrow money to repurchase common stock, or low leverage, where the company maintains its current low debt-to-equity ratio. Bruce will recommend whether or not his division should invest in a major new technology. The board is expected to accept Tammy and Bruce's recommendations.

Figure 16.4 displays the personal payoffs to Tammy and Bruce for the four possible combinations of leverage and investment. Tammy prefers low leverage and investment in the new technology, while Bruce prefers low leverage and not investing in the new technology.[16] Currently Tammy and Bruce are scheduled to make their first public disclosures

---

[16]Tammy anticipates that the new technology will increase firm value. As CFO she is evaluated based on the stock-price performance of the company. She favors low leverage because of its lower likelihood of bankruptcy. Bruce, on the other hand, views the investment as more work for him, with little direct personal benefit. Also, the new investment will reduce his division's reported profits for a few years (there are initial start-up expenses and it will take some time to build sales) and thus the size of his annual bonus. He expects to retire in three years and will not be with the firm when the division begins reporting higher profits.

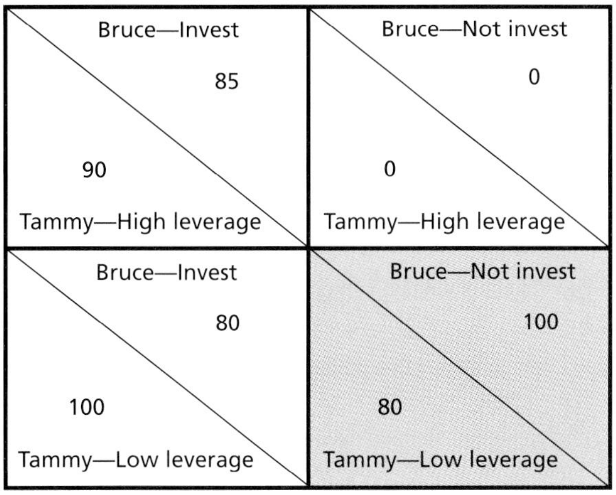

	Bruce—Invest	Bruce—Not invest
Tammy—High leverage	85 / 90	0 / 0
Tammy—Low leverage	80 / 100	100 / 80

Figure 16.4 Strategic Value of Commitment

Tammy is CFO of the GSA Company, while Bruce is the general manager of the company's largest division. At the next board meeting Tammy will recommend the degree of leverage; Bruce will recommend whether his division should invest in a new technology. If they both wait until the board meeting to announce their policy choices, the Nash equilibrium is low leverage and no investment. Tammy can motivate an outcome that she prefers—high leverage and investment—by effectively *committing* to recommend high leverage prior to the meeting.

of their recommendations at the board meeting. This schedule effectively requires Tammy and Bruce to make simultaneous announcements. Both Tammy and Bruce must prepare extensive presentations supporting their recommendations. It is unlikely that either person will want to change his or her recommendation in the middle of the board meeting—board members would view such a change as a bad signal about the person's abilities. The Nash equilibrium is for Tammy to propose low leverage and for Bruce to propose no new investment.[17]

Tammy can potentially affect Bruce's choice by *committing* to propose high leverage. Bruce views high leverage as placing the firm in a financial *crisis.* If the company does not invest in the new technology, the firm will not generate sufficient cash flow to service the debt. The firm will go bankrupt and both Tammy and Bruce will lose their jobs. The new technology, on the other hand, is likely to generate enough cash flow to avoid this outcome. If Bruce were convinced that Tammy would recommend high leverage, he would propose investing in the new technology. Tammy might effectively commit to high leverage by announcing to the financial press that she intends to make this recommendation. Bruce will realize that Tammy has "backed herself into a corner"; surely she would not alter her recommendation—it would ruin her reputation as a decisive CFO. To affect Bruce's choice, it is important that Tammy's commitment is binding. If he is not convinced, he is more likely to recommend not to invest, expecting that Tammy will recommend low leverage to the board. Bruce might also be able to influence the outcome in his favor by being the first to commit to a specific recommendation—in this case, not to invest in the new technology.

[17]Bruce knows that Tammy will recommend low leverage regardless of what she expects Bruce to do. (Holding Bruce's recommendation fixed, she always receives a higher payoff by recommending low leverage.) Thus, Bruce's optimal strategy is to recommend not to invest in the new technology.

Appendix Question

The analysis in this appendix suggests that a leader can sometimes motivate desired change by making a strong commitment to a particular action. Do you think it is always in the leader's interest to make this type of commitment? Explain.

Suggested Readings

J. Gardner (1990), *On Leadership* (Free Press: New York).

D. Kearns and D. Nadler (1992), *Prophets in the Dark* (Harper Business Press: New York).

D. Kreps (1990), "Corporate Culture and Economic Theory," in *Perspectives on Positive Political Economy,* J. Alt and K. Shepsle, eds. (Cambridge University Press: Cambridge).

J. March (1994), *A Primer on Decision Making* (Free Press: New York).

J. Pfeffer (1992), *Managing with Power* (Harvard Business School: Boston).

Review Questions

16–1. What is leadership?

16–2. It is frequently claimed that meaningful change is difficult to achieve in large companies. Why do you think this might be the case?

16–3. What does leadership have to do with organizational architecture?

16–4. What is organizational power, and where does it come from?

16–5. The PPP Company recently purchased a large chain of supermarkets (over 1,000 stores). Following this acquisition, PPP's management announced that it planned to cut labor costs dramatically so that the stores could remain competitive. Labor unions responded by saying that they would not agree to large wage cuts. After negotiating with a labor union for a short time, PPP announced that it was closing several of its most profitable stores because labor would not agree to wage cuts. On the surface, this seemed like a silly move, given that the stores were profitable. Why do you think PPP made this move?

16–6. The TRF Company has not fared well with recent increases in foreign competition. Management indicates that it must substantially cut costs to survive. Cost cutting will entail dramatic change for the company. TRF had been an all equity firm. Recently, the company borrowed nearly 90 percent of its value and used the money to repurchase shares. The required annual debt payments exceed the company's realized earnings over the past few years. What might have motivated management to make this dramatic increase in leverage, given that it placed the firm in a near "financial crisis?"

16–7. John Smith is the general manager of the textile division in a large diversified company. Recently, John argued strongly to the CEO that an expansion request by the drug division be approved. On the surface, John's actions seem strange, given that John is not affected by this decision (it does not affect his budget or his compensation). Further, John spent substantial time developing his presentation for the CEO.

  a. Why do you think John took such an active role in supporting the drug division's request?

  b. Since John is not affected by the decision, should the CEO consider John as an unbiased observer who is focused on trying to maximize company value? Explain.

16–8. Poorly performing employees in Japanese firms are sometimes punished by being sent to remote locations or placed at desks away from their colleagues. Discuss the effects that such a penalty will have on the leadership effectiveness of the punished employees.

chapter 17

Total Quality Management and Reengineering

Total quality management (TQM) and reengineering are two of the most popular management topics of the 1990s. One survey of 500 U.S. managers from large companies reports that 76 percent have used TQM and 69 percent have employed reengineering.[1] There is a coveted national award for the most successful companies applying TQM principles. Consultants argue that TQM and/or reengineering are critical and that firms must employ these techniques to survive.

While many consultants and managers endorse the importance of such techniques, a significant number of these efforts have not met expectations. A 1991 survey of 300 large companies found executive satisfaction levels with TQM was 40 percent.[2] A Gallup poll of 1,237 corporate employees reports that over half say that quality is top priority, but only one-third say their companies' programs are effective.[3] Some firms—including McDonnell Douglas and Florida Power & Light—abandoned their TQM programs. Wallace Co. won the Baldrige National Quality Award in 1990; yet filed for bankruptcy in 1992.[4] Finally, a study of 584 U.S., Canadian, German, and Japanese firms in 1991 concluded that "many businesses may waste millions of dollars a year on quality-improvement strategies that don't improve their performance and may even hamper it."[5]

The popularity of TQM and reengineering, despite their lack of widespread success, raises a number of important questions, including:

- What explains the popularity of TQM and reengineering?
- Why do they often fail to produce the desired benefits?
- Should all firms adopt TQM and/or reengineering? If not, which firms should adopt which technique: TQM or reengineering? Should some firms avoid both these techniques?
- What can managers do to increase the likelihood that TQM or reengineering will be successful?

The purpose of this chapter is to use this book's framework to answer these questions. We illustrate how this framework can be applied to provide insights into current management innovations, thereby honing a set of skills useful in analyzing future organizational proposals. New organizational innovations undoubtedly will be forthcoming. This book's analytic framework provides a powerful tool to help understand the costs and benefits of these future innovations. Since most such organizational innovations focus on a specific aspect of solving business problems, the framework helps to identify other facets of the organization that also require attention and complementary adjustments.

We begin by describing some alternative meanings of the term *quality*. We then provide a more detailed discussion of TQM and reengineering. In each case, we give a concrete example, discuss specific details of the technique, relate it to organizational architecture, and address why the technique has become popular now and not, say, 10 years ago. Next, we compare TQM and reengineering and explore their similarities and differences.

---

[1]"Missions Possible," *The Globe and Mail* (September 13, 1994), B22.

[2]*The Wall Street Journal* (July 6, 1993), A1.

[3]*The Wall Street Journal* (October 4, 1990), B1.

[4]*Newsweek* (September 7, 1992), 48–49.

[5]*The Wall Street Journal* (October 10, 1992), B7.

The final section of this chapter examines the question of why firms using these approaches often fail to achieve the desired benefits. In implementing these techniques, managers often ignore at least one leg of the three-legged stool. Also, TQM programs often fail because—despite what consultants say—quality is not free; improving quality is costly. At some point, customers are not willing to pay the extra cost for additional quality improvement. Finally, not all firms can benefit from these techniques. TQM and reengineering are investment decisions that should be adopted only when their expected benefits exceed the costs. Some firms adopt these techniques, only later to discover that the costs are greater or benefits smaller than anticipated. This discussion provides insights into whether a particular firm should use one of these techniques and if so, how it might increase the likelihood of success.

Total Quality Management

There is considerable debate surrounding what constitutes total quality management and how to define quality. Nonetheless, to most experts, TQM encompasses both improving the tangible aspects of product quality (performance, reliability, conformance to specification, durability, serviceability, aesthetics, and perceived quality) and enhancing the efficiency of the organization (lowering costs and increasing productivity). Therefore, TQM seeks to improve all aspects of the company—its products, processes, and services. Yet to apply TQM, managers must have not just a definition but a common understanding of what quality means.

What Is "Quality"?

Chapter 7 discussed implicit contracts and reputational concerns. While there are explicit warranties covering some products, most transactions occurring in markets are covered by implicit promises of product quality. If the customer expects a given level of quality and the firm shirks on that quality, the customer is more likely to switch to another supplier. Thus, the threat of losing future business creates incentives for firms to maintain promised levels of quality. The expression *caveat emptor* (buyer beware) reflects a long-standing recognition that customers must protect themselves from poor quality. Economists use the term *brand-name capital* to refer to the value the market attaches to the firm's reputation for delivering a product of a promised quality.

Ben Hogan's Brand-Name Capital

Ben Hogan, one of the most famous professional golfers of all time, began manufacturing golf equipment in 1953. "He wrote to club professionals pledging that his clubs would be made to the highest standards. When the first line of irons came out, he ordered them destroyed. One of his partners protested, arguing that it would cost the company hundreds of thousands of dollars. For Hogan, it was a matter of his reputation, not dollars, so he bought out his partner and destroyed the $150,000 worth of clubs." (Note: That $150,000 in 1953 dollars is equivalent to over $850,000 in 1995 adjusted for inflation.)

Source: D. Wade (1991), *"And Then Jack Said to Arnie"* (Contemporary Books: Chicago), 71.

Quality affects the market's demand for goods and services. In attempting to improve quality, managers must grapple with what quality means as well as how to improve it. As we will see, the term *quality* is a catchall for a number of different concepts, and the different meanings can conflict with each other. Quality can refer to *high mean, low variance, more options,* or *meeting customer expectations.* We discuss these alternative definitions in turn.

High Mean

For any good or service, consumers value particular attributes. For example, in automobiles, one attribute consumers value is acceleration. Cars of the same model and year have slightly different acceleration; testing a large sample of the same model generates a distribution of accelerations. The average (mean) acceleration of the sample is one measure of the model's quality. Chevrolet Corvettes have higher average acceleration than Toyota Corollas and hence are viewed as being of higher quality.

Low Variance

Besides calculating the automobile's average acceleration from the sample, the distribution's variance also can be computed and is another measure of quality. While Corvettes have higher mean acceleration, they might also have a greater variance than Corollas if the Corollas are subjected to tighter manufacturing tolerances. McDonald's hamburgers are higher quality than the local diner's because they taste the same whenever you buy them. The local diner's hamburgers vary from purchase to purchase depending on when and where the meat was purchased, how and by whom it was prepared, and what was last cooked on the grill.

When faced with choosing between two products, one of which has a higher mean as well as a higher variance, it is not clear which is the higher quality product. It depends on how the purchaser trades off a higher mean against a lower variance. For example, consider a fax machine. Quality can be defined in terms of how precisely the average copy reflects the original. If 1,000 pages are transmitted and each one is compared to the original, how accurately does the average copy compare to the original? This is a measure of the mean quality. A measure of quality related to variance is how badly the worst copy compares.

Reliability is often used as a synonym for quality. Toyotas are more reliable (have lower variance) than Yugos because Toyotas have fewer component failures than Yugos. Conformance to standards or requirements is another measure of quality related to variance. Quality is often measured in terms of defects. For example, a component part must be within 0.001 millimeters of standard or else it is labeled defective. If changing the machine producing the part reduces the defect rate from five per thousand to three per thousand, then quality is said to have increased.

More Options

A VCR that can be programmed for five programs is said to be of higher quality than one with only two programs. Similarly, Burger King suggests its hamburgers are of higher quality than McDonald's because at Burger King the customer "can have it your way" (that is, have more options). To some customers, product flexibility (the ability of a product to be used in a number of different ways) is an important attribute—one that is often associated with the term *quality.* For example, a video camera that can be used in low light settings is more flexible and thus of higher quality than one that requires auxiliary lights in low-light situations.

Computer Manufacturer's Quality Management Program

A large computer manufacturer redefined its business strategy as market-driven quality. The goal is "total customer satisfaction," guided by the following four market-driven principles:

- Understand our markets.
- Commit to leadership in the markets we choose to serve.
- Execute with excellence across our enterprise.
- Make customer satisfaction the final arbiter.

To implement these principles, the following initiatives have been undertaken:

- Research, understand, and segment total potential market needs; commit to market leadership and deliver the right solutions at the right time.
- Remove defects in everything we do to achieve market-driven quality.
- Reduce the total time to fulfill customer's wants/needs.
- Give employees the authority and information they need to make timely decisions and carry out the activities necessary to ensure total customer satisfaction.
- Establish achievable business targets with a particular focus on quality and customer satisfaction.

Meeting Customer Expectations

Customers have expectations with respect to all of a product's attributes, including delivery schedules, down time, operating characteristics, and service. These expectations include means, variances, *and* options. For example, a customer might expect one machine failure every three months, and when a breakdown occurs, a service technician is expected to arrive within two hours of the service request. If breakdowns occur monthly but the service technician arrives within 1.5 hours on average, the firm has met one customer expectation (mean time for arrival) but has not met another expectation (one failure every three months).

Defining quality as meeting customer expectations requires knowledge of the entire set of customer expectations, the actual realized values, as well as the importance the customer attaches to that particular expectation. Each customer views deviations from expectations in some dimensions to be more important than deviations from expectations in others. For example, missed delivery schedules might be more important than missed service times for some customers. Moreover, preferences over various product attributes vary from customer to customer. Different products can be offered to particular customer segments. For example, Fed Ex offers overnight and second day service at different prices.

When defining quality as meeting customer expectations, the term *total quality management* (TQM) includes those management processes and organizational changes necessary to meet customer expectations and to achieve continual improvement. Customers include external customers for the firm's products and services as well as internal customers. For example, the maintenance department might not have any external customers, but its internal customers consist of all the users of the firm's facilities. TQM programs seek to increase customer satisfaction by enhancing product and service quality and to increase efficiency (lower costs). Lower (marginal) costs allow price reductions, which further enhance customer satisfaction. The appendix to this chapter describes the Malcolm Baldrige quality award and how quality is measured for purposes of granting the award.

TQM: An Example[6]

Sterling Chemicals, Inc., produces commodity chemicals. It had sales in 1993 of about half a billion dollars. In the late 1980s, Sterling initiated its *Quality and Productivity Improvement* program. Once the CEO, the board of directors, and the senior management team were committed to the plan, an intensive four-day training program by outside consultants was held for the top 20 managers. Within the first two years, each of Sterling's 950 employees received a minimum of 16 hours of TQM training.

The training process involved teaching a sequence of problem-solving steps:[7]

- Analyze the symptoms.
- Theorize as to causes.
- Test the theories.
- Establish the cause(s).
- Simulate a remedy.
- Test the remedy under operating conditions.
- Establish controls to hold the gains.

The training emphasized how to brainstorm possible hypotheses, how to collect data to test the hypotheses, and how to apply simple statistical tests to reject hypotheses.

Once each employee was trained in problem-solving techniques, quality teams were formed. Any group could initiate a proposal to form a team to work on solving a particular problem. But before a team could begin working on a project, it had to recruit a management sponsor and write a one-page team charter describing the problem, the scope of the project, and performance targets. The charter had to be ratified by a Sterling quality committee. A project involving a single department could be approved by that department's quality committee; a project involving two departments in the same division required approval by the division's quality committee. Besides screening out vague or poorly conceived initiatives, the various quality committees ensured that each project team contained individuals with the likely requisite specialized knowledge to solve the problem. Sterling created three quality facilitator positions. These people were experts in applying TQM and worked with the project teams. Although Sterling's program focused on both quality and productivity improvements, the majority of the project teams worked on improving productivity and cutting costs.

Sterling employees' compensation is composed of a base salary, company stock, and profit sharing. Team performance is judged subjectively and rewarded indirectly through wage adjustments and promotions (see Chapter 13). Teams that enhance profits also share rewards through higher profit-sharing payouts and stock-price appreciation. (However, free-rider problems limit these incentives.) Another aspect of Sterling's TQM program is its no-layoff policy. Management announced that no layoffs would result from quality-team suggestions. Any head-count reductions would be implemented through attrition.

Sterling's pump-failure team illustrates how the process worked. About 15 pump failures per year occurred in one of its chemical processes. Each failure had a direct cost of $10,000. A group of engineers working for one year could not solve the problem. The maintenance engineers blamed the production people for not knowing how to operate the pumps; the production supervisors blamed poor repair work. Then a quality-improvement team was formed consisting of one mechanical engineer, three operators, four machinists, and a technical service engineer. They gathered data on pump failures and generated 57 potential reasons for the

[6]Details of this example are from S. Keating and K. Wruck (1994), "Sterling Chemicals, Inc.," Harvard Business School case 9-493-026.

[7]J. Juran (1989), *Juran on Leadership for Quality* (Free Press: New York), 59–60.

failures. Using the data, they reduced the possible causes to four. They then experimented with actual pumps and discovered that excessive vibration and pump seal installation were the causes. New procedures were developed and over the next two years, no pumps failed.

TQM and Organizational Architecture[8]

TQM programs can be viewed as a way to organize the firm. TQM programs seek to offer products that customers want and to lower operating costs. If knowledge of consumer preferences and operating cost savings resides with lower level employees in the organization, then the analysis in Chapter 9 suggests one solution is to place the decision rights with those employees. After training employees in problem-solving skills, the workers are better able to use their specific knowledge. Forming teams and assigning them decision rights is a way to assemble the specialized knowledge. Sterling Chemical illustrates one company's use of total quality management to try to increase firm value.[9]

Most TQM programs argue for empowering employees to improve product and process quality.[10] (Empowerment is another way of saying that decision rights are transferred to the person with the specialized knowledge.) But we have learned that if decision rights are repartitioned, then performance-evaluation and reward systems must also be modified to motivate the employees to use their new decision rights to maximize firm value. This section analyzes TQM in terms of how decision rights are repartitioned and how the reward and performance-evaluation systems are changed under TQM programs.

Decision Rights Assignment

As competition increases, firms face two alternatives. First, they can lower prices by reducing costs. Employees usually know how to improve the efficiency of their jobs. Second, they can compete in nonprice dimensions by satisfying more customer desires. A firm's customer base is usually heterogeneous—some valuing high means, others low variance, and others more options. TQM proponents advise "getting close to the customer," which means getting more information about the customer's demand function. One way to acquire this information is constructing an architecture that assigns decision rights to employees with this specialized knowledge.

If the potential pool of customers is changing or if technology is causing product capabilities to change, the firm's architecture also must be able to adapt the products and services it supplies to different segments of the market. No single employee is likely to see all the customers or suppliers, so firms must devise mechanisms whereby knowledge can be assembled across many individuals, each with only a limited component of the relevant knowledge. Teams can do this.

If teams of individuals with the relevant knowledge are empowered to solve problems and make decisions effectively, they must have appropriate training. As we saw with Sterling Chemicals, TQM programs generally train employees in problem-solving techniques.

[8]This section draws on the analysis in K. Wruck and M. Jensen (1994), "Science, Specific Knowledge and Total Quality Management," *Journal of Accounting and Economics* 18, 247–287.

[9]In fact, Sterling's earnings and stock price fell from 1988 through 1993; operating profits in 1993 were about 25 percent lower than in 1988, and the average annual stock price was about 70 percent smaller. While this evidence does not allow one to argue that TQM increased Sterling's firm value, it is possible that Sterling's value could have been lower had it not adopted the TQM process.

[10]Juran (1989); S. Mizuno (1988), *Company-Wide Total Quality Control* (Nordica International: Hong Kong); and K. Suzaki (1987), *The New Manufacturing Challenge: Techniques for Continuous Improvement* (Free Press: New York).

These training techniques apply the scientific method, whereby hypotheses are first generated, data is used to test the hypotheses, proposed remedies are field-tested, and finally the accepted remedy is installed. Although TQM is relatively new, it builds on the scientific method, which has evolved over centuries.

Training is costly. There is no guarantee that training costs will be recovered from the earnings by teams through lowering production costs or increasing customer demand. As we discuss further below, quality is not free. It would be naive to believe that the benefits of TQM training always exceed the costs.

Chapter 9 offered some general conditions when team decision making is most productive: There are potential synergies from working as a team; there is the ability to assemble relevant specific knowledge; and free-rider problems can be controlled. For TQM teams to be most effective, these conditions must hold. To elicit relevant specific knowledge from employees, not only must they be trained to use their knowledge, they must have incentives to recommend efficiency-enhancing staff reductions. One method of achieving this is by adopting a no-layoff policy; in fact, this guarantee frequently accompanies TQM programs. Also, free-rider problems must be controlled, normally by limiting the size of the team.

Wruck and Jensen argue against indiscriminate decentralization of decision rights to TQM teams—they caution against "team mania." At one point, Sterling Chemicals had 77 quality teams, each with 6 to 10 people. It was difficult to provide technical support to so many teams, let alone to implement their recommendations successfully. To control team mania, Sterling Chemicals established quality committees to approve each quality project. By creating a hierarchy of quality committees with the decision rights to ratify and monitor quality teams, Sterling separated decision management from decision control (recall Chapter 9). Any individual or group of individuals has the decision rights to initiate a quality project. Once a quality project is ratified by the appropriate quality committee, the team must produce an action plan, which also must be ratified by the quality committee. After approving the action plan, the quality team is responsible for its implementation and the quality committee monitors the team's performance. Following the implementation of a remedy, the quality team is disbanded.

Evaluating and Rewarding Performance of TQM Teams

To lower costs and meet customer expectations, specialized knowledge is assembled by forming quality teams. Creating and monitoring the teams requires the allocation of decision rights to the teams. To control the agency problems of the teams, performance-evaluation and reward systems must be changed. In Sterling Chemical's case, each team's performance is measured by comparing the team's action plan and stated goals (submitted to and approved by the quality committees) with actual outcomes.

Rewarding quality-team performance is often based on both nonmonetary and monetary rewards. By solving workplace problems, teams can improve their working conditions. Public recognition of quality-team achievements via plaques, jackets, and award ceremonies provides additional motivation. Participation on successful teams increases promotion opportunities. But the most controversial issue among quality experts involves the role of monetary incentives. Some argue to tie pay to team performance while others argue against such incentive schemes. One quality consultant says:

> *People really don't work for money. They go to work for it, but once the salary has been established, their concern is appreciation. Recognize their contribution publicly and noisily, but don't demean them by applying a price tag to everything.*[11]

---

[11]P. Crosby (1980), *Quality Is Free* (Mentor: New York), 218.

TQM in Government

The Office of Quality Management at the U.S. Department of Energy spent $3.5 million in 1994. A 12-person "culture team" in this office oversees a variety of training programs for the department's 20,000 federal employees. Some of the training procedures include "customer focus advocates," "customer focus coordinators," and "habits facilitators."

The Office of Quality Management also produces training videos. One, dealing with creativity and innovation, touts one innovation: an employee newsletter posted in bathroom stalls at a department's weapons plant. The newsletter is called the "Porcelain Press." The TQM training video describing the "Porcelain Press" even includes the sound of a flushing toilet and describes "this too, is the sound of communication . . . in the sanctuary of contemplation." The head of the Office of Quality Management describes the graffiti written on the posted newsletters as a "feedback feature."

A less enthusiastic Energy Department employee suggested that TQM stands for "time to quit and move."

Source: T. Noah (1994), "So, What Do People at Energy Department Do
All Day Long?" *The Wall Street Journal* (December 15), A1 and A8.

As summarized in Chapter 12, critics of incentive compensation such as Crosby ultimately argue that pay for performance does not work because poorly designed systems reward people for doing the wrong things. But on this basis one ought not to conclude that incentive pay should be discarded. Monetary and nonmonetary incentives are not mutually exclusive. Both types of rewards are valued by employees. Excluding one type of incentive reduces management flexibility.[12]

Another important motivator in TQM is the presence of a management sponsor for each quality team. Lower-level employees on the team may for the first time in their careers have direct access to a senior manager. Team members often perceive that this association will improve their future promotion possibilities or increase the likelihood of their appointment to another quality team with more access to even senior managers. The presence of the management sponsor probably increases the performance of the individual team members.

Why Quality Now?[13]

The traditional approach to ensuring product quality was to "inspect it in." Inspection stations and quality assurance inspectors were added along the production line to weed out inferior products. Statistical sampling methods were used to draw random samples from a batch and reject the entire batch if an unacceptable number of bad units were detected in the sample. (Notice that this process implicitly defines quality as low variance—meeting a certain set of specifications that might or might not be of interest to the consumer.)[14] Sections of the factory stored defects waiting to be reworked or

---

[12]G. Baker, M. Jensen, and K. Murphy (1988), "Compensation and Incentives: Practice and Theory," *Journal of Finance,* 593–616.

[13]Material in this section draws on the analysis in J. Zimmerman (1995), *Accounting for Decision Making and Control* (Richard D. Irwin: Burr Ridge, IL), Chapter 10.

[14]Statistical quality control (SQC) consists of a set of statistical methods used to determine if a particular repetitive manufacturing process is in or out of control. By employing common statistical procedures (means and standard deviations), normal variation of the process is established. If products exceed the normal bounds, the process is deemed "out of control" and subject to management investigation.

scrapped. In some cases, if market demand exceeded production in a period, marginally defective products were released. Defective products reaching the market were corrected by the field service organization under warranty arrangements.

By the 1980s, two factors combined to change the traditional approach to quality in many industries. First, the cost of detecting problems and monitoring production via computer instrumentation fell relative to the cost of maintaining quality via direct labor inspectors. The cost of labor (including fringe benefits) made the cost of manually detecting and correcting errors more expensive relative to performing these tasks electronically. Instead of manually detecting and correcting defects after production, improved instrumentation allowed earlier detection and correction of problems, often while the product was in a production process. Second, worldwide competition expanded to such nonprice forms of competition as quality. Customers had access to more reliable products. Once the Japanese automobile companies gained price competitiveness against the American auto makers, they turned their attention to achieving quality advantages. Both the lower cost of detecting defects and increased global competition fostered quality improvements.[15]

To reduce defects, companies redesigned their products to require fewer different parts, making it easier to maintain tighter controls on the quality of their suppliers. Product designers redesigned parts that failed. Production processes were redesigned to reduce defects. Robots and more instrumentation were built into manufacturing to ensure more uniform production. Firms adopted total quality management programs. While in many firms TQM programs were initially started to improve the tangible aspects of product and service quality, TQM programs have evolved to enhance products, processes, and services for both internal and external customers.

Reengineering

Reengineering—like TQM—is a popular management technique that proponents promise will revolutionize business. It too involves organizational changes that can be analyzed using the tools of this book. Michael Hammer, a leading proponent of reengineering, defines it as "the fundamental rethinking and radical redesign of business processes to achieve dramatic improvements in critical, contemporary measures of performance, such as cost, quality, service, and speed."[16] "Processes, not organizations, are the object of reengineering. Companies don't reengineer their sales or manufacturing departments; they reengineer the work the people in those departments do."[17]

Reengineering reassigns tasks to people. Chapter 9 described linking decision rights and specialized knowledge. With rapid advances in information technology, old decision-right assignments become obsolete and must be changed. Some decision rights will have to become centralized and others decentralized—there is no general prediction that information technology necessarily causes decision rights to move either up or down within the organization. However, new information technology tends to make the status quo obsolete. Reengineering is a process whereby the organization begins to search for an improved architecture by redesigning how tasks are bundled into jobs.

---

[15]Another factor contributing to TQM is factory automation and flexible manufacturing that allowed firms to broaden their product lines and to change products more rapidly. At any time, there are more products and more new products on the factory floor. This means there is likely more specific knowledge on the shop floor now.

[16]M. Hammer and J. Champy (1993), *Reengineering the Corporation: A Manifesto for Business Revolution* (Harper Business: New York), 32.

[17]Hammer and Champy (1993), 117.

Reengineering is a procedure for changing task assignments, often from a functional organization to a process organization. In Chapter 10, we described functional versus process organizations. IBM Credit Corporation was cited as an example. When IBM Credit was organized functionally, employees were assigned narrow job tasks: credit checking, contract preparation, pricing, and document preparation. After reengineering, employees at IBM Credit had broader task assignments. They were case workers and each was responsible for all the tasks necessary to process a credit application.

Functional organizations are more likely to be cost-beneficial than process organizations in environments with stable technology, where frequent communication within functional departments is relatively important and interactions across departments can be handled through rules and procedures. This is especially true where higher-level management is likely to have the relevant specific knowledge to coordinate the various functions that make up the overall process, and economies of specialization can be exploited. But in less stable environments, direct communication across functional areas can be quite important and situations more frequently arise that challenge established coordination procedures. In turn, higher-level managers are less likely to possess the relevant specific knowledge to address these challenges. The specific knowledge is more likely held by individuals throughout the firm. For example, the frequent introduction of new products increases the benefits of communication between salespeople and design engineers about customer preferences. Similarly, it is important for development and manufacturing personnel to share information when production techniques and technologies are frequently changing. Thus, in more dynamic environments, a process-oriented organization is more likely to be desirable.

This section discusses reengineering, but first we provide an example of reengineering from the health care industry called *patient-focused care* to illustrate the technique.

Reengineering: An Example[18]

Humana Hospital, a 555-bed hospital in Dallas, Texas, reengineered its organization along a "patient-focused care" model; it began this process in 1990 to enhance patient care and reduce costs. Hospital costs in the 1980s and early 1990s increased faster than inflation, thereby contributing to the health-care crisis. Insurance companies, private individuals, and employers that provided health care benefits for their employees bore the higher expenses. To stem the rising health care costs, large employers and insurance companies began pressuring their local health care providers by threatening to require their employees be treated only at those hospitals and by those physicians that better controlled their costs. Hospitals thus began to worry more about competing for patients and cost containment.

[18]Details of this example are from J. Lathrop (1991), "The Patient-Focused Hospital," *Healthcare Forum Journal* (July–August), 17–20.

Traditional Hospital Structure

Prior to reengineering, Humana employed the traditional hospital architecture whereby patient care was provided primarily by functionally organized individuals: physicians, nurses, and a score of specialists drawing blood samples and taking X rays and EKGs. A typical 650-bed hospital had the following breakdown of its health care dollar:

Medical care (direct patient care costs)	$0.16
Scheduling	0.14
Documentation (writing patient charts)	0.29
Idle labor time (waiting for patients to arrive)	0.20
Patient services (occupancy costs)	0.08
Transportation (wheelchair aides)	0.06
Management and supervision	0.07
Total	$1.00

Only $0.16 of each dollar spent in the hospital went to direct patient care.

Most large hospitals are organized around numerous, small, clinically focused nursing units with dedicated staffs and large centrally dispatched services (physical therapists, phlebotomists, transporters, and so on). They have 60 to 100 department heads, 150 responsibility centers, and seven to nine layers of management between the CEO and the bedside caregiver. Units are generally designed with excess capacity, enabling them to handle the sickest patient with the most complex needs. Yet 60 to 80 percent of all medical procedures are for routine services (chest X rays, basic lab tests, EKGs). Therefore, infrastructure costs and idle time account for up to 75 percent of the costs for simple procedures.

Patient-Focused Care

To better control costs and attract patients, the *patient-focused care* movement arose. Nursing roles were reevaluated and tasks reassigned. After the reorganization, patient care is delivered through a team approach, where two-person caregiver teams of nurses and technicians are responsible for most procedures performed on each patient. A reengineered patient-focused-care hospital has the following characteristics.[19]

Each caregiver learns to provide basic bedside nursing, basic X-ray films, respiratory care, EKGs, and the like. Routine care is provided by nurses, med-techs, lab-techs, phlebotomists, and other staff working in two-person teams assigned to patients. The team "owns" the patient; they admit the patient, document the care, serve the meals, change linen, and even clean the room after discharge. Instead of interacting with an average of 55 employees during a three-day stay, patients interact with 15. Instead of being transported throughout the hospital for routine tests and waiting for them to be performed, most tests are done in the patient's room.

Most hospitals are arranged by level of acuity and broad medical category. For example, cardiac intensive care units and orthopedic intensive care units are two separate acute care units specializing by medical category. Wireless technology (pagers and cellular phones) allows more flexibility in how patients are grouped. Patient-focused care locates patients by the type of tests, therapies, and health care resources needed. Instead of a 15- to 20-bed dedicated unit, 50- to 100-bed patient centers allow service lines to be developed.

---

[19]C. Schartner (1994), "Principles of Patient-Focused Care," *Journal of the Healthcare Information and Management Systems Society* 7, 11–15.

Productivity Job Losses Large in Service Industries

In 1987, Capital Holding Corp., a financial services company, acquired two small insurance companies to add to its group of insurance companies. Altogether, Capital had a combined administrative staff of 1,900. After reengineering in 1993, the insurance group employs 1,100 with plans to reduce the number to 800, even though its insurance business is up 25 percent.

Source: A. Ehrbar (1993), "'Re-Engineering' Gives Firms New Efficiency, Workers the Pink Slip" *The Wall Street Journal* (March 16), A1.

Large centralized service bureaucracies are dismantled and disbursed under the control of the patient centers. Each patient service center has satellite lab, radiology, and pharmacy units. The caregivers are cross-trained to perform many of the formally centralized functions. The extent to which decentralized satellites are efficient depends on the costs of the equipment. Basic X rays are decentralized, but CAT scans are not because small inexpensive, simple-to-operate X ray machines are available whereas CAT scan equipment is still very expensive and requires more specialized training to operate.

At admission, each patient is assigned to a unit and given a standard protocol (sometimes called a "care map") that details the standard set of tests and procedures to be followed by the caregivers. Instead of documenting every procedure and test performed, the staff only documents exceptions to standard protocols. Exception-based charting has reduced documentation by as much as 50 percent.

Advocates of patient-focused care emphasize that all of the above changes are necessary if the benefits are to be achieved. Unless the old hierarchy of specialized departments is eliminated and replaced with a new structure with new reporting mechanisms and incentives, most of the benefits of patient-focused care will not be realized. That is, all the elements of reorganization are complements, not substitutes.

> *The kind of improvement our health care system requires cannot be obtained by isolating a redesign initiative to any one of the patient-focused care principles. We need a more comprehensive effort that understands the complex interrelationships between the principles.*[20]

Hammer also recognizes the importance of the complementary nature of the decision-right assignments and the performance-evaluation and performance-reward systems in reengineering. "Companies that unfurl the banner (of reengineering) and march into battle without collapsing job titles, changing compensation policy, and instilling new attitudes and values get lost in the swamp."[21]

[20]Schartner (1994), 15, and P. Milgrom and J. Roberts (1995), "Complementarities and Fit: Strategy, Structure, and Organizational Change in Manufacturing," *Journal of Accounting and Economics* 19, 179–208.

[21]*The Wall Street Journal* (July 6, 1993), A1.

Reengineering Process[22]

This section describes the process of reengineering in more detail. To reengineer, Hammer lists the following guiding principles:

- *Organize around outcomes, not tasks.* One person should perform all the steps in the process. In the patient-focused care model, patients are organized around the treatments they will receive, and a two-person caregiving team provides all the basic services from nursing to X rays.
- *Have those who use the output of the process perform the process.* If the accounting department needs pencils, instead of requesting that purchasing buy the pencils, accounting buys the pencils from preapproved vendors. This reduces the overhead associated with managing the interfaces between processes since the same person performs sequential processes.
- *Subsume information processing into the work producing the information.* Scanners in supermarkets are linked to computers that maintain perpetual inventory levels. When stocks of a particular item drops below a reorder point, an electronic data interchange (EDI) sends an order to the supplier's computer to replenish the stock. As the checkout clerk scans the customers' purchases, this automatically updates the inventory records and reorders the merchandise. Likewise, in patient-focused care, the caregiver, by doing many of the tests, generates information and acts on it directly. A centralized lab technician does not have to produce the information and pass it to the caregiver for action.
- *Put the decision point where the work is performed.* Caregivers have the decision rights to follow the procedures specified in the protocols. The protocols (care maps) control the processes. Policies guide handling exceptions to the standards, which are documented and monitored.
- *Capture information once and at the source.* Prior to the implementation of patient-focused care, before a lab test could be performed, a physician had to order the test by hand-writing an order, which was then copied into the patient's chart. After the test was performed, accounting received a copy of the original order and then entered the data into the patient's account for billing purposes. With standard protocols, orders do not have to be written, charted, and reentered by accounting.
- *Treat geographically dispersed resources as though they were centralized.* Each decentralized pharmacy in the patient centers can be linked to a centralized pharmacy database that contains preapproved drugs and vendors. This allows the benefits of scale economies via large purchases while maintaining the benefits of flexibility and service.

The first five points in effect say *marry knowledge and decision rights.* Look at how tasks are assigned, and how knowledge is generated; repackage jobs to more efficiently exploit the way knowledge is generated. Caregivers in the patient-focused care hospital perform the basic functions of admitting patients, drawing blood, and performing lab tests and X rays. Therefore, they spend less time informing the next person in the sequence of what they found. In a patient-focused care hospital, tasks are reassigned to better join knowledge and decision rights. The caregiver knows that blood was last drawn out of the patient's sore left arm and so now will use the right arm.

---

[22]This section draws on the analysis in M. Hammer (1990), "Reengineering Work: Don't Automate, Obliterate," *Harvard Business Review* (July–August), 104–112.

Reengineering and Organizational Architecture

Decision-Right Assignment

Most of the contemporary writers on reengineering spend a considerable amount of time describing not only what reengineering is but also how to accomplish it. They emphasize the difficulty of the task and the importance of senior management backing the effort. Hammer and Champy have observed the following assignment of decision rights in companies that are reengineering:[23]

- *Leader.* A senior executive who authorizes and motivates the reengineering process. Consistent with our discussion of leadership in Chapter 16, the leader must set the vision and then motivate others to follow it.
- *Reengineering team.* Five to 10 people with the specialized knowledge of the process (or its parts) who analyze the existing process, redesign it, and oversee its implementation. Individuals from both inside and outside the process, working usually full time for up to a year, form the self-directed team. Individual performance evaluation while serving on the team is based on the team's achievement. Most of the team should expect to become part of the newly reengineered process.
- *Steering committee.* The policy-making board of senior managers that establishes policies, ratifies particular reengineering proposals, and monitors each team. The leader chairs this committee. The reengineering steering committee performs the same function as the quality committees in TQM. It controls team mania.
- *Reengineering czar.* The person with the specialized knowledge of reengineering methods who acts as a resource to the reengineering teams. The czar also helps to coordinate activities across the various teams.

As in the TQM process, there is separation of decision management from decision control. Both reengineering and TQM teams have decision rights to initiate and implement changes but only after ratification by the policy making and monitoring board, the steering committee.

Evaluating and Rewarding Performance of Reengineering Teams

Chapter 13 described the general issues of evaluating team performance. Both the team's total output and the individual members' performance must be evaluated. The reengineering czar often has first-hand knowledge of individual members' contributions because this person has been working closely with the team. As with TQM, the steering committee that ratifies the reengineering team's plans also monitors the team's output, including the team's proposed reengineering plan

Reengineering efforts seek to make drastic changes in the way work is done. Often, this results in substantial reductions in the work force. Those members of the reengineering team overseeing and implementing the plan usually have more job security than those not on the team. This can be a powerful motivator for the team to get its analysis right and to see its plan implemented.

[23]Hammer and Champy (1993), 103–116.

Karolinska Hospital

The Karolinska Hospital in Stockholm, facing a 20 percent budget cut in 1992, reorganized work at the hospital around patient flow. Prior to the reorganization, the average patient with an enlarged prostate gland spent 255 days after his first contact with the hospital before being treated. Only 2 percent of that time involved treatment. The remainder of the time was spent waiting for appointments. A nurse coordinator position was created whose job was to minimize the number of visits the patient must make. Now, waiting times for surgery have been cut from over six months to three weeks, and three of the 15 operating rooms have been closed, yet operations are up 25 percent.

Source: R. Jacobs (1995), "The Struggle to Create an Organization for the
21st Century," *Fortune* (April 13), 98–99.

Why Reengineering Now?

Prior to 1970, firms faced less worldwide competition. Some industries faced lower rates of technological innovation than they do now. Many industries in the U.S. were regulated (telecommunications, banking, transportation). A functional organization was more likely optimal and typically was adopted. But in the 1990s, these firms face more dynamic environments, and their senior managers realize that the old functional organization is no longer optimal. Besides increased competition and deregulation, technology has reduced the cost of transferring information throughout the organization, thereby causing the old architecture to become increasingly inefficient.

New technology makes obsolete the old ways that tasks were bundled into jobs and jobs assembled to form processes: sophisticated information systems can easily track customers and retailers, thereby opening new market opportunities; bar coding and scanners now provide enormous amounts of information about consumer purchases; and electronic data interchange (EDI) connects customers with supplier computers that automatically reorder inventory as the customer sales occur. Thus, as in the case of TQM, both increased competition and technological change cause managers to search for new organizational architectures.

TQM versus Reengineering

TQM and reengineering are both mechanisms for effecting organizational change. Both involve changes in organizational architecture. To be successful, both require coordinated and consistent changes in all three legs of the three-legged stool. Neither TQM nor reengineering is a substitute for the other. While both might be used simultaneously, such use might lead to more confusion and disruption among the work force than if the two were sequenced. This section compares and contrasts the two approaches.[24]

[24]A process related to both TQM and reengineering is value analysis. This technique dates back to when Lawrence Miles, an engineer at General Electric, sought to identify those unnecessary costs that do not add value or customer features to product quality. Examples include product rework, scrap, ordering errors, and schedule changes. (T. Dickson, "Pioneer and Prophets: Lawrence Miles," *Financial Times,* January 16, 1995).

Continuous versus Discontinuous Changes

Cost savings from either TQM or reengineering often come from reducing labor content. For example, when Ford Motor Company reengineered its accounts payable department, head count was reduced drastically (375 out of 500 clerk jobs were eliminated).

A principle some TQM consultants stress is job-security assurances. They argue that in order to motivate employees to be forthcoming with quality improvements, TQM programs must promise workers that their jobs will not be eliminated. While not all TQM programs offer such assurances, successful programs must offer employees incentives to be forthcoming with their specialized knowledge. Job security is one way to provide such assurance. On the other hand, program success does not require that all employees have job security; in extreme cases, it might be offered only to those on TQM teams. But in companies that have announced the need to downsize, a policy of job security only for TQM team members could induce team mania by creating incentives for employees to suggest numerous TQM projects to protect themselves from layoffs. Such a policy also could create strong incentives for other employees to generate large influence costs.

If firmwide job-security assurances are made, TQM productivity improvements are constrained by the rate of job attrition. If 1 out of 10 employees quits or retires each year, then only 10 percent of the jobs can be eliminated through attrition annually. And this attrition rate interacts with the firm's business growth rate to put an upper bound on the productivity savings a TQM program can produce in any given year.

Quality programs seek to improve existing processes. Reengineering does not focus on enhancing existing processes but seeks to replace them with entirely new ones. Reengineering seeks large improvements in productivity; cost reductions of successful reengineering programs exceed the attrition rate. Technological or market changes can cause an existing architecture to become obsolete quickly. Drastic job redesign is necessary and hence so are layoffs in excess of the attrition rate. In this situation, TQM coupled with job security guarantees will not produce the desired results. One way to achieve larger savings is through reengineering—which only guarantees job security to members of the reengineering team.

In addition to job guarantees, two other factors affect the willingness of employees to participate in organizational redesign programs: the firm's growth rate and the extent of job-specific human capital. Growing firms can absorb employees whose jobs are eliminated by labor productivity improvements into other parts of the firm that are growing. However, the ability to transfer these employees to the growing parts of the

Job Cuts and TQM

An article discussing TQM programs reported:

> (D)ownsizing undermines a cornerstone of TQM: employee motivation. To achieve perfect quality, said Deming, companies must "drive out fear, so that everyone may work effectively." Yet downsizing fosters fear, as Xerox, the world's biggest photocopy maker (and a Baldrige winner in 1989), has discovered. Hector Motroni, head of quality at Xerox, says the firm has been through "11 years of wrenching change" since it adopted TQM in 1983. And although Mr. Motroni credits total quality with reinvigorating the firm, he concedes that job cuts and the loss of management layers . . . has damaged motivation and made it harder to sell the TQM message.

Source: "The Straining of Quality," *The Economist* (January 14, 1995), 55.

firm depends on the extent they have job-specific human capital. If manufacturing jobs are being eliminated and software-engineering jobs are being added, high retraining costs are incurred to transfer manufacturing employees into programming positions. However, when there is lower job-specific human capital, implicit job security exists. Salespeople selling one set of products can be retrained at fairly low cost to sell a new set of products if their customer base remains similar. Thus, high-growth firms with low job-specific human capital tasks are able to offer implicit employment guarantees and will have more employee participation in organizational redesign efforts than low-growth, high job-specific human capital firms.

Distributional Consequences in Effecting Organizational Change

It is easier to implement organizational changes when some individuals are made better off and no one is made worse off than in situations where some parties gain at the expense of others (see Chapter 16). In this latter situation, there are distributional consequences of the change, and thus more opposition to the change is expected. To the extent TQM projects include fewer layoffs, they tend to have fewer distributional consequences and hence generate less resistance than reengineering programs. A reengineering program usually involves large changes in task assignment and hence either the destruction of job-specific human capital or outright job cuts.

Parties likely to be harmed by reengineering, via reduced corporate resources under their control or by job loss, might try to block the organizational change. Agents with ratification rights harmed by the reorganization are likely to lobby against it. Reengineering efforts when announced are likely to create apprehension among the work force who have incentives to sabotage the project. One solution is to establish a reengineering team that is completely separate from the existing hierarchy. This team is guaranteed job security and positions in the reengineered organization. Working full time on the project removes the team from the social pressures of their former colleagues.

Making organizational changes with distributional consequences requires the use of power. Power is derived from formal authority (senior managers with the decision rights to ratify and implement the change), control of physical and monetary resources, control of information, and friends and allies (see Chapter 16). Using a leader, team, and steering committee marshals all these elements of power. The leader, if the chief executive officer, and the steering committee, if composed of senior managers, have the formal authority to ratify and implement the change. Selecting team members with the specialized knowledge of the various parts of the process and of how the process interacts with other processes is critical to gaining control of the necessary information.

Reasons TQM and Reengineering Fail

The preceding sections have described the mechanics of TQM and reengineering and have analyzed these popular management techniques using this book's framework. TQM and reengineering are different ways of reorganizing work within firms. While most large firms have tried these methods, the evidence, casual as it is, seems to suggest that most adopters of these methods are less than completely satisfied with the results they achieve. This section suggests three reasons TQM and reengineering efforts can fall short of their anticipated outcomes.

Linking TQM to Financial Returns and Compensation

A 1992 study by the American Quality Foundation and Ernst & Young found that in 80 percent of the firms surveyed, quality performance measures aren't important in senior manager's compensation. This suggests one reason why most TQM programs fail.

Source: R. Jacob (1993), "TQM: More than a Dying Fad?" *Fortune* (October 8), 68.

Ignoring Other Legs of the Stool

To successfully restructure the organization and push decision rights down to the people with the knowledge about processes and customer preferences, the performance-evaluation and performance-reward systems must also be changed. Empowering individuals with decision rights requires systems to evaluate and reward their performance. Firms trying to implement TQM or reengineering without modifying their performance-measurement and reward systems to support the changes in decision rights are unlikely to garner the hoped-for benefits.

Juran and Gryna[25] list several reasons quality programs fail, including focusing only on measuring the costs of quality failures, transferring these charges to departments responsible for the product failures, or trying to perfect the cost of quality estimates. Notice that these reasons are analogous to focusing on just the performance-evaluation system (measuring quality costs) and ignoring the decision-rights assignment and performance rewards.

Much of the reengineering and patient-focused care literature focuses on how to design a process for reassigning decision rights.[26] It focuses on a single leg of the three-legged stool: repartitioning decision rights via task reassignment. Most of the writers mention the importance of the performance-evaluation and reward systems but offer little guidance or occasionally inappropriate advice for how the evaluation and reward systems must change. For example, Hammer and Champy[27] make the blanket assertion: "Substantial rewards for outstanding performance take the form of bonuses, not pay raises." Clearly, the compensation decision we describe in Chapters 11 and 12 is far more complex than is reflected in the Hammer and Champy suggestion.

An important part of the performance-reward system is promotions. But most reengineering articles are silent about how to create new career paths and promotion systems to motivate individuals in a process-oriented organization. Within smaller, flatter organizations, advancement opportunities are more limited. If TQM and reengineering are to work, significant effort must be expended on "reengineering" the performance-evaluation and reward systems—all three legs of the stool must be coordinated.

[25]J. M. Juran and F. Gryna, Jr. (1993), *Quality Planning and Analysis,* (McGraw-Hill, New York), 30–32.

[26]For example, see Hammer and Champy (1993), and Hammer (1990).

[27]Hammer and Champy (1993), 73.

Quality Is Not Free

One noted quality expert argues, "Quality is free. It's not a gift, but it is free. What costs money are the unquality things—all the actions that involve not doing jobs right the first time."[28] "The cost of quality . . . is . . . the cost of doing things wrong."[29] The costs of not doing things right the first time include prevention (design reviews, supplier evaluations, tool control, preventive maintenance), appraisal (prototype tests, receiving inspection and test, packaging inspection), and failure (redesign, engineering change order, rework, scrap, product warranty, product liability). It is certainly the case that if managers can at zero cost cause prevention, appraisal, or failure costs to go down, quality goes up and profits improve. In this sense, "quality is free." And if we could get oil to jump out of the ground and into our cars as gasoline, "oil is free." However, improving a product's quality requires management time and other resources. Defects must be discovered and their causes investigated and corrected. Employees must be trained in quality methods. In this sense, improving quality is costly.

Improving product quality usually lowers the cost of reworking defects along with inspection costs, warranty costs, and customer complaints. The firm's brand-name capital is higher when product quality is increased. However, improving quality (lowering the number of defects and providing products with attributes customers value) is not free.[30] Figure 17.1 illustrates the relation between quality and firm value. Firm value increases as product quality improves. This is due to two factors: lower production costs and increased consumer demand. Profit-maximizing managers will want to undertake all quality improvements where the expected benefits from enhanced quality exceed the costs of improving quality. Ultimately, customers must pay for the cost of the enhanced quality. At some point, the costs of making an additional improvement in quality will exceed what the customer is willing to pay for it. Consumers are presented with a wide variety of quality choices in most product lines. The wine lists at many restaurants contain a wide selection with a range of prices. Presumably, higher-priced wines are of higher quality. Yet, we observe few customers ordering the most expensive wines. Few diners value the additional quality of the $275 bottle over the $20 house wine.

Managers might systematically underestimate the total costs of poor quality. Given the wide range of costs of providing quality—ranging from scrap, rework, and inspection to lost customer goodwill—senior management might systematically underestimate the benefits of reducing defects. While manufacturing might optimize its production process with respect to quality, it does not take into account in its calculations the costs marketing and distribution incur having to fix problems in the field. If some managers underestimate all the benefits from improving quality, they might underinvest in programs to improve quality. They might not fully appreciate the costs of reduced consumer confidence in their products. If managers are about to retire, they may be reluctant to spend money today on quality programs that yield benefits after they retire. But this is just the standard horizon problem that occurs with all decisions where outlays occur now and the benefits span several periods; in this sense, quality programs are no different from capital investment, R&D, and advertising. Successful firms must control these horizon problems.

---

[28]Crosby (1980), 1.

[29]Crosby (1980), 15.

[30]P. Lederer and S. Rhee (1995), "Economics of Total Quality Management," *Journal of Operations Management* 12, 353–367.

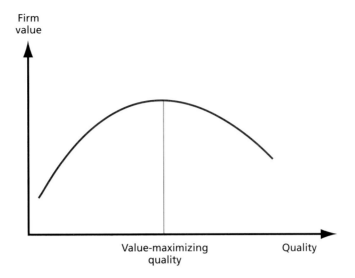

Figure 17.1 The Relation between Quality and Firm Value

Firm value increases as quality increases because consumer demand increases and manufacturing costs decline. Beyond some point, the cost of increasing quality is greater than the manufacturing cost savings and the increased consumer demand. Maximizing quality does not maximize firm value. Too much quality lowers value.

If managers are not aware of all the possible benefits of improved quality, educational programs are required. However, quality still is not free. Quality decisions, like all decisions, require accurate estimates of all the expected costs and benefits. It is just as dangerous to underestimate the benefits of quality programs as it is to underestimate the costs by arguing "quality is free." In both cases, nonfirm-value-maximizing decisions are likely to result.

While Crosby recognizes that improving quality is costly, he unambiguously believes that the benefits of improving quality exceed the costs. "If you concentrate on making quality certain, you can probably increase your profit by an amount equal to 5 to 10 percent of your sales. That is a lot of money for free."[31] In this sense, Crosby asserts that the benefits unambiguously exceed the costs for all firms. Without offering any systematic evidence other than a few anecdotal stories, he asserts that all firms (including those currently following his advice) are systematically forgoing profitable projects.

Restructurings Are Investment Decisions

Any restructuring is costly. Senior managers must devote their limited time to designing the new architecture and then implementing it. Implementation often entails confrontations with those managers in the firm made worse off by the reorganization (influence costs). When downsizings are required because of reengineering, managers bear additional costs of having to fire employees.

---

[31]Crosby (1980), 1.

The Costs of Reorganizing

Many managers face psychological stress from having to fire people because of reorganizations. One IBM manager remarked, "I came home every night worried how this one or that one was going to support himself. I snapped at my husband, I had trouble sleeping." After accepting the next early retirement package offered by IBM, she said, "Reorganization had been five years out of my life, and when I quit, I felt the biggest load in the world had been lifted from my shoulders."

One manager who had gone through several rounds of firing subordinates was described as follows: "He was smoking, had lost weight, had trouble looking me in the eye, was extremely nervous. It seemed to me that a few months of telling people they were out the door had gone a long way in destroying his personality."

Nolan Brohaugh of the Menninger Clinic, a noted psychiatric hospital, has been conducting weeklong seminars for 15 years for professionals in crisis. He says, "In my experience, they (managers) have a lot of trouble firing people who deserve to get canned."

Source: L. Smith (1994), "Burned Out Bosses" *Fortune* (July 25), 44–52.

How much a firm should invest in TQM and reengineering are investment decisions. Not all firms face the same expected benefits from restructuring. Decentralizing decision rights, even to employees with specialized knowledge, still might not be firm-value maximizing if agency costs increase. As discussed earlier, these restructurings occur because of changes in the firm's markets or technology. If firms are in stable markets and technological advances have not been rapid, the benefits of restructuring are likely to be low and, for these firms, the expected costs of restructuring are more likely to exceed the benefits. TQM and reengineering are more likely to be profitable investments where the firm's markets and technology are changing. Since firms in the same industry face similar markets and technology, you would expect firms in the same industry to restructure at approximately the same time.

Summary

TQM and reengineering are popular management techniques promising to add value to the firm. Yet, these approaches have failed to achieve many of their claimed benefits. This chapter illustrates how the analytic framework of this book can be applied to emerging management trends, in particular to total quality management and reengineering. TQM is the process whereby employees are trained in the scientific method and then use these skills to improve product quality and production efficiency by forming multidisciplinary teams. TQM involves repartitioning decision rights by empowering teams who have the knowledge to increase firm value. This is most effectively accomplished if the quality teams have the incentives to discover value-increasing changes because the performance-evaluation and reward systems (the other two legs of our three-legged stool) support the quality program. One important assurance quality teams often receive is the guarantee of job security if they discover a way to improve a process that requires layoffs. TQM is a procedure that seeks continuous, small improvements in processes. To control the quality program, a hierarchy of quality committees are created to ratify and then monitor the behavior of each quality team.

Reengineering, like TQM, is a mechanism for changing the organization's architecture. But unlike TQM, reengineering seeks drastic, radical changes in processes. Advances in information technology change where knowledge is captured in the firm and how it can be transmitted. The old architecture that attempted to link decision rights and knowledge is obsolete. Garnering the benefits of the new information technology

CASE STUDY
Software Development, Inc.

Software Development, Inc. (SDI), produces and markets software for personal computers, including spreadsheet, word processing, desktop publishing, and database management programs. SDI has annual sales of $800 million.

Producing software is a time-consuming, labor-intensive process. Software quality is an extremely important aspect of success in computer software markets. One aspect of quality is program reliability. Does the software perform as expected? Does it work with other software in terms of data transfers and interfaces? Does it terminate abnormally? In spite of extensive testing of the software, programs always contain some "bugs" (defects). Once the software is released, SDI stands behind the product with phone-in customer service consultants who answer questions and help the customer work around existing problems in the software. SDI also has a software maintenance group that fixes bugs and sends out revised versions of the programs to customers.

SDI has been tracking the relation between quality costs and quality. The quality measure it uses is the number of documented bugs in a software package. These bugs are counted when a customer calls in with a complaint and the SDI customer service representative determines that this is a new problem. The software maintenance programmers then set about fixing the program to eliminate the bug. To manage quality, SDI tracks quality costs. It has released 38 new or major revisions in existing packages in the last three years. Table 17.1 reports the number of defects documented in the first six months following release. Also listed in Table 1 is total product cost and quality cost per software package release.

Product cost includes all the costs incurred to produce and market the software, excluding the quality cost in Table 17–1. Quality cost consists of these components: training, prevention, and software maintenance and customer service costs. Training costs are those expenditures for educating the programmers and updating their training. Better educated programmers produce fewer bugs. Prevention cost includes the expenditures for testing the software before it is released. Maintenance and customer service costs are those of the programmers charged with fixing the bugs and reissuing the revised software and the customer service representatives answering phone questions. The training and prevention costs are measured over the period the software was being developed and the number of bugs, and maintenance and service costs are measured in the first six months following release.

All the numbers in Table 17.1 have been divided by lines of computer code in the particular program release. Programs with more lines of code cost more and also have more bugs. Prior studies find that lines of code is an acceptable way to control for program complexity. Thus, the numbers in Figure 17.4 are stated in terms of defects and cost per 100,000 lines of code.

Figure 17.2 plots the relation between total quality cost and number of defects. The vice president of quality of SDI likes to use Figure 17.2 to emphasize that costs and quality are inversely related. She is fond of saying, "Quality pays! Our total costs are a declining function of the number of defects. The more we spend on quality, the lower our costs."

often requires entirely new bundling of tasks into jobs. Instead of having several employees specializing by task and handing off work from one to another to complete a process, one employee now performs the entire process for routine transactions. Networked, on-line databases or expert computer systems provide the necessary support for the newly created multifunctional job.

Like TQM, reengineering requires a team of people knowledgeable about the old process being redesigned. This team has the decision rights to initiate and implement the design change. This team also requires incentives to do this, thus necessitating changes in the performance-evaluation and reward systems. But since reengineering usually results in large layoffs, only individuals on the reengineering team are normally given job-security guarantees.

	Defects	Product Cost	Training Cost	Prevention Cost	Software Maintenance and Customer Service Cost	Total Cost
1	66	$3,455	$442	$ 770	$2,160	$6,827
2	86	3,959	428	447	2,658	7,492
3	14	3,609	417	1,167	687	5,880
4	73	3,948	211	655	2,334	7,148
5	17	3,104	290	1,013	544	4,951
6	48	3,179	253	547	1,556	5,535
7	80	3,112	392	508	2,633	6,645
8	41	3,529	276	577	1,563	5,945
9	50	3,796	557	634	1,666	6,653
10	67	3,444	365	947	2,140	6,896
11	42	3,922	453	869	1,444	6,688
12	64	3,846	378	1,108	1,942	7,274
13	71	3,014	555	762	2,384	6,715
14	1	3,884	301	773	423	5,381
15	18	3,183	378	1,080	857	5,498
16	85	3,475	528	1,010	2,572	7,585
17	17	3,445	357	666	631	5,099
18	50	3,203	285	427	1,546	5,461
19	22	3,839	239	1,080	891	6,049
20	73	3,060	540	1,054	2,309	6,963
21	52	3,182	329	1,079	1,867	6,457
22	75	3,075	395	832	2,697	6,999
23	35	3,456	447	969	1,518	6,390
24	53	3,987	355	651	2,042	7,035
25	25	3,836	309	1,160	1,036	6,341
26	6	3,886	234	794	252	5,166
27	78	3,846	418	833	2,800	7,897
28	82	3,106	409	1,092	2,871	7,478
29	39	3,506	448	899	1,342	6,195
30	47	3,545	450	442	1,450	5,887
31	30	3,376	456	784	1,260	5,876
32	17	3,740	542	420	607	5,309
33	67	3,479	411	821	2,018	6,729
34	51	3,773	351	1,145	1,873	7,142
35	74	3,034	497	671	2,389	6,591
36	25	3,768	268	887	1,094	6,017
37	14	3,168	356	645	837	5,006
38	77	3,561	492	1,167	2,597	7,817
Average	48	$3,509	$390	$ 826	$1,671	$6,395

Table 17–1   SDI Defects and Costs by Program Release (per 100,000 lines of computer code)

One of the key questions posed at the beginning of this chapter is why TQM and reengineering fail to produce the desired benefits. While both involve empowering teams of employees to discover substantive improvements in the organization, managers implementing both TQM and reengineering often fail to emphasize changing the other two legs of the three-legged stool: the performance-evaluation and reward systems. Processes can be improved or radically redesigned, but changing the performance-evaluation and reward systems for the new task assignments is usually not emphasized as much as the reassignment of decision rights. Also, TQM programs will fail to maximize firm value if

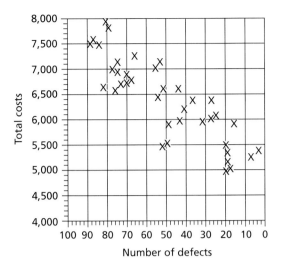

Figure 17.2 SDI Total Costs by Defects

Based on this analysis, the vice president has recommended a major investment in quality improvement, focusing specifically on prevention and training. Evaluate the vice president's analysis. What criteria should be used in deciding whether or not to invest more in quality? Do you have all the data that is necessary to evaluate such an investment proposal?

---

management overinvests in quality. Since improving quality is costly, only those quality enhancements valued by customers at more than their cost should be undertaken. Maximizing quality (or minimizing the number of defects) does not necessarily lead to maximizing firm value. Typically, the benefits of restructuring will be large in firms facing rapid changes in technology or in market competition.

APPENDIX | *Baldrige National Quality Award*

In 1987, the federal government established the Malcolm Baldrige National Quality Award to recognize quality achievement in U.S. companies. The annual awards are administered by the National Bureau of Standards of the U.S. Department of Commerce. After paying an application fee, companies wishing to apply for the award file a written report describing their company and information on 24 examination items that will be scored by an examining team from the government. These 24 items form seven categories summarized in Figure 17.3. For example, under leadership, one of the specific items is "Senior Executive Leadership." The applicant is asked to describe "how the company's senior executives set strategic directions and build and maintain a leadership system conducive to high performance, individual development, and organizational learning." The examiners then assign point scores using specific scoring criteria.

It is interesting to compare the contents of Figure 17.3 with the analytic framework developed in this book. Most of the key elements needed to ensure that the organizational architecture is designed to increase quality are present in the Baldrige criteria. The

1.   Leadership (90 pts.)

The *Leadership* category examines senior executives' personal leadership and involvement in creating and sustaining a customer focus, clear values and expectations, and a leadership system that promotes performance excellence. Also examined is how the values and expectations are integrated into the company's management system, including how the company addresses its public responsibilities and corporate citizenship.

2.   Information and Analysis (75 pts.)

The *Information and Analysis* category examines the management and effectiveness of the use of data and information to support customer-driven performance excellence and marketplace success.

3.   Strategic Quality Planning (55 pts.)

The *Strategic Quality Planning* category examines how the company sets strategic directions and how it determines key plan requirements. Also examined are how the plan requirements are translated into an effective performance management system.

4.   Human Resource Development and Management (140 pts.)

The *Human Resource Development and Management* category examines how the work force is enabled to develop and utilize its full potential, aligned with the company's performance objectives. Also examined are the company's efforts to build and maintain an environment conducive to performance excellence, full participation, and personal and organizational growth.

5.   Process Management (140 pts.)

The *Process Management* category examines the key aspects of process management, including customer-focused design, product and service delivery processes, support services, and supply management involving all work units, including research and development. The category examines how key processes are designed, effectively managed, and improved to achieve higher performance.

6.   Business Results (250 pts.)

The *Business Results* category examines the company's performance and improvement in key business areas—product and service quality, productivity and operational effectiveness, supply quality, and financial performance indicators linked to these areas. Also examined are performance levels relative to competitors.

7.   Customer Focus and Satisfaction (250 pts.)

The *Customer Focus and Satisfaction* category examines the company's systems for customer learning and for building and maintaining customer relationships. Also examined are levels and trends in key measures of business success—customer satisfaction and retention, market share, and satisfaction relative to competitors.

Figure 17.3 1995 Malcolm Baldrige National Quality Award Examination Categories (and Point Values)[32]

Points are assigned in seven categories based on how well the firm meets the stated criteria in that category. Each category has a maximum number of points that can be awarded.

firm must demonstrate that it gathers knowledge of the customer and competitors, that decision rights are partitioned to promote participation, and that employees have incentives to increase customer satisfaction.

Figure 17.4 lists the firms that have won the Baldrige award. Up to two awards in each of three categories are presented annually to companies or subsidiaries. A 1991 U.S. Government Accounting Office report studied 20 of the top-scoring companies in the 1988 and 1989 Baldrige competitions. These companies had quality programs in place for an average of two and a half years. The surveyed companies reported an increase in

---

[32]National Institute of Standards and Technology (1995), *1995 Award Criteria: Malcolm Baldrige National Quality Award* (Department of Commerce: Gaithersburg, MD).

Manufacturing Category
Motorola (1988)
Westinghouse Electric Commercial Nuclear Fuel Division (1988)
Commercial Nuclear Fuel Division (1989)
Milliken & Co. (1989)
Xerox Business Products and Systems (1989)
Cadillac (1990)
IBM Rochester, MN (1990)
Solectron Corp. (1991)
Zytec Corp. (1991)
AT&T Network Systems Group Transmission Systems (1992)
Texas Instruments Defense Systems & Electronics Group (1992)
Eastman Chemical Co. (1993)
Armstrong World Industries' Building Products Operations (1995)
Corning Telecommunications Products Division (1995)

Service Category
Federal Express (1990)
AT&T Universal Card Services (1992)
Ritz-Carlton Hotel Co. (1992)
AT&T Power Systems (1994)
GTE Corp. (1994)

Small Business Category
Globe Metallurgical Inc. (1988)
Wallace Co. (1990)
Marlow Industries (1991)
Granite Rock Co. (1992)
Ames Rubber Co. (1993)
Wainwright Industries Inc. (1994)

Figure 17.4 Malcolm Baldrige National Quality Award Winners

These companies have won the Baldrige Award in the categories shown

reliability and on-time delivery. Product defects and development time for new products dropped. Market share increased 13.7 percent a year, and profits rose 0.4 percent. Customer complaints dropped 12 percent.

Partly due to the public relations and advertising value of winning the Baldrige award, the number of applications rose from 203 for the first three years to over 180,000 requests for applications in 1990. Since 1991, the number of applicants has fallen sharply.[33] The government uses hundreds of examiners to assign the point values. Companies hire former examiners as consultants to advise them on filing applications. Once a company reaches the semifinalist stage, which includes an on-site visit, additional consulting teams, coach managers, and employees who might be chosen randomly are interviewed by the Baldrige examiners. *The Wall Street Journal*[34] reports that the Baldrige award creates consulting engagements lasting up to six months and costing as much as $175,000, and has become "the full employment act for quality consultants."

[33]R. Jacob (1993), "TQM: More than a Dying Fad?" *Fortune* (October 18), 66.
[34]S. Yadar, G. Fuchsber, and B. Stertz (December 13, 1990) "All That's Lacking Is Bert Parks Singing 'Cadilac, Cadilac'" *The Wall Street Journal*, A1.

Suggested Readings

P. Crosby (1980), *Quality Is Free* (Mentor: New York).

M. Hammer and J. Champy (1993), *Reengineering the Corporation: A Manifesto for Business Revolution* (Harper Business: New York).

J. Juran (1989), *Juran on Leadership for Quality* (Free Press: New York).

J. Juran and Gryna, Jr. (1993), *Quality Planning and Analysis* (McGraw-Hill: New York).

S. Keating and K. Wruck (1994), "Sterling Chemicals Inc.: Quality and Process Improvement Program," Harvard Business School Case 9-493-026.

K. Wruck and M. Jensen (1994), "Science, Specific Knowledge and Total Quality Management," *Journal of Accounting and Economics* 18, 247–287.

Review Questions

17–1. "Hewlett-Packard now treats TQM like any other investment: if a particular total-quality initiative doesn't show a quick return in terms of higher sales, lower costs, or happier customers, it is redesigned or scrapped."[35] Critically evaluate Hewlett-Packard's policy.

17–2. Guest Watches is a division of Guest Fashions, a large, international fashion designer. Guest Watches manufactures highly stylish watches for young adults (18–30) who are fashion conscious. It is a profit center and its senior management's compensation is tied closely to the watch division's reported profits. While Guest Watches has succeeded in capturing the fashion market, a lack of product dependability is eroding these gains. A number of retailers have dropped or are threatening to drop the Guest watch line because of customer returns. Guest Watches carry a one-year warranty and 12 percent are returned, compared to an industry average of 4 percent. Besides high warranty costs and lost sales due to reputation, Guest has higher than industry average manufacturing scrap and rework costs.

Senior management, worried about these trends and the possible erosion of its market dominance, hired a consulting firm to study the problem and make recommendations for reversing the situation. After a thorough analysis of Guest's customers, suppliers, and manufacturing facilities, the consultants recommended five possible actions, ranging from the status quo to a complete total quality management, zero defects program (Level IV). The table below outlines the various alternatives (in thousands of dollars):

	Additional Training Cost*	Additional Prevention/Compliance+
Status quo	$ 0	$ 0
Level I	80	180
Level II	200	240
Level III	350	340
Level IV	550	490

* Includes the annual costs of training employees in TQM methods.
+ All annual costs, including certifying suppliers, redesigning the product, and inspection costs to reduce defects.

The consultant emphasized that while first-year start-up costs are slightly higher than subsequent years, management must really view the cost estimates in the table as annual, ongoing costs. Given employee turnover and the assumption that supplier changes, training, prevention, and compliance costs are not likely to decline over time, the costs in the preceding table will be annual operating expenses.

[35]"The Straining of Quality," *The Economist* (January 14, 1995), 55.

The consulting firm and the newly appointed vice president for quality programs estimated that under level IV, rework and scrap would be $25,000 and warranty costs zero. Level IV was needed to get the firm to zero defects. A task force was convened, and after several meetings, it generated the following estimates of rework/scrap and warranty costs for the various levels of firm commitment:

	Total Rework/Scrap Cost*	Total Warranty Costs+
Status quo	$500	$350
Level I	300	280
Level II	150	140
Level III	75	80
Level IV	25	0

* The costs of manufacturing scrap and rework.
+ The costs of repairing and replacing products that fail in the hands of customers.

There was considerable discussion and debate about the quantitative impact of increased quality on additional sales. While no hard and fast numbers could be derived, the consensus view was that the total net cash flows (contribution margin) from additional sales as retailers and customers learn of the reduced defect rate would be:

	Contribution Margin on Additional Sales
Status quo	$ 0
Level I	600
Level II	1,000
Level III	1,200
Level IV	1,300

a. Assuming the data as presented are reasonably accurate, what should Guest Watches do about its deteriorating quality situation? Should it maintain the status quo or should it adopt the consultant's recommendation and implement Level I, II, III, or IV?

b. Critically evaluate the analysis underlying your policy recommendation in part (a). Will the senior management of the watch division make the same decision as the senior management of Guest Fashions?

17–3. According to a *New York Times* article,[36] LDS Hospital in Salt Lake City installed a computer in every hospital room in the mid-1980s. These computers replaced paper charts so everything the doctor or nurses did was entered into a database as it happened. A small number of patients get infections following surgery, which adds to the length of their hospital stay and ultimately to the cost of treating the patient. After several years, hospital personnel began using the computerized data to determine the best time to begin antibiotics for patients undergoing surgery. They found that by starting antibiotics a few hours before surgery, the rate of infections fell from 1.8 percent to 0.4 percent, saving the hospital about $9,000 per case. By using the computer system, the head of LDS's quality-control program can improve quality and cut hospital costs.

Analyze the LDS quality control program in terms of the traditional TQM program described in this chapter.

[36] *New York Times* (March 31, 1994).

17–4. LDS Hospital in Salt Lake City has a computer system that records all procedures performed on patients and all drugs administered.[37] The computer system can track which surgeons are the best and which ones are the worst in terms of length of patient stays, complications, and death rates. They found that once a new quality-improvement program was imposed after an extensive study of past practices, nearly all the doctors improved. But some did not.

The doctor in charge of the quality-improvement program said, "I have a few bad apples. And I know who they are. But for quality improvement to work, you have to construct a 'safe' environment where doctors trust you. Any time you start taking names, you're going to start a cycle of fear, and quality improvement will not occur."

When he learned of LDS tracking system, the head of the Utah medical board said, "that's a terrible indictment of them and of the practice of medicine that they are willing to sacrifice patients to unnecessary mortality, morbidity, injury and pain by these doctors. It's unconscionable!"

Using the analysis of TQM in this chapter, comment on the dilemma LDS faces in terms of using its computer system to improve quality.

17–5. A company chairman was given a ticket for a performance of Schubert's Unfinished Symphony. Since he was unable to go, he passed the invitation to the company's quality assurance manager. The next morning the chairman asked him how he enjoyed it and, instead of a few plausible observations, he was handed a memorandum which read as follows:

a. For a considerable period, the oboe players had nothing to do. Their number should be reduced, and their work spread over the whole orchestra, thus avoiding peaks of inactivity.

b. All 12 violins were playing identical notes. This seems unnecessary duplication, and the staff of this section should be drastically cut. If a large volume of sound is really required, this could be obtained through the use of an amplifier.

c. Much effort was involved in playing the demi-semiquavers. This seems an excessive refinement, and it is recommended that all notes should be rounded up to the nearest semiquaver. If this were done, it would be possible to use trainees instead of craftsmen.

d. No useful purpose is served by repeating with horns the passage that has already been handled by the strings. If all such redundant passages were eliminated, the concert could be reduced from two hours to 20 minutes.

In light of the above, one can only conclude that had Schubert given attention to these matters, he probably would have had the time to finish his symphony.

While the above was written partially in jest,[38] how would you respond?

---

[37] *New York Times*, (March 31, 1994).

[38] Doug Rathbun, Internet.

chapter 18

Ethics and Organizational Architecture*

CHAPTER OUTLINE

*Portions of this chapter were published in C. Smith (1992), "Economics and Ethics: The Case of Salomon Brothers," *Journal of Applied Corporate Finance* 5:2, 23–28, and J. Brickley, C. Smith, and J. Zimmerman (1994), "Ethics, Incentives, and Organizational Design," *Journal of Applied Corporate Finance* 7:2, 20–30.

In December 1990, the head of Salomon Brothers' government-bond trading desk, Paul W. Mozer, submitted bids for 35 percent of a four-year Treasury note auction. He also submitted another $1 billion bid under the name of Warburg Asset Management—a Salomon Brothers customer—but without the customer's authorization. The two bids, which represented 46 percent of the issue, violated the Treasury's auction rules limiting the amount sold to any one bidder to 35 percent of the issue.[1] Mozer repeated this tactic in February and April at auctions for five-year notes.

In April, Mozer apparently became concerned that the Treasury was about to uncover his bidding tactics. He admitted his illegal bid in the February auction in a meeting with Salomon Chairman John Gutfreund, President Thomas Strauss, Vice Chairman John Meriwether, and General Counsel Donald Feuerstein. They apparently accepted his confession to a one-time, not-to-be-repeated mistake and no immediate action was taken.

In May, he again employed this bidding tactic in an auction of two-year notes. In June, the Securities and Exchange Commission and the Justice Department issued subpoenas to Salomon and some of its clients for records involving bond auctions. Salomon then initiated a review of its government-bond operations and in August disclosed its illegal bids over the period between December and May.

By May 1992, the government had imposed a number of penalties on Salomon Brothers. The Treasury barred Salomon from bidding in government securities auctions for customer accounts. While allowing Salomon to retain its designation as a primary dealer, the Federal Reserve Bank of New York suspended its authority to trade with the Bank for two months. The firm agreed to pay $122 million to the Treasury for violating securities laws and $68 million for claims made by the Justice Department. It established a $100 million restitution fund for payments of private damage claims that might result from approximately 50 civil lawsuits that the firm still faced stemming from the scandal. Amounts in this fund not paid to the plaintiffs reverted to the Treasury, not Salomon.

While these legal and regulatory penalties were substantial, they represent only a fraction of the total costs borne by the firm. In the week that the information about the illegal bids was released, Salomon Brothers' stock price dropped by one-third. This $1.5 billion fall in market value suggests that the market expected Salomon to bear significant costs as a result of these actions and seems too large to simply reflect fines and other expected legal and regulatory sanctions. In addition to the penalties and decline in the market value of Salomon's stock, all of the senior officers who knew of the illegal bids but did not act swiftly were forced to leave the firm—and none of these individuals have since worked in a major securities firm. The case of Salomon Brothers illustrates that market forces can impose material sanctions on parties found engaging in unethical behavior.[2]

Over the past decade, much public attention has been devoted to the issues of business ethics and corporate social responsibility. Politicians and social critics have deplored the materialism of the 80s; the media have treated the public to sensational accounts of corporate scandal; and business schools across the country offer courses in ethics.

---

[1] In auctioning Treasury bonds, the U.S. Treasury awarded bonds first to the highest bidder at their quoted prices, then they moved to the next highest bidder. This process continued until the issue was exhausted. If the Treasury received multiple bids at the price that exhausted the issue, it allocated bonds in proportion to the bid size. But Treasury auction rules limited the amount of an issue sold to a single bidder to no more than 35 percent of the issue.

[2] For a more complete discussion of the Salomon Brothers case, see C. Smith (1992), "Economics and Ethics: The Case of Salomon Brothers," *Journal of Applied Corporate Finance* 5:2, 23–28.

In recent years, many U.S. corporations have responded by issuing formal codes of conduct, appointing ethics officers, and offering employee-training programs in ethics. Such codes and programs cover a wide range of behavior, but most emphasize the following:

- Compliance with laws and statutory regulations.
- Honesty and integrity in dealings with customers and other employees.
- The avoidance of conflicts of interest with the company.

While few would quarrel with such aims, equally few proponents of such corporate initiatives have bothered to ask questions like the following: Are such codes and programs likely to be effective in deterring unethical behavior by corporate managers and employees? And, more pointedly, is the behavior enjoined by such codes consistent with the normal incentives of employees or managers, *given the current organizational architecture* of the firm?

Although it is rarely recognized in most public discussions of the subject, corporate ethics and organizational architecture are closely related. To increase the likelihood that businesspeople will behave ethically in their roles as managers and employees, corporate performance-evaluation systems, reward systems, and assignments of decision rights can be designed to encourage such behavior.

In this chapter, we make five basic arguments:

First, the term *ethics* is elusive. It has many different meanings, and these meanings change across cultures and over time. The term *business ethics* can mean everything from corporate social responsibility to maximizing shareholder value.

Second, if the corporation is to survive in a competitive environment, it must maximize its value to its owners (primarily the stockholders). Taking care of other corporate stakeholders such as employees and local communities is important, but such care can be taken too far. If the firm reduces the owners' value, this care can endanger corporate survival.

Third, a company's reputation for ethical behavior, including its integrity in dealing with noninvestor stakeholders, is part of its brand-name capital; as such, it is reflected in the value of its securities. By the same token, individuals' human capital—that which determines their future earnings prospects—is based in large part on their reputation for ethical behavior. In this sense, private markets provide strong incentives for ethical behavior by imposing substantial costs on institutions and individuals that depart from accepted social standards. The Salomon Brothers trading scandal illustrates that the magnitude of these costs can be enormous.

Fourth, considerable emphasis in corporate ethics programs is put on misplaced efforts to change employees' preferences by attempting to persuade them to put the interests of the organization or its customers ahead of their own. Our approach, instead, accepts people's preferences as given and assumes they will follow their perceived self-interest. We focus on structuring the organization in ways that better align the incentives of managers and employees with the corporate aim of maximizing value.

Fifth, even if ethical guidelines and training programs are unlikely to alter fundamental preferences, they have the potential to add value by more explicitly communicating the firm's expectations to its employees. To be most effective, however, such guidelines must be reinforced by the firm's organizational architecture.

Ethics and Choices

People make choices. A fundamental cornerstone of this book is that individuals make choices to maximize their utility. Individuals have preferences over just about everything and choose how much to spend on food, transportation, housing, charities, and other purchases. People choose how to spend their time between work and leisure and how to allocate their time among alternate leisure activities—for example, watching television, attending church, or raising money for a local charity. Economics is the study of how people make choices; it is basically a descriptive study seeking to explain people's observed decisions. In this book, our analysis has been positive, not normative. We have not argued what decisions people should make—we have not argued that people should spend more time fundraising for their local charities and less time watching television. We have argued that given people's preferences, they will tend to select those activities that maximize their well-being (see Chapter 2).

This chapter is also about choices—in particular, choices among actions that are perceived to have ethical implications. Much of the study of ethics specifically focuses on how people should make choices—it is the study of those behaviors people should pursue. In large part, ethics is normative, not positive. When philosophers speak of ethics, they are dealing with the 25-century-old discipline that seeks to identify those behaviors that are right or wrong, good or bad, virtue or vice. Moral philosophers have been debating ethics since ancient times, and all religions involve statements of which behaviors are ethical and which are unethical. All major religions—Buddhism, Christianity, Confucianism, Hinduism, Islam, and Judaism—espouse the Golden Rule: "Do unto others as you would have them do unto you."[3] Western religions are based on the Ten Commandments, a code of ethical behavior.

Behaviors such as lying, cheating, stealing, and killing are almost universally viewed as wrong—except under mitigating circumstances (murder in self-defense is usually justifiable, for instance). However, certain behaviors are viewed as wrong by some, while others view them as right. For example, some view abortion as wrong, while others view denying women the right to choose as wrong. Similar conflicts exist regarding birth control and a person's right to die. In these cases, there simply is no universally accepted code of ethics on which one can rely to assess right and wrong.

Business ethics seeks to proscribe those behaviors in which businesses should not engage. Such actions range from the giving or taking of gifts, bribing government officials, misrepresenting data, discriminating hiring, and boycotting third parties. For example, some deemed it unethical for a company to do business in South Africa while that country practiced apartheid.

Business ethics and organizational architecture are interdependent. Organizational architecture, we have argued throughout this book, establishes incentives and thus affects the decisions managers and employees undertake. If it is important for businesspeople to behave ethically in their roles as managers and employees, it is important that the organization be structured to foster ethical behavior. In examining these issues, we first focus on "external" ethics policies controlling interaction between the firm and parties like customers, investors, and the local community. We then turn to internal ethics policies that deal with employees and managers.

Corporate Mission: Ethics and Policy Setting

What is the mission of the corporation, and does it involve ethics? Most people have a pretty good idea what they mean when they describe an individual as ethical. Most of us feel an emotional allegiance to the Golden Rule that urges us to treat others as we would have them treat us, and we value qualities such as honesty, integrity, fairness, and

---

[3]W. Shaw (1991), *Business Ethics* (Wadsworth Publishing: Belmont, CA), 12.

commitment to the task at hand. But what does it mean for a corporation to behave ethically? First, we have to understand what the term *ethical* means and then how it relates to the firm's mission.

Ethics

Ethics is a branch of philosophy. Western ethical philosophy can be traced back at least 2,500 years to Socrates, Plato, and Aristotle. These ancient Greeks searched for a generally understood set of principles of human conduct. Their treatises revolve around the terms *happiness* and *virtue.* Writing in the 13th century, St. Thomas Aquinas "argues that the first principle of thought about conduct is that good is to be done and pursued and evil avoided."[4]

There are numerous ethical theories. Ranging from egoism (an act is correct if and only if it promotes the individual's long-term interests)[5] to utilitarianism (behaviors should "produce the greatest possible balance of good over bad for everyone affected by our action").[6] Kantian ethics judges the nature of the act, not the outcome; Kant argued that only good deeds matter.[7] Adam Smith argued that through the invisible hand of market competition driven by self-interested traders, resources are directed to their most productive use and societal wealth is maximized. Ethical relativism holds "that moral principles cannot be valid for everybody; and . . . that people ought to follow the conventions of their own group."[8]

Even a cursory review of the major ethical philosophies yields two immediate observations. First, ethics is an enormous subject area that has engaged some of history's best minds. Second, despite considerable effort, there is no universally accepted philosophical consensus across time and societies as to which behaviors are ethical and which are not.

Furthermore, when it comes to defining the ethics of organizations like public corporations that encompass large groups of people, there is bound to be confusion. A corporation, after all, is simply a collection of individuals—or, more precisely, a set of contracts that bind together individuals with different, often conflicting, interests (see Chapter 7). In this sense, organizations themselves do not behave ethically or unethically—only individuals do. And if managers and employees are not pursuing their own interests, then whose interests are they serving? Their bosses'? The shareholders'? The board's? And what if there are major conflicts among these various interests?

Value Maximization

Economic Darwinism

Maximizing firm value is the mission most economists ascribe to managers. By maximizing the size of the pie, more can be distributed to each party contracting with the firm—including the shareholders, bondholders, managers, employees, customers, and suppliers. If the firm faces competition for both inputs and outputs, the prices the firm pays for its inputs and receives for its outputs will be driven to the competitive levels (Chapter 6), and the firm will

---

[4]J. Haldane (1991), "Medieval and Renaissance Ethics," in *A Companion to Ethics,* P. Singer, ed. (Basil Blackwell: Oxford), 135.

[5]K. Bair (1991), "Egoism," in *A Companion to Ethics,* 197.

[6]W. Shaw (1991), *Business Ethics,* 49.

[7]Shaw (1991), 74.

[8]R. Brandt (1970), "Ethical Relativism," in *Ethical Issues in Business: A Philosophical Approach,* T. Donaldson and P. Werhane, eds. (Prentice Hall: Englewood Cliffs, NJ), 78.

not receive any abnormal profits. Economic Darwinism and survival were discussed in Chapter 1. Long-run survival in a competitive environment dictates that firms seek to produce products at the lowest possible cost. In the absence of barriers to entry, firms that survive in the long run are the ones that deliver products consumers want at the lowest cost. This means that managers must adopt policies that maximize the value of the firm—or, what amounts to the same thing, the net present value of future cash flows distributable to the firm's investors. If managers follow other policies that raise their costs, value-maximizing competitors enter, manufacture products at lower costs, and sell them at lower prices. Eventually, firms that deviate significantly from value maximization will be shut out of the market.

Role for Regulation

There are two important cases where value maximization leads to predictable resource misallocation. First, if the firm has monopoly power, it will reduce output and set price above marginal cost (see Chapter 6). Second, if there are externalities—if firms' actions can impose costs on uninvolved third parties—the firm may have incentives to produce too much of an item (see Chapter 3). For example, because no one has easily enforceable property rights to clean air, factories may produce too much air pollution. In both cases, one limiting factor in these problems is government regulation. Thus, if appropriate regulation constrains any resource misallocation from monopolies or externalities, firms can focus on value maximization within the bounds of the regulation.[9]

Compensating Differentials

Maximizing firm value requires managers to assess all costs and benefits of proposed actions accurately. Suppose a firm is considering entering the business of disposing of hazardous wastes. Workers exposed to such hazards usually demand a compensating wage differential to offset the higher risks of illness from such work (see Chapter 11). Therefore, when evaluating whether to enter this business, value-maximizing managers must factor these compensating differentials into their estimated costs. Likewise, when considering entering businesses with ethical dimensions such as birth-control products, some employees of the firm may have personal beliefs that conflict with the new business. Some of these employees will leave the firm; some will seek transfers to another division; others may require compensating differentials to stay; and workers with strong moral beliefs opposed to the company's position may sabotage the project or misreport data to dissuade senior managers from undertaking the project. In such cases, the costs of business decisions that some view as unethical are higher because of the compensating differentials, labor turnover, agency problems, and adverse publicity associated with the decisions.

Corporate Social Responsibility

One source of confusion about the corporate mission is the concept of "corporate social responsibility," which is often used interchangeably with corporate ethics. In 1969, Ralph Nader and several other lawyers launched their Project on Corporate Responsibility with the following statement:[10]

---

[9]There are a number of issues implied by this brief discussion. In general, within the government, individuals are not always acting to maximize social welfare. Thus, even if appropriate regulation could reduce these problems in principle, there is no assurance that the regulation that is adopted will do so. G. Stigler (1971), "The Theory of Economic Regulation," *Bell Journal of Economics* 2, 3–21.

[10]J. Collins (1979), "Case Study—Campaign to Make General Motors Responsible," reprinted in *Ethical Issues in Business*, 90.

Phone Companies Charged with Electronic "Redlining"

A coalition of public-interest groups recently charged that four leading telephone companies engage in "electronic redlining" by bypassing low-income and minority communities as they begin to build advanced communication networks. These groups asked the Federal Communications Commission to clarify its rules and issue a policy statement opposing discrimination in the building of such networks. By raising charges of redlining, these groups seek to persuade the firms to provide early, subsidized service to less profitable markets. A spokesman for one firm pointed out that to achieve its plan of "wiring" half the state of California by 2000 "without raising rates," the company "must [first] bring the network to areas where it will generate some new business and revenues, so ultimately we can bring it to everyone in the state."

Source: M. Carnevale (1994), "Coalition Charges Phone Firms with 'Redlining' in Adding Networks," *The Wall Street Journal* (May 24).

> *Today we announce an effort to develop a new kind of citizenship around an old kind of private government—the large corporation. It is an effort which rises from the shared concern of many citizens over the role of the corporation in American society and the uses of its complex powers. It is an effort which is dedicated toward developing a new constituency for the corporation that will harness these powers for the fulfillment of a broader spectrum of democratic values.*

As Nader's statement suggests, the aim of advocates of corporate social responsibility is nothing less than to change the objective function of the corporation. In Nader's view, the corporation is to be transformed from a means of maximizing investor wealth into a vehicle for using private wealth to redress social ills. The corporate social responsibility movement seeks to make management responsible for upholding "a broader spectrum of democratic values." Corporate support for such values could take the form of philanthropic activities, the provision of subsidized goods and services to certain segments of the community, or the use of corporate resources on public projects such as education, environmental improvement, and crime prevention. If all firms in the world face the same social requirements, then the survival of any given firm is less of an issue. However, if some firms are exempted from redressing social ills, others' survival in a competitive environment requires that they maximize their market value.[11]

Economists' View of Social Responsibility

The conflict between Nader's and economists' views of the corporation is not quite as pronounced as it might appear. Corporations intent on maximizing firm value often find it in their interest to devote resources to noninvestor stakeholders such as employees, customers, suppliers, and local communities. For example, a company with a large plant in an inner city might decide that investing corporate resources and personnel to improve area schools leads to better-trained employees and eventually lower-cost products. Giving money to the local university might benefit the firm by improving its R&D or increasing its access to top graduates. Improving the environment lowers the company's legal exposure to damage claims and might also lower its wage bill to the extent a cleaner local environment makes it easier to attract employees.

---

[11]M. Jensen and W. Meckling (1978), "Can the Corporation Survive?" *Financial Analysis Journal* 34, 31–37.

Milton Friedman's View of Corporate Social Responsibility

What does it mean to say that the corporate executive has a "social responsibility" in his capacity as businessman? If this statement is not pure rhetoric, it must mean that he is to act in some way that is not in the interest of his employers. For example . . . that he is to make expenditures on reducing pollution beyond the amount that is in the best interests of the corporation or that is required by law in order to contribute to the social objective of improving the environment. . . .

[The problem in this case is that] the corporate executive would be spending someone else's money for a general social interest . . . [when] the stockholders or the customers or the employees could separately spend their own money on the particular action if they wished to do so.

Source: M. Friedman (1970), "The Social Responsibility of Business Is to Increase Its Profits," *New York Times Magazine* (September 13).

Maximizing firm value requires expending firm resources on members of each important corporate constituency to improve the terms on which they contract with the company, to maintain the firm's reputation, and to reduce the threat of restrictive regulation. More precisely, it means allocating corporate resources to all groups or interests that affect firm value—but only to the point where the incremental benefits from such expenditures at least equal the additional costs.

Many managers are inclined to endorse Nobel Laureate Milton Friedman's prescription that the social mission of the corporation is "to make as much money for its owners as possible while conforming to the basic rules of society." As we have noted, some companies will find it in their shareholders' interest to "invest" in social causes of various kinds, but corporate investments that systematically fail to provide adequate long-term returns to private investors are wealth transfers that end up reducing social as well as private wealth.

Absent tax benefits, it is usually more efficient for the corporation to focus on creating wealth and to let its shareholders, employees, and customers choose the beneficiaries of their charitable contributions. By maximizing their shareholders' (or owners') wealth, corporations effectively enlarge the pool of individual (noncorporate) resources available for charity.[12]

The experience of the 1980s, incidentally, is consistent with this argument. During this decade of large shareholder gains, total charitable giving—by individuals, corporations and foundations—expanded in real dollars at a compound annual growth rate of over 5 percent, a growth rate over 50 percent higher than in the previous 25 years. Moreover, private donations rose from an historic low of 2.1 percent of national income in 1979 to 2.7 percent in 1989.[13]

People who advocate ever larger corporate contributions to charities and social causes such as retraining displaced workers and environmental cleanup (without consideration of their own long-run profitability) are effectively calling for higher

[12]J. Brickley (1988), "Managerial Goals and the Court System: Some Economic Insights," *Canada-United States Law Journal* 13, 79.
[13]R. McKenzie (1991), "Decade of Greed: Far from It," *The Wall Street Journal* (July 24), A10.

Taxes and Corporate Philanthrophy

One potential benefit to the owners of a firm from having the corporation donate to charities is a reduction in taxes paid to the government. Assume that both the corporate and personal tax rate is 50 percent. Suppose a corporation has profits of $5,000 before taxes and distributes all its after-tax profits to the shareholders as dividends. The firm has four equal shareholders who collectively want to give $1,000 to a particular charity. If the firm makes the contribution, it is deductible from corporate income before taxes. Thus, the corporation has $4,000 of taxable income ($5,000 minus $1,000), of which $2,000 is paid in taxes and $2,000 is paid to the owners who pay personal taxes on the dividends they receive. After personal taxes, each shareholder has $250 ($2,000 ÷ 4 × 50%).

Now suppose the shareholders donate $250 each to the charity and the corporation makes no contribution. The firm has pre-tax profits of $5,000, pays taxes of $2,500 (50% of $5,000) and distributes $2,500, to shareholders. Each shareholder receives $625 ($2,500 ÷ 4) before personal taxes, makes the contribution ($250), has taxable income of $375 ($625 minus $250). Each pays taxes of $187.50 and has after taxes $187.50 ($625 minus $250 minus $187.50). By having the firm make the charitable contribution, each shareholder has $62.50 ($250 - $187.50) more than when the shareholder makes the charitable contribution. When the firm makes the contribution, the gift shields $1,000 from corporate taxation.

These tax-reduction gains for corporate philanthropy are most compelling when all the shareholders agree on the amount and nature of the donations. Gifts to charities not valued by some shareholders reduce these shareholders' welfare. Unfortunately, there is unlikely to be agreement among corporate stakeholders about which charities should receive corporate donations and how much. Customers, employees, or independent sales agents objecting to the firm's choice of charities may take their business or services elsewhere. Moreover, corporate managers do not obviously have a comparative advantage in choosing which charities to support. If it is time-consuming for managers to sort through charitable requests and make the selections, this is time that could have been spent on other activities that more predictably increase firm value. Thus, even with the tax advantage of corporate philanthroplogy, it is not necessarily the case that shareholders are better off by having the firm make charitable donations instead of doing it themselves.

implicit taxes on corporations. If all companies are so taxed, the taxes are ultimately borne not only by shareholders in the form of lower returns to capital but also by workers in the form of lower wages and customers in the form of higher prices. Thus, ironically, the likely social consequences of such an increase in corporate social responsibility are lower rates of economic growth, lower corporate values, higher unemployment, and overall reductions in charitable donations—reductions in donations by individuals might more than offset the increases in mandated corporate giving.

Corporate Philanthropy Comes under Fire

Pioneer Hi-bred International, the world's largest seed company, provided financial support for Planned Parenthood of Greater Iowa. But when right-to-life groups voiced strong objections in the farming communities where the firm does business, the company was forced to withdraw its sponsorship. As *The Wall Street Journal* reported:

"We were blackmailed," declares Pioneer chairman and president Thomas Urban. "But," he says, . . . "you can't put the core business at risk," even though the company concedes that canceling funding probably upset as many farmers as it appeased and the boycott didn't end.

Source: *The Wall Street Journal* (June 10, 1992), B1.

Corporate Policy Setting

Once a corporation has determined its mission, implementing the mission requires a set of operating policies. Again, ethical issues arise. It is futile to think that one can reduce excruciatingly difficult corporate policy issues to simple, universally applauded policy decisions. Consider questions like:

- Should we use laboratory animals for product testing?
- Should we market infant formula in Central Africa?
- Should we do business with a company that employs child labor in its Asian textile factory?
- Should we adopt different procedures for handling and disposing of hazardous wastes in Latin American plants than we use in the United States?
- Should we pay "fees" to expedite paperwork for export permits to an African market?
- Should our obsolete North Sea oil rig be towed to deep water and sunk?

Because there is no widely embraced definition of ethical behavior, these problems require careful analysis in establishing appropriate corporate policy. In particular, managers should be careful to collect data for estimating the total cost and benefits of alternative actions, including costs of adverse publicity, tarnished reputation, and lost customers. While we cannot solve the above problems, we can suggest steps to help craft an appropriate policy.

Teamwork

In questions with potentially contentious ethical implications, it is particularly important to obtain input from a broad cross section of potentially affected stakeholders in the firm. Here, diversity in perspective can be especially valuable in identifying potentially sensitive areas that require additional analysis prior to setting policy. Diversity in backgrounds can help the team better assess the potential total costs of alternate policies.

Legal Standards

It is important to understand the legal consequences of potential policy choices. The first, most obvious, question is—*Is it legal?* Yet this knowledge alone is generally far from sufficient to frame policy. For example, after the United States bombed Libya in 1986, some U.S. banks faced a dilemma: The U.S. Federal Reserve and the State Department required that Libyan funds in U.S. banks be frozen. But the Central Bank of Greece announced that under Greek law, any Libyan funds on deposit in Greece must be available on demand. If Libya had funds on deposit in Citibank's Athens branch and requested the funds, the bank would have to choose between violating U.S. law or Greek law. Or, consider potential consequences of hiring child labor in a textile mill in Pakistan, even if it is legal there, some customers might object because it is illegal in the United States or Europe.

Moreover, illegality may not be the determining factor. For example, it is doubtful that Federal Express would adopt a policy of firing a driver who violates the law by receiving a parking ticket. Hence, it is important to understand what sanctions might be imposed if a law is violated.

Finally, laws are not constant over time. For instance, although the 1995 Congress rolled back certain environmental regulations, some firms appear reluctant to take advantage of the entire range of newly allowed activities. They appear to be concerned that if the political pendulum swings back, they might face some future liability.

Business Norms

In the business community, there are expectations in transactions that do not have the force of law but nevertheless represent expected behavior. These norms are rarely written down; knowledge of them accumulates primarily with experience. These issues can be especially important when entering a new market.

In special cases, these norms are codified. Adopting procedures developed by an external group to handle sensitive issues can be quite useful. For example, standards for using laboratory animals in product testing are established by the U.S. Department of Agriculture, the National Institute of Health, and the Public Health Service. Most organizations that undertake animal research adhere to these standards. Nongovernmental groups also participate in this process. For instance, firms in the motion picture industry frequently voluntarily adopt standards developed by the American Society for the Prevention of Cruelty to Animals. By simply stating that you adhere to the ASPCA code, a film company may be able to deflect much criticism.

Press Standard

Another useful device managers use in determining the ethical issues in setting corporate policies involves assessing the public's likely reaction. The example of Pioneer Hi-bred International's withdrawal of support for Planned Parenthood illustrates the often important interaction among ethics, public relations, and the media. Ethics consultants regularly counsel corporate managers to apply the press standard to help determine which behaviors are ethical. This criteria suggests that to judge whether an action is ethical, ask if you would be comfortable reading about what you did on the front page of a newspaper or seeing it reported on television.[14]

Using publication of your behavior as an ethical benchmark for judging a decision highlights the linkage between ethical behavior and reputation. Below, we discuss market forces that create incentives for people and firms to behave ethically. The argument is that unethical behavior adversely affects reputation, and one way to assess a decision's reputational effects is to ask how it would read in *The New York Times*.

Mechanisms for Encouraging Ethical Behavior

Ethical lapses are a manifestation of a conflict of interest, or agency problem. As stated earlier, in most market exchanges, parties to the contracts have incentives to devise mechanisms to reduce agency costs, thereby raising the prices they receive for their products or services. For example, when taking their firms public for the first time, founders of companies frequently retain large positions in the stock and voluntarily impose restrictions on their own selling to help ensure that their interests are consistent with those of their new investors. Such arrangements effectively raise the price investors are willing to pay.

Likewise, external public auditors voluntarily prohibit themselves from owning stock in the companies they audit. By not owning any stock, auditors do not reap any gain by withholding unfavorable financial information. This increases their independence from their clients and increases the value and hence price firms are willing to pay for the audit.

As we also noted earlier, because reputational capital is an important determinant of future earnings, market forces provide incentives for firms and individuals to behave ethically.

---

[14]Thomas Jefferson offered similar advice in a letter to Peter Carr: "Whenever you are to do a thing, though it can never be known but to yourself, ask yourself how you would act were all the world looking at you, and act accordingly." T. Jefferson (1785), in *Thomas Jefferson: His Life and Words* (1986), N. Beilson, ed. (Peter Pauper Press: White Plains, NY), 47.

Adam Smith on Merchant Reputation

Of all the nations in Europe, the Dutch, the most commercial, are the most faithful to their word. The English are more so than the Scotch, but much inferior to the Dutch, and in the remote parts of this country they [are] far less so than in the commercial parts of it. This is not at all to be imputed to national character, as some pretend; there is no natural reason why an Englishman or a Scotchman should not be as punctual in performing agreements as a Dutchman. It is far more reducible to self-interest, that general principle which regulates the actions of every man, and which leads men to act in a certain manner from view of advantage, and is as deeply implanted in an Englishman as a Dutchman. A dealer is afraid of losing his character, and is scrupulous in observing every engagement. When a person makes perhaps 20 contracts a day, he cannot gain so much by endeavoring to impose on his neighbors, as the very appearance of a cheat would make him lose. When people seldom deal with one another, we find that they are somewhat disposed to cheat, because they can gain more by a smart trick than they can lose by the injury which it does to the character.

Sources: A. Smith (1964), *Lectures on Justice, Police, Revenue, and Arms*, E. Cannan, ed. (Augustus M. Kelley: New York); and P. Milgrom and J. Roberts (1992), *Economics, Organizations, and Management* (Prentice Hall: Englewood Cliffs, NJ), 257.

But the effectiveness of market forces in reducing conflicts of interest and enforcing contracts varies among different kinds of transactions. Among the most important characteristics of such transactions are the difficulty of ascertaining product quality prior to purchase and the likelihood that the transaction will be repeated.

Take the case of a buyer purchasing a product. For products whose quality can be determined at low cost prior to purchase, markets readily solve this problem. If buyers can cheaply monitor quality, they will do so. For example, a buyer negotiating a purchase of silver for Kodak can confidently and cheaply ascertain its quality by assay.

For some products, quality is virtually impossible to determine prior to purchase. For example, the quality of an airplane ticket can be known only after the plane has landed, parked at the gate, and the passengers have retrieved their luggage. Although sellers have incentives to cheat on quality when quality is expensive to measure, rational sellers will provide products of lower than promised quality only if the expected gains exceed the expected costs.

Repeat Sales

One important constraint on such cheating is the potential for future sales.[15] Moreover, corporations with established market positions and substantial franchise values face higher costs of cheating and hence are less likely to cheat than start-up firms. The costs of cheating on quality are also higher if the information about such activities is more rapidly and widely distributed to potential future customers. For example, in markets like the diamond trade in New York, which is dominated by a close-knit community of Hasidic Jews, cheating on quality is extremely rare.[16]

[15]L. G. Telser (1980), "A Theory of Self-Enforcing Agreements," *Journal of Business* 53, 27–44.

[16]Other examples of ethnic communities, like the Chinese in Singapore, support the view that confining choice of trading partners to one's own ethnic community economizes on the costs of contracting. J. Landa (1981), "A Theory of the Ethnically Homogenous Middlemen Group: An Institutional Alternative to Contract Law," *Journal of Legal Studies* 10, 349–62.

Signaling Quality by External Monitoring: Rice Aircraft

In 1991, Rice Aircraft Company became the first company in its industry to earn ISO 9002 accreditation, an international standard for quality management. This was a significant, highly visible signal of change within the firm. For in August 1989, Bruce J. Rice, CEO of Rice Aircraft, had pled guilty to fraud and was sentenced to four years in prison. The Defense Department forbade its contractors to do business with the company for five years, and annual sales fell from $15 million to $5 million. At this point, Paula DeLong Rice, Rice's wife, took over and set out to save the company by visibly and radically transforming it. She implemented a total quality initiative and provided classes in statistical process control, time management, and communications for all the company's employees.

Paula DeLong Rice's strategy appears to have been quite effective. Profit margins increased from 12 percent in 1992 to 27 percent in 1993 without benefit of price increases; order cycle time was reduced by 50 percent; and on-time deliveries increased 98 percent. Paula DeLong Rice, moreover, is now in great demand as a speaker on managing for quality.

Source: T. Pare (1994), "Rebuilding a Lost Reputation," *Fortune* (May 20), 176.

Warranties

Seller-provided product warranties are another mechanism to reduce the likelihood of cheating. Seller warranties will be most prevalent when product failures result from factors that are under the firm's control (such as manufacturing tolerances). In this case, warranties directly impose the cost of failure on the parties who have the most control over product quality or failure. However, when failures are due primarily to factors that are under the customers' control, the moral-hazard problem will be greater and warranties are less useful as a quality-assurance mechanism. Since sellers bear higher warranty costs if they cheat on quality, they have less incentive to cheat.

Third-Party Monitors

In some markets, specialized information services monitor the market, certify quality, and help to ensure contract performance. For example, *Consumer Reports* evaluates products from toasters to automobiles, the *Investment Dealer Digest* reports on activities of investment bankers, and A.M. Best Company rates insurance companies' financial conditions. These third-party information sources lower the costs for potential customers to determine quality and so increase the expected costs of cheating.

In credit markets, specialized credit-information services like Moody's and Dun & Bradstreet perform both a monitoring and an information dissemination function. The existence of such intermediaries provides an opportunity for the firm to guarantee quality. For this reason, corporate issuers pay Moody's to have their debt rated over the life of the bond issue. By issuing rated public debt, a firm lowers the cost to other potential corporate claimholders (including potential customers) of ascertaining the firm's financial condition.[17]

Disclosure

The required level of disclosure in markets can also be important in determining quality. For example, a study of two wholesale used car markets with different levels of required

---

[17]L. Wakeman (1983), "The Real Function of Bond Rating Agencies," *Chase Financial Quarterly* 1:1, 18–26.

Evidence on the Penalty from Fraud

Researchers have examined the stock market's reaction to announcements of fraud charges against corporations. They specifically focus on cases where the damaged party does business with the accused firm—thus, they focus on frauds alleged against customers, suppliers, employees, and investors (but not damages to third parties such as in pollution dumping). The evidence suggests that in the days around the first announcement in *The Wall Street Journal,* the average fall in the firm's stock price is 1.58 percent. Thus, press reports of alleged fraud are associated with statistically significant and economically material losses in value. Moreover, these losses were much too large to be explained by legal costs and fines.

Source: J. Karpoff and J. Lott (1993), "The Reputational Penalty Firms Bear from Committing Criminal Fraud," *Journal of Law & Economics* XXXVI, 757–802.

disclosure found higher prices in the market with more required disclosure.[18] The ability to "precommit" to disclose information reduces the potential information disparity between buyer and seller and so reduces that discount buyers apply to their demand prices.

Ownership Structure

Incentives to provide high-quality products vary across ownership structures. Take the case of franchise companies such as fast-food and lawn-care firms. Such companies typically franchise some units instead of owning all their stores in order to take advantage of the incentive benefits of decentralized ownership while retaining scale economies in advertising and brand-name promotion.

Outlets that have little repeat business create a special problem. The franchise owners of these stores have an incentive to cheat on quality because they can benefit from a steady stream of one-time sales while hurting the reputation of the entire organization. At these locations, the central company is more likely to own the unit than to franchise it, in part because a salaried manager has less incentive to cheat on quality.[19]

Companies with large amounts of debt in their capital structure can face a significant probability of financial distress. Such firms are more likely to cheat on quality than financially healthy firms because repeat sales are less likely. Therefore, some firms can "bond" product quality by adopting conservative financial policies. Since financial distress is more costly for firms that market products where quality is difficult to ascertain, such firms have incentives to adopt financing policies—including lower leverage, fewer leases, and more hedging—that lead to a lower probability of financial distress.

Agency Costs: Ethics and Policy Implementation

In our examples of Barings Bank (Chapter 1), Sears Auto Centers (Chapter 2), and Salomon Brothers (Chapter 18), none of these firms had formal corporate strategies of engaging in

---

[18]H. Grieve (1984), "Quality Certification in a 'Lemons' Market: An Empirical Test of Certification in Wholesale Leased-Car Auctions," working paper, University of Rochester.

[19]One study finds that franchise companies in lines of business with more repeat sales at individual units (e.g., lawn-care and beauty shops) are likely to franchise a higher percentage of total units than franchise lines with less repeat business (such as motels, car rental agencies, and restaurants). J. Brickley and F. Dark (1987), "The Choice of Organizational Form: The Case of Franchising," *Journal of Financial Economics* 18, 401–20.

unethical behavior. Rather, their ethical problems arose from controlling the behavior of individuals granted particular decision rights within the firm. They are examples of agency problems within firms. Chapter 7 described the general agency problem as the difficulty in making corporate managers and employees perform in ways consistent with the aims of the firm's owners. In addressing these internal ethical issues, this section makes two key points: First, the agency problem of shirking or opportunistic actions by the agent is often labeled an ethical lapse; and second, if all agents reduced their opportunistic actions (behaved more ethically), agency costs would be lower.

To review the agency problems that can arise with performance evaluation and monitoring, take the case of hiring someone to paint your house. Especially in performing tasks that are hard to monitor such as surface preparation (sanding, scraping, and priming), the painter has incentives to shirk—or, at least, to do a job that may not be as thorough as you might like. Of course, this same painter will also be prompted by other considerations to do a good job. It may be a matter of private conscience; that is, the painter's sense of self-worth might be tied up with the quality of the workmanship, and violating such a self-imposed standard would impose major "costs" in the form of a tarnished self-image. Or the painter is constrained by the desire to maintain his commercial reputation (and, though it might take some time for a poor job of surface preparation to show its effects, the quality will eventually reveal itself). As we noted earlier in this chapter and discussed in Chapter 7, reputation is an important contributor to the capitalized value of one's expected future earnings.

But because the prompting of conscience and the desire to maintain a reputation are neither universal nor constant, it's impossible for you to know the extent to which your painter is bound by such considerations. You face an information problem: You do not know when hiring the painter the kind of surface preparation you will get, nor will you be capable of ascertaining that until well after the job is done and the bill is paid.

To reduce your vulnerability in such circumstances of informational asymmetry, you will likely ask for a list of references (if the painter has not already provided one). Such references should give you some basis for assessing the painter's time horizon and the importance he attaches to reputation. The painter also might offer, or you might insist on, a one-or-more-year warranty on the job. (As discussed previously in this chapter, such common practices as the use of warranties, third-party references, and credit checks play an important role in reducing agency costs in the business world.)

But despite such assurances, some uncertainties about the painter's level of performance remain. For example, will he be around to make good on the warranty if the paint peels in a year? Perhaps the painter has heavy debts and is about to declare personal bankruptcy. Or perhaps yours will be the painter's last job before he embarks on a new career painting still lifes and family portraits.

As a consequence of the possibility of shirking and your own remaining uncertainty, you (as the principal) effectively reduce the price you are willing to pay. Or, to state the converse of this proposition, if there were some means for the painter to provide you with complete assurance about his level of commitment, you would be willing to pay a higher price for the job.

Three points emerge from this simple example. First, let's assume you were able to design a perfect contract; for the sake of argument, let's say you had a camera that enabled you to observe the painter's activity at random intervals (and the painter knew you had it), and that you were able to structure a pay schedule based on the observed effort. Even if you were able to devise such a monitoring and reward scheme, it would clearly not pay you to do so. The cost to you of writing, administering, and, most important, monitoring compliance with such a contract would be substantial—perhaps even greater than the value of the painting job itself. Thus, as this simple illustration is meant to point out,

A Retired CEO's View of Verbal Contracts

Most of our products were custom-made. Customers called in their orders over the phone. The orders, ranging in value from a few hundred dollars to tens of thousands of dollars, generally required delivery of goods within one or two days. It meant we would usually begin production before receiving a confirming purchase order. (This was before faxes.) The customer's word alone was enough. In my 20-year stint as CEO, not once did a customer go back on it. Unusual? Not at all. Without such trust, business couldn't be conducted. Similar transactions happen every day. . . . (W)e learned there are two ways to go: An eye for an eye, or do unto others what you would have them do unto you. In business, the latter philosophy is far more common, simply because it makes things work better.

Source: H. Aaron (1994), "The Myth of the Heartless Businessman," *The Wall Street Journal* (February 7), A14.

in most cases it does not pay to attempt to eliminate all possible shirking; because of the costs of writing and monitoring compliance with contracts, it is efficient to leave some slack in the system. As explained in Chapter 7, the *optimal* amount of shirking or opportunistic behavior by the agent is not zero.

Second, the *expected* level of opportunism or shirking—which, again, is greater than zero—is priced in the contract. Thus, the principals do not bear the full costs of opportunistic actions by their agents. Typically, at least some of these costs are shifted back to agents in the form of lower prices for their services or products.

Third, higher ethical standards among agents, whether corporate employees or participants in market exchanges, would lead (over time) to a reduction in the level of *expected* opportunistic behavior and hence a reduction in agency costs. As a result, there would be more transactions (including more jobs created) and higher prices paid to agents by principals (including higher corporate wages). This would occur not only because of a reduction in the amount of shirking but also because the costs of writing and monitoring contracts would fall. Both principals and agents would be better off. Economist Jack Hirshleifer makes this last point: "Altruism economizes on the costs of policing and enforcing contracts."[20] In discussing economic development, one writer lists low business ethics as an important factor impeding growth. During the late 19th century, such practices as confidence men selling shares, bankruptcy with concealed assets, and squandering capital increased the difficulty of raising capital to finance new ventures such as the construction of the railroads.[21]

The retired CEO's story illustrates an important point about the economic consequences of ethics: If we as a society could get everyone voluntarily to reduce opportunistic behavior such as withholding important information about product quality, then the resources devoted to monitoring and enforcing exchanges could be used in more productive pursuits.[22]

[20]J. Hirshleifer (1977), "Economics from a Biological Viewpoint," *Journal of Law and Economics* 20, 28.

[21]T. Cochran (1964), *The Inner Revolution* (Harper and Row: New York).

[22]E. Noreen (1988), "The Economics of Ethics: A New Perspective on Agency Theory," *Accounting, Organizations and Society* 13, 359–369.

Codes of Ethics

We view important aspects of the corporate ethics problem primarily as problems of reducing agency costs. And, generalizing from the above discussion, there are several potential ways to reduce them. One way to reduce agency costs would be to get corporate managers and employees to voluntarily adopt higher, more stringent ethical standards. A second is to use contracts that better align the interests of managers and employees with those of shareholders. Examples of such contracts in corporations are executive or employee stock options, bonus plans, and profit-sharing arrangements (see Chapter 12). (Such contracts also will act to reinforce voluntary codes.) Both more cost-effective incentive contracts and higher ethical standards can be expected to lead to lower agency costs, greater corporate efficiency, higher corporate values, and greater social welfare.

As mentioned earlier, many companies and most professions have written codes of conduct, and some companies also have educational programs dealing with ethics for their employees. Most codes and programs emphasize the following:[23]

- Employees must obey the laws and observe statutory regulations.
- Customer relations in terms of the reputation and integrity of the company are of great importance.
- Employees must support the company's policies to customers.
- Conflicts of interest between the company and the employee must be avoided.
- Confidential information gained in the course of business must not be used improperly.
- It is improper to conceal dishonesty and protect others in their dishonesty.
- Advice to customers should be restricted to facts about which the employee is confident.

Why have corporations adopted such codes? The most cynical view is that a corporate code of ethics is nothing more than a document that helps the firm defend itself against charges of illegality. The new sentencing guidelines issued by the U.S. Sentencing Commission in November 1991 strongly encourage corporations to establish and communicate compliance standards and procedures for employees and other agents through training programs and publications. For example, when an individual is found guilty of wrongdoing, the organization may be vulnerable to federal fines. These penalties can be reduced by more than 50 percent simply by demonstrating that the organization has a compliance program that meets the Sentencing Commission's standards.[24] A compliance program consists of at least a code of ethics and a training program. These federal sentencing guidelines have blurred the line between legal and ethical issues.

---

[23]These codes are not unique to the United States. For example, similar codes are observed in Australian firms. B. Kaye (1992), "Codes of Ethics in Australian Business," *Journal of Business Ethics*, 11.

[24]N. Gilbert (1994), "1-800-ETHICS," *Financial World* (August 16), 20–25.

But corporate ethical codes, as we have just argued, also have the potential to perform the economically valuable function of reducing the costs of monitoring and enforcing contracts. To the extent they reduce managerial and employee opportunism, better ethical standards can increase corporate brand-name capital and hence shareholder wealth.

The critical questions, however, are these: *Are ethical codes effective in deterring unethical behavior? And if they are, how or why are they effective?*

Altering Preferences

There are two basic ways to view the function of corporate codes of conduct in reducing opportunistic behavior. One way is by appealing directly to employees' consciences, attempting to instill in them loyalty to the organization and its goals. Economists describe this as an attempt to alter people's "preferences."

Now, there is undoubtedly some value to this approach. As we noted earlier, personal codes of conduct and the guilt one suffers in violating such codes are undeniably constraints on many people's behavior. As described in Chapter 2, individuals' utility functions contain many nonpecuniary factors, including conscience and guilt. As the following statement by Nobel Laureate Kenneth Arrow suggests, even subjective concepts like ethics and morality are consistent with the economist's notion of rational self-interest:

> *Certainly one way of looking at ethics and morality . . . is that these principles are agreements, conscious or, in many cases, unconscious, to supply mutual benefits . . . Societies in their evolution have developed implicit agreements to certain kinds of regard for others, agreements which are essential to the survival of the society or at least contribute greatly to the efficiency of its working. . . . [T]he fact we cannot mediate all our responsibilities to others through prices . . . makes it essential in the running of society that we have what might be called "conscience," a feeling of responsibility for the effects of one's actions on others.[25]*

The problem in applying this logic to corporate management, however, is that such "agreements to supply mutual benefits to others" are likely to be too amorphous to serve as a practicable guide to individual behavior in large public companies with diffuse stock ownership. If corporate factory workers are understandably unmoved by serving an anonymous group of "wealthy" shareholders, then who precisely are "the others" whose interests their morality is intended to serve? And what should employees do in those cases, noted earlier, where there appear to be (at least short-run) conflicts between the interests of the corporation and those of its noninvestor constituencies? After all, as we have seen earlier, the effective management of scarce resources often means saying no to the requests or desires of some employees, customers, and local communities. Moreover, the entire situation is complicated by the fact that the fundamental goal of the corporation—making money for its owners—is viewed as immoral or unethical by many advocates of corporate ethics.

Given this confusion about, and even conflict between, some professed ethical objectives and the goal of the corporation, we are skeptical about corporate attempts to instill conscience or a sense of guilt in their employees—that is, to alter employees' preferences. To the extent these corporate ethics programs are aimed at trying to change employees' preferences, they are likely to fail.

---

[25]K. Arrow (1974), *Limits of Organization* (W.W. Norton: New York), 26–27.

Consider the transfer-pricing problem faced by corporations with multiple divisions that buy and sell to one another. In Chapter 14, the firm value-maximizing solution to this problem was described as setting the transfer price to the buyer at the seller's opportunity cost of producing one more unit. But let's assume, as tends to be the case, that the selling or manufacturing division has better information about its costs than the purchasing division.

In such a situation, to the extent the manager's compensation is based on divisional profits, the selling division's manager has the incentive to set the transfer price substantially above opportunity cost. In such a case, the manufacturing division's pursuit of its own profits will come at the expense of total firmwide profits (because the buying division will purchase less than the optimal number of units).

Now, if adoption of a code of ethics somehow succeeded in inducing divisional managers to reveal their information about costs, units within the firm would be transferred at opportunity cost, and firm profits would be increased. But as long as division managers are being *paid* based on the profits of their own divisions, they are unlikely to reveal their actual costs.

Most economists generally assume that individuals' preferences are given and for the most part difficult to alter. We thus believe that managers, instead of attempting to alter preferences, should redesign the firm's architecture to change their employees' incentives to take certain actions. For example, in the above case, senior management should attempt to find a means of giving the divisional manager some stake in the profitability of the division to which he or she "sells" the product. A common, though only partly effective, solution to this problem is to give divisional managers stock options with payoffs tied to overall company value as well as bonuses for divisional performance.

Education

Even if corporate codes of ethics are unlikely to change preferences or eradicate self-interest, such codes can still play a potentially important role in modifying behavior. Up to this point, we have assumed that corporate managers and employees know what is the "right thing" to do to promote the interests of the organization. But it is unlikely that this assumption always holds. In many cases, managers' and employees' uncertainty about ethical standards—or how to live up to them in practice—may well be a greater corporate problem than their failure to work hard or to act in accordance with standards that are well established and clearly defined.

We earlier described the confusion about the corporate mission stemming from the aims and actions of the social responsibility movement. Another potential source of confusion resides in the variability of ethical standards. What may have been acceptable behavior 10 or 20 years ago may not be so today. Social changes such as those brought about by movements as different as civil rights and women's rights, on the one hand, and corporate restructuring, on the other, have clearly altered conceptions of socially accepted behavior. Moreover, the progressive globalization of corporations is increasingly forcing corporate employees to recognize and adapt to differences in national or regional cultural expectations.

Given this large and, in some ways, growing uncertainty about what constitutes ethical behavior in large organizations, corporate codes of ethics and training programs can play an important educational role by effectively communicating corporate expectations to employees and by demonstrating to them how certain kinds of behavior reduce the value of the firm. For example, misrepresentations of products and services to

The Appearance of Impropriety at Citibank, Argentina

A newspaper article reported that H. Richard Handley, the president of Citibank Argentina, had sold portions of Citibank's Argentine assets to some of his friends at "what now look like bargain prices." Citicorp spokesmen dismissed that talk as "Monday morning quarterbacking," pointing out that, at the time of the first sales, there was an equal chance that the value of Argentine investments would rise or fall thereafter.

It is not important whether the terms of this particular set of transactions were appropriate or not; they may well have been deals that furthered important business interests of Citicorp in Argentina. What this case highlights, however, are the costs associated with the *potential* for self-dealing by corporate managers, and the importance of stating and enforcing policies for business dealings on less than an arms-length basis. The structure of this deal has forced Citibank to defend its actions to employees, investors, and regulators.

Source: *Miami Herald*, April 24, 1994.

---

customers for short-term gain can be shown to reduce the value of the firm by hurting its reputation and thus lowering its brand-name capital. Moreover, in the process of globalizing and thus dealing with customers worldwide, companies may be forced to respond to the increasing cultural differences—or absence of shared expectations—among their managers and employees by providing more explicit communication of standards and expectations.

Besides issuing a clear set of rules governing employee relations with consumers, corporations are also likely to benefit from communicating guidelines for dealings among managers and employees within the firm. For example, many companies develop their executives by rotating them through a series of jobs. The resulting management turnover can undermine the "implicit" agreements among managers and employees. The explicit, corporatewide communication of expectations to employees can reduce uncertainty about the enforcement of informal agreements and thereby increase internal efficiency.

Virtually all professions such as medicine, the law, and accounting have professional ethics codes. Prospective candidates must pass entry exams that test their understanding of these codes. Most professional codes contain detailed descriptions of behaviors that reduce the value of the profession's services. For example, professional accountants are prohibited by their code of ethics from serving on the board of directors of their client firms. Such memberships reduce the appearance of independence of the auditor when rendering an opinion on the client's financial statements. If one accountant is caught not disclosing a known financial fraud, this reduces the value of other accountants' audit opinions. Thus, professions, like firms, have incentives to monitor their members for ethical breaches.

Corporate Culture

More generally, codes of conduct and training programs in ethics have the potential to contribute to the building and maintaining of a value-based corporate culture. Like corporate ethics, *corporate culture* is an ill-defined term, but as discussed in Chapter 8, it generally encompasses things such as the ways work and authority are organized within a company as well as organizational features such as customs, taboos, company slogans, heroes, and social rituals. For example, slogans like that of Federal Express—"When it absolutely positively has to be there overnight"—help communicate the message that employees are expected to focus on meeting delivery schedules and that this focus will be recognized and rewarded by the organization. Singling out role models or heroes for special awards is another way of communicating the values of the company. Similarly, social rituals such as training sessions and company parties can help disseminate information by increasing interaction among workers and encouraging discussion of ethical standards. Indeed, the *process* by which a code of ethics is produced and the training programs through which these standards are communicated are potentially more important than the code itself in developing and maintaining the desired corporate culture.

Nevertheless, to create the value-based or consumer-focused organization that many companies seek to become, these less tangible aspects of corporate culture must be reinforced by more tangible actions. That is, the more formal corporate systems that partition decision rights and evaluate and reward performance, as well as sanctions for unethical behavior, must all be internally consistent and designed to encourage firm value-increasing behavior.

Summary

Business ethics is the study of those behaviors that businesspeople should or should not follow. This book is also about business behaviors—in particular, how firms are organized to motivate and control the behavior of self-interested workers to maximize firm value. The focus of this book has been primarily descriptive. Assuming people are motivated by self-interest, how are they expected to behave under alternative organizational architectures? Ethics is primarily normative—how should people behave. Managers often endorse the ethical philosophy espoused by Adam Smith. In Smith's view, through private ownership of property, self-interest, and competition, a society's resources are put to the best use and produce the highest quantity and quality of goods and services at the lowest prices (value maximization).

Value maximization requires that all costs and benefits be considered. If a particular business decision conflicts with a worker's or customer's own personal belief, that person is worse off. If enough people are affected, costs are imposed on the firm through compensating wage differentials, higher turnover, and lost sales.

Moral philosophers and all religions have debated ethics since ancient times and yet we still do not have a universally accepted code of ethics. Witness the current debates over abortion and birth control. There is considerable confusion about the meaning of corporate ethics. It is highly unlikely that a universally accepted code of business conduct will emerge. The corporate social responsibility movement has focused less on raising corporate ethical standards than on transferring shareholder wealth to other parties such as customers, employees, and local communities. While these corporate stakeholders are important, if the corporation is to survive, it must maximize its value to its owners—a goal that in turn promotes efficient use of scarce social resources.

Many of the issues raised in this chapter are recurring themes in the popular press and will continue to be in the future. You may be called on to resolve a sexual harassment case, an environmental issue, or a product recall dispute. There is no doubt that at least once during your career you will be faced with a key decision that some will label a major ethical dilemma. This chapter seeks to demonstrate that the economic framework presented in the earlier chapters can provide guidance for understanding issues involving ethics.

There are a number of important managerial implications raised by the discussion in this chapter.

First, behaviors that others classify as unethical impose real costs on the firm by lowering the firm's brand-name capital, especially when they are reported in the media.

These costs from reduced reputation include lost sales or higher costs because parties outside the firms are less willing to contract with the firm. Many ethical problems are similar to agency problems discussed throughout the text, and much of the same analysis of agency problems can be used to analyze ethical problems.

Second, ethics has many different meanings, ranging from making firms socially responsible (transferring wealth from the firm to other parties) to trying to make workers not self-interested. Another use of ethics means informing employees that certain behaviors impose large reputational costs on the firm, and hence the firm will impose sanctions on employees engaging in such actions.

Third, mechanisms arise to constrain unethical behavior. Like agency costs, costs of unethical behavior create incentives to minimize these costs. Managers should understand these mechanisms to ascertain under what conditions ethical behavior is most likely. For example, extra care should be exerted when structuring deals with firms in financial distress.

Fourth, decisions that have major ethical dimensions almost invariably involve potential adverse publicity and a decline in the firm's brand-name capital. How the firm responds to the press affects how the public perceives the issue. In dealing with the media, the following application of this book's framework is usually helpful:

- News reporters are pursuing their own self-interest—not yours. They are trying to maximize their value, which usually means increasing their audience in order to sell more newspapers or TV and radio advertising. Reporters know more about their job than you do.
- Having access to the media is valuable. Developing brand-name capital is very costly to do through advertising. Use your access to the media to present the firm's position in a credible, honest way. Lying or misrepresenting the facts to the media is likely to backfire because reporters have the incentive and skills to uncover these misrepresentations, again because such discovered lies make juicy stories.

Fifth, when ethics programs are used to get employees to work hard on the job instead of taking on-the-job leisure, these programs try to alter people's preferences. Senior managers concerned about the ethical conduct of their employees would do better to spend less time searching, like Diogenes, for "an honest man." Instead, they should pay more attention to the incentives created by the firm's organizational architecture (the three-legged stool). As discussed in Chapter 2, it is unlikely Sears would have faced widely reported consumer indignation and legal sanctions from unnecessary auto repairs had it anticipated the (quite predictable) incentives its compensation plan would give its managers and its employees to overcharge customers. Incentives work. If the compensation plan pays employees for unethical behavior, then unethical behavior is exactly what the company will get. The approach in this book is to redesign organizational architecture, not people's preferences. Managers must structure their subordinates' incentives to ensure that they do not reduce total firm value.

Sixth, ethical guidelines can provide effective communication of behaviors that reduce firm value. Codes of conduct, rather than trying to change workers' preferences, can inform workers of firm-value-reducing actions that will not be tolerated and that can lead to sanctions imposed on the worker.

Suggested Readings

T. Cochran (1964), *The Inner Revolution* (Harper and Row: New York).

T. Donaldson and P. Werhane, eds. (1979), *Ethical Issues in Business: A Philosophical Approach* (Prentice Hall: Englewood Cliffs, NJ).

M. Jensen and W. Meckling (1978), "Can the Corporation Survive?" *Financial Analysts Journal* 34, 31–37.

L. Nash (1991), "Ethics without the Sermon," *Harvard Business Review* (November–December).

L. Newton and M. Ford (1994), *Taking Sides: Clashing Views on Controversial Issues in Business Ethics* (Duskin Publishing Group: Guilford, CT).

E. Noreen (1988), "The Economics of Ethics: A New Perspective on Agency Theory," *Accounting, Organizations and Society* 13, 359–369.

W. Shaw (1991), *Business Ethics* (Wadsworth Publishing: Belmont, CA).

W. Shaw and V. Barry (1995), *Moral Issues in Business* (Wadsworth Publishing: Belmont, CA).

C. Smith (1992), "Economics and Ethics: The Case of Salomon Brothers," *Journal of Applied Corporate Finance* 5:2, 23–28.

B. Toffler (1986), *Tough Choices: Managers Talk Ethics* (John Wiley & Sons: New York).

Review Questions

18–1. Seventh Generation, of Colchester, Vermont, manufactures and markets "environmentally friendly" household products—vegetable-based, chlorine-free laundry products and nontoxic cleaners. Seventh Generation used to sell its products through natural-food outlets and direct mail catalogs. In 1992, the CEO of Seventh Generation, Jeffrey Hollander, concluded that to continue to grow, his company had to appeal to a broader range of customers. The only way to do this was to lower his prices. He concluded, "The research that says people will pay more for socially responsible goods simply isn't true."

Hollander reformulated his products and compromised on environmental purity. Environmentally harmful phosphates and chlorines were still excluded, but cheaper petroleum-based cleaning agents were substituted. These changes allowed a dish detergent's price to be lowered from $3.50 to $2.50. While margins are lower, sales are up 20 percent. Also, the new formulas work better.

Seventh Generation is criticized by some of its old customers for paying less attention to core customers and substituting profits for idealism. Hollander says to his critics, "They not only have greater access to our products, (t)hey also can get them cheaper."

a. Do you agree with Hollander that people aren't willing to pay more for socially responsible goods? Explain why or why not.

b. Is Seventh Generation behaving ethically by substituting petroleum-based cleaners into its products?

c. What additional information would you request to help Seventh Generation address its ethical questions?

18–2. Ben and Jerry's Homemade Inc. has received much favorable press for its Rainforest Crunch ice cream. It uses official rain forest nuts and berries and all natural ingredients; it also sends a percentage of profits to charities. However, another flavor, Cherry Garcia, contains sulfur dioxide preservatives, and other flavors use margarine, not butter. What are the problems a firm faces if it is "politically correct" in some products but not others?

18–3. The Body Shop has been widely noted for its ethical stands in its business: natural cosmetics; "Products for People Tested by People"; and First World wages for Third World products. Recently, Jon Entine published an analysis of the Body Shop in *Business Ethics,* alleging false advertising and other ethical lapses. Would you expect such charges to have more or less of an impact on a company like the Body Shop that touted its business ethics than if the same charges were leveled against a competitor who made fewer claims?

18–4. The Body Shop started its business by developing an extensive network of franchisees. Recently, franchisees have complained about the company competing with their franchises through direct catalog sales. How does an expansion of direct catalog selling affect the Body Shop?

18–5. Eastman Kodak charged that the Fuji Film Company of Japan was illegally dumping film in U.S. markets. It asked the U.S. government to investigate and impose sanctions on Fuji for its unfair practices. But the world film market is dominated by Kodak and Fuji. If the government agrees to sanction Fuji, Kodak will obtain significant market power in the U.S. film market. Is it ethical for Kodak to attempt to use the government to undermine its competitor?

18–6. Wilmorite Corporation owned a large tract of land and proposed erecting a large, modern enclosed shopping mall south of town. The mall was opposed by an environmental group that argued that the land had areas with standing water that waterfowl used in their spring and fall migrations. The challenges resulted in a substantial delay in the development of the land; more extensive environmental impact statements had to be prepared and plans had to be redrawn.

  a. Was this development ethical?

  b. The largest contributor to the environmental group happened to own Southtown Mall, an older strip mall across the road from the proposed new mall. Was his contribution to the environmental group ethical?

Glossary*

Absolute performance evaluation is one which is based on a predetermined standard of performance; the employee is not evaluated on performance relative to peers, but rather against some prespecified, generally objective performance standard.

Activity-based costing assigns different categories of overhead (purchasing, engineering, inspection) costs to products by first estimating the underlying cost-drivers of the activities performed in the overhead department and then assigning these activity costs to the products that benefit from or consume activity resources.

Adverse selection refers to the tendency of individuals with private information about factors that affect a potential trading partner's benefits to make offers that are detrimental to the trading partner.

Agency problems occur within contracts because agents have incentives to take actions that increase their well-being at the expense of the principals; they occur not only in *agency relationships,* but in any type of cooperative undertaking, such as partnerships and teams.

Agency relationship is an agreement under which one party, the principal, engages another party, the agent, to perform some service on the principal's behalf.

Alienable property rights are private property rights that can be transferred (sold or given) to other individuals.

Arc elasticities are estimated between two points (elasticities also can be calculated at a point); they measure the percentage change in one variable, such as quantity, with respect to a percentage change in another variable, such as price.

Asset specificity occurs when a given asset is especially useful to one or a small number of buyers—for physical assets, this results from product design or *site specificity;* for *human capital,* it results from investments in specialized knowledge or skills.

Asymmetric information occurs when one party to a transaction has different information than another party.

Average cost (AC) is the *total cost* divided by total output; average cost can be defined for either the *long run* or the *short run.*

Average product of an input is the *total product* divided by the quantity of the input employed.

Backward (or upstream) integration occurs when an organization produces its own inputs.

Bargaining failures occur due to *asymmetric information;* parties fail to reach an agreement, even when in theory a contract could be constructed that is mutually advantageous.

Barriers to entry are factors that limit the entry of new firms to a *market,* even though the existing firms are making *economic profits.*

Benchmarking is identifying the practices of firms operating in similar environments, so that you can learn from their experience.

Boundary setting occurs when managers empower employees to make decisions within some prespecified limits.

Broad task assignment has individual employees performing a relatively large set of tasks.

---

*Italicized terms are defined elsewhere in the glossary.

Business environment includes the technology, *markets* (product and input), and regulations facing the *firm.*

Business ethics is the study of those behaviors that business people should or should not follow (however, the term also is used in ways that range from making firms socially responsible to attempting to induce employees to ignore their self-interest).

Business strategy focuses on strategy at the business-unit level; the primary consideration is whether to focus on being the low-cost producer in an industry or to develop differentiated products for which customers are willing to pay a price premium.

Cafeteria-style benefit plans (menu plans) are plans where individual employees allocate a fixed-dollar fringe-benefit allowance among a variety of choices.

Career earnings are the total wages that employees expect to earn over their entire careers.

Cartels consist of formal agreements among a set of firms to cooperate in setting prices and output levels.

Centralized decision system is one which assigns most major decisions to executives at the top of the organization.

Certainty equivalent is the certain income that an individual considers equivalent to an activity with risky payoffs.

Changes in demand are movements of the *demand curve* motivated by factors other than changes in the good's own price (such as changes in income or changes in the prices of related goods).

Changes in the quantity demanded are movements along a *demand curve* that are motivated by changes in the good's own price, holding all other factors constant.

Coase Theorem states that the ultimate resource allocation will be efficient, regardless of the initial assignment of property rights, as long as the *transaction costs* are sufficiently low, *property rights* are clearly assigned, and these rights can be exchanged.

Comparative advantage is when one party can produce a good relatively more efficiently than other parties (relative efficiency means that alternative products which could have been produced from the same inputs are less valuable). It is conceptually possible for a party to have an absolute advantage in producing all goods (meaning that it can produce all goods with fewer inputs); however, it cannot have a comparative advantage in all goods. Aggregate output is increased if parties specialize in producing products in which they have a comparative advantage.

Compensating wage differential is the extra wage that is paid to attract an individual to a less desirable *job.*

Competitive market is a *market structure* where no buyer or seller has market power (all trades are made at the going *market price*); it is characterized by a large number of potential buyers and sellers, low costs of entry and exit, product homogeneity, and rapid dissemination of accurate information at low cost.

Complementarities exist when doing more of one activity either increases the benefits or reduces the costs of doing another activity.

Complements are products that tend to be consumed together; a price increase of one good will tend to reduce the consumption or use of the other good.

Complete contracts are contracts which specify exactly what is expected of each party under all possible future contingencies.

Constant returns to scale occur when a one-percent change in all inputs results in a one-percent change in output.

Consumer surplus is the difference between what the consumer would be willing to pay for a product and what the consumer actually pays when buying it.

Contracting costs are the out-of-pocket and *opportunity costs* of negotiating, drafting, and enforcing contracts; they include search and information costs, bargaining and decision costs, and policing and enforcement costs, and the efficiency losses that result because incentive conflicts are not completely resolved.

Corporate culture is the set of explicit and implicit expectations of behavior within the *firm;* it usually encompasses the ways work and authority are organized, the ways people are rewarded and controlled, as well as organizational features such as customs, taboos, company slogans, heroes, and social rituals.

Corporate strategy focuses on strategy at the firm level; the primary consideration is on the scope of the *firm*—the number of different products that the firm sells.

Cost centers are business units whose performance is evaluated based on the efficiency of production.

Cournot model examines producer interaction assuming each *firm* treats the output level of its competitor as fixed and then decides how much to produce.

Cross elasticity is the percentage change in the demand of a good, given a percentage change in the price of some other good.

Cross-training is training employees to complete more than one task or *function.*

Cumulative production is the total output produced by the firm in all previous production periods.

Decentralized system is one which assigns many important decision rights to lower-level employees.

Decision control is the *ratification* and *monitoring* of decisions.

Decision management is the *initiation* and *implementation* of decisions.

Decreasing returns to scale occur when a one-percent change in all inputs results in a less than one-percent change in output.

Dedicated assets are those whose purchase is necessitated only by the requirements of one or a few buyers.

Demand curve pictures the relation between the quantity of a product that will be purchased at each price over a stated period of time, holding all other factors fixed; demand curves slope downward because customers typically buy more if the price is lower.

Demand function is the relation between the quantity demanded of a product and all factors that influence this demand.

Double markups are the increments in the product's price above *marginal cost* first by the manufacturer and then by the distributor.

Downstream integration—see *forward integration.*

Economic Darwinism is the economic counterpart of the biological theory of natural selection; an organization selects features that increase its ability to survive within its environment; the basic idea is that only those organizations that are relatively most efficient can survive in a competitive marketplace.

Economic profit is an above-competitive rate of return on assets; economic profits are eroded in a competitive market.

Economic Value Added (registered trademark of Stern Stewart) is a measure of *residual income;* it is the after-tax operating profit of the division minus the total annual cost of capital invested in the division.

Economies of scale occur in industries where *average cost* declines over a broad range of output.

Economies of scope occur when the cost of producing a joint set of products within one firm is less than the cost of producing the products separately in independent firms.

Efficiency wages are wage premiums paid to reduce shirking because employees are afraid that if they are caught, they will be fired and lose this premium; efficiency wages also discourage employees turnover.

Elastic demand is when the *price elasticity* is greater than one; a small increase in price is associated with a decrease in total revenue.

Equilibrium refers to a stable situation where no party has a reason to change its strategy; in a competitive market, this occurs when the quantity supplied of a product equals the quantity demanded.

Ethics is the study of those behaviors that people should or should not follow.

Exclusive territories grant individual distributors the exclusive rights to operate within a stipulated market area.

Expense centers are business units that are given fixed budgets and asked to maximize some hard-to-measure service or output; it is a *cost center* that does not produce an easily measurable output.

Experience goods are those which must be tried by the customer to ascertain *quality.*

Explicit contracts are formal written agreements with a party to the firm—for example, employees, customers, suppliers, capital providers.

Externalities are costs of or benefits from the actions of one party that affect the *utility* or production possibilities of another party.

Factor demand curves picture the relation between the quantity of an input the firm demands and its price, holding other factors constant.

Firm is a focal point for a set of contracts.

Firm-specific assets are assets that are significantly more valuable in their current use within the firm than in their next best alternative use outside the firm.

First-degree price discrimination is when the producer extracts all potential consumer surplus from each potential customer.

First-mover advantages are the expected benefits derived by the first firm to introduce a product.

Fixed costs are those that do not vary with output within the time horizon of the analysis.

Formal authority is the power that comes from the explicitly assigned decision rights within the organization.

Forward (or downstream) integration occurs when the firm begins to conduct additional finishing work or to market its own goods.

Franchise agreements are contracts between the franchisor (parent) and the franchisee that grant to the franchisee the rights to use the parent's name, reputation, and business format at a particular location or within a stipulated market area.

Free cash flow problems are incentive conflicts between owners and managers over retaining cash within the firm beyond that necessary to fund profitable investment projects—the managers prefer to empire build, rather than to distribute the cash to owners.

Free-rider problems occur in team efforts; each member of the team has an incentive to shirk because each receives the full benefit from shirking, but only bears a part of the costs.

Fringe benefits are compensation that is either in-kind or deferred—such as medical insurance and pensions.

Full-cost transfer prices use full cost to value goods exchanged between business units; full cost is the sum of fixed and variable cost.

Function refers to a primary activity within the process that a firm employs to provide a product to customers; major functions include research, manufacturing, finance, marketing, sales, and service.

Functional myopia occurs when employees focus on their individual *function* at the expense of the overall process.

Functional subunits group all jobs performing the same *function* into the same department.

General human capital consists of training and education that is useful across a wide variety of different firms.

General knowledge is that which is relatively inexpensive to transfer.

Goal-based system is a one in which each employee is given a set of goals for the year and evaluated based on whether or not they are achieved.

Group incentive pay bases employee compensation on group performance.

Historical costs reflect the original purchase price of resources and not necessarily their current *opportunity cost;* historical costs are generally not relevant for decision making (except for their tax effects).

Hold-up problems can occur when parties invest in specific assets; for example, after the investment is made the buyer might be able to force a price concession, since it will be in the interests of the seller to continue to operate as long as *variable costs* are covered.

Horizon problems are the incentive conflicts that can arise between owners and employees due to differential horizons with the firm; employees' claims on the firm are generally tied to their tenure with the firm, but owners are interested in the present value of cash flows over the life of the firm.

Human capital is a term that characterizes individuals as having a set of skills that can be "rented" to employers.

Human asset specificity—see *asset specificity.*

Identification problem is a statistical problem that arises in separating the effects of simultaneous equations; for example, separating supply versus demand shifts in explaining the observed changes in market prices and quantities.

Implementation rights involve the execution of ratified decisions.

Implicit contracts consist of promises and shared understandings that are not expressed by formal legal documents.

Incentive coefficients are weights that the compensation plan places on the various tasks assigned to an employee.

Income elasticity is the percentage change in the *demand* for a good, given a percentage change in income.

Incomplete contracts do not specify actions under all possible contingencies.

Increasing returns to scale occur when a one-percent change in all inputs results in a greater than one-percent change in output.

Indifference curves picture all the combinations of goods that yield the same *utility*.

Inelastic demand is when the *price elasticity* is less than one; a small increase in price raises total revenue.

Inferior goods are goods for which *demand* declines with income.

Influence costs include those nonproductive activities in which employees engage to influence decisions.

Informativeness principle states that it is typically desirable to include in the compensation plan all performance indicators that provide incremental information about the employee's effort—assuming the measures are available at low cost.

Initiation rights are the decision rights to generate proposals for resource utilization or contract structure.

Internal labor markets fill most non-entry-level jobs from within the firm; employees typically spend a significant fraction of their careers with the firm.

Investment centers are business units that have all the decision rights of *cost centers* and *profit centers* as well as the decision rights over the amount of capital to be invested.

Isocost lines picture all combinations of the factors of production that cost the same.

Isoquants picture all possible ways to produce the same quantity (iso meaning the same, quant from quantity).

Jobs define the basic roles and responsibilities of employees; jobs have at least two important dimensions: the variety of tasks that the employee is asked to complete and the decision authority that is granted to the individual to complete the tasks.

Joint ventures establish new firms that are jointly owned by two or more independent firms.

Keiretsu is a form of *network organization* employed in Japan; it consists of an affiliation of quasi-independent firms with ongoing, fluid relationships; typically, the firms have cross holdings in each others' common stock.

Law of demand states that normal *demand curves* slope downward to the right—quantity demanded varies inversely with price.

Law of diminishing returns (law of diminishing marginal product) states that the *marginal product* of a variable factor will eventually decline as the use of the factor is increased.

Leadership is the process of persuasion or example by which an individual induces a group to pursue objectives held by the leader; it has at least two important components: establishing goals and motivating others.

Learning curve pictures the relation between *average cost* and cumulative volume of production; learning-curve effects refer to average cost falling as production experience accumulates.

Logroll consists of a coalition of individuals who are largely indifferent to each other's demands, but agree to support each other's requests so that each can get what he wants.

Long run is the period of time over which the firm has complete flexibility—no inputs are fixed.

Malcolm Baldrige National Quality Award

was instituted in 1987 by the U.S. government to recognize quality achievement by U.S. companies.

Marginal analysis considers only the incremental costs and benefits in making a decision; costs and benefits that do not vary with the decision are sunk and hence are irrelevant.

Marginal benefits are the incremental benefits associated with making a decision.

Marginal cost (MC) is the change in total costs associated with a one-unit change in output— marginal costs can be defined for either the *long run* or the *short run*.

Marginal-cost transfer prices use marginal production cost to value goods exchanged between business units.

Marginal product of an input is the change in total output associated with a one-unit change in the input, holding other inputs fixed.

Marginal revenue (MR) is the change in total revenue given a one-unit change in quantity.

Marginal revenue product (MRP) is the incremental revenue that the firm obtains from employing one more unit of the input (the incremental output times the incremental revenue).

Market consists of all firms and individuals who are willing and able to buy or sell a particular product.

Market-based transfer prices use external market prices to value goods exchanged between business units.

Market-clearing price is the price at which the quantity supplied of a product is equal to the quantity demanded.

Market structure refers to the basic characteristics of the market environment, including: (1) the number and size of buyers, sellers, and potential entrants, (2) the degree of product differentiation, (3) the amount and cost of information about product price and quality, and (4) the conditions for entry and exit.

Matrix organizations are those which are characterized by intersecting lines of authority; they have functional departments (such as finance, manufacturing, and development), but employees from these functional departments are also assigned to subunits organized around product, geography, or some special project—individuals report to both a functional manager and a product manager. See *function* and *functional subunits*.

Minimum efficient scale is the plant size at which *long-run average cost* first reaches its minimum.

Monitoring rights involve determining whether the contractual obligations of another party have been met.

Monopolistic competition is a *market structure* that is a hybrid between *competitive markets* and *monopoly;* firms have downward sloping *demand curves* for their differentiated products, but *economic profits* are limited by entry and competition (examples include the markets for toothpaste and golf balls).

Monopoly is a *market structure* where there is only one firm in the industry; here, industry and firm *demand curves* are the same.

Moral-hazard problems—see *postcontractual information* problems.

Motion studies involve the systematic analysis of work methods considering the raw materials, the design of the product or process, the process or order of work, the tools, and the activity of each step.

Multitask principal-agent model examines the incentive problems that arise when an employee is assigned multiple tasks.

Multicollinearity is a statistical problem which arises when the factors that affect a dependent variable in a regression are highly correlated (tend to move together); it can make it difficult to estimate the individual effects of the explanatory variables with much precision.

Multidivisional form (M-form) of firm organization groups jobs into a collection of business units based on factors such as product or geographic area; operating decisions such as product offerings and pricing are decentralized to the business-unit and each business unit has its own *functional subunits*.

Nash equilibrium

is when each firm is doing the best it can given the actions of its rivals.

Negotiated transfer prices use prices set by negotiation between the two business units to value goods exchanged between them.

Network organizations are those which are organized into work groups based on *function,* geography, or some other dimension; the relationships among these work groups are determined by the demands of specific projects and work activities, rather than by formal lines of authority; these relationships are fluid and frequently change with changes in the business environment.

Normal goods are those for which demand increases with income.

Objective performance measure is a measure that is easily observable and quantifiable.

Oligopolistic market is a *market structure* that has only a few firms which account for most of the production in the market; products may or may not be differentiated; firms can earn economic profits.

Omitted variables problem is a statistical problem which arises from estimating equations without all the relevant explanatory variables.

Operating cost curves are used in making near-term production and pricing decisions.

Opportunity cost is the value of the good in its next best alternative use.

Organizational architecture comprises the three critical aspects of corporate organization: (1) the assignment of decision rights within the company; (2) the methods of rewarding individuals; and (3) the structure of systems to evaluate the performance of both individuals and business units.

Outsourcing is moving an activity outside the firm that formerly was done within the *firm;* it can also refer to an outgoing arrangement for using external firms either to supply inputs or distribute products.

Pareto efficiency occurs when there is no feasible alternative that keeps all individuals at least as well off but makes at least one person better off.

Physical asset specificity—see *asset specificity.*

Planning curves are the same as *long-run cost curves;* they play a key role in longer-run planning decisions relating to plant size and equipment acquisitions.

Postcontractual information problems are agency problems that occur because of *asymmetric*

information after the contract is negotiated; individuals have incentives to deviate from the contract and take self-interested actions because the other party has insufficient information to know whether the contract was honored (some refer to these problems as *moral-hazard problems*).

Potential entrants are all firms that pose a sufficiently credible threat of market entry to affect the pricing and output decisions of incumbent firms.

Precontractual information problems are contracting problems that occur because of *asymmetric information* at the time the contract is being negotiated; these problems include *adverse selection* and *bargaining failures.*

Price discrimination occurs whenever a firm's prices in different markets are not related to differentials in production and distribution costs.

Price elasticity of demand measures the percentage change in quantity demanded from a percentage change in price; it is conventionally stated in terms of its absolute value—it is actually a negative number.

Principal/agent model examines incentive problems among contracting parties, especially within organizations.

Prisoners' dilemma is a game-theory model which examines the tension between group interest and individual self interest; the *equilibrium* is for the two prisoners to confess, even though it is in their joint interest not to confess.

Product attributes are the various characteristics of a product that buyers value.

Product life cycle is the pattern in the demand for products over their life cycles; it is divided into four stages: introduction, growth, maturity, and decline. Typically, the demand for a successful product increases rapidly through the growth phase; the demand tends to level off during the maturity phase; it eventually drops when the product enters the decline phase.

Production function specifies the maximum feasible output that can be produced for given quantities of inputs.

Profit centers are business units whose managers are given decision rights for input mix, product mix, and selling prices (or output quantities) and asked to maximize profits given a fixed capital budget.

Profit-maximizing level of production occurs when marginal revenue equals marginal cost.

Property right is an enforceable right to select the uses of a good.

Quality can refer to high mean, low variance, more options, or meeting customer expectations.

Ratchet effect refers to basing next year's performance standard on this year's actual performance; such standard setting can induce employees to restrict production in the current period in order to limit the increase in their future performance benchmarks.

Ratification rights are those which involve the choice of the decision initiatives to be implemented.

Reaction curve pictures one firm's optimal output given the output choice of another firm.

Reengineering is a management technique defined as the fundamental rethinking and radical redesign of business processes to achieve improvements in measures of performance, such as cost, *quality,* service, and speed.

Relative-performance evaluation measures employees' performance relative to peers.

Relative price is the price of one good as compared to another.

Repeated relationship is where two parties expect to interact with each other over time; sometimes it is possible for the parties to cooperate in a repeated relationship, even though they would not cooperate in a one-time interaction due to incentive conflicts.

Reservation price is the maximum price that the buyer is willing to pay; or the minimum that the seller is willing to accept.

Reservation utility is the *utility* that the employee can obtain in the next best alternative; the employee must be paid his reservation utility or he will not work for the firm.

Residual claimants have the legal rights to the profits of the enterprise once the fixed claimants of the firm (for example, bondholders and employees) are paid.

Residual income measures business-unit performance by subtracting a stated return on investment from division profits.

Residual loss is the dollar equivalent of the remaining loss in value that results because *agency problems* have not been completely resolved by out-of-pocket expenditures on monitoring and bonding.

Residual use rights for an asset are the rights to select any use that does conflict with prior contract, custom, or law.

Return on investment (ROI) is a commonly used investment-center performance measure; ROI is the ratio of accounting net income generated by the investment center divided by total assets invested in the *investment center.*

Returns to a factor define the relation between output and the variation in only one input, holding other inputs fixed.

Returns to scale is the relation between output and a proportional variation of all inputs taken together.

Revenue centers are business units that evaluate performance based on revenue generation.

Risk-averse individuals prefer a lower level of risk, holding the expected payoff fixed.

Risk premium is the difference between the expected value of a risky income stream and its *certainty equivalent.*

Risk-neutral individuals care only about expected value and are indifferent to the level of risk.

Second-degree price discrimination involves setting prices based on quantity purchased; prices are often blocked with a high price charged for the first unit or block of units purchased, and lower prices set for successive units or blocks.

Self selection occurs when people with differential private information identify themselves to outsiders by choosing contracts that best fit with their private information.

Short run is the operating period during which at least one input (frequently capital) is fixed in supply.

Short-run profit maximization occurs when *marginal revenue* equals *short-run marginal cost.*

Shortage occurs when the price in the market is lower than the *market-clearing price;* therefore, quantity demanded is greater than quantity supplied.

Shut-down condition in the *short-run* is where price is less than *average variable cost;* in the *long-run* it is where price is less than *long-run average cost.*

Site specificity is when an asset is located in a particular place that makes it useful only to a small number of buyers or suppliers and it cannot be moved easily. See *asset specificity.*

Specialized task assignments are those in which individual employees concentrate on a limited set of tasks.

Specific assets are those which are worth more in their current use than in alternative uses.

Specific human capital is created by learning things that are expected to be useful only within a specific contractual relationship.

Specific knowledge is that which is relatively expensive to transfer.

Spot market is one where the exchange is made immediately at the current market price with no long-term commitment between the buyer and the seller.

Standard rating scales require the performance evaluator to rank the employee on a number of different performance factors using a scale (for example: far exceeds requirements, exceeds requirements, meets all requirements, partially meets requirements, does not meet requirements).

Strategic alliances are any of a variety of agreements between independent firms to cooperate in the development and/or marketing of products.

Subjective performance evaluation is an evaluation that is based on the personal opinion of the supervisor (rather than some objective measure, such as the quantity of output).

Substitutes are goods that compete with each other; if the price of one good is increased the consumer will tend to shift purchases to the other good.

Substitution effect is when the firm shifts among inputs in producing a product due to changes in the relative prices of the inputs.

Sunk costs are those costs that have already been incurred and have no alternative use.

Supply curve pictures the quantity producers are willing to sell at each price; the curve typically slopes upward—at higher prices producers are able and willing to produce and sell more units.

Surplus is when quantity supplied is greater than quantity demanded; this happens when the price in the market is higher than the *market-clearing price.*

Survival of the fittest is a principle implied by the concept of *Economic Darwinism;* companies have the greatest chance of survival if they are organized efficiently given their particular environment.

Team mania is when teams are formed indiscriminately as a result of *TQM* programs.

Telecommuting is employees working out of their homes and communicating with the central office via fax, computer, or telephone.

Third-degree price discrimination results when a firm separates its customers into several classes and sets a different price for each class.

Three legs of a stool is an analogy used to characterize *organizational architecture;* like a balanced stool, a well-designed organization should have an architecture where the three components (the assignment of *decision rights,* the *reward system* and the *performance-evaluation system*) match each other.

Time studies are a wide variety of techniques employed for determining the duration a particular activity requires under certain standard conditions.

Total cost curve pictures the relation between total costs (total fixed costs plus total variable costs) and output.

Total product of an input is the schedule of output obtained as the input increases, holding other inputs fixed.

Total quality management (TQM) includes those management processes and organizational changes necessary to meet customer expectations and to achieve continual improvement.

Transaction costs—see *contracting costs* (note that this term sometimes is used to refer only to out-of-pocket contracting costs).

Transfer price is the price established to value goods and services that are exchanged between business units.

Two-part tariff is a *price discrimination* mechanism in which the customer pays an up-front fee for the right to buy the product and then pays additional fees for each unit of the product consumed; two-part pricing is sometimes used in contracts between manufacturers and distributors.

Unitary elastic demand is when the *price elasticity* is equal to one; a small increase in price is associated with no change in total revenue.

Unitary organization (U-form) of firm organization groups *jobs* by *function* (engineering, design, sales, finance, and so on); it places each primary function in one major subunit (rather than in multiple subunits).

Upstream integration—see *backward integration*.

Utility is an index of personal well-being.

Utility function is the relation between an individual's well-being (*utility*) and the level of goods consumed.

Variable costs are costs which change with the level of output.

Vertical chain of production is the series of steps in the production process.

Vertically integrated firms are those that participate in more than one successive stage in the *vertical chain of production*.

Vision refers to a course of action for the firm (see *corporate strategy*).

Work sampling is one type of *time study* which involves selecting a large number of observations taken at random intervals and observing how long employees take in performing various components of the *job*.

Index